Motivation
and Work Behavior

McGraw-Hill Series in Management

KEITH DAVIS AND FRED LUTHANS, CONSULTING EDITORS

Motivation and Work Behavior

Second Edition

Richard M. Steers
University of Oregon

Lyman W. Porter
University of California, Irvine

McGraw-Hill Book Company

New York   St. Louis   San Francisco   Auckland   Bogotá   Düsseldorf   Johannesburg
London   Madrid   Mexico   Montreal   New Delhi   Panama   Paris   São Paulo
Singapore   Sydney   Tokyo   Toronto

Library of Congress Cataloging in Publication Data

Steers, Richard M   comp.
    Motivation and work behavior.

    (McGraw-Hill series in management)
    Includes index.
        1.   Employee motivation—Addresses, essays,
lectures.   2.   Psychology, Industrial—Addresses,
essays, lectures.   I.   Porter, Lyman W.   II.   Title.
HF5549.5.M63S73   1979   658.31′4   78–17142
ISBN 0–07–060941–1

MOTIVATION AND WORK BEHAVIOR

1 2 3 4 5 6 7 8 9 0   FGRFGR   7 8 3 2 1 0 9 8

This book was set in Times Roman by Offset Composition Services, Inc. The editor was William J. Kane; the cover was designed by Scott Chelius; the production supervisor was Donna Piligra.

Fairfield Graphics was printer and binder.

Contents

2

CONTEMPORARY THEORIES AND RESEARCH

3

CENTRAL ISSUES IN MOTIVATION AT WORK

4

MOTIVATION THEORY IN PERSPECTIVE

Preface

Interest in the topic of motivation in work organizations has escalated dramatically in recent years. If we consider the level of knowledge and research in the area just over 20 years ago, we can see that it largely consisted of classic, though singular, efforts to set forth some basic theoretical generalizations based on only fragmentary research data. Beginning in the early 1960s, however, interest in motivational problems of organizations increased significantly, and this trend has continued through the 1970s. It is difficult to pick up a current research journal in organizational behavior, industrial psychology, or the general area of management without finding at least one selection dealing with motivational problems at work.

Such intense interest in the field is a healthy sign that increased knowledge will be gained on this important topic. Simultaneously, however, a potential problem exists in ensuring that the various research efforts are somehow integrated and synthesized so that we can maximize our understanding of the main issues involved. This book is largely the result of our concern for this potential problem. Several major theories of motivation have been "floating around" over the past decade, but few attempts have been made to study them in a comparative fashion. Moreover, while a great deal has been written concerning the relation of motivational processes to various other important organizational factors (such as job design, group dynamics, and so on), this literature has also been largely fragmentary. Our hope in organizing this book, then, is to bring together in one volume the major contemporary theories, research, and applications in the area of motivation and work behavior.

It is our belief that a thorough knowledge of motivation as it affects organizational processes requires at least three important inputs. First, the reader must gain a general knowledge of what is meant by the concept of motivation, as well as of historical approaches to the study of motivation. Moreover, the reader needs a fairly comprehensive framework for analyzing the various theories and applications that exist. We have attempted to deal with these matters in Part One of the book. Second, it is our contention that the serious student of motivation must be conversant with the major theories that exist in the field today. These theories—and the research associated with them—are described in Part Two. This section has been enhanced in the second edition by the addition of a chapter on behavior modification in organizations. Finally, we feel that theories alone are of little value unless the student can understand how motivational processes relate to other organizational variables. Such interrelationships are covered in detail in Parts Three and Four. In Part Three of this second edition, greater attention has been given to the role of group processes (including the role of leadership) in organizational behavior. Moreover, the chapter on Attachment to Organizations now contains models of both the turnover and absenteeism process. Part Four then attempts to review and synthesize what has been learned concerning the role of motivation in organizational settings.

Throughout the second edition, readings have been updated. This second edition includes 23 new selections. Moreover, the text has also been updated and expanded somewhat.

The approach taken here is to integrate text materials with selections authored by some of the foremost scholars in the field. The major focus in the text and readings is on a blend of theoretical formulations with practical applications. Thus, chapters generally contain some major theoretical propositions, some research evidence relevant to the theories, and some examples of how such models have been or could be applied in existing organizations. Furthermore, each chapter contains suggested additional readings for students desiring a greater in-depth study of a particular topic, as well as questions to stimulate discussion and analysis of the major issues.

This book is designed primarily for students of organizational behavior, industrial psychology, and general management. It should also be useful for managers who wish to gain an increased understanding of problems of work motivation. It is assumed that the reader has had some previous exposure to organizational behavior, perhaps through an introductory course. This book attempts to build upon such knowledge and to analyze general organizational processes, using the concept of motivation as the basic unit of analysis.

We wish to express our sincere appreciation to all those who have contributed to the realization of this project. In particular, our thanks go to Daniel N. Braunstein, Keith Davis, Richard T. Mowday, and Eugene F. Stone for their helpful comments and suggestions on earlier drafts of the manuscript. We are also indebted to Mary Beth Corrigan, Daniel G. Spencer, Thom McDade, and Dorothy Wynkoop for their valuable assistance in preparing the manuscript for publication. In addition, we are grateful to our respective schools, the University of Oregon and the University of California, Irvine, for providing stimulating motivational environments in which to work. Finally, a special note of appreciation is due our wives, Sheila and Meredith, for their support and encouragement throughout the project.

Richard M. Steers
Lyman W. Porter

Part One

Initial Considerations

Chapter 1

The Role of Motivation in Organizations

The topic of motivation at work has received considerable and sustained attention in recent years among both practicing managers and organizational researchers. One has only to ask first-level supervisors what their most taxing work problems are for evidence of the importance of the concept to management. Likewise one can observe the large number of empirical articles relating to the topic in psychological and management journals for evidence of its importance to researchers. Several factors appear to account for the prominence of this topic as a focal point of interest.

To begin with, managers and organizational researchers cannot avoid a concern with the *behavioral* requirements of an organization. In addition to the necessity to acquire financial and physical resources, every organization needs people in order to function. More specifically, Katz and Kahn (1966) have posited that organizations have three behavioral requirements in this regard: (1) people must be attracted not only to join the organization but also to remain in it; (2) people must perform the tasks for which they are hired, and must do so in a dependable manner; and (3) people must go beyond this dependable role performance and engage in some form of creative, spontaneous, and innovative behavior at work (Katz, 1964; Katz & Kahn, 1966). In other words, for an organization to be effective, according to this reasoning, it must come to grips with the motivational problems of stimulating both the decision to participate and the decision to produce at work (March & Simon, 1958).

A second and related reason behind the attention directed toward motivation centers around the pervasive nature of the concept itself. Motivation as a concept represents a highly complex phenomenon that affects, and is affected by, a multitude of factors in the organizational milieu. A comprehensive understanding of the way in which organizations function requires that at least some attention be directed toward the question of why people behave as they do on the job (that is, the determinants of employee work behavior *and* the ramifications of such behavior for an organization). An understanding of the topic of motivation is thus essential in order to comprehend more fully the effects of variations in other factors (such as leadership style, job redesign, and salary systems) as they relate to performance, satisfaction, and so forth.

Third, given the ever-tightening constraints placed on organizations by unions, governmental agencies, increased foreign and domestic competition, citizens' lobbies, and the like, management has had to look for new mechanisms to increase—and in some cases just to maintain—its level of organizational effectiveness and efficiency. Much of the "slack" that organizations could depend upon in the past is rapidly disappearing in the face of these new environmental type of constraints. Because of this, management must ensure that it is deriving full potential benefit from those resources—including human resources—that it does have at its disposal. Thus, organizational effectiveness becomes to some degree a question of management's ability to motivate its employees to direct at least a reasonable effort toward the goals of the organization.

A fourth reason can be found in the nature of present and future technology required for production. As technology increases in complexity, machines tend to become necessary *yet insufficient* vehicles of effective and efficient operations. Modern technology can no longer be considered synonomous with the term "automation." Consider the example of the highly technologically based space program in the United States. While mastery of the technological and mechanical aspects of aerospace engineering was requisite for placing a man on the moon or for developing Skylab, a second and equally important ingredient was the ability of an organization (in this case NASA) to bring together thousands of employees who would work at peak capacity to *apply* the technology required for success. In other words, it becomes necessary for an organization to ensure that it has employees who are both capable of using—*and willing to use*—the advanced technology to achieve organizational objectives.

Finally, while organizations have for some time viewed their financial and physical resources from a long-term perspective, only recently have they begun seriously to apply this same perspective to their human resources. Many organizations are now beginning to pay increasing attention to developing their employees as future resources (a "talent bank") upon which they can draw as they grow and develop. Evidence for such concern can be seen in the recent growth of management and organization development programs, in the increased popularity of "assessment center" appraisals, in recent attention to manpower planning, and in the emergence of "human resource accounting" systems. More concern is being directed, in addition, toward stimulating employees to enlarge their job skills (through training, job design, job rotation, and so on) at both the blue-collar and the white-collar levels in an effort to ensure a continual reservoir of well-trained and highly motivated people.

In summary, then, there appear to be several reasons why the topic of motivation has been receiving increased attention by both those who study organizations and those who manage them. The old simplistic, prescriptive guidelines concerning "economic man" are simply no longer sufficient as a basis for understanding human behavior at work. New approaches and greater understanding are called for to deal with the complexities of contemporary organizations.

Toward this end, this book will attempt to assist the serious student of motivation to obtain a more comprehensive and empirically based knowledge of motivation at work. This will be done through a combination of explanatory text and readings on current theories, research, and applications in the field. Before discussing some of the more current approaches to motivation, however, some consideration is in order concerning the nature of basic motivational processes. This consideration is followed by a brief history of early psychological and managerial approaches to the topic. Finally, a conceptual framework is presented to aid in the comprehension and evaluation of the various theories and models that follow. Throughout this book, emphasis is placed on the comparative approach; that is, we are primarily concerned with similarities among—and differences between—the various theories and models rather than with the presentation and defense of one particular theory. Moreover, because of the pervasive nature of the topic, we feel that the concept of motivation can best be understood only by considering its role as it affects—and is affected by—other important variables which constitute the work environment. Thus, special emphasis is placed throughout on the study of *relationships* between major variables (for example, motivation as it relates to job design and the work environment) rather than on the simple enumeration of facts or theories.

THE NATURE OF MOTIVATION

The term "motivation" was originally derived from the Latin word *movere*, which means "to move." However, this one word is obviously an inadequate definition for our purposes here. What is needed is a description which sufficiently covers the various aspects inherent in the process by which human behavior is activated. A brief selection of representative definitions indicates how the term has been used:

> . . . the contemporary (immediate) influences on the direction, vigor, and persistence of action. (Atkinson, 1964)
> . . . how behavior gets started, is energized, is sustained, is directed, is stopped,

and what kind of subjective reaction is present in the organism while all this is going on. (Jones, 1955)

. . . a process governing choices made by persons or lower organisms among alternative forms of voluntary activity. (Vroom, 1964)

. . . motivation has to do with a set of independent/dependent variable relationships that explain the direction, amplitude, and persistence of an individual's behavior, holding constant the effects of aptitude, skill, and understanding of the task, and the constraints operating in the environment. (Campbell & Pritchard, 1976)

These definitions appear generally to have three common denominators which may be said to characterize the phenomenon of motivation. That is, when we discuss motivation, we are primarily concerned with: (1) what energizes human behavior; (2) what directs or channels such behavior; and (3) how this behavior is maintained or sustained. Each of these three components represents an important factor in our understanding of human behavior at work. First, this conceptualization points to energetic forces within individuals that "drive" them to behave in certain ways and to environmental forces that often trigger these drives. Second, there is the notion of goal orientation on the part of individuals; their behavior is directed *toward* something. Third, this way of viewing motivation contains a *systems orientation*; that is, it considers those forces in the individuals and in their surrounding environments that feed back to the individuals either to reinforce the intensity of their drive and the direction of their energy or to dissuade them from their course of action and redirect their efforts. These three components of motivation appear again and again in the theories and research that follow.

THE MOTIVATIONAL PROCESS: BASIC CONSIDERATIONS

Building upon this definition, we can now diagram a *general* model of the motivational process. While such a model is an oversimplification of far more complex relationships, it should serve here to represent schematically the major sets of variables involved in the process. Later, we can add to this model to depict how additional factors may affect human behavior at work.

The basic building blocks of a generalized model of motivation are: (1) needs or expectations; (2) behavior; (3) goals; and (4) some form of feedback. The interaction of these variables is shown in Exhibit 1. Basically, this model posits that individuals possess in varying strengths a multitude of needs, desires, and expectations. For example, they may have a high need for affiliation, a strong desire for additional income, or an expectation that increased effort on the job would lead to a promotion. These "activators" are generally characterized by two phenomena. First, the emergence of such a need, desire, or expectation generally creates a state of disequilibrium within the individuals which they will try to reduce; hence, the energetic component of our definition above. Second, the presence of such needs, desires, or expectations is generally associated with an anticipation or belief that certain actions will lead to the

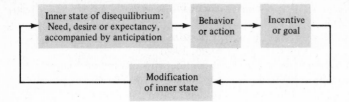

Exhibit 1   A generalized model of the basic motivation process. (*After Dunnette & Kirchner, 1965.*)

reduction of this disequilibrium; hence, the goal-orientation component of our definition.

In theory, the following is presumed to be the chain of events: Based on some combination of this desire to reduce the internal state of disequilibrium and the anticipation or belief that certain actions should serve this purpose, individuals act or behave in a certain manner that they believe will lead to the desired goal. The initiation of this action then sets up a series of cues, either within the individuals or from their external environment, which feeds information back to the individuals concerning the impact of their behavior. Such cues may lead them to modify (or cease) their present behavior or they may reassure them that their present course of action is correct.

An example should clarify this process. Individuals who have a strong desire to be with others (that is, have a high "need for affiliation") may attempt to increase their interactions with those around them (behavior) in the hope of gaining their friendship and support (goal). Based on these interactions, they may eventually reach a point where they feel they have enough friends and may then direct their energies toward other goals. Or, conversely, they may receive consistent negative feedback that informs them that their behavior is not successful for goal attainment and they may then decide to modify such behavior. In either case, we can see the important moderating function of feedback on subsequent behavior and goals.

The general model of the motivational process appears fairly simple and straightforward. Such is not the case, however. Several complexities exist which tend to complicate the theoretical simplicity. Dunnette and Kirchner (1965) and others have identified four such complications. First, motives can really only be *inferred*; they cannot be seen. Thus, when we observe individuals putting in a great deal of overtime, we really do not know whether they are doing it because of the extra income they receive or simply because they enjoy their work. In fact, at least five reasons have been identified for why it is difficult to infer motives from observed behavior: (1) any single act may express several motives; (2) motives may appear in disguised forms; (3) several motives may be expressed through similar or identical acts; (4) similar motives may be expressed in different behavior; and (5) cultural and personal variations may significantly moderate the modes of expression of certain motives (Hilgard & Atkinson, 1967).

A second complication of the model centers around the dynamic nature of motives. Any individual at any one time usually has a host of needs, desires, and expectations. Not only do these motives change but they may also be in conflict with each other. A desire to put in extra hours at the office to "get ahead" may be in direct conflict with a desire to spend more time with one's family. Thus, given the changing nature of an individual's particular set of motives, and given their often conflicting nature, it becomes exceedingly difficult to observe or measure them with much certainty.

Third, considerable differences can exist among individuals concerning the manner in which they select certain motives over others and the intensity with which they pursue such motives. A salesperson who has a strong need for achievement may in large measure satisfy this need by one big sale and then turn his or her attention to other needs or desires. A second salesperson, however, may be spurred on by such a sale to increase his or her achievement motive and to try for an even bigger sale in the near future. Or, as found by Atkinson and Reitman (1956), a high need for achievement may be related to performance only when certain other needs (such as need for affiliation) were not aroused. In other words, it is important to realize that individual differences exist among employees which can significantly affect what they desire and how they pursue such desires.

A final complication of the model is the impact of goal attainment on subsequent motives and behavior. The intensity of certain motives (such as hunger, thirst, sex) is generally considerably reduced upon gratification. When this happens, other motives come to the forefront as primary motivating factors. However, the attainment of certain other goals may lead to an *increase* in the intensity of some motives. For example, as Herzberg, Mausner, and Snyderman (1959) and others have argued, giving a person a pay raise does not long "satisfy" the desire for more money; in fact, it may even heighten this desire. Similarly, promoting an employee to a new and more challenging job may intensify the drive to work harder in anticipation of the *next* promotion. Thus, while the gratification of certain needs, desires, and expectations may at times lead individuals to shift their focus of attention toward different motives, at other times such gratification can serve to increase the strength of the motive.

In conclusion, it must be remembered that the above description of motivational processes represents a very general model of human behavior. As will be seen in the following chapters, considerable research has been done in an attempt to more rigorously define the nature of the relationships between the major variables in this process, particularly as they relate to behavior in the work situation. We have reviewed this general model in an effort to provide a basic framework for the understanding and analysis of the more specific theories that follow. However, before proceeding with these theories, we shall first review very briefly some early psychological approaches to motivation, and then follow our review with a discussion of some traditional management approaches to motivating employees.

PSYCHOLOGICAL APPROACHES TO MOTIVATION

Most psychological theories of motivation, both early and contemporary, have their roots—at least to some extent—in the principle of *hedonism*.[1] This principle, briefly defined, states that individuals tend to seek pleasure and avoid pain. Hedonism assumes a certain degree of conscious behavior on the part of individuals whereby they make intentional decisions or choices concerning future actions. In theory, people rationally consider the behavioral alternatives available to them and act to maximize positive results and to minimize negative results. The concept of hedonism dates back to the early Greek philosophers; it later reemerged as a popular explanation of behavior in the eighteenth and nineteenth centuries, as seen in the works of such philosophers as Locke, Bentham, Mill, and Helvetius. Bentham even went so far as to coin the term "hedonic calculus" in 1789 to describe the process by which individuals calculate the pros and cons of various acts of behavior.

Toward the end of the nineteenth century, motivation theory began moving from the realm of philosophy toward the more empirically based science of psychology. As consideration of this important topic grew, it became apparent to those who attempted to use the philosophically based concept of hedonism that several serious problems existed. Vroom explained this dilemma as follows:

> There was in the doctrine no clear-cut specification of the type of events which were pleasurable or painful, or even how these events could be determined for a particular individual; nor did it make clear how persons acquired their conceptions of ways of attaining pleasure and pain, or how the source of pleasure and pain might be modified by experience. In short the hedonistic assumption has no empirical content and was untestable. Any form of behavior could be explained, after the fact, by postulating particular sources of pleasure or pain, but no form of behavior could be predicted in advance [1964, p. 10].

In an effort to fill in this void, several theories of motivation began evolving which attempted to formulate empirically verifiable relationships among sets of variables which could be used to predict behavior. The earliest such theory centered around the concept of instinct.

Instinct Theories

While not rejecting the notion of hedonism, psychologists like James, Freud, and McDougall argued that a more comprehensive explanation of behavior was necessary than simply assuming a rational person pursuing his or her own best interest. In short, they posited that two additional variables were crucial to our understanding of behavior: instinct and unconscious motivation.

Instead of seeing behavior as being highly rational, these theorists saw much of it as resulting from instinct. McDougall, writing in 1908, defined an

[1]For a more detailed discussion of early psychological models of motivation, see Cofer & Appley (1964) and Atkinson (1964).

instinct as "an inherited or innate psychophysical disposition which determines its possessor to perceive, or pay attention to, objects of a certain class, to experience an emotional excitement of a particular quality upon perceiving such an object, and to act in regard to it in a particular manner, or at least, to experience an impulse to such an action." However, while McDougall saw instinct as purposive and goal directed, other instinct theorists, like James, defined the concept more in terms of blind and mechanical action. James (1890) included in his list of instincts the following; locomotion, curiosity, sociability, love, fear, jealousy, and sympathy. Each person was thought by James and McDougall to have such instincts in greater or lesser degree and these instincts were thought to be the prime determinants of behavior. In other words, individuals were seen as possessing automatic *predispositions* to behave in certain ways, depending on internal and external cues.

The second major concept associated with instinct theories is that of unconscious motivation. While the notion of unconscious motivation is implicit in the writings of James, it was Freud (1915) who most ardently advocated the existence of such a phenomenon. Based upon his clinical observations, Freud argued that the most potent behavioral tendencies were not necessarily those that individuals *consciously* determined would be in their best interests. Individuals were not always aware of all of their desires and needs. Rather, such unconscious phenomena as dreams, slips of the tongue ("Freudian slips"), and neurotic symptoms were seen by Freud as manifestations of the hedonistic principle on an *unconscious* level. Thus, a major factor in human motivation was seen here as resulting from forces unknown even to the individual himself.

The instinct theory of motivation was fairly widely accepted during the first quarter of this century. Then, beginning in the early 1920s, it came under increasing attack on several grounds (Hilgard & Atkinson, 1967; Morgan & King, 1966). First, there was the disturbing fact that the list of instincts continued to grow, reaching nearly six thousand in number. The sheer length of such a list seriously jeopardized any attempt at parsimony in the explanation of motivation. Second, the contention that individuals varied greatly in the strengths or intensities of their motivational dispositions was becoming increasingly accepted among psychologists, adding a further complication to the ability of instinct theory to fully explain behavior. Third, some researchers found that at times there may be little relation between the strengths of certain motives and subsequent behavior. Fourth, some psychologists came to question whether the unconscious motives as described by Freud were really instinctive or whether they were *learned* behavior. In fact, this fourth criticism formed the basis of the second "school" of motivation theorists who later became known as "drive" theorists.

Drive and Reinforcement Theories

Researchers who have been associated with drive theory typically base their work on the influence that learning has on subsequent behavior. Thus, such theories have a historical component which led Allport (1954) to refer to them as "hedonism of the past"; that is, drive theories generally assume that decisions concerning present behavior are based in large part on the consequences or rewards of past behavior. Where past actions led to positive consequences, individuals would tend to repeat such actions; where past actions led to negative consequences or punishment, individuals would tend to avoid repeating them. This position was first elaborated by Thorndike in his "law of effect." Basing his "law" on experimental observations of animal behavior, Thorndike posited:

> Of several responses made to the same situation, those which are accompanied or closely followed by satisfaction to the animal will, other things being equal, be more firmly connected with the situation, so that when it recurs, they will be more likely to occur; those which are accompanied or closely followed by discomfort to the animal will, other things being equal, have their connections with that situation weakened, so that when it recurs, they will be less likely to occur. The greater the satisfaction or discomfort, the greater is the strengthening or weakening of the bond [1911, p. 244].

While this law of effect did not explain why some actions were pleasurable or satisfying and others were not, it did go a long way toward setting forth an empirically verifiable theory of motivation. Past learning and previous "stimulus-response" connections were viewed as the major causal variables of behavior.

The term "drive" was first introduced by Woodworth (1918) to describe the reservoir of energy that impels an organism to behave in certain ways. While Woodworth intended the term to mean a general supply of energy within an organism, others soon modified this definition to refer to a host of specific energizers (such as hunger, thirst, sex) toward or away from certain goals. With the introduction of the concept of drive, it now became possible for psychologists to predict in advance—at least in theory—not only what goals an individual would strive toward but also the strength of the motivation toward such goals. Thus, it became feasible for researchers to attempt to test the theory in a fairly rigorous fashion, a task that was virtually impossible for the earlier theories of hedonism and instinct.

A major theoretical advance in drive theory came from the work of Cannon in the early 1930s. Cannon (1939) introduced the concept of "homeostasis" to describe a state of disequilibrium within an organism which existed whenever internal conditions deviated from their normal state. When such disequilibrium occurred (as when an organism felt hunger), the organism was motivated by internal drives to reduce the disequilibrium and to return to its normal state. Inherent in Cannon's notion was the idea that organisms exist in a dynamic environment and that the determining motives for behavior constantly change, depending upon where the disequilibrium exists within the system. Thus, certain drives, or motives, may move to the forefront and then, once satisfied, retreat while other drives become paramount. This concept can be seen to a large extent in the later works of Maslow and Murray (see Chapter 2).

The first comprehensive—and experimentally specific—elaboration of drive theory was put forth by Hull. In his major work *Principles of Behavior*, published in 1943, Hull set down a specific equation to explain an organism's "impetus to respond": Effort = Drive × Habit. "Drive" was defined by Hull as an energizing influence which determined the intensity of behavior, and which theoretically increased along with the level of deprivation. "Habit" was seen as the strength of relationship between past stimulus and response (S-R). Hull hypothesized that habit strength depended not only upon the closeness of the S-R event to reinforcement but also upon the magnitude and number of such reinforcements. Thus, Hull's concept of habit draws very heavily upon Thorndike's law of effect. Hull argued that resulting effort, or motivational force, was a *multiplicative* function of these two central variables.

If we apply Hull's theory to an organization setting, we can use the following example to clarify how drive theory would be used to predict behavior. A person who has been out of work for some time (high deprivation level) would generally have a strong need or desire to seek some means to support himself or herself (goal). If, based upon *previous* experience, this person draws a close association between the securing of income and the act of taking a job, we would expect him or her to search ardently for employment. Thus, the motivation to seek employment would be seen, according to this theory, as a multiplicative function of the intensity of the need for money (drive) and the strength of the feeling that work has been associated with the receipt of money in the past (habit).

Later, in response to empirical evidence which was inconsistent with the theory, Hull (1952) modified his position somewhat. Instead of positing that behavior was wholly a function of antecedent conditions (such as past experiences), he added an incentive variable to his equation. His later formulation thus read: Effort = Drive × Habit × Incentive. This incentive factor, added in large measure in response to the attack by the cognitive theorists (see below), was defined in terms of anticipatory reactions to future goals. It was thus hypothesized that one factor in the motivation equation was the size of, or attraction to, future potential rewards. As the size of the reward varied, so too would the motivation to seek such a reward. This major revision by Hull (as amplified by Spence, 1956) brought drive theory into fairly close agreement with the third major category of motivational theories, the cognitive theories. However, while cognitive theories have generally been applied to humans, including humans at work, drive theory research has continued by and large to study animal behavior in the laboratory.

Just as drive theory draws upon Thorndike's "law of effect," so do modern reinforcement approaches (e.g., Skinner, 1953). The difference is that the former theory emphasizes an internal state (i.e., drive) as a necessary variable to take into account, while reinforcement theory does not. Rather, the reinforcement model places total emphasis on the *consequences* of behavior. Behavior initiated by the individual (for whatever reason) that produces an effect or consequence is called *operant* behavior (i.e., the individual has "operated" on the environment), and the theory deals with the contingent relationships between this operant behavior and the pattern of consequences. It ignores the inner state of the individual and concentrates solely on what happens to a person when he or she takes some action. Thus, strictly speaking, reinforcement theory is not a theory of motivation because it does not concern itself with what energizes or initiates behavior. Nevertheless, since a reinforcement approach provides a powerful means of analysis of what controls behavior (its direction and maintenance), it is typically considered in discussions of motivation and will be given prominent attention later in this book (Chapter 4).

Cognitive Theories

The third major line of development in psychological approaches to motivation is the cognitive theories. Whereas drive theories viewed behavior largely as a function of what happened in the past, cognitive theories saw motivation as a sort of "hedonism of the future." The basic tenet of this theory is that a major determinant of human behavior is the beliefs, expectations, and anticipations individuals have concerning future events. Behavior is thus seen as purposeful and goal directed, and based on conscious intentions.

Two of the most prominent early researchers in this field were Edward Tolman and Kurt Lewin. While Tolman studied animal behavior and Lewin human behavior, both took the position that organisms make conscious decisions concerning future behavior based on cues from their environment. Such a theory is largely *ahistorical* in nature, as opposed to the historical notion inherent in drive theory. Tolman (1932) argued, for example, that learning resulted more from changes in beliefs about the environment than from changes in the strengths of past habits. Cognitive theorists did not entirely reject the concept that past events may be important for present behavior, however. Lewin (1938), whose work is characterized by an ahistorical approach, noted that the historical and ahistorical approaches were in some ways complementary. Past occurrences could have an impact on present behavior to the extent that they modified present conditions. For example, the past experience of a child who burned a finger on a hot stove may very likely carry over into the present to influence behavior. In general, however, the cognitive theorists posit that it is the "events of the day" that largely influence behavior; past events are important only to the extent that they affect present and future beliefs and expectations.

In general, cognitive theories, or expectancy/valence theories as they later became known (see Chapter 5), view motivational force as a multiplicative function of two key variables: expectancies and valences. "Expectancies" were seen by Lewin (1938) and Tolman (1959) as beliefs individuals had that particular actions on their part would lead to certain outcomes. "Valence" denoted the amount of positive or negative value placed on the outcomes by an individual. Individuals were viewed as engaging in some form of choice behavior where they first determined the potential outcomes of various acts of behavior and the value they attached to each of these outcomes. Tolman (1959) refers to this as a "belief-value matrix." Next, individuals selected that mode of behavior which maximized their potential benefits. When put into equation form, such a formulation reads: Effort = Expectancy $\times$ Valence.

This conceptualization of the motivational process differs from drive theory in several respects. First, as has already been mentioned, while drive theory emphasizes past stimulus-response connections in the determination of present behavior, expectancy/valence theory stresses anticipation of response-outcome connections.

Second, as pointed out by Atkinson (1964), a difference exists between the two theories with regard to what is activated by a drive (in drive theory) or expectation (in expectancy/valence theory). In drive theory, the magnitude of the goal is seen as a source of *general* excitement; that is, it represents a nonselective influence on performance. In expectancy/valence theory, on the other hand, *positively* valent outcomes are seen as acting *selectively* to stimulate particular forms of behavior that should lead to these outcomes.

Third, a subtle difference exists concerning the nature in which outcomes and rewards acquire their positive or negative connotations. This difference has been described by Porter and Lawler as follows:

> For drive theory, this has traditionally come about through their ability to reduce the tension associated with the deprivation of certain physiologically based drives. It also states that some outcomes acquire their rewarding or adverse properties through their association with primary reinforcers. Outcomes that gain their values this way are typically referred to as secondary reinforcers. Expectancy theory has been much less explicit on this point. However, expectancy theorists seem typically to have included more than just physiological factors as determinants of valence. For example, needs for esteem, recognition, and self-actualization have been talked about by expectancy theory with explaining performance. Drive theory, on the other hand, has focused largely on learning rather than performance and has not found it necessary to deal with motives like self-actualization in order to explain this learning [1968, p. 11].

However, while several differences can thus be found between drive theories and cognitive theories, Atkinson (1964) has emphasized that the two approaches actually share many of the same concepts. Both stress the importance of some form of goal orientation; that is, both posit the existence of some reward or outcome that is desired and sought. Moreover, both theories include the notion of a learned connection between central variables; drive theory posits a learned stimulus-response association, while cognitive theories see a learned association between behavior and outcome.

Just as there has been an evolutionary process in psychological theories of motivation, so too have there been major developments and trends in the way managers in work organizations approach motivation in the work situation. With these general psychological theories in mind, we shall now shift our attention to the workplace and review some of these early managerial approaches to motivating employees. It will be noted in the discussion below that, although psychological and managerial models of motivation developed, roughly, during the same period, there are few signs of any cross-fertilization of ideas until very recently.

MANAGERIAL APPROACHES TO MOTIVATION AT WORK

Despite the fact that large-scale, complex organizations have existed for several hundreds of years, managerial attention to the role of motivation in such organizations is a most recent phenomenon. Before the industrial revolution, the major form of "motivation" took the form of fear of punishment—physical, financial, or social. However, as manufacturing processes became more complex, large-scale factories emerged which destroyed many of the social and exchange relationships which had existed under the "home industries," or "putting-out," system of small manufacturing. These traditional patterns of behavior between workers and their "patron" were replaced by the more sterile and tenuous relationship between employees and their company. Thus, the industrial revolution was not only a revolution in a production sense but also in a social sense.

The genesis of this *social* revolution can be traced to several factors. First, the increased capital investment necessary for factory operation required a high degree of efficiency in order to maintain an adequate return on investment. This meant that an organization had to have an efficient work force. Second, and somewhat relatedly, the sheer size of these new operations increased the degree of impersonalization in superior-subordinate relationships, necessitating new forms of supervising people. Third, and partly as a justification of the new depersonalized factory system, the concept of social Darwinism came into vogue. In brief, this philosophy argued that no person held responsibility for other people and that naturally superior people were destined to rise in society, while naturally inferior ones would eventually be selected out of it. In other words, it was "every man for himself" in the workplace.

These new social forces brought about the need for a fairly well-defined *philosophy* of management. Many of the more intrinsic motivational factors of the home industry system were replaced by more extrinsic factors. Workers— or, more specifically, "good" workers—were seen as pursuing their own best economic self-interests. The end result of this new approach in management was what has been termed the "traditional" model of motivation.

Traditional Model

This model is best characterized by the writings of Frederick W. Taylor (1911) and his associates in the scientific management school. Far from being exploitative in intent, these writers viewed scientific management as an economic boon to the worker as well as to management. Taylor saw the problem of inefficient production as a problem primarily with management, not workers. It was management's responsibility to find suitable people for a job and then to train them in the most efficient methods for their work. The workers having been thus well trained, management's next responsibility was to install a wage incentive system whereby workers could maximize their income by doing exactly what management told them to do and doing it as rapidly as possible. Thus, in theory, scientific management represented a joint venture of management and workers to the mutual benefit of both. If production problems arose, they could be solved either by altering the technology of the job or by modifying the wage incentive program.

This approach to motivation rested on several very basic contemporary assumptions about the nature of human beings. Specifically, workers were viewed as being typically lazy, often dishonest, aimless, dull, and, most of all, mercenary. To get them into the factories and to keep them there, an organization had to pay a "decent" wage, thus outbidding alternative forms of livelihood (e.g., farming). To get workers to produce, tasks were to be simple and repetitive, output controls were to be externally set, and workers were to be paid bonuses for beating their quotas. The manager's major task was thus seen as closely supervising workers to ensure that they met their production quotas and adhered to company rules. In short, the underlying motivational assumption of the traditional model was that, for a price, workers would tolerate the routinized, highly fractionated jobs of the factory. These assumptions and expectations, along with their implied managerial strategies, are summarized in Exhibit 2.

As this model became increasingly applied in organizations, several problems began to arise. To begin with, managers, in their quest for profits, began modifying the basic system. While jobs were made more and more routine and specialized (and "efficient" from a mass-production standpoint), management began putting severe constraints on the incentive system, thereby limiting worker income. Soon, workers discovered that, although their output was increasing, their wages were not (at least not proportionately). Simultaneously, fear of job security arose. As factories became more "efficient," fewer workers were needed to do the job and layoffs and terminations became commonplace. Workers responded to the situation through elaborate and covert methods of restriction of output in an attempt to optimize their incomes, while at the same time protecting their jobs. Unionism began to rise, and the unparalleled growth and efficiency that had occurred under scientific management began to subside.

In an effort to overcome such problems, some organizations began to reexamine the simplicity of their motivational assumptions about employees and to look for new methods to increase production and maintain a steady work force. It should be pointed out, however, that the primary economic assumption of the traditional model was not eliminated in the newer approaches and that it remains a central concept of many motivational approaches today. Recent studies among both managers and workers indicate that money is a primary motivational force and that many workers will, in fact, select jobs based more upon salary prospects than job content (Mahoney, 1964; Opinion Research Corporation, 1947; Opsahl & Dunnette, 1966). (See Chapter 11.) However,

Exhibit 2   General Patterns of Managerial Approaches to Motivation (*After Miles, Porter, & Craft, 1966*)

Traditional model	Human relations model	Human resources model
Assumptions	**Assumptions**	**Assumptions**
1 Work is inherently distasteful to most people.	1 People want to feel useful and important.	1 Work is not inherently distasteful. People want to contribute to meaningful goals which they have helped establish.
2 What they do is less important than what they earn for doing it.	2 People desire to belong and to be recognized as individuals.	
3 Few want or can handle work which requires creativity, self-direction, or self-control.	3 These needs are more important than money in motivating people to work.	2 Most people can exercise far more creative, responsible self-direction and self-control than their present jobs demand.
Policies	**Policies**	**Policies**
1 The manager's basic task is to closely supervise and control subordinates.	1 The manager's basic task is to make each worker feel useful and important.	1 The manager's basic task is to make use of "untapped" human resources.
2 He or she must break tasks down into simple, repetitive, easily learned operations.	2 He or she should keep subordinates informed and listen to their objections to his plans.	2 He or she must create an environment in which all members may contribute to the limits of their ability.
3 He or she must establish detailed work routines and procedures, and enforce these firmly but fairly.	3 The manager should allow subordinates to exercise some self-direction and self-control on routine matters.	3 He or she must encourage full participation on important matters, continually broadening subordinate self-direction and control.
Expectations	**Expectations**	**Expectations**
1 People can tolerate work if the pay is decent and the boss is fair.	1 Sharing information with subordinates and involving them in routine decisions will satisfy their basic needs to belong and to feel important.	1 Expanding subordinate influence, self-direction, and self-control will lead to direct improvements in operating efficiency.
2 If tasks are simple enough and people are closely controlled, they will produce up to standard.	2 Satisfying these needs will improve morale and reduce resistance to formal authority— subordinates will "willingly cooperate."	2 Work satisfaction may improve as a "by-product" of subordinates making full use of their resources.

newer approaches have tended to view the role of money in more complex terms as it affects motivational force. Moreover, these newer theories argue that additional factors are also important inputs into the decision to produce. One such revisionist approach to motivation at work is the "human relations" model.

Human Relations Model

Beginning in the late 1920s, initial efforts were begun to discover why the traditional model was inadequate for motivating people. The earliest such work, carried out by Mayo (1933, 1945) and Roethlisberger and Dickson (1939), pointed the way to what was to become the human relations school of management by arguing that it was necessary to consider the "whole person" on the job. These researchers posited that the increased routinization of tasks brought about by the industrial revolution had served to drastically reduce the possibilities of finding satisfaction in the task itself. It was believed that, because of this change, workers began seeking satisfaction elsewhere (such as from their fellow workers). Based on this early research, some managers began replacing many of the traditional assumptions with a new set of propositions concerning the nature of human beings (see Exhibit 2). Bendix (1956, p. 294) best summarized this evolution in managerial thinking by noting that the "failure to treat workers as human beings came to be regarded as the cause of low morale, poor craftsmanship, unresponsiveness, and confusion."

The new assumptions concerning the "best" method of motivating workers were characterized by a strong social emphasis. It was argued here that management had a responsibility to make employees *feel* useful and important on the job, to provide recognition, and generally to facilitate the satisfaction of workers' social needs. Attention was shifted away from the study of man-machine relations and toward a more thorough understanding of interpersonal and group relations at work. Behavioral research into factors affecting motivation began in earnest, and morale surveys came into vogue in an attempt to measure and maintain job satisfaction. The basic ingredient that typically was *not* changed was the nature of the required tasks on the job.

The motivational strategies which emerged from such assumptions were several. First, as noted above, management felt it had a new responsibility to make workers feel important. Second, many organizations attempted to open up vertical communication channels so employees would know more about the organization and would have greater opportunity to have their opinions heard by management. Company newsletters emerged as one source of downward communication; employee "gripe sessions" were begun as one source of upward communication. Third, workers were increasingly allowed to make routine decisions concerning their own jobs. Finally, as managers began to realize the existence of informal groups with their own norms and role prescriptions, greater attention was paid to employing *group* incentive systems. Underlying all four of these developments was the presumed necessity of viewing motivation as largely a social process. Supervisory training programs began emphasizing that a supervisor's role was no longer simply that of a taskmaster. In addition, supervisors had to be understanding and sympathetic to the needs and desires of their subordinates. However, as pointed out by Miles (1965), the basic goal of management under this strategy remained much the same as it had been under the traditional model; that is, both strategies aimed at securing employee compliance with managerial authority.

Human Resources Models

More recently, the assumptions of the human relations model have been challenged, not only for being an oversimplified and incomplete statement of human behavior at work, but also for being as manipulative as the traditional model. These newest models have been proposed under various titles, including McGregor's (1960) "Theory Y," Likert's (1967) "System 4," Schein's (1972) "Complex Man," and Miles' (1965) "Human Resources model." We shall adopt the latter term here as being more descriptive of the underlying philosophy inherent in these newer approaches.

Human resources models generally view humans as being motivated by a complex set of interrelated factors (such as money, need for affiliation, need for achievement, desire for meaningful work). It is assumed that different employees often seek quite different goals in a job and have a diversity of talent to offer. Under this conceptualization, employees are looked upon as reservoirs of potential talent and management's responsibility is to learn how best to tap such resources.

Inherent in such a philosophy are several fairly basic assumptions about the nature of people. First, it is assumed that people want to contribute on the job. In this sense, employees are viewed as being somewhat "premotivated" to perform. In fact, the more people become involved in their work, the more meaningful the job can often become. Second, it is assumed that work does not necessarily have to be distasteful. Many of the current efforts at job enrichment and job redesign are aimed at increasing the potential meaningfulness of work by adding greater amounts of task variety, autonomy, responsibility, and so on. Third, it is argued that employees are quite capable of making significant and rational decisions affecting their work and that allowing greater latitude in employee decision making is actually in the best interests of the organization. Finally, it is assumed that this increased self-control and direction allowed on the job, plus the completion of more meaningful tasks, can in large measure determine the level of satisfaction on the job. In other words, it is generally assumed that good and meaningful performance leads to job satisfaction and not the reverse, as is assumed in the human relations model.

Certain implied managerial strategies follow naturally from this set of assumptions. In general, this approach would hold that it is management's responsibility to first understand the complex nature of motivational patterns. Based upon such knowledge, management should attempt to determine how best to use the potential resources available to it through its work force. It should assist employees in meeting some of their own *personal* goals within the organizational context. Moreover, such a philosophy implies a greater degree of participation by employees in relevant decision-making activities, as well as increased autonomy over task accomplishment. Thus, in contrast to the traditional and human relations models, management's task is seen not so much as one of manipulating employees to accept managerial authority as it is of setting up conditions so that employees can meet their own goals at the same time as meeting the organization's goals.

In conclusion, it should be pointed out that the human resources approach to motivation has only lately begun to receive concentrated attention. Many organizations have attempted to implement one or more aspects of it, but full-scale adoptions of such models, including the multitude of strategic implications for managers, are still relatively rare. In fact, when one looks across organizations, it becomes readily apparent that all three models have their advocates, and empirical evidence supportive of a given approach can be offered in defense of one's preferred strategy (Schein, 1972). In recent years, in fact, the notion of a multiple strategy—using all three approaches at one time or another depending upon the nature of the organization, its technology, its people, and its goals and priorities—has come to be labeled a "contingency approach" to management. In effect, a contingency perspective allows one to dispense with the unlikely assumption that a single approach will be equally effective under any and all circumstances, and rather substitutes an emphasis on diagnosis of the situation to determine which approach will be most useful and appropriate under the *particular* circumstances.

A FRAMEWORK FOR ANALYSIS

Before proceeding to a consideration of some of the more highly developed or widely accepted contemporary theories of motivation, we should place this complex topic within some meaningful conceptual framework. Such a framework would serve as a vehicle not only for organizing our thoughts concerning human behavior at work but also for evaluating the ability of each of the theories that follows to deal adequately with all the factors in the work situation. In other words, it should provide a useful beginning for later analyses by pointing to several important factors to look for in the theoretical approaches that follow.

The conceptual model we wish to pose here (after Porter & Miles, 1974) consists of two parts. First, it assumes that motivation is a complex phenomenon that can best be understood within a multivariate framework: that is *several* important—and often quite distinct—factors must be taken into account when explaining motivational processes. Second, the model proposed here argues that these motivationally relevant factors must be viewed within a systems framework; we must concern ourselves with interrelationships and interactive effects among the various factors. It is our belief, then, that a full comprehension of the intricacies of human behavior at work requires the student of motivation to consider both parts of this equation: a multivariate conceptual approach and an integrating systems framework. Let us briefly examine each part of this proposed framework for analysis.

Multivariate Conceptual Approach

If motivation is concerned with those factors which energize, direct, and sustain human behavior, it would appear that a comprehensive theory of motivation at work must address itself to at least three important sets of variables which constitute the work situation. First, some consideration must be given to the characteristics of the individual; second, some thought should be directed toward the behavioral implications of the required job tasks; and third, some concern should be shown for the impact of the larger organizational environment. These three sets of variables, along with examples of each, are depicted in Exhibit 3.

Characteristics of the Individual   The natural starting point for any theory of motivation is the nature of the individual himself. We are concerned here with what the employee *brings to* the work situation. Considerable research (see, for example, Atkinson, 1964; Vroom, 1964) has demonstrated that differences in individuals can at times account for a good deal of the variance in effort and performance on a job. Thus, when we examine the factors comprising the motivational force equation, we must ask how large an input is made by these variations within people themselves. At least three major categories of individual difference characteristics have been shown to affect the motivational process: interests, attitudes, and needs.

"Interests" refers to the direction of one's attention. It appears likely that the nature of an employee's interests would affect both the manner and the extent to which external stimuli (like money) would affect his behavior. Consider the example of two people working side by side on the same job and earning

Exhibit 3   Variable Affecting the Motivational Process in Organizational Settings (*After Porter & Miles,* 1974)

I. Individual characteristics	II. Job characteristics (examples)	III. Work environment characteristics
1 Interests	Types of intrinsic rewards	1 Immediate work environment
2 Attitudes (examples)	Degree of autonomy	• Peers
• Toward self	Amount of direct performance feedback	• Supervisor(s)
• Toward job	Degree of variety in tasks	2 Organizational actions
• Toward aspects of the work situation		• Reward practices
3 Needs (examples)		System-wide rewards
• Security		Individual rewards
• Social		• Organizational climate
• Achievement		

Note: These lists are not intended to be exhaustive, they are meant to indicate some of the more important variables influencing employee motivation.

identical salaries. Person A is highly interested in the work; person B is not. In this example, person A can be seen as "self-motivated" to some degree because he or she is pursuing a central interest (his or her work), and we would expect this person to derive considerable satisfaction from the activity. If person A were offered a pay raise to take a less interesting job, he or she would be faced with making a decision of whether to keep the more interesting job or to earn more money, and it is not inconceivable that the intrinsic rewards of the present job would be motivation enough *not* to accept the transfer. Person B, however, who is not interested in the work, has no such conflict of choice in our simplified example; there is no motivation to stay on the present job and the added income of the new job could be a strong incentive for change. Some empirical research exists in support of our hypothetical example. Several studies have shown that an employee's motivation to participate (stay on the job) is to a large extent determined by the degree of fit between his or her vocational interests and the realities of the job. Thus, interests may be considered one factor that individuals generally bring to the organization that, at least to some extent, can affect how they behave at work.

In addition to interests, employees' attitudes or beliefs may also play an important role in their motivation to perform. Individuals who are very dissatisfied with their jobs, or with their supervisor, or any number of other things, may have little desire to put forth much effort. Several theories of motivation have encompassed the notion of attitudes as they relate to performance behavior at work. For example, Korman (1970, 1971) has proposed a theory of motivation centering around one's attitudes about oneself (that is, one's self-image). This theory posits that individuals attempt to behave in a fashion consistent with their own self-image. If employees see themselves as failures on the job, they will not put forth much effort and their resulting performance will probably be poor. Such action will then reinforce the negative self-image. Two important points can be made here. First, various attitudes (in this case, attitudes about oneself) can play an important role in motivational force to perform. Second, in this example, there is a specific implied managerial strategy to improve employee effort: The manager should attempt to modify the employees' self-image. If the employees in our example were proud to work for the XYZ Company and if they saw themselves as effective contributors to the company's goals, they would, in theory, be more likely to perform at a higher level.

The individual characteristic that has received the most widespread attention in terms of motivation theory and research is the concept of "needs." A need may be defined as an internal state of disequilibrium which causes individuals to pursue certain courses of action in an effort to regain internal equilibrium. For example, individuals who have a high need for achievement might be motivated to engage in competitive acts with others so they can "win," thereby satisfying this need. The theories of Maslow and of McClelland and Atkinson use this concept of need as the basic unit of analysis. While further discussion of these types of theories is reserved for the following chapter, suffice it to say that variations in human needs can be significant factors in the determination of effort and performance.

Characteristics of the Job   A second set of variables to be considered when viewing the motivational process involves those factors relating to the attributes of an individual's job. We are concerned here with what an employee does at work. Factors such as the variety of activities required to do the job, the significance of the tasks, and the type of feedback one receives as a consequence of performing the job all have a role to play in motivation. Later in the book (Chapter 9) a model developed by Hackman and Oldham (1976) will be presented that attempts to provide a theoretical explanation of how these types of job-related variables interact to affect motivation and performance. Other parts of that chapter will provide additional evidence on the role that job design changes can play in determining employee behavior. In effect, whether jobs are designed well or poorly (from either the organization's or the employee's point of view), they are crucial in their impact on the motivational process in the work setting.

Characteristics of the Work Environment   The final set of variables under our analytical framework that appears to be relevant to the motivational process is concerned with the nature of the organizational, or work, environment. Work environment factors can be divided for our purposes into two major categories: those associated with the immediate work environment (the work group), and those associated with the larger problem of organizationwide actions. Both categories, however, focus primarily on *what happens to* the employee at work.

As indicated in Exhibit 3, there are at least two major factors in the immediate work environment which can affect work behavior. The first is the quality of peer-group interactions. Research dating from the Hawthorne studies (Roethlisberger & Dickson, 1939) indicates that peer-group influence can significantly influence an employee's effort. Such influence can occur at both ends of the productivity continuum: peers can exert pressure on "laggards" to contribute their fair share of output, or they can act to curb the high productivity of the "rate-buster." These considerations are discussed in Chapter 8. Similarly, supervisory or leadership style can influence effort and performance under certain circumstances. Immediate supervisors can play an important role in motivation because of their control over desired rewards (such as bonuses, raises, feedback) and because of their central role in the structuring of work activities. In other words, supervisors have considerable influence over the ability or freedom of employees to pursue their own personal goals on the job.

The second major category of work environment variables—organization-wide actions—are concerned with several factors which are common throughout the organization and are largely determined by the organization itself. Such factors would include both systemwide rewards (like fringe benefits) and individual rewards (such as overall salary system and allocation of status). Moreover, the emergent organizational climate that pervades the work environment would also fall into this category (see Chapter 8). Factors such as openness of communication, perceived relative emphasis on rewards versus punishment, degree of interdepartmental cooperation, and so forth, may at times influence individuals' decisions to produce on the job.

Interactive Effects

Based on the foregoing discussion, it becomes apparent that a multitude of variables throughout the organizational milieu can be important inputs into the motivational force equation. Such a conclusion forces us to take a broad perspective when we attempt to understand or explain why employees behave as they do at work. However, this simple enumeration of motivationally relevant factors fails to recognize how these variables may interact with one another within a systems type of framework to determine work behavior. In other words, the second half of our conceptual framework stresses the fact that we must consider motivational models from a dynamic perspective. For example, an individual may have a strong desire to perform well on the job, but he or she may lack a clear understanding of his or her proper role. The employee may thus waste or misdirect effort and thereby fail to receive expected rewards. Similarly, an employee may truly want to perform at a high level, but simply lack the necessary ability for good performance on his or her particular job. The important point here is that, when viewing various approaches to motivation, it becomes clear that one must be aware of the interactive or "system" dynamics between major sets of variables that may influence resulting effort and performance.

Each of the theories of work motivation that will be considered in the following chapters has focused on *at least* one of these three major factors: the individual, the job, or the organizational environment. Several of the theories have included more than one factor. Moreover, some of the more highly developed models have placed such variables within a systems framework and have studied the interactive effects between the major sets of variables. Hopefully, the framework for analysis presented here will aid in understanding the pervasive nature of motivation and in evaluating the adequacy of each of the major theories to explain human behavior at work.

A note of caution is in order, however. When evaluating the theories and the research evidence that follow, the student of motivation must determine whether it is helpful to try to find the "one best way" to motivate individuals in the work situation or whether different approaches may be more or less relevant, depending upon the uses for which the theory is employed. That is, as with theories of management in general, both practicing managers and organizational researchers must decide whether they want to search for an ultimate universal theory of motivation which can be applied in all types of situations, or whether they want to adopt a contingency approach and select that theory which appears most pertinent to the specific problem at hand. In this connection, it is well to keep in mind that many of the theories, concepts, and approaches that will be discussed throughout the book are in fact complementary to one another, and therefore the search for understanding and for practical application is as much one of trying to seek out integration as it is one of making choices.

PLAN OF BOOK

The remainder of this book consists of three parts. Part Two introduces the student to four major contemporary theories of motivation as they relate to the work situation. Each chapter includes an introductory section which lays the foundation for an understanding of the articles that follow. This introduction includes suggested additional readings for the student who wishes to study the subject in greater detail. The particular articles within each chapter have been selected so as to cover not only the theoretical propositions of each model but also to review some of the research associated with each theory. The articles, when taken together, will, it is hoped, present both the strengths and weaknesses of the various theories.

Part Three concentrates on the study of the relationship of motivation to various other important phenomena found in the work situation. Emphasis is placed on interrelationships among various factors (e.g., the relation between job design and motivation), and each chapter presents a broad survey of the relevant theories and research on the topic. Again, introductory material, suggested additional readings, and several theoretical or empirical articles accompany each chapter.

Finally, in Part Four we summarize and integrate what has, hopefully, been learned here. Consideration is given not only to how the various issues in motivation relate to one another, but also how they relate to the broader concerns of organizational behavior. The implications of such information for managerial practice is also discussed.

REFERENCES AND SUGGESTED ADDITIONAL READINGS

Allport, G. W. The historical background of modern social psychology. In G. Lindzey (Ed.), *Handbook of social psychology*. Cambridge, Mass.: Addison-Wesley, 1954.

Atkinson, J. W. *An introduction to motivation*. Princeton, N.J.: Van Nostrand, 1964.

Atkinson, J. W., & Reitman, W. R. Performance as a function of motive strength and expectancy of goal attainment. *Journal of Abnormal Social Psychology*, 1956, **53**, 361–366.

Bendix, R. *Work and authority in industry*. New York: Wiley, 1956.

Campbell, J. P., & Pritchard, R. D. Motivation theory in industrial and organizational psychology. In M. D. Dunnette (Ed.), *Handbook of industrial and organizational psychology*. Chicago: Rand McNally, 1976.

Cannon, W. B. *The wisdom of the body*. New York: Norton, 1939.

Cofer, C. N., & Appley, M. H. *Motivation: Theory and research*. New York: Wiley, 1964.

Dunnette, M. D., & Kirchner, W. K. *Psychology applied to industry*. New York: Appleton-Century-Crofts, 1965.

Freud, S. The unconscious. In *Collected papers of Sigmund Freud*, Vol. IV (Riviere, J., trans.) London: Hogarth Press, 1949. (Original edition, 1915.)

Hackman, J. R., & Oldham, G. R. Motivation through the design of work: Test of a theory. *Organizational Behavior and Human Performance*, 1976, **16**, 250–279.

Hilgard, E. R., & Atkinson, R. C. *Introduction to psychology*. New York: Harcourt, Brace & World, 1967.

Hull, C. L. *Principles of behavior*. New York: Appleton-Century-Crofts, 1943.

Hull, C. L. *A behavior system: An introduction to behavior theory concerning the individual organism*. New Haven: Yale University Press, 1952.

James, W. *The principles of psychology*. Vols. I and II. New York: Henry Holt, 1890.

Jones, M. R. (Ed.) *Nebraska symposium on motivation*. Lincoln: University of Nebraska Press, 1955.

Katz, D. The motivational basis of organizational behavior. *Behavioral Science*, 1964, **9**, 131–146.

Katz, D., & Kahn, R. *The social psychology of organizations*. New York: Wiley, 1966.

Korman, A. K. Toward an hypothesis of work behavior. *Journal of Applied Psychology*, 1970, **54**, 31–41.

Korman, A. K. Expectancies as determinants of performance. *Journal of Applied Psychology*, 1971, **55**, 218–222.

Lewin, K. *A dynamic theory of personality*. New York: McGraw-Hill, 1935.

Lewin, K. *The conceptual representation and the measurement of psychological forces*. Durham, N.C.: Duke University Press, 1938.

Likert, R. *The human organization*. New York: McGraw-Hill, 1967.

Mahoney, T. A. Compensation preference of managers. *Industrial Relations*, 1964, **3**, 135–144.

March, J. G., & Simon, H. A. *Organizations*. New York: Wiley, 1958.

Mayo, E. *The human problems of an industrial civilization*. New York: Macmillan, 1933.

Mayo, E. *The social problems of an industrial civilization*. Boston: Harvard University Press, 1945.

McDougall, W. *An introduction to social psychology*. London: Methuen, 1908.

McGregor, D. *The human side of enterprise*. New York: McGraw-Hill, 1960.

Miles, R. E. Human relations or human resources? *Harvard Business Review*, 1965, **43**(4), 148–163.

Miles, R. E., Porter, L. W., & Craft, J. A. Leadership attitudes among public health officials. *American Journal of Public Health*, 1966, **56**, 1990–2005.

Morgan, C. T., & King, R. A. *Introduction to psychology*. New York: McGraw-Hill, 1966.

Opinion Research Corporation. *Public opinion index for industry*, 1947.

Opsahl, R. L., & Dunnette, M. D. The role of financial compensation in industrial motivation. *Psychological Bulletin*, 1966, **66**, 94–118.

Porter, L. W., & Lawler, E. E., III. *Managerial attitudes and performance*. Homewood, Ill.: Irwin, 1968.

Porter, L. W., & Miles, R. E. Motivation and management. In J. W. McGuire (Ed.), *Contemporary management: Issues and viewpoints*. Englewood Cliffs, N.J.: Prentice-Hall, 1974.

Porter, L. W., & Steers, R. M. Organizational, work and personal factors in employee turnover and absenteeism. *Psychological Bulletin*, 1973, **80**, 151–176.

Roethlisberger, F., & Dickson, W. J. *Management and the worker*. Cambridge, Mass.: Harvard University Press, 1939.

Schein, E. *Organizational psychology*. Englewood Cliffs, N.J.: Prentice-Hall, 1972.

Skinner, B. F. *Science and human behavior*. New York: Macmillan, 1953.

Spence, K. W. *Behavior theory and conditioning*. New Haven: Yale University Press, 1956.

Taylor, F. W. *Scientific management*. New York: Harper and Brothers, 1911.

Thorndike, E. L. *Animal intelligence: Experimental studies*. New York: Macmillan, 1911.
Tolman, E. C. *Purposive behavior in animals and men*. New York: Appleton-Century-Crofts, 1932.
Tolman, E. C. Principles of purposive behavior. In S. Koch (Ed.), *Psychology: A study of a science*. Vol. 2. New York: McGraw-Hill, 1959.
Vroom, V. H. *Work and motivation*. New York: Wiley, 1964.
Woodworth, R. S. *Dynamic psychology*. New York: Columbia University Press, 1918.

QUESTIONS FOR DISCUSSION

1. Exactly what is meant by the term "motivation"?
2. Describe the basic motivational process.
3. What similarities are there in the development of psychological theories of motivation compared to managerial theories? What differences?
4. What are the basic differences between drive or reinforcement models of motivation and cognitive models? Which approach seems more applicable to motivation in work settings?
5. What is really different between the human resources model and the earlier human relations model?
6. What value is there from a managerial standpoint in taking a comprehensive approach to motivational problems, as suggested in this chapter?

include the desire to move toward beauty and away from ugliness. These two needs were not included in Maslow's hierarchical arrangement, however, and have generally been omitted from discussions of his concepts as they relate to organizational settings.

ALDERFER'S MODIFIED NEED HIERARCHY THEORY

In response to criticism of the original formulation (see Wahba and Bridwell review), Clayton Alderfer has proposed a modified need hierarchy theory that essentially collapses Maslow's five hierarchical levels into three. This model has become known as the ERG theory (or existence-relatedness-growth theory). Specifically, Alderfer (1969) suggests the three need levels:

1 *Existence needs* These needs include those needs required to sustain human existence. As such, this category would include both physiological and safety needs.
2 *Relatedness needs* This category concerns how people relate to their surrounding social environment and includes the needs for meaningful social and interpersonal relationships.
3 *Growth needs* This category, thought to be the highest need category, includes the needs for self-esteem and self-actualization.

In general, then, Alderfer suggests that individuals move up the hierarchy from existence needs to relatedness needs to growth needs, as the lower-level needs become satisfied. In this respect, Alderfer's model is quite similar to that proposed by Maslow.

Alderfer's theory differs from Maslow's original formulation, however, in two important respects. First, Maslow argued that progression from one level in the hierarchy to the next was based on the satisfaction of the lower-order need; hence, individuals progress up the hierarchy as a result of satisfaction. Alderfer's ERG theory, in contrast, suggests that in addition to this satisfaction-progression process, there is also a frustration-regression process, as shown in Exhibit 1. That is, when an individual is continually frustrated in his attempts to satisfy his growth needs, relatedness needs may reemerge as primary and the individual may redirect his efforts toward these lower-order needs.

A second major difference is that unlike Maslow's original formulation, Alderfer's model suggests that more than one need may be operative, or activated, at the same point in time. This assumption suggests a less rigid model of the motivational process and bears a resemblance in this regard to Murray's manifest needs model.

MURRAY'S MANIFEST NEEDS THEORY

In addition to the models of Maslow and Alderfer, there is a third theory which uses the concept of human needs as the basic unit of analysis. This is Murray's

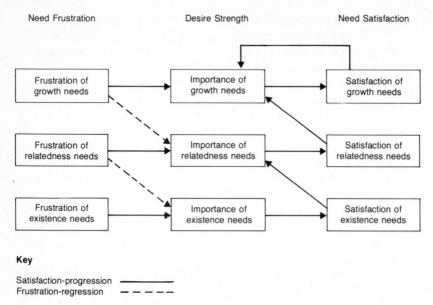

Need Frustration   Desire Strength   Need Satisfaction

Key

Satisfaction-progression ————————
Frustration-regression   — — — — —

Exhibit 1   Satisfaction-progression, frustration-regression components of ERG theory.

manifest needs theory. This model has its origin in the early work of Henry A. Murray and his associates at the Harvard Psychological Clinic during the 1930s. Based on several years of clinical observations, Murray (1938) wrote his classic *Explorations in Personality* in which he argued that individuals could be classified according to the strengths of various personality-need variables. These needs were believed to represent a central motivating force, both in terms of the intensity and the direction of goal-directed behavior. A need was defined as "a construct . . . which stands for a force . . . in the brain region, a force which organizes perception, apperception, intellection, conation and action in such a way as to transform in a certain direction an existing, unsatisfying situation" (1938, p. 123). A somewhat briefer definition has been offered by McClelland (1971, p. 13): "a recurrent concern for a goal state." Needs were not something that could be observed by the researcher. On the contrary, Murray (1938, p. 54) stated that the anlysis of such needs was "a hypothetical process, the occurrence of which is imagined in order to account for certain objective and subjective facts." In other words, one could only *infer* needs from observed behavior.

Moreover, needs were viewed as largely learned behavior—rather than innate tendencies—which were activated by cues from the external environment. This conception closely resembles the concepts of "motive" and "drive" and can be likened to a state of disequilibrium. According to Murray, each need was composed of two factors: (1) a qualitative or directional component which represents the object toward which the motive is directed; and (2) a quantitative or energetic component which represents the strength or intensity of the motive toward the object.

While much of the research attention relating to this theory has concerned the need for achievement, it is important to point out that Murray viewed an individual's personality as being composed of many divergent, and often conflicting, needs which had the potential of motivating human behavior. This list of needs included the needs for achievement, affiliation, power, autonomy, nurturance, and deference (see Exhibit 2). Thus, for example, individuals with a strongly aroused need for achievement would typically attempt to engage in activities where they could excel and accomplish something important to them. According to this model, needs may be manifest ("activated") or latent. A latent need does not imply that the need is not strong, only that it has been inhibited and has found no overt form of expression. Thus, a person may have a high need for achievement but such a need may not be strongly aroused because of impediments in the environment (such as the lack of a challenging task). The result would theoretically be poor performance. If sufficient arousal of the need were attained (by providing a challenging job), we would expect the resulting drive to energize achievement-oriented behavior.

While Murray was concerned with an entire set of needs, most current research in this area has focused on the specific need for achievement, particularly as it relates to performance in organizational settings. (Some recent research has also been carried out on the needs for power and affiliation.) The two most prominent contemporary investigators in the need for achievement (abbreviated "n Ach") research are David C. McClelland and John Atkinson. McClelland and Atkinson view the achievement motive as a relatively stable predisposition to strive for success. More specifically, n Ach is defined as "behavior toward competition with a standard of excellence" (McClelland, Atkinson, Clark, & Lowell, 1953). The basis or reward for such a motive is posited to be the positive affect associated with successful performance. McClelland, Atkinson, and their associates present a series of primarily laboratory studies indicative of a strong positive relation between high need for achievement and high levels of performance and executive success (Atkinson, 1958; Atkinson & Feather, 1966; McClelland, 1951; McClelland et al., 1953). More recent studies both in the field and in the laboratory have tended to support such a conclusion (Cummin, 1967; Hundal, 1971; Steers, 1975b; Steers & Spencer, 1977; Wainer & Rubin, 1969; Weiner & Kukla, 1970). However, Cofer and Appley (1964, p. 374) caution that "the theory McClelland and his coworkers have developed is neither compelled by nor directly derived from their data, but is presumably consistent with the data."

Murray versus Maslow   Murray's conceptualization, based on multiple needs, bears a strong resemblance to Maslow's theory in at least two respects. First, both theories posit the existence of a set of needs or goals toward which behavior is directed. Second, both theories represent hypothetical constructs designed to describe behavior and were based initially on clinical observations, not empirical research.

The major distinction between the two theories is that Murray, in contrast

Exhibit 2   Murray's needs

Need	Characteristics
Achievement	Aspires to accomplish difficult tasks; maintains high standards and is willing to work toward distant goals; responds positively to competition; willing to put forth effort to attain excellence.
Affiliation	Enjoys being with friends and people in general; accepts people readily; makes efforts to win friendships and maintain associations with people.
Aggression	Enjoys combat and argument; easily annoyed; sometimes willing to hurt people to get his or her way; may seek to "get even" with people perceived as having harmed him or her.
Autonomy	Tries to break away from restraints, confinement, or restrictions of any kind; enjoys being unattached, free, not tied to people, places, or obligations; may be rebellious when faced with restraints.
Endurance	Willing to work long hours; doesn't give up quickly on a problem; persevering, even in the face of great difficulty; patient and unrelenting in his work habits.
Exhibition	Wants to be the center of attention; enjoys having an audience; engages in behavior which wins the notice of others; may enjoy being dramatic or witty.
Harmavoidance	Does not enjoy exciting activities, especially if danger is involved; avoids risk of bodily harm; seeks to maximize personal safety.
Impulsivity	Tends to act on the "spur of the moment" and without deliberation; gives vent readily to feelings and wishes; speaks freely; may be volatile in emotional expression.
Nurturance	Gives sympathy and comfort; assists others whenever possible; interested in caring for children, the disabled, or the infirm; offers a "helping hand" to those in need; readily performs favors for others.
Order	Concerned with keeping personal effects and surroundings neat and organized; dislikes clutter, confusion, lack of organization; interested in developing methods for keeping materials methodically organized.
Power	Attempts to control the environment and to influence or direct other people; expresses opinions forcefully; enjoys the role of leader and may assume it spontaneously.
Succorance	Frequently seeks the sympathy, protection, love, advice, and reassurance of other people; may feel insecure or helpless without such support; confides difficulties readily to a receptive person.
Understanding	Wants to understand many areas of knowledge; values synthesis of ideas, verifiable generalization, logical thought, particularly when directed at satisfying intellectual curiosity.

Source: Adapted from D. N. Jackson, *Personality Research Form Manual*. Goshen, N. Y.: Research Psychologists Press, 1967.

to Maslow (or Alderfer), does not suggest a hierarchical relationship between the various needs. Hence, according to Murray, an individual may be described as having a high need for achievement, a high need for power, and a low need for affiliation *at the same time*. This multivariate approach to need structures allows for more flexibility and specificity in describing individuals than simply saying an individual has strong esteem needs. It is perhaps this increased specificity or precision of description that has caused Murray's model to maintain its popularity in research on work motivation in the face of the many criticisms of Maslow's model.

THE MOTIVE ACQUISITION PROCESS

It is generally believed that motives and needs are learned at a very early age. Once these needs are formed, it is very difficult to change them. One major effort to discover how such motives *can* be changed has been under way for some time by McClelland (1965). McClelland believes it is possible to alter need states and to train people to increase need strengths. Most of his work in this regard has dealt with need for achievement and how it can be learned.

McClelland's (1965) research led to the identification of several ''propositions'' concerning the nature of motive acquisition. While a detailed examination of these propositions, and the evidence in support of them, is beyond the scope of our interest here, it is possible to briefly summarize several of the major points. First, it is believed that the motive acquisition process is facilitated by an individual's beliefs concerning the desirability to acquire the motive. That is, the more an individual believes he or she *should* and *can* acquire a high need for achievement, for example, the greater his or her willingness to work to develop the motive.

Second, the acquisition of the achievement motive is facilitated to the extent that the individual thoroughly understands the nature and underlying processes relating to the motive, as well as how this motive relates to other actions and behaviors. Moreover, motive acquisition is also facilitated when individuals see the new motive as a way to enhance their self-image, when feedback on progress toward acquiring the motive is provided, and when the learning environment for the new motive is a warm and nonthreatening one.

To the extent that such conditions are present, we would expect the individual to be receptive to influences to change his or her motive strength. In this way, McClelland argues, it is possible to train managers and entrepreneurs to have higher needs for achievement, to strive more for success, and, ultimately, to improve their level of performance on the job.

IMPLICATIONS FOR MANAGEMENT

Although Maslow's original concern centered around the development of a model that was generally descriptive of the relation between motivation and personality, he later focused his attention specifically on the motivational problems of employees in work settings (Maslow, 1965). When the need hierarchy concept is applied to work organizations, the implications for managerial actions become obvious. Managers have the responsibility, according to this line of reasoning, to create a "proper climate" in which employees can develop to their fullest potential. This proper climate might include increasing the opportunities for greater autonomy, variety, responsibility, and so forth, so that employees could work toward higher-order need satisfaction. Failure to provide such a climate would theoretically increase employee frustration and could result in poorer performance, lower job satisfaction, and increased withdrawal from the organization.

Somewhat similarly, the achievement motivation model of Murray, McClelland, and Atkinson focuses largely on individual characteristics as they relate to motivational force. The implicit managerial strategy here would be to design the work environment so that it "cues" the achievement motive. Hence, as noted in the third reading selection in this chapter, high n Ach employees should be given challenging work assignments. Such assignments provide them with opportunities to accomplish something with a standard of excellence, thereby leading to need satisfaction. On the other hand, other motivational strategies may be more appropriate for motivating those with low needs for achievement (see Chapter 4 for a discussion on behavior modification).

In addition, some research suggests that need for achievement can influence the relationship between performance and job satisfaction (Steers, 1975a). Specifically, it was found in one study among managers that a fairly strong relationship existed between performance and satisfaction for employees high in need for achievement. No such relationship was found for low n Ach employees. These findings suggest that good performance represents one form of need satisfaction for high need achievers, thus leading to feelings of general job satisfaction. For low need achievers, on the other hand, other needs (like affiliation or power) are probably more important and there is little reason to believe that good performance would necessarily help satisfy these other needs. One implication of these findings concerns supervisory style. That is, low n Ach employees may require closer supervison than high n Ach employees because high n Ach employees are motivated by need level to perform. They are "self"-motivated. Other techniques (e.g., closer supervision, incentive systems) may be necessary to a greater extent to insure good task performance for low n Ach employees.

Finally, in a separate field study, it was found that managers who have a high need for achievement also tend to be more participative; that is, they tend to allow their subordinates to have a greater voice in decisions affecting their jobs (Steers, 1977). No such findings emerged for employees with high needs for affiliation or power. This finding suggests that when successful task accomplishment requires the coordinated efforts of several people (such as in a research laboratory), it would be important to select a group manager who had a high need for achievement and who would work through others to insure task accomplishment.

OVERVIEW

Five reading selections follow. The first, by Maslow, presents the early developmental work on the need hierarchy theory. This is followed by a review of the research relating to Maslow's model by Wahba and Bridwell. Next, Litwin and Stringer discuss the manifest needs theory, focusing on the three needs for achievement, affiliation, and power. In addition, a fairly sophisticated achievement motivation model (by Atkinson) is reviewed. Finally, two recent articles (by Salancik and Pfeffer and by Alderfer) nicely summarize many of the current controversies surrounding need theories of motivation. Salancik and Pfeffer argue that such theories are of little value in explaining employee behavior in complex organizations, while Alderfer provides a rejoinder.

REFERENCES AND SUGGESTED ADDITIONAL READINGS

Alderfer, C. P. A new theory of human needs. *Organizational Behavior and Human Performance*, 1969, **4**, 142–175.

Alderfer, C. P. *Existence, relatedness, and growth*. New York: Free Press, 1972.

Atkinson, J. W. Motivational determinants of risk-taking behavior. *Psychological Review*, 1957, **64**, 359–372.

Atkinson, J. W. *An introduction to motivation*. Princeton, N. J.: Van Nostrand, 1964.

Atkinson, J. W., & Feather, N. T. *A theory of achievement motivation*. New York: Wiley, 1966.

Cofer, C. N., & Appley, M. H. *Motivation: Theory and research*. New York: Wiley, 1964.

Cummin, P. C. TAT correlates of executive performance. *Journal of Applied Psychology*, 1967, **51**, 78–81.

Ghiselli, E. E., & Johnson, D. A. Need satisfaction, managerial success, and organizational structure. *Personnel Psychology*, 1970, **23**, 569–576.

Hall, D. T., & Nougaim, K. E. An examination of Maslow's need hierarchy in an organizational setting. *Organizational Behavior and Human Performance*, 1968, **3**, 12–35.

Heckhausen, H. *The anatomy of achievement motivation*. New York: Academic Press, 1967.

Hundal, P. S. A study of entrepreneurial motivation: Comparison of fast- and slow-progressing small-scale industrial entrepreneurs in Punjab, India. *Journal of Applied Psychology*, 1971, **55**, 317–323.

Lawler, E. E., III, & Suttle, J. L. A causal correlational test of the need hierarchy concept. *Organizational Behavior and Human Performance*, 1972, **7**, 265–287.

Litwin, G., & Stringer, R. A. *Motivation and organizational climate*. Boston: Graduate School of Business Administration, Harvard University, 1968.

Maslow, A. H. A theory of human motivation. *Psychological Review*, 1943, **50**, 370–396.

Maslow, A. H. *Motivation and personality*. New York: Harper, 1954.

Maslow, A. H. *Eupsychian management*. Homewood, Ill.: Irwin, 1965.

Maslow, A. H. *Toward a psychology of being*. New York: Van Nostrand Reinhold, 1968.

McClelland, D. C. *Personality*. New York: Dryden Press, 1951.

McClelland, D. C. *The achieving society*. Princeton, N. J.: Van Nostrand, 1961.

McClelland, D. C. Business drive and national achievement. *Harvard Business Review*, 1962, **40**(4), 99–112.

McClelland, D. C. Toward a theory of motive acquisition. *American Psychologist*, 1965, **20**, 321–333.

McClelland, D. C. *Assessing human motivation*. New York: General Learning Press, 1971.

McClelland, D. C., Atkinson, J. W., Clark, R. A., & Lowell, E.L. *The achievement motive*. New York: Appleton-Century-Crofts, 1953.

McClelland, D. C., & Winter, D. G. *Motivating economic achievement*. New York: Free Press, 1971.

McGregor, D. *The human side of enterprise*. New York: McGraw-Hill, 1960.

McGregor, D. *The professional manager*. New York: McGraw-Hill, 1967.

Miner, J. B., & Dachler, H. P. Personnel attitudes and motivation. In P. H. Mussen and M. R. Rosenzweig (Eds.), *Annual review of psychology*. Palo Alto, Calif.: Annual Reviews, Inc., 1973.

Mitchell, V. F. Need satisfactions of military commanders and staff. *Journal of Applied Psychology*, 1970, **54**, 282–287.

Mitchell, V. M., & Moudgill, P. Measurement of Maslow's need hierarchy. *Organizational Behavior and Human Performance*, 1976, **16**, 334–349.

Murray, H. A. *Explorations in personality*. New York: Oxford University Press, 1938.

Payne, R. Factor analysis of a Maslow-type need satisfaction questionnaire. *Personnel Psychology*, 1970, **23**, 251–268.

Porter, L. W. A study of perceived need satisfaction in bottom and middle management jobs. *Journal of Applied Psychology*, 1961, **45**, 1–10.

Porter, L. W. Job attitudes in management: I. Perceived deficiencies in need fulfillment as a function of job level. *Journal of Applied Psychology*, 1962, **46**, 375–384.

Porter, L. W. Job attitudes in management: II. Perceived importance of needs as a function of job level. *Journal of Applied Psychology*, 1963, **47**, 141–148.

Schneider, B., & Alderfer, C. P. Three studies of measures of need satisfaction in organizations. *Administrative Science Quarterly*, 1973, **18**, 489–505.

Steers, R. M. Effects of need for achievement on the job performance-job attitude relationship. *Journal of Applied Psychology*, 1975, **60**, 678–682. (a)

Steers, R. M. Task-goal attributes, n achievement, and supervisory performance. *Organizational Behavior and Human Performance*, 1975, **13**, 392–403. (b)

Steers, R. M. Factors affecting job attitudes in a goal-setting environment. *Academy of Management Journal*, 1976, **19**, 6–16.

Steers, R. M. Antecedents and outcomes of organizational commitment. *Administrative Science Quarterly*, 1977, **22**, 46–56.

Steers, R. M. Individual differences in participative decision-making. *Human Relations*, 1977, **30**, 837–847.

Steers, R. M., & Braunstein, D. N. A behaviorally-based measure of manifest needs in work settings. *Journal of Vocational Behavior*, 1976, **9**, 251–266.

Steers, R. M., & Spencer, D. G. The role of achievement motivation in job design. *Journal of Applied Psychology*, 1977, **62**, 472–479.

Stone, E. F., Mowday, R. T., & Porter, L. W. Higher-order need strengths as moderators of the job scope-job satisfaction relationship. *Journal of Applied Psychology*, 1977, **62**, 468–473.

Wainer, H. A., & Rubin, I. M. Motivation of research and development enterpreneurs. *Journal of Applied Psychology*, 1969, **53**, 178–184.

Wahba, M. A., & Bridwell, L. Maslow reconsidered: A review of research on the need hierarchy theory. *Organizational Behavior and Human Performance*, 1976, **15**, 212–240.

Wanous, J. P., & Zwany, A. A cross-sectional test of need hierarchy theory. *Organizational Behavior and Human Performance*, 1977, **18**, 38–97.

Weiner, B., & Kukla, A. An attributional analysis of achievement motivation. *Journal of Personality and Social Psychology*, 1970, **15**, 1–20.

Wofford, J. C. The motivational bases of job satisfaction and job performance. *Personnel Psychology*, 1971, **24**, 501–518.

Wolf, M. G. Need gratification theory: A theoretical reformulation of job satisfaction/dissatisfaction and job motivation. *Journal of Applied Psychology*, 1970, **54**, 87–94.

A Theory of Human Motivation

A. H. Maslow

DYNAMICS OF THE BASIC NEEDS

The "Physiological" Needs

The needs that are usually taken as the starting point for motivation theory are the so-called physiological drives. . . .

Undoubtedly these physiological needs are the most prepotent of all needs. What this means specifically is that, in the human being who is missing everything in life in an extreme fashion, it is most likely that the major motivation would be the physiological needs rather than any others. A person who is lacking food, safety, love, and esteem would most probably hunger for food more strongly than for anything else.

If all the needs are unsatisfied, and the organism is then dominated by the physiological needs, all other needs may become simply non-existent or be pushed into the background. It is then fair to characterize the whole organism by saying simply that it is hungry, for consciousness is almost completely pre-empted by hunger. All capacities are put into the service of hunger-satisfaction, and the organization of these capacities is almost entirely determined by the one purpose of satisfying hunger. The receptors and effectors, the intelligence, memory, habits, all may now be defined simply as hunger-gratifying tools. Capacities that are not useful for this purpose lie dormant or are pushed into the background. . . .

Abridged from the *Psychological Review*, 1943, **50**, 370–396, by permission of the American Psychological Association.

Obviously a good way to obscure the "higher" motivations, and to get a lopsided view of human capacities and human nature, is to make the organism extremely and chronically hungry or thirsty. Anyone who attempts to make an emergency picture into a typical one and who will measure all of man's goals and desires by his behavior during extreme physiological deprivation is certainly being blind to many things. It is quite true that man lives by bread alone—when there is no bread. But what happens to man's desires when there *is* plenty of bread and when his belly is chronically filled?

At once other (and "higher") needs emerge and these, rather than physiological hungers, dominate the organism. And when these in turn are satisfied, again new (and still "higher") needs emerge and so on. This is what we mean by saying that the basic human needs are organized into a hierarchy of relative prepotency.

One main implication of this phrasing is that gratification becomes as important a concept as deprivation in motivation theory, for it releases the organism from the domination of a relatively more physiological need, permitting thereby the emergence of other more social goals. The physiological needs, along with their partial goals, when chronically gratified cease to exist as active determinants or organizers of behavior. They now exist only in a potential fashion in the sense that they may emerge again to dominate the organism if they are thwarted. But a want that is satisfied is no longer a want. The organism is dominated and its behavior organized only by unsatisfied needs. If hunger is satisfied, it becomes unimportant in the current dynamics of the individual.

This statement is somewhat qualified by a hypothesis to be discussed more fully later, namely, that it is precisely those individuals in whom a certain need has always been satisfied who are best equipped to tolerate deprivation of that need in the future; furthermore, those who have been deprived in the past will react to current satisfactions differently from the one who has never been deprived.

The Safety Needs

If the physiological needs are relatively well gratified, there then emerges a new set of needs, which we may categorize roughly as the safety needs. All that has been said of the physiological needs is equally true, although in lesser degree, of these desires. The organism may equally well be wholly dominated by them. They may serve as the almost exclusive organizers of behavior, recruiting all the capacities that they are primarily safety-seeking tools. Again, as in the hungry man, we find that the dominating goal is a strong determinant not only of his current world-outlook and philosophy but also of his philosophy of the future. Practically everything looks less important than safety (even sometimes the physiological needs which being satisfied, are now underestimated). A man, in this state, if it is extreme enough and chronic enough, may be characterized as living almost for safety alone. . . .

The healthy, normal, fortunate adult in our culture is largely satisfied in his safety needs. The peaceful, smoothly running, "good" society ordinarily makes its members feel safe enough from wild animals, extremes of temperature, criminals, assault and murder, tyranny, etc. Therefore, in a very real sense, they no longer have any safety needs as active motivators. Just as a sated man no longer feels hungry, a safe man no longer feels endangered. If we wish to see these needs directly and clearly we must turn to neurotic or near-neurotic individuals, and to the economic and social underdogs. In between these extremes, we can perceive the expressions of safety needs only in such phenomena as, for instance, the common preference for a job with tenure and protection, the desire for a savings account, and for insurance of various kinds (medical, dental, unemployment, disability, old age). . . .

The Love Needs

If both the physiological and the safety needs are fairly well gratified, then there will emerge the love and affection and belongingness needs, and the whole cycle already described will repeat itself with this new center. Now the person will feel keenly, as never before, the absence of friends or a sweetheart or a wife or children. He will hunger for affectionate relations with people in general, namely, for a place in his group, and he will strive with great intensity to achieve this goal. He will want to attain such a place more than anything else in the world and may even forget that once, when he was hungry, he sneered at love.

In our society the thwarting of these needs is the most commonly found core in cases of maladjustment and more severe psychopathology. Love and affection, as well as their possible expression in sexuality, are generally looked upon with ambivalence and are customarily hedged about with many restrictions and inhibitions. Practically all theorists of psychopathology have stressed thwarting of the love needs as basic in the picture of maladjustment. Many clinical studies have therefore been made of this need and we know more about it perhaps than any of the other needs except the physiological ones.

One thing that must be stressed at this point is that love is not synonymous with sex. Sex may be studied as a purely physiological need. Ordinarily sexual behavior is multi-determined, that is to say, determined not only by sexual but also by other needs, chief among which are the love and affection needs. Also not to be overlooked is the fact that the love needs involve both giving *and* receiving love.

The Esteem Needs

All people in our society (with a few pathological exceptions) have a need or desire for a stable, firmly based, (usually) high evaluation of themselves, for self-respect, or self-esteem, and for the esteem of others. By firmly based self-esteem, we mean that which is soundly based upon real capacity, achievement, and respect from others. These needs may be classified into two subsidiary sets. These are, first, the desire for strength, for achievement, for adequacy, for confidence in the face of the world, and for independence and freedom. Second, we have what we may call the desire for reputation or prestige (defining it as respect or esteem from other people), recognition, attention, importance, or appreciation. These needs have been relatively stressed by Alfred Adler and his followers, and have been relatively neglected by Freud and the psycho-analysts. More and more today, however, there is appearing widespread ap-preciation of their central importance.

Satisfaction of the self-esteem need leads to feelings of self-confidence, worth, strength, capability, and adequacy, of being useful and necessary in the world. But thwarting of these needs produces feelings of inferiority, of weak-ness, and of helplessness. These feelings in turn give rise to either basic dis-couragement or else compensatory or neurotic trends. An appreciation of the necessity of basic self-confidence and an understanding of how helpless people are without it can be easily gained from a study of severe traumatic neurosis.

The Need for Self-Actualization

Even if all these needs are satisfied, we may still often (if not always) expect that a new discontent and restlessness will soon develop, unless the individual is doing what he is fitted for. A musician must make music, an artist must paint, a poet must write, if he is to be ultimately happy. What a man *can* be, he *must* be. This need we may call self-actualization.

This term, first coined by Kurt Goldstein, is being used in this paper in a much more specific and limited fashion. It refers to the desire for self-fulfillment, namely, to the tendency for one to become actualized in what one is potentially. This tendency might be phrased as the desire to become more and more what one is, to become everything that one is capable of becoming.

The specific form that these needs take will of course vary greatly from person to person. In one individual it may be expressed maternally, as the desire to be an ideal mother, in another athletically, in still another aesthetically, in the painting of pictures, and in another inventively in the creation of new contrivances. It is not necessarily a creative urge although in people who have any capabilities for creation it will take this form.

The clear emergence of these needs rests upon prior satisfaction of the physiological, safety, love and esteem needs. We shall call people who are satisfied in these needs, basically satisfied people, and it is from these that we may expect the fullest (and healthiest) creativeness. Since, in our society, basically satisfied people are the exception, we do not know much about self-actualization, either experimentally or clinically. It remains a challenging prob-lem for research. . . .

Degrees of Relative Satisfaction

So far, our theoretical discussion may have given the impression that these five sets of needs are somehow in a stepwise, all-or-none relationship to one another. We have spoken in such terms as the following: "If one need is satisfied, then another emerges." This statement might give the false impression that a need must be satisfied 100 per cent before the next need emerges. In actual fact, most members of our society who are normal are partially satisfied in all their basic needs and partially unsatisfied in all their basic needs at the same time. A more realistic description of the hierarchy would be in terms of decreasing percentages of satisfaction as we go up the hierarchy of prepotency. For instance, if I may assign arbitrary figures for the sake of illustration, it is as if the average citizen is satisfied perhaps 85 per cent in his physiological needs, 70 per cent in his safety needs, 50 per cent in his love needs, 40 per cent in his self-esteem needs, and 10 per cent in his self-actualization needs.

As for the concept of emergence of a new need after satisfaction of the prepotent need, this emergence is not a sudden, saltatory phenomenon but rather a gradual emergence by slow degrees from nothingness. For instance, if prepotent need A is satisfied only 10 per cent then need B may not be visible at all. However, as this need A becomes satisfied 25 per cent, need B may emerge 5 per cent; as need A becomes satisfied 75 per cent, need B may emerge 90 per cent; and so on.

Unconscious Character of Needs

These needs are neither necessarily conscious nor unconscious. On the whole, however, in the average person, they are more often unconscious. It is not necessary at this point to overhaul the tremendous mass of evidence which indicates the crucial importance of unconscious motivation. It would by now be expected, on a priori grounds alone, that unconscious motivations would on the whole be rather more important than the conscious motivations. What we have called the basic needs are very often largely unconscious although they may, with suitable techniques and with sophisticated people, become conscious. . . .

SUMMARY

1 There are at least five sets of goals which we may call basic needs. These are briefly physiological, safety, love, esteem, and self-actualization. In addition, we are motivated by the desire to achieve or maintain the various conditions on which these basic satisfactions rest and by certain more intellectual desires.

2 These basic goals are related to one another, being arranged in a hierarchy of prepotency. This means that the most prepotent goal will monopolize consciousness and will tend of itself to organize the recruitment of the various capacities of the organism. The less prepotent needs are minimized, even forgotten or denied. But when a need is fairly well satisfied, the next prepotent ("higher") need emerges, in turn to dominate the conscious life and to serve as the center of organization of behavior, since gratified needs are not active motivators.

Thus man is a perpetually wanting animal. Ordinarily the satisfaction of these wants is not altogether mutually exclusive but only tends to be. The average member of our society is most often partially satisfied and partially unsatisfied in all of his wants. The hierarchy principle is usually empirically observed in terms of increasing percentages of non-satisfaction as we go up the hierarchy. Reversals of the average order of the hierarchy are sometimes observed. Also it has been observed that an individual may permanently lose the higher wants in the hierarchy under special conditions. There are not only ordinarily multiple motivations for usual behavior but, in addition, many determinants other than motives.

3   Any thwarting or possibility of thwarting of these basic human goals, or danger to the defenses which protect them or to the conditions upon which they rest, is considered to be a psychological threat. With a few exceptions, all psychopathology may be partially traced to such threats. A basically thwarted man may actually be defined as a "sick" man.

4   It is such basic threats which bring about the general emergency reactions.

5   Certain other basic problems have not been dealt with because of limitations of space. Among these are (a) the problem of values in any definitive motivation theory, (b) the relation between appetites, desires, needs and what is "good" for the organism, (c) the etiology of the basic needs and their possible derivation in early childhood, (d) redefinition of motivational concepts, i.e., drive, desire, wish, need, goal, (e) implication of our theory for hedonistic theory, (f) the nature of the uncompleted act, of success and failure, and of aspiration-level, (g) the role of association, habit, and conditioning, (h) relation to the theory of interpersonal relations, (i) implications for psychotherapy, (j) implication for theory of society, (k) the theory of selfishness, (l) the relation between needs and cultural patterns, (m) the relation between this theory and Allport's theory of functional autonomy. These as well as certain other less important questions must be considered as motivation theory attempts to become definitive.

Maslow Reconsidered:
A Review of Research on the Need
Hierarchy Theory

Mahmoud A. Wahba
Lawrence G. Bridwell

PURPOSE AND BACKGROUND

Maslow's Need Hierarchy Theory [references 21; 22; 24] presents the student of work motivation with an interesting paradox: the theory is widely accepted, but there is little research evidence to support it. Since Maslow first published his theory thirty years ago, it has become one of the most popular theories of motivation in the management and organizational behavior literature. Furthermore, the theory has provided an a priori conceptual framework to explain diverse research findings. [26] Such widespread acceptance of the Need Hierarchy Theory is rather surprising in light of the fact that until the mid-sixties [1; 7; 14] little empirical evidence existed that tested predictions of the theory. It has become a tradition for writers to point out the discrepancy between the popularity of the theory and the lack of clear and consistent empirical evidence to support it. [6; 9; 10; 30]

Recently, the interest in Maslow's Need Hierarchy Theory has been revived, due to the publication of a number of empirical studies testing some predictions of the theory. As yet, however, no known review of the literature compares and integrates the findings of these studies. The purpose of this paper is to review and evaluate the empirical research related to Maslow's Need Hierarchy Theory, thereby assessing the empirical validity of the theory itself.

Several constraints were imposed on this review. First, the review will deal only with the test of Maslow's theory in the work situation. [For a review of the empirical evidence in other situations, see reference 10.] Second, this review will include only studies that used statistical rather than clinical methodology. [25] Third, this review will deal only with what is considered to be the core or the main elements of Maslow's theory as it relates to work motivation.

MASLOW'S NEED HIERARCHY THEORY:
A BRIEF DESCRIPTION

Part of the appeal of Maslow's Need Hierarchy Theory is that it provides both a theory of human *motives* by classifying basic human needs in a hierarchy, and a theory of *human motivation* that relates these needs to general behavior. As a theory of motives or needs, Maslow proposed that basic needs are structured in a hierarchy of prepotency and probability of appearance. The hierarchy of needs is as follows (in ascending order of prepotency): the physiological

From Proceedings of the Thirty-third Annual Meeting of the Academy of Management, 1973, 514–520. Reprinted by permission of the Academy of Management and the authors.

needs, the safety needs, the belongingness or love needs, the esteem needs, and the need for self-actualization.

As a theory of motivation, Maslow utilized the two concepts of deprivation and gratification to provide the dynamic forces that linked needs to general behavior. He used the deprivation concept to establish "dominance" within his hierarchy of needs. He postulated that deprivation or dissatisfaction of a need of high prepotency will lead to the domination of this need over the organism's personality.

Following the satisfaction of a dominating need, the second element of the dynamic force in Maslow's Theory will then take place. Relative gratification of a given need submerges it and "activates" the next higher need in the hierarchy. The activated need then dominates and organizes the individual's personality and capacities so that instead of the individual's being hunger obsessed, he now becomes safety obsessed.

This process of deprivation → domination → gratification → activation continues until the physiological, safety, affiliation and esteem needs have all been gratified and the self-actualization need has been activated. In a later work [23], Maslow modified the gratification/activation idea by proposing that gratification of the self-actualization need causes an increase in its importance rather than a decrease. Maslow also acknowledged numerous exceptions to his theory. Notably, he pointed out that long deprivation of a given need may create a fixation for that need. Also, higher needs may emerge not after gratification, but rather after long deprivation, renunciation, or suppression of lower needs. Maslow emphasized again and again that behavior is multi-determined and multi-motivated. From this general approach Maslow dealt with a wide range of consequences to his theory.

The present paper will review the research literature that attempted to test Maslow's theory or parts of it. The review will be divided into three related sections, each section dealing with one main element of Maslow's Need Hierarchy Theory. These elements are:

1   Maslow's Need Classification scheme;
2   The Deprivation/Domination proposition;
3   The Gratification/Activation proposition.

Maslow's Need Classification Scheme

Most of the research dealing with Maslow's need classification scheme has utilized factor analytic techniques. In the literature, eight factor analytic studies attempted explicitly to test Maslow's need classification scheme. These studies raised three related questions:

1   Does the factor analysis yield five factors that can be interpreted conceptually in terms of Maslow's five need categories?

2   Are Maslow's need categories independent from each other or do they overlap? What is the pattern of overlapping? Is the overlapping between adjacent or non-adjacent categories?

3   Are Maslow's need categories independent from supposedly unrelated items or factors?

The samples in these studies were composed of various groups (professionals, nonprofessionals, students, managers, males, and females) and four different measuring scales were used. A modified Porter [27] Need Satisfaction Questionnaire (NSQ) was the research instrument in four studies. Although it was designed basically to reflect Maslow's need classification scheme, the NSQ appears to suffer from a number of methodological problems particularly due to response bias. Subjects filling out the instrument give the fulfillment and importance ratings almost simultaneously. This produces a high correlation between fulfillment and importance. [3] Also, Lawler and Suttle [19] pointed out that the correlations among the NSQ items in the same category were not high and that all items correlated with each other. As a result the NSQ may not accurately reflect Maslow's need classification scheme.

Three researchers [3; 5; 17] used three different scales. Huizinga's 24-item questionnaire appears to be the best designed scale for several reasons. One, it reflects all of Maslow's categories including the physiological needs. Two, the questionnaire is oriented to work motivation in general rather than being specific to the employee's present job. The questions were placed in the context of how important each of the items would be in the respondent's evaluation of *any* job. Unlike the NSQ, this minimizes the situational aspects of the current job affecting the answers of respondents. Three, it contains both positive and negative items to reflect the concepts of gratification and deprivation. Fourth, the scale was well validated by various methods. However, the scale did have one weakness; no reliability figures were reported.

The following conclusions can be drawn from the results of the factor analytic studies testing Maslow's need classification scheme.

1   None of the studies has shown *all* of Maslow's five need categories as independent factors. Only Beer's study showed four independent factors reflecting four needs; the fifth need overlapped with an unrelated factor.

2   In some studies, lower-order needs and higher-order needs clustered together independently from each other.

3   Self-actualization needs emerged as an independent factor in some studies, and in other studies, they overlapped with other need categories.

4   Two studies using two samples each showed no support for Maslow's need categories.

Another type of evidence related to the test of Maslow's need classification scheme comes from studies that attempted to classify human needs empirically by factor analysis techniques without an a priori theoretical framework. [8; 12; 28] These studies do not show need categories similar to those proposed by Maslow.

Taken together, the empirical results of the factor analytic studies provide no consistent support for Maslow's need classification as a whole. There is no clear evidence that human needs are classified into five distinct categories, or that these categories are structured in a special hierarchy. Some evidence exists for possibly two types of needs, higher- and lower-order needs, even though this categorization is not always operative. Self-actualization needs may emerge as an independent category. However, it is not possible to assess from the studies reviewed whether self-actualization is, in fact, a need or simply a social desirability response resulting from certain cultural values. [6] There is some empirical evidence to substantiate this latter conclusion. [17]

The Deprivation/Domination Proposition

The deprivation/domination proposition is closely related to the gratification/activation proposition. Consequently, some studies have provided a test of both propositions at the same time. However, to allow for careful examination of both propositions, it was decided to review each proposition independently.

The deprivation/domination proposition can be interpreted as follows: the higher the deprivation or deficiency of a given need, the higher its importance, strength, or desirability. Deficiency is usually measured as the difference between what is expected and what is attained. The evidence to test this proposition is derived from two groups of studies. The first group of studies utilizes the Porter NSQ in the measurement of job satisfaction, and the second group of studies investigates the relationship between satisfaction and the judged importance of environmental and job characteristics.

The samples for the first group of studies consisted mostly of managers. These studies utilized the Porter NSQ or a modified variation of it. Although these studies were not originally designed to test Maslow's ideas, they provide the necessary data to test the deprivation/domination proposition. In particular, these studies present a measure of need deficiency and a measure of need importance. According to Maslow's theory, the most deficient need should be the most dominant or important need. Consequently, the rank in order of both need deficiency and need importance should correspond to each other. In particular, the most deficient need should be ranked as the most important need. The results generally showed that the deprivation/domination proposition is partially supported with regard to self-actualization and autonomy needs; but the results do not support the proposition with regard to security, social and esteem needs. Findings of other studies utilizing different scales or methodologies are generally consistent with the Porter type studies. [1; 2; 3; 14; 17; 19; 29] These studies show directly or indirectly that the proposition of deprivation/domination is not always supported.

It is difficult to assess whether the higher order needs (autonomy and self-actualization) are ranked more important in the Porter type studies because they are deficient, or reported deficient because they are important. Some evidence for the latter conclusion comes from another group of studies dealing with satisfaction and the judged importance of environmental and job characteristics. Two studies [13; 20] showed a V-curve relationship between satisfaction and judged importance. That is, the higher the satisfaction *or* the dissatisfaction, the higher the ranked importance. Another study [11] showed that this relationship is limited to cases where a Likert-type scale is used. Under an alternative scale of measurement (e.g., Job Descriptive Index) only high satisfaction is correlated to importance which is the opposite of Maslow's hypothesis. These studies indicate that the issue of need deprivation and the domination of behavior may not be as simple as suggested by Maslow.

The Gratification/Activation Proposition

The gratification/activation proposition has been mostly operationalized in two ways:

1 Need satisfaction should be generally decreasing going up in the Maslow need hierarchy:
2 The higher the satisfaction with a given need:
   a the lower the importance of the need, *and*
   b the higher the importance of the need at the next level of the hierarchy.

Several studies that used the original or modified version of the NSQ provide a test of the idea that need satisfaction should decrease going up in Maslow's need hierarchy. The samples consisted mostly of managers and also included professionals and workers. The results indicate that either self-actualization or security are the least satisfied needs, and social needs are the most satisfied. The degree of satisfaction of other needs varies widely: it is difficult to determine their general pattern. These trends are not in agreement with those proposed by Maslow.

Four cross-sectional studies explicitly tested the proposition, the higher the satisfaction with a given need, the lower the importance of this need *and* the higher the importance of the need at the next level in the hierarchy. Two studies [29; 32] produced findings opposite to Maslow's proposition. Two others [2; 3] showed limited support for individual needs of the hierarchy, and no support for other needs.

Two longitudinal studies [14; 19] also tested the gratification/activation proposition. The longitudinal studies are based on the assumption that changes in need satisfaction and need strength or importance can only be studied over time using longitudinal data. The proposition tested is that the satisfaction of needs in one category should correlate negatively with the importance of these same needs and positively with the importance of needs in the next higher level of the hierarchy. The longitudinal studies used a cross-lagged correlational analysis in addition to static correlational analysis. The former technique makes it possible to test with some confidence the strength and direction of causal relationships by using longitudinal data and correlational analysis. The two longitudinal studies indicate no support for Maslow's propositions. The two studies, however, provide the most appropriate methodology to test Maslow's theory in general and its dynamic aspects in particular.

General Evaluation and Conclusion

This literature review shows that Maslow's Need Hierarchy Theory has received little clear or consistent support from the available research findings. Some of Maslow's propositions are totally rejected, while others receive mixed and questionable support at best. The descriptive validity of Maslow's Need Classification scheme is not established, although there are some indications that low-order and high-order needs may form some kind of hierarchy. However, this two-level hierarchy is not always operative, nor is it based upon the domination or gratification concepts. No strong evidence supports the deprivation/domination proposition except with regard to self-actualization. Self-actualization, however, may not be a basic need, but rather a romantic throwback to the eigteenth century notion of the "noble savage." [6] That is, it may be based more on wishes of what man should be than on what he actually is. Furthermore, a number of competing theories explain self-actualization with more rigor than does Maslow's theory. [10] Longitudinal data does not support Maslow's gratification/activation proposition, and the limited support received from cross-sectional studies is questionable because of numerous measurement and control problems.

Do these findings invalidate Maslow's Need Hierarchy Theory? The answer to this question is rather difficult, partly because of the nature of the theory, which defies empirical testing, and partly because of the conceptual, methodological and measurement problems of the research reviewed. Maslow's Need Hierarchy Theory is almost a non-testable theory. This is evident by the relatively limited research that has sought to test it, and the difficulty of interpreting and operationalizing its concepts. For example, what behavior should or should not be included in each need category? How can a need be gratified out of existence? What does dominance of a given need mean? What are the conditions under which the theory is operative? How does the shift from one need to another take place? Do people also go down the hierarchy as they go up in it? Is there an independent hierarchy for each situation or do people develop a general hierarchy for all situations? What is the time span for the unfolding of the hierarchy? These and similar questions are not answered by Maslow and are open for many interpretations.

The most problematic aspect of Maslow's theory, however, is that dealing with the concept of need itself. There is ample evidence that people seek objects and engage in behavior that are in no way related to the satisfaction of needs. [15; 31] Cofer and Appley [10] concluded that this is probably true also for animals. Vroom [30] does not use the concept of needs in his discussion of motivation. Lawler [18] limits the use of the term to certain stimuli (or outcomes) that can be grouped together because they are sought by people. Even if we accept such a limited view of needs, the remaining question should be, why should needs be structured in a fixed hierarchy? Does this hierarchy vary for different people? What happens to the hierarchy over time? How can we have a fixed hierarchy when behavior is multi-determinate? These and other logical arguments have been raised about Maslow's theory by many writers [e.g., 6] and have resulted in some attempts to reformulate the theory which have shown some validity. [e.g., 1; 2; 3; 4; 16]

The research reviewed in this paper is not free from weakness. In particular, there are two drawbacks in most of the research reviewed: the interpretation and operationalization of the theory, and the measurement problems. The variations in interpretations are evident by the hypotheses and the operational definitions attached to Maslow's main concepts by different authors. Methodologically, Maslow's theory is a clinically derived theory and its unit of analysis is the individual. Most of the research used the group as the unit of analysis. The theory is a dynamic theory, while most of the research, except the two longitudinal studies, dealt with the theory as a static theory. Maslow's theory is based upon a causal logic, while most of the studies were correlational (again except for the dynamic correlations used by the two longitudinal studies). The dependent variables in most of the research varied and were measured usually by self-reporting techniques, but none of the studies included observable behavior. Although there are six different scales designed especially to reflect Maslow's ideas, there are many measurement problems associated with these scales. Some of the scales do not show acceptable reliability coefficients and their construct validity is questionable.

Future research dealing with Maslow's theory should concentrate upon the areas that show some promise and ignore those areas that received little support. It is possible to develop further some of the ideas that received some support from the empiric research and improve its predictive validity, e.g., two-level hierarchy, gratification concept, and self-actualization needs. These areas should be clarified and operationalized to facilitate the formulation of testable hypotheses. The dynamic aspects of the theory should be subjected to further tests, and scales of measurements should be more refined to allow more reliable and valid tests of the theory.

REFERENCES

1 Alderfer, C. P. Differential importance of human needs as a function of satisfaction obtained in the organization. Ph.D. diss., Yale University, 1966.
2 Alderfer, C. P. An empirical test of a new theory of human needs. *Organizational Behavior and Human Performance*, 1969, 4, 142–75.
3 Alderfer, C. P. *Existence, relatedness, and growth*. New York: Free Press, 1972.

4   Barnes, L. B. *Organizational systems and engineering groups*. Boston: Harvard
     Graduate School of Business, 1960.
5   Beer, M. *Leadership, employee needs and motivation*. Columbus: Bureau of Busi-
     ness Research, Ohio State University, 1966.
6   Berkowitz, L. Social motivation. In Lindzey, G., and Aronson, E. (Eds.), *Handbook
     of social psychology*, 2nd ed., vol. 3. Reading, Mass.: Addison-Wesley, 1969.
7   Blai, B., Jr. An occupational study of job satisfaction and need satisfaction. *Journal
     of Experimental Education*, 1964, 32, 383–88.
8   Centers, R. Motivational aspects of occupational stratification. *Journal of Social
     Psychology*, 1948, 28, 187–217.
9   Clark, J. B. Motivation in work groups: A tentative view. *Human Organization*,
     1960–61, 13, 198–208.
10 Cofer, C. N., and Appley, M. H. *Motivation: Theory and research*. New York:
     Wiley, 1964.
11 Dachler, H. P., and Hulin, C. L. A reconsideration of the relationship between
     satisfaction and judged importance of environmental and job characteristics. *Or-
     ganizational Behavior and Human Performance*, 1969, 4, 252–66.
12 Friedlander, F. Underlying sources of job satisfaction. *Journal of Applied Psy-
     chology*, 1963, 47, 246–50.
13 Friedlander, F. Comparative work value systems. *Personnel Psychology*, 1965,
     18, 1–20.
14 Hall, D. T., and Nougaim, K. E. An examination of Maslow's need hierarchy in
     an organizational setting. *Organizational Behavior and Human Performance*, 1968,
     3, 12–35.
15 Harlow, H. F. Mice, monkeys, men, and motives. *Psychological Review*, 1953,
     60, 23–32.
16 Harrison, R. *A conceptual framework for laboratory training*. Unpublished man-
     uscript, 1966.
17 Huizinga, G. *Maslow's need hierarchy in the work situation*. The Netherlands:
     Wolters-Noordhoff nv Groningen, 1970.
18 Lawler, E. E. *Pay and organizational effectiveness: A psychological review*. New
     York: McGraw-Hill, 1971.
19 Lawler, E. E., and Suttle, J. L. A causal correlation test of the need hierarchy
     concept. *Organizational Behavior and Human Performance*, 1972, 7, 265–87.
20 Locke, E. A. Importance and satisfaction in several job areas. Paper delivered at
     American Psychological Association convention, New York, 1961.
21 Maslow, A. H. A theory of human motivation. *Psychological Review*, 1943, 50,
     370–96.
22 Maslow, A. H. *Motivation and personality*. New York: Harper, 1954.
23 Maslow, A. H. *Eupsychian management*. Homewood, Ill.: Irwin-Dorsey, 1965.
24 Maslow, A. H. *Motivation and personality*, 2nd ed. New York: Harper and Row,
     1970.
25 Meehl, P. E. *Clinical vs. statistical prediction*. Minneapolis: University of Min-
     nesota Press, 1954.
26 Miner, J. B., and Dachler, H. P. Personnel attitudes and motivation. *Annual Review
     of Psychology* (in press).
27 Porter, L. W. Job attitudes in management: I. Perceived deficiencies in need ful-
     fillment as a function of job level. *Journal of Applied Psychology*, 1962, 46, 375–
     84.

28   Schaffer, R. H. Job satisfaction as related to need satisfaction in work. *Psychological Monographs*, 1953, 47, Whole no. 364.

29   Trexler, J. T., and Schuh, A. J. Longitudinal verification of Maslow's motivation hierarchy in a military environment. *Experimental Publication System*. Washington, D.C.: American Psychological Association, 1969, Manuscript no. 020A.

30   Vroom, V. H. *Work and motivation*. New York: Wiley, 1964.

31   White, R. W. Motivation reconsidered: The concept of competence. *Psychological Review*, 1959, 66, 297–333.

32   Wofford, J. C. The motivational basis of job satisfaction and job performance. *Personnel Psychology*, 1971, 24, 501–18.

Motivation and Behavior

George H. Litwin
Robert A. Stringer, Jr.

THE ATKINSON MODEL

In his *Introduction to Motivation* (1964), Atkinson presents a formal theory or model of motivated behavior, utilizing a number of principles of motivation which have emerged from the research in this field. We will state the principles embodied in this theory or model, using a simple mechanistic analogy, and then proceed to examine some technical details of the Atkinson model. The basic principles are summarized below:[1]

1   All reasonably healthy adults have a considerable *reservoir of potential energy*. Studies thus far have not indicated that differences in the total amount of potential energy are important determinants of motivation.

2   All adults have a number of basic "motives" or "needs" which can be thought of as valves or outlets that channel and regulate the flow of potential energy from this reservoir.

3   Although most adults within a given culture may have the same set of motives or energy outlets, they will differ greatly in the relative strength or "readiness" of various motives. A strong motive may be thought of as a valve or energy outlet that opens easily and has a larger aperture for energy flow (due, usually, to frequent use). A weak motive can be thought of as a tight, sticky valve that, even when open, allows only limited energy flow.

4   Whether or not a motive is "actualized," that is, whether energy flows through *this* outlet into behavior and useful work, depends on the specific situation in which the person finds himself.

From *Motivation and organizational climate*, Boston: Division of Research, Graduate School of Business Administration, Harvard University, 1968, 10–27, Reprinted by permission.

[1]The mechanical analogy and the language are our own. Neither David McClelland nor John Atkinson should bear any responsibility for this oversimplified description.

5 Certain characteristics of the situation arouse or trigger different motives, opening different valves or energy outlets. Each motive or energy outlet is responsive to a different set of situational characteristics.

6 Since various motives are directed toward different kinds of satisfaction, the pattern of behavior that results from arousal of a motive (and the opening of that energy outlet) is quite distinct for each motive. That is, each motive leads to a different pattern of behavior.

7 By changing the nature of the situational characteristics or stimuli, different motives are aroused or actualized, resulting in the energizing of distinct and different patterns of behavior.

In other words, all adults carry around with them the potential energy to behave in a variety of ways. Whether they behave in these ways depends on: (a) the relative strength or readiness of the various motives a person has; and (b) the situational characteristics or stimuli presented by the situation determine, in large part, which motives will be aroused and what kind of behavior will be generated.

For example, an employee may be used to working in small informal work groups. He is dependent on the group for much of his work satisfaction. We might say that this employee is motivated by a *need for affiliation*. His affiliation energy outlet seems to be wide open when he is allowed to do his job around other people. If the situation was changed, and the worker had to work alone, or if talking was prohibited, or if fellow workers were unfriendly, there would be little opportunity for social interaction. In this new environment, this worker's affiliation energy outlet would not be used. Other motives may be stimulated by the new situation, but we can see how the worker's overall pattern of motivation and behavior would be changed.

Specifically, the Atkinson model holds that *aroused motivation* (to strive for a particular kind of satisfaction or goal) is a joint multiplicative function of (a) the *strength of the basic motive* [M], (b) the *expectancy* of attaining the goal [E], and (c) the *perceived incentive value* of the particular goal [I]. In other words, a person's aroused motivation to behave in a particular way is said to depend on the strength or readiness of his motives, and on two kinds of perceptions of the situation: his expectancies of goal-attainment and the incentive values he attaches to the goals presented. The model can be summarized as follows:

$$\text{Aroused Motivation} = M \times E \times I$$

Motives are conceived here as dispositions to strive for general and often internalized goals. They are presumably acquired in childhood and are relatively enduring and stable over periods of time. Expectancies and incentive values depend on the person's experience in specific situations like the one he now confronts, and they change as the person moves about from one situation to another or as the situation itself is altered.

This theory or model of motivation is closely related to the field theory of behavior proposed by Kurt Lewin (1938) and to several other prominent theories of motivation and behavior (see Feather, 1959; Atkinson, 1964, pp. 274–275). These theories all state that the tendency to act in a certain way depends on the strength of the expentancy or belief that the act will lead to a particular outcome or goal and on the value of that outcome or goal to the person.

The Atkinson model was developed to explain behavior and performance related to the *need for achievement* (*n* Achievement), which is defined as a need to excel in relation to competitive or internalized standards. More recently the model has been extended to explain behavior related to the *need for power* (*n* Power), defined as a need for control and influence over others, and the *need for affiliation* (*n* Affiliation), defined as a need for warm, friendly relationships. All these qualities of motivation have been shown to be important determinants of performance and success in business and government organizations (see McClelland, 1961; Vroom, 1964; and Andrews, 1967).

MEASUREMENT OF MOTIVE STRENGTH

The presence and strength of these motives are assessed through thematic apperceptive methods. This basic method, called the TAT (Thematic Apperception Test), was developed by Murray (1938). Present methods are derivations of the original TAT, aimed at the study of particular motives and suited to particular populations (e.g., college students, business men, Negro Americans). The subject is shown a series of pictures, usually of people in fairly ambiguous social and work situations, and he is asked to make up an imaginative story suggested by each picture of the series. These stories are written (by the subject) or recorded (by the experimenter) and analyzed in detail for evidence of the different kinds of imagery associated with various motives.

Such tests are often referred to as projective tests because the subject "projects" into his story his own thoughts, feelings, and attitudes. What the tests actually do is provide us with samples of the kinds of things a person spends his time thinking and daydreaming about when he is not under pressure to think about anything in particular. What do his thoughts turn to when he is by himself and not engaged in a special job? Does he think about his family and friends, about relaxing and watching the Rose Bowl on TV, about getting a particular customer or colleague off his back? Or does he spend his time thinking and planning how he will sell a customer on a new product, cut production costs, or invent a better steam trap, toothpaste tube, or guidance system?

NEED FOR ACHIEVEMENT[2]

If a man spends his time thinking about doing his job better, accomplishing something unusual and important, or advancing his career, the psychologist says he has a high *need for achievement*, often written *n* Achievement—he is

[2]The material in this section is adapted from "Business Drive and National Achievement" by David C. McClelland (1962).

concerned with achievement and derives considerable satisfaction from striving for achievement. A man with a strong *need for achievement* thinks not only about the achievement goals, but about how he can attain them, what obstacles or blocks he might encounter, and how he will feel if he succeeds or fails.

What are people with a strong *need for achievement* good for? Evidence indicates that they seek out, enjoy, and do well at jobs that are entrepreneurial in character. They make good business executives, particularly in challenging or developing industries. They enjoy activity and often become salesmen, sales managers, consultants, or fund raisers. Years of careful empirical research have made possible an understanding of why a man with a strong *need for achievement* exhibits such characteristics in his behavior.

1. *He likes situations in which he takes personal responsibility for finding solutions to problems*. The reason is obvious. Otherwise, he could get little personal achievement satisfaction from the successful outcome. Not a gambler, he does not prefer situations the outcome of which depends on chance or other factors beyond his control, rather than on his abilities and efforts. For example:

Some business school students in one study played a game in which they had to choose between two options, each of which afforded only one chance in three of succeeding. For one option they rolled a die, and if it came up at either of two of the six possibilities, they won. For the other option they had to work on a difficult business problem which they knew that only one out of three people on the average had been able to solve in the time allotted.

Under these conditions, the men with high *n* Achievement consistently chose to work on the business problem, even though they knew the odds of success were statistically the same for rolling the die.

To men strong in achievement concern, the idea of winning by chance simply does not produce the same achievement satisfaction as winning by their own personal efforts. Obviously, such a concern for taking personal responsibility is useful in a business executive. He may not be faced very often with the alternative of rolling dice to determine the outcome of a decision, but there are many other ways by which he could avoid taking personal responsibility, such as passing the buck or trying to get someone else (or a committee) to take the responsibility for getting something done.

The famed self-confidence of good executives (which, actually, is related to high achievement motivation) is also involved here. He thinks it can be done if he takes responsibility, and very often he is right because he has spent so much time thinking about how to do it that he does it better.

2. *Another characteristic of a man with a strong achievement concern is his tendency to set moderate achievement goals and to take calculated risks*. Again his strategy is well suited to his needs. Only by taking on moderately difficult tasks is he likely to get the achievement satisfaction he wants. If he takes on an easy or routine problem, he will succeed but will get very little satisfaction out of his success, the mere simplicity of the task not affording adequate opportunity to prove his ability and achievement. If he takes on an extremely difficult problem, he is unlikely to get any satisfaction because he

may not succeed. Such an eventuality might disprove his ability and frustrate rather than satisfy his need to achieve. In between these two extremes, he stands the best chance of maximizing both his sense of personal achievement and his likelihood of succeeding.

Applying Atkinson's model, it is only the moderate risk situation which simultaneously maximizes his expectancy of success and the incentive value associated with that success, thereby allowing maximal satisfaction of the need. The point can be made with the children's game of ring toss, a variant of which we have used with individuals of all ages, to discover how a person with *high need for achievement* approaches it. To illustrate:

The child is told that he scores when he succeeds in throwing a ring over a peg on the floor and that he can choose to stand anywhere he pleases. Obviously, if he stands next to the peg, he can score a ringer every time, but if he stands a long distance away, he will hardly ever get a ringer. The curious fact is that children with high concern for achievement quite consistently stand at moderate distances from the peg where they are most apt to get achievement satisfaction (or, to be more precise, where the decreasing probability-of-success curve crosses the increasing satisfaction-from-success curve). The ones with low concern for achievement, on the other hand, distribute their choices of where to stand quite randomly over the entire distance. In other words, people with high *need for achievement* prefer a situation where there is a challenge, where there is some real risk of not succeeding, but where that risk is not so great that they might not overcome it by their own efforts.

We waste our time feeling sorry for the entrepreneur whose constant complaints are that he is overworking, that he has more problems than he knows how to deal with, that he is doomed to ulcers because of overwork, and so on. The bald truth is that he has high *need for achievement*—that he loves the very challenges he complains about. In fact, a careful study might well show that he creates most of them for himself. He may talk about quitting business and living on his investments, but if he did, he might then really get ulcers. The state of mind of being a little overextended is precisely the one he seeks, since overcoming difficulties gives him achievement satisfaction. His real problem is that of keeping the difficulties from getting too big for him, which explains in part why he talks so much about them—it is a nagging problem for him to keep them at a level he can handle.

3. *The man who has a strong concern for achievement also wants concrete feedback as to how well he is doing.* Otherwise, how could he get any satisfaction out of what he had done? Business is almost unique in the amount of feedback it provides in the form of sales, cost, production, and profit figures. It is no accident that the symbol of the businessman in popular cartoons is a wall chart with a line on it going up or down. The businessman, sooner or later, knows how well he is doing; salesmen will often know their success from day to day. There is a concreteness in this knowledge of results which is by and large missing from the kind of feedback professionals get.

The teacher will serve as a representative example of such a professional.

His job is to transmit certain attitudes and certain kinds of information to his students. He does get some degree of feedback as to how well he has done his job, but results are fairly imprecise and hardly concrete. His students, colleagues, and even his institution's administration may indicate that they like his teaching, but he still has no real objective or precise evidence that his students have learned anything from him. Many of his students do well on examinations, but he knows from past experience that they will forget much of what they have written in a year or two. If he has high *need for achievement* and is really concerned about whether he has done his job well, he must be satisfied with sketchy, occasional evidence that his former pupils did absorb some of his ideas and attitudes. Most likely, however, he is *not* a person with high *need for achievement* and is quite satisfied with the affection and recognition that he gets for his work. These feedback measures will gratify needs other than his *need for achievement*.

Obviously not everyone likes to work in situations where the feedback is concrete. It can prove him right, but it also can prove him wrong. The person with high *n* Achievement has a compelling interest to know whether he was right or wrong. He thrives and is happier when this condition is satisfied by the situation than when it is not, as is usually the case in the professional situation. When an individual with a high *need for achievement* does involve himself in a professional situation, furthermore, he usually seeks out a role where more concrete feedback on performance is provided, such as that of a trial lawyer, a doctor who establishes a clinic, or a professor who becomes a fund raiser.

NEED FOR POWER

If a man spends his time thinking about the influences and control he has over others, and how he can use this influence, say, to win an argument, to change other people's behavior, or to gain a position of authority and status, then the psychologist says he has a high *need for power*, often written *n* Power. He derives satisfaction from controlling the means of influence over others.

Men with a strong need for power will usually attempt to influence others directly—by making suggestions, by giving their opinions and evaluations, and by trying to talk others into things. They seek positions of leadership in group activities; whether they become leaders or are seen only as "dominating individuals" depends on other attributes such as ability and sociability. They are usually verbally fluent, often talkative, sometimes argumentative. Men with a strong *need for power* are seen by others as forceful and outspoken, but also as hard-headed and demanding.

As should be expected, men with a strong concern for power prefer positions which allow the exercise of power. They enjoy roles requiring persuasion, such as teaching and public speaking. In addition, a man with a high concern for power will seek out positions which involve control of the means of influencing others, such as political office or top management slots. Studies of the motivation of managers have shown that although strong achievement motivation distinguishes the successful manager or entrepreneur from other people, the men in top management, and particularly organization presidents, are strongly motivated by the *need for power*.

For the past 20 years, social scientists have been involved in the study of influence and power. Much of this research deals with topics such as "Authoritarian Personality" and "Fascism," and represents largely a kind of social criticism regarding the use of power rather than a genuine scientific exploration of power motivation. In a democracy, matters relating to the accumulation of personal power are inevitably treated with suspicion and dread, and some scientists have been quick to interpret the natural concerns with influence, control, and power which develop in society as a dangerous threat to our democratic institutions and way of life.

What research has been done indicates clearly that men with strong *need for power* do not always gain power and that even when they do, what use they make of this power is determined by *other needs and values*. A man with a strong *n* Power, little concern for warm, affiliative relationships, and strong authoritarian values would certainly tend toward autocratic and dictatorial action. On the other hand, a man with strong *n* Power, considerable sensitivity to others' feelings, and a desire to give service to others would probably make an excellent Peace Corps worker or missionary. This polarity in the use of power is illustrated in a study by Andrews (1967) of two Mexican companies. One of these was a dynamic and rapidly growing organization whose employees were enthusiastic about their work; the other organization, despite a large initial investment and favorable market, had shown almost no growth and had serious problems of dissatisfaction and turnover, particularly in the management ranks. Assessment of personnel motivation in both these companies showed that those in the upper management of the more dynamic organization were much higher in *n* Achievement than either their own subordinates or those in the upper management of the static organization. The presidents of both of these companies were *very high* in the *need for power*. In the case of the dynamic organization, the president's *need for power*, combined with a moderate *need for achievement* and a strong commitment to achievement values had helped create a thriving successful business. In the other case, the president's *need for power* and rather authoritarian values led him to dominate every other person in the organization, make all the decisions himself, and leave almost no room for individual responsibility.

Politics as an activity represents one of the clearest theaters for expression of the *need for power*, and men who run for political office characteristically demonstrate very strong power motivation. Here the explicit goal is control of the means of influencing others (e.g., law enforcement, executive position), and this goal can only be reached by influencing many others (e.g., the voters). The various writings on the American Presidency may be the richest literature available on the phenomenology of power, how power is gained, and how it affects men who have it. The following two passages, from Theodore H. White's *The Making of the President 1960*, are very vivid descriptions of the phenomenology of power—how power is experienced by the man who seeks and gains it:

Shortly before he died in 1950, the great Henry L. Stimson was asked which of the many Presidents of his acquaintance had been the best. Stimson, according to the man from whom I heard the tale, reflected a minute or two, for his career stretched over half a century of American history. He had known intimately or served importantly more Presidents, Democratic and Republican, than any other citizen of his age—from Theodore Roosevelt through Taft, Wilson, Coolidge and Hoover to Franklin D. Roosevelt and Harry S. Truman. After reflection, Stimson replied to his friend:

If, by the phrase "best President," the friend meant who had been the most efficient President—why, of course, the answer would be William Howard Taft. Under Taft, the Cabinet met in order, affairs marched to the agenda of the meeting, responsibility was clearly deputized, and when each man rose from the Cabinet table he knew exactly what he was to do and to whom he was to report. Yes, Taft certainly was the most efficient. If, however, continued Stimson, by the "best President" one meant the "greatest President," then the answer must be different. The name would, without doubt, be Roosevelt—but he was not sure whether the first name was Theodore or Franklin. For both of these gentlemen, you see, not only understood the *use* of power, they knew the *enjoyment* of power, too. And that was the important thing.

Whether a man is burdened by power or enjoys power; whether he is trapped by responsibility or made free by it; whether he is moved by other people and other forces or moves them—this is of the essence of leadership.

A one-time personal aide of President Truman once put the matter to me in this way: "The most startling thing a new President discovers is that his world is *not* monolithic. In the world of the Presidency, giving an order does *not* end the matter. You can pound your fist on the table or you can get mad or you can blow it all and go out to the golf course. But nothing gets done except by endless follow-up, endless kissing and coaxing, endless threatening and compelling. There are all those thousands of people in Washington working for you in the government—and every one is watching you, waiting, trying to guess what you mean, trying to get your number. Can they fool you? Can they outwait you? Will you be mad when you hear it isn't done yet? And Congress keeps shoving more and more power into the President's lap—the Formosa resolution gives the President power to declare war all by himself; and Congress keeps setting up new regulatory agencies, and you have to hire and fire the men who run them. And they're all testing you. How much can they get away with? How much authority can they take? How much authority do *you* want them to have? And once you choose your men—you have to keep them; which means the endless attrition of *your* will against their will, because some of them will be damned good men . . . (White, 1965, pp. 366–367).

NEED FOR AFFILIATION

If a man spends his time thinking about the warm, friendly, companionate relationships he has, or would like to have, the psychologist says he has a *need for affiliation*, often written *n* Affiliation. Thoughts about restoring close relationships that have been disrupted, consoling or helping someone, or participating in friendly, companionate activities such as bull sessions, reunions, and parties are regarded as evidence of affiliation motivation.

Since they want others to like them, men with a strong *need for affiliation* are likely to pay attention to the feelings of others. In group meetings they make efforts to establish friendly relationships, often by agreeing or giving emotional support. Men with strong *need for affiliation* seek out jobs which offer opportunities for friendly interaction. In business, these men often take supervisory jobs where maintaining good relationships is more important than decision making. People who have institutionalized helping roles, such as teachers, nurses, and counselors, also demonstrate strong *need for affiliation*.

While strong *n* Affiliation does not seem to be important for effective managerial performance, and might well be detrimental, recent research has suggested that some minimal concern with the feelings of others and with the companionate quality of relationships is necessary for superior managerial and executive capability. It is reasonable to assume that such basic affiliative concern is critical in understanding others and in building good working relationships with both superiors and subordinates—this affiliative concern is a means to attain other, broader kinds of satisfaction and might well be labeled *interpersonal competence*. Moment and Zaleznik give a graphic description of this kind of behavior:

> People need each other to get work done and to live full lives. The fullness of life is measured by achievements. Communicating with people is the ultimate achievement process. Something new is created through talking and working with people. The ultimate achievement is the creation of new and better resolutions of social and technical problems.
>
> Although there are standards of excellence for individuals' contributions, real resolutions of problems are tested in the communication process. . . .
>
> . . . his behavior clearly communicates his feelings. He also communicates his confidence in himself; he will unapologetically defend his positions, but he will also change his position in accordance with what he is learning in the process. He acknowledges in his behavior that he is communicating with specific people, rather than thinking out loud about ideas separated from people. His behavior says that the other persons as individuals, as well as sources of ideas, are bound up in the problem-solving process (Moment and Zaleznik, 1963, pp. 120–121).

Compare this with Moment and Zaleznik's description of the "social specialists," which we would characterize as men with strong *need for affiliation*:

> People need each other for support. Feeling lonely, disliked, and disrespected by people is the worst thing that could happen to a person. Living together in harmony is the ultimate value. One must work hard and do a good job in order to be accepted by others. But work should not be allowed to interfere with harmony, respect, and affection.
>
> One learns from experience that being close and friendly with people is more

important than career success. Having friends and being friendly are necessary to support and encourage a person through periods of disappointment and hardship.

Satisfaction is derived from being liked and accepted in the group. Argument and conflict are frustrating and make for an unhappy experience (Moment and Zaleznik, 1963, pp. 123–124).

SUMMARY

In this chapter a theory of motivation developed out of more than 20 years of laboratory and field research has been presented. Some emphasis was placed on a recent formal model, the Atkinson model, which states that aroused motivation (to strive for a particular goal) is a function of the strength of the basic need and two situationally determined factors, the expectancy of goal-attainment and the perceived incentive value of the goal.

We have tried to describe the three kinds of motivation that we will focus on in this monograph—achievement motivation, power motivation, and affiliation motivation. There are at least three ways of describing these motivational tendencies, all of which we have employed. First, we have tried to define the nature of the basic need or goal, particularly in terms of the kind of satisfaction that is desired. Second, we have described the quality of aroused motivation, in terms of the thoughts and feelings of the motivated person. Third, we have identified patterns of behavior which stem from arousal of the *need for achievement*, the *need for power*, and the *need for affiliation*. It is not always possible to distinguish among these levels of description without being overly tedious. However, the reader should try to keep in mind the very important difference between *motive*, which is a relatively stable personality characteristic, and *aroused motivation*, which is a situationally influenced action tendency. The reader should also keep in mind that aroused motivation can be described in terms of a *pattern of thoughts and feelings*, which is a situationally influenced action tendency. The reader should also keep in mind that aroused motivation can be described in terms of a *pattern of thoughts and feelings*, such as would be revealed in thematic apperceptive stories, or in terms of a *pattern of behavior* which is likely to result from motive arousal.

The specific scoring procedures which are used to analyze thematic apperceptive stories, and which allow us to measure the relative strength of *n* Achievement, *n* Power, and *n* Affiliation have not been dealt with. These scoring procedures are described in detail in Atkinson's *Motives in Fantasy, Action, and Society* (1958). Nonprofessional scorers can use these procedures to derive specific scores which provide objective measures of the strength of aroused motivation. The objectivity of these measures is demonstrated by the high agreement that is possible among scorers working independently. Recent attempts to develop computer programs to do this scoring have been quite successful, providing definite evidence of the objectivity of these scoring procedures (see Litwin, 1965).

The *n* Achievement, *n* Power and *n* Affiliation scores derived from thematic apperceptive tests through application of the scoring procedures described by Atkinson (1958) are assumed to represent the strength of aroused motivation. That is, they are products of motive strength *and* of situational factors. Under certain circumstances, these scores can also provide a useful index of the strength of the basic motives. When a group of people with similar backgrounds and experiences (and, presumably, perceptions) are in the same constant situation, differences in motivation scores can be assumed to represent differences in the strength of basic motives—the subjective or idiosyncratic elements are assumed to cancel each other out. That is, the situational influences are held constant and relative differences in score represent differences in motive strength.

The administrative implications of the kind of motivation theory we have described are quite dramatic. By identifying and learning to influence particular expectancies and incentives associated with a motive network, it is possible to strengthen the aroused motivation or behavior tendency. Though the role of reinforcement in the Atkinson model has not been clearly specified, the effects of reinforcement on aroused motivation are well established. Using our oversimplified, hydraulic model of the Atkinson theory, reinforcement can be represented as an enlargement of the valve capacity associated with any particular motive. Just as water enlarged the proverbial hole through which the little Dutch boy stuck his finger, so the repeated passage of energy through these motivational values tends to wear away at their edges, making them larger and more easily opened, increasing their total capacity for energy flow. By tying the expectancies and incentives to as many consistent cues as possible in the business environment, the likelihood of a particular pattern of behavior can be increased.

Since different motives lead to different behavior patterns, it is important that the manager learn to identify, at least in a rough way, different kinds of basic motives or needs. He must also be able to "fit" the demands of a job to a pattern of behavior that will result from and provide satisfaction for the arousal of a given motive. He can create this fit by the selection and appropriate placement of people with different motives, by altering somewhat the demands of a given job, or by *selectively* arousing, satisfying, and thereby reinforcing the kind of motivation that will lead to the most appropriate job behavior. Once he has obtained what he considers a reasonable fit, he can proceed to build into the work situation the kinds of expectancies and incentives that will arouse the desired motivation and assure persistent patterns of behavior.

REFERENCES

Andrews, J. (1967)"The Achievement Motive in Two Types of Organizations," *Journal of Personality and Social Psychology*, **6**: 163–168.
Atkinson, J. W., ed. (1958) *Motives in Fantasy, Action and Society*. Princeton: D. Van Nostrand Company.

Atkinson, J. W. (1964) *An Introduction to Motivation*. Princeton: D. Van Nostrand Company.

Feather, N. T. (1950) "Subjective Probability and Decision under Uncertainty," *Psychological Review*, **66**: 150–164.

Herzberg, F. (1966) *Work and the Nature of Man*. Cleveland: World Publishing Company.

Lewin, K. (1938) *The Conceptual Representation and the Measurement of Psychological Forces*. Durham: Duke University Press.

Litwin, G. H. (1965) "The Language of Achievement: An Analysis of Achievement-Related Themes in Fantasy Using Mechanical Methods," unpublished doctoral dissertation, Harvard University.

McClelland, D. C. (1961) *The Achieving Society*. Princeton: D. Van Nostrand Company.

McClelland, D. C. (1962) "Business Drive and National Achievement," *Harvard Business Review*, **40**: July-August, 99–112.

Moment, D., and A. Zaleznik (1963) *Role Development and Interpersonal Competence*. Boston: Division of Research, Harvard Business School.

Murray, H. A. (1938) *Explorations in Personality*. New York: Oxford University Press.

Myers, M. S. (1966) "Conditions for Manager Motivation," *Harvard Business Review*, **44**: January-February, 58–71.

Vroom, V. H. (1964) *Work and Motivation*. New York: John Wiley and Sons.

White, T. H. (1965) *The Making of the President 1960*. New York: Atheneum Publishers.

An Examination of Need-Satisfaction Models of Job Attitudes[1]

Gerald R. Salancik
Jeffrey Pfeffer

One of the most prominent areas of study in organizational behavior is job attitudes, or how people feel about what they do when they work. This interest in job satisfaction persists to attract research attention. Affective responses to job conditions are the bases for several different organizational development strategies (Bowers, 1973) and an important component of recent interest in work and job design (Hackman and Suttle, 1977).

It is fair to state that a need-satisfaction model has been the theoretical framework almost universally applied to understand job satisfaction and, occasionally, motivation. The purpose of this examination is to analyze the nature of need-satisfaction models and their usefulness for understanding individuals' reactions to their jobs. Both the specific methodological issues that are involved in research on such models, and, more importantly, the fundamental assumptions about behavior implicit in the theoretical structure of such models are

Reprinted from: *Administrative Science Quarterly*, 1977, **22**, 427–456. Reprinted by permission.

1. In the process of preparing this paper, we were aided by the contributions of several individuals. We thank them all, particularly George Strauss, Barry Staw, Karlene Roberts, Charles O'Reilly, Greg Oldham, and Jeanne Herman.

considered. In conclusion, it is shown that the basic, theoretical assumptions of such models fundamentally conflict with recent research findings about attitudes and information processing. . . .

Two other introductory notes are in order. First, because of the large number of studies dealing with need satisfaction, comprehensive summaries and citations of every one shall not be made. Nor shall each particular abridgement of need models be noted. The purpose of this examination is not to attack the authors who have worked so hard to refine theories of needs and the effects on job attitudes and behavior. Rather it is to question the validity and value of fundamental conceptions of needs and jobs. Second, an alternative perspective on job attitudes and task design is proposed.

THE NEED-SATISFACTION MODEL

The need-satisfaction model, in its basic structure, is quite simple (see Figure 1). The model posits that persons have basic, stable, relatively unchanging and identifiable attributes, including needs (and personality [Argyris, 1957]). The model also assumes that jobs have a stable, identifiable set of characteristics that are relevant to those needs of individuals. Job attitudes and, occasionally, motivation, are presumed to result from the correspondence between the needs of the individual and the characteristics of the job or the job situation. When the characteristics of the job are compatible with the person's needs, the assumption is made that the person is satisfied and, on occasion, the further

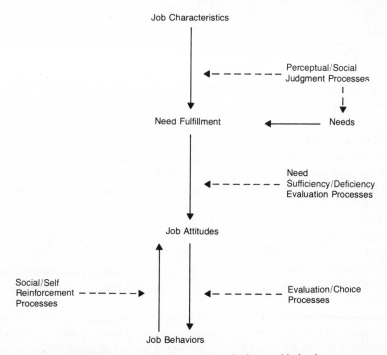

Figure 1 A need-satisfaction model of jobs, needs, attitudes, and behaviors.

argument is made that the person will be more motivated to perform the job. Jobs which fulfill a person's needs are satisfying; those that do not are not satisfying. If the person is satisfied with his job, it is presumably because the job has characteristics compatible with his needs. If the person is unhappy with his job, it is because the job is presumably not satisfying his needs.

Components of the Need-Satisfaction Model

While the basic model is relatively simple, there are a variety of assumptions embedded in its components. To consider alternative formulations, the components of the need-satisfaction model are summarized graphically.

The first component of the need-satisfaction model is an assumption of causality. The presumed sequence of causality begins with the job and its characteristics. Job characteristics are considered the stimuli which elicit an attitude from the person. In assuming that job characteristics cause attitudes, need-satisfaction models have neglected attitude following from the characteristics. If a person likes the job for whatever reason, we are arguing, the possibility exists that he or she may impute desirable characteristics to the job as a consequence.

A second component of the need-satisfaction model is that attitudes are conceived of as reactions by people to their environment. Some authors argue that the reaction is affective, involving a component of arousal. Others postulate a behavioral reaction, involving some approach or avoidance to the job. For instance, absenteeism has been considered as an indicator of a person's attitude toward the job (Hackman and Lawler, 1971; Hrebiniak and Roteman, 1973; Porter and Steers, 1973). Still others have thought of the reaction as cognitive, involving a component of evaluation.

While the need-satisfaction model itself does not distinguish among these possible reactions, it is important to keep in mind that presumed reactions to job characteristics are measured and conceived of differently by different authors. The validity of any assumption about which particular reactions reflect an underlying attitude can affect critically the ability to predict the implications of the need-satisfaction model for a given situation. For example, if absenteeism does not reflect a person's attitude toward the job, then any test of the need-satisfaction model using such a measure is hampered.

There is a presumed, implicit attitude-behavior causal link in most need-satisfaction formulations. Certainly in the use of absenteeism as an indicator of job attitudes, there is the presumption that the unsatisfied worker will manifest his feelings by staying off the job. Some formulations have begun to define motivation in terms of attitudes, as did Oldham (1976: 559): "Internal work motivation refers to the degree to which an individual experiences positive internal feelings when performing effectively on the job." Oldham further defines motivation in terms of satisfaction with work, and since motivation presumably leads to behavior, the attitude-behavior sequence has motivation as an intervening construct. There is enough controversy about the validity of the attitude-behavior causal linkage (Wicker, 1969; Calder and Ross, 1973; Schuman and Johnson, 1976) to call into question this portion of the need-satisfaction formulation. This controversy has been largely ignored in the development of the job-attitude literature.

A third feature of need-satisfaction models is that needs are conceptualized as relatively stable characteristics of persons. In predicting the reaction of an individual to his job, needs are the filter through which reactions distill. For example, Wanous (1974) studied three different ways of characterizing individuals in an attempt to identify what moderates the relation between the presence of certain job characteristics and individual reactions to these characteristics. There are differences among versions concerning the ubiquity of needs across the population and also some difference in the extent to which needs are viewed as changeable. Even those who view needs as something changeable or learned (McClelland, 1961), however, give needs the property of being relatively stable, fixed dimensions of persons, particularly in the case of adults who, more fully socialized, are attributed with stable personalities.

Although need models imply relatively stable, fixed characterizations of needs the implication here is not meant to be that none of the models consider the possibility that need strength changes. Many theorists do argue that need strengths change. Argyris (1957) suggested that a personality can be stunted when confronted with a constant environment lacking challenge. Alderfer (1972) assumed that the desire for need fulfillment diminished with the actual fulfillment. His findings are consistent with Maslow's (1954) view of needs arranged hierarchically, so that as one need becomes fulfilled, its strength diminishes while the strength of the next need up the hierarchy increases. While some authors argue that there are changes in need strength, the perspective underlying need-satisfaction models assumes that the needs themselves are fixed characteristics of individuals. Furthermore, the structure of the theories and tests of them require the assumption of needs fixed over some time period. Studies presume to predict reactions to job characteristics on the basis of needs. Such a formulation clearly implies that needs are stable at least over the period from the time the needs are measured to the time when the events (attitude, motivation) predicted by the theory are to occur.

A fourth feature of need-satisfaction models is the conceptualization of job characteristics. Job characteristics are taken as realities in the environment to which the individual responds. Jobs have particular and fixed characteristics, and, further, such characteristics bear some relation to a person's needs. Jobs can be routine, provide feedback, give workers freedom, require a variety of skills, and so forth (Hackman and Lawler, 1971). Newman (1975) has argued that organizational context affects workers' responses through the mediating construct of the perceived work environment. In Newman's formulation, there are objective, structural features which, in turn, affect the perceived environment, and this, in turn, affects attitudes toward the job and the organization. What is interesting about Newman's study is that there were relatively low (though frequently statistically significant) correlations between dummy variables representing the department and the work group and perceived environment characteristics (1975: 380). In only one case was more than 25 percent of the variance in perceived work environment characteristics explained by the respondents' location in the organization. Present need-satisfaction models do not seriously consider the possibility that job characteristics are socially constructed realities, mediated by the individual's social environment, rather than inherent characteristics of the objective situation. . . .

The fifth component of need-satisfaction models is the functional relation among needs, job characteristics, and attitudes. If attitudes result from the interaction of a person's needs with the objective job characteristics, some calculus is still required to specify just how such attitudes are related to needs and characteristics. One model used is a discrepancy model, based on Porter's (1961; 1962; 1963) need deficiency conceptualization. In this model, persons are asked to rate the importance of characteristics presently associated with their jobs and how much of each characteristic they would prefer to have connected with the job (Hrebiniak and Roteman, 1973). The individual need deficiencies can be correlated with satisfaction or some behavioral measure presumed to reflect satisfaction, such as absenteeism. Alternately, the scores can be totaled and then correlated with the criterion measure. Given the moderate correlations occasionally found between the various items in the Porter need-deficiency scale (Herman and Hulin, 1973: 122), other possible combinations of such scores to predict the criterion could be constructed, such as sums over a few of the items, or using subscale scores.

The second model, for measuring the interrelationship of need, job characteristics, and attitude, suggests that attitudes are a function of the presence or absence of positively valued job characteristics. This means the higher the person's need for a certain characteristic, the higher the correlation between the presence of that characteristic and motivation or job satisfaction (Hackman and Lawler, 1971; Brief and Aldag, 1975). Instead of asking people their desired job characteristics and how much of each characteristic they perceive in their current jobs, this latter formulation asks the respondents about their jobs, about their satisfaction, and about their higher-order needs, presumably met by the various job characteristics also measured. An interaction is posited between higher-order need strength and the relation between job characteristics and job satisfaction, though this interaction has only rarely been explicitly tested in the research. Furthermore, the studies reported seldom use any form of multivariate analysis. Job satisfaction measures are correlated with individual job characteristics. The question is left open as to whether attitudes are a function of the number of job characteristics present, whether job characteristics interact to affect attitudes, or whether the importance of various characteristics varies.

Thus, in spite of the large number of studies conducted from the need-satisfaction framework, there has been little precise specification of the additive, interactive, or disjunctive effects of either need deficiencies or job characteristics on satisfaction. One exception is the study by Hackman and Oldham (1976) on the effects of job design, in which they explicated a precise multiplicative relationship of the various job features to individual motivations. The analysis of the data indicated that an additive function provided a better fit than their multiplicative model, thereby challenging that aspect of the theory.

IMPLICATIONS OF NEED-SATISFACTION MODELS
FOR MANAGEMENT

The implications of the need-satisfaction model for the management of job attitudes are, of course, logical consequences of the basic assumptions of the model. Thus, a model that posits stable needs and fixed job characteristics leads only to strategies of either matching needs with characteristics or changing characteristics of the job to fit the needs of the job holders. Since assumptions made about how job attitudes develop are critical to determining the strategies used to change such attitudes, it is necessary to test these assumptions occasionally and abandon them when they do not hold. To refute an assumption, however, one must attempt to violate it. This procedure is not often followed by researchers; more often, the search is for support of beliefs than tests of their validity.

If one's assumptions become more flexible about the permanence of needs and the reality of job characteristics, a variety of strategies for managing job attitudes becomes possible. Some of the strategies include: 1. redesigning or changing people to have different needs (as in socialization or consciousness-raising); 2. affecting a person's awareness, comprehension, or interpretation of job characteristics; 3. altering the context of the job to develop desired attitudes; 4. affecting the relationship of the person to the job (such as expected length of tenure, or degree of commitment) to obtain desired attitudes; or, 5. affecting behavior or the conditions of behavior to provoke, create, or change attitudes. The evidence for the effectiveness of such strategies is precisely evidence against the assumptions associated with the need-satisfaction model, and, therefore, evidence that invalidates the model. . . .

THE POPULARITY OF NEED-SATISFACTION MODELS

The need-satisfaction model, in one of its versions, is virtually ubiquitous in writing about job attitudes. To reduce the hold of a need-satisfaction perspective, one must first understand some of its sources of persistence as a theoretical framework for thinking about persons in the work situation.

Need-satisfaction models, are consistent with other models of human behavior that promote beliefs about human rationality. As Mitchell and Biglan (1971) noted, expectancy models are to be found not only in organizational behavior but also in marketing, in the studies of attitudes (Fishbein, 1963), and in theories of rational decision making (Edwards, 1959). The need-satisfaction model is similar to the rational-economic man model of decision making, which argues that people make decisions consistent with the extent to which choice alternatives satisfy or do not satisfy their preferences or self interest. By suggesting that individuals develop preferences according to the manner in which states of the world satisfy their needs, it is suggested that individual responses are rationally linked to the environment. The idea suggests that people pursue their interests and shape their behavior and attitudes to achieve their goals.

Thus, the underlying structure of need-satisfaction models presumes rational action. In this, they are consistent in important respects with other models of rational choice.

Need-satisfaction models also have the benefit of attributing potency and freedom to individuals. The idea that individuals shape their actions to satisfy their needs gives individual activity purpose and direction. While a person is, to some extent, a captive to his needs, he is pictured as directing activities according to his needs, and potentially, choosing situations in which his needs will be more or less well met. A person has the freedom to decide and, through his decisions, to attain need satisfaction.

Although need-satisfaction models apparently attribute freedom to an individual, in one important respect they also deny a person freedom to behave. Implicit in the idea that a person is motivated to satisfy his needs is that needs serve as inevitable determinants of action. Maslow (1943) even speaks of self-actualizing behavior as a somewhat compulsive thing, as musicians who *must* make music, and artists who *must* paint. Such a formulation provides a ready explanation for behavior—I had to do it—and can aid in maintaining the behaviors in the face of negative reactions about their worth or acceptability. In other words, needs make it acceptable not to change. Children who fail at a task have been found to avoid trying further if they attribute their failure to unchangeable personal characteristics (Dweck, 1975). Thus needs, by providing explanations for behavior, help to stabilize individual action and provide continuity.

Need-satisfaction models offer the further advantage of being simple, easily expressed views of human behavior. And, as with most persistent theories, need-satisfaction models, if carefully formulated, are almost impossible to disprove, and can provide an explanation for behavior that is almost as pervasive as the idea of motivation (Weick, 1969). Needs, used for explanation by scientists and lay people alike, are indeed a seductive concept.

Because of the ubiquity and appeal of need models, it is appropriate to discuss the conditions of reality with which such models are consistent and inconsistent. The Table [Table 1] displays various possible states of the world confronting an experimenter studying only two subjects. The subjects can have similar or dissimilar measured needs or need strengths, confront similar or dissimilar job characteristics, and have the same or different attitudinal reactions. Since there are two possible conditions for each of the three variables (needs, job characteristics, and attitudinal reactions), there are a total of eight possible states of the world. The Table illustrates why, by chance alone, need-satisfaction models are easily confirmed.

In condition 1, individuals have the same needs, face the same job characteristics, and have the same reactions. This outcome is consistent with the need-satisfaction model. But so are the conditions in which the individuals have different needs, face the same jobs, and have different attitudes; face different jobs, have different needs, and have the same attitudes; or face different jobs, have different needs, and have different attitudes. Further, the need-satisfaction

Table 1 Possible Combinations of Needs, Job Characteristics, and Attitudes for Two Individuals

Condition	Needs	Job characteristics	Attitudinal reaction
1	Same	Same	Same
2*	Same	Same	Different
3	Same	Different	Same
4	Same	Different	Different
5	Different	Same	Same
6	Different	Same	Different
7	Different	Different	Same
8	Different	Different	Different

*This condition provides the only clear instance in which the need-satisfaction model is refuted.

model is compatible with the condition in which individuals have the same needs, have different jobs, and have different attitudes.

Conditions 3 and 5 are slightly more difficult for the model to handle. Can individuals have the same attitudes if they have the same needs but face different jobs, or have different needs but face the same job? The answer depends on what assumptions are made about the mapping of attitudes and needs to job characteristics. If a person processes all job characteristics relevant to his needs, the answer is no, for people with the same needs will have the same attitudes only if the jobs have identically experienced characteristics. The answer also depends on the assumed relationship of needs to characteristics; if two individuals with different needs can each select those characteristics appropriate to their needs, then they may have similar attitudes. Since there is scarcely a precise mapping of job characteristics with needs and attitudes provided in the existing literature, perhaps most need models could be constructed consistent with conditions 3 and 5.

That leaves condition 2 as the only unambiguous condition which could potentially refute the need-satisfaction model. If persons with the same needs face jobs with identical characteristics but have different attitudes, data have been generated inconsistent with the need-satisfaction model. The reason is clear: If different attitudes can be generated from equivalent need-job contingencies, then the attitudes cannot be described as being determined by needs. The concept of need would be unnecessary to explain attitudes. The condition is then a strong source for refuting need models. It occurs in only one out of eight circumstances, however, and is a circumstance that frequently is not sought by researchers. Thus, by chance, it is likely that data will be produced consistent with the need-satisfaction formulation. An adequate test of the model would attempt to produce the circumstances of condition 2. If this were to prove impossible, then there would be strong support for the validity of the model.

Need-satisfaction models are also accepted more readily because of certain cognitive biases affecting observations of human behavior. Recent research in attribution theory has suggested that there is a tendency for observers of action to attribute the cause of the action to internal states of the actors (Jones and Harris, 1967; Jones and Nisbett, 1971). A number of studies further demonstrate that, while observers tend to make internal attributions of a person's behavior, the person himself tends to attribute his behavior to external causes (cf. Jones and Nisbett, 1971). One explanation for this phenomenon is that actors and observers possess different information (Jones and Nisbett, 1971). The actor sees the environment more than he sees himself behaving and, thus, is likely to select information from the environment which explains his behavior because of its relative saliency. The observer, on the other hand, is exposed primarily to the actor, with his attention focused on the action itself. This leads observers to attribute causality to characteristics of the actor. The tendency to attribute causality to a person's internal characteristics is similar to attributing needs to individuals as explanations for their behavior. Thus, the saliency of information and cognitive processes tends to support an attribution process consistent with the need-satisfaction framework.

The tendency to attribute action to personal characteristics is not limited to observers. Such attributions are also relevant for the actor's understanding of his own behavior. If a person behaves in a situation for which there are no salient external cues consistent with the behavior, he will tend to use a personal construct (such as attitude) to explain and justify that behavior. This effect, of course, is the core of Bem's (1972) self-perception theory, which has been experimentally tested numerous times.

Although need-satisfaction models postulate generally pleasing characteristics to persons—such as, rationality and freedom—are difficult to disprove, and are supported by cognitive biases to attribute personal causes to actions, need-satisfaction models implicitly deny one important human potential—adaptability, the ability to cope with a variety of circumstances. Need models assume that individuals react to external realities in the context of relatively unchanging needs. Need-satisfaction models do not allow for the possibility that instead of reacting to environments which include job characteristics, individuals enact environments (Weick, 1969). According to need-satisfaction models, when the external environment is incompatible with an individual's needs, the person is doomed to dissatisfaction. That person can, of course, try to find another environment or change the features of the present one, but failing in those two efforts, dissatisfaction must follow.

The need-satisfaction model ultimately denies persons the creative capacity to cope with their environment, in part, by constructing meaning that makes the context more satisfying, and, in part, by redefining the situation and attending to selected aspects of the situation. The function of producing satisfaction is delegated to outsiders, those who design the environment. Individuals are presumed to be incapable of perceiving their environments to create their own satisfaction. Thus, need-satisfaction models imply that individuals are tightly linked to their environments (cf. Weick, 1976). Individuals register the objective environment, and respond in terms of their needs. In such a formulation, the probability of dissatisfaction is necessarily high. All mismatches between a person's needs and the situation will cause dissatisfaction. Since many needs, or the characteristics they imply, are empirically (if not logically) incompatible, such as desires for freedom and equality, then a person will confront dissatisfaction most of the time. If it is further assumed that a person is motivated to reduce dissatisfaction, then the person must be either dissatisfied always and in constant search for better conditions, or the world must be assumed to be an unusually perfect place. The evidence indicates that there is not much job dissatisfaction, nor that such dissatisfaction is increasing greatly (Strauss, 1974). Perhaps, persons are not tightly linked through their needs to an objective environment after all.

THEORETICAL DIFFICULTIES CONFRONTING NEED-SATISFACTION MODELS

When the principal features of the need-satisfaction model were outlined, an allusion was made to some conceptual ambiguities facing this perspective, such as the calculus by which needs, job characteristics, and attitudes were interrelated. The major theoretical problems confronting need-satisfaction models, however, have to do with the two basic components of these models, the concepts of needs and job characteristics. Given the relatively large number of studies devoted to job attitudes, it is reasonable to expect that the theoretical problems inherent in the use of concepts such as needs and job characteristics would have been addressed long ago. Such is not the case, and any critique of the model must proceed from an examination of these two major building blocks.

The Concept of Needs

The concept of needs is a concept that has been widely used in psychology. One irreverent observer has commented that psychologists must have a need to construct lists of needs. The idea of needs is one of the basic foundations of the need-satisfaction model. Whether the needs are arranged in a hierarchy, in categories, are widely distributed through the population, are acquired in childhood or are instinctual, need-satisfaction models all assume that persons have needs. Most models assert hypotheses about needs as if these hypotheses were established truths, and then move quickly on to the interesting problem of the interrelationship of needs, jobs, and attitudes.

Such a cavalier attitude is scarcely warranted. The concept of needs may be potentially misleading and unnecessary for the development of theories of human behavior. The first question to be asked about needs is their origin. As noted, some believe that virtually all needs are instinctual (for example, Maslow, 1970), and most psychologists believe that at least some needs are instinctual.

If some needs are instinctual and some are learned, then an interesting issue becomes which needs are acquired and which are inherent. One general finding of the research on the concept of instinct is that the further the inquiries progress, less tends to be attributed to instinct. Such is the case with the concept of human needs as well. Even the presumably basic human needs such as hunger, thirst, and sex are, in part, socially conditioned, as is evidenced from the research on obesity and human sexual dysfunctions. It is difficult to maintain the position that needs, particularly higher-order needs, are instinctual in the face of little evidence for the generality of needs (Turner and Lawrence, 1965; Hulin and Blood, 1968) and of the convincing social learning literature (Bandura, 1969) which argues that most behavioral dispositions are acquired through learning.

Needs must be relatively stable if they are to have any explanatory power over time, and, therefore, theorists who do argue that needs are learned tend to argue that such learning occurs early in a person's life. For example, McClelland (1961) believed that the need for achievement could be inculcated to affect future economic development in a nation, and even undertook programs in developing nations to change the level of the need for achievement. Yet, McClelland stressed the inculcation of this need in childhood, and did not address the issue of the extent to which the need for achievement varies over short periods during a person's adult life. In this case, it is difficult to distinguish between needs and cultural expectations for behavior. Furthermore, even if needs are learned, there is a question as to the mechanism by which such learning takes place. According to theories of operant conditioning, for instance, it is behaviors that are conditioned. While one such behavior could be the expression of an attitude or some other affective statement (Insko and Cialdini, 1971), such learning involves the learning of a need or an attitude only to the extent one is willing to accept the idea that the expression of the statement or the acting of the behavior is equivalent to having the need. For instance, one indicator of the need for achievement is the distance an individual stands from the target in a ring-tossing game, while another indicator is derived from a content analysis of the stories told about pictures the subjects is shown. While either positioning behavior or verbal behavior can clearly be conditioned or socially reinforced, does such conditioning involve the actual change of fundamental, individual characteristics?

An additional difficulty with the learned-needs concept is to be found in the idea that such learning is terminated relatively early in life. Operant conditioning has been used on persons of all ages, and there is little theoretical justification for believing that learning terminates at pubescence. As long as there is some possibility that learning continues, including the learning of needs, then need models must attempt to incorporate changes in needs and acknowledge the cause of such changes over time.

But the concept of needs faces an even greater problem than the mystery of origin and development. The descriptions of the needs most frequently used to explain job-related behavior are frequently ambiguous. This is the case with Maslow's arrangement of need hierarchy. The sequence in which the needs are activated also represents a sequence of increasing ambiguity and indefiniteness. The basic physiological needs of hunger and thirst are well defined. Deprivation can be measured and metered physiologically, and, more importantly, there are precise objects associated with need satisfaction. Such precision in definition is lost as the need hierarchy is ascended. Self-actualization is a concept so poorly articulated that there continue to be debates about its essential properties: Is it an ever increasing need or can it be satisfied like the lower-order needs? What is the precise distinction between self-actualization and esteem (competence needs)? Is self-actualization the most intrinsically controlled need? To the extent that needs are loosely defined, it becomes difficult to do research that has any chance of refuting their applicability. The ambiguity of need concepts facilitates the finding of support for the need-satisfaction model. It is much easier to find empirical support for a concept which is vague.

The difficulties with the need concept are apparent in research attempts which, of necessity, must realize the concept. It is generally difficult to create statements which reflect concepts such as self-actualization, growth, or fulfillment. For instance, Schneider and Alderfer (1973) tried to write statements which represented Maslow's five needs. The number of words used to express the need concept increased log linearly with the position of the need in Maslow's hierarchy. While 8 words were required for security items, and social items required 22, higher-order need questions took 31, 44, and 34 words to present. These longer explanations may, in part, reflect the difficulty encountered in communicating the concept, a function of its ambiguity. These authors also attempted three factor analyses of needs, finding little convergence in their operationalizations in two of the three studies. In the third study, Schneider and Alderfer obtained convergence on items when they were written expressly so that more specific items could be subsumed under more abstract and general items.

If needs are poorly specified, particularly higher-order needs, then the need satisfier is also poorly specified. Rather than being an abstraction with some psychological reality, needs can be considered as constructs invented by individuals and their observers as a means of organizing their thinking and reactions to the environment. It is reasonable to presume that the need to develop the concept of need to explain behavior is affected by the environment in which the behavior occurs. If there are plausible, salient alternate explanations for the behavior, then allusions to needs are not made. Thus, if a person works hard on the job under a threat of being fired and he requires money to pay for an operation to save his child's life, a situation of convincing external cues for behavior is clear. When a person works hard and it is more difficult to locate the external agents controlling the behavior, there is more likely an effort to develop explanations relying on unobserved and potentially unobservable concepts such as needs to explain the behavior. The definition of a need as ambiguous is, therefore, an advantage, because it permits use of the concept as an almost universal explanation for behavior. From a scientific point of view, however, the fact that the concept of need is ambiguous on the points of the origins of needs, the development of needs, and even the meaning and measurement of needs makes the possibility of empirical refutation remote and the concept, in its present stage of development, of limited utility.

The Concept of Job Characteristics

Needs are related to attitudes through the experience of the individual on the job. Thus, theories of need satisfaction must define jobs in terms of characteristics that could then be related somehow to need satisfaction. There have been two major approaches to developing job characteristics—asking people directly about what makes them happy, and hypothesizing about what should make them happy. Herzberg, Mausner, and Snyderman's (1959) approach was to ask people to describe what made them feel good and what did not make them feel good about their job. When people described what they liked about work, they tended to use concepts relating to accomplishment, achievement, and personal growth. When they described what they disliked about their job, they tended to use concepts such as poor pay, company rules, working conditions, and characteristics of their supervisor. The generalization Herzberg, Mausner, and Snyderman drew, though not perfectly consistent with the data they reported, was that persons tended to describe good feelings toward factors intrinsic to themselves or toward their work activities, while bad feelings were due to things outside of themselves or their immediate job. This tendency is similar to the common attributional phenomenon of attributing success to personal causes and failure to external causes as noted by Weiner and Sierad (1975).

Though it has been argued by Vroom (1964), no one has investigated the possibility that Herzberg, Mausner, and Snyderman's results could be an outcome of an attributional process. Some relevant studies do indicate that this process may account for the observed data. Staw (1975) has noted that when individuals are led to believe their performance has been successful, they tend to attribute various pleasing characteristics to the work group. Furukawa (1972) showed that regardless of the supervisor's behavior, manipulated to be structuring or considerate, when a work group does well it tends to see the leader as considerate. In short, people select characteristics on the basis of their outcomes.

The second approach to developing dimensions for characterizing jobs involves proceeding from thinking of human needs and uncovering job characteristics that would appear to be, a priori, relevant to these needs. The lists of job characteristics developed have tended to emphasize the higher-order needs from Maslow's hierarchy. Turner and Lawrence (1965) developed the Requisite Task Attribute Index which included the job attributes of variety, autonomy, required interaction, optional interaction, knowledge and skill required, and responsibility. Hackman and Lawler (1971) described jobs in terms of their variety, autonomy, task identity, feedback, opportunity for dealing with others, and friendship opportunities. More recently, Hackman and Oldham (1975) developed the Job Diagnostic Survey, measuring the five dimensions of skill variety, task identity, task significance, autonomy, and feedback, as well as a dimension measuring the extent to which the job facilitates dealing with others. The important contribution of this second approach is that a theory is used to generate the list of job characteristics and, therefore, can be tested. If the defined job characteristics do provide for the satisfaction of higher-order needs, then individuals with those needs should be more or less satisfied to the extent the jobs have those characteristics. This is what has been empirically found (Hackman and Lawler, 1971) to some extent.

Regardless of the strategy used to develop a list of job characteristics, there are some problems with the concept and its operationalization. First and most important, the reader should recognize that the characterization of jobs is a process. When one sees well-developed lists of job characteristics, one is tempted to take such lists as descriptions of reality and forget to ask how the lists were developed in the first place. Saying that a job has certain characteristics orients the reader and the researcher to the characteristics, and the characteristics therefore become real and meaningful. However, if one asks the question of how did particular characteristics come to be identified with a job, one recognizes that the characteristics are defined into the situation by someone. Characterization of jobs, therefore, is a process which says as much about the researcher as it does about the jobs.

If jobs can be characterized in multiple ways, then the selection of those dimensions becomes problematic. Hackman and his colleagues solved this problem by reference to a presumed need structure of people. We have already suggested that this assumption of human needs, is, itself, open to question. Second, there is the problem of who is to characterize the job: the worker, the supervisor, the researcher, the naive observer? The possibility that others may assist in characterizing jobs means that characterizations developed by the worker are themselves affected by his social environment. Hackman and Lawler (1971: 268) presented data indicating that for several dimensions, there are high and significant correlations among job dimensions as rated by employees, supervisors, and the researchers. However, not all intercorrelations are large, particularly on the dimension of feedback, and, moreover, this procedure in part begs the question. Saying that when given a set of specified dimensions, several groups will assess different jobs in comparable fashion is somewhat different than saying that without any external cueing, persons will spontaneously choose similar dimensions to characterize jobs. If the way individuals characterize jobs can be controlled by experimental procedures, then jobs have no fixed characteristics. As a result, there will be no necessary relation to the individual's needs or job attitudes, thus undercutting one of the premises of job design for job satisfaction.

A third issue in characterizing jobs is how much of the job situation is included and captured by the dimensions? The nature of the work itself is, of course, included, but there are other job dimensions such as the company, pay, status, outcomes of the task, supervision, pace of the task, and physical surroundings. Any or all of these dimensions might affect an individual's reaction to the job situation. A recent book by Studs Terkel (1974) suggests that many different dimensions affect employee attitudes. When individuals were invited to be expansive and descriptive about their work, they provided elaborate and rich descriptions of the things they thought about. For some, the work was a way of obtaining prestige in the community, for others, a way of getting out of the house, for still others, a source of friendship. The point is that the job is itself embedded in a rich social setting which affects how people characterize and feel about their work.

The problem with the concept of job characteristics is that it must ultimately be arbitrarily defined. Inevitably, jobs can be characterized along multiple dimensions, and the choice of the dimensions used may affect what the researcher observes. The fact that job characterization is a process, providing information about the observer, also implies that job characterization is a process with information about the worker and his social context. Characteristics are imputed to jobs, and this imputation may be a consequence of a social process.

An important research task is to discover the factors which determine what selections individuals make in characterizing their jobs. We have already alluded to Herzberg's finding that attributions differ when outcomes differ. Research from cognitive psychology and dissonance theory shows different factors affect the perceptions of the environment. To the extent that job dimensions are cognitively constructed and behaviorally enacted (Weick, 1977), additional research on the processes is required to understand individual behaviors in work settings.

METHODOLOGICAL PROBLEMS IN NEED-SATISFACTION RESEARCH

The formulation of a model that accommodates almost every conceivable state of the world is an important constraint on testing it. There are few cases that can refute the model. Unless researchers attempt to produce these states, some support for the model will emerge by chance because of its inclusive formulation. The support may be illusory, however, for the only means of testing the model is by studying conditions where refutation is possible. If such conditions can be shown to occur, the model can be rejected.

Need-satisfaction models face two other methodological problems as well. First, as will be briefly reviewed, need-satisfaction models have seldom been able to account for substantial proportions of variance in behaviors or attitudes. And, more importantly, the findings of many need-satisfaction studies are open to alternate interpretations as the procedures used to observe correlations between job characteristics and satisfaction may produce consistency and priming artifacts.

The evidence gathered to test the need-satisfaction model is open to alternate interpretations or, in other words, is consistent with psychological theories different from the need-satisfaction model. The most prevalent form of testing the need-satisfaction model is to ask individuals to describe their needs on scales presented to them, to describe their jobs along attribution scales presented to them, and then to describe their satisfaction with those jobs, also presented on attitude scales. This method may create attitudes as much as measure them.

Response Artifacts: Consistency

One alternate interpretation of many studies of job attitudes is that responses are generated by tendencies toward consistency prompted by the procedures used to ask people about their jobs. Consistency effects refers to the phenomenon in which individuals, when interviewed about their attitudes and beliefs, tend to organize information in consistent ways. This effect has sometimes been called the Socratic effect (McGuire, 1968; Wyer, 1974) after the logical process used by Socrates to instruct his students. Consistency effects come from an individual's awareness of his own responses to questions. In answering questions, a person presents to himself as well as to the researcher information that may not have been as salient before. Being aware of answers to past questions, the person tends to answer additional questions so as to be consistent with these past answers or with the implications of the interview situation itself. Consistency effects are not the same as demand characteristics, in which a respondent can be expected to provide responses to conform with certain assumed or explicit expectations of the researcher (Orne, 1962; Webb, *et al.*, 1966). . . .

Response Artifacts: Priming

Another alternate explanation for the results reported in the job attitude studies is that a priming effect produced the observed data. Priming means that in questioning a person about his activities or beliefs, the interviewer orients the respondent's attention to particular information. While related to the consistency effect, the priming effect is somewhat different. Consistency presupposes a person's tendency to be logical in his statements about the world and is concerned as to how he processes information; the priming effect occurs in the questioning process when various aspects of the situation are made more salient than they might otherwise be. It affects the attending to more than the processing of information. Langer and Abelson (1972), in an elegant study of human behavior, illustrated the priming effect by asking busy passersby one of two forms of a question about their willingness to help. One form of the question was, "I need help, can you do me a favor?" The other form was, "Are you busy, can you do me a favor?" The first form invites the listener to center his attention on the distressed enquirer, while the second causes the listener to focus on his own situation. If the questioner in fact appears to need legimate help, the first question produces more aid. If, however, the questioner does not appear in need, the second form of the question elicits more assistance than the first.

In the questioning process, the investigator causes the respondent to concentrate on certain features of the situation. Priming, coupled with tendencies toward consistency, offers a powerful tool for shaping attitudes. Thus, when a worker is asked. "Does your job have challenging characteristics?", the worker reflects on the job itself, rather than on such features as pay, location, and colleagues. When the worker is then asked about his satisfaction, he will answer in terms of the former dimension, not because satisfaction is necessarily related to challenging work, but because that feature of the job has been made most salient at that point in time.

The effect of priming on attitude statements is probably immense. In one study, Salancik and Conway (1975) asked college students about their religious behavior. To affect the content of their thoughts, some people were asked to respond to questions of the form, "I frequently do X," others to the form, "I occasionally do X," where X was some religious behavior such as going to church, having a Bible, and so forth. It was assumed and proved that individuals would more easily recall instances of their behavior in support of the "occasionally" statements than the "frequently" statements, and therefore, that those people would have more information available suggesting they were religious. Moreover, when the adverb forms were paired with antireligious behavior, the individuals exposed to the "occasionally" form of the questions expressed more negative attitudes toward religion. In another study of priming (Salancik and Conway, 1975) students were interviewed about their attitudes toward a course recently completed. Some students were primed to think about positive, course-related behaviors and others to think about negative, course-related behaviors. Attitudes predictably followed the priming manipulation, with liking for the course varying from 5.38 to 3.85 on a seven point scale.

The priming phenomenon is based on the idea that an individual's attitude is derived from whatever information is available when asked about the attitude. The theory is that it is possible to present a standard set of information to individuals and then manipulate their recall of that information so that the basis of their attitudes can be varied systematically. In a demonstration of this, Salancik (1974) induced students to think about their behaviors in a course through a series of questions. Following this, some students were led to think about intrinsic features of the course and others were to consider extrinsic features, with the cognitive sets being induced through the linguistic form of the questions presented. Attitudes of students were then measured, with the results indicating that attitudes were based on different information about behavior depending on which cognitive set was induced. For example, the extrinsic set subjects developed attitudes that were highly correlated with the extent to which they fulfilled course requirements, while the intrinsic set subjects' attitudes were more highly correlated with talking about the course with their friends. More importantly, the extrinsic-set subjects' attitudes were highly correlated with the grade received ($R = .94$), while grade had virtually no effect on the attitude of intrinsic-set students ($R = -.16$).

Studies of job attitudes based on need-satisfaction theories are likely to introduce priming effects by using standard research methods. Questionnaires typically ask the individual to recall information about his job situation. This information is related to the investigator's own model of needs and job characteristics as these relate to attitudes. If a person is asked to describe his job in terms that are of interest to the investigator, he can do so. But if the individual is then asked how he feels about the job, he has few options but to respond using the information the investigator has made salient. The correlation between job characteristics and attitudes from such a study is not only unremarkable, but provides little information about the need-satisfaction model being tested. . . .

Consistency and priming effects offer alternate explanations for data gathered and interpreted as supporting the need-satisfaction model. At the same time, the possibility exists that needs themselves are perceptions that can be manipulated like other perceptions. One must begin to question the concept of need if this is, in fact, the case. An implication of the argument is that needs are not independent of satisfaction and are not the fixed and given characteristics of persons from which satisfaction is derived but, rather, can be determined by satisfaction. Presumably, it is possible to induce a feeling of satisfaction in a person and then present the person with needs consistent with the satisfaction. The person would perceive a given need and would then provide activities to meet the need.

The Amount of Explained Variance

Given the consistency and priming effects which appear to be present in most need-satisfaction studies, the striking thing is that the amount of explained variance, even with these artifacts operating, is relatively small. A close inspection of the evidence indicates less support for the need-satisfaction model than might be expected. This can be illustrated by considering some well known direct tests of the need-satisfaction framework.

Hackman and Lawler (1971) used the four job characteristics of variety, autonomy, task identity, and feedback in an attempt to explain the level of intrinsic motivation to rate performance on quality, quantity, and overall effectiveness dimensions, general job satisfaction and job involvement, absenteeism, and specific job satisfaction. As noted, only two of the four job characteristics were even statistically significantly related to absenteeism. The greatest amount of variance explained was less than 5 percent. Even with the attitudinal items, and given the artifacts in the research arising from consistency and priming effects, the amount of explained variance was not large. The amount of explained variance for general job satisfaction was 15.2 percent; level of intrinsic motivation, 10.2 percent; quantity of performance, 1.7 percent; quality of performance, 2.9 percent; and job involvement, 5.8 percent. The highest amount of explained variance in all the specific satisfaction items was 38.4 percent, for the relationship between job autonomy and satisfaction with the amount of independent thought and action permitted. When Hackman and Lawler (1971: 279) split the sample and examined only the one-third with the highest higher-order need strength compared to the one-third with the lowest amount of higher-order need strength, the results were not improved significantly. The largest amount of variance in absenteeism explained is only about 8 percent. Of even more importance, in comparing the correlations between subjects with higher order need strength in great amounts with those with less higher-order need strength, none of the differences are statistically significant except on some specific satisfaction items. The difference between those with high-need strength and those with low-need strength on overall job satisfaction was only 0.08.

These results were replicated in the study by Brief and Aldag (1975). The highest amount of variance explained in satisfaction was 26 percent, which is the variance explained by job autonomy in both general job satisfaction and work satisfaction. Several of the correlations were not statistically significant, and, in most cases, less than 10 percent of the variance was explained. The attempt to split the sample into those with high and low amounts of higher-order need strength was particularly revealing (Brief and Aldag, 1975: 184). Only 3 of 32 correlations were significantly different between groups in the expected direction at the 0.05 level of probability. Even the authors concluded that questions are raised as to the effect of higher-order need strength as a moderator of job characteristic-job satisfaction relationships. Wanous (1974: 619) was able to explain as much as 34 percent of the variance in job satisfaction with the job dimension of autonomy when the sample was split in terms of the amount of higher-order need strength.

It is fair to conclude that in spite of consistency and priming effects, studies of need satisfaction seldom explain more than 10 percent of the variance, and the amount of variance in job satisfaction explained almost never exceeds 40 percent. There is, at best, a tremendous amount of variance left unexplained by the need-satisfaction formulation, and this formulation does even more poorly when attempting to explain non-attitudinal variables such as absenteeism or performance ratings. Moreover, the differences predicted between persons' reactions to their jobs depending on their need strength are seldom observed, and when observed, are not very substantial.

CONCLUSION

The evidence and argument in this examination indicate that the need-satisfaction model must be seriously reexamined, and does not warrant the unquestioning acceptance it has attained in organizational psychology literature. As the model is formulated, it is difficult to disprove, as shown in the Table. Researchers have seldom attempted to disprove the model, and thus, have not really subjected it to testing. The principal concepts of the model—needs and job characteristics—are both open to serious questioning and to alternate interpretations. The calculus relating needs to job satisfaction, through the mechanism of job characteristics, has not been well specified. Where needs originate, their stability and their usefulness as concepts for explaining behavior in a predictive fashion, remain important questions. The possibility that job characteristics are socially constructed realities, and the issue of who characterizes jobs for research purposes both diminish the usefulness of the view that jobs have fixed specific characteristics. And, consistency and priming effects provide potent alternate explanations for the observed results. Even with these effects, only small amounts of variance are explained by the formulation.

Need-satisfaction models have survived, more because of their aesthetics than because of their scientific utility. Yet, even here, there are problems. While need-satisfaction models posit rationality and the possibility of individual action, they do not give humans credit for much adaptability in the pursuit of satisfaction.

A separate issue, not even broached in this argument, is whether one should be interested in job attitudes at all. Webb, *et al.* (1966) and Bem (1967) have taken psychology to task for being concerned with epiphenomena rather than behavior. Given that there is interest in job attitudes, however, the existing theoretical, methodological, and empirical weaknesses of the need-satisfaction formulation require that an attempt be made to develop an alternate explanation for job attitudes.

REFERENCES

Abelson, Robert P., and Milton J. Rosenberg
1958   "Symbolic psycho-logic: a model of attitudinal cognition." Behavioral Science, 3: 1–13.
Alderfer, Clayton P.
1969a   "Job enlargement and the organizational context." Personnel Psychology, 22: 418–426.
1969b   "An empirical test of a new theory of human needs." Organizational Behavior and Human Performance, 4: 142–175.
1972   Human Needs in Organizational Settings. New York: The Free Press of Glencoe.
Argyris, Chris
1957   Personality and Organization. New York: Harper.
1973   "Personality and organization theory revisited." Administrative Science Quarterly, 18: 141–167.
Bandura, Albert
1969   Principles of Behavior Modification. New York: Holt, Rinehart and Winston.
Bem, Daryl J.
1967   "Self-perception: the dependent variable of human performance." Organizational Behavior and Human Performance, 2: 105–121.
1972   "Self-perception theory." In L. Berkowitz (ed.), Advances in Experimental Social Psychology, Vol. 6: 1–62. New York: Academic Press.
Blauner, Robert
1964   Alienation and Freedom. Chicago: University of Chicago Press.
Bowers, David G.
1973   "OD techniques and their results in 23 organizations: the Michigan ICL study." Journal of Applied Behavioral Science, 9: 21–43.
Brayfield, Arthur H., and Walter H. Crockett
1955   "Employee attitudes and performance." Psychological Bulletin, 52: 396–428.
Brief, Arthur P., and Ramon J. Aldag
1975   "Employee reactions to job characteristics: a constructive replication." Journal of Applied Psychology, 60: 182–186.
Calder, Bobby J., and Michael Ross
1973   Attitudes and Behavior. Morristown, NJ: General Learning Press.

Dunnette, Marvin D., John P. Campbell, and Milton D. Hakel
1967   "Factors contributing to job satisfaction and dissatisfaction in six occupational
        groups." Organizational Behavior and Human Performance, 2: 143–174.

Dweck, C. S.
1975   "The role of expectations and attributions in the alleviation of learned helpless-
        ness." Journal of Personality and Social Psychology, 31: 674–685.

Edwards, Ward
1959   "The theory of decision making." Psychological Bulletin, 51: 380–414.

Fishbein, Martin
1963   "An investigation of the relationship between beliefs about an object and the
        attitude toward that object." Human Relations, 16: 233–240.

Furukawa, Hisataka
1972   "The effect of success or failure evaluation upon followers' morale and perception
        of leadership function." Japanese Journal of Experimental Social Psychology,
        11: 133–147.

Gallagher, William E., Jr., and Hillel J. Einhorn
1976   "Motivation theory and job design." Journal of Business, 49: 358–373.

Hackman, J. Richard, and Edward E. Lawler III
1971   "Employee reactions to job characteristics." Journal of Applied Psychology, 55:
        259–286.

Hackman, J. Richard, and Greg R. Oldham
1975   "Development of the job diagnostic survey." Journal of Applied Psychology, 60:
        159–170.
1976   "Motivation through the design of work: test of a theory." Organizational Be-
        havior and Human Performance, 16: 250–279.

Hackman, J. Richard, and J. L. Suttle
1977   Improving Life at Work: Behavioral Science Approaches to Organizational
        Change. Santa Monica, CA: Goodyear.

Hall, Douglas T., and Khalil E. Nougaim
1968   "An examination of Maslow's need hierarchy in an organizational setting." Or-
        ganizational Behavior and Human Performance, 3: 12–35.

Herman, Jeanne Brett, and Charles L. Hulin
1972   "Studying organizational attitudes from individual and organizational frames of
        reference." Organizational Behavior and Human Performance, 8: 84–108.
1973   "Managerial satisfactions and organizational roles: an investigation of Porter's
        need deficiency scales." Journal of Applied Psychology, 57: 118–124.

Herzberg, Frederick
1966   Work and the Nature of Man. Cleveland: World.

Herzberg, Frederick, Bernard Mausner, and Barbara Bloch Snyderman
1959   The Motivation to Work. New York: Wiley.

Hinton, Bernard L.
1968   "An empirical investigation of the Herzberg methodology and two-factor theory."
        Organizational Behavior and Human Performance, 3: 286–309.

Hrebiniak, Lawrence G., and Michael R. Roteman
1973   "A study of the relationship between need satisfaction and absenteeism among
        managerial personnel." Journal of Applied Psychology, 58: 381–383.

Hulin, Charles L., and Milton R. Blood
1968   "Job enlargement, individual differences, and worker responses." Psychological
       Bulletin, 69: 41–55.

Insko, Chester A., and R. B. Cialdini
1971   Interpersonal Influence in a Controlled Setting: The Verbal Reinforcement of
       Attitude. New York: General Learning Press.

Jones, Edward E., and Victor A. Harris
1967   "The attribution of attitudes." Journal of Experimental Social Psychology, 3: 1–
       24.

Jones, Edward E., and Richard Nisbett
1971   The Actor and the Observer: Divergent Perceptions of the Causes of Behavior.
       Morristown, NJ: General Learning Press.

Kahn, Robert L., D. M. Wolfe, R. P. Quinn, J. D. Snoek, and Robert A. Rosenthal
1964   Organizational Stress. New York: Wiley.

King, Nathan
1970   "A clarification and evaluation of the two-factor theory of job satisfaction."
       Psychological Bulletin, 74: 18–31

Langer, Ellen J., and Robert P. Abelson
1972   "The semantics of asking a favor: how to succeed in getting help without really
       dying." Journal of Personality and Social Psychology, 24: 26–32.

Lawler, Edward E., III
1969   "Job design and employee motivation." Personnel Psychology, 22: 426–435.

Lawler, Edward E., III, and Lyman W. Porter
1967   "Antecedent attitudes of effective managerial performance." Organizational
       Behavior and Human Performance, 2: 122–142.

Maslow, Abraham H.
1943   "A theory of human motivation." Psychological Review, 50: 370–396.
1954   Motivation and Personality. New York: Harper.
1970   Motivation and Personality, 2nd ed. New York: Harper and Row.

McClelland, David Clarence
1961   The Achieving Society. Princeton: Van Nostrand.

McGuire, William J.
1968   "A syllogistic analysis of cognitive relationships." In M. J. Rosenberg, C. I.
       Hovland, W. J. McGuire, R. P. Abelson, and J. W. Brehm (eds.), Attitude
       Organization and Change: 65–111. New Haven: Yale University Press.

Mitchell, Terence R., and Anthony Biglan
1971   "Instrumentality theories: current uses in psychology." Psychological Bulletin,
       76: 432–454.

Newman, John E.
1975   "Understanding the organizational structure-job attitude relationship through
       perceptions of the work environment." Organizational Behavior and Human
       Performance, 14: 371–397.

Oldham, Greg R.
1976   "Job characteristics and internal motivation: the moderating effect of interper-
       sonal and individual variables." Human Relations, 29: 559–569.

Oldham, Greg R., J. Richard Hackman, and Jone L. Pearce
1976   "Conditions under which employees respond positively to enriched work." Journal of Applied Psychology, 61: 395–403.

O'Reilly, Charles A.
1977   "Personality-job fit: implications for individual attitudes and performance." Organizational Behavior and Human Performance, 18: 36–46.

Orne, Martin T.
1962   "On the social psychology of the psychological experiment: with particular reference to demand characteristics and their implications." American Psychologist, 17: 776–783.

Porter, Lyman W.
1961   "A study of perceived need satisfaction in bottom and middle management jobs." Journal of Applied Psychology, 45: 1–10.
1962   "Job attitudes in management: I. perceived deficiencies in need fulfillment as a function of job level." Journal of Applied Psychology, 46: 375–384.
1963   "Job attitudes in management: II. perceived importance of needs as a function of job level." Journal of Applied Psychology, 47: 141–148.

Porter, Lyman, and Richard Steers
1973   "Organizational, work and personal factors in employee turnover and absenteeism." Psychological Bulletin, 80: 151–176.

Pritchard, Robert D., and Lawrence H. Peters
1974   "Job duties and job interests as predictors of intrinsic and extrinsic satisfaction." Organizational Behavior and Human Performance, 12: 315–330.

Rush, Harold M. F.
1971   Job Design for Motivation. New York: The Conference Board.

Salancik, Gerald R., and Mary Conway
1975   "Attitude inferences from salient and relevant cognitive content about behavior." Journal of Personality and Social Psychology, 32: 829–840.

Salancik, G. R.
1974   "Inference of one's attitude from behavior recalled under linguistically manipulated cognitive sets." Journal of Experimental Social Psychology, 10: 415–427.

Salancik, G. R., and Bobby J. Calder
1974   "A non-predispositional information analysis of attitude expressions." Urbana: Department of Business Administration, University of Illinois (Unpublished manuscript).

Schneider, Benjamin, and Clayton P. Alderfer
1973   "Three studies of needs satisfaction in organizations." Administrative Science Quarterly, 18: 489–505.

Schneider, Joseph, and Edwin A. Locke
1971   "A critique of Herzberg's incident classification system and a suggested revision." Organizational Behavior and Human Performance, 6: 441–457.

Schuman, H., and M. P. Johnson
1976   "Attitudes and behavior." Annual Review of Sociology, 2: 161–207.

Schwab, Donald P., and Larry L. Cummings
1970   "Theories of performance and satisfaction: a review." Industrial Relations, 9: 408–430.

Staw, Barry M.
1975   "Attribution of the 'causes' of performance: a new, alternative interpretation of

cross-sectional research on organizations." Organizational Behavior and Human Performance, 13: 414–432.
1976   Intrinsic and Extrinsic Motivation. Morristown, NJ: General Learning Press.
Strauss, George
1974   "Job satisfaction, motivation, and job redesign." In G. Strauss, R. E. Miles, C. C. Snow, and A. S. Tannenbaum (eds.), Organizational Behavior: Research and Issues: 19–49. Madison, WI: Industrial Relations Research Association.
Terkel, Louis (Studs)
1974   Working. New York: Pantheon.
Turner, Arthur Nicholson, and Paul R. Lawrence
1965   Industrial Jobs and the Worker. Boston: Harvard Graduate School of Business Administration.
Umstot, Denis D., Cecil H. Bell, Jr., and Terence R. Mitchell
1976   "Effects of job enrichment and task goals on satisfaction and productivity: implications for job design." Journal of Applied Psychology, 61: 379–394.
Useem, Michael
1976   "Government influence on the social science paradigm." The Sociological Quarterly, 17: 146–161.
Vroom, Victor
1964   Work and Motivation. New York: Wiley.
Wahba, M. A., and L. G. Bridwell
1976   "Maslow reconsidered: a review of research on the need hierarchy theory." Organizational Behavior and Human Performance, 15: 212–240.
Wanous, John P.
1974   "Individual differences and reactions to job characteristics." Journal of Applied Psychology, 59: 616–622.
Watts, William A., and Lewis E. Holt
1970   "Logical relationships among beliefs and timing as factors in persuasion." Journal of Personality and Social Psychology, 16: 571–582.
Webb, Eugene J., Donald T. Campbell, Richard D. Schwartz, and Lee Sechrest
1966   Unobtrusive Measures: Nonreactive Research in the Social Sciences. Chicago: Rand McNally.
Weick, Karl E.
1969   The Social Psychology of Organizing. Reading, MA: Addison-Wesley.
1976   "Educational organizations as loosely coupled systems." Administrative Science Quarterly, 21: 1–19.
Weiner, Bernard and Jack Sierad
1975   "Misattribution for failure and enhancement of achievement strivings." Journal of Personality and Social Psychology, 31: 415–421.
White, J. Kenneth, and Robert A. Ruh
1973   "The effects of personal values on the relationship between participation and job attitudes." Administrative Science Quarterly, 18: 506–514.
Wicker, Alan W.
1969   "Attitudes vs. actions: the relationship of verbal and overt behavioral responses to attitude objects." Journal of Social Issues, 25: 41–78.
Wyer, Robert S., Jr.
1974   Cognitive Organization and Change: An Information Processing Approach. Potomac, MD: Erlbaum.

A Critique of Salancik and Pfeffer's Examination of Need-Satisfaction Theories

Clayton P. Alderfer

THEORETICAL AND METATHEORETICAL PROBLEMS

Need-satisfaction models of job attitudes consist of two basic bodies of theory: expectancy theory and need theory. It is also possible to examine the *intersection* of expectancy theory and need theory. The phrase "need-satisfaction theories of job attitudes" does not make it clear whether Salancik and Pfeffer wish to discuss expectancy theory, need theory, expectancy theory and need theory in combination, or all of the above. In the issues they raise throughout the paper, they do not clarify this problem. Some of the problems they raise are relevant (though not necessarily correct) to one of the theories but not the other. Other issues are appropriate (though again not necessarily correct) only if you take the two bodies of theory in combination.

Salancik and Pfeffer are not alone in their confusion about the relationship between expectancy theory and need theory. Other investigators have shown a similar difficulty. One position is taken by Hunt and Hill (1969), who have "compared" the two bodies of theory, and emerged from the comparison favoring expectancy over need theory. The other position is to view the two bodies of theory as complementary, recognizing that the two frameworks concern themselves with conceptually distinct, though pragmatically related, phenomena. Campbell, Dunnette, Lawler, and Weick (1970) advocate this second position. They distinguish between "mechanical" theories of motivation which attempt to explain motivated behavior and "content" theories of motivation which are concerned with what in the individual or environment energizes and sustains behavior. According to this view expectancy theory is a mechanical theory, and need theory is a content theory. Viewing expectancy theory and need theory as complementary means that one does not have to choose one theory over the other. They are useful separately and together depending on what is to be predicted or explained. Porter and Lawler (1968), Hackman and Lawler (1971), and Hackman and Oldham (1976) have used the two bodies of theory complementarily to analyze the motivational problems associated with pay and job design.

Theories are in conflict when they make directly contradictory predictions about the same phenomena. Expectancy theory and need theory refer to two classes of theory which I believe are complementary rather than contradictory. However, within the broad classes of expectancy theory and need theory, there are different versions of each type, and they may conflict with one another. The Vroom (1964) version of expectancy theory, for example, is somewhat different than the Porter and Lawler (1968) proposal. As far as I know, these theorists have not examined whether their respective versions lead to different

Reprinted from *Administrative Science Quarterly*, 1977, **22**, 658–669. Reprinted by permission.

predictions. It is likely that they would, however, because some terms appear in the Porter and Lawler (1968) version which are not found in the Vroom (1964) model. Need theory has two clear alternatives: Maslow's (1954) well-known hierarchy and Alderfer's (1972) ERG model. There has been an effort to specify the similarities and differences between Maslow and the ERG model (Alderfer, 1972: 21–29). In addition to not recognizing the distinction between expectancy and need theories, Salancik and Pfeffer do not indicate awareness of the differences among the varieties of expectancy and need theories. They write as if there are no important differences.

The proposition shared by most versions of expectancy theory is that the motivational force to perform an act is the sum of products between valences and expectancies (probabilities). In mathematical notation:

$$\text{Motivational Force}_{\,i} = f\left[\ \sum_j (v_i p_{ij})\right] \left\{ \begin{array}{l} {}_i \text{ refers to act }_i \\ {}_j \text{ refers to outcome }_j \end{array}\right\}$$

Expectancy theories reason that performing an act produces outcomes. Each outcome has a value (valence), which may vary in magnitude and sign, and a probability of being associated with the act. The force on a person to perform the act is the sum of the valences times probabilities for all outcomes associated with the act.

The link between expectancy theory and need theory arises with the valence term in the equation. An expectancy theorist might employ a need theory to determine what types of valences are relevant to a particular act, whether the act will produce positive or negative valences, and whether valences will increase or decrease in strength from satisfactions produced by the act. Hackman and Lawler (1971) borrow part of need theory (that is, growth needs) to combine with expectancy theory in forming their theory of job motivation. But an expectancy theorist does not necessarily have to call upon need theory to identify the valences of particular outcomes. Another approach is to proceed inductively by asking people to list outcomes, the values of those outcomes, and their probabilities. Hackman and Porter (1968) used this research strategy.

Expectancy theory is based on a view that human beings are subjectively rational. When Salancik and Pfeffer say that an attraction of the need-satisfaction models is based on their subjective rationality, they should be clearer that it is expectancy theory, *not* need theory, that promotes a subjectively rational view of people. Need theory, separate from expectancy theory, does not imply a subjectively rational view of human beings. The question of rationality is not in the domain of need theory.

Need theory, by itself, is concerned with the subjective experiences of individuals interacting with complex environments. The theory has two classes of terms—satisfactions and desires—and is concerned with how satisfaction affects desire and how desire influences satisfaction (Alderfer, 1972). Salancik and Pfeffer misinterpret need theory when, in the context of pointing out a number of methodological problems in attitude research, they say (p. 83), "One must begin to question the concept of need if this is, in fact, the case.

An implication of this argument is that needs are not independent of satisfaction . . . but, rather, can be determined by satisfaction.'' Half or more of what
need theory is about is how satisfaction affects desire. Thus Salancik and
Pfeffer, while seeming to make a case against need theory, are led to one of
the theory's basic assumptions.

Need theory is *not* a theory about job attitudes in the way the term ''attitude'' is normally used by social psychologists. The questionnaire and interview measures developed to test need theory ask people to *describe subjective
experiences* (as a measure of satisfaction/frustration) and to express preferences
(as measures of desires). It is a simple exercise to form a linear model with
''job satisfaction'' as the dependent measure and the various need satisfactions
as independent measures. Although investigators have done research of this
kind, it is not directly relevant to need theory. Expectancy theory, however,
with or without need theory complementing it, has been used as a basis for
predicting job satisfaction (Vroom, 1964: 276–288; Porter and Lawler, 1968:
15–40).

A general characteristic Salancik and Pfeffer exhibit in their paper is that
they misunderstand when theories are in conflict and when they are complementary. Nor are Salancik and Pfeffer clear about the possible relationships
between need theory and expectancy theory. As a result they smooth over
important theoretical differences, such as among variations of expectancy theory and between versions of need theory, and they attempt to provoke a fight
between their hypothetical model, ''the need-satisfaction model of job attitudes,'' and a new position which emphasizes the impact of social influence
and information processing on the formation of attitudes. There are issues about
job attitudes and motivation which are not covered by expectancy theory, need
theory, or the two in combination. Salancik and Pfeffer identify a number of
these issues including how attitudes are formed, how social reality is constructed, and how individuals cognitively cope with their frustrations and other
dilemmas. Other theoretical perspectives can be proposed to deal with such
phenomena. Need theory and expectancy theory are incomplete because they
do not deal with these phenomena, but they are not wrong because of their
incompleteness. They do not have to be put aside in order for different perspectives to emerge. Blackburn (1971) has discussed how such complementary
theories have been found in the history of physical science (such as physicists
simultaneously holding wave and corpuscular theories of light). It already exists
in the domain entered by Salancik and Pfeffer in the relationship between
expectancy theory and need theory. It should exist among expectancy theory,
need theory, and social-information-processing theory.

A MORE COMPLETE VIEW OF NEED THEORY

Salancik and Pfeffer base a substantial portion of their argument on what I
think is a highly simplified and, in many cases, inaccurate view of need theory.
They ignore the interaction between theory and data that has characterized

work in this area. In some cases they misinterpret reports of empirical results. As one whose work has included sustained efforts in the need-theory domain, I feel that these problems in their examination should not be ignored.

According to Salancik and Pfeffer (p. 69), need theory assumes that "needs are conceptualized as relatively stable characteristics of persons." They repeat a version of this assertion several times throughout their paper. Assuming all people have certain needs does *not* assume all people have the same strength of all needs. Need theory does not contradict the principles of individual differences. If anything, it enhances the understanding of individual differences by specifying some conditions that explain how individuals evolve their differences in need strength. Salancik and Pfeffer are confusing on this point. They cite work by Turner and Lawrence (1965) and by Hulin and Blood (1968), which shows that individuals differ in strength of needs, as if that demonstrates that there are not needs in common to all people. If Joe just finished eating and Harry hasn't eaten for two days, need theory predicts that Harry's desire for food will be higher than Joe's. It assumes that both have existence needs including the need for food, as a property of their common human condition. It does not assume they have the same strength of existence needs, either over time for each, or at a particular time for the two of them.

Assuming that there is a set of needs differing in strength common to all people is based upon careful review of empirical evidence and can in principle be disconfirmed. The case for using need constructs, and particularly those of existence, relatedness, and growth is thoroughly grounded in an extensive review of empirical literature (Alderfer, 1972: 31–44). There are two kinds of arguments for each need category. First, some degree of need satisfaction is necessary for survival and nonpathological functioning of the human organism. Second, there must be evidence that the needs conceptualized by the theory are basic to the human organism independent of learning.

A wide variety of literature supports the first point in each case of existence, relatedness, and growth needs, and findings of this sort continue to accumulate. The most recent example is a book by James Lynch, *The Broken Heart* (1977), which links loneliness (that is, absence of relatedness satisfaction) to the on-slaught of a variety of major illnesses including heart disease, cancer, and mental illness. Similar evidence exists for the other major need categories.

For the second argument, the evidence is experimental, ruling out learning as the sole mechanism for explaining the presence of certain classes of desires. When learning is ruled out as the sole explanation for relatedness and growth needs, one is in a strong position to infer that certain "needs" are basic to the naturally functioning organism. Harlow and Harlow's (1962) well-known studies of desire for affection among monkeys make this case for relatedness needs. White's (1959) review of the case for competence motivations draws together a vast array of experimental evidence making the case for independent growth need energies.

Thus the Salancik and Pfeffer assertion about the position of need theory with respect to the assumption of the universality of certain classes of human needs is oversimplified. It misstates the position of the ERG theory, and it ignores much empirical evidence which supports the use of need constructs.

Salancik and Pfeffer seem to have an aversion to the idea that human beings have psychological properties that might be conceptualized as basic needs. I doubt if they find the idea that people have two arms, two legs, and one head as objectionable. Why are they bothered by analogous assertions about the psychological structure of human beings?

Salancik and Pfeffer assert (p. 68) that the need-satisfaction model assumes that "causality begins with the job" (not the person). This view is in direct contradiction to explicit propositions in ERG theory (for example, Alderfer, 1972: 20):

> In challenging discretionary settings, then the higher chronic growth desires, the more growth satisfaction.

They also ignore evidence reported in Alderfer (1972: 141) supporting the proposition as stated. Thus, propositions inconsistent with the Salancik and Pfeffer view of need theory exist. There is evidence to support some of the propositions. They overlook both the propositions and the evidence.

Another argument proposed by Salancik and Pfeffer is that need theory is constructed in such a way that it cannot be disproved, disconfirmed, or refuted (p. 72). In the context of their argument, Salancik and Pfeffer do not distinguish among the terms disprove, disconfirm, and refute, although most social science investigators do. To address their concerns in this area it is important to make these distinctions, and then discuss the position of need theory in relation to each.

Issues of proof and disproof in the context of research usually refer to the logical-mathematical relations among theoretical terms. Given assumptions A and B, does conclusion C follow logically from them? Questions of proof and disproof do not pertain to the relationship between theory and data. It is possible to make deductive predictions from need theory, expectancy theory, and the two theories in combination. Nonetheless, the two bodies of theory as used in the field of organizational psychology are largely verbal, not mathematical, in their formulation. Depending on one's perspective this may or may not be viewed as a problem. It is a property that need theory and expectancy theory share with many other social science theories, including the formulation proposed by Salancik and Pfeffer.

The question of confirmation and disconfirmation is different than the problem of proof. Confirmation and disconfirmation refer to the relation between theory and data. Here the question is whether data are collected in such a way as to allow for findings that are inconsistent with theoretical predictions. Research on need theory shows many instances of testing comparative predictions. Results of these investigations provide empirical reasons for favoring one theory over another (for example, ERG vs. Maslow) or for altering and rejecting aspects of existing theories (such as, the prepotency assumption in need theory).

Three published reports showing this mode of investigation are described below.

First, the most complete presentation of ERG theory is contained in Alderfer (1972). In that book, ERG theory is presented in its own terms and contrasted with two other theoretical positions—Maslow's theory and the "simple frustration hypothesis." Specific testable hypotheses from all three positions are formulated, and explicit attention is given to specifying where ERG theory makes different predictions than Maslow's theory and/or the simple frustration hypothesis (Alderfer, 1972: 102–131). Further evidence that need theory can be disconfirmed is found in the final chapter of the ERG book where the theory is reformulated based on the empirical results contained in earlier chapters (Alderfer, 1972: 145–150).

Second, Alderfer, Kaplan, and Smith (1974) reported a laboratory experiment testing propositions from the reformulated ERG theory and comparing these predictions with more conventional views concerning a deprivation-satiation function for social approval (Eisenberger, 1970). Results from this study were consistent with the hypothesized curvilinear relationship between relatedness satisfaction and desire. They also forged a link between the field results reported in Alderfer (1972) and laboratory findings, and showed that the original theory can be modified and substantiated based upon empirical findings.

Third, there is the Schneider and Alderfer (1973) study, which is explicitly discussed by Salancik and Pfeffer. This research is especially interesting because it was designed to correct for investigator bias when comparing Maslow's concepts and the ERG model. Schneider was the advocate for Maslow's theory in the construction of instruments and in the interpretation of results, while Alderfer was the spokesperson for ERG theory. Salancik and Pfeffer do not mention that the study was designed to explore differences between need theories, nor do they indicate that the evidence seems to favor one theory over the other. Instead they chose to report the number of words used to express items for different need categories, and state (p. 77), "The number of words used to express the need concept increased log linearly with the position of the need in Maslow's hierarchy. . . . These longer explanations may, in part, reflect the difficulty encountered in communicating the concept, a function of its ambiguity. . . ." In presenting a count of the number of words used to express scale items Salancik and Pfeffer sum across items; they do not take the number of words per item. There are more words used to express higher order needs because Porter wrote more items to measure these concepts. In fact, the *average* number of words per item is 11 for each of social, esteem, autonomy, and self-actualization needs. The *single* security item has 8 words. Moreover, they choose to do their counting from the Porter scales for measuring Maslow's concepts when it is clear to a reader of the Schneider and Alderfer (1973) article that Porter's scales have the poorest psychometric properties of any scales used. The case that Salancik and Pfeffer attempt to make by confusing a sum with an average and by selecting the poorest example of need satisfaction measurement in three studies is that higher order needs (i.e., self-actualization or growth) are difficult to operationalize because of the ambiguity of the concept. In fact, the empirical data contained in the Schneider and Alderfer report (1973) as well as others make just the opposite case. Even Porter's scales, which do rather poorly for lower level needs, show the highest loadings for two of three self-actualization items (see Table 1 in Schneider and Alderfer, 1973: 492). Across each of the Porter, Schneider, and Alderfer scales the self-actualization or growth scales consistently show clarity and more than acceptable internal consistency. The area where there is *least* conceptual *dis*agreement between Maslow and ERG theory is with respect to self-actualization and/or growth needs. Salancik and Pfeffer do not comment on the conceptual agreement, and their brief report of the empirical findings distorts the empirical data relevant to the point they discuss.

Salancik and Pfeffer discuss the question of whether need-satisfaction theories can be refuted in Table 1 and the related discussion (pp. 72–73). Although stated more generally Table 1 is aligned very closely to the Hackman and Oldham (1976) theory of job design. If the table were to be formulated to deal with need theory, the three columns would have to be relabeled respectively "need constellation" (to take account of the various combinations of chronic need strength people have), "environmental targets" (to take account of the various environmental sources of potential need satisfaction, including but not restricted to "job characteristics") and "need satisfaction." Even if formulated in this manner Table 1 would be relevant only to a portion of the phenomena explained by need theory. If modified as suggested it deals with the aspect of need theory that is concerned with how desires affect satisfaction. The theory is also concerned with how satisfaction influences desire, and this portion of the theory, which some people may view as the most crucial, is omitted from the table. Thus in its formulation, the table is both too general and too specific. It is not directly tied to the job design theories to which it is most relevant, and it is substantially incomplete with respect to need theory.

The point of Table 1 is to argue that need-satisfaction theories have not been tested under conditions most likely to refute them. For Salancik and Pfeffer this is "condition 2" where individuals with the same needs face the same job characteristics and have different attitudinal reactions. Anyone familiar with the empirical literature in this area knows that there has been variance left unaccounted for in need-satisfaction research. Not every individual with the same needs (or need strength) facing the same job characteristics (or other environmental conditions) has the same attitudinal reactions (or need satisfaction). Salancik and Pfeffer make this point in another section of their paper. As I see it therefore condition 2 has been found in need-satisfaction research and reduces to the question of whether need-satisfaction theories account for all the variance in attitudinal reaction. Neither theoretical positions nor empirical reports make this case. Unexplained variance is partly due to imperfect reliability of measurement, but it is also due to the incompletenesses of need and expectancy theories as explanatory frameworks. This incompleteness does not refute the theories. It does argue for improved measurement and additional explanatory propositions.

Salancik and Pfeffer also point out a number of important measurement issues in assessing the results of empirical research on need-satisfaction models. Consistency and priming effects could be important artifacts confounding the interpretation of need satisfaction studies. A variety of design features in ERG studies have been introduced to minimize these effects. The original ERG scales, for example, were validated against content coded responses to open end interview questions coded blindly and given in advance of questionnaire administration (Alderfer, 1967). A laboratory experiment designed to test for a curvilinear function between relatedness satisfaction and desire used a repeated measures design and fully counterbalanced for the order of satisfaction conditions across subjects (Alderfer, Kaplan, and Smith, 1974). And, as they suggest, desire measures used to predict satisfaction were taken both two weeks and two months in advance of satisfaction measures in two studies (Alderfer, 1972: 140–142). So on this matter I agree with their concerns and point out that some need satisfaction research has been designed with those methodological problems in mind. The strength of the empirical findings was not weakened by correcting for these potential measurement artifacts. Indeed there was confirmation across studies (see especially, Alderfer, Kaplan, and Smith, 1974).

Salancik and Pfeffer propose that investigators should be more explicit in reporting the order in which various measures are taken. I agree, and just for the reasons they cite. I think researchers should also be expected to report about the nature of the relationship they create with respondents in field and laboratory settings. Frequently in field studies investigators administer monotonous questionnaires in a cold and distant manner. The effect of this "methodological error" could reduce scale reliability and thereby make it more difficult to find support for predicted relationships. In laboratory studies, particularly those associated with the tradition of dissonance theory, investigators are notorious for their deception of subjects. How can laboratory researchers who deceive their subjects ever be sure that their results are not the effects of counter deception in return? As organizational researchers, Salancik and Pfeffer should be aware that many of those studies took place within the "social reality" of sophomore psychology courses. Some of the work cited by Salancik and Pfeffer to support arguments for information salience and conformity processes arise from a research tradition steeped in the deception of subjects. They should be aware of these measurement problems, as well as priming and consistency efforts, as we all strive to design artifact-free studies.

A general property of the Salancik and Pfeffer paper is being very imprecise in their references to need theory research, both theory and data. I undoubtedly notice their imprecision more because of my involvement in this area of research. Nevertheless, the list of misleading reports of need-theory research is long. It raises serious questions about the soundness of their general arguments against need-satisfaction theories.

PRAGMATIC AND VALUE QUESTIONS

In their examination of need-satisfaction models Salancik and Pfeffer do not limit themselves to scientific issues of data and theory. They also raise questions about human values and suggest ways that need-satisfaction models enter business and governmental influence processes. By doing this, they join an increasing number of social scientists who are willing to deal with the complex value questions implied by their work. As Salancik and Pfeffer raise value issues with the need-satisfaction model, they also create some with respect to their own views.

They write (p. 74), "The need-satisfaction model ultimately denies persons the creative capacity to cope with their environment, in part, by constructing meaning that makes the context more satisfying, and, in part, by redefining the situation and attending to selected aspects of the situation." In the language of psychoanalytic theory, they recognize that neither expectancy theory nor need theory has constructs that explain the phenomena Anna Freud (1946) called "defenses." It is not clear to me that the need-satisfaction model denies defensive coping. Argyris (1957), one of the people cited by Salancik and Pfeffer, does deal with psychological defenses in his analysis. But for the most part these constructs are missing from the other writings reviewed by Salancik and Pfeffer. This is an area where the need-satisfaction models could be complemented by the kinds of constructs Salancik and Pfeffer propose. With that I have no quarrel.

Their proposals become troublesome, however, when one sees how their theory is used to influence people in organizations. In another article, Salancik (1977: 79) writes, "We are trying to have people who report substantial absenteeism from work to attribute the absences to extrinsic and situational circumstances, such as the severe winter weather. Our expectation is that this will eventually lead to a decrease in their absences." By changing how people understand causality and in this case by inducing an attribution of external causation, they expect to change behavior. From a purely academic point of view, this is an interesting idea. But Salancik seems to show little concern that in doing so he is engaging in deception. In another section of the same article he provides managers with some advice about how to co-opt opinions in a group meeting. He says (1977: 78), "Thus the chairperson of the meeting might say, 'I think we can all agree,' and from that point go on to state a position that those attending had not thought about before."

It is of course an open question as to what kinds of people under what circumstances would be affected in what ways by such tactics. I believe there are many situations where such behavior would create mistrust and strong reactions against the influencer. Conceptually Salancik does not distinguish between overt and covert aspects of influence. In the same article, he asks (1977: 62), "How do you manage—the more precise word is 'manipulate'—commitment in organizations?" For me the term "manipulate" is not just a synonym for influence or manage. It also implies that the influence process is covert and/or counter to the best interests of the people subject to the influence. In overt influence attempts, the influencer acknowledges his aims. In the preceding examples, the overt influencer, would say: (a) "I want you to believe that the severe weather is the reason for your absence," and (b) "I am saying 'we' so that everyone will believe he or she is part of this idea." In that way the influencees are in a better position to judge what is in their interests than if the influencer does not explicitly state his objectives. Salancik is thoughtful in identifying how a sense of choice is crucial to commitment. He does not seem to recognize that people also make up their own minds about whether they can trust individuals who present choices to them. And he seems unaware of the possible ethical issues involved in a professional behavioral scientist promoting covert influence strategies (Kelman, 1968).

This problem arises in part because of the exclusive reliance on a social influence model for shaping attitudes. While I agree that information salience and conformity processes do influence attitudes, I believe people are also capable of knowing their own reactions to organizational stresses without behavioral scientists telling them what to think. In the realm of values and pragmatics of organizational life, need theory provides a basis against which one can measure the psychological violence done to people by inhumane forces in organizations.

Salancik and Pfeffer suggest that funding considerations have led researchers to emphasize mental health over performance considerations in justifying organizational research. I have no doubt that for some investigators this is true. But Salancik and Pfeffer fail to entertain the possibility that after many years of research, funding agencies have begun to get the message that organizational life can be hazardous to people. Theories and research about human needs have been a force in that influence process. I am impressed that society has become more open to that knowledge. Now that the change has occurred, however, there is a problem that some people may exploit it cynically.

CONCLUSION

In summary, a variety of problems with the Salancik and Pfeffer examination of need-satisfaction theories of job attitudes have been identified. On a theoretical level they failed to distinguish adequately between expectancy theory and need theory, and to specify those problems for which these bodies of theory are complementary to one another and those for which they are irrelevant to each other. On a metatheoretical level they do not seem to understand the difference between conflicting theories, which make contradicting predictions about common phenomena, and complementary theories which make different predictions about phenomena that are not in the domain of both theories. In addition, their understanding of need theory is limited. They attribute properties to need theory that it does not have (or which not all versions of the theory have), and they propose solutions to certain perceived problems of need theory that are already characteristic of some versions of the theory. Their report of the empirical bases of need theory and of tests of hypotheses derived from the theory is significantly incomplete. They present highly erroneous accounts of empirical need-theory studies. Their inclination to replace (rather than to complement) need-satisfaction models of job attitudes with another theory raises a number of value questions about the nature of psychological reality for members of organizations and about how academic theories might be used in the disservice of human beings in organizations.

Pointing out the wide range of difficulties with the Salancik and Pfeffer examination, however, is not to say that expectancy and need theories—either separately or together—deal adequately with all the important issues in the area of job attitudes, or more broadly, in the conceptually rich area of subjective and intellectual reactions of individuals to their encounters with organizations. They do not. And Salancik and Pfeffer do identify important areas where expectancy and need theories are incomplete. This incompleteness is an opportunity for other theories to be proposed, which I believe is what Salancik and Pfeffer intend to do.

For the person interested in the philosophy and social psychology of organizational behavior, the Salancik and Pfeffer paper poses an additional question, which goes beyond the substantive questions they discuss: Why did they so persistently misinterpret need-satisfaction theories of job attitudes? I would like to suggest that their criticism may be traced to intergroup conflicts within the field of organizational behavior. Nor am I immune from these conflicts. I doubt if there are many people who would have been as interested in pointing out the conceptual and empirical errors in their treatment of need theory as I have been.

Stimulated by the works of "participants" and "observers" scientists are beginning to accept the role of their own subjectivity in the process of practicing science. Feuer (1974), for example, has recently made a very provocative and, to me, rather convincing case that a substantial portion of the energy for the theoretical advances in physics made at the start of the twentieth century was found in the generational conflict among physicists. In another context, I have shown how male and female scholars differed markedly in their views of the social psychology of female-male relations (Alderfer, 1976). It has been shown repeatedly that intergroup conflict is associated with cognitive distortions among the parties. If intergroup tensions explain some of Salancik and Pfeffer's behavior in examining need-satisfaction theories of job attitudes, it would strengthen their own case for the importance of social influence on information processing, including their own. Have we as social scientists reached the point where we can apply our theories explicitly to ourselves when we are practicing social science? Most professional change agents accept this proposition and spend years learning how to implement it in practice. I believe we would have a richer, more profound study of organizational behavior if we were able to do the same thing as physicists.

REFERENCES

Alderfer, Clayton P.
1967   "Convergent and discriminant validation of satisfaction and desire measures by interviews and questionnaires." Journal of Applied Psychology, 51: 509–520.
1972   Existence, Relatedness, and Growth: Human Needs in Organizational Settings. New York: Free Press.
1976   "Group and intergroup relations." In J. R. Hackman and J. L. Suttle (eds.), Improving Life at Work: Behavioral Science Approaches to Organizational Change: 227–296. Santa Monica, CA: Goodyear.

Alderfer, Clayton P., Robert E. Kaplan, and Ken K. Smith
1974   "The effect of variations in relatedness need satisfaction on relatedness desires." Administrative Science Quarterly, 19: 507–532.

Argyris, Chris
1957   Personality and Organization, New York: Harper.

Blackburn, T. R.
1971   "Sensuous-intellectual complementarity in science." Science, 172: 1003–1007.

Campbell, John P., M. D. Dunnette, E. E. Lawler III, and Karl E. Weick, Jr.
1970   Managerial Behavior, Performance and Effectiveness. New York: McGraw-Hill.

Eisenberger, R.
1970   "Is there a deprivation-satiation function for social approval?" Psychological Bulletin, 74: 255–275.

Feuer, Lewis S.
1974   Einstein and the Generations of Science. New York: Basic Books.

Freud, Anna
1946   The Ego and the Mechanisms of Defense. New York: International University Press.

Hackman, J. Richard, and E. E. Lawler, III
1971   "Employee reactions to job characteristics." Journal of Applied Psychology, 55: 259–286.

Hackman, J. R., and G. R. Oldham
1976   "Motivation through the design of work: test of a theory." Organizational Behavior and Human Performance, 16: 250–279.

Hackman, J. R., and L. W. Porter
1968   "Expectancy theory predictions of work effectiveness." Organizational Behavior and Human Performance, 3: 417–426.

Harlow, Harry F., and M. K. Harlow
1962   "Social deprivation in monkeys." Scientific American, 207: 136–146.

Hulin, Charles C., and M. R. Blood
1968   "Job enlargement, individual differences, and worker responses." Psychological Bulletin, 69: 41–55.

Hunt, J. G., and J.W. Hill
1969 "The new look in motivation theory for organization research." Human Orga-
      nization, 28: 100–109.
Kelman, Herbert C.
1968 A Time to Speak. San Francisco: Jossey-Bass.
Lynch, James J.
1977 The Broken Heart: The Medical Consequences of Loneliness. New York: Basic
      Books.
Maslow, Abraham H.
1954 Motivation and Personality. New York: Harper.
Porter, Lyman W., and E. E. Lawler III
1968 Managerial Attitudes and Performance. Homewood, IL: Irwin-Dorsey.
Salancik, Gerald R.
1977 "Commitment is too easy!" Organization Dynamics, 6: 62–80.
Salancik, Gerald R., and Jeffrey Pfeffer
1977 "An examination of need-satisfaction models of job attitudes." Administrative
      Science Quarterly, 22: 427–456.
Schneider, Benjamin, and C. P. Alderfer
1973 "Three studies of measures of need satisfaction in organizations." Administrative
      Science Quarterly, 18: 489–505.
Turner, Arthur N., and P. R. Lawrence
1965 Industrial Jobs and the Worker. Cambridge, MA: Harvard Graduate School of
      Business Administration.
Vroom, Victor H.
1964 Work and Motivation. New York: Wiley.
White, Robert W.
1959 "Motivation reconsidered: the concept of competence." Psychological Review,
      66: 297–333.

QUESTIONS FOR DISCUSSION

1 How does Alderfer's ERG theory of motivation differ from that of Maslow?
2 In what way does Murray's manifest need theory differ from both Maslow and
   Alderfer? What importance would you attach to that difference?
3 How can managers make use of McClelland's ideas concerning the motive acquisition process in organizational settings?
4 Why do you think Maslow's theory of motivation has been so popular among both
   managers and organizational researchers?
5 What research evidence is offered by Maslow in support of his theory?
6 How useful a concept is Maslow's basic theory as it applies to work settings?
7 Is Maslow's need hierarchy model a theory of motivation or a theory of personality?
8 Specifically, how could you redesign a typical blue-collar job so as to assist employees in meeting their higher-order needs? What about white-collar workers'
   jobs?
9 Do you think it is generally easier for managers to self-actualize than workers? Why
   or why not?

10 If a person's job failed to facilitate his pursuit of self-actualization, what courses of action might he or she take?

11 Would you classify Murray's basic model of motivation as an instinct theory, a drive theory, or a cognitive theory? Why?

12 In what ways have Atkinson and McClelland modified and extended Murray's original formulation of the model?

13 Researchers have often found that persons with high needs for achievement simultaneously have low needs for affiliation. What factors might explain such findings?

14 How would you go about improving the performance of an employee who has a low need for achievement?

15 If high need achievement people tend to be superior performers, why could a manager not increase organizational performance simply by hiring only high n Ach employees?

16 What uses might a line manager make of achievement motivation theory?

17 What is the basic argument advanced by Salancik and Pfeffer against need theories of motivation and satisfaction? Do you agree or disagree with this argument?

18 Evaluate the adequacy of Alderfer's response to the Salancik and Pfeffer critique.

Chapter 3

Equity Theory

Several related theories of motivation have emerged during the past 20 years that deal with social comparison processes. These theories generally suggest that an individual's motivation is largely influenced by how the individual feels he or she is being treated compared to those around him or her. These theories are referred to by various names, including "distributive justice" or "exchange theory" (Homans, 1961; Jaques, 1961; Patchen, 1961), and "equity theory" (Adams, 1963, 1965; Weick, 1964).

GENERAL FRAMEWORK OF EQUITY THEORY

While each of these models differs in some respects from the others, the general thrust of all of them is similar. Specifically, such theories argue that a major determinant of job effort, performance, and satisfaction is the degree of equity or inequity that an individual perceives in the work situation. The degree of equity is defined in terms of a ratio of an individual's inputs (such as level of effort on the job) to outcomes (such as pay) *as compared with* a similar ratio for a relevant "other." Because of this comparative aspect, the theory has also been called "social comparison" theory. In our discussions below, we shall concentrate on Adams's formulation of equity theory as an example. This variation of the general model appears to be the most highly developed and heavily researched statement on the topic.

This social comparison, or equity, aspect of the model contrasts sharply with the need theories discussed earlier. The previous theories were largely individually based theories. Equity theory, on the other hand, places considerable emphasis on group influences and individuals' perceptions of others.

There is also a second important distinction between equity theory and the earlier models. While the earlier theories focus on the identification of specific factors in the individual which determine behavior, equity theory (as well as expectancy/valence theory, to be discussed later) concentrates on an understanding of the *processes* by which behavior is energized and sustained. It is thus a more dynamic approach to the study of motivationally relevant variables in a work situation. Because of this, equity theory has been called a "process" theory by Campbell et al. (1970), while the relatively more static need theories of Maslow, Alderfer, and Murray have been termed "content" theories.

A third major distinction that differentiates equity theory from the models discussed earlier is that this theory posits that a major share of motivated behavior is based on the *perceived* situation and not necessarily on the actual set of circumstances. Where Maslow and Murray saw behavior largely as a result of personality-need variables, equity theory generally argues that it is the perceived equity of the situation that stimulates behavior and satisfaction. In other words, if an employee "thinks" he or she is being paid less than coworkers for the same amount and quality of work, the person would, according to this model, be dissatisfied and move to reduce the inequity through various means. Such an hypothesis is particularly interesting in view of several findings that indicate that workers generally tend to overestimate the salaries of others (Lawler, 1971).

IMPLICATIONS FOR MANAGEMENT

As the above discussion suggests, equity theory leads to quite different managerial implications than the earlier models of motivation. Specifically, equity theory emphasizes the necessity for managers to be aware of social processes in organizations and to view motivation in dynamic, changing terms. Hence, redesigning someone's job may not increase motivation if such efforts are not seen by the individual as changing the inputs-outcomes mix. If the employee still believed he or she was inequitably treated (perhaps paid at a lower rate than comparable others), there is little reason to believe that such an individual would be motivated to increase effort.

Inherent in the social comparison process, then, is the notion of equity. Managers must, according to this theory, find ways to insure that employees believe they are being fairly treated. Employee perceptions of the situation are more important here than objective "reality." The fact that a particular employee is actually overpaid for his or her services compared with others means little in terms of employee motivation unless the employee feels the same way.

Finally, equity theory tends to place a great deal of emphasis on monetary rewards. While this emphasis may not have been intended originally, money is one of the few outcomes, or rewards, that people can clearly see and assess. Hence, when we talk about equity, it is easier to talk about pay equity than equity in task design, promotional opportunities, or recognition. Moreover, as will be seen in the selections that follow, most of the research on equity theory uses money as the primary treatment variable. Therefore, a manager interested in using equity theory in work organizations is to a large extent assuming a monetarily based motivational strategy.

OVERVIEW

Two articles on equity theory are presented below. The first, by Adams, includes both a fairly well-developed statement of the theory and a discussion of how the theory works in a variety of situations. Adams also reviews several studies that either support or are consistent with the model as formulated. In a second and more recent article, Mowday reviews the research evidence as it relates to the theory. The notion of equity is discussed not only as it relates to pay, but also as it relates to a variety of social processes, such as leader behavior. As will be noted in both articles, the vast majority of evidence supportive of equity theory is laboratory-based. The interested reader is specifically referred to Lawler (1968), Pritchard (1969), and Goodman (1977) for three additional excellent reviews of research and theoretical issues relating to this model.

REFERENCES AND SUGGESTED ADDITIONAL READINGS

Adams, J. S. Toward an understanding of inequity. *Journal of Abnormal and Social Psychology*, 1963, **67**, 422–436.

Adams, J. S. Injustice in social exchange. In L. Berkowitz (Ed.), *Advances in experimental social psychology*, vol. 2. New York: Academic Press, 1965.

Campbell, J. P., Dunnette, M. D., Lawler, E. E., III, & Weick, K. E., Jr. *Managerial behavior, performance, and effectiveness*. New York: McGraw-Hill, 1970.

Festinger, L. *A theory of cognitive dissonance*. Evanston, Ill.: Row, Peterson, 1957.

Goodman, P. S. Social comparison processes in organizations. In B. M. Staw and G. R. Salancik (Eds.), *New directions in organizational behavior*. Chicago: St. Clair Press, 1977. Pp. 97–132.

Heider, R. *The psychology of interpersonal relations*. New York: Wiley, 1958.

Homans, G. *Social behavior*. New York: Harcourt, Brace & World, 1961.

Jaques, E. *Equitable payment*. New York: Wiley, 1961.

Lawler, E. E., III. *Pay and organizational effectiveness: A psychological view*. New York: McGraw-Hill, 1971.

Lawler, E. E., III, & O'Gara, P. W. Effects of inequity produced by underpayment on work output, work quality, and attitudes toward the work. *Journal of Applied Psychology*, 1967, **51**, 403–410.

Patchen, M. *The choice of wage comparisons*. Englewood Cliffs, N. J.: Prentice-Hall, 1961.

Pritchard, R. D. Equity theory: A review and critique. *Organizational Behavior and Human Performance*, 1969, **4**, 176–211.

Pritchard, R. D., Dunnette, M. D., & Jorgenson, D. O. Effects of perceptions of equity and inequity on worker performance and satisfaction. *Journal of Applied Psychology*, 1972, **56**, 75–94.

Telly, C. S., French, W. L., & Scott, W. G. The relationship of inequity to turnover among hourly workers. *Administrative Science Quarterly*, 1971, **16**, 164–172.

Tornow, W. W. The development and application of an input-outcome moderator test on the perception and reduction of inequity. *Organizational Behavior and Human Performance*, 1971, **6**, 614–638.

Weick, K. E., Jr. Reduction of cognitive dissonance through task enhancement and effort expenditure. *Journal of Abnormal and Social Psychology*, 1964, **68**, 533–539.

Weick, K. E., Jr. The concept of equity in the perception of pay. *Administrative Science Quarterly*, 1966, **11**, 414–439.

Wiener, Y. The effects of task and ego-oriented performance on two kinds of overcompensation inequity. *Organizational Behavior and Human Performance*, 1970, **5**, 191–208.

Inequity in Social Exchange

J. Stacy Adams

In what follows it is hoped that a fairly comprehensive theory of inequity will be elaborated. The term *inequity* is used instead of *injustice* first, because the author has used this term before (Adams and Rosenbaum, 1962; Adams, 1963a,b, 1965; Adams and Jacobsen, 1964), second, to avoid the confusion of the many connotative meanings associated with the term *justice*, and third, to emphasize that the primary concern is with the causes and consequences of the absence of equity in human exchange relationships. In developing the theory, major variables affecting perceptions of inequity in an exchange will be described. A formal definition of inequity will then be proposed. From this point the effects of inequity upon behavior and cognitive processes will be discussed and research giving evidence of the effects will be presented. For heuristic purposes employee-employer exchanges will be a focus because such relations are within the experience of almost everyone and constitute a significant aspect of human intercourse. Moreover, much empirical research relating to inequity has been undertaken in business and industrial spheres or in simulated employment situations. It should be evident, however, that the theoretical notions offered are quite as relevant to any social situation in which an exchange takes place, explicitly or implicity, whether between teammates, teacher and student, lovers, child and parent, patient and therapist, or opponents or even enemies, for between all there are expectations of what is fair exchange.

A ANTECEDENTS OF INEQUITY

Whenever two individuals exchange anything, there is the possibility that one or both of them will feel that the exchange was inequitable. Such is frequently the case when a man exchanges his services for pay. On the man's side of the exchange are his education, intelligence, experience, training, skill, seniority, age, sex, ethnic background, social status, and, of course, the effort he expends on the job. Under special circumstances other attributes will be relevant. These may be personal appearance or attractiveness, health, possession of certain tools, the characteristics of one's spouse, and so on. They are what a man perceives as his contributions to the exchange, for which he expects a just return. As noted earlier, these are the same as Homans' (1961) investments. A man brings them into an exchange, and henceforth they will be referred to as his *inputs*. These inputs, let us emphasize, are *as perceived by their contributor* and are not necessarily isomorphic with those perceived by the other party to the exchange. This suggests two conceptually distinct characteristics of inputs, *recognition* and *relevance*.

The possessor of an attribute, or the other party to the exchange, or both, may recognize the existence of the attribute in the possessor. If either the possessor or both members of the exchange recognizes its existence, the attribute has the potentiality of being an input. If only the nonpossessor recognizes its existence, it cannot be considered psychologically an input so far as the possesssor is concerned. Whether or not an attribute having the potential of being an input is in fact an input is contingent upon the possessor's perception of its relevance to the exchange. If he perceives it to be relevant, if he expects a just return for it, it is an input. Problems of inequity arise if only the possessor of the attribute considers it relevant to the exchange, or if the other party to the exchange considers it irrelevant and acts accordingly. Thus, unless prohibited from doing so by contract terms, an employer may consider seniority irrelevant in granting promotions, thinking it wiser to consider merit alone, whereas the employee may believe that seniority is highly relevant. In consequence, the employee may feel that injustice has been done. Conversely, the employer who is compelled to use seniority rather than merit as a promotion criterion may well feel that he has been forced into an inequitable exchange. In a personal communication Crozier (1960) made a relevant observation. Paris-born bank clerks worked side by side with clerks who did identical work and earned identical wages but who were born in the provinces. The Parisians were dissatisfied with their wages, for they considered that a Parisian upbringing was an input deserving recognition. The bank management, although recognizing that place of birth distinguished the two groups, did not, of course, consider birthplace relevant in the exchange of services for pay.

The principal inputs that have been listed vary in type and in their degree of relationship to one another. Some variables such as age are clearly continuous; others, such as sex and ethnicity, are not. Some are intercorrelated: seniority and age, for example. Sex, on the other hand, is largely independent of the other variables, with the possible exception of education and some kinds of effort. Although these intercorrelations, or the lack of them, exist in a state of nature, it is probable that the individual cognitively treats all input variables as independent. Thus, for example, if he were assessing the sum of his inputs, he might well "score" age and seniority separately. It is as if he thought, "I am older and have been with Acem longer than Joe," without taking account of the fact that the two attributes are correlated. This excursion into the "black box" should not imply, as Homans (1961) seems to imply, that men assess various components of an exchange on an ordinal scale. If the work of Jaques on equitable payment (1956, 1961a) is taken at face value, there is reason to believe in this respect that men employ interval and ratio scales, or that, at the very least, they are capable of making quite fine ordinal discriminations.

On the other side of an exchange are an individual's receipts. These *outcomes*, as they will be termed, include in an employee-employer exchange pay, rewards intrinsic to the job, satisfying supervision, seniority benefits, fringe benefits, job status and status symbols, and a variety of formally and informally sanctioned perquisites, such as the right of a higher-status person to park his car in a privileged location. These are examples of positively valent outcomes. But outcomes may have negative valence. Poor working conditions, monotony, fate uncertainty, and the many "dissatisfiers" listed by Herzberg *et al.* (1959) are no less "received" than, say, wages and are negatively valent. They would be avoided, rather than approached, if it were possible. As in the case of job inputs, job outcomes are often intercorrelated. For example, greater pay and higher job status are likely to go hand-in-hand.

In other than employee-employer exchanges, though they are not precluded from these exchanges, relevant positive outcomes for one or both parties may consist of affection, love, formal courtesies, expressions of friendship, fair value (as in merchandise), and reliability (as part of the purchase of a service). Insult, rudeness, and rejection are the other side of the coin. It may be noted that in a vast array of social relations reciprocity is a functional element of the relation. What is in fact referred to by reciprocity is equality of exchange. The infinitive "to reciprocate" is commonly used to denote an obligation to give someone equal, positively valent outcomes in return for outcomes received. When a housewife says "John, we must have the Browns over, to reciprocate," she means to maintain a social relationship by reestablishing a parity in the outcomes of the two families. In this connection, it can be observed that reciprocation is usually "in kind." That is, there is a deliberate effort to match outcomes, to give equal value for value received. People who undershoot or overshoot the mark are called "cheapskates" or "uppish" and pretentious, repectively.

In a manner analogous to inputs, outcomes are *as perceived*, and, again, they should be characterized in terms of recognition and relevance. If the recipient or both the recipient and giver of an outcome in an exchange recognize its existence, it has the potentiality of being an outcome psychologically. If the recipient considers it relevant to the exchange and it has some marginal utility for him, it *is* an outcome. Not infrequently the giver may give or yield something which, though of some cost to him, is either irrelevant or of no marginal utility to the recipient. An employer may give an employee a carpet for his office in lieu, say, of a salary increment and find that the employee is dissatisfied, perhaps because in the subculture of that office a rug has no meaning, no psychological utility. Conversely, a salary increment may be inadequate, if formalized status recognition was what was wanted and what had greater utility. Or, in another context, the gift of a toy to a child may be effectively irrelevant as reciprocation for a demonstration of affection on his part if he seeks affection. Fortunately, in the process of socialization, through the reinforcing behavior of others and of the "verbal community" (Skinner, 1957), the human organism learns not only what is appropriate reciprocation, but he learns also to assess the marginal utility of a variety of outcomes to others. In the absence of this ability, interpersonal relations would be chaotic, if not impossible. An idea of the problems that would exist may be had by observing travelers in a foreign culture. Appropriate or relevant reciprocation of outcomes is difficult, even in such mundane exchanges as tipping for services.

In classifying some variables as inputs and others as outcomes, it is not implied that they are independent, except conceptually. Inputs and outcomes are, in fact, intercorrelated, but imperfectly so. Indeed, it is because they are imperfectly correlated that there need be concern with inequity. There exist normative expectations of what constitute "fair" correlations between inputs and outcomes. The expectations are formed—learned—during the process of socialization, at home, at school, at work. They are based by observation of the correlations obtaining for a reference person or group—a co-worker or a colleague, a relative or neighbor, a group of co-workers, a craft group, an industry-wide pattern. A bank clerk, for example, may determine whether her outcomes and inputs are fairly correlated, in balance so to speak, by comparing them with the ratio of the outcomes to the inputs of other female clerks in her section. The sole punch-press operator in a manufacturing plant may base his judgment on what he believes are the inputs and outcomes of other operators in the community or region. For a particular professor the relevant reference group may be professors in the same discipline and of the same academic "vintage." While it is clearly important to be able to specify theoretically the appropriate reference person or group, this will not be done here, as the task is beyond the scope of the paper and is discussed by others (e.g., Festinger, 1954; Hyman, 1942; Merton and Kitt, 1950; Patchen, 1961). For present purposes, it will be assumed that the reference person or group will be one comparable to the comparer on one or more attributes. This is usually a co-worker in industrial situations, according to Livernash (1953), but, as Sayles (1958) points out, this generalization requires verification, as plausible as it may appear.

When the normative expectations of the person making social comparisons are violated, when he finds that his outcomes and inputs are not in balance in relation to those of others, feelings of inequity result. But before a formal definition of inequity is offered, two terms of reference will be introduced to facilitate later discussion, *Person* and *Other*. *Person* is any individual for whom equity or inequity exists. *Other* is any individual with whom Person is in an exchange relationship, or with whom Person compares himself when both he and Other are in an exchange relationship with a third party, such as an employer, or with third parties who are considered by Person as being comparable, such as employers in a particular industry or geographic location. Other is usually a different individual, but may be Person in another job or in another social role. Thus, Other might be Person in a job he held previously, in which case he might compare his present and past outcomes and inputs and determine whether or not the exchange with his employer, present or past, was equitable. The terms Person and Other may also refer to groups rather than to individuals, as when a class of jobs (e.g., toolmakers) is out of line with another class (e.g., lathe operators), or when the circumstances of one ethnic group are incongruous with those of another. In such cases, it is convenient to deal with the class as a whole rather than with individual members of the class.

B   DEFINITION OF INEQUITY

Inequity exists for Person whenever he perceives that the ratio of his outcomes to inputs and the ratio of Other's outcomes to Other's inputs are unequal. This may happen either (a) when he and Other are in a direct exchange relationship or (b) when both are in an exchange relationship with a third party and Person compares himself to Other. The values of outcomes and inputs are, of course, as perceived by Person. Schematically, inequality is experienced when either

$$\frac{O_p}{I_p} < \frac{O_a}{I_a}$$

or

$$\frac{O_p}{I_p} > \frac{O_a}{I_a}$$

where $O = \Sigma_{oi}$, $I = \Sigma_{oi}$ and p and a are subscripts denoting Person and Other, respectively. A condition of equity exists when

$$\frac{O_p}{I_p} = \frac{O_a}{I_a}$$

The outcomes and inputs in each of the ratios are conceived as being the sum of such outcomes and inputs as are perceived to be relevant to a particular exchange. Furthermore, each sum is conceived of as a weighted sum, on the assumption that individuals probably do not weight elemental outcomes or inputs equally. The work of Herzberg *et al.* (1959) on job "satisfiers" and "dissatisfiers" implies strongly that different outcomes, as they are labeled here, have widely varying utilities, negative as well as positive. It also appears reasonable to assume that inputs as diverse as seniority, skill, effort, and sex are not weighted equally. Zaleznik *et al.* (1958), in attempting to test some predictions from distributive justice theory in an industrial corporation, gave equal weight to five factors which correspond to inputs as defined here—age, seniority, education, ethnicity, and sex—but were unable to sustain their hypotheses. In retrospect, they believe (Zaleznik *et al.*, 1958) that weighting these inputs equally may have represented an inadequate assumption of the manner in which their respondents summed their inputs.

From the definition of inequity it follows that inequity results for Person not only when he is, so to speak, relatively underpaid, but also when he is relatively overpaid. Person, will, for example, feel inequity exists not only when his effort is high and his pay low, while Other's effort and pay are high, but also when his effort is low and his pay high, while Other's effort and pay are low. This proposition receives direct support from experiments by Adams and Rosenbaum (1962), Adams (1963a), and Adams and Jacobsen (1964) in which subjects were inequitably overpaid. It receives some support also from an observation by Thibaut (1950) that subjects in whose favor the experimenter discriminated displayed "guilty smirks" and "sheepishness." The magnitude of the inequity experienced will be a monotomically increasing function of the size of the discrepancy between the ratios of outcomes to inputs. The discrepancy will be zero, and equity will exist, under two circumstances: first, when Person's and Other's outcomes are equal and their inputs are equal. This would be the case, for example, when Person perceived that Other's wages, job, and working conditions were the same as his and that Other was equal to him on such relevant dimensions as sex, skill, seniority, education, age, effort expended, physical fitness, and risk incurred (risk of personal injury, of being fired for errors committed, for instance). Secondly, the ratios will be equal when Person perceives that Other's outcomes are higher (or lower) than his and that Other's inputs are correspondingly higher (or lower). A subordinate who compares himself to his supervisor or work group leader typically does not feel that he is unjustly treated by the company that employs them both, because the supervisor's greater monetary compensation, better working conditions, and more interesting, more varied job are matched on the input side of the ratio by more education, wider range of skills, greater responsibility and personal risk, more maturity and experience, and longer service.

Although there is no direct, reliable, evidence on this point, it is probable, as Homans (1961) conjectured, that the thresholds for inequity are different (in absolute terms from a base of equity) in cases of under- and overreward.

The threshold would be higher presumably in cases of overreward, for a certain amount of incongruity in these cases can be acceptably rationalized as "good fortune" without attendant discomfort. In his work on pay differentials, Jaques (1961b) notes that in instances of undercompensation, British workers paid 10% less than the equitable level show "an active sense of grievance, complaints or the desire to complain, and, if no redress is given, an active desire to change jobs, or to take action . . ." (p. 26). He states further, "The results suggest that it is not necessarily the case that each one is simply out to get as much as he can for his work. There appear to be equally strong desires that each one should earn the right amount—a fair and reasonable amount relative to others" (p. 26).

   In the preceding discussion, Person has been the focus of attention. It should be clear, however, that when Person and Other are in an exchange interaction, Other will suffer inequity if Person does, but the nature of his experience will be opposite to that of Person. If the outcome-input ratio discrepancy is unfavorable to Person, it will be favorable to Other, and vice versa. This will hold provided Person's and Other's perceptions of outcomes and inputs are equivalent and provided that the outcome-input ratio discrepancy attains threshold level. When Person and Other are not engaged in an exchange with one another but stand in an exchange relationship with a third party, Other may or may not experience inequity when Person does. Given the prerequisites mentioned above, he will experience inequity if he compares himself to Person with respect to the same question as induces Person to use Other as a referent (e.g., "Am I being paid fairly?").

C CONSEQUENCES OF INEQUITY

Although there can be little doubt that inequity results in dissatisfaction, in an unpleasant emotional state, be it anger or guilt, there will be other effects. A major purpose of this paper is to specify these in terms that permit specific predictions to be made. Before turning to this task, two general postulates are presented, closely following propositions from cognitive dissonance theory (Festinger, 1957). First, the presence of inequity in Person creates tension in him. The tension is proportional to the magnitude of inequity present. Second, the tension created in Person will motivate him to eliminate or reduce it. The strength of the motivation is proportional to the tension created. In short, the presence of inequity will motivate Person to achieve equity or to reduce inequity, and the strength of motivation to do so will vary directly with the magnitude of inequity experienced. From these postulates and from the theory of cognitive dissonance (Festinger, 1957; Brehm and Cohen, 1962), means of reducing inequity will be derived and presented. As each method of reduction is discussed, evidence demonstrating usage of the method will be presented. Some of the evidence is experimental; some of it is the result of field studies, either of a survey or observational character.

1 Person Altering His Inputs

Person may vary his inputs, either increasing them or decreasing them, depending on whether the inequity is advantageous or disadvantageous. Increasing inputs will reduce felt inequity, if

$$\frac{O_p}{I_p} > \frac{O_a}{I_a}$$

Conversely, decreasing inputs will be effective, if

$$\frac{O_p}{I_p} < \frac{O_a}{I_a}$$

In the former instance, Person might increase either his productivity or the quality of his work, provided that it is possible, which is not always the case. In the second instance, Person might engage in "production restriction," for example. Whether Person does, or can, reduce inequity by altering his inputs is partially contingent upon whether relevant inputs are susceptible to change. Sex, age, seniority, and ethnicity are not modifiable. Education and skill are more easily altered, but changing these requires time. Varying inputs will also be a function of Person's perception of the principal "cause" of the inequity. If the discrepancy between outcome-input ratios is primarily a function of his inputs being at variance with those of Other, Person is more likely to alter them than if the discrepancy is largely a result of differences in outcomes. Additionally, it is postulated that given equal opportunity to alter inputs and outcomes, Person will be more likely to lower his inputs when

$$\frac{O_p}{I_p} < \frac{O_a}{I_a}$$

than he is to increase his inputs when

$$\frac{O_p}{I_p} > \frac{O_a}{I_a}$$

This is derived from two assumptions: first, the assumption stated earlier that the threshold for the perception of inequity is higher when Person is overrewarded than when he is underrewarded; secondly, the assumption that Person is motivated to minimize his costs and to maximize his gains. By the second assumption, Person will reduce inequity, insofar as possible, in a manner that will yield him the largest outcomes.

Altering certain inputs has the corollary effect of altering the outcomes of Other. A change in the quality and amount of work performed, for instance, will usually affect the outcomes of Other. When this is the case, the effect of both changes will operate in the same direction in the service of inequity reduction. It follows, therefore, that *less* a change in inputs is required to eliminate inequity than if the change had no effect on Other's outcomes. Inputs, a change in which would have no or very little impact on Other's outcomes, are attributes such as education, age, and seniority—at least to the extent that they are uncorrelated with performance.

Several experiments have been conducted specifically to test the hypothesis that Person will reduce inequity by altering his inputs (Adams and Rosenbaum, 1962; Adams, 1963a; Adams and Jacobsen, 1964).

2 Person Altering His Outcomes

Person may vary his outcomes, either decreasing or increasing them, depending on whether the inequity is advantageous or disadvantageous to him. Increasing outcomes will reduce inequity, if

$$\frac{O_p}{I_p} < \frac{O_a}{I_a}$$

Conversely, decreasing outcomes will serve the same function, if

$$\frac{O_p}{I_p} > \frac{O_a}{I_a}$$

Of these two possibilities, the second is far less likely, and there is no good evidence of the use of this means of reducing inequity, though some may be available in the clinical literature. There are, however, data bearing on attempts to increase outcomes, data other than those related to wage increase demands in union-management negotiations, probably only a part of which are directly traceable to wage inequities.

In the experiment by Thibaut (1950), to which reference was made earlier, teams of 5 or 6 boys made up of approximately equal numbers of popular and unpopular boys were assigned either high- or low-status roles in playing a series of four games. The low-status teams were unfairly treated in that, although they were comparable in their characteristics (i.e., their inputs) to the high-status teams, they were forced to adopt an inferior, unpleasant role vis-a-vis the other team. For example, in one game they formed a human chain against which the other team bucked; in another, they held the target and retrieved thrown bean bags. Thus, since their inputs were equal to, and their outcomes lower than, those of the high-status teams, they were clearly suffering the disadvantages of inequity. From Thibaut's report of the behavior of the low-status teams, it is evident that at least four means of reducing the inequity were used by them: lowering the high-status team members' outcomes by fighting with them and displaying other forms of hostility; lowering their inputs by not playing the games as required, which would also have had the effect of lowering the outcomes of the high-status team members; by leaving the field, that is, withdrawing and crying; and by trying to interchange roles with the high-status teams. The latter is the relevant one for purposes of discussion here.

Thibaut (1950) reports that about halfway through the second game the participants had come to understand the experimenter's intention, i.e., that the status differentiation was to be permanent. At this stage of the experiment low-status subjects began to express mobility aspirations, asking the experimenter that the roles of the two teams be reversed. This may be interpreted as an attempt to establish equity by increasing outcomes, since assumption of high status would have been accompanied by pleasurable activities. Interestingly, though the report is not entirely clear on this point, there is the suggestion that, when the attempt of low-status subjects to increase their outcomes was rejected by the experimenter, they desisted and, instead, engaged more in withdrawal.

Also giving evidence that increasing outcomes will serve to reduce inequity is a study of unfair wages among clerical workers by Homans (1953). Two groups of female clerical workers in a utilities company, cash posters and ledger clerks, worked in the same, large room. Cash posting consisted of recording daily the amounts customers paid on their bills, and management insisted that posting be precisely up to date. It required that cash posters pull customer cards from the many files and make appropriate entries on them. The job was highly repetitive and comparatively monotonous, and required little thought but a good deal of walking about. Ledger clerks, in contrast, performed a variety of tasks on customer accounts, such as recording address changes, making breakdowns of over and underpayments, and supplying information on accounts to customers and others on the telephone. In addition, toward the end of the day, they were required by their supervisor to assist with "cleaning up" cash posting in order that it be current. Compared to the cash posters, ledger clerks performed a number of nonrepetitive clerical jobs requiring some thought; they had a more *responsible* job; they were considered to be of higher status, since promotion took place from cash poster to ledger clerk; and they were older and had more seniority and experience. Their weekly pay, however, was identical.

Summarizing in the terms of the inequity model, cash posters had distinctly lower inputs than ledger clerks (i.e., they were younger, and had less experience, less seniority, and less responsibility). With respect to outcomes they received equal wages, but their jobs were somewhat more monotonous and less interesting. On the other hand, the ledger clerks' inputs were superior with respect to age, experience, seniority, skill, responsibility, and versatility (they were required to know and do cash posting in addition to their own jobs). Their earnings were equal to the cash posters', but they were required to "clean up" (note connotation) posting each day, an activity that would deflate self-esteem and would, therefore, be a negative outcome. In the balance, then, the net outcomes of ledger clerks and cash posters were approximately of the same magnitude, but the inputs of the clerks were definitely greater. From this it would be predicted that the ledger clerks felt unfairly treated and that they would try to increase their outcomes.

The evidence reported by Homans (1953) is that the ledger clerks felt the inequity and that they felt they ought to get a few dollars more per week to show that their jobs were more important—that their greater inputs ought to be matched by greater outcomes. On the whole, these clerks seemed not to have done much to reduce inequity, though a few complained to the union representative, with, apparently, little effect. However, the workers in this division voted to abandon their independent union for the CIO, and Homans intimates that the reason may have been the independent union's inability to force a resolution of the inequity.

The field studies of dissatisfaction with status and promotions by Stouffer *et al.* (1949) and the experiments by Spector (1956), in which expectation of promotion and morale, which were described in Section II, may also be interpreted as cases of inequity in which dissatisfactions were expressions of attempts by Persons to increase their outcomes.

3 Person Distorting His Inputs and Outcomes Cognitively

Person may cognitively distort his inputs and outcomes, the direction of the distortion being the same as if he had actually altered his inputs and outcomes, as discussed above. Since most individuals are heavily influenced by reality, substantial distortion is generally difficult. It is pretty difficult to distort to oneself, to change one's cognitions about the fact, for example, that one has a BA degree, that one has been an accountant for seven years, and that one's salary is $700 per month. However, it is possible, within limits, to alter the utility of these. For example, State College is a small, backwoods school with no reputation, or, alternatively, State College has one of the best business schools in the state and the dean is an adviser to the Bureau of the Budget. Or, one can consider the fact that $700 per month will buy all of the essential things of life and a few luxuries, or, conversely, that it will never permit one to purchase a Wyeth oil painting or an Aston Martin DB5. There is ample evidence in the psychological literature, especially that related to cognitive dissonance theory, that individuals do modify or rearrange their cognitions in an effort to reduce perceived incongruities (for a review, see Brehm and Cohen, 1962). Since it has been postulated that the experience of inequity is equivalent to the experience of dissonance, it is reasonable to believe that cognitive distortion may be adopted as a means of reducing inequity. In a variety of work situations, for example in paced production line jobs, actually altering one's inputs and outcomes may be difficult; as a consequence these may be cognitively changed in relatively subtle ways.

Although not a cognitive change in inputs and outcomes per se, related methods of reducing inequity are for Person to alter the *importance* and the *relevance* of his inputs and outcomes. If, for example, age were a relevant input, its relative importance could be changed to bring about less perceived inequity. Person could convince himself that age was either more or less important than he thought originally. In terms of the statement made earlier that net inputs (and outcomes) were a weighted sum of inputs, changing the importance of inputs would be equivalent to changing the weights associated with them. Altering the relevance of inputs and outcomes is conceived of as more of an all-or-none process: Present ones are made irrelevant or new ones are made relevant. For instance, if Person perceived that the discrepancy between his and Other's outcome-input ratios were principally a result of his outcomes being too low, he might become "aware" of one or more outcomes he had not recognized as being relevant before, perhaps that his job had variety absent from Other's job. Obviously, importance and relevance of inputs and outcomes are not completely independent. An outcome suddenly perceived as being relevant automatically assumes some importance; conversely, one that is made irrelevant in the service of inequity reduction assumes an importance of zero. Nevertheless, the psychological processes appear to be different and it is useful, therefore, to keep them conceptually distinct. . . .

4 Person Leaving the Field

Leaving the field may take any of several ways of severing social relationships. Quitting a job, obtaining a transfer, and absenteeism are common forms of leaving the field in an employment situation. These are fairly radical means of coping with inequity. The probability of using them is assumed to increase with magnitude of inequity and to decrease with the availability of other means.

Data substantiating the occurrence of leaving the field as a mode of reducing inequity is sparse. In the aforementioned study by Thibaut (1950), it was observed that low-status team members withdrew from the games as it became increasingly clear what their fate was and as, it must be presumed, the felt injustice mounted. In a study by Patchen (1959) it was observed that men who said their pay should be higher had more absences than men who said the pay for jobs was fair. This relationship between perceived fairness of pay and absenteeism was independent of actual wage level. That absenteeism in this study was a form of withdrawal is strongly supported by the fact that men with high absence rates were significantly more likely than men with low rates to say that they would not go on working at their job, if they should chance to inherit enough money to live comfortably without working.

5 Person Acting on Other

In the face of injustice, Person may attempt to alter or cognitively distort Other's inputs and outcomes, or try to force Other to leave the field. These means of reducing inequity vary in the ease of their use. Getting Other to accept greater outcomes, which was a possible interpretation of some of the findings by Leventhal et al. (1964), would obviously be easier than the opposite. Similarly, inducing Other to lower his inputs may be easier than the reverse. For example, all other things being equal, such as work group cohesiveness and the needs and ability of an individual worker, it is probably easier to induce a "rate buster" to lower his inputs than to get a laggard to increase them. The direction of the change attempted in the inputs and outcomes of Other is the reverse of the change that Person would make in his own inputs and outcomes, whether the change be actual or cognitive. By way of illustration, if Person experienced feelings of inequity because he lacked job experience compared to Other, he could try to induce Other to decrease a relevant input instead of increasing his own inputs.

Cognitive distortion of Other's inputs and outcomes may be somewhat less difficult than distortion of one's own, since cognitions about Other are probably less well anchored than are those concerning oneself. This assumption is consistent with the finding that "where alternatives to change in central attitudes are possible, they will be selected" (Pilisuk, 1962, p. 102). Acceptable evidence that inequity, as such, is reduced by cognitive distortion of Other's inputs or outcomes is nonexistent, although there is ample evidence that cognitive dissonance may be reduced by perceptual distortion (e.g., Bramel, 1962; Brehm and Cohen, 1962; Steiner and Peters, 1958). An observation made while pretesting procedures for an unpublished study by Adams (1961) is little better than anecdotal. To test some hypotheses from inequity theory, he paired a subject and a stooge at a "partner's desk." Each performed sequentially one part of the preparation of a personnel payroll. In one condition the subject was paid $1.40 per hour and performed the relatively complex task of looking in various tables for standard and overtime rates, looking up in other tables the products of pay rates and hours worked, and recording the products on a payroll form. The stooge, whose pay was announced as being $2.10 per hour, performed the presumably much easier task of summing products on a machine and recording the totals on the form the subject passed to him across the desk. In addition, the stooge was programmed to be slightly ahead of the subject in his work, so that his task appeared fairly easy. It was hoped that these conditions would lead the subject to perceive that, compared to the stooge, he had higher inputs and lower outcomes. Nothing of the sort happened. Most subjects pretested felt that the relationship was equitable, and this appeared to result from the fact that they distorted cognitively the stooge's inputs in an upward direction. Specifically, they convinced themselves that the stooge was performing a "mathematical task." Simple *adding* on a machine became *mathematics*.

Forcing Other to leave the field, while theoretically possible, is probably difficult to realize and would, no doubt, be accompanied by anxiety about potential consequences or simply by the discomfort of having done something socially unpleasant. This aspect makes it costly to Person; it lowers his outcomes to some extent. Firing an individual in an employer-employee exchange and some divorces and separations are common examples of this means put to use. Somewhat though barely more subtle is the practice of creating an inequity by withholding expected outcomes (e.g., salary increases, promotions) to the point where an individual leaves the field "voluntarily."

6 Person Changing the Object of His Comparison

Person may change Other with whom he compares himself when he experiences inequity and he and Other stand in an exchange relationship with a third party. This mode is limited to the relationship specified; it is not applicable when

Person and Other are in a direct exchange. Changing the object of comparison in the latter situation would reduce to severing the relationship.

The resolution of inequity by changing comparison object is undoubtedly difficult to accomplish, particularly if Person has been comparing himself to Other for some time. Person would need to be able to make himself noncomparable to Other on one or more dimensions. For instance, if Other, whose outcome-input ratio was previously equal to Person's received a salary increase without any apparent increment in inputs, Person could try to reduce the resulting feeling of inequity by conceiving of Other as belonging now to a different organizational level. But this would likely meet with little success, at least in this culture. A cognitive change of this sort would be extremely unstable, unless it were accompanied by changes in the perception of Other's inputs: for instance, that Other had assumed greater responsibility when his salary was increased. But this involves a process of inequity reduction already referred to.

In the initial stages of comparison processes, as when a man first comes on the job, it probably is relatively easy to choose as comparison Others individuals who provide the most equitable comparisons. This does not necessarily entail making comparisons with men whose outcomes and inputs are the same as one's own; it is sufficient that their outcome input ratio be equal to one's own. In a study of the choice of wage comparison, Patchen (1961) asked oil refinery workers to name someone whose yearly earnings were *different* from theirs and then proceeded to ask them questions about the resulting wage comparisons and about their satisfaction with them. Of the workers who named someone earning *more* than they, 60% indicated satisfaction with the comparison and only 17.6% reported dissatisfaction. Among those who were satisfied, 44.6% stated they were satisfied because they had financial or other advantages, i.e., compensating outcomes, and 55.8% indicated satisfaction with the upward comparison because the person with higher earnings had more education, skill, experience, seniority and the like, i.e., higher inputs. Patchen's data may be recast and reanalyzed to make a different point. Among the men who chose comparison persons whose outcome-input ratios seemingly were equal to theirs, approximately 85% were satisfied with the comparison and only about 4% were dissatisfied. While Patchen's study does not bear directly either on what wage comparisons men actually make in their day-to-day relations with other or on changes in comparison persons when inequity arises, it gives clear evidence that comparisons are made on the basis of the equality of the outcome-input ratios of the comparer and comparison person and that such comparisons prove satisfying i.e., are, at least, judged to be not inequitable.

7 Choice Among Modes of Inequity Reduction

Although reference has been made previously to conditions that may affect the use of one or another method of reducing inequity, there is need for a general statement of conditions that will govern the adoption of one method over another. Given the existence of inequity, any of the means of reduction described earlier are potentially available to Person. He may alter or attempt to alter any of the four terms in the inequality formula or change his cognitions about any of them, or he may leave the field and change his comparison Other, but it is improbable that each of the methods are equally available to him *psychologically* (no reference is made to environmental constraints that may affect the availability of methods), as the work of Steiner and his colleagues on alternative methods of dissonance reduction suggests (Steiner, 1960; Steiner and Johnson, 1964; Steiner and Peters, 1958; Steiner and Rogers, 1963).

Set forth below are some propositions about conditions determining the choice of modes by Person. As will be noted, the propositions are not all independent of one another, and each should be prefaced by the condition, *ceteris paribus*.

a Person will maximize positively valent outcomes and the valence of outcomes.

b He will minimize increasing inputs that are effortful and costly to change.

c He will resist real and cognitive changes in inputs that are central to his self-concept and to his self-esteem. To the extent that any of Person's outcomes are related to his self-concept and to his self-esteem, this proposition is extended to cover his outcomes.

d He will be more resistant to changing cognitions about his own outcomes and inputs than to changing his cognitions about Other's outcomes and inputs.

e Leaving the field will be resorted to only when the magnitude of inequity experienced is high and other means of reducing it are unavailable. Partial withdrawal, such as absenteeism, will occur more frequently and under conditions of lower inequity.

f Person will be highly resistant to changing the object of his comparisons, Other, once it has stabilized over time and, in effect, has become an anchor.

These propositions are, admittedly, fairly crude, but they permit, nevertheless, a degree of prediction not available otherwise. In the resolution of a particular injustice, two or more of the processes proposed may be pitted one against the other. To propose which would be dominant is not possible at this stage of the development of the theory. One might propose that protection of self-esteem would dominate maximization of outcomes, but it would be conjecture in the absence of evidence.

CONCLUSION

Dissatisfaction is both so commonplace and such an irritant, particularly in industrial and other large organizations, that it has been the subject of widespread research (see Vroom, 1964, for a recent, thorough review). Despite prima facie evidence that feelings of injustice underlay a significant proportion of cases of dissatisfaction, thorough behavioral analyses of injustice were not made until recently. In the classic Hawthorne studies (Roethlisberger and Dickson, 1939), there was ample evidence that much of the dissatisfaction observed among Western Electric Company employees was precipitated by felt injustice. Describing complaints, the authors referred frequently to reports by workers that wages were not in keeping with seniority, that rates were too low, that ability was not rewarded, and the like, as distinguished from reports that, for example, equipment was not working and that the workshop was hot. They stated that "no physical or logical operations exist which can be agreed upon as defining them" (p. 259), and they sought "personal or social situations" (p. 269) that would explain the complaints parsimoniously. Yet, the notion of injustice was not advanced as an explanatory concept.

It is not contended here, of course, that all dissatisfaction and low morale are related to a person's suffering injustice in social exchanges. But it should be clear from the research described that a significant portion of cases can be usefully explained by invoking injustice as an explanatory concept. More importantly, much more than dissatisfaction may be predicted once the concept of injustice is analyzed theoretically.

In the theory of inequity that has been developed in this chapter, both the antecedents and consequences of perceived injustice have been stated in terms that permit quite specific predictions to be made about the behavior of persons entering social exchanges. On the whole, empirical support for the theory is gratifying, but it falls short of what is desirable. More research is required. This is particularly so because some of the support comes from data leading to the formulation of parts of the theory. Needed are direct tests of propositions made in the theory, as well as empirical tests of novel derivations from the theory. Some research filling these needs is under way. Being tested, for example, is the hypothesis that overpaid workers for whom an increase in inputs is impossible will reduce inequity by decreasing their outcomes, specifically by developing unfavorable attitudes toward their employer, their working conditions, the pay rates, and so on.

In order for more refined predictions to be made from the theory, theoretical, methodological, and empirical work are also required in at least two areas related to it. First, additional thought must be given to social comparison processes. The works of Festinger (1954), Hyman (1942), Merton and Kitt (1950), Newcomb (1943), and Patchen (1961) are signal contributions but still do not allow sufficiently fine predictions to be made about whom Person will choose as a comparison Other when both are in exchange relationship with a third party. For example, as a function of what variables will one man compare himself to a person on the basis of age similarities and another man compare himself on the basis of attitude similarities? Second, psychometric research is needed to determine how individuals aggregate their own outcomes and inputs and those of others. Is the assumptive model that net outcomes are the algebraic sum of elemental outcomes weighted by their importance a valid one?

The need for much additional research notwithstanding, the theoretical analyses that have been made of injustice in social exchanges should result not only in a better general understanding of the phenomenon, but should lead to a degree of social control not previously possible. The experience of injustice need not be an accepted fact of life.

REFERENCES

Adams, J. S. (1961). Wage inequities in a clerical task. Unpublished study. General Electric Company, New York.

Adams, J. S. (1963a). Toward an understanding of inequity. *J. abnorm. soc. Psychol.* **67**, 422–436.

Adams, J. S. (1963b). Wage inequities, productivity, and work quality. *Industr. Relat.* **3**, 9–16.

Adams, J. S. (1965). Etudes expérimentales en matière d'inégalités de salaires, de productivité et de qualité du travail. *Synopsis,* **7**, 25–34.

Adams, J. S., and Jacobsen, Patricia R. (1964). Effects of wage inequities on work quality. *J. abnorm. soc. Psychol.* **69**, 19–25.

Adams, J. S., and Rosenbaum, W. B. (1962). The relationship of worker productivity to cognitive dissonance about wage inequities. *J. appl. Psychol.* **46**, 161–164.

Bramel, D. (1962). A dissonance theory approach to defensive projection. *J. abnorm. soc. Psychol.* **64**, 121–129.

Brehm, J. W., and Cohen, A. R. (1962). *Explorations in cognitive dissonance.* New York: Wiley.

Clark, J. V. (1958). A preliminary investigation of some unconscious assumptions affecting labor efficiency in eight supermarkets. Unpublished doctoral dissertation (Grad. Sch. Business Admin.). Harvard Univer.

Crozier, M. (1960). Personal communication to the author.

Festinger, L. (1954). A theory of social comparison processes. *Hum. Relat.* 7, 117–140.

Festinger, L. (1957). *A theory of cognitive dissonance.* Evanston, Ill.: Row, Peterson.

Herzberg, F., Mausner, B., and Snyderman, Barbara B. (1959). *The motivation to work.* New York: Wiley.

Homans, G. C. (1950). *The human group.* New York: Harcourt, Brace.

Homans, G. C. (1963). Status among clerical workers. *Hum. Organiz.* **12**, 5–10.

Homans, G. C. (1961). *Social behavior: its elementary forms.* New York: Harcourt, Brace.

Hyman, H. (1942). The psychology of status. *Arch. Psychol.* **38**, No. 269.

Jaques, E. (1956). *Measurement of responsibility.* London: Tavistock.

Jaques, E. (1961a). *Equitable payment.* New York: Wiley.

Jaques, E. (1961b). An objective approach to pay differentials. *Time Motion Study* **10**, 25–28.

Leventhal, G., Reilly, Ellen, and Lehrer, P. (1964). Change in reward as a determinant of satisfaction and reward expectancy. Paper read at West. Psychol. Assoc. Portland, Ore.

Livernash, E. R. (1953). Job evaluation. In W. S. Woytinsky *et al.* (Eds.), *Employment and wages in the United States.* New York: Twentieth Century Fund, pp. 427–435.

Merton, R. K., and Kitt, Alice S. (1950). Contributions to the theory of reference group behavior. In *Continuities in social research.* R. K. Merton and P. F. Lazarsfeld (Eds.), Glencoe, Ill.: Free Press, pp. 40–105.

Newcomb, T. M. (1943). *Personality and social change: attitude formation in a student community*. New York: Dryden.

Patchen, M. (1959). Study of work and life satisfaction, Report No. II: absences and attitudes toward work experience. Inst. for Social Res., Ann Arbor, Mich.

Patchen, M. (1961). *The choice of wage comparisons*. Englewood Cliffs, N.J.: Prentice-Hall.

Roethlisberger, F. J., and Dickson, W. J. (1939). *Management and the worker*. Cambridge, Mass.: Harvard Univer. Press.

Sayles, L. R. (1958). *Behavior of industrial work groups: prediction and control*. New York: Wiley.

Skinner, B. F. (1957). *Verbal behavior*. New York: Appleton.

Spector, A. J. (1956). Expectations, fulfillment, and morale. *J. abnor. soc. Psychol.* **52**, 51–56.

Steiner, I. D. (1960). Sex differences in the resolution of A-B-X conflicts. *J. Pers.* **28**, 118–128.

Steiner, I. D., and Johnson, H. H. (1964). Relationships among dissonance reducing responses. *J. abnorm. soc. Psychol.* **68**, 38–44.

Steiner, I. D., and Peters, S. C. (1958). Conformity and the A-B-X model. *J. Pers.* **26**, 229–242.

Steiner, I. D., and Rogers, E. D. (1963). Alternative responses to dissonance. *J. abnorm. soc. Psychol.* **66**, 128–136.

Stouffer, S. A., Suchman, E. A., DeVinney, L. C., Starr, Shirley A., and Williams R. M., Jr. (1949). *The American soldier: adjustment during army life*. Vol. 1. Princeton, N.J.: Princeton Univer. Press.

Thibaut, J. (1950). An experimental study of the cohesiveness of underprivileged groups. *Hum. Relat.* **3**, 251–278.

Vroom, V. H. (1964). *Work and motivation*. New York: Wiley.

Weick, K. E. (1964). Reduction of cognitive dissonance through task enhancement and effort expenditure. *J. abnor. soc. Psychol.* **66**, 533–539.

Zaleznik, A., Christensen, C. R., and Roethlisberger, F. J. (1958). The motivation, productivity, and satisfaction of workers. A prediction study (Grad. Sch. Business Admin.) Harvard Univer.

Equity Theory Predictions of Behavior in Organizations

Richard T. Mowday

Employees are seldom passive observers of the events that occur in the workplace.[1] They form impressions of others and the events that affect them and cognitively or behaviorally respond based on their positive or negative evaluations. A great deal of theory and research in the social sciences has been

[1] This paper was written especially for this volume. Support for the preparation of the manuscript was partially provided by a grant from the Office of Naval Research, Contract No. N00014-76-C-0164, NR 170-812. The assistance of Thom McDade in the early stages of preparing the paper is gratefully acknowledged.

devoted to understanding these evaluative processes. More specifically, research has attempted to uncover the major influences on individual reactions in social situations and the processes through which these reactions are formed. One useful framework for understanding how social interactions in the workplace influence employee reactions to their jobs and participation in the organization is provided by theories of social exchange processes (Adams, 1965; Homans, 1961; Jaques, 1961; Patchen, 1961; Simpson, 1972).

Exchange theories are based on two simple assumptions about human behavior. First, there is an assumed similarity between the process through which individuals evaluate their social relationships and economic transactions in the market. Social relationships can be viewed as exchange processes in which individuals make contributions (investments) for which they expect certain outcomes. Individuals are assumed to have expectations about the outcomes that should result when they contribute their time or resources in interaction with others.

The second assumption concerns the process through which individuals decide whether or not a particular exchange is satisfactory. Most exchange theories assign a central role to social comparison processes in terms of how individuals evaluate exchange relationships. Information gained through interaction with others is used to determine whether an exchange has been advantageous. For example, individuals may compare their outcomes and contributions in an exchange with the outcomes and contributions of the person with whom they are interacting. Where there is relative equality between the outcomes and contributions of both parties to an exchange, satisfaction is likely to result from the interaction.

The popularity of social exchange theories may be attributable to their agreement with commonsense observations about human behavior in social situations. Exchange theories suggest that individuals in social interaction behave in a manner similar to the "economic man" of classical economics. Most theories of motivation assume that individuals are motivated to maximize their rewards and minimize their costs (Vroom, 1964; Walster, Bercheid & Walster, 1976). The major difference between assumptions made about economic man and social exchange theories is that the latter recognize that individuals exist in environments characterized by limited and imperfect information. The ambiguity present in most social situations results in individuals relying heavily on information provided by others to evaluate their actions and those of others (Darley & Darley, 1973). Social interactions therefore play a central role in providing information to individuals on the quality of their relationships with others. Our reliance upon others for valued information, however, may place constraints on how we behave in our interactions with others. In order to maintain our social relationships it may be necessary to conform to certain social norms that prevent us from maximizing our outcomes without regard to the outcome of others.

The purpose of this paper is to examine one prominent theory of social exchange processes: Adams' (1963a, 1965) theory of equity. Although Adams' theory is only one of several exchange theories that have been developed, it deserves special attention for several reasons. First, Adams' theory is perhaps the most rigorously developed statement of how individuals evaluate social exchange relationships. The careful formulation of the theory has led to considerable research interest in testing its specific predictions. The large number of studies available on equity theory provides evidence upon which to evaluate the adequacy of social exchange models. Second, the majority of research on equity theory has investigated employee reactions to compensation in employer-employee exchange relationships. The theory and supporting resarch are therefore highly relevant to increasing our understanding of behavior in organizational settings.

In the sections that follow, Adams' equity theory will be briefly summarized and the research evidence reviewed. The major empirical and conceptual questions surrounding the theory will then be discussed. Finally, the generalizability of the theory will be considered and suggestions made for applying equity theory to several previously neglected areas of organizational behavior.

EQUITY THEORY

Antecedents of Inequity

The major components of exchange relationships in Adams' theory are inputs and outcomes. Inputs or investments are those things a person contributes to the exchange. In a situation where a person exchanges his or her services for pay, inputs may include previous work experience, education, effort on the job, and training. Outcomes are those things that result from the exchange. In the employment situation, the most important outcome is likely to be pay. In addition, other outcomes such as supervisory treatment, job assignments, fringe benefits, and status symbols may also be considered in evaluating the exchange. To be considered in evaluating exchange relationships, inputs and outcomes must meet two conditions. First, the existence of an input or outcome must be recognized by one or both parties to the exchange. Second, an input or outcome must be considered relevant to the exchange (i.e., have some marginal utility). Unless inputs or outcomes are both recognized and considered relevant, they will not be considered in evaluating an exchange relationship.

Adams suggests that individuals weight their inputs and outcomes by their importance to the individual. Summary evaluation of inputs and outcomes are developed by separately summing the weighted inputs and weighted outcomes. In the summation process, inputs and outcomes are treated as independent even though they may be highly related (e.g., age and previous work experience would be considered as separate inputs). The ratio of an individual's (called "person's") outcomes to inputs is compared to the ratio of outcomes to inputs of another individual or group (called "other"). Other may be a person with whom you are engaged in a direct exchange, another individual engaged in an exchange with a common third party, or person in a previous or anticipated work situation. The selection of comparison others is discussed in more detail below. The important consideration at this point is that person evaluates his or her outcomes and inputs by comparing them with those of others.

Equity is said to exist whenever the ratio of person's outcomes to inputs is equal to the ratio of other's outcomes and inputs.

$$\frac{O_p}{I_p} = \frac{O_o}{I_o}$$

Inequity exists whenever the two ratios are unequal.

$$\frac{O_p}{I_p} < \frac{O_o}{I_o} \quad \text{or} \quad \frac{O_p}{I_p} > \frac{O_o}{I_o}$$

Several important aspects of this definition should be recognized. First, the conditions necessary to produce equity or inequity are based on the individual's perceptions of inputs and outcomes. In behavioral terms, the objective characteristics of the situation are of less importance than the person's perceptions. Second, inequity is a relative phenomenon. Inequity does not necessarily exist if person has high inputs and low outcomes as long as the comparison other has a similar ratio. Employees may therefore exhibit satisfaction on a job that demands a great deal and for which they receive very little if their comparison other is in a similar position. Third, inequity exists when a person is relatively underpaid and relatively overpaid. It is this implication of Adams' theory that has generated the most attention since it suggests that people will react in a counterintuitive fashion when they are overpaid. Research evidence indicates, however, that the threshold for underpayment is lower than that associated with overpayment (Levanthal, Weiss, & Long, 1969). As might be expected, individuals are somwhat more willing to accept overpayment in an exchange relationship than they are to accept underpayment. The relationship between the ratios of outcomes to inputs of person and other might best be considered along a continuum reflecting different degrees of inequity ranging from overpayment on one extreme to underpayment on the other. The midpoint of the continuum represents the point at which the two ratios are equal. Equity is defined as a zone which is asymmetric about the midpoint. The asymmetry reflects the fact that the thresholds for overpayment and underpayment may differ.

One final aspect of Adams' formulation should be mentioned. Walster et al. (1976) have shown that the formula relating the two ratios of person and other is inadequate in situations where inputs might be negative. Following their example, consider the situation where person's inputs have a value of 5 and outcomes are -10 while other's inputs and outcomes are -5 and 10, respectively. Using Adams' formula, these two ratios are equal and thus a condition of equity would be said to exist.

$$\frac{O_p}{I_p} = \frac{-10}{5} = -2 \text{ and } \frac{O_o}{I_o} = \frac{10}{-5} = -2$$

Obviously, a situation in which person makes positive inputs but receives negative outcomes is inequitable when compared to another who makes negative inputs but receives positive outcomes. Walster et al. (1976) have proposed an alternative formulation that overcomes this problem. Equity and inequity are defined by the following relationship.

$$\frac{\text{Outcomes}_p - \text{Inputs}_p}{(|\text{Inputs}_p|)^k_p} \text{ compared with } \frac{\text{Outcomes}_o - \text{Inputs}_o}{(|\text{Inputs}_o|)^k_o}$$

The reader interested in pursuing this subject further can find a more detailed discussion of this formula and its terms in Walster et al. (1976).

Consequences of Inequity

The motivational aspects of Adams' theory are derived from the hypothesized consequences of perceived inequity. The major postulates of the theory can be summarized simply: (1) perceived inequity creates tension in the individual; (2) the amount of tension is proportional to the magnitude of the inequity; (3) the tension created in the individual will motivate him or her to reduce it; and (4) the strength of the motivation to reduce inequity is proportional to the perceived inequity (Adams, 1965). In other words, the presence of inequity motivates the individual to change the situation through behavioral or cognitive means to return to a condition of equity.

The methods through which individuals reduce inequity are referred to as methods of inequity resolution. Adams describes six alternative methods of restoring equity: (1) altering inputs; (2) altering outcomes; (3) cognitively distorting inputs or outcomes; (4) leaving the field; (5) taking actions designed to change the inputs or outcomes of the comparison other; or (6) changing the comparison other. The choice of a particular method of restoring equity will depend upon the characteristics of the inequitable situation. Adams suggests, however, that the person will attempt to maximize positively valent outcomes and minimize increasingly effortful inputs in restoring equity. In addition, person will resist changing the object of comparison and distorting inputs that are considered central to the self-concept. In general, it is considered easier to distort other's inputs and outcomes than the person's own inputs or outcomes. Finally, leaving the field (e.g., turnover from an organization) as a method of reducing inequity will only be considered in extreme cases of inequity.

RESEARCH ON EQUITY THEORY PREDICTIONS OF EMPLOYEE REACTIONS TO PAY

Considerable research interest has been generated in testing predictions from Adams' theory. The most recent review of equity theory research summarized the results from over 160 investigations (Adams & Freedman, 1976). Although equity considerations are relevant to a number of different types of social relationships (cf., Walster et al., 1976), most early research focused attention on the employer-employee exchange relationship. These studies were generally laboratory investigations in which subjects were hired to perform relatively simple tasks such as proofreading or interviewing. The simple nature of the tasks suggests that differences found between subjects in the quantity or quality of performance would be attributable to motivation levels rather than differences in skills or abilities. Perceived inequity was induced by either manipulating the subject's perceived qualifications to be hired for the task (qualifications manipulation) or by actual differences in pay rates (manipulation by circumstances).

Predictions from equity theory about employee reactions to pay distinguish between two conditions of inequity (underpayment versus overpayment) and two methods of compensation (hourly versus piece rate). Specific predictions are summarized for each condition in Table 1. The methodology and results of selected studies designed to test these predictions are presented in Table 2. More extensive reviews of this literature can found in Adams and Freedman (1976), Campbell and Pritchard (1976), Goodman and Friedman (1971), Lawler (1968a), Opsahl and Dunnette (1966), and Pritchard (1969).

A review of the studies summarized in Table 2 suggests general support for equity theory predictions. In the overpayment-hourly condition, a number of studies have provided some support for the prediction that overpaid subjects will produce higher quantity than equitably paid subjects (Adams & Rosenbaum, 1962; Arrowood, 1961; Goodman & Friedman, 1968; Lawler, 1968b; Pritchard, Dunnette & Jorgenson, 1972; Wiener, 1970). Several studies have either failed to support or provided mixed support for equity theory predictions in this condition, although they often differed from the supporting studies in the manner in which perceived inequity was experimentally manipulated (Anderson & Shelly, 1970; Evans & Simmons, 1969; Friedman & Goodman, 1967; Valenzi & Andrews, 1971). In the overpayment–piece-rate condition, support for the theory has been found by Adams (1963b), Adams and Jacobsen (1964), Adams and Rosenbaum (1962), Andrews (1967), and Goodman and Friedman (1969).

Table 1 Equity Theory Predictions of Employee Reactions to Inequitable Payment

	Underpayment	Overpayment
Hourly payment	Subjects underpaid by the hour produce less or poorer-quality output than equitably paid subjects	Subjects overpaid by the hour produce more or ‚ higher-quality output than equitably paid subjects
Piece-rate payment	Subjects underpaid by piece rate will produce a large number of low-quality units in comparison with equitably paid subjects	Subjects overpaid by piece rate will produce fewer units of higher quality than equitably paid subjects

Table 2   Summary of Equity Theory Research on Employee Reactions to Pay

Study	Equity condition	Method of induction	Task	Dependent variables	Results
Adams (1963b)	Overpayment: hourly and piece rate	Qualifications	Interviewing	Productivity, work quality	Hourly-overpaid subjects produced greater quantity and piece-rate–overpaid subjects produced higher quality and lower quantity than equitably paid subjects.
Adams and Jacobsen (1964)	Overpayment: piece rate	Qualifications	Proofreading	Productivity, work quality	Overpaid subjects produced less quantity of higher quality.
Adams and Rosenbaum (1962)	Overpayment: hourly and piece rate	Qualifications	Interviewing	Productivity	Hourly-overpaid subjects produced more quantity while piece-rate–overpaid subjects produced less quantity.
Anderson and Shelly (1970)	Overpayment: hourly	Qualifications, importance of task	Proofreading	Productivity, work quality	No differences were found between groups
Andrews (1967)	Overpayment and underpayment: piece rate	Circumstances, previous wage experiences	Interviewing Data checking	Productivity, work quality	Overpaid subjects produced higher quality and underpaid subjects produced greater quantity and lower quality.
Arrowood (1961)	Overpayment: hourly	Qualifications, work returned	Interviewing	Productivity	Overpaid subjects had higher productivity.
Evans and Simmons (1969)	Overpayment and underpayment: hourly	Competence, authority	Proofreading	Productivity, work quality	Underpaid subjects produced more of poorer quality in competence condition. No differences found in other conditions.

Study	Equity condition	Method of induction	Task	Dependent variables	Results
Friedman and Goodman (1967)	Overpayment: hourly	Qualifications	Interviewing	Productivity	Qualifications induction did not affect productivity. When subjects were classified by perceived qualifications, unqualified subjects produced less than qualified subjects.
Goodman and Friedman (1968)	Overpayment and underpayment: hourly	Qualifications, quantity versus quality emphasis	Questionnaire coding	Productivity, work quality	Overpaid subjects produced more than equitably paid subjects. Emphasis on quantity versus quality affected performance.
Goodman and Friedman (1969)	Overpayment: piece rate	Qualifications, quantity versus quality emphasis	Questionnaire scoring	Productivity, work quality	Overpaid subjects increased productivity or work quality, depending upon induction.
Lawler (1968b)	Overpayment: hourly	Qualifications, circumstances	Interviewing	Productivity, work quality	Overpaid (unqualified) subjects produced more of lower quality. Subjects overpaid by circumstances did not differ from equitably paid group.
Lawler, Koplin, Young, and Fadem (1968)	Overpayment: piece rate	Qualifications	Interviewing	Productivity, work quality	Overpaid subjects produced less of higher quality in initial work session. In later sessions, subject's perceived qualifications and productivity increased. The need for money was related to productivity for both groups.
Lawler and O'Gara (1967)	Underpayment: piece rate	Circumstances	Interviewing	Productivity, work quality	Underpaid subjects produced more of lower quality and also perceived their job as more interesting but less important and complex.

Table 2 Summary of Equity Theory Research on Employee Reactions to Pay (Continued)

Study	Equity condition	Method of induction	Task	Dependent variables	Results
Pritchard, Dunnette, and Jorgenson (1972)	Overpayment and underpayment: hourly and piece rate	Circumstances, actual change in payment	Clerical task	Performance satisfaction	Circumstances induction did not result in performance differences for piece rate, but some support was found for hourly overpay and underpay. Changes in pay rate supported hourly predictions. Some support found for piece-rate–overpayment prediction but not for underpayment.
Valenzi and Andrews (1971)	Overpayment and underpayment: hourly	Circumstances	Clerical task	Productivity, work quality	No significant differences found between conditions. 27 percent of underpaid subjects quit. No other subjects in other conditions quit.
Wiener (1970)	Overpayment: hourly	Qualifications, inputs versus outcomes, ego-oriented versus task-oriented	Word manipulation	Productivity, work quality	Outcome-overpayment subjects produced more. Input-overpaid subjects produced more only on ego-oriented task.
Wood and Lawler (1970)	Overpayment: piece rate	Qualifications	Reading	Amount of time reading, quality	Overpaid subjects produced less, but this could not be attributed to striving for higher quality.

Mixed or marginal support for the theory was provided by Lawler, Koplin, Young and Fadem (1968) and Wood and Lawler (1970). Although fewer studies have examined the underpayment conditions, support for both the hourly and piece-rate predictions have been reported (Andrews, 1967; Evans & Simmons, 1969; Lawler & O'Gara, 1967; Pritchard et al., 1972).

Although the support for Adams' theory appears impressive, several questions concerning the interpretation of the study results need to be considered. Following Vroom (1964), Goodman and Friedman (1971) suggest that the following concepts must be operationalized to provide a complete and unambiguous test of equity theory: (1) person's evaluation of his or her inputs; (2) person's perception of the relevance of the inputs for task performance; (3) person's perception of the experimenter's perception of the inputs; (4) person's perception of other's outcome-input ratio; (5) person's perception of future outcomes; (6) person's perception of the outcomes relative to alternative outcomes (e.g., past outcomes); and (7) relative importance person attaches to using 4, 5, and 6 as comparison objects. Control over these factors is central to ensuring a high degree of internal validity for the results of experimental studies. To the extent these factors may remain uncontrolled, conclusive tests of the theory become very difficult and alternative explanations for the study results can be raised. It should be apparent that many of these factors remain uncontrolled in even the most rigorous laboratory experiment. For example, Goodman and Friedman (1971) point out that the comparison other used by subjects is ambiguous in most studies. To the extent subjects use different comparison others than intended by the experimenter, interpretation of the study results becomes problematic.

A number of writers have been critical of research on equity theory precisely because several alternative explanations may exist for observed differences in the performance of subjects, particularly in the overpayment condition (Campbell & Pritchard, 1976; Goodman & Friedman, 1971; Lawler, 1968a; Pritchard, 1969). Two problems are commonly raised in interpreting the results of research on overpayment inequity, and both have to do with experimental manipulations of perceived inequity. Inequity is commonly induced in subjects by challenging their qualifications for the job. Subjects are led to believe they do not possess the necessary experience or training to qualify for the rate of pay they are to receive. Although seldom verified, it is assumed that this will result in experienced overpayment inequity (i.e., subjects believe they are being paid more than they should receive given their qualifications).

Challenging the qualifications of subjects, however, may also be experienced as threatening their self-esteem or perceived job security. Subjects may therefore work harder to prove to themselves (and to the experimenter) that they are capable of performing the task or to protect their job security. In other words, subjects may perform as predicted by the theory for reasons related to the experimental treatment but not to perceived inequity. Support for these alternative explanations for results of research on overpayment inequity comes from several sources. Andrews and Valenzi (1970) had subjects role-play an overpayment inequity situation in which subject qualifications to perform the task were challenged. When asked to indicate how they would respond in this situation, none of the subjects reponded in terms of wage inequity. A majority of subjects, however, responded in terms of their self-image as a worker. In another study, Wiener (1970) found that overpaid subjects produced more than equitably paid subjects only when the task was ego-involving (i.e., task performance was central to the self-concept). Based on this finding, he argued that the performance of subjects in the overpayment condition was more highly attributable to devalued self-esteem brought about by challenges to their qualifications than to feelings of inequity. In studies where perceived inequity has been manipulated by means other than challenging the subject's qualifications (e.g., by actual changes in pay rates), less support is commonly found for equity theory predictions (Evans & Simmons, 1969; Pritchard et al., 1972; Valenzi & Andrews, 1971).

Several writers have seriously questioned the extent to which overpayment in work organizations may lead to perceived inequity. Locke (1976), for example, argues that employees are seldom told they are overpaid or made to feel incompetent to perform their job duties as is the case in laboratory experiments. He argues that employees are more likely to simply adjust their idea of equitable payment to justify what they are getting. This raises the possibility that employees in organizations use their pay rates as a primary source of information about their contributions (e.g., "if the organization is willing to pay this much, I must be making a valuable contribution"). Campbell and Pritchard (1976) also point out that employer-employee exchange relationships are highly impersonal when compared to exchanges between two close friends. Perceived overpayment inequity may be more likely in the latter exchange relationship than in the former. Individuals may react to overpayment inequity only when they believe their actions have led to someone else's being treated unfairly (Campbell & Pritchard, 1976; Walster et al., 1976). From the employee's standpoint in work organizations, there may be little objective evidence that the organization feels it is being treated unfairly.

In summary, predictions from Adams' theory about employee reactions to wage inequities have received some support in the research literature. Research support for the theory appears to be strongest for predictions about underpayment inequity. Although there are fewer studies of underpayment than of overpayment, results of research on underpayment are relatively consistent and subject to fewer alternative explanations. There are both theoretical and empirical grounds for being cautious in generalizing the results of research on overpayment inequity to employee behavior in work organizations. Where such studies have manipulated perceived inequity by challenging subjects' qualifications for the job, observed differences in performance can be explained in ways that have little to do with inequity. Where other methods of inducing overpayment inequity are used, considerably less support is often found for the theory. Predicted differences in productivity and satisfaction due to overpayment inequity are often in the predicted direction but fail to reach acceptable levels of statistical significance.

Conceptual Issues in Equity Theory

In addition to the methodological considerations discussed with respect to research on equity theory, several writers have also raised questions about the conceptual adequacy of the theory (e.g., Weick, 1967). Since theories or models of social processes are ways of making sense out of our environment by simplifying relationships between variables, it should not be surprising that any given theory fails to capture the complexity we know to exist in the real world. Consequently, there are usually a number of limitations that can be pointed out in any given theory, and equity theory is no different from other motivation approaches in this regard. The conceptual issues to be discussed below point to several limitations of the present formulation of equity theory, and they should be viewed as areas in which the theory may be clarified or extended through further research.

Concept of Equity

The concept of equity is most often interpreted in work organizations as a positive association between an employee's effort or performance on the job and the pay he or she receives (Goodman, 1977). In other words, it is believed that employees who contribute more to the organization should receive higher amounts of the rewards the organization has to offer. This belief is often referred to as the "equity norm." Adams (1965) suggests that individual expectations about equity or "fair" correlations between inputs and outcomes are learned during the process of socialization (e.g., in the home or at work) and through comparison with the inputs and outcomes of others. Although few would question the existence of an equity norm governing social relationships, the derivation of this norm and its pervasiveness remain somewhat unclear. In addition, it is important to determine the extent to which the equity norm is defined by an individual's effort and performance or by other types of contributions they may make to organizations.

Walster et al. (1976) suggest the norm of equity originates in societal attempts to develop methods of allocating rewards that maximize the amount of collective reward. Through evolving ways to "equitably" distribute rewards and costs among its members, groups or organizations can maximize the total rewards available. Groups therefore induce their members to behave equitably and establish reinforcement systems to ensure this norm is followed in social relationships. It should be apparent, however, that groups or society in general frequently deviate from the equity norm in distributing rewards. Social welfare programs and old-age medical assistance, for example, are instances in which resources are distributed on the basis of need rather than an assessment of the individual's contribution to the larger group.

The equity norm appears to be only one of several norms that govern the distribution of rewards in social relationships. An important question concerns what factors influence the extent to which rewards are distributed equitably or allocated on some other basis. In an analysis of reward allocation in small groups, Leventhal (1976) suggests that the particular distribution rule adopted in allocating rewards is related to both the goals of the reward system and characteristics of the allocator. Table 3 contrasts three decision rules that can be used in allocating rewards (equity, equality, and responsiveness to needs) and the situations where each rule is most likely to be used. The equity norm appears to be most closely associated with the goal of maximizing productivity in a group, while rewards are most likely to be distributed equally when the goal is to minimize group conflict.

Distribution rules represent an important concept in understanding reward systems (Cook, 1975; Goodman, 1977). Distribution rules identify the association between any dimension of evaluation and the levels of outcomes to be distributed. A consideration of distribution rules suggests both that different norms may govern the distribution of rewards in organizations and that different factors may weight more heavily in allocating rewards using any given norm. For example, in organizations where an equity norm is followed, it is common to find that an individual's contribution in terms of seniority is a more important basis for rewards than is actual job performance. Our ability to predict how individuals react to reward systems therefore depends upon identifying the particular norm they believe should be followed and the specific dimension (i.e., input) they feel is most important in allocating rewards. Equity theory often assumes that rewards should be given in relation to a person's contribution and, further, that performance is the most important contribution in the work setting. The accuracy of our predictions of employee reactions to reward systems can be increased, however, by recognizing the existence of several norms governing the distribution of rewards and the differential importance that may be attached to employee inputs.

Choice of a Method of Inequity Resolution

Although the several factors Adams (1965) suggested individuals will take into consideration in choosing among alternative methods of reducing inequity make the theory more testable, they do not allow a totally unequivocal set of predictions to be made from the theory (Wicklund & Brehm, 1976). In any situation, a given method of restoring inequity may satisfy one of these rules while at the same time violating another. Cognitively distorting inputs as a method of reducing inequity, for example, may allow the individual to maximize positively valent outcomes, but at the expense of threatening aspects central to his or her self-concept. When such a conflict occurs, it is difficult to specify how an individual will react to inequity. Opsahl and Dunnette (1966) have pointed out that the inability to predict how individuals will react to inequity makes conclusive tests of the theory problematic. If an overcompensated group fails to respond to inequity by increasing inputs, can this be interpreted as a disconfirmation of the theory or as an instance in which other methods of reducing inequity (e.g., cognitively distorting your own or other's inputs or outcomes) are being used? This ambiguity associated with equity theory appears to result in a situation where almost any result of empirical research can be explained in terms of the theory.

Table 3   Distribution Rules for Allocating Rewards

Distribution rule	Situations where distribution rule is likely to be used	Factors affecting use of distribution rule
Equity/contributions (outcomes should match contributions)	1 Goal is to maximize group productivity. 2 A low degree of cooperation is required for task performance.	1 What receiver is expected to do 2 What others receive 3 Outcomes and contributions of person allocating rewards 4 Task difficulty and perceived ability 5 Personal characteristics of person allocating rewards and person performing
Social responsibility/needs (outcomes distributed on the basis of needs)	1 Allocator of rewards is a close friend of the receiver, feels responsible for the well-being of the receiver, or is successful or feels competent.	1 Perceived legitimacy of needs 2 Origin of need (e.g., beyond control of the individual)
Equality (equal outcomes given to all participants)	1 Goal is to maximize harmony, minimize conflict in group. 2 Task of judging performer's needs or contribution is difficult. 3 Person allocating rewards has a low cognitive capacity. 4 A high degree of cooperation is required for task performance. 5 Allocator anticipates future interactions with low-input member.	1 Sex of person allocating rewards (e.g., females more likely to allocate rewards equally than males) 2 Nature of task

Source: Adapted from Leventhal (1976).

Many of the studies of equity theory have failed to capture the complexity of inequity resolution processes (Adams & Freedman, 1976). It is common in such studies to set up an inequitable situation and determine the extent to which subjects reduce inequity by changing work quantity or quality. In more personal exchange relationships, however, the method of reducing inequity chosen may be sensitive to cues from the other party to the exchange (Adams & Freedman, 1976). For example, in overpayment situations, an organization may suggest employees increase their skills and abilities through further education rather than increasing their effort on the job. Research also suggests that strategies for reducing inequity are dynamic and may change over time. Lawler et al. (1968) found that subjects reduced overpayment–piece-rate inequity by increasing work quality in an initial work session but increased their perceived qualifications to perform the task in subsequent sessions. Cognitively changing perceived inputs (qualifications) may have allowed subjects to reduce the overpayment inequity in a manner that permitted increased quantity of production and thus increased rewards to be received.

The way in which individuals reduce perceived inequity appears to be a complex process. A greater understanding of this process is essential to increasing the accuracy of predictions from equity theory.

Choice of a Comparison Other

One area of recent concern in equity theory is to develop a greater understanding of how individuals choose comparison standards against which to evaluate inputs and outcomes. Adams (1965) suggested that comparison others may be the other party to the exchange or another individual involved in an exchange with the same third party. Until recently, little has been known about the actual comparison standards people use or the process through which alternative comparisons are chosen.

Goodman (1974) differentiated between three classes of referents: (1) others, (2) self-standards, and (3) system referents. Others are people who may be involved in a similar exchange either with the same organization or with some other organization. Self-standards are unique to the individual but different from his or her current ratio of outcomes and inputs; for example, individuals may compare their current ratio against inputs and outcomes associated with an earlier job. System referents are implicit or explicit contractual expectations between an employer and employee. At the time of being hired, an employee may be promised future rewards and this can become a basis for evaluating the exchange. In a study of 217 managers, Goodman (1974) found each of these referents was used in determining the degree of satisfaction with pay. Perhaps his most important finding was that a majority of managers reported using multiple referents in assessing their satisfaction. For example, 28 per cent of the managers indicated they compared their present situation against both those of others and self-standards. He also found that higher levels of education were associated with choosing a comparison referent outside the organization.

Based on his research, Goodman (1977) has developed a model of the factors that may influence the selection of comparison person or standard. This model is presented in Figure 1. He postulates that the choice of a referent is a function of both the availability of information about the referent and the relevance or attractiveness of the referent for the comparison. Availability of information about referents is primarily determined by the individual's propensity to search and his or her position in an organization (i.e., access to information). The relevance or attractiveness of a referent is determined jointly by the instrumentality of the referent for satisfying the individual's comparison needs and the number and strength of needs related to a referent. A more detailed discussion of this model can be found in Goodman (1977).

Goodman's (1974, 1977) work represents an important step in increasing our understanding of how social comparison processes are made. If his model is supported by subsequent research, it will provide an important tool for both researchers and managers in determining who or what employees use in making comparisons about their present level of rewards.

Individual and Situational Differences in Reactions to Inequity

One area of research on equity theory that has received little attention is the impact of individual and situational differences on employee perceptions and reactions to inequity. The importance of considering individual differences was first demonstrated by Tornow (1971). Recognizing that the classification of

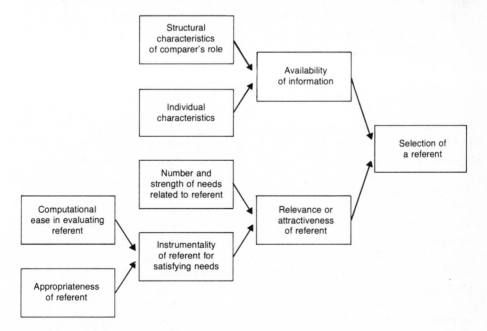

Figure 1 Factors influencing the selection of a referent in social comparison processes. (*Adapted from Goodman, 1977.*)

something as an input or an outcome is often ambiguous in equity comparisons, he suggested that individuals may have a stable tendency to classify ambiguous job elements as either inputs or outcomes. Using the data collected by Pritchard et al. (1972), he subsequently classified subjects as either input- or outcome-oriented and found this factor had an impact on their reactions to inequity. For example, outcome-oriented individuals were found to be more sensitive to overpayment than were subjects with an input orientation. Individual differences were therefore having an effect on how individuals reacted to perceived inequity. This is an area in which more research is needed to isolate the stable traits of individuals that can affect inequity perceptions. One variable that may be promising is the individual's level of internal/external control (Rotter, 1966). It is possible that individuals who believe events that happen to them are under their control (internals) would have a greater propensity to attempt to reduce perceived inequity than individuals who believe events are largely beyond their control (externals).

The importance of considering situational factors in employee reactions to inequity has already been noted in discussing Campbell and Pritchard's (1976) personal-impersonal exchange continuum. In the overpayment situation, employees may not react strongly to perceived inequity since the exchange with the larger organization is quite impersonal. However, where exchanges are between two close friends, both parties to the exchange may be highly sensitive to any inequities. Walster et al. (1976) have noted that an individual who feels responsible for an inequitable situation may express greater tension than someone who inadvertently finds himself or herself in an inequitable relationship. The locus of cause for a perceived inequity may therefore represent an important consideration in how individuals react to perceived inequity, particularly when the inequity is favorable to themselves.

RELATIONSHIP OF EQUITY THEORY
TO EXPECTANCY THEORY

Much of the original interest in equity theory came from the fact that it made predictions about individual behavior that were difficult to incorporate into existing theories of motivation (Weick, 1967). For example, in the overpayment–piece-rate situation equity theory predicted that employees will increase quality and reduce quantity of performance. In contrast, expectancy theory appears to suggest that individuals attempt to maximize the attainment of valued outcomes and that motivation levels should be high whenever attractive outcomes (e.g., pay) are made directly contingent upon performance. Considerable research interest has been generated in trying to test these seemingly competing predictions.

Lawler (1968a) was one of the first to suggest that equity theory and expectancy theory may not be irreconcilable in terms of their predictions. A review of the equity theory literature led Lawler to conclude that the results of studies of the hourly payment condition could be explained equally well by expectancy theory. In the piece-rate conditions, expectancy theory could make the same predictions as equity theory if it was assumed that perceived inequity influenced the valence or attractiveness of rewards. It is possible that increasingly large piece-rate rewards have a decreasing valence for employees and that the amount of reward that has been received influences the valence of additional amounts of the reward. Lawler felt that if perceived equity were explicitly recognized as one of the factors affecting the valence of outcomes, expectancy theory could explain the results of equity theory research. Lawler (1973) and others (Campbell & Pritchard, 1976) have therefore concluded that equity considerations could be subsumed under the more general expectancy theory of motivation.

Although the two theories do not really appear to be in conflict, it is unclear whether this reflects genuine similarity or the ambiguity with which the theories are stated. As noted by Campbell and Pritchard (1976), both theories are somewhat ambiguous and thus it always is possible to come up with some previously unrecognized outcome that will reconcile competing predictions. In addition, the effects of perceived inequity on the valence of outcomes remains to be demonstrated. Although Lawler et al. (1968) found that the need for money correlated more highly with productivity for overpaid subjects than for equitably paid subjects, need for money was not experimentally manipulated and thus the direction of causality is difficult to establish. In addition, a composite measure of need for money was constructed based on measures taken both before and after the manipulation of perceived overpayment. Consequently, the effects of the inequity manipulation on the subject's need for money (an indicator of valence of money) cannot be determined.

In view of the ambiguity surrounding the two theories and the lack of evidence concerning the effects of perceived inequity on the valence of outcomes, it is perhaps premature to conclude that equity theory can be incorporated into expectancy theory. As Adams (1968) has argued, it may be less useful to debate which theory can be incorporated into the other than to identify the conditions in which individual behavior is guided by either equity or expectancy considerations.

CONCLUSIONS AND DIRECTIONS FOR FUTURE RESEARCH

Evaluating the current status of equity theory presents something of a dilemma; depending upon the particular body of literature one examines, very different conclusions can be drawn. On the one hand, researchers interested in organizations have largely moved away from equity theory to other motivation approaches in explaining behavior in the workplace. After a high level of initial research interest, organization researchers appear to have followed the arguments of Lawler (1973) and others that equity theory can be incorporated into expectancy theory. Consequently, research involving applications of equity theory to organizational settings has decreased in recent years. If the current literature in social psychology is examined, on the other hand, a very different picture emerges. Walster et al. (1976) recently introduced a reformulation of Adams' original theory, and it has been heralded as a general theory of social behavior capable of integrating a number of the minitheories (e.g., reinforcement theory, cognitive consistency theory) that currently exist. Berkowitz and Walster (1976, p. xi) go so far as to talk about "a new mood of optimism" emerging in social psychology, at least in part attributable to the promise of equity theory for developing a more comprehensive understanding of social behavior.

Has equity theory largely outlived its usefulness as a theory of motivation in organizations, or is it a theory capable of providing general explanations of behavior in a number of different social settings? This is a difficult question to answer at the present time. However, it appears that equity theory has more to contribute to our understanding of organizational behavior than previous research would suggest. The early emphasis of organizational research on equity theory predictions of employee reactions to pay was perhaps both its greatest strength and weakness. On the positive side, focusing on monetary rewards provided a research setting in which the variables were easily quantifiable and the predictions were relatively unambiguous (or so it seemed at the time). On the negative side, exclusive interest in employee reactions to pay prevented the extension of equity theory to other areas of social relationships in organizations. Adams (1965) was careful to note that equity theory was relevant to any social situations in which exchanges may take place (e.g., between co-workers, between superiors and subordinates, etc.). With the exception of Goodman's (1977) recent work on social comparison process in organizations, the extension of the theory to a broad range of social relationships has been left to social psychologists (see Berkowitz & Walster, 1976). Several areas of behavior in organizations that might profitably be examined in equity theory terms are discussed below.

Previous research on equity theory has largely been concerned with individual reactions to perceived inequity. What appears to have been neglected are the instrumental uses of inequity in interpersonal relationships (Adams & Freedman, 1976). Individuals in organizations, for example, may purposely create perceived inequity in social relationships as a way of improving their situation or achieving certain goals. Supervisors may routinely attempt to convince employees that they are not contributing as much as another employee or at a level expected for the pay they receive. Creating perceptions of overpayment inequity may therefore be viewed as a strategy designed to increase the level of employee performance. Just as routinely, employees may attempt the same strategy, but in reverse. Ingratiation attempts (Wortman & Linsenmeier, 1977) may be viewed as strategies on the part of lower-status employees to increase the outcomes of those in higher level positions. To the extent that those in higher positions perceive an inequity in their social relationships with lower-level employees, they will feel obligated to reciprocate. Research evidence that individuals may create perceived inequity in social relationships as a means of accomplishing certain objectives was presented by Leventhal and Bergman (1969). They found that subjects who were moderately underrewarded attempted to reduce the inequity by taking some of their partner's money when given the opportunity. Subjects who were extremely underrewarded, however, increased the discrepancy between their own rewards and those of their partner by increasing his or her advantage. By intensifying the inequity, subjects may have been following a deliberate strategy designed to convince their partner that a more equitable distribution of rewards was necessary.

Campbell, Dunnette, Lawler, and Weick (1970) have suggested the importance of viewing leadership processes in terms of exchanges between superiors and subordinates. In describing what they call the "unilateral fiction" in leadership research, they point out that managers are most often viewed as initiating the action of others and that superior-subordinate interactions are assumed to end when the manager issues a directive. Relationships between superiors and subordinates in organizations, however, are more accurately characterized by reciprocal-influence processes. A great deal of interaction between managers and employees in organizations may involve bargaining processes in which the terms of an exchange are established to the satisfaction of each party. When the manager issues a directive that is carried out by the employee, it is reasonable to assume that expectations of repayment are formed in the employee. Furthermore, when employees do a favor for the manager it may result in a perceived obligation to reciprocate on the part of the manager. Reciprocal relationships between managers and employees can be described in terms of equity theory; taking such a perspective may increase our understanding of the leadership process.

Equity theory appears to offer a useful approach to understanding a wide variety of social relationships in the workplace. Additional research is needed to extend predictions from the theory beyond simple questions about how employees react to their pay. As Goodman and Friedman (1971) have noted, equity theory predictions about employee performance levels may be one of the less interesting and useful applications of the theory. The effects of perceived inequity on employee performance levels are often slight and of limited time duration. The utility of equity theory may be greatest for increasing our understanding of interpersonal interactions at work (e.g., supervisory-subordinate relationships). In this regard, researchers interested in organizations may want to follow the lead of social psychologists in extending applications of the theory.

REFERENCES

Adams, J. S. Toward an understanding of inequity. *Journal of Abnormal and Social Psychology*, 1963, **67**, 422–436. (a)

Adams, J. S. Wage inequities, productivity and work quality. *Industrial Relations*, 1963, **3**, 9–16. (b)

Adams, J. S. Inequity in social exchange. In L. Berkowitz (Ed.), *Advances in experimental social psychology*. Vol. 2. New York: Academic Press, 1965. Pp. 267–299.

Adams, J. S. Effects of overpayment: Two comments on Lawler's paper. *Journal of Personality and Social Psychology*, 1968, **10**, 315–316.

Adams, J. S., & Freedman, S. Equity theory revisited: Comments and annotated bibliography. In L. Berkowitz & E. Walster (Eds.), *Advances in experimental social psychology*, Vol. 9. New York: Academic Press, 1976. Pp. 43–90.

Adams, J. S., & Jacobsen, P. R. Effects of wage inequities on work quality. *Journal of Applied Psychology,* 1964, **69,** 19–25.

Adams, J. S., & Rosenbaum, W. B. The relationship of worker productivity to cognitive dissonance about wage inequities. *Journal of Applied Psychology*, 1962, **46,** 161–164.

Anderson, B., & Shelly, R. K. Reactions to inequity, II: A replication of the Adams experiment and a theoretical reformulation. *Acta Sociologica*, 1970, **13,** 1–10.

Andrews, I. R. Wage inequity and job performance: An experimental study. *Journal of Applied Psychology*, 1967, **51,** 39–45.

Andrews, I. R., & Valenzi, E. Overpay inequity or self-image as a worker: a critical examination of an experimental induction procedure. *Organizational Behavior and Human Performance*, 1970, **53,** 22–27.

Arrowood, A. J. Some effects on productivity of justified and unjustified levels of reward under public and private conditions. Unpublished doctoral dissertation, University of Minnesota, 1961.

Berkowitz, L., & Walster, E. (Eds.). *Advances in experimental social psychology,* Vol. 9. New York: Academic Press, 1976.

Campbell, J. P., Dunnette, M. D., Lawler, E. E., & Weick, K. E. *Managerial behavior, performance, and effectiveness*. New York: McGraw-Hill, 1970.

Campbell, J., & Pritchard, R. D. Motivation theory in industrial and organizational psychology. In M. Dunnette (Ed.), *Handbook of industrial and organizational psychology*. Chicago: Rand McNally, 1976. Pp. 63–130.

Cook, K. S. Expectations, evaluations and equity. *American Sociological Review*, 1975, **40,** 372–388.

Darley, J. M., & Darley, S. A. *Conformity and deviation*. Morristown, N.J.: General Learning Press, 1973.

Evans, W. M., & Simmons, R. G. Organizational effects of inequitable rewards: Two experiments in status inconsistency. *Administrative Science Quarterly*, 1969, **14,** 224–237.

Friedman, A., & Goodman, P. Wage inequity, self-qualifications, and productivity. *Organizational Behavior and Human Performance*, 1967, **2,** 406–417.

Goodman, P. S. An examination of referents used in the evaluation of pay. *Organizational Behavior and Human Performance*, 1974, **12,** 170–195.

Goodman, P. S. Social comparison processes in organizations. In B. Staw & G. Salancik (Eds.), *New directions in organizational behavior*. Chicago: St. Clair, 1977. Pp. 97–132.

Goodman, P. S., & Friedman, A. An examination of the effect of wage inequity in the hourly condition. *Organizational Behavior and Human Performance*, 1968, **3,** 340–352.

Goodman, P. S., & Friedman, A. An examination of quantity and quality of performance under conditions of overpayment in piece-rate. *Organizational Behavior and Human Performance*, 1969, **4,** 365–374.

Goodman, P. S., & Friedman, A. An examination of Adams' theory of inequity. *Administrative Science Quarterly*, 1971, **16,** 271–288.

Homans, G. C. *Social behavior: Its elementary forms*. New York: Harcourt, Brace & World, 1961.

Jaques, E. *Equitable payment*. New York: Wiley, 1961.

Lawler, E. E. Equity theory as a predictor of productivity and work quality. *Psychological Bulletin*, 1968, **70**, 596–610. (a)

Lawler, E. E. Effects of hourly overpayment on productivity and work quality. *Journal of Personality and Social Psychology*, 1968, **10**, 306–313. (b)

Lawler, E. E. *Motivation in work organizations*. Belmont, Calif.: Brooks/Cole, 1973.

Lawler, E. E., Koplin, C. A., Young, T. F., & Fadem, J. A. Inequity reduction over time in an induced overpayment situation. *Organizational Behavior and Human Performance*, 1968, **3**, 253–268.

Lawler, E. E., & O'Gara, P. W. Effects of inequity produced by underpayment on work output, work quality, and attitudes toward the work. *Journal of Applied Psychology*, 1967, **51**, 403–410.

Leventhal, G. S. Fairness in social relationships. In J. Thibaut, J. Spence, & R. Carson (Eds.), *Contemporary topics in social psychology*. Morristown, N.J.: General Learning Press, 1976.

Leventhal, G. S., & Bergman, J. T. Self-depriving behavior as a response to unprofitable inequity. *Journal of Experimental Social Psychology*, 1969, **5**, 153–171.

Leventhal, G. S., Weiss, T., & Long, G. Equity, reciprocity, and reallocating rewards in the dyad. *Journal of Personality and Social Psychology*, 1969, **13**, 300–305.

Locke, E. A. The nature and causes of job satisfaction. In M. Dunnette (Ed.), *Handbook of industrial and organizational psychology*. Chicago: Rand McNally, 1976. Pp. 1297–1349.

Opsahl, R. L., & Dunnette, M. The role of financial compensation in industrial motivation. *Psychological Bulletin*, 1966, **66**, 94–118.

Patchen, M. *The choice of wage comparisons*. Englewood Cliffs, N.J.: Prentice-Hall, 1961.

Pritchard, R. D. Equity theory: A review and critique. *Organizational Behavior and Human Performance*, 1969, **4**, 176–211.

Pritchard, R. D., Dunnette, M. D., & Jorgenson, D. O. Effects of perceptions of equity and inequity on worker performance and satisfaction. *Journal of Applied Psychology*, 1972, **56**, 75–94.

Rotter, J. B. Generalized expectancies for internal versus external control of reinforcement. *Psychological Monographs*, 1966, **80** (1, Whole No. 609).

Simpson, R. L. *Theories of social exchange*. Morristown, N.J.: General Learning Press, 1972.

Tornow, W. W. The development and application of an input-outcome moderator test on the perception and reduction of inequity. *Organizational Behavior and Human Performance*, 1971, **6**, 614–638.

Valenzi, E. R., & Andrews, I. R. Effect of hourly overpay and underpay inequity when tested with a new induction procedure. *Journal of Applied Psychology*, 1971, **55**, 22–27.

Vroom, V. H. *Work and motivation*. New York: Wiley, 1964.

Walster, E., Bercheid, E., & Walster, G. W. New directions in equity research. In L. Berkowitz & E. Walster (Eds.), *Advances in experimental social psychology*, Vol. 9. New York: Academic Press, 1976. Pp. 1–42.

Weick, K. E. The concept of equity in the perception of pay. *Administrative Science Quarterly*, 1967, **2**, 414–439.

Wicklund, R. A., & Brehm, J. W. *Perspectives on cognitive dissonance*. Hillsdale, N.J.: Lawrence Erlbaum, 1976.

Wiener, Y. The effects of "task-" and "ego-oriented" performance on 2 kinds of overcompensation inequity. *Organizational Behavior and Human Performance*, 1970, **5**, 191–208.

Wood, I., & Lawler, E. E. Effects of piece-rate overpayment on productivity. *Journal of Applied Psychology*, 1970, **54**, 234–238.

Wortman, C. B., & Linsenmeier, J. A. W. Interpersonal attraction and methods of ingratiation in organizational settings. In B. M. Staw & G. R. Salancik (Eds.), *New directions in organizational behavior*. Chicago: St. Clair, 1977. Pp. 133–178.

QUESTIONS FOR DISCUSSION

1 Using the analytical framework proposed in Chapter 1, how would you evaluate Adams's theory of inequity?
2 How would you compare equity theory to need theories of motivation?
3 How would you evaluate the research evidence in support of equity theory?
4 Under this theoretical formulation, why would one's peers be so important in determining individual job satisfaction?
5 Why has equity theory been largely ignored by many managers and writers in organizational behavior?
6 What can line managers learn from equity theory that could help them to improve their supervisory abilities?
7 Suggest some new applications for equity theory in work organizations in addition to the area of pay.

Chapter 4

Reinforcement Theory and Behavior Modification

Although Skinner's (1953) research on the effects of positive reinforcement, or behavior modification, on behavior have been widely publicized in the psychological literature, it is only recently that attention has been paid to the application of such principles to work settings in organizations. Only in the last several years have management researchers attempted to experiment with these techniques in such diverse areas as job design, compensation, organizational climate, and so forth.

The results claimed by those organizations that have attempted such experiments with behavior modification are impressive—at least on the surface. An air freight firm, for example, estimates that its new performance-improvement system, which is largely based on Skinnerian principles, has saved the company over $2 million during a 3-year period (*Psychology Today*, 1972). And in a large Midwest public utility, operant conditioning techniques were used to attack the problem of absenteeism, with the result that the rate dropped from 7½ to 4½ percent (*Business Week*, 1972). Other positive results, using more rigorous measurement procedures, have been reported by Adam (1972), Jablonsky and DeVries (1972), and Hamner and Hamner (1976).

NATURE OF POSITIVE REINFORCEMENT

The basic concept of behavior modification is simple. Briefly, it assumes that human behavior can be engineered, shaped, or altered by manipulating the reward structures of various forms of behavior. This process is called "positive reinforcement." Performance standards are clearly set, and improvement re-sults—at least in theory—from the application of frequent *positive* feedback and from recognition for satisfactory behavior. Negative feedback is not gen-erally used. It is assumed that the employee's desire for the rewards of positive feedback and recognition will in large measure motivate him or her to perform satisfactorily in anticipation of such rewards.

According to Luthans and Kreitner (1975), three fundamental principles underlie behavior modification: First, it is necessary to deal exclusively with observable behavioral events, not attitudes, perceptions, or feelings. Second, one should measure behavior in terms of response frequency, or the extent to which desired behaviors are repeated by individuals. Third, since behavior is viewed as a function of its consequences (according to advocates of behavior modification), clear contingency relationships must be established for employ-ees between acts or behaviors and subsequent rewards or outcomes. The ram-ifications of these three principles are discussed in detail in the reading selec-tions in this chapter.

IMPLICATIONS FOR MANAGEMENT

Advocates of behavior modification point to several advantages that purport-edly result from the use of operant conditioning techniques. For such benefits to result, however, major responsibility is placed on managers to control the work environment and reward contingencies. Without such control, the major benefits of the program are lost. Hence, managerial behavior is seen as crucial for the success of such programs.

A variety of managerial implications emerge from recent work on behavior modification (Luthans & Kreitner, 1975; Hamner & Hamner, 1976). First, it is important that managers clearly inform subordinates concerning which be-haviors are desirable and get rewarded and which behaviors do not get rewarded.

Second, performance can be improved by providing continuous feedback to employees concerning the nature and quality of their work. This would include pointing out errors made by employees as well as noting ways of overcoming such errors.

Third, it is important that the rewards or consequences offered for good performance equal behaviors exhibited by employees. That is, if an employee is doing a good job, he or she should be told this. Supervisors often find this hard to do, but the importance of recognizing good behavior is crucial to behavior modification.

Fourth, managers should ensure that all employees are not rewarded equally; that is, rewards should be differentiated by performance levels. If employees fail to see a clear relationship between performance and rewards, there is little reason to believe they will exert increased energies for task accomplishment.

As can be seen from these managerial implications, behavior modification as a theory of work motivation requires significant administrative effort in managing reward contingencies. When examining this approach, it would be useful to compare both the theory and the managerial implications with the more cognitive theories of motivation, such as expectancy/valence theory (Chapter 5) and the goal-setting model (Chapter 10).

RESERVATIONS CONCERNING THE THEORY

While behavior modification in work organizations may appear appealing on the surface, it has not been universally accepted. Whyte (1972), for example, points out that most of the research in support of Skinner's theory is laboratory-based, primarily using animals under highly controlled conditions. He argues that such principles may not apply when one attempts to use them in the more complex world of organizations. While not completely rejecting Skinner, Whyte raises four problems with applying his principles to "real-life" behavior.

First, much of Skinner's research has ignored complex social processes that can moderate any incentive system. (See, for example, the discussion of group influences on performance in Chapter 8.) If group performance norms are set in contravention to the positive reinforcement incentive system for improving performance, such incentives may have little impact.

Second, there is the problem of conflicting stimuli. For example, the use of positive reinforcement to gain increased productivity may stimulate employees' desires to improve output, yet simultaneously arouse their fears that this improved output will only lead to the permanent establishment of still higher performance standards.

Third, there is the traditional problem of obtaining employees' belief that management is truly acting with the employees' interests in mind and not simply trying to exploit them.

Fourth, there is what Whyte terms the "one-body problem." An employee is motivated by experiences and anticipations that come from a variety of sources (family, friends, coworkers, and so on). If behavior modification principles are to be effectively implemented, Whyte argues, all these forms of input would need to be controlled simultaneously so that a unified system of positive reinforcement could be attained. This would certainly be no easy task.

OVERVIEW

Even so, the recent work on behavior modification in work organizations is impressive in terms of results. Many of these results are reviewed in the selections that follow. First, Hamner discusses the nature of learning theory that underlies behavior modification. The notion of positive reinforcement, schedules of reinforcement, and the role of management are discussed. Following this, Hamner and Hamner review some recent field applications of behavior modification. Finally, Locke suggests some possible shortcomings of the behavior modification approach, including critiques of both the theory and applications.

REFERENCES AND SUGGESTED ADDITIONAL READINGS

Adam, E. E., Jr. An analysis of changes in performance quality with operant conditioning procedures. *Journal of Applied Psychology,* 1972, **56,** 480–486.

Adam, E. E., Jr., & Scott, W. E., Jr. The application of behavioral conditioning procedures to the problems of quality control. *Academy of Management Journal,* 1971, **14,** 175–193.

Aldis, O. Of pigeons and men. *Harvard Business Review,* 1961, **39**(4), 59–63.

Bandura, A. *Principles of behavior modification.* New York: Holt, Rinehart & Winston, 1969.

Business Week. Where Skinner's theories work. December 2, 1972, No. 2257, 64–65.

Hamner, W. C., & Hamner, E. P. Behavior modification on the bottom line. *Organizational Dynamics,* Spring 1976, **4**(4), 3–21.

Jablonsky, S. F., & DeVries, D. L. Operant conditioning principles extrapolated to the theory of management. *Organizational Behavior and Human Performance,* 1972, **7,** 340–358.

Luthans, F., & Kreitner, R. *Organizational behavior modification.* Glenview, Ill.: Scott, Foresman, 1975.

Luthans, F., & White, D. D., Jr. Behavior modification: Application to manpower management. *Personnel Administration,* 1971, **34,** 41–47.

Nord, W. R. Beyond the teaching machine: The neglected area of operant conditioning in the theory and practice of management. *Organizational Behavior and Human Performance,* 1969, **4,** 352–377.

Organizational Dynamics. At Emery Air Freight: Positive reinforcement boosts performance. Winter 1973.

Psychology Today. New tool: Reinforcement for good work. April 1972, 68–69.

Reynolds, G. S. *A primer of operant conditioning.* Glenview, Ill.: Scott, Foresman, 1968.

Skinner, B. F. *Science and human behavior.* New York: Free Press, 1953.

Spielberger, C. D., & De Nike, L. D. Descriptive behaviorism versus cognitive theory in verbal operant conditioning. *Psychological Review,* 1966, **73,** 306–325.

Whyte, W. F. Skinnerian theory in organizations. *Psychology Today,* April 1972, 67–68, 96, 98, 100.

Reinforcement Theory and Contingency Management in Organizational Settings

W. Clay Hamner

Traditionally management has been defined as the process of getting things done through other people. The succinctness of this definition is misleading in that, while it may be easy to say *what* a manager does, it is difficult to describe the determinants of behavior, i.e. to tell *how* the behavior of the manager influences the behavior of the employee toward accomplishment of a task. Human behavior in organizational settings has always been a phenomenon of interest and concern. However, it has only been in recent years that a concerted effort has been made by social scientists to describe the principles of reinforcement and their implications for describing the determinants of behavior as they relate to the theory and practice of management (e.g. see Nord, 1969; Wiard, 1972; Whyte, 1972; Jablonsky and DeVries, 1972; Hersey and Blanchard, 1972; and Behling, Schriesheim, and Tolliver, in press).[1]

Organizational leaders must resort to environmental changes as a means of influencing behavior. Reinforcement principles are the most useful method for this purpose because they indicate to the leader how he might proceed in designing or modifying the work environment in order to effect specific changes in behavior (Scott and Cummings, 1973). A reinforcement approach to management does not consist of a bag of tricks to be applied indiscriminately for the purpose of coercing unwilling people (Michael & Meyerson, 1962). Unfortunately, many people who think of Skinnerian applications (Skinner, 1969) in the field of management and personnel think of manipulation and adverse control over employees. Increased knowledge available today of the positive aspects of conditioning as applied to worker performance should help to dispel these notions.

The purpose of this paper is to describe the determinants of behavior as seen from a reinforcement theory point of view, and to describe how the management of the contingencies of reinforcement in organizational settings is a key to successful management. Hopefully, this paper will enable the manager to understand how his behavior affects the behavior of his subordinates and to see that in most cases the failure or success of the worker at the performance of a task is a direct function of the manager's own behavior. Since a large portion of the manager's time is spent in the process of modifying behavior patterns and shaping them so that they will be more goal oriented, it is appropriate that this paper begin by describing the processes and principles that govern behavior.

LEARNING AS A PREREQUISITE FOR BEHAVIOR

Learning is such a common phenomenon that we tend to fail to recognize its occurrence. Nevertheless, one of the major premises of reinforcement theory is that all behavior is learned—a worker's skill, a supervisor's attitude and a secretary's manners. The importance of learning in organizational settings is asserted by Costello and Zalkind when they conclude:

> Every aspect of human behavior is responsive to learning experiences. Knowledge, language, and skills, of course; but also attitudes, value systems, and personality characteristics. All the individual's activities in the organization—his loyalties, awareness of organizational goals, job performance, even his safety record have been learned in the largest sense of that term (1963, p. 205).

There seems to be general agreement among social scientists that learning can be defined as *a relatively permanent change in behavior potentiality that results from reinforced practice or experience.* Note that this definition states that there is change in behavior potentiality and not necessarily in behavior itself. The reason for this distinction rests on the fact that we can observe other people responding to their environments, see the consequences which accrue to them, and be vicariously conditioned. For example, a boy can watch his older sister burn her hand on a hot stove and "learn" that pain is the result of touching a hot stove. This definition therefore allows us to account for "no-trial" learning. Bandura (1969) describes this as imitative learning and says that while behavior can be *acquired* by observing, reading, or other vicarious methods, "*performance* of observationally learned responses will depend to a great extent upon the nature of the reinforcing consequences to the model or to the observer" (p. 128).

Luthans (1973, p. 362) says that we need to consider the following points when we define the learning process:

1   Learning involves a change, though not necessarily an improvement, in behavior. Learning generally has the connotation of improved performance, but under this definition bad habits, prejudices, stereotypes, and work restrictions are learned.

2   The change in behavior must be relatively permanent in order to be considered learning. This qualification rules out behavioral changes resulting from fatigue or temporary adaptations as learning.

3   Some form of practice or experience is necessary for learning to occur.

4   Finally, practice or experience must be reinforced in order for learning to occur. If reinforcement does not accompany the practice or experience, the behavior will eventually disappear.

From this discussion, we can conclude that learning is the acquisition of knowledge, and performance is the translation of knowledge into practice. The primary effect of reinforcement is to strengthen and intensify certain aspects of ensuing behavior. Behavior that has become highly differentiated (shaped) can be understood and accounted for only in terms of the history of reinforcement of that behavior (Morse, 1966). Reinforcement generates a reproducible behavior process in time. A response occurs and is followed by a reinforcer, and further responses occur with a characteristic temporal patterning. When a response is reinforced it subsequently occurs more frequently than before it was reinforced. Reinforcement may be assumed to have a characteristic and reproducible effect on a particular behavior, and usually it will enhance and intensify that behavior (Skinner, 1938; 1953).

TWO BASIC LEARNING PROCESSES

Before discussing in any detail exactly how the general laws or principles of reinforcement can be used to predict and influence behavior, we must differentiate between two types of behavior. One kind is known as *voluntary* or *operant* behavior, and the other is known as *reflex* or *respondent* behavior. Respondent behavior takes in all responses of human beings that are *elicited* by special stimulus changes in the environment. An example would be when a person turns a light on in a dark room (stimulus change), his eyes contract (respondent behavior).

Operant behavior includes an even greater amount of human activity. It takes in all the responses of a person that may at some time be said to have an effect upon or do something to the person's outside world (Keller, 1969). Operant behavior *operates* on this world either directly or indirectly. For example, when a person presses the up button at the elevator entrance to "call" the elevator, he is operating on his environment.

The process of learning or acquiring reflex behavior is different from the processes of learning or acquiring voluntary behavior. The two basic and distinct learning processes are known as *classical conditioning* and *operant conditioning*. It is from studying these two learning processes that much of our knowledge of individual behavior has emerged.

Classical Conditioning[2]

Pavlov (1902) noticed, while studying the automatic reflexes associated with digestion, that his laboratory dog salivated (unconditioned response) not only when food (unconditioned stimulus) was placed in the dog's mouth, but also when other stimuli were presented before food was placed in the dog's mouth. In other words, by presenting a neutral stimulus (ringing of a bell) every time food was presented to the dog, Pavlov was able to get the dog to salivate to the bell alone.

A stimulus which is not a part of a reflex relationship (the bell in Pavlov's experiment) becomes a *conditioned stimulus* for the response by repeated, temporal pairing with an *unconditioned* stimulus (food) which already elicits the response. This new relationship is known as a conditioned reflex, and the pairing procedure is known as classical conditioning.

While it is important to understand that reflex behavior is conditioned by a different process than is voluntary behavior, classical conditioning principles are of little use to the practicing manager. Most of the behavior that is of interest to society does not fit in the paradigm of reflex behavior (Michael and Meyerson, 1962). Nevertheless, the ability to generalize from one stimulus setting to another is very important in human learning and problem solving, and for this reason, knowledge of the classical conditioning process is important.

Operant Conditioning[3]

The basic distinction between classical and operant conditioning procedures is in terms of the *consequences* of the conditioned response. In classical conditioning, the sequence of events is independent of the subject's behavior. In operant conditioning, consequences (rewards and punishments) are made to occur as a consequence of the subject's response or failure to respond. The distinction between these two methods is shown in Figure 1.

In Figure 1, we see that classical conditioning involves a three stage process. In the diagram, let S refer to *stimulus* and R to *response*. We see that in stage 1, the unconditioned stimulus (food) elicits an unconditioned response (salivation). In stage 2, a neutral stimulus (bell) elicits no known response. However, in stage 3, after the ringing of the bell is repeatedly paired with the presence of food, the bell alone becomes a conditioned stimulus and elicits a conditioned response (salivation). The subject has no control over the unconditioned or conditioned response, but is "at the mercy" of his environment and his past conditioning history.

Note however, that for voluntary behavior, the consequence is dependent on the behavior of the individual in a given stimulus setting. Such behavior can be said to "operate" (Skinner, 1969) on the environment, in contrast to behavior which is "respondent" to prior eliciting stimuli (Michael and Meyerson, 1962). Reinforcement is not given every time the stimulus is presented, but is *only* given when the correct response is made. For example, if an employee taking

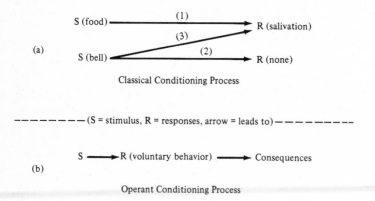

Figure 1   Classical vs. operant conditioning.

a work break puts a penny (R) in the soft drink machine (S), nothing happens (consequence). However, if he puts a quarter (R) in the machine (S), he gets the soft drink (consequence). In other words, the employee's behavior is *instrumental* in determining the consequences which accrue to him.

The interrelationships between the three components of (1) *stimulus* or environment, (2) *response* or performance, and (3) consequences or *reinforcements* are known as the *contingencies* of reinforcement. Skinner (1969) says "The class of responses upon which a reinforcer is *contingent* is called an operant, to suggest the action on the environment followed by reinforcements (p. 7)." Operant conditioning presupposes that human beings explore their environment and act upon it. This behavior, randomly emitted at first, can be constructed as an operant by making a reinforcement contingent on a response. Any stimulus present when an operant is reinforced acquires control in the sense that the rate of response for that individual will be higher when it is present. "Such a stimulus does not act as a *goal*; it does not elicit the response (as was the case in classical conditioning of reflex behavior)[4] in the sense of forcing it to occur. It is simply an essential aspect of the occasion upon which response is made and reinforced (Skinner, 1969, p. 7)."

Therefore, an adequate formulation of the interaction between an individual and his environment must always specify three things: (1) the occasion upon which a response occurs, (2) the response itself and (3) the reinforcing consequences. Skinner holds that the consequences determine the likelihood that a given operant will be performed in the future. Thus to change behavior, the consequences of the behavior must be changed, i.e. the contingencies must be rearranged (the ways in which the consequences are related to the behavior) (Behling, *et al.*, in press). For Skinner, this behavior generated by a given set of contingencies can be accounted for without appealing to hypothetical inner states (e.g. awareness or expectancies). "If a conspicuous stimulus does not have an effect, it is not because the organism has not attended to it or because some central gatekeeper has screened it out, but because the stimulus plays no important role in the prevailing contingencies (Skinner 1969, p. 8)."

Arrangement of the Contingencies of Reinforcement

In order to *understand* and *interpret* behavior, we must look at the interrelationship among the components of the contingencies of behavior. If one expects to influence behavior, he must also be able to manipulate the consequences of the behavior (Skinner, 1969). Haire (1964) reports the importance of being able to manipulate the consequences when he says,

> Indeed, whether he is conscious of it or not, the superior is bound to be constantly shaping the behavior of his subordinates by the way in which he utilizes the rewards that are at his disposal, and he will inevitably modify the behavior patterns of his work group thereby. For this reason, it is important to see as clearly as possible what is going on, so that the changes can be planned and chosen in advance, rather than simply accepted after the fact.

After appropriate reinforcers that have sufficient incentive value to maintain stable responsiveness have been chosen, the contingencies between specific performances and reinforcing stimuli must be arranged (Bandura, 1969). Employers intuitively use rewards in their attempt to modify and influence behavior, but their efforts often produce limited results because the methods are used improperly, inconsistently, or inefficiently. In many instances considerable rewards are bestowed upon the workers, but they are not made conditional or contingent on the behavior the manager wishes to promote. Also, "long delays often intervene between the occurrence of the desired behavior and its intended consequences; special privileges, activities, and rewards are generally furnished according to fixed time schedules rather than performance requirements; and in many cases, positive reinforcers are inadvertently made contingent upon the wrong type of behavior (Bandura, 1969, pp. 229–230)."

One of the primary reasons that managers fail to "motivate" workers to perform in the desired manner is due to a lack of understanding of the power of the contingencies of reinforcement over the employee and of the manager's role in arranging these contingencies. The laws or principles for arranging the contingencies are not hard to understand, and if students of behavior grasp them firmly, they are powerful managerial tools which can be used to increase supervisory effectiveness.

As we have said, operant conditioning is the process by which behavior is modified by manipulation of the contingencies of the behavior. To understand how this works, we will first look at various *types* (arrangements) of contingencies, and then at various *schedules* of the contingencies available. Rachlin (1970) described the four basic ways available to the manager of arranging the contingencies—*positive reinforcement, avoidance learning, extinction*, and *punishment*. The difference among these types of contingencies depends on the consequence which results from the behavioral act. Positive reinforcement and avoidance learning are methods of strengthening *desired* behavior, and extinction and punishment are methods of weakening *undesired* behavior.

Positive Reinforcement   "A positive reinforcer is a stimulus which, when added to a situation, strengthens the probability of an operant response (Skinner, 1953, p. 73)." The reason it strengthens the response is explained by Thorndike's (1911) Law of Effect. This law states simply that behavior which appears to lead to a positive consequence tends to be repeated, while behavior which appears to lead to a negative consequence tends not to be repeated. A positive consequence is called a reward.

Reinforcers, either positive or negative, are classified as either: (1) unconditioned or primary reinforcers, or (2) conditioned or secondary reinforcers. Primary reinforcers such as food, water, and sex are of biological importance in that they are innately rewarding and have effects which are independent of past experiences. Secondary reinforcers such as job advancement, praise, recognition, and money derive their effects from a consistent pairing with other reinforcers (i.e., they are conditioned). Secondary reinforcement, therefore, depends on the individual and his past reinforcement history. What is rewarding to one person may not be rewarding to another. Managers should look for a reward system which has maximal reinforcing consequences to the group he is supervising.

Regardless of whether the positive reinforcer is primary or secondary in nature, once it has been determined that the consequence has reward value to the worker, it can be used to increase the worker's performance. So the *first step* in the successful application of reinforcement procedures is to select reinforcers that are sufficiently powerful and durable to "maintain responsiveness while complex patterns of behavior are being established and strengthened" (Bandura, 1969, p. 225).

The *second step* is to design the contingencies in such a way that the reinforcing events are made contingent upon the desired behavior. This is the rule of reinforcement which is most often violated. Rewards must result from performance, and the greater the degree of performance by an employee, the greater should be his reward. Money as a reinforcer will be discussed later, but it should be noted that money is not the only reward available. In fact, for unionized employees, the supervisor has virtually no way to tie money to performance. Nevertheless, other forms of rewards, such as recognition, promotion and job assignments, can be made contingent on good performance. Unless a manager is willing to discriminate between employees based on their level of performance, the effectiveness of his power over the employee is nil.

The arrangement of positive reinforcement contingencies can be pictured as follows:

Stimulus $\rightarrow$ Desired response $\rightarrow$ Positive consequences
$(S \rightarrow R \rightarrow R^+)$

The stimulus is the work environment which leads to a response (some level of performance). If this response leads to positive consequences, then the probability of that response being emitted again increases (Law of Effect). Now, if the behavior is undesired, then the supervisor is conditioning or teaching the employee that undesired behavior will lead to a desired reward. It is important therefore that the reward administered be equal to the performance input of the employee. Homans (1950) labels this as the rule of distributive justice and stated that this reciprocal norm applies in both formal (work) and informal (friendship) relationships. In other words, the employee *exchanges* his services for the rewards of the organization. In order to maintain desired performance, it is important that the manager design the reward system so that the level of reward administered is proportionately contingent on the level of performance emitted.

The *third step* is to design the contingencies in such a way that a reliable procedure for eliciting or inducing the desired response patterns is established; otherwise, if they never occur there will be few opportunities to influence the desired behavior through contingent management. If the behavior that a manager wishes to strengthen is already present, and occurs with some frequency, then contingent applications of incentives can, from the outset, increase and maintain the desired performance patterns at a high level. However, as Bandura (1969) states, "When the initial level of the desired behavior is extremely low, if the criterion for reinforcement is initially set too high, most, if not all, of the person's responses go unrewarded, so that his efforts are gradually extinguished and his motivation diminished (p. 232)."

The nature of the learning process is such that acquiring the new response patterns can be easily established. The principle of operant conditioning says that an operant followed by a positive reinforcement is more likely to occur under similar conditions in the future. Through the process of *generalization*, the more nearly alike the new situation or stimulus is to the original one, the more the old behavior is likely to be emitted in the new environment. For example, if you contract with an electrician to rewire your house, he is able to bring with him enough old behavioral patterns which he generalized to this unfamiliar, but similar, stimulus setting (the house) in order to accomplish the task. He has learned through his past reinforcement history that, when in a new environment, one way to speed up the correct behavior needed to obtain reward is to generalize from similar settings with which he has had experience. Perhaps one reason an employer wants a person with work experience is because the probability of that person emitting the correct behavior is greater and thus the job of managing that person simplified.

Just as generalization is the ability to react to similarities in the environment, *discrimination* is the ability to react to differences in a new environmental setting. Usually when an employee moves from one environment (a job, a city, an office) to another he finds that only certain dimensions of the stimulus conditions change. While all of the responses of the employee in this new setting will not be correct, by skilled use of the procedures of reinforcement currently being discussed, we can bring about the more precise type of stimulus control called discrimination. When we purchase a new car, we do not have to relearn how to drive a car (generalizable stimulus). Instead we need only learn the differences in the new car and the old car so that we can respond to these differences in order to get reinforced. This procedure is called *discrimination training*. "If in the presence of a stimulus a response is reinforced, and in the absence of this stimulus it is extinguished, the stimulus will control the probability of the response in high degree. Such a stimulus is called a *discriminative stimulus* (Michael and Meyerson, 1962)."

The development of effective discriminative repertoires is important for dealing with many different people on an interpersonal basis. Effective training techniques will allow the supervisor to develop the necessary discriminative repertoires in his new employees (e.g. see Bass and Vaughan, 1966, *Training in Industry: The Management of Learning*).

Using the principles of generalization and discrimination in a well-designed training program allows the manager to accomplish the third goal of eliciting or inducing the desired response patterns. Training is a method of *shaping* desired behavior so that it can be conditioned to come under the control of the reinforcement stimuli. Shaping behavior is necessary when the response to be learned is not currently in the individual's repertoire and when it is a fairly complex behavior. In shaping, we teach a desired response by reinforcing the series of successive steps which lead to the final response. This method is essentially the one your parents used when they first taught you to drive. You were first taught how to adjust the seat and mirror, fasten the seat belt, turn on the lights and windshield wipers, and then how to start the engine. Each time you successfully completed each stage you were positively reinforced by some comment. You then were allowed to practice driving on back roads and in empty lots. By focusing on one of these aspects at a time and reinforcing proper responses, your parents were able to shape your driving behavior until you reached the final stage of being able to drive. After your behavior was shaped, driving other cars or driving in new territories was accomplished successfully by the process of generalization and discrimination. This same process is used with a management trainee who is rotated from department to department for a period of time until he has "learned the ropes." After his managerial behavior has been minimally shaped, he is transferred to a managerial position where, using the principles of generalization and discrimination, he is able to adjust to the contingencies of the work environment.

Avoidance Learning   The second type of contingency arrangement available to the manager is called escape, or avoidance learning. Just as with positive reinforcement, this is a method of strengthening desired behavior. A contingency arrangement in which an individual's performance can terminate an already noxious stimulus is called *escape* learning. When behavior can prevent the onset of a noxious stimulus the procedure is called *avoidance learning*. In both cases, the result is the development and maintenance of the desired operant behavior (Michael and Meyerson, 1962).

An example of this kind of control can be easily found in a work environment. Punctuality of employees is often maintained by avoidance learning. The noxious stimulus is the criticism by the shop steward or office manager for being late. In order to avoid criticism other employees make a special effort to come to work on time. A supervisor begins criticizing a worker for "goofing off." Other workers may intensify their efforts to escape the criticism of the supervisor.

The arrangement of an escape reinforcement contingency can be diagrammed as follows:

Noxious stimulus $\rightarrow$ Desired response $\rightarrow$ Removal of noxious stimulus
$(S^- \rightarrow R \not\rightarrow S^-)$

The distinction between the process of strengthening behavior by means of positive reinforcement techniques and avoidance learning techniques should be noted carefully. In one case, the individual works hard to gain the consequences from the environment which results from good work, and in the second case, the individual works hard to avoid the noxious aspects of the environment itself. In both cases the same behavior is strengthened.

While Skinner (1953) recognizes that avoidance learning techniques can be used to condition desired behavior, he does not advocate their use. Instead a Skinnerian approach to operant conditioning is primarily based on the principles of positive reinforcement.

Extinction While positive reinforcement and avoidance learning techniques can be used by managers to strengthen desired behavior, extinction and punishment techniques are methods available to managers for reducing undesired behavior. When positive reinforcement for a learned or previously conditioned response is withheld, individuals will continue to exhibit that behavior for an extended period of time. Under repeated nonreinforcement, the behavior decreases and eventually disappears. This decline in response rate as a result of nonrewarded repetition of a task is defined as *extinction*.

The diagram of the arrangement of the contingency of extinction can be shown as follows:

(1) Stimulus → Response → Positive consequences
$(S → R → R^+)$

(2) Stimulus → Response → Withholding of positive consequences
$(S → R \nrightarrow R +)$

(3) Stimulus → Withholding of response
$(S \nrightarrow R)$

The behavior which was previously reinforced because (a) it was desired or (b) by poor reinforcement practices is no longer desired. To extinguish this behavior in a naturally recurring situation, response patterns sustained by positive reinforcement (Stage 1) are frequently eliminated (Stage 3) by discontinuing the rewards (Stage 2) that ordinarily produce the behavior. This method when combined with a positive reinforcement method is the procedure of behavior modification recommended by Skinner (1953). It leads to the least negative side effects and when the two methods are used together, it allows the employee to get the rewards he desires and allows the organization to eliminate the undesired behavior.

Punishment A second method of reducing the frequency of undesired behavior is through the use of punishment. Punishment is the most controversial method of behavior modification, and most of the ethical questions about operant methods of control center around this technique. "One of the principal objections to aversive control stems from the widespread belief that internal, and often unconscious, forces are the major determinant of behavior. From this perspective, punishment may temporarily suppress certain expressions, but the underlying impulses retain their strength and press continuously for discharge through alternative actions (Bandura, 1969, p. 292).'' While Skinner (1953) discounts the internal state hypothesis, he recommends that extinction rather than punishment be used to decrease the probability of the occurrence of a particular behavior.

Punishment is defined as presenting an aversive or noxious consequence contingent upon a response, or removing a positive consequence contingent upon a response. Based on the Law of Effect, as rewards strengthen behavior, punishment weakens it. This process can be shown as follows:

(1) Stimulus → Undesired behavior → Noxious consequence or withold-
$\quad$ (S → R → R$^-$) $\qquad\qquad\qquad$ ing of positive consequence
$\quad$ ($\quad$ or $\not\to$ R$^+$)

(2) Stimulus → Undesired behavior
$\quad$ (S $\not\to$ R)

Notice carefully the difference in the withholding of rewards in the punishment process and the withholding of rewards in the extinction process. In the extinction process, we withhold rewards for behavior that has previously been administered the rewards because the behavior was desired. In punishment, we withhold a reward because the behavior is undesired, has never been associated with the reward before, and is in fact a noxious consequence. For example, if your young son began imitating an older neighborhood boy's use of profanity and you thought it was "cute," you might reinforce the behavior by laughing or by calling public attention to it. Soon, the son learns one way to get the recognition he craves is to use profanity—even though he may have no concept of its meaning. As the child reaches an accountable age, you decide that his use of profanity is no longer as cute as it once was. To stop the behavior you can do one of three things: (1) You can withhold the previous recognition you gave the child by ignoring him (extinction), (2) You can give the child a spanking (punishment by noxious consequence), or (3) You can withhold his allowance or refuse to let him watch television (punishment by withholding of positive consequences not previously connected with the act.)

It should be noted that method 2 and perhaps method 3 would be considered cruel because of the parent's own inconsistencies. Punishment should rarely be used to extinguish behavior that has previously been reinforced if the person administering the punishment is the same person who previously reinforced the behavior. However, had the parent failed to extinguish the use of profanity prior to sending the child out in society (e.g. school, church), it is possible that the society may punish the child for behavior that the parent is reinforcing or at least tolerating. It is often argued therefore that the failure to use punishment early in the life of a child for socially unacceptable behavior (e.g. stealing, driving at excessive speeds, poor table manners) is more cruel than the punishment itself, simply because the society will withhold rewards or administer aversive consequences for the behavior which the parents should have extinguished.

The use of aversive control is frequently questioned on the assumption that it produces undesirable by-products. In many cases this concern is warranted. Bandura (1969) states that it depends on the circumstances and on the past reinforcement history of the reinforcement agent and the reinforcement target as to whether punishment or extinction should be used. He says:

> Many of the unfavorable effects, however, that are sometimes associated with punishment are not necessarily inherent in the methods themselves but result from the faulty manner in which they are applied. A great deal of human behavior is, in fact, modified and closely regulated by natural aversive contingencies without any ill effects. On the basis of negative consequences people learn to avoid or to protect themselves against hazardous falls, flaming or scalding objects, deafening sounds, and other hurtful stimuli. . . . In instances where certain activities can have injurious effects, aversive contingencies *must* be socially arranged to ensure survival. Punishment is rarely indicated for ineffectiveness or deleterious side effects when used, for example, to teach young children not to insert metal objects into electrical outlets, not to cross busy thoroughfares . . . Certain types of negative sanctions, if applied considerately, can likewise aid in eliminating self-defeating and socially detrimental behavior without creating any special problems (p. 294).

Rules for Using Operant Conditioning Techniques

Several rules concerning the arrangement of the contingencies of reinforcement should be discussed. While these rules have common sense appeal, the research findings indicate that these rules are often violated by managers when they design control systems.

Rule 1. Don't reward all people the same. In other words, differentiate the rewards based on performance as compared to some defined objective or standard. We know that people compare their own performance to that of their peers to determine how well they are doing ("Social Comparison Theory," Festinger, 1954) and they compare their rewards to the rewards of their peers ("Equity Theory," Adams, 1965) in order to determine how to evaluate their rewards. While some managers seem to think that the fairest system of compensation is one where everyone in the same job classification gets the same pay, employees want differentiation so that they know their importance to the organization. Based on social comparison and equity theory assumptions, it can be argued that managers who reward all people the same are encouraging, at best, only average performance. Behavior of high performance workers is being extinguished (ignored) while the behavior of average performance and poor performance workers is being strengthened by positive reinforcement.

Rule 2. Failure to respond has reinforcing consequences. Managers who find the job of differentiating between workers so unpleasant that they fail to respond must recognize that failure to respond modifies behavior. "Indeed, whether he is conscious of it or not, the superior is bound to be constantly shaping the behavior of his subordinates by the way in which he utilizes the rewards that are at his disposal, and he will inevitably modify the behavior of his work group (Haire, 1964)," Managers must be careful that they examine the performance consequence of their non-action as well as their action.

Rule 3. Be sure to tell a person what he can do to get reinforced. By making clear the contingencies of reinforcement to the worker, a manager may be actually increasing the individual freedom of the worker. The employee who has a standard against which to measure his job will have a built-in feedback system which allows him to make judgements about his own work. The awarding of the reinforcement in an organization where the worker's goal is specified will be associated with the performance of the worker and not based on the biases of the supervisor. The assumption is that the supervisor rates the employee accurately (see Scott and Hamner, 1973a) and that he then reinforces the employee based on his ratings (see Scott and Hamner, 1973b). If the supervisor fails to rate accurately or administer rewards based on performance, then the stated goals for the worker will lose stimulus control, and the worker will be forced to search for the "true" contingencies, i.e., what behavior should he perform in order to get rewarded (e.g., ingratiation? loyalty? positive attitude?).

Rule 4. Be sure to tell a person what he is doing wrong. As a general rule, very few people find the act of failing rewarding. One assumption of behavior therefore is that a worker wants to be rewarded in a positive manner. A supervisor should never use extinction or punishment as a sole method for modifying behavior, but if used judiciously in conjunction with other techniques designed to promote more effective response options (Rule 3) such combined procedures can hasten the change process. If the supervisor fails to specify why a reward is being withheld, the employee may associate it with past desired behavior instead of the undesired behavior that the supervisor is trying to extinguish. The supervisor then extinguishes good performance while having no effect on the undesired behavior.

Rules 3 and 4, when used in combination, should allow the manager to control behavior in the best interest of reaching organizational goals. At the same time they should give the employee the clarity he needs to see that his own behavior and not the behavior of the supervisor controls his outcomes.

Rule 5. Don't punish in front of others. The reason for this rule is quite simple. The punishment (e.g., reprimand) should be enough to extinguish the undesired behavior. By administering the punishment in front of the work group, the worker is doubly punished in the sense that he is also put out of face (Goffman, 1959). This additional punishment may lead to negative side-effects in three ways. First, the worker whose self-image is damaged may feel that he must retaliate in order to protect himself. Therefore, the supervisor has actually increased undesired responses. Secondly, the work group may misunderstand the reason for the punishment and through "avoidance learning" may modify their own behavior in ways not intended by the supervisor. Third, the work group is also being punished in the sense that observing a member of their team being reprimanded has noxious or aversive properties for most people. This may result in a decrease in the performance of the total work group.

Rule 6. Make the consequences equal to the behavior. In other words be fair. Don't cheat the worker out of his just rewards. If he is a good worker, tell him. Many supervisors find it very difficult to praise an employee. Others find it very difficult to counsel an employee about what he is doing wrong. When a manager fails to use these reinforcement tools, he is actually reducing his effectiveness. When a worker is overrewarded he may feel guilty (Adams, 1965) and based on the principles of reinforcement, the worker's current level of performance is being conditioned. If his performance level is less than others who get the same reward, he has no reason to increase his output. When a worker is underrewarded, he becomes angry with the system (Adams, 1965). His behavior is being extinguished and the company may be forcing the good employee (underrewarded) to seek employment elsewhere while encouraging the poor employee (overrewarded) to stay.

An Argument for Positive Reinforcement

Most workers enter the work place willingly if not eagerly. They have a sense of right and wrong and have been thoroughly conditioned by their parents and by society. By the time they reach adulthood, it can be assumed that they are mature. For these reasons, it is argued here as well as by others (Skinner, 1953; Wiard, 1972), that the only tool needed for worker motivation is the presence or absence of positive reinforcement. In other words, managers do not, as a general rule, need to use avoidance learning or punishment techniques in order to control behavior.

Whyte (1972) says "positive reinforcers generally are more effective than negative reinforcers in the production and maintenance of behavior" (p. 67). Wiard (1972) points out, "There may be cases where the use of punishment has resulted in improved performance, but they are few and far between. The pitfalls of punishment can be encountered with any indirect approach" (p. 16). However, a positive reinforcement program is geared toward the desired results. It emphasizes what needs to be done, rather than what should not be done. A positive reinforcement program is result oriented, rather than process oriented. A well designed program encourages individual growth and freedom, whereas negative approach (avoidance learning and punishment) encourages immaturity in the individual and therefore eventually in the organization itself.

The reason organizations are ineffective according to Skinner (1969) is because they insist on using avoidance learning or punishment techniques, and because they fail to use a positive reinforcement program in an effective manner. He says:

> The contingencies of positive reinforcement arranged by governmental and religious agencies are primitive, and the agencies continue to lean heavily on the puritanical solution. Economic reinforcement might seem to represent an environmental solution, but it is badly programmed and the results are unsatisfactory for both the employer (since not much is done) and the employee (since work is still work).

Education and the management of retardates and psychotics are still largely aversive. In short, as we have seen, the most powerful forces bearing on human behavior are not being effectively used. . . . Men are happy in an environment in which active, productive, and creative behavior is reinforced in effective ways (pp. 63–64).

Schedules of Positive Reinforcement

The previous discussion was primarily concerned with methods of arranging the contingencies of reinforcement in order to modify behavior. Two major points were discussed. First, some type of reinforcement is necessary in order to produce a change in behavior. Second, a combined program of positive reinforcement and extinction are more effective for use in organizations than are programs using punishment and/or avoidance learning techniques. The previous discussion thus tells what causes behavior and why it is important information for the manager, but it does not discuss the several important issues dealing with the scheduling or administering of positive reinforcement.

According to Costello and Zalkind (1963), "The speed with which learning takes place and also how lasting its effects will be is determined by the timing of reinforcement" (p. 193). In other words, the effectiveness varies as a function of the schedule of its administration. A reinforcement schedule is a more-or-less formal specification of the occurrence of a reinforcer in relation to the behavioral sequence to be conditioned, and effectiveness of the reinforcer depends as much upon its scheduling as upon any of its other features (magnitude, quality and degree of association with the behavioral act) (Adam and Scott, 1971).

There are many conceivable arrangements of a positive reinforcement schedule which managers can use to reward workers (Ferster and Skinner, 1957). Aldis (1961) identifies two basic types of schedules which have the most promise concerning possible worker motivation. These schedules are *continuous* and *partial reinforcement* schedules.

Continuous Reinforcement Schedule   Under this schedule, every time the correct operant is emitted by the worker, it is followed by a reinforcer. With this schedule, behavior increases very rapidly but when the reinforcer is removed (extinction) performance decreases rapidly. For this reason it is not recommended for use by the manager over a long period of time. It is also difficult or impossible for a manager to reward the employee continuously for emitting desired behavior. Therefore a manager should generally consider using one or more of the partial reinforcement schedules when he administers both financial and nonfinancial rewards.

Partial Reinforcement Schedules   Partial reinforcement, where reinforcement does not occur after every correct operant, leads to slower learning but stronger retention of a response than total or continuous reinforcement. "In other words, *learning is more permanent when we reward correct behavior only part of the time*" (Bass and Vaughan, 1966, p. 20). This factor is extremely relevant to the observed strong resistance to changes in attitudes, values, norms, and the like.

Ferster and Skinner (1957) have described four basic types of partial reinforcement schedules for operant learning situations. They are:

1 Fixed Interval Schedule   Under this schedule a reinforcer is administered only when the desired response occurs after the passage of a specified period of time since the previous reinforcement. Thus a worker paid on a weekly basis would receive a full pay check every Friday, assuming that the worker was performing minimally acceptable behavior. This method offers the least motivation for hard work among employees (Aldis, 1961). The kind of behavior often observed with fixed interval schedules is a pause after reinforcement and then an increase in rate of responding until a high rate of performance occurs just as the interval is about to end. Suppose the plant manager visits the shipping department each day at approximately 10:00 A.M. This fixed schedule of supervisory recognition will probably cause performance to be at its highest just prior to the plant manager's visit and then performance will probably steadily decline thereafter and not reach its peak again until the next morning's visit.

2 Variable Interval Schedule   Under this schedule, reinforcement is administered at some variable interval of time around some average. This schedule is not recommended for use with a pay plan (Aldis, 1961), but it is an ideal method to use for administering praise, promotions, and supervisory visits. Since the reinforcers are dispensed unpredictably, variable schedules generate higher rates of response and more stable and consistent performance (Bandura, 1969). Suppose our plant manager visits the shipping department on an *average* of once a day but at randomly selected time intervals, i.e., twice on Monday, once on Tuesday, not on Wednesday, not on Thursday, and twice on Friday, all at different times during the day. Performance will be higher and have less fluctuation than under the fixed interval schedule.

3 Fixed Ratio Schedule   Here a reward is delivered only when a fixed number of desired responses take place. This is essentially the piece-work schedule for pay. The response level here is significantly higher than that obtained under any of the interval (or time-based) schedules.

4 Variable Ratio Schedule   Under this schedule, a reward is delivered only after a number of desired responses with the number of desired responses changing from the occurrence of one reinforcer to the next, around an average. Thus a person working on a 15 to 1 variable ratio schedule might receive reinforcement after ten responses, then twenty responses, then fifteen responses, etc., to an average of one reinforcer per fifteen responses. Gambling is an example of a variable ratio reward schedule. Research evidence reveals that of all the variations in scheduling procedures available, this is the most powerful in sustaining behavior (Jablonsky and DeVries, 1972). In industry, this plan would be impossible to use as the only plan for scheduling reinforcement. However, Aldis (1961) suggests how this method could be used to supplement other monetary reward schedules:

Take the annual Christmas bonus as an example. In many instances, this "surprise" gift has become nothing more than a ritualized annual salary supplement which everybody expects. Therefore, its incentive-building value is largely lost. Now suppose that the total bonus were distributed at irregular intervals throughout the year and in small sums dependent upon the amount of work done. Wouldn't the workers find their urge to work increased? (p. 63)

An important point to remember is that to be effective a schedule should always include the specification of a contingency between the behavior desired and the occurrence of a reinforcer. In many cases it may be necessary to use each of the various schedules for administering rewards—for example, base pay on a fixed interval schedule, promotions and raises on a variable interval schedule, recognition of above average performance with a piece-rate plan (fixed ratio) and supplementary bonuses on a variable ratio schedule. The effect of each of the types of reinforcement schedules and the various methods of arranging reinforcement contingencies on worker performance is summarized in Table 1.

Table 1   Operant Conditioning Summary

Arrangement of reinforcement contingencies	Schedule of reinforcement contingencies	Effect on behavior when applied to the individual	Effect on behavior when removed from the individual
	Continuous reinforcement	Fastest method to establish a new behavior	Fastest method to extinguish a new behavior
	Partial reinforcement	Slowest method to establish a new behavior	Slowest method to extinguish a new behavior
	Variable partial reinforcement	More consistent response frequencies	Slower extinction rate
	Fixed partial reinforcement	Less consistent response frequencies	Faster extinction rate
Positive reinforcement Avoidance reinforcement		Increased frequency over preconditioning level	Return to preconditioning level
Punishment extinction		Decreased frequency over preconditioning level	Return to preconditioning level

Source. Adapted from Behling et al., reprinted with permission of the author from "Present Theories and New Directions in Theories of Work Effort," *Journal Supplement and Abstract Service* of the American Psychological Corporation.

The necessity for arranging appropriate reinforcement contingencies is dramatically illustrated by several studies in which rewards were shifted from a response-contingent (ratio) to a time-contingent basis (interval). During the period in which rewards were made conditional upon occurrence of the desired behavior, the appropriate response patterns were exhibited at a consistently high level. When the same rewards were given based on time and independent of the worker's behavior, there was a marked drop in the desired behavior. The reinstatement of the performance-contingent reward schedule promptly restored the high level of responsiveness (Lovaas, Berberich, Perloff, and Schaeffer, 1966; Baer, Peterson, and Sherman, 1967). Similar declines in performance were obtained when workers were provided rewards in advance without performance requirements (Ayllon and Azrin, 1965; Bandura and Perloff, 1967).

Aldis (1961) encourages businessmen to recognize the importance of a positive reinforcement program. He also says that experimentation with various schedules of positive reinforcement is the key to reducing job boredom and increasing worker satisfaction. He concludes:

> Most of us fully realize that a large proportion of all workers hold jobs that are boring and repetitive and that these employees are motivated to work not by positive rewards but by various oblique forms of threat. . . . The challenge is to motivate men by positive rewards rather than by negative punishments or threats of punishments. . . . Businessmen should recognize how much their conventional wage and salary systems essentially rely on negative reinforcement.
>
> Thus the promise of newer methods of wage payments which rely on more immediate rewards, on piece-rate pay, and greater randomization does not lie only in the increase in productivity that might follow. The greater promise is that such experiments may lead to happier workers as well (p. 63).

MANAGEMENT AND THE DISSEMINATION OF KNOWLEDGE

Previously we defined *learning* as the acquisition of knowledge (by the process of operant conditioning), and performance as the translation of knowledge into behavior (depending on the consequences). It can be argued therefore that what managers do is disseminate knowledge to those they manage in order to gain the desired level of performance. The question that remains to be answered is "What is knowledge, i.e., what information should one disseminate to control behavior?"

There are two types of knowledge according to Skinner (1969). *Private knowledge* (Polanyi, 1960; Bridgeman, 1959) is knowledge established through experience with the contingencies of reinforcement. Skinner says, "The world which establishes contingencies of reinforcement of the sort studied in an operant analysis is presumably 'what knowledge is about.' A person comes to know that world and how to behave in it in the sense that he acquires behavior which satisfies the contingencies it maintains" (1969, p. 156). The behavior which results from private knowledge is called *contingency-shaped* behavior. This is the knowledge which one must possess in order to perform correctly in order to get rewarded. This knowledge does not assume any awareness on the part of the person but is based entirely on the person's past reinforcement history. A person can "know how" to play golf, for example, as indicated by a series of low scores—yet it is an entirely different thing to be able to tell others how to play golf. A machine operator may be an excellent employee, but make a poor foreman. One reason may be that, while he possesses private knowledge about his job, he is unable to verbalize the contingencies to other people.

Public knowledge, then, is the ability to derive rules from the contingencies, in the form of injunctions or descriptions which specify occasions, responses, and consequences (Skinner, 1969, p. 160). The behavior which results from public knowledge is called *rule-governed* behavior.

The reason the possession of public knowledge is important to the manager is simple. The employee looks to the manager for information about what behavior is required, how to perform the desired behavior, and what the consequences of the desired behavior will be. Before a manager can give correct answers to these questions, he must understand the true contingencies himself, since his business is not in doing, but in telling others how to do. The point is to be able to analyze the contingencies of reinforcement found in the organization and "to formulate rules or laws which make it unnecessary to be exposed to them in order to behave appropriately" (Skinner, 1969, p. 166).

After living in a large city for a long time, a person is able to go from Point A to Point B with little trouble. The knowledge of how to get around in the city was shaped by the past history with the environment. This behavior is an example of contingency-shaped behavior. If a stranger arrives in the same city and desires to go from Point A to Point B he too will have little trouble. He will look at a map of the city, and follow the path specified by the map. This behavior is an example of rule-governed behavior. Whether or not a person will continue to follow the map (rule) in the future is dependent on the consequences of following the map in the past. If the rule specified the correct contingencies, he probably will continue to use the map, but if a person found the map to be in error, then he will probably look to other sources of information (e.g., asking someone with private knowledge). The same thing happens in industry. If a manager is correct in the specification of the rules, i.e., the new worker follows the rules and receives a reward, then the worker will probably follow the other rules specified by the manager. If the manager specifies incorrect rules, then the worker may look to his peers or to other sources for information (e.g., the union steward) and specification of rules which describe behavior that will be rewarded.

There are two kinds of rules the manager can specify to the employee. A command or *mand* is a rule that specifies behavior and consequences of the behavior, where the consequences are arranged by the person giving the command. The specified or implied consequences for failure to act are usually aversive in nature and the judgment of the correctness of the behavior is made by the person given the command. A foreman who tells the worker to be on time for work is giving the worker a command. The implied consequence is that if the employee fails to report on time, the foreman will take action.

Advice and warnings are called *tacts* and involve rules which specify the reinforcements contingent on prior stimulation from rules, or laws. They specify the same contingencies which would directly shape behavior (private knowledge). The specification of the tact speeds up the conditioning process. If a secretary tells her boss he should take an umbrella when he goes to lunch she is describing a tact. She has no control over the consequences (getting wet) of the behavior (not carrying the umbrella). Instead it is determined by the environment itself (weather). Skinner (1969 says:

> *Go west, young man* is an example of advice (tacting) when the behavior it specifies will be reinforced by certain consequences which do not result from action taken by the advisor. We tend to follow advice because previous behavior in response to similar verbal stimuli has been reinforced. Go west, young man is a command when some consequences of the specified action are arranged by the commander— say, the aversive consequences arranged by an official charged with relocating the inhabitants of a region. When maxims, rules, and laws are advice, the governed behavior is reinforced by consequences which might have shaped the same behavior directly in the absence of the maxims, rules, and laws. When they are commands, they are effective only because special reinforcements have been made contingent upon them (p. 148).

While a manager must possess public knowledge as well as private knowledge in order to accomplish his task of "getting things done through other people" in keeping with a plea for positive reinforcement and unbiased reward systems, tacting is the method of rule specification recommended. Skinner (1969) recommends that by specifying the contingencies in such a way that the consequences are positive in nature and failure to respond is met with the withholding of a reward rather than by aversive stimuli, "the 'mand' may be replaced by a 'tact' describing conditions under which specific behavior on the part of the listener will be reinforced (p. 158)." Instead of saying "Give me that report" say "I need the report." "The craftsman begins by ordering his apprentice to behave in a given way; but he may later achieve the same effect simply by describing the relation between what the apprentice does and the consequences" (Skinner, 1969, p. 158). Thus, the technique which managers use to direct the employee can make a lot of difference in the acceptance of the rule by the employee. A mand operates from an avoidance learning base while a tact operates from a positive reinforcement base. A tact is more impersonal and gives the employee freedom in that it does not "enjoin anyone to behave in a given way, it simply describes the contingencies under which certain kinds of behavior will have certain kinds of consequences" (Skinner, 1969, p. 158).

CONTROVERSIES SURROUNDING AN OPERANT APPROACH
TO MANAGEMENT

The reinforcement approach to the study and control of human behavior has met with resistance and criticism, primarily through a lack of understanding of its recommended uses and limitations. Goodman (1964) said, "Learning theory has two simple points to make and does so with talmudic ingenuity, variability, intricacy, and insistence. They are reinforcement and extinction. What has to be left out . . . is thought."

While the criticisms would be too numerous to mention here, an attempt will be made to examine three of the major controversies surrounding an operant approach to the management of people in organizational settings.

1 *The application of operant conditioning techniques ignores the individuality of man.* Ashby (1967) said "now the chief weakness of programmed instruction is that it rewards rote learning, and worse than that—it rewards only those responses which are in agreement with the programme." Proponents of an operant approach to contingency management recognize that a poorly designed program can lead to rigidity in behavior. This is one of the major reasons that they recommend a program of reinforcement, which best fits the group or individuals being supervised. It is untrue, however, that behaviorists ignore the individuality of man. Each man is unique based on his past reinforcement history. When personnel psychologists build sophisticated selection models to predict future performance, they are actually trying to identify those applicants who will perform well under the contingencies of that particular organization. That does not mean that a person rejected cannot be motivated, but only that the current reward system of that organization is better suited for another applicant.[5]

In other words, the problem a manager faces is not to design contingencies that will be liked by all men, "but a way of life which will be liked by those who live it" (Skinner, 1969, p. 41). As Hersey and Blanchard (1972) point out, "Positive reinforcement is anything that is rewarding to the individual being reinforced. Reinforcement, therefore, depends on the individual (p. 22)." What is reinforcing to one may not be reinforcing to someone else based on the person's past history of satiation, deprivation and conditioning operations. A manager can do two things to insure that the contingencies of reinforcement are designed to support the individuality of the worker. First, as noted earlier he can strive to hire the worker who desires the rewards offered by the firm; i.e., can the person be happy or satisfed with this firm? Secondly, if it seems that the contingencies are ineffective, the manager can change the contingencies by using a democratic process—letting the employees design their own reward structure within the limits set by the organization. "Democracy is an effort to solve the problem by letting the people design the contingencies under which they are to live or—to put it another way—by insisting that the designer himself live under the contingencies he designs" (Skinner, 1969, p. 43).

In summary, therefore, it can be concluded that in a voluntary society, where man has freedom to move from one organization to another, operant methods of control should not ignore the individuality of man. Instead man should seek work where his individuality can best be appreciated and industries should select employees who can best be motivated by the contingencies available to them. It should be noted, however, that through the unethical application of conditioning principles, some employers may exploit workers. The overall evidence would seem to indicate that this is not due to the weakness in behavioral theory, but due to the weakness of man himself.

2   *The application of operant conditioning techniques restricts freedom of choice.*

> Discussion of the moral implications of behavioral control almost always emphasizes the Machiavellian role of change agents and the self-protective maneuvers of controllers. . . . The tendency to exaggerate the powers of behavioral control by psychological methods alone, irrespective of willing cooperation by the client, and the failure to recognize the reciprocal nature of interpersonal control obscure both the ethical issues and the nature of the social influence processes (Bandura, 1969, p. 85).

Kelman (1965) noted that the primary criterion that one might apply in judging the ethical implications of social influence approaches is the degree to which they promote freedom of choice. If individualism is to be guaranteed, it must be tempered by a sense of social obligation by the individual and by the organization.

Bandura (1969) noted that a person is considered free insofar as he can partly influence future events by managing his own behavior. A person in a voluntary society can within limits exert some control over the variables that govern his own choices. Skinner (1969) noted that "Men are happy in an environment in which active, productive, and creative behavior is reinforced in effective ways" (p. 64). One method of effectively reinforcing behavior is by allowing the employee some determination in the design of the reinforcement contingencies. Another method is to design self-control reinforcement systems in which individuals regulate their own activities (Ferster, Nurenberger and Levitt, 1962; Harris, 1969).

While it cannot be denied that reinforcers which are "all too abundant and powerful" (Skinner, 1966) can restrict freedom of choice, it is not true that a behavioral or Skinnerian approach is against freedom of choice; the opposite is true. As Bandura noted, "Contrary to common belief, behavioral approaches not only support a humanistic morality, but because of their relative effectiveness in establishing self-determination these methods hold much greater promise than traditional procedures for enhancement of behavioral freedom and fulfillment of human capabilities" (p. 88).

3   *Operant theory, through its advocacy of an external reward system, ignores the fact that individuals can be motivated by the job itself.* Deci (1971, 1972) among others (Likert, 1967; Vroom and Deci, 1970) criticizes behaviorists for advocating a system of employee motivation that only utilizes externally mediated rewards, i.e., rewards such as money and praise administered by someone other than the employee himself. In so doing, according to Deci, management is attempting to control the employee's behavior so he will do what he is told. The limitations of this method of worker motivation, for Deci, is that it only satisfies man's "lower-order" needs (Maslow, 1943) and does not take into account man's "higher-order" needs for self-esteem and self-actualization. Deci states, "It follows that there are many important motivators of human behavior which are not under the direct control of managers and, therefore, cannot be contingently administered in a system of piece-rate payments" (1972, p. 218).

Deci recommends that we should move away from a method of external control, and toward a system where individuals can be motivated by the job itself. He says that this approach will allow managers to focus on higher-order needs where the rewards are mediated by the person himself (intrinsically motivated). To motivate employees intrinsically, tasks should be designed which are interesting, creative and resourceful, and workers should have some say in decisions which concern them "so they will feel like causal agents in the activities which they engage in" (Deci, 1972, p. 219). Deci concludes his argument against a contingency approach to management by saying:

> . . . It is possible to pay workers and still have them intrinsically motivated. Hence the writer favors the prescription that we concentrate on structuring situations and jobs to arouse intrinsic motivation, rather than trying to structure piece-rate and other contingency payment schemes. Workers would be intrinsically motivated and would seek to satisfy their higher-order needs through effective performance. The noncontingent payments (or salaries) would help to satisfy the workers and keep them on the job, especially if the pay were equitable (Adams, 1965; Pritchard, 1969) (1972, p. 227).

Deci levels criticism at a positive reinforcement contingency approach on the basis of four issues: (1) advocating that external rewards be administered by someone else, (2) ignoring the importance of the task environment, (3) ignoring the importance of internal rewards, and (4) advocating a contingent payment plan. Deci makes two errors, from a reinforcement theory point of view, when he advocates noncontingent equitable pay plans. First, equity theory (Adams, 1965) assumes that rewards are based on performance. If they weren't, then the pay would be equal, not equitable. Second, and more crucial, is Deci's assumption that a pay plan can be noncontingent. Bandura notes that "all behavior is inevitably controlled, and the operation of psychological laws cannot be suspended by romantic conceptions of human behavior, any more than indignant rejection of the law of gravity as antihumanistic can stop people from falling" (1969, p. 85). Homme and Tosti (1965) made the point that, "either one manages the contingencies or they get managed by accident. Either way there will be contingencies, and they will have their effect" (p. 16). In other words, if managers instituted a pay plan that was "noncontingent," they would in fact be rewarding poor performance and extinguishing good performance (see Rules 1, 2, and 6).

The assertion that a contingency approach advocates that the rewards always be administered by someone else is false. Skinner specifically (1969, p. 158) recommends that manding behavior be replaced by tacting methods for achieving the same effect. Skinner suggested that one safeguard against exploitation is to make sure that the design of the contingencies never controls. In addition to recommending that the contingencies be so designed that they are controlled by the environment (tacting), operant theories have advocated self-control processes in which individuals regulate their own behavior by arranging appropriate contingencies for themselves (Ferster, Nurenberger and Levitt, 1962). Bandura (1969) concluded that:

> The selection of well-defined objectives, both intermediate and ultimate, is an essential aspect of any self-directed program of change. The goals that individuals choose for themselves must be specified in sufficiently detailed behavioral terms to provide adequate guidance for the actions that must be taken daily to attain desired outcomes. . . . Individuals can, therefore, utilize objective records of behavioral changes as an additional source of reinforcement for their self-controlling behavior (p. 255).

Studies which have explored the effect of self-reinforcement on performance have shown that systems which allowed workers to keep a record of their own output to use as a continuous feedback system and for reinforcement purposes helped the workers to increase their performance (Kolb, Winter and Berlew, 1968; Fox, 1966). Michigan Bell Telephone Company and the Emery Air Freight Corporation are two of several firms which are currently using self-reinforcement programs in order to increase worker motivation and performance. Both programs have been immensely successful (see *Business Week*, December 18, 1971; and December 2, 1972).

It should be noted that even though the individual is determining his own reward in the self-feedback program, the reinforcers are both externally (money, recognition, praise) and internally (self-feedback) mediated. According to Skinner (1957) and Bem (1967) the self-report feedback is a "tract" or description of an internal feeling state. In both cases, the rewards must be contingent on performance for effective control of the behavior to take place.

Deci's recommendation that jobs should be designed so that they are interesting, creative, and resourceful is wholeheartedly supported by proponents of a positive reinforcement program. Skinner (1969) warns managers that too much dependency on force and a poorly designed monetary reward system may actually reduce performance, while designing the task so that it is automatically reinforcing can have positive effects on performance. Skinner says:

> The behavior of an employee is important to the employer, who gains when the employee works industriously and carefully. How is he to be induced to do so? The standard answer was once physical force: men worked to avoid punishment

or death. The by-products were troublesome, however, and economics is perhaps the first field in which an explicit change was made to positive reinforcement. Most men now work, as we say, 'for money.'

Money is not a natural reinforcer; it must be conditioned as such. Delayed reinforcement, as in a weekly wage, raises a special problem. No one works on Monday morning because he is reinforced by a paycheck on Friday afternoon. The employee who is paid by the week works during the week to avoid losing the standard of living which depends on a weekly system. Rate of work is determined by the supervisor (with or without the pacing stimuli of a production line), and special aversive contingencies maintain quality. The pattern is therefore still aversive. It has often been pointed out that the attitude of the production-line worker toward his work differs conspicuously from that of the craftsman, who is envied by workers and industrial managers alike. One explanation is that the craftsman is reinforced by more than monetary consequences, but another important difference is that when a craftsman spends a week completing a given set object, each of the parts produced during the week is likely to be automatically reinforcing because of its place in the completed object (p. 18).

Skinner (1969) also agrees with Deci that the piece-rate may actually reduce performance in that it is so powerful it is most often misused, and "it is generally opposed by those concerned with the welfare of the worker (and by workers themselves when, for example, they set daily quotas)'' (p. 19).

It appears therefore, that critics of operant conditioning methods misunderstand the recommendations of behaviorists in the area of worker motivation. Operant theory does advocate interesting job design and self-reinforcement feedback systems, where possible. It does not advocate force or try to control the employee's behavior by making the employee "do what he is told." It is not against humanistic morality; rather it advocates that workers be rewarded on their performance and not on their needs alone.

While other controversies about operant conditioning could be reviewed, the examination of these three issues should give the reader a flavor of the criticisms which surround the use of a contingency approach to behavioral control.

ETHICAL IMPLICATIONS FOR WORKER CONTROL

The deliberate use of positive and negative reinforcers often gives rise to ethical concern about harmful effects which may result from such practices. Poorly designed reward structures can interfere with the development of spontaneity and creativity. Reinforcement systems which are deceptive and manipulative are an insult to the integrity of man. The employee should be a willing party to the influence attempt, with both parties benefiting from the relationship.

The question of whether man should try to control human behavior is covered in a classic paper by Rogers and Skinner (1956). The central issue discussed was one of personal values. Rogers contends that "values" emerge from the individual's "freedom of choice," a realm unavailable to science. Skinner, in rebuttal, points out that the scientific view of man does not allow for such exceptions, and that choice and the resulting values are, like all behavior, a function of man's biology and his environment. Since biology and environment lie within the realm of science, "choice" and "value" must be accessible to scientific inquiry. Skinner and Rogers are both concerned with abuse of the power held by scientists, but Skinner is optimistic that good judgment will continue to prevail. Krasner (1964) agrees with Skinner that we should apply scientific means to control behavior, but warns that behavioral control can be horribly misused unless we are constantly alert to what is taking place in society.

Probably few managers deliberately misuse their power to control behavior. Managers should realize that the mismanagement of the contingencies of reinforcement is actually self-defeating. Workers will no longer allow themselves to be pushed around, but instead will insist that the work environment be designed in such a way that they have a chance at a better life. The effective use of a positive reinforcing program is one of the most critical challenges facing modern management.

The first step in the ethical use of behavioral control in organizations is the understanding by managers of the determinants of behavior. Since reinforcement is the single most important concept in the learning process, managers must learn how to design effective reinforcement programs that will encourage creative, productive, satisfied employees. This paper has attempted to outline the knowledge available for this endeavor.

NOTES

1   The author is indebted to Professor William E. Scott, Jr., Graduate School of Business, Indiana University for sharing with him his Skinnerian philosophy.

2   Classical conditioning is also known as respondent conditioning and Pavlovian conditioning.

3   Operant conditioning is also known as instrumental conditioning and Skinnerian conditioning.

4   Parentheses added.

5   This is true because the criterion variable is some measure of performance, and performance is directly tied to the reinforcement consequences for the current employees used to derive the selection model.

REFERENCES

Adam, E. E., and Scott, W. E., The application of behavioral conditioning procedures to the problems of quality control, *Academy of Management Journal*, 1971, **14**, 175–193.

Adams, J. S., Inequity in social exchange, in L. Berkowitz (ed.), *Advances in Experimental Psychology*, Academic Press, 1965, 157–189.

Aldis, O., Of pigeons and men, *Harvard Business Review*, 1961, **39**, 59–63.

Ayllon, T., and Azrin, N. H., The measurement and reinforcement of behavior of psychotics, *Journal of the Experimental Analysis of Behavior*, 1965, **8**, 357–383.

Ashby, Sir Eric, Can education be machine made?, *New Scientist*, February 2, 1967.

Baer, D. M., Peterson, R. F., and Sherman, J. A., The development of imitation by reinforcing behavioral similarity to a model, *Journal of the Experimental Analysis of Behavior*, 1967, **10**, 405–416.

Bandura, A., and Perloff, B., The efficacy of self-monitoring reinforcement systems, *Journal of Personality and Social Psychology*, 1967, **7**, 111–116.

Bandura, A., *Principles of Behavior Modification*, Holt, Rinehart and Winston, Inc., New York, 1969.

Bass, B. M., and Vaughan, J. A., *Training in Industry: The Management of Learning*, Wadsworth Publishing Company, Belmont, Calif., 1966.

Behling, O., Schriesheim, C., and Tolliver, J., Present theories and new directions in theories of work effort, *Journal Supplement Abstract Service* of the American Psychological Corporation, in press.

Bem, D. J., Self-perception: An alternative interpretation of cognitive dissonance phenomena, *Psychological Review*, 1967, **74**, 184–200.

Bridgeman, D. W., *The Way Things Are*, Harvard Press, Cambridge, Mass., 1959.

Costello, T. W., and Zalkind, S. S., *Psychology in Administration*, Prentice-Hall, Inc., Englewood Cliffs, N.J., 1963.

Deci, E. L., The effects of contingent and noncontingent rewards and controls on intrinsic motivation, *Organizational Behavior and Human Performance*, 1972, **8**, 217–229.

Deci, E. L., The effects of externally mediated rewards on intrinsic motivation, *Journal of Personality and Social Psychology*, 1971, **18**, 105–115.

Festinger, L., A theory of social comparison processes, *Human Relations*, 1954, **7**, 117–140.

Ferster, C. B., and Skinner, B. F., *Schedules of Reinforcement*, Appleton-Century-Crofts, New York, 1957.

Ferster, C. B., Nurenberger, J. I., and Levitt, E. B., The control of eating, *Journal of Mathematics*, 1962, **1**, 87–109.

Fox, L., The use of efficient study habits, In R. Ulrich, T. Stachnik, and J. Mabry (Eds.), *Control of Human Behavior*, Scott, Foresman, Glenview, Ill., 1966, 85–93.

Goffman, E., *The Presentation of Self in Everyday Life*, Doubleday, New York, 1959.

Goodman, Paul, *Compulsory Mis-education*, Horizon Press, New York, 1964.

Haire, Mason, *Psychology in Management*, 2nd ed., McGraw-Hill, New York, 1964.

Harris, M. B., A self-directed program for weight control: a pilot study, *Journal of Abnormal Psychology*, 1969, **74**, 263–270.

Henry, Jules, Review of human behavior: An inventory of scientific findings by Bernard Berelson and Gary A. Steiner, *Scientific American*, July, 1964.

Hersey, P., and Blanchard, K. H., The management of change: Part 2, *Training and Development Journal*, February, 1972, 20–24.

Hilgard, E. R., *Theories of Learning*, 2nd ed., Appleton-Century-Crofts, New York, 1956.

Homme, L. E., and Tosti, D. T., Contingency management and motivation, *Journal of the National Society for Programmed Instruction*, 1965, **4**, 14–16.

Jablonsky, S., and DeVries, D., Operant conditioning principles extrapolated to the theory of management, *Organizational Behavior and Human Performance*, 1972, **7**, 340–358.

Keller, F. S., *Learning: Reinforcement Theory*, Random House, New York, 1969.

Kelman, H. C., Manipulation of human behavior: An ethical dilemma for the social scientist, *Journal of Social Issues*, 1965, **21**, 31–46.

Kolb, D. A., Winter, S. K., and Berlew, D. E., Self-directed change: Two studies, *Journal of Applied Behavioral Science*, 1968, **4**, 453–471.

Krasner, L., Behavior control and social responsibility, *American Psychologist*, 1964, **17**, 199–204.

Likert, R., *New Patterns of Management*, McGraw-Hill, New York, 1961.

Lovaas, O. I., Berberich, J. P., Perloff, B. F., and Schaeffer, B., Acquisition of imitative speech for schizophrenic children, *Science*, 1966, **151**, 705–707.

Luthans, F., *Organizational Behavior*, McGraw-Hill, New York, 1973.

Maslow, A. H., A theory of human motivation, *Psychological Review*, 1943, **50**, 370–396.

McGregor, D., *The Human Side of Enterprise*, New York, McGraw-Hill, 1960.

Michael, J., and Meyerson, L., A behavioral approach to counseling and guidance, *Harvard Educational Review*, 1962, **32**, 382–402.

Morse, W. H., Intermittent reinforcement, in W. K. Honig (Ed.), *Operant Behavior*, Appleton-Century-Crofts, New York, 1966.

New tool: Reinforcement for good work, *Business Week*, December 18, 1971, 68–69.

Nord, W. R., Beyond the teaching machine: The neglected area of operant conditioning in the theory and practice of management, *Organizational Behavior and Human Performance*, 1969, 375–401.

Pavlov, I. P., *The Work of the Digestive Glands* (translated by W. H. Thompson), Charles Griffin, London, 1902.

Polanyi, M., *Personal Knowledge*, Univ. of Chicago Press, 1960.

Rachlin, H., *Modern Behaviorism*, W. H. Freeman and Co., New York, 1970.

Rogers, Carl R., and Skinner, B. F., Some issues concerning the control of human behavior: A symposium, *Science*, 1956, **124**, 1057–1066.

Scott, W. E., and Cummings, L. L., *Readings in Organizational Behavior and Human Performance*, Revised Edition, Irwin, Homewood, Ill., 1973.

Scott, W. E., and Hamner, W. Clay, The effects of order and variance in performance on supervisory ratings of workers, Paper presented at the *45th Annual Meeting*, Midwestern Psychological Association, Chicago, 1973.

Scott, W. E., and Hamner, W. Clay, The effect of order and variance in performance on the rewards given workers by supervisory personnel, mimeo, Indiana University, 1973.

Scott, W. E., Activation theory and task design, *Organizational Behavior and Human Performance*, 1966, **1**, 3–30.

Skinner, B. F., *The Behavior of Organisms*, New York: Appleton-Century, 1938.

Skinner, B. F., *Walden Two*, New York: The Macmillan Company, 1948.

Skinner, B. F., Are theories of learning necessary? *Psychological Review*, 1950, **57**, 193–216.

Skinner, B. F., *Science and Human Behavior*, New York: The Macmillan Company, 1953.

Skinner, B. F., Freedom and the control of men, *American Scholar*, 1956, **25**, 47–65.

Skinner, B. F., Some issues concerning the control of human behavior, *Science*, 1956, **124**, 1056–1066.

Skinner, B. F., *Verbal Behavior*, New York: Appleton-Century-Crofts, 1957.

Skinner, B. F., Behaviorism at fifty, *Science*, 1963a, **134**, 566–602.

Skinner, B. F., Operant behavior, *American Psychologist*, 1963b, **18**, 503–515.

Skinner, B. F., *Contingencies of Reinforcement*, Appleton-Century-Crofts, New York, 1969.
Skinner, B. F., *Beyond Freedom and Dignity*, Alfred A. Knopf, New York, 1971.
Thorndike, E. L., *Animal Intelligence*, Macmillan, New York, 1911.
Vroom, V. H., and Deci, E. L., An overview of work motivation. In V. H. Vroom and E. L. Deci (eds.), *Management and Motivation*, Penguin Press, Baltimore, 1970, 9–19.
Wiard, H., Why manage behavior? A case for positive reinforcement, *Human Resource Management*, Summer, 1972, 15–20.
Where Skinner's theories work, *Business Week*, December, 1972, 64–65.
Whyte, W. F., Skinnerian theory in organizations, *Psychology Today*, April, 1972, 67–68, 96, 98, 100.

Behavior Modification on the Bottom Line

W. Clay Hamner
Ellen P. Hamner

SETTING UP A POSITIVE REINFORCEMENT PROGRAM IN INDUSTRY

Many organizations are setting up formal motivational programs in an attempt to use the principles of positive reinforcement to increase employee productivity.

A positive reinforcement approach to management differs from traditional motivational theories in two basic ways. First, . . . a positive reinforcement program calls for the maximum use of reinforcement and the minimum use of punishment. Punishment tends to leave the individual feeling controlled and coerced. Second, a positive reinforcement program avoids psychological probing into the worker's attitudes as a possible cause of behavior. Instead, the work situation itself is analyzed, with the focus on the reward contingencies that cause a worker to act the way in which he does.

A positive reinforcement program, therefore, is results-oriented rather than process-oriented. Geary A. Rummler, president of Praxis Corporation, a management consultant firm, claims that the motivational theories of such behavioral scientists as Herzberg and Maslow, which stress workers' psychological needs, are impractical. "They can't be made operative. While they help classify a problem, a positive reinforcement program leads to solutions."

STAGES IN PROGRAM DEVELOPMENT

Positive reinforcement programs currently used in industry generally involve at least four stages. The *first stage*, according to Edward J. Feeney, formerly

Abridged and reprinted by permission of the publisher from *Organizational Dynamics*, Spring 1976, **4** (4), 8–21. © 1976 by AMACOM, a division of American Management Associations.

vice-president, systems, of Emery Air Freight Corporation, is to define the behavioral aspects of performance and do a performance audit. This step is potentially one of the most difficult, since some companies do not have a formal performance evaluation program, especially for nonmanagerial employees, and those that do have a program often rate the employee's behavior on nonjob-related measures (such as friendliness, loyalty, cooperation, overall attitude, and so on). But once these behavioral aspects are defined, the task of convincing managers that improvement is needed and of persuading them to cooperate with such a program is simplified. Feeney asserts, "Most managers genuinely think that operations in their bailiwick are doing well; a performance audit that proves they're not comes as a real and unpleasant surprise."

The *second stage* in developing a working positive reinforcement program is to develop and set specific goals for each worker. Failure to specify concrete behavioral goals is a major reason many programs do not work. Goals should be expressed in such terms as "decreased employee turnover" or "schedules met," rather than only in terms of "better identification with the company" or "increased job satisfaction." The goals set, therefore, should be in the same terms as those defined in the performance audit, goals that specifically relate to the task at hand. Goals should be reasonable—that is, set somewhere between "where you are" (as spelled out in the performnce audit) and some ideal.

While it is important for the manager to set goals, it is also important for the employee to accept them. An approach that tends to build in goal acceptance is to allow employees to work with management in setting work goals. According to John C. Emery, president of Emery Air Freight Corporation, the use of a participatory management technique to enlist the ideas of those performing the job not only results in their acceptance of goals, but also stimulates them to come up with goals.

The *third stage* in a positive reinforcement program is to allow the employee to keep a record of his or her own work. This process of self-feedback maintains a continuous schedule of reinforcement for the worker and helps him obtain intrinsic reinforcement from the task itself. Where employees can total their own results, they can see whether they are meeting their goals and whether they are improving over their previous performance level (as measured in the performance audit stage). In other words, the worker has two chances of being successful—either by beating his previous record or by beating both his previous record and his established goal. E. D. Grady, general manager-operator services for Michigan Bell, maintains that the manager should set up the work environment in such a way that people have a chance to succeed. One way to do this, he says, is to "shorten the success interval." Grady says, "If you're looking for success, keep shortening the interval of measurement so you can get a greater chance of success which you can latch on to for positive reinforcements." Instead of setting monthly or quarterly goals, for example, set weekly or daily goals.

The *fourth stage*—the most important step in a positive reinforcement program—is one that separates it from all other motivation plans. The supervisor looks at the self-feedback report of the employee and/or other indications of performance (sales records, for example) and then praises the positive aspects of the employee's performance (as determined by the performance audit and subsequent goal setting). This extrinsic reinforcement should strengthen the desired performance, while the withholding of praise for substandard performance should give the employee incentive to improve that performance level. Since the worker already knows the areas of his or her deficiencies, there is no reason for the supervisor to criticize the employee. In other words, negative feedback is self-induced, whereas positive feedback comes from both internal and external sources.

. . . This approach to feedback follows the teachings of B. F. Skinner, who believes that use of positive reinforcement leads to a greater feeling of self-control, while the avoidance of negative reinforcement keeps the individual from feeling controlled or coerced. Skinner says, "You can get the same effect if the supervisor simply discovers things being done right and says something like 'Good, I see you're doing it the way that works best.' "

While the feedback initially used in step four of the positive reinforcement program is praise, it is important to note that other forms of reinforcement can have the same effect. M. W. Warren, the director of organization and management development at the Questor Corporation, says that the five "reinforcers" he finds most effective are (1) money (but only when it is a consequence of a specific performance and when the relation to the performance is known); (2) praise or recognition; (3) freedom to choose one's own activity; (4) opportunity to see oneself become better, more important, or more useful; and (5) power to influence both co-workers and management. Warren states, "By building these reinforcers into programs at various facilities, Questor is getting results." The need for using more than praise after the positive reinforcement program has proved effective is discussed by Skinner.

> It does not cost the company anything to use praise rather than blame, but if the company then makes a great deal more money that way, the worker may seem to be getting gypped. However, the welfare of the worker depends on the welfare of the company, and if the company is smart enough to distribute some of the fruits of positive reinforcement in the form of higher wages and better fringe benefits, everybody gains from the supervisor's use of positive reinforcements (*Organizational Dynamics*, Winter, 1973, p. 35).

EARLY RESULTS OF POSITIVE REINFORCEMENT PROGRAMS IN ORGANIZATIONS, 1969–73

Companies that claimed to be implementing and using positive reinforcement programs such as the one described above include Emery Air Freight, Michigan Bell Telephone, Questor Corporation, Cole National Company in Cleveland, Ford Motor Company, American Can, Upjohn, United Air Lines, Warner-Lambert, Addressograph-Multigraph, Allis-Chalmers, Bethlehem Steel, Chase Manhattan Bank, IBM, IT&T, Proctor and Gamble, PPG Industries, Standard

Oil of Ohio, Westinghouse, and Wheeling-Pittsburgh Steel Corporation (see *Business Week*, December 18, 1971, and December 2, 1972). Because such programs are relatively new in industrial settings (most have begun since 1968), few statements of their relative effectiveness have been reported. In the Winter 1973 issue of *Organizational Dynamics* (p. 49), it was stated that "there's little objective evidence available, and what evidence there is abound in caveats— the technique will work under the proper circumstances, the parameters of which are usually not easily apparent."

In the area of employee training, Northern Systems Company, General Electric Corporation, and Emery Air Freight claim that positive reinforcement has improved the speed and efficiency of their training program. In their pro- grammed learning program, the Northern Systems Company structures the feedback system in such a way that the trainee receives positive feedback only when he demonstrates correct performance at the tool station. The absence of feedback is experienced by the trainee when he fails to perform correctly. Therefore, through positive reinforcements, he quickly perceives that correct behaviors obtain for him the satisfaction of his needs, and that incorrect be- haviors do not. Emery has designed a similar program for sales trainees. *Busi- ness Week* reported the success of the program by saying:

> It is a carefully engineered, step-by-step program, with frequent feedback questions and answers to let the salesman know how he is doing. The course contrasts with movies and lectures in which, Feeney says, the salesman is unable to gauge what he has learned. The aim is to get the customer on each sales call to take some kind of action indicating that he will use Emery services. Significantly, in 1968, the first full year after the new course was launched, sales jumped from $62.4 million to $79.8 million, a gain of 27.8 percent compared with an 11.3 percent rise the year before.

Since 1969, Emery has instituted a positive reinforcement program for all of its employees and credits the program with direct savings to the company of over $3 million in the first three years and indirectly with pushing 1973 sales over the $160 million mark. While Emery Air Freight is and remains the biggest success story for a positive reinforcement program to date, other companies also claim improvements as a result of initiating similar programs. At Michigan Bell's Detroit office, 2,000 employees in 1973 participated in a positive rein- forcement program. Michigan Bell credits the program with reducing absen- teeism from 11 percent to 6.5 percent in one group, from 7.5 percent to 4.5 percent in another group, and from 3.3 percent to 2.6 percent for all employees. In addition, the program has resulted in the correct completion of reports on time 90 percent of the time as compared with 20 percent of the time before the program's implementation. The Wheeling-Pittsburgh Steel Corporation credits its feedback program with saving $200,000 a month in scrap costs.

In an attempt to reduce the number of employees who constantly violated plant rules, General Motors implemented a plan in one plant that gave employees opportunities to improve or clear their records by going through varying periods of time without committing further shop violations. They credit this positive reinforcement plan with reducing the number of punitive actions for shop-rule infractions by two-thirds from 1969 to 1972 and the number of production-standard grievances by 70 percent during the same period.

While there was a great deal of interest in applying behavior modification in industrial settings after the successes of Emery Air Freight and others who followed suit were made known in 1971, the critics of this approach to worker motivation predicted that it would be short-lived. Any success would owe more to a "Hawthorne Effect" (the positive consequences of paying special attention to employees) than to any real long-term increase in productivity and/or worker satisfaction. The critics pointed out—quite legitimately, we might add—that most of the claims were testimonial in nature and that the length of experience between 1969–73 was too short to allow enough data to accumulate to determine the true successes of positive reinforcement in improving morale and productivity. With this in mind, we surveyed ten organizations, all of which currently use a behavior modification approach, to see if the "fad" created by Emery Air Freight had died or had persisted and extended its gains.

Specifically, we were interested in knowing (1) how many employees were covered; (2) the kinds of employees covered; (3) specific goals (stages 1 & 2); (4) frequency of self-feedback (stage 3); (5) the kinds of reinforcers used (stage 4); and (6) results of the program. A summary of companies surveyed and the information gained is shown in Figure 1.

CURRENT RESULTS OF POSITIVE REINFORCEMENT PROGRAMS IN ORGANIZATIONS

The ten organizations surveyed included Emery Air Freight, Michigan Bell-Operator Services, Michigan Bell-Maintenance Services, Connecticut General Life Insurance Company, General Electric, Standard Oil of Ohio, Weyerhaeuser, City of Detroit, B. F. Goodrich Chemical Company, and ACDC Electronics. In our interviews with each of the managers, we tried to determine both the successes and the failures they attributed to the use of behavior modification or positive reinforcement techniques. We were also interested in whether the managers saw this as a fad or as a legitimate management technique for improving the productivity and quality of work life among employees.

Emery Air Freight

Figure 1 shows Emery Air Freight still using positive reinforcement as a motivational tool. John C. Emery commented: "Positive reinforcement, always linked to feedback systems, plays a central role in performance improvement at Emery Air Freight. *All* managers and supervisors are being trained via self-instructional, programmed instruction texts—one on reinforcement and one on feedback. No formal off-the-job training is needed. Once he has studied the

Figure 1 Results of positive reinforcement and similar behavior modification programs in organizations in 1976.

Organization & person surveyed	Length of program	Number of employees covered/total employees	Type of employees	Specific goals	Frequency of feedback	Reinforcers used	Results
Emery Air Freight John C. Emery, Jr., President Paul F. Hammond, Manager—Systems Performance	1969– 1976	500/2,800	Entire workforce	(a) Increase productivity (b) Improve quality of service	Immediate to monthly, depending on task	Previously only praise and recognition; others now being introduced	Cost savings can be directly attributed to the program
Michigan Bell— Operator Services E. D. Grady, General Manager— Operator Services	1972– 1976	2,000/5,500	Employees at all levels in operator services	(a) Decrease turnover & absenteeism (b) Increase productivity (c) Improve union-management relations	(a) Lower level— weekly & daily (b) Higher level— monthly & quarterly	(a) Praise & recognition (b) Opportunity to see oneself become better	(a) Attendance performance has improved by 50% (b) Productivity and efficiency has continued to be above standard in areas where positive reinforcement (PR) is used
Michigan Bell— Maintenance Services Donald E. Burwell. Division Superintendent Maintenance & Services Dr. W. Clay Hamner, Consultant	1974– 1976	220/5,500	Maintenance workers, mechanics, & first & second-level supervisors	Improve (a) productivity (b) quality (c) safety (d) customer-employee relations	Daily, weekly, and quarterly	(a) Self-feedback (b) Supervisory feedback	(a) Cost efficiency increase (b) Safety improved (c) Service improved (d) No change in absenteeism (e) Satisfaction with superior & coworkers improved (f) Satisfaction with pay decreased

Figure 1 Results of positive reinforcement and similar behavior modification programs in organizations in 1976. (Continued)

Organization	Years	Number	Target population	Objectives	Timing	Reinforcers	Results
Connecticut General Life Insurance Co. Donald D. Illig, Director of Personnel Administration	1941–1976	3,000/13,500	Clerical employees & first-line supervisors	(a) Decrease absenteeism (b) Decrease lateness	Immediate	(a) Self-feedback (b) System-feedback (c) Earned time off	(a) Chronic absenteeism & lateness has been drastically reduced (b) Some divisions refuse to use PR because it is "outdated"
General Electric[1] Melvin Sorcher, Ph.D., formerly Director of Personnel Research Now Director of Management Development, Richardson-Merrell, Inc.	1973–1976	1,000	Employees at all levels	(a) Meet EEO objectives (b) Decrease absenteeism & turnover (c) Improve training (d) Increase productivity	Immediate—uses modeling & role playing as training tools to teach interpersonal exchanges & behavior requirements	Social reinforcers (praise, rewards, & constructive feedback)	(a) Cost savings can be directly attributed to the program (b) Productivity has increased (c) Worked extremely well in training minority groups and raising their self-esteem (d) Direct labor cost decreased
Standard Oil of Ohio T. E. Standings, Ph.D., Manager of Psychological Services	1974	28	Supervisors	Increase supervisor competence	Weekly over 5 weeks (25-hour) training period	Feedback	(a) Improved supervisory ability to give feedback judiciously (b) Discontinued because of lack of overall success

1. Similar programs are now being implemented at Richardson-Merrell under the direction of Dr. Sorcher and at AT&T under the direction of Douglas W. Bray, Ph.D., director of management selection and development, along with several other smaller organizations (see A. P. Goldstein, Ph.D. & Melvin Sorcher, Ph.D. *Changing Supervisor Behavior*, Pergamon Press. 1974).

Figure 1 Results of positive reinforcement and similar behavior modification programs in organizations in 1976. (Continued)

Organization & person surveyed	Length of program	Number of employees covered/total employees	Type of employees	Specific goals	Frequency of feedback	Reinforcers used	Results
Weyerhaeuser Company Gary P. Latham, Ph.D., Manager of Human Resource Research	1974– 1976	500/40,000	Clerical production (tree planters) & middle-level management & scientists	(a) To teach managers to minimize criticism & to maximize praise (b) To teach managers to make rewards contingent on specified performance levels (c) To use optimal schedule to increase productivity	Immediate—daily & quarterly	(a) Pay (b) Praise & recognition	(a) Using money, obtained 33% increase in productivity with one group of workers, and 18% increase with a second group, and an 8% decrease in a third group (b) Currently experimenting with goal setting & praise and/or money at various levels in organization (c) With a lottery-type bonus, the cultural & religious values of workers must be taken into account
City of Detroit Garbage Collectors[2]	1973– 1975	1,122/1,930	Garbage collectors	(a) Reduction in paid man-hour per ton (b) Reduction on overtime (c) 90% of routes completed	Daily & quarterly based on formula negotiated by city & sanitation union	Bonus (profit sharing) & praise	(a) Citizen complaints declined significantly (b) City saved $1,654,000 first year after bonus paid (c) Worker bonus =

Organization	Years	No./Total	Level covered	Objectives	Feedback	Rewards	Results
B. F. Goodrich Chemical Co. Donald J. Barnicki, Production Manager	1972–1976	100/420	Manufacturing employees at all levels	(a) Better meeting of schedules (b) Increase productivity ... by standard (d) Effectiveness (quality)	Weekly	Praise & recognition; freedom to choose one's own activity	Production has increased over 300% ... $307,000 first year or $350 annually per man (d) Union somewhat dissatisfied with productivity measure and is pushing for more bonus to employee (e) 1975 results not yet available
ACDC Electronics Division of Emerson Electronics Edward J. Feeney, Consultant	1974–1976	350/350	All levels	(a) 96% attendance (b) 90% engineering specifications met (c) Daily production objectives met 95% of time (d) Cost reduced by 10%	Daily & weekly feedback from foreman to company president	Positive feedback	(a) Profit up 25% over forecast (b) $550,000 cost reduction on $10M sales (c) Return of 1900% on investment including consultant fees (d) Turnaround time on repairs went from 30 to 10 days (e) Attendance is now 98.2% (from 93.5%)

2. From *Improving Municipal Productivity: The Detroit Refuse Incentive Plan.* The National Commission on Productivity, April 1974.

texts, the supervisor is encouraged immediately to apply the learning to the performance area for which he is responsible.''

Paul F. Hammond, Emery's manager of system performance and the person currently in charge of the positive reinforcement program, said that there are a considerable number of company areas in which quantifiable success has been attained over the last six or seven years. Apart from the well-publicized container savings illustration (results of which stood at $600,000 gross savings in 1970 and over $2,000,000 in 1975), several other recent success stories were noted by Emery and Hammond. They include:

- Standards for customer service on the telephone had been set up and service was running 60 to 70 percent of standard. A program very heavily involved with feedback and reinforcement was introduced a few years ago and increased performance to 90 percent of objectives within three months—a level that has been maintained ever since.
- Several offices have installed a program in which specified planned reinforcements are provided when targeted levels of shipment volume are requested by Emery customers. All offices have increased revenue substantially; one office doubled the number of export shipments handled, and another averages an additional $60,000 of revenue per month.
- A program of measuring dimensions of certain lightweight shipments to rate them by volume rather than weight uses reinforcement and feedback extensively. All measures have increased dramatically since its inception five years ago, not the least of which is an increase in revenue from $400,000 per year to well over $2,000,000 per year.

While this latest information indicates that positive reinforcement is more than a fad at Emery Air Freight, Emery pointed out that a major flaw in the program had to be overcome. He said, ''Inasmuch as praise is the most readily available no-cost reinforcer, it tends to be the reinforcer used most frequently. However, the result has been to *dull* its effect as a reinforcer through its sheer repetition, even to risk making praise an *irritant* to the receiver.'' To counter this potential difficulty, Emery managers and supervisors have been taught and encouraged to expand their reinforcers beyond praise. Among the recommended reinforcers have been formal recognition such as a public letter or a letter home, being given a more enjoyable task after completing a less enjoyable one, invitations to business luncheons or meetings, delegating responsibility and decision making, and tying such requests as special time off or any other deviation from normal procedure to performance. Thus it seems that Skinner's prediction made in 1973 about the need for using more than praise after the reinforcement program has been around for a while has been vindicated at Emery Air Freight.

Michigan Bell-Operator Service

The operator services division is still actively using positive reinforcement feedback as a motivational tool. E. D. Grady, general manager for Operator

Services said, "We have found through experience that when standards and feedback are not provided, workers generally feel their performance is at about the 95 percent level. When the performance is then compared with clearly-defined standards, it is usually found to meet only the 50th percentile in performance. It has been our experience, over the past ten years, that when standards are set and feedback provided in a positive manner, performance will reach very high levels—perhaps in the upper 90th percentile in a very short period of time. . . . We have also found that when positive reinforcement is discontinued, performance returns to levels that existed prior to the establishment of feedback." Grady said that while he was not able at this time to put a specific dollar appraisal on the cost savings from using a positive reinforcement program, the savings were continuing to increase and the program was being expanded.

In one recent experiment, Michigan Bell found that when goal setting and positive reinforcement were used in a low-productivity inner-city operator group, service promptness (time to answer call) went from 94 percent to 99 percent of standard, average work time per call (time taken to give information) decreased from 60 units of work time to 43 units of work time, the percentage of work time completed within ideal limits went from 50 percent to 93 percent of ideal time (standard was 80 percent of ideal), and the percentage of time operators made proper use of references went from 80 percent to 94 percent. This led to an overall productivity index score for these operators that was significantly higher than that found in the control group where positive reinforcement was not being used, even though the control group of operators had previously (six months earlier) been one of the highest producing units.

Michigan Bell-Maintenance Services

Donald E. Burwell, Division Superintendent of Maintenance and Services at Michigan Bell, established a goal-setting and positive reinforcement program in early 1974. He said, "After assignment to my present area of responsibility in January, I found that my new department of 220 employees (maintenance, mechanics, and janitorial services), including managers, possessed generally good morale. However, I soon became aware that 1973 performances were generally lower than the 1973 objectives. In some cases objectives were either ambiguous or nonexistent."

With the help of a consultant, Burwell overcame the problem by establishing a four-step positive reinforcement program similar to the one described earlier in this article. As a result, the 1974 year-end results showed significant improvements over the 1973 base-year average in all areas, including safety (from 75.6 to 89.0), service (from 76.4 to 83.0), cost performance/hour (from 27.9 to 21.2, indexed), attendance (from 4.7 to 4.0) and worker satisfaction and cooperation (3.01 to 3.51 on a scale of 5), and worker satisfaction with the supervisors (2.88 to 3.70, also on a scale of 5); 1975 figures reflect continuing success.

While Burwell is extremely pleased with the results of this program to date, he adds a word of caution to other managers thinking of implementing such a program: "I would advise against accepting any one method, including positive reinforcement, as a panacea for all the negative performance trends that confront managers. On the other hand, positive reinforcement has aided substantially in performance improvement for marketing, production, and service operators. Nevertheless, the manager needs to know when the positive effects of the reinforcement program have begun to plateau and what steps he should consider taking to maintain his positive performance trends."

Connecticut General Life Insurance Company

The Director of Personnel Administration at Connecticut General Life Insurance Company, Donald D. Illig, stated that Connecticut General has been using positive reinforcement in the form of an attendance bonus system for 25 years with over 3,200 clerical employees. Employees receive one extra day off for each ten weeks of perfect attendance. The results have been outstanding. Chronic absenteeism and lateness have been drastically reduced, and the employees are very happy with the system. Illig noted, however, that, "Our property and casualty company, with less than half the number of clerical employees countrywide, has not had an attendance-bonus system . . . and wants no part of it. At the crux of the problem is an anti-Skinnerian feeling, which looks at positive reinforcement—and thus an attendance-bonus system— as being overly manipulative and old-fashioned in light of current theories of motivation."

General Electric

A unique program of behavior modification has been introduced quite successfully at General Electric as well as several other organizations by Melvin Sorcher, formerly director of personnel research at G.E. The behavior modification program used at G.E. involves using positive reinforcement and feedback in training employees. While the first program centered primarily on teaching male supervisors how to interact and communicate with minority and female employees and on teaching minority and female employees how to become successful by improving their self-images, subsequent programs focused on the relationship between supervisors and employees in general. By using a reinforcement technique known as behavior modeling, Sorcher goes beyond the traditional positive reinforcement ("PR") program. The employee is shown a videotape of a model (someone with his own characteristics—that is, male or female, black or white, subordinate or superior) who is performing in a correct or desired manner. Then, through the process of role playing, the employee is encouraged to act in the successful or desired manner shown on the film (that is, he is asked to model the behavior). Positive reinforcement is given when the goal of successful display of this behavior is made in the role-playing session.

Sorcher notes that this method has been successfully used with over 1,000 G.E. supervisors. As a result, productivity has increased, the self-esteem of hard-core employees has increased, and EEO objectives are being met. He says, "The positive results have been the gratifying changes or improvements that have occurred, especially improvements that increase over time as opposed to the usual erosion of effort after most training programs have passed their peak. . . . On the negative side, some people and organizations are calling their training 'behavior modeling' when it does not fit the criteria originally defined for such a program. For example, some programs not only neglect self-esteem as a component, but show little evidence of how to shape new behaviors. . . . Regarding the more general area of behavior modification and positive reinforcement, there is still a need for better research. There's not a lot taking place at present, which is unfortunate because on the surface these processes seem to have a lot of validity."

Standard Oil of Ohio

T. E. Standings, manager of psychological services at SOHIO, tried a training program similar to the one used by Sorcher at General Electric. After 28 supervisors had completed five weeks of training, Standings disbanded the program even though there were some short-term successes. He said, "My feelings at this point are that reinforcement cannot be taught at a conceptual level in a brief period of time. (Of course, the same comments can no doubt be made about Theory Y, MBO, and TA.) I see two alternatives: (1) Identify common problem situations, structure an appropriate reinforcement response for the supervisor, and teach the response through the behavioral model, or (2) alter reinforcement contingencies affecting defined behaviors through direct alternatives in procedural and/or informational systems without going through the supervisor directly."

Weyerhaeuser Company

Whereas Emery Air Freight has the longest history with applied reinforcement theory, Weyerhaeuser probably has the most experience with controlled experiments using goal setting and PR techniques. The human Resource Research Center at Weyerhaeuser, under the direction of G. P. Latham, is actively seeking ways to improve the productivity of all levels of employees using the goal-setting, PR feedback technique.

According to Dr. Latham, "The purpose of our positive reinforcement program is threefold: (1) To teach managers to embrace the philosophy that 'the glass is half-full rather than half-empty.' In other words, our objective is to teach managers to minimize criticism (which is often self-defeating since it can fixate the employee's attention on ineffective job behavior and thus reinforce it) and to maximize praise and hence fixate both their and the employee's attention on effective job behavior. (2) To teach managers that praise by itself may increase job satisfaction, but that it will have little or no effect on productivity unless it is made contingent upon specified job behaviors. Telling an employee that he is doing a good job in no way conveys to him what he is doing correctly. Such blanket praise can inadvertently reinforce the very things that the employee is doing in a mediocre way. (3) To teach managers to determine the optimum schedule for administering a reinforcer—be it praise, a smile, or money in the employee's pocket.''

Weyerhaeuser has found that by using money as a reinforcer (that is, as a bonus over and above the worker's hourly rate), they obtained a 33 percent increase in productivity with one group of workers, an 18 percent increase in productivity with a second group of workers, and an 8 percent decrease in productivity with a third group of workers. Latham says, ''These findings point out the need to measure and document the effectiveness of any human resource program. The results obtained in one industrial setting cannot necessarily be expected in another setting.''

Latham notes that because of its current success with PR, Weyerhaeuser is currently applying reinforcement principles with tree planters in the rural South as well as with engineers and scientists at their corporate headquarters. In the latter case, they are comparing different forms of goal setting (assigned, participative, and a generalized goal of ''do your best'') with three different forms of reinforcement (praise or private recognition from a supervisor, public recognition in terms of a citation for excellence, and a monetary reward). Latham adds, ''The purpose of the program is to motivate scientists to attain excellence. Excellence is defined in terms of the frequency with which an individual displays specific behaviors that have been identified by the engineers/ scientists themselves as making the difference between success and failure in fulfilling the requirements of their job.''

City of Detroit, Garbage Collectors

In December, 1972, the City of Detroit instituted a unique productivity bonus system for sanitation workers engaged in refuse collection. The plan, which provides for sharing the savings for productivity improvements efforts, was designed to save money for the city while rewarding workers for increased efficiency. The city's Labor Relations Bureau negotiated the productivity contract with the two unions concerned with refuse collection: The American Federation of State, County and Municipal Employees (AFSCME), representing sanitation laborers (loaders), and the Teamsters Union, representing drivers. The two agreements took effect on July 1, 1973.

The bonus system was based on savings gained in productivity (reductions in paid man-hours per ton of refuse collected, reduction in the total hours of overtime, percentage of routes completed on schedule, and effectiveness or cleanliness). A bonus pool was established and the sanitation laborers share 50-50 in the pool with the city—each worker's portion being determined by the number of hours worked under the productivity bonus pool, exclusive of overtime.

By any measure, this program was a success. Citizen complaints decreased dramatically. During 1974, the city saved $1,654,000 after the bonus of $307,000 ($350 per man) was paid. The bonus system is still in effect, but the unions are currently disputing with the city the question of what constitutes a fair day's work. Both unions involved have expressed doubts about the accuracy of the data used to compute the productivity index or, to be more precise, how the data are gathered and the index and bonus computed. Given this expected prenegotiation tactic by the unions, the city and the customers both agree that the plan has worked.

B. F. Goodrich Chemical Company

In 1972, one of the production sections in the B.F. Goodrich Chemical plant in Avon Lake, Ohio, as measured by standard accounting procedures, was failing. At that time, Donald J. Barnicki, the production manager, introduced a positive reinforcement program that included goal setting and feedback about scheduling, targets, costs, and problem areas. This program gave the information directly to the foreman on a once-a-week basis. In addition, daily meetings were held to discuss problems and describe how each group was doing. For the first time the foreman and their employees were told about costs that were incurred by their group. Charts were published that showed area achievements in terms of sales, cost, and productivity as compared with targets. Films were made that showed top management what the employees were doing, and these films were shown to the workers so they would know what management was being told.

According to Barnicki, this program of positive reinforcement turned the plant around. "Our productivity has increased 300 percent over the past five years. Costs are down. We had our best startup time in 1976 and passed our daily production level from last year the second day after we returned from the holidays."

ACDC Electronics

Edward J. Feeney, of Emery Air Freight fame, now heads a consulting firm that works with such firms as General Electric, Xerox, Braniff Airways, and General Atomic in the area of positive reinforcement programs. One of Mr. Feeney's current clients is the ACDC Electronics Company (a division of Emerson Electronics). After establishing a program that incorporated the four-step approach outlined earlier in this article, the ACDC Company experienced a profit increase of 25 percent over the forecast; a $550,000 cost reduction on $10 million in sales; a return of 1,900 percent on investment, including consultant fees; a reduction in turnaround time on repairs from 30 to 10 days; and a significant increase in attendance.

According to Ken Kilpatrick, ACDC President, "The results were as dramatic as those that Feeney had described. We found out output increased 30–40 percent almost immediately and has stayed at that high level for well over a year." The results were not accomplished, however, without initial problems, according to Feeney. "With some managers there were problems of inertia, disbelief, lack of time to implement, interest, difficulty in defining output for hard-to-measure areas, setting standards, measuring past performance, estimating economic payoffs, and failure to apply all feedback or reinforcement principles." Nevertheless, after positive results began to surface and initial problems were overcome, the ACDC management became enthused about the program.

CONCLUSION

This article has attempted to explain how reinforcement theory can be applied in organizational settings. We have argued that the arrangement of the contingencies of reinforcement is crucial in influencing behavior. Different ways of arranging these contingencies were explained, followed by a recommendation that the use of positive reinforcement combined with oral explanations of incorrect behaviors, when applied correctly, is an underestimated and powerful tool of management. The correct application includes three conditions. *First*, reinforcers must be selected that are sufficiently powerful and durable to establish and strengthen behavior; *second*, the manager must design the contingencies in such a way that the reinforcing events are made contingent on the desired level of performance; *third*, the program must be designed in such a way that it is possible to establish a reliable training procedure for inducing the desired response patterns.

To meet these three conditions for effective contingency management, many firms have set up a formal positive reinforcement motivational program. These include firms such as Emery Air Freight, Michigan Bell, Standard Oil of Ohio, General Electric, and B. F. Goodrich, among others. Typically, these firms employ a four-stage approach in designing their programs: (1) A performance audit is conducted in order to determine what performance patterns are desired and to measure the current levels of that performance; (2) specific and reasonable goals are set for each worker; (3) each employee is generally instructed to keep a record of his or her own work; and (4) positive aspects of the employee's performance are positively reinforced by the supervisor. Under this four-stage program, the employee has two chances of being successful— he can beat his previous level of performance or he can beat that plus his own goal. Also under this system, negative feedback routinely comes only from the employee (since he knows when he failed to meet the objective), whereas positive feedback comes from both the employee and his supervisor.

While we noted that many firms have credited this approach with improving morale and increasing profits, several points of concern and potential shortcomings of this approach should also be cited. Many people claim that you cannot teach reinforcement principles to lower-level managers very easily and unless you get managers to understand the principles, you certainly risk misusing these tools. Poorly designed reward systems can interfere with the development of spontaneity and creativity. Reinforcement systems that are deceptive and manipulative are an insult to employees.

One way in which a positive reinforcement program based solely on praise can be deceptive and manipulative occurs when productivity continues to increase month after month and year after year, and the company's profits increase as well, but employee salaries do not reflect their contributions. This seems obviously unethical and contradictory. It is unethical because the workers are being exploited and praise by itself will not have any long-term effect on performance. Emery Air Freight, for example, has begun to experience this backlash effect. It is contradictory because the manager is saying he believes in the principle of making intangible rewards contingent on performance but at the same time refuses to make the tangible monetary reward contingent on performance. Often the excuse given is that "our employees are unionized." Well, this is not always the case. Many firms that are without unions, such as Emery, refuse to pay on performance. Many other firms with unions have a contingent bonus plan. Skinner in 1969 warned managers that a poorly designed monetary reward system may actually reduce performance. The employee should be a willing party to the influence attempt, with both parties benefitting from the relationship.

Peter Drucker's concern is different. He worries that perhaps positive reinforcers may be misused by management to the detriment of the economy. He says, "The carrot of material rewards has not, like the stick of fear, lost its potency. On the contrary, it has become so potent that it threatens to destroy the earth's finite resources if it does not first destroy more economies through inflation that reflects rising expectations." In other words, positive reinforcement can be too effective as used by firms concerned solely with their own personal gains.

Skinner in an interview in *Organizational Dynamics* stated that a feedback system alone may not be enough. He recommended that the organization should design feedback and incentive systems in such a way that the dual objective of getting things done and making work enjoyable is met. He says what must be accomplished, and what he believes is currently lacking, is an effective training program for managers. "In the not-too-distant future, however, a new breed of industrial managers may be able to apply the principles of operant conditioning effectively."

We have evidence in at least a few organizational settings that Skinner's hopes are on the way to realization, that a new breed of industrial managers are indeed applying the principles of operant conditioning effectively.

SELECTED BIBLIOGRAPHY

For an understandable view of Skinner's basic ideas in his own words, see B. F. Skinner's *Contingencies of Reinforcement* (Appleton-Century-Crofts, 1969) and Carl R. Rogers and B. F. Skinner's "Some Issues Concerning the Control of Human Behavior" (*Science*, 1965, Vol. 24, pp. 1057–1066). For Skinner's views on the applications of his ideas in industry see "An Interview with B. F. Skinner" (*Organizational Dynamics*, Winter 1973, pp. 31–40).

For an account of Skinner's ideas in action, see the same issue of *Organizational Dynamics* (pp. 41–50) and "Where Skinner's Theories Work" (*Business Week*, December 2, 1972, pp. 64–69).

An article highly critical of the application of Skinner's ideas in industry is W. F. Whyte's "Pigeons, Persons, and Piece Rates" (*Psychology Today*, April 1972, pp. 67–68). For a more sympathetic and more systematic treatment see W. R. Nord's "Beyond the Teaching Machine: The Negative Area of Operant Conditioning" in *The Theory and Practice of Management, Organizational Behavior and Human Performance* (1969, No. 4, pp. 375–401).

For comments on behavior modification by the author, see W. Clay Hamner's "Reinforcement Theory and Contingency Management" in L. Tosi and W. Clay Hamner, eds., *Organizational Behavior and Management: A Contingency Approach* (St. Clair Press, 1974, pp. 188–204) and W. Clay Hamner's "Worker Motivation Programs: Importance of Climate Structure and Performance Consequences" in this chapter.

Last, the best discussion of the general subject of pay and performance is Edward E. Lawler III's *Pay and Organizational Effectiveness* (McGraw-Hill, 1971).

The Myths of Behavior Mod in Organizations[1]

Edwin A. Locke

Behavior modification, the application of behavioristic conditioning principles to practical problems, has proliferated in the last decade. While the earliest applications were to such fields as education, clinical psychology (psychotherapy), and behavior management in institutions (e.g., mental hospitals, homes for delinquents), recent attempts have been made to apply these ideas to management of employees in work organizations (13, 16, 28, 29, 30, 43, 52). One article claims: "The long range potential for behavior modification seems limitless" (31, p. 46).

Behaviorism asserts that human behavior can be understood without reference to states or actions of consciousness (54, 55). Its basic premises are:

1   Determinism: With respect to their choices, beliefs, and actions individuals are ruled by forces beyond their control (according to behaviorism, these forces are environmental). Individuals are totally devoid of volition.

2   Epiphenomenalism: People's minds have no causal efficacy; their thoughts are mere by-products of environmental conditioning and affect neither their other thoughts nor their observable actions.

Reprinted from *Academy of Management Review*, 1977, **2**, 543–553, Reprinted by permission.

[1]A shorter version of this paper was delivered at the Academy of Management meetings, New Orleans, August, 1975. The author is indebted to Professor Harry Binswanger of Hunter College for his helpful comments and suggestions.

3   Rejection of introspection as a scientific method. It is unscientific, and its results (the identification of people's mental contents and processes) are irrelevant to understanding their actions (23).

The major theoretical concept in Skinner's (54) version of behaviorism, the one most often applied to industry, is that of reinforcement. Behavior, Skinner argues, is controlled by its consequences. A reinforcer is some consequence which follows a response and makes similar responses more likely in the future. To change the probability of a given response, one merely modifies either the contingency between the response and the reinforcer or the reinforcer itself. The concept of reinforcement is, by design, devoid of any theoretical base, e.g., the experiences of pleasure and pain. The term is defined by its effects on behavior and only by these effects. Reinforcements modify responses automatically, independent of the organism's values, beliefs or mental processes, i.e., independent of consciousness.

While this theory of behavior may be appealing in its simplicity, the facts of human behavior do not correspond to it. All behavior is not controlled by reinforcements given to an acting organism. People can learn a new response by seeing other people get reinforced for that response; this is called "vicarious reinforcement" (17). People sometimes learn by imitating others who are not reinforced for their actions; this is called "vicarious learning" (33). Some behaviorists now acknowledge that people can control their own thoughts and actions by "talking to themselves," i.e., thinking. This is called "self-reinforcement" (18) or "self-instruction." These last two concepts flatly contradict the assumption of determinism.

Recent experiments and reviews of the learning literature have further undermined the behaviorist position. Not only do an individual's values, knowledge and intentions have a profound effect on behavior (9, 22), but even the simplest forms of learning may not occur in the absence of conscious awareness on the part of the learner (8).

Studies of actual practices of behavior modifiers show that their techniques implicitly contradict all the main premises of behaviorism. For example, the procedures employed by behavioral psychotherapists assume that: (a) patients are conscious; (b) they can understand the meaning of words and can think; (c) they can introspect; and (d) they can control the actions of their own minds and bodies (6, 23, 32).

In view of conclusions drawn about behavior modification in other areas, will the same hold true when behavior modification principles are applied to industrial-organizational settings? One thesis to be explored here is that "behavior mod" applications to industry do not actually rest on behaviorist premises—they do not ignore the employee's consciousness and/or assume it to be irrelevant to the employee's behavior.

If true, this thesis would mean that, since organizational changes do not automatically condition the employee's response, attention must be paid to what the employee *thinks* about such changes. Are they wanted? Are they understood? What are they expected to lead to, etc.?

A second issue concerns the originality of the techniques used by behavior mod practitioners in industry. Because the concept of reinforcement is defined solely by its consequences, if an alleged reinforcer does not reinforce, it is not a reinforcer. If it does, it is. Since the concept of reinforcement itself has no content (no defining characteristics independent of its effects on behavior), how are behavior modifiers to know what to use as reinforcers? In practice, behaviorists must use rewards and incentives which they observe people already acting to gain and/or keep; they must cash in on what they already know or believe people value or need. Thus when it comes to the choice of reinforcers, behavior mod can offer nothing new (4). A second thesis is that the actual techniques used by behavior modifiers in industry to "reinforce" behavior are no different from the rewards and incentives already used by non-behaviorist practitioners in this field or related fields.

If this thesis is true, then the claims of originality by behavior mod practitioners are spurious and the attention of researchers would be focused best on further development of existing approaches to motivating employees (e.g., human relations, job enrichment, incentives).

Behavior mod advocates might reply that even if the particular reinforcers they use are not new, they do have something original to offer the practicing manager, namely, the idea of contingency. While the contingency idea is emphasized strongly in behaviorism, it is certainly not new. It has been used, if inconsistently, for centuries by animal trainers, parents, diplomats, and employers. Furthermore the principle does not work unless the individual is aware of the contingency (8). Finally, the principle is of limited usefulness in real life work situations where the manager cannot control everything that happens to subordinates (4).

Supporters of behavior mod might also argue that an original aspect of the behavior mod approach to management is its exclusive emphasis on the use of positive rewards and the avoidance of punishment. Such an argument would be misleading, since behaviorists are by no means averse to the use of punishment. Electric shock is often used to change the habits of unruly, disturbed children and to "cure" homosexuals. Furthermore, there is an element of arbitrariness in the behaviorist definition of this and related terms. Punishment is defined as an aversive stimulus which decreases the frequency of a response when it follows the response. Withholding a positive reinforcer, such as food, is not called punishment but extinction. A starving schizophrenic who is told, "No work, no food" might see the withholding of food as very punishing, despite the benign label "extinction" which the behaviorists attach to the process. Similarly, "negative reinforcement," the removal of an aversive stimulus when the organism does what you want, may be viewed justifiably as very punishing and coercive.

Most industrial-organizational practices claiming to represent the application of behavior modification principles fall into one of four categories: programmed instruction; modeling; performance standards with feedback; and monetary incentives, including lotteries. Each of these will be considered in turn from the standpoint of two issues: Are the techniques actually behavioristic? Are they original to behavior mod?

PROGRAMMED INSTRUCTION

The concept of programmed instruction (PI) was first popularized by Skinner (53). The four crucial elements of PI are: small units, presented in a logical, hierarchical sequence; active involvement (overt response); immediate confirmation (knowledge of results); and reinforcement (reward), although this is not usually distinguished from confirmation.

These individual elements of PI are certainly not new. Task analysis, including breaking down tasks into smaller units for training purposes, was a mainstay of Scientific Management (10), has been used for decades in military training (11), and has been recognized for centuries as a basic principle of all training. Similarly, knowledge of results and reward have long been recognized as facilitators of learning (2, 58). Overt responding is similar in meaning to the concept of practice which has always been acknowledged as essential to skill development.

In fairness to the developers of PI, the particular combination of elements which comprise the essence of PI were relatively original, although Pressey had laid the groundwork for this development over two decades previously.

The most startling result of recent research on the effectiveness of PI is the finding that none of its particular elements seem to be necessary for learning to occur. The most recent review of the PI literature concludes:

1   Knowledge of results [of the type used in PI] is not necessary for learning.
2   Delayed knowledge of results may be more effective than immediate knowledge of results.
3   [Extrinsic] Rewards seem not always to function to improve learning. . . .
4   Learning by a sequence of small steps may be less effective than learning by larger jumps (35, p. 186).

Gagné (11) concludes that standard principles of laboratory learning are largely irrelevant to successful training in applied settings. He does favor breaking the task down into its elements, providing the elements are then re-integrated, a procedure which is omitted in typical PI programs. Pressey (49) and Locke (25) emphasize the importance of mental integrations in learning. Such integrations, Pressey claims, are actually retarded by the use of small, discrete frames characteristic of PI.

Gagné (11) and Annett (3) argue that knowledge of results, while helpful, does not automatically facilitate learning. Locke, Cartledge and Koeppel (27) show that certain types of knowledge of results do not produce improved performance unless they lead to the setting of explicit improvement or performance goals.

A number of studies show that making an overt response in a PI program is no better than making a "covert" response, i.e., practicing the answer mentally (45, 59).

Bolles (7) asserts that what is learned when a response is allegedly "reinforced" is not a stimulus-response connection but rather an expectancy. Expectancy is a concept referring to a conscious state of anticipation. A comprehensive review of the academic learning literature by Brewer (8) concludes that there is no such thing as automatic conditioning through reinforcement. The evidence shows that human learning requires the operation of consciousness.

To the degree that PI does encourage learning, it is probably the element of "forced" rehearsal or practice, including the mental integrations which accompany it, which is most responsible. Of course, rehearsal can also occur at the option of the learner in the absence of a PI format, and can occur "covertly," in the mind, as well as overtly.

Recent research throws increasing doubt on the claim that the PI format is superior to other methods of presenting didactic material. A thorough review of PI studies in applied settings by Nash, Muczyk and Vettori (41) concludes that PI is not practically superior to other forms of instruction, especially with respect to retention. They also found that the more carefully designed the study, the less favorable the results are to the PI method. For example, although PI takes about one third less time than the conventional methods with which it is usually compared, typical comparisons are biased by the fact that PI and non-PI programs nearly always differ with respect to content. When content is controlled, so that PI can be compared with other *methods* of instruction, this superiority not only vanishes but is reversed. Jabara (15) found that material presented in the form of a text was completed two to three times faster than the *identical material* presented in a PI format and was no less effective in terms of learning.

MODELING

The term modeling is similar in meaning to imitation, although its proponents claim that it is something more. Meichenbaum writes:

> the exposure to a modeling display permits the discrimination and organized memory of relatively complex and integrated behavior chains which may then be retrieved to satisfy environmental demands. . . . the information which observers gain from models is converted to covert perceptual-cognitive images and covert mediating rehearsal responses that are retained by the observer and later used by him as symbolic cues to overt behaviors (36).

Stripped of their behavioristic jargon, these statements assert that modeling involves the learning (mental integration) of complex actions which are stored in memory and called out on order based on the individual's perception of what is appropriate to the situation.

The main industrial application of modeling has been to training supervisors (12, 29, 39, 40, 56). Supervisory trainees are shown video-taped illustrations of models coping successfully with simulated real-life problems involving subordinates. This is often followed by role playing sessions in which the trainees attempt to apply the same principles and are given feedback by the trainer and/or by video-tape. Application then proceeds to the trainee's actual job situation. This may be accompanied by discussions of one's experience with other trainees during periodic follow-up meetings.

The formal use of modeling for supervisory training is certainly new, although it has long been used in motor skill training and sports. De facto modeling has probably always existed in hierarchical organizations. The content of the model's actions in formal supervisory training emphasizes principles derived from the "Human Relations" school of thought—"elicit[ing] the employee's ideas for improving the situation" (39, p. 5).

Whatever the status of modeling with respect to originality, by no stretch of the imagination can it be called behavioristic. Modeling, even according to its proponents, requires perception, imagination, memory, mental rehearsal ("reviewing in one's own mind the enactment of the displayed behaviors," 12, p. 30), and thinking. All these are actions of consciousness which ultimately are presumed to regulate the individual's overt behavior.

Despite some behaviorists' implicit admission that modeling assumes the existence of conscious, thinking trainees, its proponents do not seem to fully understand what modeling is. This writer believes that modeling is a technique for translating abstractions into concretes, for learning the application of general principles to specific situations. Since such applications require that the individual correctly perceive the situation, clearly understand which principle or principles apply to it, and know how to translate these principles into action, learning such applications can be extremely difficult. Modeling, in effect, shows trainees how it is done, and thus helps them to translate abstract knowledge into actions appropriate to specific situations. It provides a useful bridge between theoretical understanding and actual practice.

There is insufficient evidence to evaluate the usefulness of modeling as a training technique. One issue that is not clear from descriptions of this process is the degree to which principles of effective supervision are explicitly given to the trainees—as opposed to requiring them to discover the principles through induction. Since many people have neither the capacity nor the inclination to perform complex inductions, the former procedure should be more effective than the latter. For example, an emphasis on making the principles explicit should facilitate transfer from the observed (modeled) situations to the greater variety of situations the trainees will encounter in their own experience.

PERFORMANCE STANDARDS WITH FEEDBACK

Perhaps the most well known applications of behavior mod to industry are Feeney's quasi-experiments at Emery Air Freight (5, 42, 48, 60, 61). Related ideas are presented by Hersey and Blanchard (14) and Morasky (38). Feeney's basic procedure is to:

1 Specify the desired level or standard of performance, preferably in quantitative terms. The concept of "performance standard" in this context is clearly a behavioristic euphemism for "goal."

2 Provide immediate, quantitative feedback informing employees of their level of performance in relation to the standard (preferably this feedback will come directly to the employees such as through performance records which they keep themselves).

3 Provide positive reinforcement in cases where the feedback indicates that performance meets the standard, and encouragement in cases where it does not meet the standard. Praise is recommended as the most practical positive reinforcer.

The evidence indicates that praise is not essential to achieve output gains. When the frequency of praise is decreased, no performance decrement results; but when feedback is eliminated, performance immediately drops to its previous level. According to Feeney, "feedback is the critical variable in explaining the success of the program" (5, p. 45). Another writer offers a feedback explanation to explain the productivity increases observed in the Hawthorne studies (46).

Both writers favor a behavioristic interpretation of the effects of feedback. They argue that feedback automatically reinforces the behavior which precedes it, and that the existence of the feedback explains the results of the foregoing studies.

Taken literally, this claim is absurd. If feedback *as such* automatically reinforced previous behavior, people should never change since the feedback would reinforce whatever they did previously. (Feeney's methods actually violate good behaviorist technique since the feedback is not contingent on high performance.)

Parson's (46) hypothesis about the Hawthorne studies is refuted by findings obtained in one of those very studies. In the Bank-Wiring Observation Room individual output was recorded daily; "each man seemed to know just where he stood at any time [during the day]" (51, p. 428). In spite of this, output among these workers did not go up; it remained at a fairly constant level because the employees were deliberately restricting their output.

There are additional facts that do not coincide with the behavioristic interpretation of the effects of feedback. In Feeney's studies (5), performance in the customer service offices improved "rapidly"—in one case from 30 percent to 95 percent of standard in a single day! In the container departments, container use jumped from 45 percent to 95 percent, and in 70 percent of the cases this improvement also occurred within a day (42). Since genuine conditioning is asserted to be a gradual process, the very speed of these improvements militates against a conditioning explanation of the results. More likely what occurred was a conscious *redefinition of the job* resulting from the new standards and the more accurate feedback regarding performance in relation to those standards.

Further support for this interpretation comes from the extensive research on feedback and knowledge of results which do *not* automatically lead to performance improvement (3, 26, 27). The effects of feedback on subsequent performance depend upon such factors as: (a) amount and usefulness of information (knowledge) provided by the feedback; (b) degree to which the information source is trusted; and (c) utilization of the feedback to set goals and/or to regulate one's performance in relation to these goals.

The results obtained by Feeney are more logically explained by the joint operation of explicit goal-setting and feedback regarding performance in relation to the goals, i.e., by the employee's conscious, self-regulation of action, than by the concept of automatic conditioning through reinforcement.

Another study claiming to illustrate the positive effects of behavior mod in improving employee performance can be interpreted similarly. Adam (1) instructed the line supervisors of a die-casting department to meet with each operator weekly and to provide him or her with feedback concerning performance quantity and quality, either on an absolute basis or in relation to set standards, as well as in relation to the shift and department averages. Operators with average or below average quality scores were asked explicitly to improve, although the supervisors evidently stressed quantity more than quality during their daily interactions with the operators. The use of goal-setting led to a significant increase in work quantity but no change in quality.

The concepts of goal and feedback or knowledge of results are in no sense behavioristic concepts. The term goal, as used in industrial contexts, refers to the *consciously* held aim of an action, e.g., a work norm or an output standard. The concept of knowledge refers to the *awareness* of some fact of reality. Both concepts refer to states or actions of consciousness.

Furthermore, the concepts of goal and feedback are not new, not even as applied to industry. There is little difference between Feeney's ideas and some key elements of Scientific Management presented more than 60 years ago by Taylor (57). Taylor's central concept, the task, which consisted of an assigned work goal (with the work methods also specified), is virtually identical in meaning to Feeney's concept of a "performance standard," a term which also was used by advocates of Scientific Management. Similarly, Taylor argued that work should be measured continually and the results fed back to employees so that they could correct errors and improve or maintain their quantity of output. Taylor favored a monetary bonus as a reward for increased productivity while Feeney's results indicate that this may not be necessary.

Latham and his colleagues also obtained dramatic results in industry by the use of goals and feedback without monetary incentives (19, 20, 21). Their work was based on the results of laboratory studies of goal setting which had an explicit non-behavioristic base (22).

Two additional concepts occasionally used by Feeney are praise and participation. Both are taken directly from the Human Relations school of management.

MONETARY INCENTIVES

The effectiveness of monetary incentives in improving work performance has long been recognized in industry. The use of large bonus payments for reaching assigned tasks or work goals was a cornerstone of Scientific Management (57), although the use of piece-rate payment systems was common even before the turn of the century.

Payment programs designed explicitly around behavior mod principles and employing behavior mod terminology have been rare in industrial settings. Yukl and Latham (62) compared the effect of continuous and variable ratio piece-rate bonuses among tree planters. Contrary to predictions, the continuous schedule yielded the highest level of performance. One reason for less effectiveness of the variable ratio schedules was that some members of work groups receiving those schedules were consciously opposed to the program, some on the grounds that "gambling" was immoral, and some due to general distrust. Clearly the effect of the so-called reinforcers was far from automatic.

Other studies have used monetary reinforcers or their equivalent (e.g., valued prizes such as appliances) to reduce absenteeism (44, 47). Either payments were made to all individuals showing perfect attendance for a given time period, or rewards were based on lottery drawings with only those with perfect attendance being eligible.

Nord (44) observed that such systems may become progressively less effective with time, although no explanation was offered for this finding. Presumably the reinforcers are no longer as reinforcing, but this does not explain anything (24).

A striking finding of the Pedalino and Gamboa (47) study was that employees in the experimental, lottery group showed a significant reduction in absenteeism during the very first week of the program, *before anyone in the group had been, or could have been, reinforced* (34).

The concept of conditioning through reinforcement cannot account for these results since the behavior change *preceded* the reinforcement. Obviously the employees' expectations of and desire for the reward caused their change in behavior. Expectation and desire are not behavioristic concepts since they refer to states and actions of consciousness. Furthermore, these expectations were not, according to any evidence presented, generated by past reinforcements (lottery experiences) but by the explanation of the proposed incentive system to the employees.

CONCLUSION

The conclusion is inescapable that behavior mod in industry is neither new nor behavioristic. The specific techniques employed by behavior mod advocates have long been used in industry and other fields. What the behaviorists call reinforcers do not condition behavior automatically, but affect action through and in conjunction with the individual's mental contents and processes (integrations, goals, expectancies, etc.). While operant conditioning principles avoid the necessity of dealing with phenomena which are not directly observable, such as the minds of others, for this very reason they lack the capacity to explain human action (24).

The typical behaviorist response to arguments like the foregoing is, in effect, "Who cares why the procedures work, so long as they work?" (60). This is the kind of pragmatic answer one might expect from primitive witch doctors who are challenged to explain their "cures." One has the right to expect more from a modern day scientist.

Unless one knows why and how something "works," one does not know *when* it will work or even *that* it will work in a given circumstance. Many things which behaviorists do to change behavior, do, in fact, change it. But many of them do not, and most behaviorists do not have the slightest idea what accounts for these inconsistencies. Post-hoc speculations about past conditioning or improper scheduling of the reinforcements do not solve this problem.

Skinner has long argued that resorting to mentalistic concepts tends to prematurely cut off the search for the real causes of behavior (55). While this may be true if the mentalistic concepts involved are pseudo-scientific, semi-mystical constructs like Freud's "id," the opposite is the case if the mentalistic concepts are clearly definable and verifiable through introspection. It is empty behavioristic concepts like "reinforcement" which delude investigators into thinking they understand the organism's behavior, and thus cut off the search for the real causes, i.e., those characteristics of the organism, including its mental contents and processes, which explain why it reacted as it did in response to, or in the absence of, the so-called reinforcements (24).

As Argyris (4) and Mitchell (37) have pointed out, there are numerous contextual assumptions which are untrue, non-universal or inappropriate in most applied settings, which behaviorists make when applying their techniques. Examples are the assumptions that individuals are basically passive responders to external stimulation; and that when subjects are being exposed to reinforcers, they will not think about what is happening, talk to anyone else about it, focus on the long term implications or consider their own goals.

There is a common element in the above assumptions, a premise which underlies and unites all of the behaviorist theories of human behavior and of management. It is the premise that *humans do not possess a conceptual faculty*. The frequently made distinction between metaphysical and methodological behaviorism does not contradict this characterization of behaviorism since, in practice, both versions amount to the same thing. While Skinner does not openly deny that people have minds, he does assert that the environment is the ultimate cause of all thinking and action (54, 55). *But if mind is an epiphenomenon, then, for all practical purposes, it does not exist.*

Only if humans were by nature limited to the perceptual level of functioning, like dogs or cats, could one reasonably argue that they were passive responders to outside influences and that they would do nothing that they were not conditioned to do.[2] To quote Ayn Rand, a critic of behaviorism, on the issue of human nature:

> Man's sense organs function automatically; man's brain integrates his sense data into percepts automatically; but the process of integrating percepts into concepts— the process of abstraction and of concept-formation—is *not* automatic.
>
> The process of concept-formation does not consist merely of grasping a few simple abstractions, such as "chair," "table," "hot," "cold," and of learning to speak. It consists of a method of using one's consciousness, best designated by the term "conceptualizing." It is not a passive state of registering random impressions. It is an actively sustained process of identifying one's impressions in conceptual terms, of integrating every event and every observation into a conceptual context, of grasping relationships, differences, similarities in one's perceptual material and of abstracting them into new concepts, of drawing inferences, of making deductions, of reaching conclusions, of asking new questions and discovering new answers and expanding one's knowledge into an ever-growing sum. The faculty that directs this process, the faculty that works by means of concepts, is: *reason*. The process is *thinking*.
>
> Reason is the faculty that perceives, identifies, and integrates the material provided by man's senses. It is a faculty that man has to exercise *by choice*. Thinking is not an automatic function. In any hour and issue of his life, man is free to think or to evade that effort. Thinking requires a state of full, focused awareness. The act of focusing one's consciousness is volitional. Man can focus his mind to a full, active, purposefully directed awareness of reality—or he can unfocus it and let himself drift in a semi-conscious daze, merely reacting to any chance stimulus of the immediate moment, at the mercy of his undirected sensory-perceptual mechanism and of any random, associational connections it might happen to make (50, pp. 20–21).

Since people can choose to think (a fact which can be validated by introspection), the behaviorist view of human nature is false. Thus the claim that behaviorism, taken literally, can serve as a valid guide to understanding and modifying human behavior in organizations is a myth.

REFERENCES

1 Adam, E. E. "Behavior Modification in Quality Control," *Academy of Management Journal,* Vol. 18 (1975), 662–679.
2 Ammons, R. B. "Effects of Knowledge of Performance: A Survey and Tentative Theoretical Formulation," *Journal of General Psychology*, Vol. 54 (1956), 279–299.
3 Annett, J. *Feedback and Human Behaviour* (Baltimore: Penguin, 1969).
4 Argyris, C. "Beyond Freedom and Dignity by B. F. Skinner (An Essay Review)," *Harvard Educational Review*, Vol. 41, No. 4 (1971), 550–567.

[2]Even the assertion that animals are passive organisms is misleading. While animals lack free will (i.e., they cannot choose to think), they are still motivated by internal states (e.g., needs, wants, experiences of pleasure and pain). They are only passive by comparison to humans in that they cannot (through thinking) choose their wants nor means of achieving them. Nor can they reflect on the significance of what they are doing. Thus through arranging suitable external conditions, much of their behavior can be controlled.

5 "At Emery Air Freight: Positive Reinforcement Boosts Performance," *Organizational Dynamics*, Vol. 1, No. 3 (1973), 41–50.

6 Bergin, A. E., and R. M. Suinn, "Individual Psychotherapy and Behavior Therapy," *Annual Review of Psychology*, Vol. 26 (1975), 509–556.

7 Bolles, R. C. "Reinforcement, Expectancy, and Learning," *Psychological Review*, Vol. 79 (1972), 394–409.

8 Brewer, W. F. "There Is No Convincing Evidence for Operant or Classical Conditioning in Adult Humans," in W. B. Weimer and D. S. Palermo (Eds.), *Cognition and the Symbolic Processes* (Hillsdale, N.J.: L. Erlbaum, 1974), pp. 1–42.

9 Dulany, D. E. "Awareness, Rules and Propositional Control: A Confrontation with S-R Behavior Theory," in T. R. Dixon and D. L. Horton (Eds.), *Verbal Behavior and General Behavior Theory* (Englewood Cliffs, N.J.: Prentice-Hall, 1968), pp. 340–387.

10 Fry, F. L. "Operant Conditioning in Organizational Settings: Of Mice or Men?" *Personnel* (July-August 1974), 17–24.

11 Gagné, R. M. "Military Training and Principles of Learning," *American Psychologist*, Vol. 17 (1962), 83–91.

12 Goldstein, A. P., and M. Sorcher. *Changing Supervisory Behavior* (Elmsford, N.Y.: Pergamon Press, 1974).

13 Hamner, W. C. "Reinforcement Theory and Contingency Management in Organizational Settings," in R. M. Steers and L. W. Porter (Eds.), *Motivation and Work Behavior* (New York: McGraw-Hill, 1975), pp. 477–504.

14 Hersey, P., and K. H. Blanchard. "The Management of Change," *Training and Development Journal*, Vol. 29, No. 2 (1972), 20–24.

15 Jabara, R. F. *A Comparison of Programmed Instruction and Text Methods of Presentation, With Time Controlled* (Master's Thesis, University of Maryland, College Park, 1970).

16 Jablonsky, S. F., and D. L. DeVries. "Operant Conditioning Principles Extrapolated to the Theory of Management," *Organizational Behavior and Human Performance*, Vol. 7 (1972), 340–358.

17 Kanfer, F. H. "Vicarious Human Reinforcement: A Glimpse into the Black Box," in L. Krasner and L. P. Ullman (Eds.), *Research in Behavior Modification* (New York: Holt, Rinehart and Winston, 1965), pp. 244–267.

18 Kanfer, F. H., and P. Karoly. "Self-Control: A Behavioristic Excursion into the Lion's Den," *Behavior Therapy*, Vol. 3 (1972), 398–416.

19 Latham, G. P., and J. J. Baldes. "The 'Practical Significance' of Locke's Theory of Goal-Setting," *Journal of Applied Psychology*, Vol. 60 (1975), 122–124.

20 Latham, G. P., and S. B. Kinne. "Improving Job Performance Through Training in Goal-Setting," *Journal of Applied Psychology*, Vol. 59 (1974), 187–191.

21 Latham, G. P., and G. A. Yukl. "Assigned Versus Participative Goal Setting with Educated and Uneducated Woods Workers," *Journal of Applied Psychology*, Vol. 60 (1975), 299–302.

22 Locke, E. A. "Toward a Theory of Task Motivation and Incentives," *Organizational Behavior and Human Performance*, Vol. 3 (1968), 157–189.

23 Locke, E. A. "Is 'Behavior Therapy' Behavioristic? (An Analysis of Wople's Psychotherapeutic Methods)," *Psychological Bulletin*, Vol. 76 (1971), 318–327.

24 Locke, E. A. "Critical Analysis of the Concept of Causality in Behavioristic Psychology," *Psychological Reports*, Vol. 31 (1972), 175–197.

25 Locke, E. A. *A Guide to Effective Study* (New York: Springer, 1975).

26 Locke, E. A., and J. F. Bryan. "The Directing Function of Goals in Task Performance," *Organizational Behavior and Human Performance*, Vol. 4 (1969), 35–42.

27 Locke, E. A., N. Cartledge, and J. Koeppel. "Motivational Effects of Knowledge of Results: A Goal-Setting Phenomenon?" *Psychological Bulletin*, Vol. 70 (1968), 474–485.

28 Luthans, F. "An Organizational Behavior Modification (O. B. Mod) Approach to O. D." Paper presented at the National Academy of Management, Seattle, 1974.

29 Luthans, F., and R. Kreitner. "The Management of Behavioral Contingencies," *Personnel* (July-August 1974), 7–16.

30 Luthans, F., and R. Kreitner. *Organizational Behavior Modification* (Glenview, Ill.: Scott Foresman, 1975).

31 Luthans, F., and D. D. White. "Behavior Modification: Application to Manpower Management," *Personnel Administration*, Vol. 34, No. 4 (1971), 41–47.

32 Mahoney, M. J. *Cognition and Behavior Modification* (Cambridge, Mass.: Ballinger, 1974).

33 Marlatt, G. A. "A Comparison of Vicarious and Direct Reinforcement Control of Verbal Behavior in an Interview Setting," *Journal of Personality and Social Psychology*, Vol. 16 (1970), 695–703.

34 Mawhinney, T. C. "Operant Terms and Concepts in the Description of Individual Work Behavior: Some Problems of Interpretation, Application, and Evaluation," *Journal of Applied Psychology*, Vol. 60 (1975), 704–712.

35 McKeachie, W. J. "Instructional Psychology," *Annual Review of Psychology*, Vol. 25 (1974), 161–193.

36 Meichenbaum, D. "Self-Instructional Methods," in F. H. Kanfer and A. P. Goldstein (Eds.), *Helping People Change* (Elmsford, N.Y.: Pergamon, 1974).

37 Mitchell, T. R. "Cognitions and Skinner: Some Questions about Behavioral Determinism." Paper presented at the National Academy of Management, Seattle, 1974.

38 Morasky, R. L. "Self-Shaping Training Systems and Flexible-Model Behavior, i.e., Sales Interviewing," *Educational Technology*, Vol. 11, No. 5 (1971), 57–59.

39 Moses, J. E. "A Behavioral Method of Evaluating Training or: A Light at the End of the Tunnel." Paper presented at National Society for Performance and Instruction, New York, 1974.

40 Moses, J., and D. Ritchie. "Assessment Center Used to Evaluate an Interaction Modeling Program," *Assessment and Development*, Vol. 2, No. 2 (1975), 1–2.

41 Nash, A. N., J. P. Muczyk, and F. L. Vettori. "The Relative Practical Effectiveness of Programmed Instruction," *Personnel Psychology*, Vol. 24 (1971), 397–418.

42 "New Tool: 'Reinforcement' for Good Work," *Business Week*, December 18, 1971, 76–77.

43 Nord, W. R. "Beyond the Teaching Machine: The Neglected Area of Operant Conditioning in the Theory and Practice of Management," *Organizational Behavior and Human Performance*, Vol. 4 (1969), 375–401.

44 Nord, W. R. "Improving Attendance Through Rewards," *Personnel Administration*, Vol. 33, No. 6 (1970), 37–41.

45 O'Day, E. F., R. W. Kulhavy, W. Anderson, and R. J. Malczynski. *Programmed Instruction, Techniques and Trends* (New York: Appleton-Century-Crofts, 1971).

46 Parsons, H. M. "What Happened at Hawthorne?" *Science*, Vol. 183 (1974), 922–932.

47 Pedalino, E., and V. U. Gamboa. "Behavior Modification and Absenteeism: Intervention in One Industrial Setting," *Journal of Applied Psychology*, Vol. 59 (1974), 694–698.

48 "Performance Audit Feedback, and Positive Reinforcement," *Training and Development Journal*, Vol. 29, No. 11 (1972), 8–13.

49 Pressey, S. L. "Teaching Machine (and Learning Theory) Crisis," *Journal of Applied Psychology*, Vol. 47 (1963), 1–6.

50 Rand, A. "The Objectivist Ethics," in A. Rand, *The Virtue of Selfishness* (New York: New American Library, 1964), pp. 13–35.

51 Roethlisberger, F. J., and W. J. Dickson. *Management and the Worker* (Cambridge, Mass.: Harvard, 1956).

52 Schneier, C. E. "Behavior Modification in Management: A Review and Critique," *Academy of Management Journal*, Vol. 17 (1974), 528–548.

53 Skinner, B. F. "Teaching Machines," *Science*, Vol. 128 (1958), 969–977.

54 Skinner, B. F. *Beyond Freedom and Dignity* (New York: Alfred A. Knopf, 1971).

55 Skinner, B. F. "The Steep and Thorny Way to a Science of Behavior," *American Psychologist*, Vol. 30 (1975), 42–49.

56 Sorcher, M., and A. P. Goldstein. "A Behavior Modeling Approach to Training," *Personnel Administration*, Vol. 35, No. 2 (1972), 35–41.

57 Taylor, F. W. *The Principles of Scientific Management*, 1911 (New York: Norton, 1967).

58 Thorndike, E. L. *Human Learning*, 1931 (Cambridge, Mass.: M.I.T. Press, 1966).

59 Welsh, P., J. A. Antoinetti, and P. W. Thayer. "An Industrywide Study of Programmed Instruction," *Journal of Applied Psychology*, Vol. 49 (1965), 61–73.

60 "Where Skinner's Theories Work," *Business Week*, Dec. 2, 1972, 64–65.

61 Wiard, H. "Why Manage Behavior? A Case for Positive Reinforcement," *Human Resource Management*, Vol. 11, No. 2 (1972), 15–20.

62 Yukl, G. A., and G. P. Latham. "Consequences of Reinforcement Schedules and Incentive Magnitudes for Employee Performance: Problems Encountered in an Industrial Setting," *Journal of Applied Psychology*, Vol. 60 (1975), 294–298.

QUESTIONS FOR DISCUSSION

1 Why do operant conditioning principles stress the necessity of avoiding negative feedback?

2 From a managerial standpoint, what is really new and innovative about operant conditioning?

3 How might you employ operant conditioning principles in designing an MBO program?

4 What potential drawbacks exist when you attempt to use operant conditioning at work?

5 Would operant conditioning tend to work better among blue- or white-collar employees? Why?

6 Would the general principles of operant conditioning be as applicable to solving the problems of turnover and absenteeism as they would to solving those of performance? Why or why not? Cite examples to illustrate your answer.

7 What effects might operant conditioning have on organizational climate? Explain.

8 How could a manager tie operant conditioning principles to achievement motivation theory?

9 How would you respond to Locke's criticisms of the use of behavior modification in organization settings?

Chapter 5

Expectancy/Valence Theory

We now come to the fourth and final major theory of motivation and work behavior to be reviewed here. This theory also goes under several names, including expectancy theory, instrumentality theory, path-goal theory, and valence-instrumentality-expectancy (VIE) theory. We shall use the term "expectancy/valence theory" as being more descriptive of the two major variables of the formulation.

Expectancy/valence theory is the second "process" theory to be considered in this book (after equity theory). It can be classified as a process theory—in contrast to a content theory—primarily because it attempts to identify relationships among variables in a dynamic state as they affect individual behavior. This systems orientation is in direct contrast to the content theories, which have attempted largely to specify correlates of motivated behavior. In expectancy/valence theory, like equity theory, it is the relationship among inputs rather than the inputs themselves that is the focal point.

The expectancy/valence model is also a cognitive theory of motivation (see Chapter 1). Individuals are viewed as thinking, reasoning beings who have beliefs and anticipations concerning future events in their lives. Drawing heavily on the earlier works of Lewin, Tolman, and Peak, this theory posits that human behavior is to a considerable extent a function of the interactive processes between the characteristics of an individual (such as personality traits, attitudes, needs, and values) and his or her perceived environment (such as supervisor's style, job or task requirements, and organization climate). In fact, it is the assumed existence of these anticipations, based on the individual-environment interaction, that differentiates expectancy/valence theory most markedly from other theories of work motivation.

DETERMINANTS OF PERFORMANCE

Let us begin our discussion of this theory by considering on a general level the major hypothesized determinants of performance (Cummings & Schwab, 1973; Porter & Lawler, 1968; Vroom, 1960). Performance in organization settings appears to be a function of at least three important variables: motivational level, abilities and traits, and role perceptions. First, an individual must *want* to perform. Otherwise he or she will, at best, carry out a task only halfheartedly and, at worst, may refuse to do anything at all. We are speaking here of intentional behavior, that is, behavior directed toward specific tasks or outcomes. Thus, a basic prerequisite to task performance on most jobs becomes the desire—or motivation—of the employee to do the assigned tasks.

But motivation alone will not ensure task performance. A person must also have the necessary abilities and skills. Such is the purpose of education and training both before the person begins the job and while he or she holds it. Similarly, it is important to have personality traits that are at least somewhat compatible with the job requirements. For example, it is usually thought that a salesperson must be something of an extrovert. More introverted persons, it is assumed, are not "aggressive" enough to get the sales. Organizations have for decades used various personality and vocational interest tests in an effort to improve the match between individual and job, thereby hoping to affect resulting performance.

Finally, a third important factor in performance is role clarity. A person must usually have an accurate understanding of what the job requirements are if he or she is to be expected to devote full and efficient energy to them. A misunderstanding can lead to a considerable waste of effort—and poor performance—even if the person is highly motivated and has the required abilities. Thus, there appear to be at least three factors that significantly influence performance: one must be motivated, one must have the necessary abilities and traits, and one must have fairly clear role prescriptions.

DETERMINANTS OF MOTIVATION

Most of the theoretical and empirical work by expectancy/valence theorists has focused on the "motivation" variable of the above equation. Put most simply, this theory argues that motivational force to perform—or effort—is a multiplicative function of the expectancies, or beliefs, that individuals have concerning future outcomes *times* the value they place on those outcomes. Vroom (1964,

p. 18) defines "expectancy" as "an action-outcome association." It is a statement of the extent to which an individual believes that a certain action will result in a particular outcome. Theoretically, an expectancy can take on a mathematical value of from 0 (absolutely no belief that an outcome will follow a particular action) to 1 (complete certainty that an outcome will follow a particular action). Usually, however, an expectancy would take on a probability value somewhere between these two extremes.

More recently, the generalized concept of expectancy has been divided into two specific types: "$E \rightarrow P$ expectancy" and "$P \rightarrow O$ expectancies" (Campbell et al., 1970; Lawler, 1973). An $E \rightarrow P$ expectancy represents a belief that effort, such as a salesperson's increasing the number of calls made per day, will lead to desired performance, namely, increased sales. That is, the closer the *perceived* relationship between effort and resulting job performance, the greater the $E \rightarrow P$ expectancy. $P \rightarrow O$ expectancies, on the other hand, are beliefs or anticipations that an individual has concerning the likelihood that performance will, in fact, lead to particular outcomes. A salesperson, for example, may be almost certain of receiving a raise or a bonus if he or she succeeds in increasing sales (that is, high $P \rightarrow O$ expectancy); or conversely, he or she may feel that such success would probably go unrewarded (low $P \rightarrow O$ expectancy). The multiplicative combination of these two types of expectancies, then, determines the expectancy part of the expectancy/valence equation.

Valence, the second major component of the theory, can be defined as the value, or preference, which an individual places on a particular outcome. Valences may take on theoretical values of from $+1.0$ to -1.0. That is, a person may be very strongly attracted to a particular outcome, such as a pay raise, and may assign the outcome a high positive value, or the person may very strongly want to avoid the outcome, such as being fired, and may assign a negative valence to it.

Under the expectancy/valence model, then, we would determine an individual's motivational force to perform (effort) by multiplying the $E \rightarrow P$ expectancy *times* the $P \rightarrow O$ expectancies *times* the outcome valences. Perhaps a very simple example will clarify this relationship. If the salesperson of our previous example places a high probability (let us say 8 out of 10) on increased sales resulting from increased effort, we would say he or she has a high $E \rightarrow P$ expectancy. Moreover, if this person strongly believes (at the same probability) that such a sales increase would lead to a bonus or a pay raise, we would say he or she has a high $P \rightarrow O$ expectancy. Finally, if our salesperson truly values the receipt of this bonus or pay raise, he or she would be described as placing a high valence, such as 0.9, on such a reward. When these three factors are combined in a multiplicative fashion ($0.8 \times 0.8 \times 0.9 = 0.58$), we can see that under this theory our person would have a strong motivational force to perform. If ability as a salesperson is also high and if role prescription is clear, we would then expect to see success in job performance. On the other hand, if expectancies were high (0.8 and 0.8, respectively) but there was little genuine desire for the pay raise (for whatever reasons), the valence would be fairly low (let us say 0.1 instead of 0.9). Again computing the motivational force ($0.8 \times 0.8 \times 0.1 = 0.06$), we can see that in this latter case our salesperson would have little desire to perform.

EXPECTANCY/VALENCE THEORY VERSUS BEHAVIOR MODIFICATION

Recent attention has focused on how expectancy/valence theory differs from behavior modification as a theory of work motivation. These two theories are probably the most popular comprehensive models in use today and each has its proponents and opponents. Hence, it is useful to summarize several major differences between the two models.

The first major difference concerns the assumptions that are made about the nature of people. Expectancy/valence theory assumes that individuals are largely autonomous beings who independently determine expectancies, instrumentalities, and valences for various types of behavior. Behavior modification, on the other hand, suggests that individuals are much more prone to respond passively to forces in their environment.

Second, expectancy/valence theory is primarily concerned with ahistorical and conscious choice behavior. It represents a cognitive theory that asserts that people make conscious choices about present and future behavior based on the information that is available to them. Behavior modification, on the other hand, is an operant theory that is primarily concerned with the effects of previous (historical) events on present behavior. It emphasizes the importance of learned stimulus-response bonds as they affect one's decisions concerning behavior. (See distinction between drive theory and cognitive theory in Chapter 1.)

Third, major differences exist concerning their implication for reward scheduling. While expectancy/valence theory advocates sometime argue for continuous reinforcement (that is, a direct relationship between performance and rewards), behavior modification suggests a variable or partial reinforcement interval. Behavior modification proponents argue with some support (see Yukl, Wexley, & Seymore, 1972) that variable reinforcement leads to more sustained effort on the job. (The importance of reward scheduling was covered in detail in the previous chapter.)

Despite these differences, it should be noted that both theories place strong emphasis on the role of rewards and performance-reward contingencies as they affect subsequent performance. Thus, while differences do exist, both theories can help understand the intricacies of managing employee motivation and facilitating improved performance. Indeed, it may be that the two models are not entirely incompatible. Combining historical and ahistorical influences on effort and performance may increase our ability to structure rewarding environments to the benefit of both organizations and their employees.

IMPLICATIONS FOR MANAGEMENT

From a managerial perspective, expectancy theory offers a wide range of recommendations for increasing employee motivation. Since these are discussed
in detail in the reading selection by Nadler and Lawler, it is not necessary to
repeat them here. Suffice it to say that expectancy theory identifies several
specific strategies for managers by allowing them to raise questions about what
they want from their subordinates and what their subordinates want from the
organization. Expectancy theory also makes a strong argument in favor of
having rewards contingent upon successful performance. Moreover, the theory
emphasizes the need to take a systematic view of how several personal and
organizational variables interact to influence motivation and performance. In
all, then, expectancy theory represents a comprehensive approach to understanding motivational processes in work organizations that does appear to hold
promise for managers.

OVERVIEW

Several aspects of expectancy theory are examined in the selections that follow.
First, Nadler and Lawler review the basic assumptions underlying the model.
The theory itself is then presented, both in a simplified form and in a more
comprehensive form (see appendix to article). Finally, implications for both
managers and organizations are discussed.

The second selection, by Campbell and Pritchard, provides a current review
of the available research evidence as it pertains to expectancy theory. Research
relating to each aspect of the model is discussed separately. In addition, several
problems with the model are discussed; these problems suggest new avenues
of research on the topic as well as pointing to areas of management concern.

Taken together, these two selections give a comprehensive review of ex-
pectancy/valence theory. A key factor, present in both the selections, is the
developmental nature of the theory itself—which has, over the past decade,
evolved into a fairly well-developed theory of work motivation. However, as
is evident, a good deal more testing and modeling work is necessary, for the
theory, although it shows definite promise, still requires a firmer empirical-
analytical base that can come only from further thought and investigation.

REFERENCES AND SUGGESTED ADDITIONAL READINGS

Behling, O., Schriesheim, C., & Tolliver, J. Alternatives to expectancy theories of work
    motivation. *Decision Sciences*, 1975, **6**, 449–461.
Campbell, J. P., Dunnette, M. D., Lawler, E. E., III, & Weick, K. E. *Managerial
    behavior, performance, and effectiveness*. New York: McGraw-Hill, 1970.
Cummings, L. L., & Schwab, D. P. *Performance in organizations*. Glenview, Ill.:
    Scott. Foresman, 1973.

Galbraith, J., & Cummings, L. L. An empirical investigation of the motivational determinants of task performance: Interactive effects between valence-instrumentality and motivation-ability. *Organizational Behavior and Human Performance*, 1967, **2**, 237–258.

Georgopoulos, B. S., Mahoney, G. M., & Jones, N. W., Jr. A path-goal approach to productivity. *Journal of Applied Psychology*, 1957, **41**, 345–353.

Graen, G. Instrumentality theory of work motivation: Some experimental results and suggested modifications. *Journal of Applied Psychology Monograph*, 1969, **53**, (2, Part 2).

Heneman, H. G., III, & Schwab, D. P. Evaluation of research on expectancy theory predictions of employee performance. *Psychological Bulletin*, 1972, **78**, 1–9.

Lawler, E. E., III. A correlational-causal analysis of the relationship between expectancy attitudes and job performance. *Journal of Applied Psychology*, 1968, **52**, 462–468.

Lawler, E. E., III. *Motivation in work organizations*. Monterey, Calif.: Brooks/Cole, 1973.

Lawler, E. E., III, & Porter, L. W. Antecedent attitudes of effective managerial performance. *Organizational Behavior and Human Performance*, 1967, **2**, 122–142.

Lawler, E. E., III, & Porter, L. W. The effects of performance on job satisfaction. *Industrial Relations*, 1967, **7**(1), 20–28.

Mitchell, T. R. Expectancy models of job satisfaction, occupational preference and effort: A theoretical, methodological and empirical appraisal. *Psychological Bulletin*, 1974, **81**, 1096–1112.

Mitchell, T. R., & Nebeker, D. M. Expectancy theory predictions of academic effort and performance. *Journal of Applied Psychology*, 1973, **57**, 61–67.

Porter, L. W., & Lawler, E. E., III. *Managerial attitudes and performance*. Homewood, Ill.: Irwin, 1968.

Porter, L. W., & Lawler, E. E., III. What job attitudes tell us about motivation. *Harvard Business Review*, 1968, **46**(1), 118–126.

Pritchard, R. D., & Sanders, M. S. The influence of valence, instrumentality, and expectancy on effort and performance. *Journal of Applied Psychology*, 1973, **57**, 55–60.

Vroom, V. H. *Some personality determinants of the effects of participation*. Englewood Cliffs, N. J.: Prentice-Hall, 1960.

Vroom, V. H. *Work and motivation*. New York: Wiley, 1964.

Wahba, M. A., & House, R. J. Expectancy theory in work and motivation: Some logical and methodological issues. *Human Relations*, 1974, **27**, 121–147.

Yukl, G., Wexley, K. N., & Seymore, J. D. Effectiveness of pay incentives under variable ratio and continuous reinforcement schedules. *Journal of Applied Psychology*, 1972, **56**, 19–23.

Motivation: A Diagnostic Approach

David A. Nadler
Edward E. Lawler III

- What makes some people work hard while others do as little as possible?
- How can I, as a manager, influence the performance of people who work for me?
- Why do people turn over, show up late to work, and miss work entirely?

These important questions about employees' behavior can only be answered by managers who have a grasp of what motivates people. Specifically, a good understanding of motivation can serve as a valuable tool for *understanding* the causes of behavior in organizations, for *predicting* the effects of any managerial action, and for *directing* behavior so that organizational and individual goals can be achieved.

EXISTING APPROACHES

During the past twenty years, managers have been bombarded with a number of different approaches to motivation. The terms associated with these approaches are well known—"human relations," "scientific management," "job enrichment," "need hierarchy," "self-actualization," etc. Each of these approaches has something to offer. On the other hand, each of these different approaches also has its problems in both theory and practice. Running through almost all of the approaches with which managers are familiar are a series of implicit but clearly erroneous assumptions.

Assumption 1: All Employees Are Alike Different theories present different ways of looking at people, but each of them assumes that all employees are basically similar in their makeup: Employees all want economic gains, or all want a pleasant climate, or all aspire to be self-actualizing, etc.

Assumption 2: All Situations Are Alike Most theories assume that all managerial situations are alike, and that the managerial course of action for motivation (for example, participation, job enlargement, etc.) is applicable in all situations.

Assumption 3: One Best Way Out of the other two assumptions there emerges a basic principle that there is "one best way" to motivate employees.

When these "one best way" approaches are tried in the "correct" situation they will work. However, all of them are bound to fail in some situations. They are therefore not adequate managerial tools.

From Hackman, J. R., Lawler, E. E., and Porter, L. W., *Perspectives on behavior in organizations.* New York, McGraw-Hill, 1977, 26–36. Used by permission.

A NEW APPROACH

During the past ten years, a great deal of research has been done on a new approach to looking at motivation. This approach, frequently called "expectancy theory," still needs further testing, refining, and extending. However, enough is known that many behavioral scientists have concluded that it represents the most comprehensive, valid, and useful approach to understanding motivation. Further, it is apparent that it is a very useful tool for understanding motivation in organizations.

The theory is based on a number of specific assumptions about the causes of behavior in organizations.

Assumption 1: Behavior Is Determined by a Combination of Forces in the Individual and Forces in the Environment Neither the individual nor the environment alone determines behavior. Individuals come into organizations with certain "psychological baggage." They have past experiences and a developmental history which has given them unique sets of needs, ways of looking at the world, and expectations about how organizations will treat them. These all influence how individuals respond to their work environment. The work environment provides structures (such as a pay system or a supervisor) which influence the behavior of people. Different environments tend to produce different behavior in similar people just as dissimilar people tend to behave differently in similar environments.

Assumption 2: People Make Decisions about Their Own Behavior in Organizations While there are many constraints on the behavior of individuals in organizations, most of the behavior that is observed is the result of individuals' conscious decisions. These decisions usually fall into two categories. First, individuals make decisions about *membership behavior*—coming to work, staying at work, and in other ways being a member of the organization. Second, individuals make decisions about the amount of effort they will direct *towards performing their jobs*. This includes decisions about how hard to work, how much to produce, at what quality, etc.

Assumption 3: Different People Have Different Types of Needs, Desires and Goals Individuals differ on what kinds of outcomes (or rewards) they desire. These differences are not random; they can be examined systematically by an understanding of the differences in the strength of individuals' needs.

Assumption 4: People Make Decisions among Alternative Plans of Behavior Based on Their Perceptions (Expectancies) of the Degree to Which a Given Behavior Will Lead to Desired Outcomes In simple terms, people tend to do those things which they see as leading to outcomes (which can also be called "rewards") they desire and avoid doing those things they see as leading to outcomes that are not desired.

In general, the approach used here views people as having their own needs and mental maps of what the world is like. They use these maps to make decisions about how they will behave, behaving in those ways which their mental maps indicate will lead to outcomes that will satisfy their needs. Therefore, they are inherently neither motivated nor unmotivated; motivation depends on the situation they are in, and how it fits their needs.

THE THEORY

Based on these general assumptions, expectancy theory states a number of propositions about the process by which people make decisions about their own behavior in organizational settings. While the theory is complex at first view, it is in fact made of a series of fairly straightforward observations about behavior. (The theory is presented in more technical terms in Appendix A.) Three concepts serve as the key building blocks of the theory:

Performance-Outcome Expectancy Every behavior has associated with it, in an individual's mind, certain outcomes (rewards or punishments). In other words, the individual believes or expects that if he or she behaves in a certain way, he or she will get certain things.

Examples of expectancies can easily be described. An individual may have an expectancy that if he produces ten units he will receive his normal hourly rate while if he produces fifteen units he will receive his hourly pay rate plus a bonus. Similarly an individual may believe that certain levels of performance will lead to approval or disapproval from members of her work group or from her supervisor. Each performance can be seen as leading to a number of different kinds of outcomes and outcomes can differ in their types.

Valence Each outcome has a "valence" (value, worth, attractiveness) to a specific individual. Outcomes have different valences for different individuals. This comes about because valences result from individual needs and perceptions, which differ because they in turn reflect other factors in the individual's life.

For example, some individuals may value an opportunity for promotion or advancement because of their needs for achievement or power, while others may not want to be promoted and leave their current work group because of needs for affiliation with others. Similarly, a fringe benefit such as a pension plan may have great valence for an older worker but little valence for a young employee on his first job.

Effort-Performance Expectancy Each behavior also has associated with it in the individual's mind a certain expectancy or probability of success. This expectancy represents the individual's perception of how hard it will be to achieve such behavior and the probability of his or her successful achievement of that behavior.

For example, you may have a strong expectancy that if you put forth effort, you can produce ten units an hour, but that you have only a fifty-fifty chance of producing fifteen units an hour if you try.

Putting these concepts together, it is possible to make a basic statement about motivation. In general, the motivation to attempt to behave in a certain way is greatest when:

a The individual believes that the behavior will lead to outcomes (performance-outcome expectancy)

b The individual believes that these outcomes have positive value for him or her (valence)

c The individual believes that he or she is able to perform at the desired level (effort-performance expectancy)

Given a number of alternative levels of behavior (ten, fifteen, and twenty units of production per hour, for example) the individual will choose that level of performance which has the greatest motivational force associated with it, as indicated by the expectancies, outcomes, and valences.

In other words, when faced with choices about behavior, the individual goes through a process of considering questions such as, "Can I perform at that level if I try?" "If I perform at that level, what will happen?" "How do I feel about those things that will happen?" The individual then decides to behave in that way which seems to have the best chance of producing positive, desired outcomes.

A General Model

On the basis of these concepts, it is possible to construct a general model of behavior in organizational settings (see Figure 1). Working from left to right

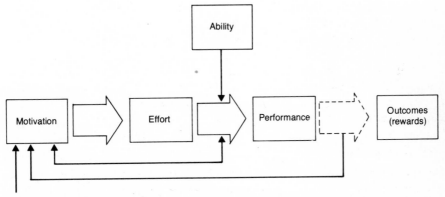

A person's motivation is a function of:

a. Effort-to-performance expectancies
b. Performance-to-outcome expectancies
c. Perceived valence of outcomes

Figure 1 The basic motivation-behavior sequence.

in the model, motivation is seen as the force on the individual to expend effort. Motivation leads to an observed level of effort by the individual. Effort, alone, however, is not enough. Performance results from a combination of the effort that an individual puts forth *and* the level of ability which he or she has (reflecting skills, training, information, etc.).Effort thus combines with ability to produce a given level of performance. As a result of performance, the individual attains certain outcomes. The model indicates this relationship in a dotted line, reflecting the fact that sometimes people perform but do not get desired outcomes. As this process of performance-reward occurs, time after time, the actual events serve to provide information which influences the individual's perceptions (particularly expectancies) and thus influences motivation in the future.

Outcomes, or rewards, fall into two major categories. First, the individual obtains outcomes from the environment. When an individual performs at a given level he or she can receive positive or negative outcomes from supervisors, coworkers, the organization's rewards systems, or other sources. These environmental rewards are thus one source of outcomes for the individual. A second source of outcomes is the individual. These include outcomes which occur purely from the performance of the task itself (feelings of accomplishment, personal worth, achievement, etc.). In a sense, the individual gives these rewards to himself or herself. The environment cannot give them or take them away directly; it can only make them possible.

Supporting Evidence

Over fifty studies have been done to test the validity of the expectancy-theory approach to predicting employee behavior.[1] Almost without exception, the studies have confirmed the predictions of the theory. As the theory predicts, the best performers in organizations tend to see a strong relationship between performing their jobs well and receiving rewards they value. In addition they have clear performance goals and feel they can perform well. Similarly, studies using the expectancy theory to predict how people choose jobs also show that individuals tend to interview for and actually take those jobs which they feel will provide the rewards they value. One study, for example, was able to correctly predict for 80 percent of the people studied which of several jobs they would take.[2] Finally, the theory correctly predicts that beliefs about the outcomes associated with performance (expectancies) will be better predictors of performance than will feelings of job satisfaction since expectancies are the critical causes of performance and satisfaction is not.

[1]For reviews of the expectancy theory research see Mitchell, T. R. Expectancy models of job satisfaction, occupational preference and effort: A theoretical methodological, and empirical appraisal. *Psychological Bulletin*, 1974, **81**, 1053–1077. For a more general discussion of expectancy theory and other approaches to motivation see Lawler, E. E. *Motivation in work organizations*, Belmont Calif.: Brooks/Cole, 1973.

[2]Lawler, E. E., Kuleck, W. J., Rhode, J. G. & Sorenson, J. E. Job choice and post-decision dissonance. *Organizational Behavior and Human Performance*, 1975, **13**, 133–145.

Questions about the Model

Although the results so far have been encouraging, they also indicate some problems with the model. These problems do not critically affect the managerial implications of the model, but they should be noted. The model is based on the assumption that individuals make very rational decisions after a thorough exploration of all the available alternatives and on weighing the possible outcomes of all these alternatives. When we talk to or observe individuals, however, we find that their decision processes are frequently less thorough. People often stop considering alternative behavior plans when they find one that is at least moderately satisfying, even though more rewarding plans remain to be examined.

People are also limited in the amount of information they can handle at one time, and therefore the model may indicate a process that is much more complex than the one that actually takes place. On the other hand, the model does provide enough information and is consistent enough with reality to present some clear implications for managers who are concerned with the question of how to motivate the people who work for them.

Implications for Managers

The first set of implications is directed toward the individual manager who has a group of people working for him or her and is concerned with how to motivate good performance. Since behavior is a result of forces both in the person and in the environment, you as manager need to look at and diagnose both the person and the environment. Specifically, you need to do the following:

Figure Out What Outcomes Each Employee Values As a first step, it is important to determine what kinds of outcomes or rewards have valence for your employees. For each employee you need to determine "what turns him or her on." There are various ways of finding this out, including (a) finding out employees' desires through some structured method of data collection, such as a questionnaire, (b) observing the employees' reactions to different situations or rewards, or (c) the fairly simple act of asking them what kinds of rewards they want, what kind of career goals they have, or "what's in it for them." It is important to stress here that it is very difficult to change what people want, but fairly easy to find out what they want. Thus, the skillful manager emphasizes diagnosis of needs, not changing the individuals themselves.

Determine What Kinds of Behavior You Desire Managers frequently talk about "good performance" without really defining what good performance is. An important step in motivating is for you yourself to figure out what kinds of performance are required and what are adequate measures or indicators of performance (quantity, quality, etc.). There is also a need to be able to define those performances in fairly specific terms so that observable and measurable behavior can be defined and subordinates can understand what is desired of them (e.g., produce ten products of a certain quality standard—rather than only produce at a high rate).

Make Sure Desired Levels of Performance Are Reachable   The model states that motivation is determined not only by the performance-to-outcome expectancy, but also by the effort-to-performance expectancy. The implication of this is that the levels of performance which are set as the points at which individuals receive desired outcomes must be reachable or attainable by these individuals. If the employees feel that the level of performance required to get a reward is higher than they can reasonably achieve, then their motivation to perform well will be relatively low.

Link Desired Outcomes to Desired Performances   The next step is to directly, clearly, and explicitly link those outcomes desired by employees to the specific performances desired by you. If your employee values external rewards, then the emphasis should be on the rewards systems concerned with promotion, pay, and approval. While the linking of these rewards can be initiated through your making statements to your employees, it is extremely important that employees see a clear example of the reward process working in a fairly short period of time if the motivating "expectancies" are to be created in the employees' minds. The linking must be done by some concrete public acts, in addition to statements of intent.

If your employee values internal rewards (e.g., achievement), then you should concentrate on changing the nature of the persons' job, for he or she is likely to respond well to such things as increased autonomy, feedback, and challenge, because these things will lead to a situation where good job performance is inherently rewarding. The best way to check on the adequacy of the internal and external reward system is to ask people what their perceptions of the situation are. Remember it is the perceptions of people that determine their motivation, not reality. It doesn't matter for example whether you feel a subordinate's pay is related to his or her motivation. Motivation will be present only if the subordinate sees the relationship. Many managers are misled about the behavior of their subordinates because they rely on their own perceptions of the situation and forget to find out what their subordinates feel. There is only one way to do this: ask. Questionnaires can be used here, as can personal interviews.

Analyze the Total Situation for Conflicting Expectancies   Having set up positive expectancies for employees, you then need to look at the entire situation to see if other factors (informal work groups, other managers, the organization's reward systems) have set up conflicting expectancies in the minds of the employees. Motivation will only be high when people see a number of rewards associated with good performance and few negative outcomes. Again, you can often gather this kind of information by asking your subordinates. If there are major conflicts, you need to make adjustments, either in your own performance and reward structure, or in the other sources of rewards or punishments in the environment.

Make Sure Changes in Outcomes Are Large Enough   In examining the motivational system, it is important to make sure that changes in outcomes or rewards are large enough to motivate significant behavior. Trivial rewards will result in trivial amounts of effort and thus trivial improvements in performance. Rewards must be large enough to motivate individuals to put forth the effort required to bring about significant changes in performance.

Check the System for Its Equity   The model is based on the idea that individuals are different and therefore different rewards will need to be used to motivate different individuals. On the other hand, for a motivational system to work it must be a fair one—one that has equity (not equality). Good performers should see that they get more desired rewards than do poor performers, and others in the system should see that also. Equity should not be confused with a system of equality where all are rewarded equally, with no regard to their performance. A system of equality is guaranteed to produce low motivation.

Implications for Organizations

Expectancy theory has some clear messages for those who run large organizations. It suggests how organizational structures can be designed so that they increase rather than decrease levels of motivation of organization members. While there are many different implications, a few of the major ones are as follows:

Implication 1: The Design of Pay and Reward Systems   Organizations usually get what they reward, not what they want. This can be seen in many situations, and pay systems are a good example.[3] Frequently, organizations reward people for membership (through pay tied to seniority, for example) rather than for performance. Little wonder that what the organization gets is behavior oriented towards "safe," secure employment rather than effort directed at performing well. In addition, even where organizations do pay for performance as a motivational device, they frequently negate the motivational value of the system by keeping pay secret, therefore preventing people from observing the pay-to-performance relationship that would serve to create positive, clear, and strong performance-to-reward expectancies. The implication is that organizations should put more effort into rewarding people (through pay, promotion, better job opportunities, etc.) for the performances which are desired, and that to keep these rewards secret is clearly self-defeating. In addition, it underscores the importance of the frequently ignored performance evaluation or appraisal process and the need to evaluate people based on how they perform clearly defined specific behaviors, rather than on how they score on ratings of general traits such as "honesty," "cleanliness," and other, similar terms which frequently appear as part of the performance appraisal form.

---

[3]For a detailed discussion of the implications of expectancy theory for pay and reward systems, see Lawler, E. E. *Pay and organizational effectiveness: A psychological view*. New York: McGraw-Hill, 1971.

Implication 2: The Design of Tasks, Jobs, and Roles   One source of desired outcomes is the work itself. The expectancy-theory model supports much of the job enrichment literature, in saying that by designing jobs which enable people to get their needs fulfilled, organizations can bring about higher levels of motivation.[4] The major difference between the traditional approaches to job enlargement or enrichment and the expectancy-theory approach is the recognition by the expectancy theory that different people have different needs and, therefore, some people may not want enlarged or enriched jobs. Thus, while the design of tasks that have more autonomy, variety, feedback, meaningfulness, etc., will lead to higher motivation in some, the organization needs to build in the opportunity for individuals to make choices about the kind of work they will do so that not everyone is forced to experience job enrichment.

Implication 3: The Importance of Group Structures   Groups, both formal and informal, are powerful and potent sources of desired outcomes for individuals. Groups can provide or withhold acceptance, approval, affection, skill training, needed information, assistance, etc. They are a powerful force in the total motivational environment of individuals. Several implications emerge from the importance of groups. First, organizations should consider the structuring of at least a portion of rewards around group performance rather than individual performance. This is particularly important where group members have to cooperate with each other to produce a group product or service, and where the individual's contribution is often hard to determine. Second, the organization needs to train managers to be aware of how groups can influence individual behavior and to be sensitive to the kinds of expectancies which informal groups set up and their conflict or consistency with the expectancies that the organization attempts to create.

Implication 4: The Supervisor's Role   The immediate supervisor has an important role in creating, monitoring, and maintaining the expectancies and reward structures which will lead to good performance. The supervisor's role in the motivation process becomes one of defining clear goals, setting clear reward expectancies, and providing the right rewards for different people (which could include both organizational rewards and personal rewards such as recognition, approval, or support from the supervisor). Thus, organizations need to provide supervisors with an awareness of the nature of motivation as well as the tools (control over organizational rewards, skill in administering those rewards) to create positive motivation.

Implication 5: Measuring Motivation   If things like expectancies, the nature of the job, supervisor-controlled outcomes, satisfaction, etc., are important in understanding how well people are being motivated, then organizations need to monitor employee perceptions along these lines. One relatively cheap

---

[4]A good discussion of job design with an expectancy theory perspective is in Hackman, J. R., Oldham, G. R., Janson, R., & Purdy, K. A new strategy for job enrichment. *California Management Review*, Summer, 1975, p. 57.

and reliable method of doing this is through standardized employee question-naires. A number of organizations already use such techniques, surveying employees' perceptions and attitudes at regular intervals (ranging from once a month to once every year-and-a-half) using either standardized surveys or surveys developed specifically for the organization. Such information is useful both to the individual manager and to top management in assessing the state of human resources and the effectiveness of the organization's motivational systems.[5]

Implication 6: Individualizing Organizations   Expectancy theory leads to a final general implication about a possible future direction for the design of organizations. Because different people have different needs and therefore have different valences, effective motivation must come through the recognition that not all employees are alike and that organizations need to be flexible in order to accommodate individual differences. This implies the "building in" of choice for employees in many areas, such as reward systems, fringe benefits, job assignments, etc., where employees previously have had little say. A success-ful example of the building in of such choice can be seen in the experiments at TRW and the Educational Testing Service with "cafeteria fringe-benefits plans" which allow employees to choose the fringe benefits they want, rather than taking the expensive and often unwanted benefits which the company frequently provides to everyone.[6]

SUMMARY

Expectancy theory provides a more complex model of man for managers to work with. At the same time, it is a model which holds promise for the more effective motivation of individuals and the more effective design of organiza-tional systems. It implies, however, the need for more exacting and thorough diagnosis by the manager to determine (a) the relevant forces in the individual, and (b) the relevant forces in the environment, both of which combine to motivate different kinds of behavior. Following diagnosis, the model implies a need to act—to develop a system of pay, promotion, job assignments, group structures, supervision, etc.—to bring about effective motivation by providing different outcomes for different individuals.

Performance of individuals is a critical issue in making organizations work effectively. If a manager is to influence work behavior and performance, he or she must have an understanding of motivation and the factors which influence an individual's motivation to come to work, to work hard, and to work well. While simple models offer easy answers, it is the more complex models which

[5]The use of questionnaires for understanding and changing organizational behavior is dis-cussed in Nadler, D. A. *Feedback and organizational development: Using data-based methods.* Reading, Mass.: Addison-Wesley, 1977.

[6]The whole issue of individualizing organizations is examined in Lawler. E. E. The indi-vidualized organization: Problems and promise. *California Management Review*, 1974, **17** (2), 31–39.

seem to offer more promise. Managers can use models (like expectancy theory) to understand the nature of behavior and build more effective organizations.

APPENDIX A: The Expectancy Theory Model in More Technical Terms

A person's motivation to exert effort towards a specific level of performance is based on his or her perceptions of associations between actions and outcomes. The critical perceptions which contribute to motivation are graphically presented in Figure 2. These perceptions can be defined as follows:

   a The effort-to-performance expectancy ($E \rightarrow P$): This refers to the person's subjective probability about the likelihood that he or she can perform at a given level, or that effort on his or her part will lead to successful performance. This term can be thought of as varying from 0 to 1. In general, the less likely a person feels that he or she can perform at a given level, the less likely he or she will be to try to perform at that level. A person's $E \rightarrow P$ probabilities are also strongly influenced by each situation and by previous experience in that and similar situations.

   b The performance-to-outcomes expectancy ($P \rightarrow O$) and valence (V): This refers to a combination of a number of beliefs about what the outcomes of successful performance will be and the value or attractiveness of these

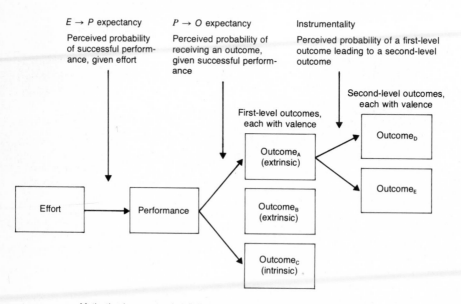

Motivation is expressed as follows: $M = [E \rightarrow P] \times \Sigma [(P \rightarrow O)(V)]$

Figure 2 Major terms in expectancy theory.

outcomes to the individual. Valence is considered to vary from $+1$ (very desirable) to -1 (very undesirable) and the performance-to-outcomes probabilities vary from $+1$ (performance sure to lead to outcome) to 0 (performance not related to outcome). In general, the more likely a person feels that performance will lead to valent outcomes, the more likely he or she will be to try to perform at the required level.

c Instrumentality: As Figure 2 indicates, a single level of performance can be associated with a number of different outcomes, each having a certain degree of valence. Some outcomes are valent because they have direct value or attractiveness. Some outcomes, however, have valence because they are seen as leading to (or being "instrumental" for) the attainment of other "second level" outcomes which have direct value or attractiveness.

d Intrinsic and extrinsic outcomes: Some outcomes are seen as occurring directly as a result of performing the task itself and are outcomes which the individual thus gives to himself (i.e., feelings of accomplishment, creativity, etc.). These are called "intrinsic" outcomes. Other outcomes that are associated with performance are provided or mediated by external factors (the organization, the supervisor, the work group, etc.). These outcomes are called "extrinsic" outcomes.

Along with the graphic representation of these terms presented in Figure 2, there is a simplified formula for combining these perceptions to arrive at a term expressing the relative level of motivation to exert effort towards performance at a given level. The formula expresses these relationships:

a The person's motivation to perform is determined by the $P \rightarrow O$ expectancy multiplied by the valence (V) of the outcome. The valence of the first order outcome subsumes the instrumentalities and valences of second order outcomes. The relationship is multiplicative since there is no motivation to perform if either of the terms is zero.

b Since a level of performance has multiple outcomes associated with it, the products of all probability-times-valence combinations are added together for all the outcomes that are seen as related to the specific performance.

c This term (the summed $P \rightarrow O$ expectancies times valences) is then multiplied by the $E \rightarrow P$ expectancy. Again the multiplicative relationship indicates that if either term is zero, motivation is zero.

d In summary, the strength of a person's motivation to perform effectively is influenced by (1) the person's belief that effort can be converted into performance, and (2) the net attractiveness of the events that are perceived to stem from good performance.

So far, all the terms have referred to the individual's perceptions which result in motivation and thus an intention to behave in a certain way. Figure 3 is a simplified representation of the total model, showing how these intentions get translated into actual behavior.[7] The model envisions the following sequence of events:

a   First, the strength of a person's motivation to perform correctly is most directly reflected in his or her effort—how hard he or she works. This effort expenditure may or may not result in good performance, since at least two factors must be right if effort is to be converted into performance. First, the person must possess the necessary abilities in order to perform the job well. Unless both ability and effort are high, there cannot be good performance. A second factor is the person's perception of how his or her effort can best be converted into performance. It is assumed that this perception is learned by the individual on the basis of previous experience in similar situations. This "how to do it" perception can obviously vary widely in accuracy, and—where erroneous perceptions exist—performance is low even though effort or motivation may be high.

b   Second, when performance occurs, certain amounts of outcomes are obtained by the individual. Intrinsic outcomes, not being mediated by outside forces, tend to occur regularly as a result of performance, while extrinsic outcomes may or may not accrue to the individual (indicated by the wavy line in the model).

c   Third, as a result of the obtaining of outcomes and the perceptions of

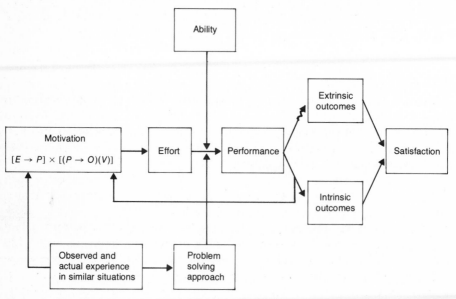

Figure 3   Simplified expectancy-theory model of behavior.

[7]For a more detailed statement of the model see Lawler, E. E. Job attitudes and employee motivation: Theory, research and practice. *Personnel Psychology*, 1970, 23, 223–237.

the relative value of the outcomes obtained, the individual has a positive or negative affective response (a level of satisfaction or dissatisfaction).

   d   Fourth, the model indicates that events which occur influence future behavior by altering the $E \to P$, $P \to O$, and V perceptions. This process is represented by the feedback loops running from actual behavior back to motivation.

Research Evidence Pertaining to Expectancy-Instrumentality-Valence Theory

John P. Campbell
Robert D. Pritchard

We would like to consider briefly the present state of empirical research relative to expectancy-valence theory. This is in no sense meant to be a comprehensive literature review, but is intended to give, in rather Spartan fashion, a representative sample of the prevailing empirical winds and the methods by which the theory has been operationalized. More detailed treatments can be found in Vroom (1964, 1965), Campbell, Dunnette, Lawler, and Weick (1970), Lawler (1971, 1973), Heneman and Schwab (1972), Dachler and Mobley (1973), Mitchell and Biglan (1971), House and Wahba (1972), Miner and Dachler (1973), and Mitchell (1974).

Kinds of Studies

Before discussing specific findings we would like to outline two basic parameters that we think are important for distinguishing among studies. The first has to do with the research setting in which the study was done and whether it was experimental or correlational in nature. A cross-classification of setting and metholology yields five principal varieties.

   1   A few investigators have conducted laboratory experiments using students as subjects (e.g., Arvey, 1972; Motowidlo, Loehr, & Dunnette, 1972; Pritchard & DeLeo, 1973). Keep in mind that VIE theory deals with perceptions as determinants of behavior and even though expectancy, instrumentality, valence or some combination thereof might be manipulated experimentally, the model says that the subject's perceptions of the manipulated situation must then be obtained and related to behavior. Not all experimental studies purporting to "test" VIE theory have done that.

From Campbell, J. P., & Pritchard, R. D., Motivation theory in industrial and organizational psychology. In M. D. Dunnette (ed.), *Handbook of industrial and organizational psychology*, Chicago: Rand McNally, 1976, 84–95. Used by permission.

2 There have been at least two attempts to manipulate VIE components experimentally in simulated organizations (e.g., Graen, 1969; Jorgenson, Dunnette, & Pritchard, 1973). Both of these set up temporary "employer overload" type organizations and "hired" subjects to work on a very short term basis. Such studies preserve the controls necessary for a true experiment but also add a great deal of realism in the task content.

3 There has been only one study (Pritchard, DeLeo, & VonBergen, 1974) to date that has approached the nature of a true field experiment in which VIE variables were experimentally manipulated in an ongoing organizational setting.

4 Perhaps the bulk of the studies pertaining to the VIE model are correlational field studies in which existing perceptions of expectancy, instrumentality, and valence are assessed via a questionnaire instrument and the resulting scores and combinations of scores are correlated with the dependent variable (e.g., Arvey & Neil, 1972; Dachler & Mobley, 1975; Gavin, 1970; Hackman & Porter, 1968; Lawler, 1968a; Lawler & Porter, 1967; Mitchell & Albright, 1972; Mitchell & Nebeker, 1973; Schuster, Clark, & Rogers, 1971).

5 A subset of the above would be a correlational field study which attempts to measure the independent and dependent variables at two points in time and then employs a panel design or path analysis in an attempt to gain some insights into the causal relationship. The Lawler and Suttle (1973) study is an example of such a design.

The second major parameter pertains to the way in which the dependent variable has been operationalized. Consider the following list:

1 A few studies have used occupational or job preference as a dependent variable (e.g., Holmstrom & Beach, 1973; Mitchell & Knudsen, 1973; Sheard, 1970; Vroom, 1966; Wanous, 1972). However, this is analogous to using the valence of specific task goal or performance level as a dependent variable and only one study (Sheridan, Richards & Slocum, 1974) has attempted to predict an individual's actual choice of a job.

2 A number of studies have used "rated" effort as a dependent variable (e.g., Hackman & Porter, 1968; Lawler & Porter, 1967; Mitchell & Albright, 1972; Mitchell & Nebeker, 1973; Pritchard & Sanders, 1973; Schuster, Clark & Rogers, 1971). Almost all of these studies have been carried out in a field setting, but there is a major distinction between studies that have employed self-ratings of effort versus those that have used supervisor or peer ratings.

3 Several experimental laboratory or simulation studies used measures of task performance (e.g., Arvey, 1972; Cartledge, 1972; Graen, 1969; Jorgenson, Dunnette, & Pritchard, 1973; Motowidlo, Loehr, & Dunnette, 1972). Strictly speaking, the expectancy model does not try to explain performance, since there are many other determinants of performance besides motivational ones. However, for the most part, the laboratory and simulation studies have chosen very simple and repetitive tasks for which the explicit or implicit assumption has been that individual differences in performance should reflect primarily effort differences and not differences in skill, aptitude or task understanding. Everyone should have more than enough skill to perform well. For example, Graen (1969) and Jorgenson et al. (1973) had subjects search for simple errors in computer printouts, and Arvey (1972) and Motowidlo et al. (1972) asked subjects to add two digit numbers. The field study reported by Dachler and Mobley (1973) also focused on simple production tasks, but for real jobs in two different manufacturing operations.

4 Finally, other studies have used the VIE model to predict performance or job satisfaction in relatively complex jobs. Again, these dependent variables are outside the confines of the VIE model, but a number of investigators have used them anyway.

Valence and Behavior

While a few data do exist pertaining to relation between valence and effort and between valence and performance; the results are quite mixed. In several managerial samples Porter and Lawler (1968) found in general that the greater the importance attributed to pay, the higher were the individual's performance evaluations and ratings of effort. In a study by Pritchard and Sanders (1973), 148 employees in a government agency who were learning a new job completed a questionnaire that included measures of valence of job outcomes and performance-outcome instrumentalities. The criteria consisted of self and supervisors' ratings of effort for different aspects of the training program. The sum of the valence ratings correlated .54 with self-reported effort and .21 with supervisors' ratings of effort.

There are also some negative findings, Hackman and Porter (1968), in a survey of telephone operators found that the medium correlation between measures of performance and valence of outcomes was only .16. However, when valence was multiplied by instrumentality to get an overall prediction, significant correlations with performance were obtained even though correlations of instrumentality with performance were also low. Further negative evidence comes from an experimental study by Jorgenson, Dunnette, and Pritchard (1973). Although the design was complex, the essential elements consisted of hiring subjects for what they felt was a real job and paying them on a high performance-outcome instrumentality pay system (a semi-piece rate) for six days. The valence of outcomes portion of the model would predict that for subjects on such a pay system, there should be positive correlation between the valence of pay and performance. However, this was not the case. Correlations between rated importance of pay and job performance ranged from −.18 to .15 for the six days, with a median of .05.

The predominant impression generated by these data is that no definite conclusions can be drawn regarding the predictive utility of the valence of outcomes portion of the model. However, three conditions must hold for the valence of outcomes to be related to effort or performance. Performance outcome instrumentalities must be greater than zero, effort-performance expectancy must be greater than zero, and there must be some variability in the valence of outcomes.

Low correlations between valence of outcomes and effort or performance cannot in themselves be taken as negative evidence for the influence of valence of outcomes, if the research effort was not specifically designed to control for these factors. It is also apparent that methods used to measure valence have been of the crudest sort. In spite of the fact that the measurement of the utility of an outcome to an individual has consistently been shown to be one of the most difficult problems in the investigation of human choice behavior (e.g., Becker & McClintock, 1967), organizational psychologists have exhibited little sense of urgency about the matter. The difficulty is illustrated by asking simply, "What is the utility to an individual of a $500 salary increase?" The analogous question for other outcomes presents even more problems. Assuming they can put them all on a common dimension, asking subjects to rate the importance or desirability of various outcomes produces a weak ordering at best, yet the model requires a utility scale with substantial interval or perhaps even ratio properties. All of which argues that we should spend more time developing better measures of valence.

It would seem unwise to conclude that valences don't affect behavior since the literature in experimental psychology is quite clear in showing the significant influence of reward magnitude on subsequent behavior.

Performance/Outcome Contingency (Instrumentality)

The literature on this component of the model is fairly extensive and offers consistent support for the effects of the component on effort and performance. The crucial question concerns the form of the relationship.

The classic study by Georgopoulos, Mahoney, and Jones (1957) surveyed 621 production employees on an incentive system in a unionized household appliance factory. Via questionnaire they measured both the instrumentality of high and low performance for the attainment of the three outcomes of making more money in the long run, getting along well with the work group, and promotion to a higher salary rate. The results indicated that subjects who reported high instrumentalities tended to be higher producers.

A number of other correlational studies have supported the link between instrumentality and behavior. Lawler and Porter (1967) used a three-item composite measure of instrumentality which included two items dealing with performance-outcome instrumentality and one item dealing with effort-outcome instrumentality and found low positive relationships between this composite instrumentality measure and ratings of effort (median $r = .18$), but little relationship between the instrumentality measure and ratings of performance (median $r = .11$). In a more extensive study (Porter & Lawler, 1968), using a similar instrumentality measure, they found instrumentality generally related to ratings of performance, and even more strongly related to ratings of effort. Using the Lawler and Porter questionnaire with male and female managerial candidates, Gavin (1970) found that instrumentality was positively and significantly related to supervisors' ratings of performance for both males and females (median $r = .27$). Schuster, Clark, and Rogers (1971) also used the Lawler and Porter measures in a survey of professional workers. They found that subjects who saw work quality and productivity as very important determinants of pay were rated as higher performers. Spitzer (1964) obtained uncross-validated multiple correlations of .40–.50 when the perceived instrumentalities for nine outcomes were used to predict five different productivity criteria. However, there were only ninety-six subjects (production foremen) and the lack of cross-validation is critical. Wofford (1971) found a correlation of .43 between the performance-outcome instrumentality averaged across outcomes and supervisory ratings of performance. However, the carefully done field study by Dachler and Mobley (1973) could find only small correlations between average instrumentality and performance, even when the research site was one using an incentive pay system.

In addition to these correlational studies, several experimental investigation studies of performance-outcome instrumentality have been reported. Jorgenson, Dunnette, and Pritchard (1973) manipulated performance-outcome instrumentality by paying employees in a temporary organization created for purposes of the experiment on either an hourly basis (low instrumentality) or a type of piece rate (high instrumentality). After individuals had worked for three four-hour days under their respective pay systems, each group switched to the other system and worked for three more days. The data indicated that people under the high instrumentality pay system performed higher than those under the low instrumentality pay system for the first three days. Furthermore, immediately following the shift in pay systems, and for all three subsequent days, the performance of subjects who were shifted to the high instrumentality system was higher than their own performance under the low instrumentality system and higher than the performance of those subjects who were shifted to the low instrumentality system. Results similar to Jorgenson et al. were obtained previously by Graen (1969) who also hired subjects to work in a temporary organization. In Graen's study the subjects were females hired to find errors in batches of computer output. Changes in outcomes produced changes in performance only if outcomes were contingent on performance. Similar results in a laboratory simulation study were obtained by Pritchard and DeLeo (1973) who compared an hourly and incentive pay system.

An experimental study by Arvey (1972) manipulated performance-outcome instrumentality by giving subjects who worked on an arithmetic task differing chances to "win" extra subject participation points for their introductory psychology course. In the high instrumentality condition, subjects who were high performers had a .75 probability of getting the extra points while in the low instrumentality condition subjects had a .25 probability. The results did not support the hypothesis since there was no difference in performance between the two levels of performance-outcome instrumentality.

One unfortunate characteristic of almost all the experimental studies that have manipulated the performance-outcome instrumentality is that only two levels of instrumentality have been used. A good Skinnerian should be furious, since with only two data points we cannot distinguish a linear from a nonlinear relationship between performance and instrumentality, and it very well may be the latter.

In a laboratory study where female undergraduates were first paid an hourly wage for scoring test answer sheets and then were switched to an incentive condition, Yukl, Wexley, and Seymore (1972) were able to show that performance was higher when subjects were paid 25¢ per sheet on the basis of a coin flip (i.e., expected value of payoff probability = .50) than when they were paid 25¢ for every sheet completed. On the surface this appears to argue that effort is not maximized when instrumentality = 1.0.

Another source of data on performance-outcome instrumentality comes from the literature on the effects of incentive pay, since an incentive pay system is one where the instrumentality of performance for a financial outcome should be perceived as high.

Several reviews of this literature were made some time ago (Marriott, 1957; Viteles, 1953) and the general conclusion seems to be that incentive plans tend to increase peformance for non-salaried personnel but "may not realize their full potential in increasing performance because of the 'rate restriction' phenomenon . . ." (Campbell et al., 1970, p. 366). These results are very much in line with the model since increases in performance-outcome instrumentality should result in increases in performance but high instrumentalities for peer sanctions and for lowered piece rate wage would tend to decrease effort and performance.

Effort/Performance Contingency (Expectancy)

While there is not a great deal of literature on the perceived degree of relationship between effort and performance, the bulk of the evidence seems to support it as a useful component. Schuster, Clark, and Rogers (1971) compared the performance ratings of those subjects who were higher in perceived effort-performance expectancy to the performance of subjects lower in effort-performance expectancy. While the difference was not statistically significant, it was in the predicted direction. In the experimental study by Arvey (1972) described above, subjects working on the arithmetic task were told they were in competition with other members of their group and that only a certain proportion of them would be designated as "top performers." Expectancy was manipulated by varying the proportion of subjects who would be designated as top performers from one fifth (low expectancy), to one half (medium expectancy), to three-quarters (high expectancy). The results of the study offered support for the expectancy model in that subjects in the low-expectancy condition performed lower than subjects in the high expectancy condition. This finding was supported in a similar study reported by Motowidlo, Loehr, and Dunnette (1972).

Somewhat less direct evidence comes from studies which do not explicitly measure effort-performance expectancy, but rather measure the perceived degree of relationship between effort and outcomes. Such a measure combines effort-performance expectancy and performance-outcome instrumentality. All the studies using such a measure (Hackman & Porter, 1968; Lawler & Porter, 1967; Porter & Lawler, 1968) reported positive relationships between this expectancy-instrumentality composite and measures of performance, but the confounding of these two variables does not permit any direct assessment of the effects of perceived effort-performance expectancy.

Rather negative evidence comes from the study described above of government workers learning a new task (Pritchard & Sanders, 1973). Measuring effort performance expectancy by questionnaire, it was found that expectancy correlated .14 with self-reports of effort, and this correlation dropped to .02 when expectancy was compared with supervisory ratings of effort.

In sum, while the effort-performance expectancy variable shows consistently significant results (at least in a statistical sense), there is still considerable inconsistency in how this variable should be conceptualized and measured. While the question is most often posed in terms of asking the subject for a subjective probability estimate, the object of the question (i.e., what's meant by performance) varies considerably.

Multiplicative Composites of VIE Components

The literature we have reviewed so far seems to indicate that each component separately shows at least some moderate relationship to effort or performance, but another question is whether their combination increases the level of prediction over and above what each one does separately.

Considering first the combination of the valence of outcomes and the performance-outcome instrumentality, Lawler and Porter (1967) found in their sample of managers from five different organizations that predictions of performance and effort using instrumentality alone resulted in correlations from .17 to .32 with a median of .23. When outcome valences were multiplied by instrumentalities the correlations ranged from .18 to .44 with a median of .29. Correlational studies by Spitzer (1964) and Evans (1976) also showed only a small increment in correlations as a result of multiplying performance-outcome instrumentalities by the importance or desirability of outcomes. Similar, but generally stronger, differences were obtained by Hackman and Porter (1968), Porter and Lawler (1968), Galbraith and Cummings (1967), and Mitchell and Pollard (1973). In contrast, two other studies (Gavin, 1970; Pritchard & Sanders, 1973) found no increase in the accuracy of prediction when the two elements were combined. However, the Gavin (1970) study found a correlation of .91 between measures of instrumentality and measures of valence and thus it would be highly unlikely for any combination of the two elements to increase prediction over each used alone. This correlation raises the issue of whether instrumentality and valence are independent events. The multiplicative VIE model implicitly assumes they are independent, but it also seems reasonable that they are not. Moreover, it is not unreasonable that for some people there is a positive relationship (i.e., the higher the instrumentality the higher the anticipated value of the reward) and for others the correlation may be negative.

There have been a number of studies which have combined all three major components in an attempt to predict individual effort, or performance on repetitive tasks. One of the most elaborate studies to date is reported by Dachler and Mobley (1973). It was a correlational field study carried out in each of two research sites using semiskilled operatives as subjects. Both sites were manufacturing operations but individuals were on an hourly pay plan in one plant and an incentive system in the other. The researchers took considerable care to identify as many of the relevant outcomes in the two situations as they could. Through interviews and questionnaires they eventually assembled a list of forty-five relevant outcomes. Rather than asking subjects to estimate correlations between effort and performance and between performance and outcomes they broke performance and valence into specific levels and asked the subjects to estimate the appropriate conditional properties. Their overall finding was that the multiplicative combination of expectancies, instrumentalities, and valences was the single best predictor of performance, but the correlation was only significant for the plant which used the incentive system; that is, where at least some outcomes were directly contingent on performance level. The correlation of .30 is in line with the previously cited research. The most important single component in the Dachler and Mobley study was the expectancy variable and combining expectancy with the valence of performance levels, which in turn was a function of outcome valences and the instrumentality of that performance level, did not increase the correlations much. This finding is also consistent with previous findings.

An exceptionally thorough correlational field study utilizing a panel design is reported by Lawler and Suttle (1973). The subjects were sixty-nine retail managers each of whom was measured twice. Half the sample was remeasured after a six-month interval and the remainder after a twelve-month interval, which unfortunately resulted in a rather small N for the cross-lagged correlations. The questionnaire focused on eighteen outcomes and obtained data on their valences, the rated instrumentality of "good job performance" for each of the eighteen outcomes, the rated expectancy that "working hard" would lead to each of the eighteen outcomes, and the expectancy that "working hard" would lead to "good job performance." The dependent variables consisted of peer, superior, and self-ratings of effort and performance, and an objective performance measure consisting of sales data for the manager's department adjusted to correct for certain obvious biases. In an attempt to account for additional determinants of performance, data were also obtained on the subjects' role perceptions. In addition, the verbal, quantitative, and total scores from the *Thurstone Test of Mental Alertness* were available from company files. The analysis was thorough and consisted of calculating the static and cross-lagged correlations (for both six- and twelve-month intervals) of every VIE component, and combination of components, with each dependent variable. For our current purposes, the correlations with effort ratings are the crucial ones. For the static analysis, the correlations of the VIE components and component combinations range from approximately .30–.40 for self-rated effort, from .20–.30 for superior rating of effort, and from .10–.20 for peer ratings of effort, and there is little advantage to one combination over the other. Weighting instrumentalities and/or expectancies by valence did not increase the correlations. The correlations for the "full" model are .39, .27, and .15 respectively. The results of the cross-lagged correlations gave only slight support to a causal analysis.

A number of other studies (e.g., Arvey & Neil, 1972; Galbraith & Cummings, 1967; Mitchell & Albright, 1972; Mitchell & Nebeker, 1973; Pritchard & Sanders, 1973) also attempted to determine via correlational field studies the correlation between a multiplicative combination of the components in the complete VIE model and ratings of effort and performance. Although their instrumentation was generally less elaborate than either Dachler and Mobley or Lawler and Suttle the obtained results are quite consistent with these two studies.

Summary of Expectancy Theory Research

As of this date there have been approximately thirty-five published studies that have some relevance as "a test" of expectancy theory predictions. What summary statements can be made about the data themselves? We offer the following:

1 Almost all of the studies purporting to test the full model have been correlational field studies and the correlational "ceiling" seems to be approximately .30 when independent ratings of effort are used as the criterion. The mode seems to be closer to .25. Virtually the only time r's exceed this ceiling is when self-rated effort is used as a dependent variable. However, this introduces so much method variance into the correlation that interpretation of such a coefficient would be quite risky.

2 While a multiplicative combination of expectancy, instrumentality, and outcome valence typically yields a higher correlation than that for the individual components or simpler combinations of components, the differences are usually not very great. Expectancy or instrumentality usually accounts for most of the variance that is to be accounted for and multiplying by valence seldom makes much difference. To date, it does not seem possible to choose sides between effort-performance expectancy and performance-outcome instrumentality as the more potent variable.

3 The results from the experimental studies do not seriously contradict the correlational investigations. That is, the variance in the dependent variable accounted for by the experimental treatment does not exceed $.30^2$. One additional characteristic of the experimental studies is that significant interactions were not typically found (e.g., Arvey, 1972; Pritchard & DeLeo, 1973) which further supports the lack of advantage attributed to the multiplicative combinations. However, we should also point out that most of the experimental studies did not deal with *perceptions* of the VIE components as independent variables, as an expectancy theory says should be the case, but focused on the experimenters' manipulation. The Arvey (1972) and Motowidlo et al. (1972) experiments are exceptions, but their results do not change the overall conclusion.

4   In those experimental studies which used performance on a simple repetitive task as a dependent variable and which also obtained measures of ability, a brief aptitude or general intelligence test almost always accounted for much more variance in performance than did the motivational variables (Dunnette, 1972). However, keep in mind that this was not the case in the Lawler and Suttle (1973) correlational field study which used rated effort and performance on a managerial job as dependent variables.

5   The attempts to account for additional variance in performance by some multiplicative combination of motivational and ability variables have been singularly unsuccessful. However, the performance = ability × motivation formulation is a muddled one at best and perhaps little else could have been expected.

6   There is a slight hint in the literature that performance-outcome relationships attached to internally mediated outcomes are more potent than those attached to externally mediated outcomes (e.g., Lawler & Suttle, 1973).

7   Although we did not review any of the evidence on this question, the available research comparing a multiplicative versus additive combination of the VIE components (e.g., Hackman & Porter, 1968; Porter & Lawler, 1968; Pritchard & Sanders, 1973) tends to show a slight advantage for the multiplicative formulation, but the differences are neither startling nor easy to interpret (Mitchell, 1974).

In sum, the available data do not portray the VIE model as a very powerful explainer of behavior. However, the above conclusion begs a number of questions and we would like now to turn to a discussion of various problems that plague both conceptual and research activity in this area. When all is said and done, we think the heuristic value of the expectancy framework will remain as a powerful force in organizational psychology even though its empirical house is certainly not in order.

Difficulties with VIE Theory and Research

The expectancy point of view has not been without its critics and a number of conceptual, measurement, and inferential problems have been pointed out (e.g., see Behling & Starke, 1973; Heneman & Schwab, 1972; Mitchell, 1974; Schmidt, 1973; Wahba & House, in press). Perhaps it would be wise to briefly list the problems that confront anyone who wishes to use the full VIE model as an explanation of effort or choice behavior in organizations. In total, we think these problems constitute a strong indictment of the full multiplicative model, but we also think they point the way to more fruitful avenues of research on motivational issues.

1   One major problem is with the dependent variable itself. The model attempts to predict choice or effort and most of the research activity has been directed at the latter. However, organizational psychology is without any clear specification of the meaning of effort and consequently there is no operationalization of the variable that possesses even a modicum of construct validity. The most frequently used measures are self, peer, or supervisor ratings of overall effort after some attempt has been made to distinguish between performance and effort in the instructions for the rater. Most often this consists of reminding the rater that the amount of energy, concentration, and perhaps time, that an individual puts into a task is not synonymous with the performance outcome that results and that the latter is also a product of skills, task understanding, and whatever constraints may be operating. On the basis of this reminder, it is hoped that the rater will use these two factors in some fashion approximating their arrangement in the "true" factor space, even though we, as yet, do not have even the beginnings of a theory that would suggest what such a factor space might look like. Obviously, or perhaps not so obviously, the problem can be better handled in a laboratory setting where the dependent variable can be "sanitized" in various ways. However, a careful experimental operationalization of effort may destroy the ecological validity of the variable for translation to field settings. It is in the measurement of effort in situ where we are really hurting and it would be well worth our while to start an in depth look at the meaning and measurement of just this variable.

Aside from the overall conceptual vacuum, or perhaps because of it, the use of self and superior ratings of effort are each beset by a number of problems. For example, the supervisor simply may not know how the individual spends time; and even if the individual were observed constantly, by what indicator does an individual signal a high effort or a low effort input? Hand in hand with some intelligent conceptual analyses as to what effort might mean, it would also be worthwhile to employ some policy capturing techniques in an attempt to "recover" the indicators that lead various kinds of raters to judgments of high effort or low effort.

Self-ratings of effort present special problems since the same individual provides ratings of the independent variables (i.e., expectancy, valence, and instrumentality) and the dependent variable. The method variance door is wide open and the two measures are not experimentally independent. It's no wonder the "model" correlates higher with self-rated effort than with independent ratings. In our opinion, self-ratings of effort should not be used in motivation research until we know more about them.

Practically the only systematic investigation of effort measures in a field setting is a multi-trait-multimethod study by Williams and Seiler (1973) who obtained self and superior ratings of both effort and performance for a sample of engineers. Two measures of each were used, a global rating and a dimensionalized set of scales constructed via the method of scaled expectations. The correlations among these variables suggested that (a) effort ratings obtained from independent observers correlated hardly at all (i.e., .24 and .33), (b) performance ratings show more convergent and discriminate validity than effort ratings, (c) effort ratings don't show any discriminate validity at all, and (d) superior ratings of effort exhibit more halo than self-ratings. This study and previous literature suggest that self-ratings of effort and performance correlate about .40−.50 while superior ratings of the same two correlate about .55−.65. Obviously, there are many explanations for why these correlations are not 1.00 besides the fact that there are real differences between the two factors.

2   An allied problem concerns the methods that have been used to measure the independent variables. Most often these have been questionnaire items using summated ratings (i.e., Likert) response formats and almost no effort (*sic*) has been devoted to testing (via some kind of process analysis or scaling technology) whether the subjects are using the variable the way the researcher has in mind. A few studies (e.g., Sheridan, Richards, & Slocum, 1974) have used paired comparison methods, which at least permit a transitivity test, but that's about as far as we have progressed.

Someone must get busy and try to find out what subjects are really doing when they generate "scores" on these variables. For example, data gathered by the decision theorists in gambling situations (Slovic & Lichtenstein, 1968) suggests that when subjective probabilities are compared to objective probabilities, people tend to underestimate the probability of almost certain events and overestimate the probability of rare events. Does the same thing happen in an employment setting?

3   Mitchell (1974) points out that Vroom's theory was originally designed to make *within* individual not *between* individual predictions. That is, the basic question is what task or effort level would an individual choose from among a range of alternatives? As Mitchell also points out, almost all the research designed to test VIE theory has used *between* individuals comparisons. We have already alluded to the trade-offs involved. If a study is meant to be a within subjects analysis, as the Dachler and Mobley (1973) study was in part, then estimates of expectancy and instrumentality must be obtained for several effort levels and several performance outcomes and the number of questions the subject must be asked quickly escalates. If a between subjects analysis is to be used, then the meaning of a variable must be the same across subjects. Serious response biases (e.g., tendency to use extremes) or differing underlying utility functions would confuse the between people comparisons and confuse the observed relationships.

4   Without citing chapter and verse (see Mitchell, 1974, for a partial review), the available data concerning the reliability with which VIE components are measured suggests that while internal consistency estimates are reasonably high, any estimate obtained by measuring the variable at two different times is usually quite low (i.e., .30–.50). We do not wish to get into a long argument as to what kind of reliability should be demanded of VIE variables, but it seems to us that the theory requires the true score to be relatively stable across at least relatively short time periods. This is not to say that the true scores could not change drastically as the result of some new informational input. After all, accommodating such an event is one of the virtues of a cognitive theory. However, in an ongoing work setting which is relatively stable in character, we might expect the expectancy and instrumentality estimates to be relatively stable. In general, they have not been and this does present problems

for the model. It suggests that the high internal consistency estimates may be partially the result of common method variance rather than common substantive variance.

5   Another issue concerns the precise nature of the predictions to be made. The major focus of the model is really on the *change* in the dependent variable as a function of changes in the independent variables. However, to test the model, researchers have relied primarily on relating predicted effort to ratings of effort and performance via static correlations.

6   The available studies have also relied primarily on subjects from a single organization, who were all doing the same job. It would seem quite possible that data collection from one job in one organization could result in a serious restriction in range in expectancies and instrumentalities.

7   Yet another issue concerns the specific first level outcomes for which valence measurements should be obtained. The VIE model is a process theory and it does not specify which outcomes are relevant for particular people in a particular situation. Such specifications are left to the ingenuity of the individual researcher. As a consequence, negative results or unsupported predictions can almost always be explained on the grounds that all the relevant outcomes operating on the subjects were not included in the study. Mitchell (1974) argues that the problem of outcomes breaks down into three sub-questions. How many should be used? How specific should they be? What is their content? There are as yet no systematic answers to these questions.

8   Most versions of the full VIE model contain sums of cross-products between valences and expectancies and between valences and instrumentalities. Computing such cross-products makes several assumptions. First, for the multiplication to make sense, the two terms being multiplied must be independent. That is, the model assumes no interaction between valence and expectancy or between valence and instrumentality, or between instrumentality and expectancy. This may or may not be the case but it seems hardly likely that such zero interactions are always true. For example, as Atkinson (1965) suggests, the outcome of, "I will feel a high sense of achievment if I accomplish task X" may be dependent on the individual's estimate of his/her probability of success on task X. Also, a drastic increase in the instrumentality of performance for obtaining some outcome may influence its perceived value. For example, outcomes that have a very low contingency on performance may be devalued. Recall the previous study by Gavin (1970) which obtained a correlation of .91 between instrumentality and valence.

9   Strictly speaking, variables must also be measured on a ratio scale if the scores are subsequently to be multiplied together. In a pointed discussion of this matter, Schmidt (1973) shows that the correlations of sums of cross-products generated by VIE type operations with other variables can be changed drastically by transformations that would be invariant if the scales possessed ratio properties. This problem is an old one in psychology, and it remains to be seen whether the use of a scaling technology that is consistent with the multiplicative requirements of the theory will appreciably change the results

it generates. Schmidt suspects that it will and worries that using "weak" measures with a very demanding theory may be very misleading.

10   Most versions of the model also carry the assumption that outcome valences are additive in some sense. However, perhaps individuals at work do not really sum valences, but combine them in some other fashion, such as focusing on a dominant outcome under certain conditions and forgetting about the rest.

11   There is inherent in the model a general notion that the world is built in a linear or at least monotonic fashion. The higher the expectancy the greater the force, the greater the instrumentality the greater the force, and the greater the valence the greater the force. All these linearity assumptions are grounds for debate, and to the extent they do not mirror reality, the predictions of the model are weakened. Atkinson (1965) and reinforcement theorists (e.g., Bolles, 1967) would challenge such an assumption for expectancy and instrumentality respectively. Certain "need" theorists (e.g., Maslow, 1954) . . . might also challenge the assumption as it pertains to valence. For example, the valence of pay might change as we go up the pay scale because the need outcomes for which it is instrumental change as a function of amount. The valence of a salary increase at a high salary level may be much higher or much lower than a salary increase at a lower pay level because some people might see it as instrumental for status or some other powerful need, while for others pay is instrumental for nothing besides food, clothing, and shelter.

12   Finally, in the tradition of Spearman, the research using expectancy models has tended to adopt a general factor plus specifics as its view of the "structure" of expectancy, instrumentality, and valence. That is, instrumentality is a general factor that is made up of a number of specific instrumentalities, expectancy is a general factor made up of a number of specific expectancies, and so on. However, it may be the case, for example, that the components of an individual's expectancy estimate attributable to general self-esteem versus that attributable to specific task characteristics may relate to behavior in different functional ways and some tasks may elicit more of the self-esteem component than others.

Some versions of the model do speak to a distinction between internally and externally mediated outcomes (rewards) and some studies have analyzed results separately for these two sub-general factors. However, what about positive versus negative outcomes (e.g., Reitz, 1971) and the nature of the instrumentalities attached to internal versus external or positive versus negative outcomes? Since internally mediated outcomes are under the control of the individual, perhaps the instrumentality of task accomplishment for obtaining these outcomes is nearly always 1.00.

A SUMMARY COMMENT

In general what message does this list of problems seem to convey? We think it says quite clearly that the VIE model is a simple appearing formulation that encompasses a highly complex and poorly understood set of variables and variable dynamics. Rather than strive for large scale studies that provide a complete test of the "full" model with superficial measures of poorly understood variables, we think researchers could better spend their time studying the individual components in depth. For example, a host of questions surround the expectancy variable. We shall talk about a few of these later on. We think it would be far better to ask what is expectancy and how does it relate to well defined variables than to ask what is the correlation between $E \cdot \Sigma(V \times I)$ and a global rating of effort.

REFERENCES

Arvey, R. D. Task performance as a function of perceived effort-performance and performance-reward contingencies. *Organizational Behavior and Human Performance*, 1972, **8**, 423–433.

Arvey, R. D., & Neil, C. W. Testing expectancy theory predictions using behaviorally based measures of motivational effort for engineers. Mimeograph, University of Tennessee, Knoxville, 1972.

Atkinson, J. W. Some general implications of conceptual developments in the study of achievement oriented behavior. In M. R. Jones (Ed.), *Human motivation: A symposium*. Lincoln: University of Nebraska Press, 1965.

Becker, G. M., & McClintock, C. G. Value: Behavioral decision theory. In P. R. Farnsworth (Ed.), *Annual review of psychology*, vol. 18. Palo Alto, Calif.: Annual Reviews, 1967.

Behling, O., & Starke, F. A. Some limits on expectancy theories of work effort. Proceedings, Midwest Meeting, American Institute of Decision Sciences, 1973.

Bolles, R. C. *Theory of motivation*. New York: Harper and Row, 1967.

Campbell, J. P., Dunnette, M. D., Lawler, E. E. III, & Weick, K. E. Jr. *Managerial behavior, performance, and effectiveness*. New York: McGraw-Hill, 1970.

Cartledge, N. D. An experimental study of the relationship between expectancies, goal utility, goals and task performance. Unpublished doctoral dissertation, University of Maryland, College Park, 1972.

Dachler, H. P., & Mobley, W. H. Construct validation of an instrumentality-expectancy-task-goal model of work motivation: Some theoretical boundary conditions. *Journal of Applied Psychology*, 1973, **58**, 397–418.

Dunnette, M. D. Performance equals ability and what? Mimeographed paper, University of Minnesota, Minneapolis, 1972.

Evans, M. G. The effects of supervisory behavior on the path-goal relationship. *Organizational Behavior and Human Performance*, 1970, **54**, 105–114.

Galbraith, J., & Cummings, L. L. An empirical investigation of the motivational determinants of task performance: Interactive effects between instrumentality-valence and motivation-ability. *Organizational Behavior and Human Performance*, 1967, **2**, 237–257.

Gavin, J. F. Ability, effort, and role perception as antecedents of job performance. *Experimental Publication System*, 1970, **5**, Ms. No. 190A, 1–26.

Georgopoulos, B. S., Mahoney, G. M., & Jones, N. W. A path-goal approach to productivity. *Journal of Applied Psychology*, 1957, **41**, 345–353.

Graen, G. Instrumentality theory of work motivation: Some experimental results and suggested modifications. *Journal of Applied Psychology Monograph*, 1969, **53**, 1–25.

Hackman, J. R., & Porter, L. W. Expectancy theory predictions of work effectiveness. *Organizational Behavior and Human Performance*, 1968, **3**, 417–426.

Heneman, H. G. III, & Schwab, D. P. An evaluation of research on expectancy theory predictions of employee performance. *Psychological Bulletin*, 1972, **78**, 1–9.

Holmstrom, V. L., & Beach, L. R. Subjective expected utility and career preferences. *Organizational Behavior and Human Performance*, 1973, **10**, 201–207.

House, R. J., & Wahba, M. A. Expectancy theory in industrial and organizational psychology: An integrative model and a review of literature. Paper presented at the meetings of the American Psychological Association, Honolulu, Hawaii, 1972.

Jorgenson, D. O., Dunnette, M. D., & Pritchard, R. D. Effects of the manipulation of a performance-reward contingency on behavior in a simulated work setting. *Journal of Applied Psychology*, 1973, **57**, 271–280.

Lawler, E. E. A causal correlation analysis of the relationship between expectancy attitudes and job performance. *Journal of Applied Psychology*, 1968, **52**, 462–468.

Lawler, E. E. *Pay and organizational-effectiveness: A psychological view*. New York: McGraw-Hill, 1971.

Lawler, E. E. *Motivation in work organizations*. Belmont, Calif.: Brooks/Cole, 1973.

Lawler, E. E., & Porter, L. W. Antecedent attitudes of effective managerial performance. *Organizational Behavior and Human Performance*, 1967, **2**, 122–142.

Lawler, E. E., & Suttle, J. L. Expectancy theory and job behavior. *Organizational Behavior and Human Performance*, 1973, **9**, 482–503.

Marriott, R. *Incentive payment systems: A review of research and opinion*. London: Stapler Press, 1957.

Maslow, A. H. *Motivation and personality*. New York: Harper and Row, 1954.

Miner, J. B., & Dachler, H. P. Personnel attitudes and motivation. In P. H. Mussen & M. R. Rosenzweig (Eds.), *Annual review of psychology*, vol. 24. Palo Alto, Calif.: Annual Reviews, 1973.

Mitchell, T. R. Expectancy models of satisfaction, occupational preference, and effort: A theoretical, methodological, and empirical appraisal. Unpublished paper, University of Washington, Seattle, 1974.

Mitchell, T. R., & Albright, D. W. Expectancy theory predictions of the satisfaction, effort, performance and retention of naval aviation officers. *Organizational Behavior and Human Performance*, 1972, **8**, 1–20.

Mitchell, T. R., & Biglan, A. Instrumentality theories: Current uses in psychology. *Psychological Bulletin*, 1971, **76**, 432–454.

Mitchell, T. R., & Knudsen, B. W. Instrumentality theory predictions of students' attitudes towards business and their choice of business as an occupation. *Academy of Management Journal*, 1973, **16**, 41–51.

Mitchell, T. R., & Nebeker, D. M. Expectancy theory predictions of academic effort and performance. *Journal of Applied Psychology*, 1973, **57**, 61–67.

Mitchell, T. R., & Pollard, W. E. Instrumentality theory predictions of academic behavior. *Journal of Social Psychology*, 1973, **89**, 34–45.

Motowidlo, S. J., Loehr, V., & Dunnette, M. D. The effect of goal specificity on the relationship between expectancy and task performance. Minneapolis: University of Minnesota, Technical Report No. 4008, 1972.

Porter, L. W., & Lawler, E. E. *Managerial attitudes and performance*. Homewood, Ill. Dorsey Press, 1968.

Pritchard, R. D., & DeLeo, P. J. Experimental test of the valence-instrumentality relationship in job performance. *Journal of Applied Psychology*, 1973, **57**, 264–270.

Pritchard, R. D., & Sanders, M. S. The influence of valence, instrumentality, and expectancy on effort and performance. *Journal of Applied Psychology*, 1973, **57**, 55–60.

Pritchard, R. D., DeLeo, P. J., & VonBergen, C. W. An evaluation of incentive motivation techniques in Air Force technical training. Air Force Human Resources Laboratory Technical Report, Purdue University, Lafayette, Ind., 1974.

Reitz, H. J. Managerial attitudes and perceived contingencies between performance and organizational responses. Proceedings of the 31st Annual Meeting of the Academy of Management, 1971, 227–238.

Schmidt, F. L. Implications of a measurement problem for expectancy theory research. *Organizational Behavior and Human Performance*, 1973, **10**, 243–251.

Schuster, J. R., Clark, B., & Rogers, M. Testing portions of the Porter and Lawler model regarding the motivational role of pay. *Journal of Applied Psychology*, 1971, **55**, 187–195.

Sheard, J. L. Intrasubject prediction of preferences for organizational types. *Journal of Applied Psychology*, 1970, **54**, No. 3, 248–252.

Sheridan, J. E., Richards, M. D., & Slocum, J. W. A longitudinal test of expectancy and heuristic models of job selection. Unpublished manuscript, Wayne State University, Detroit, 1974.

Slovic, P., & Lichtenstein, S. C. The relative importance of probabilities and payoffs in risk taking. *Journal of Experimental Psychology Monograph Supplement*, 1968, **78** (3, Part 2).

Spitzer, M. E. Goal attainment, job satisfaction, and behavior. Unpublished doctoral dissertation, New York University, New York City, 1964.

Viteles, M. S. *Motivation and morale in industry*. New York: W. W. Norton, 1953.

Vroom, V. H. *Work and motivation*. New York: Wiley, 1964.

Vroom, V. H. *Motivation in management*. New York: American Foundation for Management Research, 1965.

Vroom, V. H. Organizational choice: A study of pre- and post-decision processes. *Organizational Behavior and Human Performance*, 1966, **1**, 212–225.

Wahba, M. A., & House, R. J. Expectancy theory in work and motivation: Some logical and methodological issues. *Human Relations*, in press.

Wanous, J. P., & Lawler, E. E. Measurement and meaning of job satisfaction. *Journal of Applied Psychology*, 1972, **56**, 95–105.

Williams, W. E., & Seiler, D. A. Relationship between measures of effort and job performance. *Journal of Applied Psychology*, 1973, **57**, 49–54.

Wofford, J. C. The motivational bases of job satisfaction and job performance. *Personnel Psychology*, 1971, **24**, 501–518.

Yukl, G., Wexley, K. N., & Seymore, J. D. Effectiveness of pay incentives under variable ratio and continuous reinforcement schedules. *Journal of Applied Psychology*, 1972, **56**, 19–23.

QUESTIONS FOR DISCUSSION

1   Compare and contrast equity theory and expectancy/valence theory.
2   Why is expectancy/valence theory a multiplicative model?

3 Evaluate the research evidence in support of the expectancy/valence model of motivation.
4 What, if anything, is really different about expectancy/valence theory of motivation?
5 What factors might possibly affect the valence levels attached to various outcomes by individuals?
6 If managers wanted to increase the motivational levels of their subordinates, would it generally be easier for them to manipulate their subordinates' expectancies or their valences? Why?
7 How can various rewards, like money, affect motivational processes under expectancy/valence theory?
8 When studying the expectancy/valence model of motivation, what benefits can be derived from dividing expectancies into two "types" ($E \rightarrow P$ and $P \rightarrow O$)?
9 Of what practical value is the expectancy/valence model for line managers? What can managers learn from the model that would improve their effectivness on the job?
10 In what respects does expectancy/valence theory differ from behavior modification?

Part Three

Central Issues in Motivation at Work

Chapter 6

Performance, Rewards, and Satisfaction

This chapter deals with several related aspects of the relationship between employee performance, rewards, and job satisfaction. As such, much of the material covered here will transcend many of the work motivation theories discussed earlier. Specifically, we shall examine the nature of intrinsic and extrinsic motivation, the nature of job attitudes (particularly job satisfaction), and the moderating effects of rewards on the performance-satisfaction relationship.

INTRINSIC AND EXTRINSIC MOTIVATION

Up to this point, little attempt has been made to distinguish among varying types of motivation. However, if we are to succeed in understanding basic motivational processes, it is useful to distinguish at least two types: *intrinsic* and *extrinsic*. Intrinsic motivation is thought to be motivation that results from an individual's need to be competent and self-determining (Deci, 1975a). Kruglanski, Alon, and Lewis (1972) point out that intrinsically motivated tasks are those that are interesting and enjoyable to perform—irrespective of possible external rewards. The clearest example of intrinsic motivation can be seen in job enrichment efforts, where it is felt that providing more challenging tasks will increase one's intrinsic desire to perform. (Job enrichment will be discussed in detail in Chapter 9.) Extrinsic motivation, on the other hand, deals with behaviors that are motivated by factors external to the individual. Examples of extrinsic motivators are pay, coworkers' pressures to perform, supervisory behavior, and so forth.

Much of the current conceptual work on intrinsic motivation is incorporated in the recent work of Deci (1975a,b) and his *cognitive evaluation theory*. Briefly, this theory argues that an individual's level of effort on a task is largely determined by the nature of the rewards available for task accomplishment. Two processes by which rewards influence intrinsic motivation can be identified.

First, there is the notion of *locus of causality*. When behavior is intrinsically motivated, an individual's perceived locus of causality is thought to be internal; that is, individuals feel that task accomplishment is under their own control. Under such circumstances, they will engage in activities for *intrinsic* rewards. On the other hand, when individuals receive *extrinsic* rewards for task behavior, they will perceive their locus of causality to be external and will engage in those activities only when they believe that extrinsic rewards will be forthcoming. The important point here is that, according to Deci, providing extrinsic rewards on an intrinsically satisfying task leads to a shift from internal to external locus of causality. As Deci (1972) states:

> Interpreting these results in relation to theories of work motivation, it seems clear that the effects of intrinsic motivation and extrinsic motivation are not additive. While extrinsic rewards such as money can certainly motivate behavior, they appear to be doing so at the expense of intrinsic motivation; as a result, contingent pay systems do not appear to be compatible with participative management systems (pp. 224–225).

Second, rewards can also influence intrinsic motivation through changes in feelings of *competence* and *self-determination*. Rewards or outcomes that reassure people they are competent or self-determining tend to increase their intrinsic motivation to perform. However, rewards or outcomes that convince people they are not competent or self-determining tend to decrease intrinsic motivation.

This distinction between intrinsic and extrinsic motivation is examined in detail in the selection by Staw that follows. Several refinements on the model and implications for management are also discussed.

JOB ATTITUDES AND JOB BEHAVIOR

The relationship between job attitudes and job behavior has long been a topic of interest to both managers and organizational researchers. Such interest dates back at least to the human relations movement of the 1930s, when it was generally felt that a happy worker was a productive one. A causal relationship was largely assumed during this time whereby job satisfaction "caused" improved job performance. The managerial implication was thus quite simple: keep your employees satisfied.

As time went on, however, research evidence began to call into question the veracity of this simple pronouncement. Based on an extensive review of investigations in the area, Brayfield and Crockett (1955) concluded that little evidence existed of any simple or even appreciable relation between job satisfaction and resulting performance. Somewhat later, Vroom (1964) analyzed the results of twenty studies which measured both satisfaction and performance and found that the two variables had a median correlation of .14. Correlation coefficients ranged from $+.86$ to $-.31$ across these studies.

These revelations sparked considerable controversy concerning the causal relationship—if any—between these variables. Did job satisfaction in fact lead to job performance or was the reverse true? Or was there a third alternative? Was it possible, for example, that other important intervening variables served to moderate the relationship? The nature of this controversy is the subject of the second two selections in this chapter (by Lawler and by Greene and Craft). Before examining this controversy, however, it should prove useful to consider on a general level the nature of job attitudes.

NATURE OF JOB ATTITUDES

Initially, we should consider what is meant by the concept of *attitude*. Briefly defined, an attitude represents a predisposition to respond in a favorable or unfavorable way to persons or objects in one's environment. When we say we "like" something or "dislike" something, we are in effect expressing our attitudes toward the person or object. When we look at the specific attitude of "job satisfaction," we are considering the extent to which one's job or job experiences are pleasurable or unpleasurable.

There are three important assumptions that help to explain the concept of attitude. To begin with, an attitude is a hypothetical construct. Hence, while the consequences (in terms of behavior) can be observed, the attitude itself cannot. No one "sees" an attitude. We simply infer attitudes from people's statements and behaviors. Second, an attitude is a unidimensional construct; it ranges from very positive to very negative. As such, an attitude can be measured along a continuum. Third, attitudes are generally believed to be somewhat related to subsequent behavior. While the relationship is clearly not a direct one, we would generally expect people's attitudes to be predictive of their behaviors *assuming* they have control over that behavior (Herman, 1973).

Fishbein (1967; Fishbein & Ajzen, 1975) has suggested that one useful way to conceptualize the notion of attitude is to subdivide it into three related parts: (1) beliefs about the job, (2) the attitude itself, and (3) the behavioral intentions that result from the attitude. This process is diagrammed in Exhibit 1. As shown in this diagram, *beliefs* about one's job (e.g., this job is dull, dirty, etc.) lead to negative *job attitudes* (e.g., job dissatisfaction) which, in turn, lead to the *behavioral intentions* to leave or to reduce effort on the job. These behavioral intentions are then translated into actual *behavior*, assuming the individual is able to carry out his or her intentions.

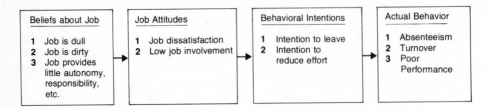

Exhibit 1   A Conceptual Model of Job Attitudes. (*After Fishbein, 1967.*)

OVERVIEW

With this as a background, we are now in a position to take a closer look at the theories and research relating to motivation, performance, rewards, and satisfaction. The three selections that follow provide fairly broad coverage of this topic, including both the controversies in the literature and possible resolutions for these controversies. Throughout, the implications of the major findings for the practice of management are considered.

The first selection, by Staw, examines the dynamics of intrinsic and extrinsic motivation. Following this, Greene reviews the evidence concerning the role of rewards in determining performance and job satisfaction. Finally, Lawler focuses on the concept of job satisfaction and reviews major influences on satisfaction as well as major outcomes.

REFERENCES AND SUGGESTED ADDITIONAL READINGS

Brayfield, A. H., & Crockett, W. H. Employee attitudes and employee performance. *Psychological Bulletin*, 1955, **52**, 396–424.

Deci, E. L. The effects of contingent and non-contingent rewards and controls on intrinsic motivation. *Organizational Behavior and Human Performance*, 1972, **8**, 217–229.

Deci, E. L. *Intrinsic motivation.* New York: Plenum, 1975. (a)

Deci, E. L. Notes on the theory and metatheory of intrinsic motivation. *Organizational Behavior and Human Performance*, 1975, **15**, 130–145. (b)

Fishbein, M. (Ed.). *Readings in attitude theory and measurement.* New York: Wiley, 1967.

Fishbein, M., & Ajzen, I. *Belief, attitude, intention, and behavior: An introduction to theory and research.* Reading, Mass.: Addison-Wesley, 1975.

Hamner, W. C., & Foster, L. W. Are intrinsic and extrinsic rewards additive: A test of Deci's cognitive evaluation theory of task motivation. *Organizational Behavior and Human Performance*, 1975, **14**, 398–415.

Herman, J. B. Are situational contingencies limiting job attitude-job performance relationships? *Organizational Behavior and Human Performance*, 1973, **10**, 208–224.

Herzberg, F., Mausner, B., Peterson, R. O., & Capwell, D. *Job attitudes: Review of research and opinion*. Pittsburgh: Psychological Service of Pittsburgh, 1957.

Kruglanski, A. W., Alon, S., & Lewis, T. Retrospective mis-attribution and task enjoyment. *Journal of Experimental Social Psychology*, 1972, **8**, 493–501.

Lawler, E. E., III, & Porter, L. W. The effect of performance on job satisfaction. *Industrial Relations*, 1967, 7(1), 20–28.

Porter, L. W., & Lawler, E. E., III. *Managerial attitudes and performance*. Homewood, Ill.: Irwin, 1968.

Porter, L. W., & Lawler, E. E., III. What job attitudes tell us about motivation. *Harvard Business Review*, 1968, **46**(1), 118–126.

Vroom, V. H. *Work and motivation*. New York: Wiley, 1964.

The Self-Perception of Motivation

Barry M. Staw

Within the area of interpersonal perception, it has been noted (Heider, 1958) that an individual may infer the causes of another's actions to be a function of personal and environmental force:

Action = f (personal force + environmental force)

This is quite close to saying that individuals attempt to determine whether another person is intrinsically motivated to perform an activity (action due to personal force), or extrinsically motivated (action due to environmental force), or both. The extent to which an individual will infer intrinsic motivation on the part of another is predicted to be affected by the clarity and strength of external forces within the situation (Jones & Davis, 1965; Jones & Nisbett, 1971; Kelley 1967). When there are strong forces bearing on the individual to perform an activity, there is little reason to assume that a behavior is self-determined, whereas a high level of intrinsic motivation might be inferred if environmental force is minimal. Several studies dealing with interpersonal perception have supported this general conclusion (Jones, Davis, & Gergen, 1961; Jones & Harris, 1967; Strickland, 1958; Thibaut & Riecken, 1955).

Bem (1967a, b) extrapolated this interpersonal theory of causal attribution to the study of self-perception or how one views his *own* behavior within a social context. Bem hypothesized that the extent to which external pressures are sufficiently strong to account for one's behavior will determine the likelihood that a person will attribute his own actions to internal causes. Thus if a person acts under strong external rewards or punishments, he is likely to assume that his behavior is under external control. However, if extrinsic contingencies are not strong or salient, the individual is likely to assume that his behavior is due to his own interest in the activity or that his behavior is intrinsically motivated. De Charms has made a similar point in his discussion of individuals' perception of personal causation (1968, p. 328):

> As a first approximation, we propose that whenever a person experiences himself to be the locus of causality for his own behavior (to be an Origin), he will consider himself to be intrinsically motivated. Conversely, when a person perceives the locus of causality for his behavior to be external to himself (that he is a Pawn), he will consider himself to be extrinsically motivated.

De Charms emphasized that the individual may attempt psychologically to label his actions on the basis of whether or not he has been instrumental in affecting his own behavior; that is, whether his behavior has been intrinsically or extrinsically motivated.

THE CASE FOR A NEGATIVE RELATIONSHIP BETWEEN INTRINSIC AND EXTRINSIC MOTIVATION

The self-perception approach to intrinsic and extrinsic motivation leads to the conclusion that there may be a negative interrelationship between these two motivational factors. The basis for this prediction stems from the assumption that individuals may work backward from their own actions in inferring sources of causation (Bem, 1967a, b; 1972). For example, if external pressures on an individual are so high that they would ordinarily cause him to perform a given task regardless of the internal characteristics of the activity, then the individual might logically infer that he is extrinsically motivated. In contrast, if external reward contingencies are extremely low or nonsalient, the individual might then infer that his behavior is intrinsically motivated. What is important is the fact that a person, in performing an activity, may *seek out* the probable cause of his own actions. Since behavior has no doubt been caused by something, it makes pragmatic, if not scientific, sense for the person to conclude that the cause is personal (intrinsic) rather than extrinsic if he can find no external reasons for his actions.

Two particular situations provide robust tests of the self-perception prediction. One is a situation in which there is insufficient justification for a person's actions, a situation in which the intrinsic rewards for an activity are very low (e.g., a dull task) and there are no compensating extrinsic rewards (e.g., monetary payment, verbal praise). Although rationally, one ordinarily tries to avoid these situations, there are occasions when one is faced with the difficult question of "why did I do that?" The self-perception theory predicts that in situations of insufficient justification, the individual may cognitively reevaluate the intrinsic characteristics of an activity in order to justify or explain his own behavior. For example, if the individual performed a dull task for no external reward, he may "explain" his behavior by thinking that the task was not really so bad after all.

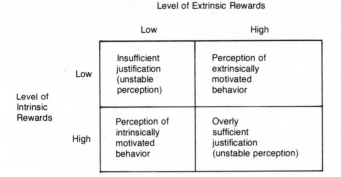

Figure 1   A conceptual framework of self-perception theory.

Sometimes a person may also be fortunate enough to be in a situation in which his behavior is oversufficiently justified. For example, a person may be asked to perform an interesting task and at the same time be lavishly paid for his efforts. In such situations, the self-perception theory predicts that the individual may actually reevaluate the activity in a downward direction. Since the external reward would be sufficient to motivate behavior by itself, the individual may mistakenly infer that he was extrinsically motivated to perform the activity. He may conclude that since he was forced to perform the task by an external reward, the task probably was not terribly satisfying in and of itself.

Figure 1 graphically depicts the situations of insufficient and overly sufficient justification. From the figure, we can see that the conceptual framework supporting self-perception theory raises several interesting issues. First, it appears from this analysis that there are only two fully stable attributions of behavior: (1) the perception of extrinsically motivated behavior in which the internal rewards associated with performing an activity are low while external rewards are high; and (2) the perception of intrinsically motivated behavior in which the task is inherently rewarding but external rewards are low. Furthermore, it appears that situations of insufficient justification (where intrinsic and extrinsic rewards are both low) and oversufficient justification (where intrinsic and extrinsic rewards are both high) involve unstable attribution states. As shown in Figure 2, individuals apparently resolve this attributional instability by altering their perceptions of intrinsic rewards associated with the task.

An interesting question posed by the self-perception analysis is why individuals are predicted to resolve an unstable attribution state by cognitively reevaluating a task in terms of its intrinsic rewards rather than changing their perceptions of extrinsic factors. The answer to this question may lie in the relative clarity of extrinsic as compared with intrinsic rewards, and the individual's relative ability to distort the two aspects of the situation. Within many settings (and especially within laboratory experiments) extrinsic rewards are generally quite salient and specific, whereas an individual must judge the intrinsic nature of a task for himself. Any shifts in the perception of intrinsic and extrinsic rewards may therefore be more likely to occur in the intrinsic

Perceived Extrinsic Rewards

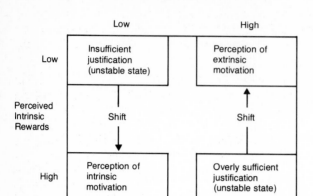

Figure 2   A schematic analysis of the self-perception of intrinsic and extrinsic motivation.

factor. As shown in Figure 2 it is these predicted shifts in perceived intrinsic rewards that may theoretically underlie a negative relationship between intrinsic and extrinsic motivation.

Empirical Evidence: Insufficient Justification

Several studies have shown that when an individual is induced to commit an unpleasant act for little or no external justification, he may subsequently conclude that the act was not so unpleasant after all. Actually, the first scientific attempt to account for this phenomenon was the theory of cognitive dissonance (Festinger, 1957). It was predicted by dissonance theorists (Aronson, 1966; Festinger, 1957) that, since performing an unpleasant act for little or no reward would be an inconsistent (and seemingly irrational) thing to do, an individual might subsequently change his attitude toward the act in order to reduce the inconsistency or to appear rational. Bem's self-perception theory yields the same predictions but does not require one to posit that there is a motivating state such as dissonance reduction or self-rationalization. To Bem, since the individual examines his own behavior in light of the forces around him, he is simply more likely to come to the conclusion that his actions were intrinsically satisfying if they were performed under minimal external force.

   In general, two types of experiments have been designed to assess the consequences of insufficient justification. One type of design has involved the performance of a dull task with varied levels of reward (Brehm & Cohen, 1962; Freedman, 1963; Weick, 1964; Weick & Penner, 1965). A second and more popular design has involved some form of counterattitudinal advocacy, either in terms of lying to a fellow subject about the nature of an experiment or writing an essay against one's position on an important issue (Carlsmith, Collins, & Helmreich, 1966; Festinger & Carlsmith, 1959; Linder, Cooper, & Jones, 1967).

Fundamentally, the two types of designs are not vastly different. Both require subjects to perform an intrinsically dissatisfying act under varied levels of external inducement, and both predict that, in the low payment condition, the subject will change his attitude toward the activity (i.e., think more favorably of the task or begin to believe the position advocated).

The most well-known experiment designed to test the insufficient justification paradigm was conducted by Festinger and Carlsmith (1959). Subjects participated in a repetitive and dull task (putting spools on trays and turning pegs) and were asked to tell other waiting subjects that the experiment was enjoyable, interesting, and exciting. Half the experimental subjects were paid $1, and half were paid $20 for the counterattitudinal advocacy (and to be "on call" in the future), while control subjects were not paid and did not perform the counterattitudinal act. As predicted, the smaller the reward used to induce subjects to perform the counterattitudinal act, the greater the positive change in their attitudes toward the task. Although the interpretation of the results of this study have been actively debated (e.g., between dissonance and self-perception theorists) the basic findings have been replicated by a number of different researchers. It should be noted, however, that several mediating variables have also been isolated as being necessary for the attainment of this dissonance or self-perception effect: free choice (Linder, Cooper, & Jones, 1967), commitment or irrevocability of behavior (Brehm & Cohen, 1962), and substantial adverse consequences (Calder, Ross, & Insko, 1973; Collins & Hoyt, 1972).

Recently, a strong test of the insufficient justification paradigm was also conducted outside the laboratory (Staw, 1974a). A natural field experiment was made possible by the fact that many young men had joined an organization (Army ROTC) in order to avoid being drafted, *and* these same young men subsequently received information (a draft lottery number) that changed the value of this organizational reward. Of particular relevance was the fact that those who joined ROTC did so not because of their intrinsic interest in the activities involved (e.g., drills, classes, and summer camp), but because they anticipated a substantial extrinsic reward (draft avoidance). As a result, those who received draft numbers that exempted them from military service subsequently faced a situation of low extrinsic as well as intrinsic rewards, a situation of insufficient justification. In contrast, persons who received draft numbers that made them vulnerable to military call-up found their participation in ROTC perfectly justified—they were still successfully avoiding the draft by remaining in the organization. To test the insufficient justification effect, both the attitudes and the performance of ROTC cadets were analyzed by draft number before and after the national draft lottery. The results showed that those in the insufficient justification situation enhanced their perception of ROTC and even performed somewhat better in ROTC courses after the lottery. It should be recognized, however, that this task enhancement occurred only under circumstances very similar to those previously found necessary for the dissonance or self-perception effect (i.e., high commitment, free choice, and adverse consequences).

Empirical Evidence: Overly Sufficient Justification

There have been several empirical studies designed to test the self-perception prediction within the context of overly sufficient justification. Generally, a situation in which an extrinsic reward is added to an intrinsically rewarding task has been experimentally contrived for this purpose. Following self-perception theory, it is predicted that an increase in external justification will cause individuals to lose confidence in their intrinsic interest in the experimental task. Since dissonance theory cannot make this prediction (it is neither irrational nor inconsistent to perform an activity for too many rewards), the literature on overly sufficient justification provides the most important data on the self-perception prediction. For this reason, we will examine the experimental evidence in some detail.

In an experiment specifically designed to test the effect of overly sufficient justification on intrinsic motivation, Deci (1971) enlisted a number of college students to participate in a problem-solving study. All the students were asked to work on a series of intrinsically interesting puzzles for three experimental sessions. After the first session, however, half of the students (the experimental group) were told that they would also be given an extrinsic reward (money) for correctly solving the second set of puzzles, while the other students (the control group) were not told anything about the reward. In the third session, neither the experimental nor the control subjects were rewarded. This design is schematically outlined below:

Basic Design of Deci (1971) Study

	Time 1	Time 2	Time 3
Experimental group	No payment	Payment	No payment
Control group	No payment	No payment	No payment

Deci had hypothesized that the payment of money in the second experimental session might decrease subjects' intrinsic motivation to perform the task. That is, the introduction of an external force (money) might cause participants to alter their self-perception about why they were working on the puzzles. Instead of being intrinsically motivated to solve the interesting puzzles, they might find themselves working primarily to get the money provided by the experimenter. Thus Deci's goal in conducting the study was to compare the changes in subjects' intrinsic motivation from the first to third sessions for both the experimental and control groups. If the self-perception hypothesis was correct, the intrinsic motivation of the previously paid experimental subjects would decrease in the third session, whereas the intrinsic motivation of the unpaid controls should remain unchanged.

As a measure of intrinsic motivation, Deci used the amount of free time participants spent on the puzzle task. To obtain this measure, the experimenter left the room during each session, supposedly to feed some data into the computer. As the experimenter left the room, he told the subjects they could do anything they wanted with their free time. In addition to the puzzles, current issues of *Time, The New Yorker*, and *Playboy* were placed near the subjects. However, while the first experimenter was out of the laboratory, a second experimenter, unknown to the subjects, observed their behavior through a one-way mirror. It was reasoned that if the subject worked on the puzzles during this free time period, he must be intrinsically motivated to perform the task. As shown in Table 1, the amount of free time spent on the task decreased for those who were previously paid to perform the activity, while there was a slight increase for the unpaid controls. Although the difference between the experimental and control groups was only marginally significant, the results are suggestive of the fact that an overly sufficient extrinsic reward may decrease one's intrinsic motivation to perform a task.

Lepper, Greene, and Nisbett (1973) also conducted a study that tested the self-perception prediction in a situation of overly sufficient justification. Their study involved having nursery school children perform an interesting activity (playing with Magic Markers) with and without the expectation of an additional extrinsic reward. Some children were induced to draw pictures with the markers by promising them a Good Player Award consisting of a big gold star, a bright red ribbon, and a place to print their name. Other children either performed the activity without any reward or were told about the reward only after completing the activity. Children who participated in these three experimental conditions (expected reward, no reward, unexpected reward) were then covertly observed during the following week in a free-play period. As in the Deci (1971) study, the amount of time children spent on the activity when they could do other interesting things (i.e., playing with other toys) was taken to be an indicator of intrinsic motivation.

The findings of the Lepper, Greene, and Nisbett study showed that the introduction of an extrinsic reward for performing an already interesting activity caused a significant decrease in intrinsic motivation. Children who played with Magic Markers with the expectation of receiving the external reward did not spend as much subsequent free time on the activity as did children who were not given a reward or those who were unexpectedly offered the reward. Moreover, the rated quality of drawings made by children with the markers was

Table 1   Mean Number of Seconds Spent Working on the Puzzles during the Free Time Periods

Group	Time 1	Time 2	Time 3	Time 3 − Time 1
Experimental (n = 12)	248.2	313.9	198.5	−49.7
Control (n = 12)	213.9	202.7	241.8	27.9

Source: E. L. Deci, "The Effects of Externally Mediated Rewards on Intrinsic Motivation," *Journal of Personality and Social Psychology* 18 (1971): 105–15. Copyright 1971 by the American Psychological Association. Reprinted by permission.

significantly poorer in the expected-reward group than either the no-reward or unexpected-reward groups.

The results of the Lepper et al. study help to increase our confidence in the findings of the earlier Deci experiment. Not only are the earlier findings replicated with a different task and subject population, but an important methodological problem is minimized. By reexamining Table 1, we can see that the second time period in the Deci experiment was the period in which payment was expected by subjects for solving the puzzles. However, we can also see that in time 2 there was a whopping increase in the free time subjects spent on the puzzles. Deci explained this increase as an attempt by subjects to practice puzzle solving to increase their chances of earning money. However, what Deci did not discuss is the possibility that the subsequent decrease in time 3 was due not to the prior administration of rewards but to the effect of satiation or fatigue. One contribution of the Lepper et al. study is that its results are not easily explained by this alternative. In the Lepper et al. experiment, there was over one week's time between the session in which an extrinsic reward was administered and the final observation period.

Although both the Deci and Lepper et al. studies support the notion that the expectation of an extrinsic reward may decrease intrinsic interest in an activity, there is still one important source of ambiguity in both these studies. You may have noticed that the decrease in intrinsic motivation follows not only the prior administration of an extrinsic reward, but also the withdrawal of this reward. For example, in the Deci study, subjects were not paid in the third experimental session in which the decrease in intrinsic motivation was reported. Likewise, subjects were not rewarded when the final observation of intrinsic motivation was taken by Lepper, Greene, and Nisbett. It is therefore difficult to determine whether the decrease in intrinsic interest is due to a change in the self-perception of motivation following the application of an extrinsic reward or merely to frustration following the removal of the reward. An experiment by Kruglanski, Freedman, and Zeevi (1971) helps to resolve this ambiguity.

Kruglanski et al. induced a number of teenagers to volunteer for some creativity and memory tasks. To manipulate extrinsic rewards, the experimenters told half the participants that because they had volunteered for the study, they would be taken on an interesting tour of the psychology laboratory; the other participants were not offered this extrinsic reward. The results showed that teenagers offered the reward were less satisfied with the experimental tasks and were less likely to volunteer for future experiments of a similar nature than were teenagers who were not offered the extrinsic reward. In addition, the extrinsically rewarded group did not perform as well on the experimental task (in terms of recall, creativity, and the Zeigarnik effect) as the nonrewarded group. These findings are similar to those of Deci (1971) and Lepper et al. (1973), but they cannot be as easily explained by a frustration effect. Since in the Kruglanski et al. study the reward was never withdrawn for the experimental group, the differences between the experimental (reward) and control (no reward) conditions are better explained by a change in self-perception than by a frustration effect.

The designs of the three overly sufficient justification studies described above have varying strengths and weaknesses (Calder & Staw, 1975a), but taken together, their results can be interpreted as supporting the notion that extrinsic rewards added to an already interesting task can decrease intrinsic motivation. This effect, if true, has important ramifications for educational, industrial, and other work settings. There are many situations in which people are offered extrinsic rewards (grades, money, special privileges) for accomplishing a task which may already be intrinsically interesting. The self-perception effect means that, by offering external rewards, we may sometimes be sacrificing an important source of task motivation and not necessarily increasing either the satisfaction or the performance of the participant. Obviously, because the practical implications of the self-perception effect are large, we should proceed with caution. Thus, in addition to scrutinizing the validity of the findings themselves (as we have done above), we should also attempt to determine the exact conditions under which they might be expected to hold.

Earlier, Deci (1971, 1972) had hypothesized that only rewards contingent on a high level of task performance are likely to have an adverse effect on intrinsic motivation. He had reasoned that a reward contingent upon specific behavioral demands is most likely to cause an individual to infer that his behavior is extrinsically rather than intrinsically motivated and that a decrease in intrinsic motivation may result from this change in self-perception. Although this assumption seems reasonable, there is not a great deal of empirical support for it. Certainly in the Kruglanski et al. and Lepper et al. studies all that was necessary to cause a decrease in intrinsic motivation was for rewards to be contingent upon the completion of an activity. In each of these studies what seemed to be important was the cognition that one was performing an activity *in order to get an extrinsic reward* rather than a prescribed goal for a particular level of output. Thus as long as it is salient, a reward contingency based upon the completion of an activity may decrease intrinsic motivation just like a reward contingency based on the quality or quantity of performance.

Ross (1975) recently conducted two experiments that dealt specifically with the effect of the salience of rewards on changes in intrinsic motivation. In one study, children were asked to play a musical instrument (drums) for either no reward, a nonsalient reward, or a salient reward. The results showed that intrinsic motivation, as measured by the amount of time spent on the drums versus other activities in a free play situation, was lowest for the salient reward condition. Similar results were found in a second study in which some children were asked to think either of the reward (marshmallows) while playing a musical instrument, think of an extraneous object (snow), or not think of anything in particular. The data for this second study showed that intrinsic motivation was lowest when children consciously thought about the reward while performing the task.

In addition to the salience of an external reward, there has been empirical research on one other factor mediating the self-perception effect, the existing norms of the task situation. In examining the prior research using situations of overly sufficient justification, Staw, Calder, and Hess (1976) reasoned that there is one common element which stands out. Always, the extrinsic reward appears to be administered in a situation in which persons are not normally paid or otherwise reimbursed for their actions. For example, students are not normally paid for laboratory participation, but the Deci (1971) and Kruglanski et al. (1971) subjects were. Likewise, nursery school children are not normally enticed by special recognition or rewards to play with an interesting new toy, but both the Lepper et al. (1973) and Ross (1975) subjects were. Thus Staw, Calder, and Hess (1976) manipulated norms for payments as well as the actual payment of money for performing an interesting task. They found an interaction of norms and payment such that the introduction of an extrinsic reward decreased intrinsic interest in a task only when there existed a situational norm for no payment. From these data and the findings of the Ross study, it thus appears that an extrinsic reward must be both salient and situationally inappropriate for there to be a reduction in intrinsic interest.

Reassessing the Self-perception Effect

At present there is growing empirical support for the notion that intrinsic and extrinsic motivation *can* be negatively interrelated. The effect of extrinsic rewards on intrinsic motivation has been replicated by several researchers using different classes of subjects (males, females, children, college students) and different activities (puzzles, toys), and the basic results appear to be internally valid. As we have seen, however, the effect of extrinsic rewards is predicated on certain necessary conditions (e.g., situational norms and reward salience), as is often the case with psychological findings subjected to close examination.

To date, the primary data supporting the self-perception prediction have come from situations of insufficient and overly sufficient justification. Empirical findings have shown that individuals may cognitively reevaluate intrinsic rewards in an upward direction when their behavior is insufficiently justified and in a downward direction when there is overly sufficient justification. In general, it can be said that the data of these two situations are consistent with the self-perception hypothesis. Still, theoretically, it is not immediately clear why previous research has been restricted to these two particular contexts. No doubt it is easier to show an increase in intrinsic motivation when intrinsic interest is initially low (as under insufficient justification) or a decrease when intrinsic interest is initially high (as under overly sufficient justification). Nevertheless, the theory should support a negative interrelationship of intrinsic and extrinsic factors at *all levels*, since it makes the rather general prediction that the greater the extrinsic rewards, the less likely is the individual to infer that he is intrinsically motivated.

One recent empirical study has tested the self-perception hypothesis by manipulating *both* intrinsic and extrinsic motivation. Calder and Staw (1975b) experimentally manipulated both the intrinsic characteristics of a task as well as intrinsic rewards in an attempt to examine the interrelationship of these two factors at more than one level. In the study male college students were asked to solve one of two sets of puzzles identical in all respects except the potential for intrinsic interest. One set of puzzles contained an assortment of pictures highly rated by students (chiefly from *Life* magazine but including several *Playboy* centerfolds); another set of puzzles was blank and rated more neutrally. To manipulate extrinsic rewards, half the subjects were promised $1 for their 20 minutes of labor (and the dollar was placed prominently in view), while for half of the subjects, money was neither mentioned nor displayed. After completing the task, subjects were asked to fill out a questionnaire on their reactions to the puzzle-solving activity. The two primary dependent variables included in the questionnaire were a measure of task satisfaction and a measure of subjects' willingness to volunteer for additional puzzle-solving exercises. The latter consisted of a sign-up sheet on which subjects could indicate the amount of time they would be willing to spend (without pay or additional course credit) in future experiments of a similar nature.

The results of the Calder and Staw experiment showed a significant interaction between task and payment on subjects' satisfaction with the activity and a marginally significant interaction on subjects' willingness to volunteer for additional work without extrinsic reward. These data provided empirical support for the self-perception effect in a situation of overly sufficient justification, but not under other conditions. Specifically, when the task was initially interesting (i.e., using the picture puzzle activity), the introduction of money caused a reduction of task satisfaction and volunteering. However, when the task was initially more neutral (i.e., using the blank puzzle activity), the introduction of money increased satisfaction and subjects' intentions to volunteer for additional work. Thus if we consider Calder and Staw's dependent measures as indicators of intrinsic interest, the first finding is in accord with the self-perception hypothesis, while the latter result is similar to what one might predict from a reinforcement theory. The implications of these data, together with previous findings, are graphically depicted in Figure 3.

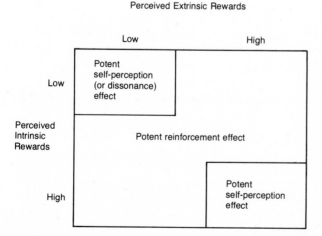

Figure 3 The relative potency of self-perception and reinforcement mechanisms.

As shown in the figure, self-perception effects have been found *only* at the extremes of insufficient and overly sufficient justification. Thus it may be prudent to withhold judgment on the general hypothesis that there is a uniformly negative relationship between intrinsic and extrinsic motivation. Perhaps we should no longer broadly posit that the greater external rewards and pressures, the weaker the perception of intrinsic interest in an activity; and the lower external pressures, the stronger intrinsic interest. Certainly, under conditions other than insufficient and overly sufficient justification, reinforcement effects of extrinsic rewards on intrinsic task satisfaction have readily been found (Cherrington, 1978; Cherrington, Reitz, & Scott, 1971; Greene, 1974).

At present it appears that only in situations of insufficient or overly sufficient reward will there be attributional instability of such magnitude that shifts will occur in the perception of intrinsic rewards. We might therefore speculate that either no attributional instability is evoked in other situations or it is just not strong enough to overcome a countervailing force. This writer would place his confidence in the latter theoretical position. It seems likely that both self-perception *and* reinforcement mechanisms hold true, but that their relative influence over an individual's task attitudes and behavior varies according to the situational context. For example, only in situations with insufficient or overly sufficient justification will the need to resolve attributional instability probably be strong enough for external rewards to produce a decrease in intrinsic motivation. In other situations we might reasonably expect a more positive relationship between intrinsic and extrinsic factors, as predicted by reinforcement theory.

Although this new view of the interrelationship between intrinsic and extrinsic motivation remains speculative, it does seem reasonable in light of recent theoretical and empirical work. Figure 4 graphically elaborates this model and shows how the level of intrinsic and extrinsic motivation may depend on the characteristics of the situation. In the figure, secondary reinforcement is depicted to be a general force for producing a positive relationship between intrinsic and extrinsic motivation. However, under situations of insufficient and oversufficient justification, self-perception (and dissonance) effects are shown to provide a second but still potentially effective determinant of a negative interrelationship between intrinsic and extrinsic motivation. Figure 4 shows the joint operation of these two theoretical mechanisms and illustrates their ultimate effect on individuals' satisfaction, persistence, and performance on a task.

IMPLICATIONS OF INTRINSIC AND EXTRINSIC MOTIVATION

In this discussion we have noted that the administration of both intrinsic and extrinsic rewards can have important effects on a person's task attitudes and behavior. Individually, extrinsic rewards may direct and control a person's activity on a task and provide an important source of satisfaction. By themselves, intrinsic rewards can also motivate task-related behavior and bring gratification to the individual. As we have seen, however, the joint effect of

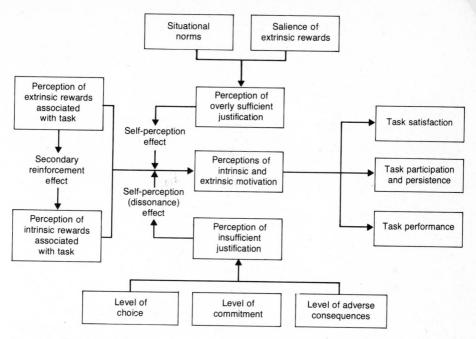

Figure 4 The interrelationship of intrinsic and extrinsic motivation as a function of situational characteristics.

intrinsic and extrinsic rewards may be quite complex. Not only may intrinsic and extrinsic factors not be additive in their overall effect on motivation and satisfaction, but the interaction of intrinsic and extrinsic factors may under some conditions be positive and under other conditions negative. As illustrated in Figures 3 and 4, a potent reinforcement effect will often cause intrinsic and extrinsic motivation to be positively interrelated, although on occasion a self-perception mechanism may be so powerful as to create a negative relationship between these two factors.

The reinforcement predictions of Figures 3 and 4 are consistent with our common sense. In practice, extrinsic rewards are relied upon heavily to induce desired behaviors, and most allocators of rewards (administrators, teachers, parents) operate on the theory that extrinsic rewards will positively affect an individual's intrinsic interest in a task. We should therefore concentrate on those situations in which our common sense may be in error—those situations in which there may in fact be a negative relationship between intrinsic and extrinsic motivation. . . .

Motivation in Work Organizations

Voluntary work organizations are very much like educational organizations: their members are often intrinsically motivated to perform certain tasks and extrinsic rewards are generally not necessary to induce the performance of many desired behaviors. Moreover, if for some reason extrinsic rewards were

to voluntary workers for performing their services we would
..d, as in the educational setting, a decrease in intrinsic motivation.
..1e educational context, we would expect an external reward to decrease
,elf-motivated (or voluntary) behavior in settings free from external reinforcement, although the specific behaviors which are reinforced might be increased.
As a concrete example, let us imagine a political candidate who decides to
"motivate" his volunteer campaign workers by paying them for distributing
flyers to prospective voters. In this situation, we might expect that the administration of an extrinsic reward will increase the number of flyers distributed.
However, the political workers' subsequent interest in performing other campaign activities *without pay* may subsequently be diminished. Similarly, the
volunteer hospital worker who becomes salaried may no longer have the same
intrinsic interest in his work. Although the newly professionalized worker may
exert a good ideal of effort on the job and be relatively satisfied with it, his
satisfaction may stem from extrinsic rather than intrinsic sources of reward.

Let us now turn to the implications of intrinsic and extrinsic motivation
for nonvoluntary work organizations. Deci (1972), in reviewing his research on
intrinsic motivation, cautioned strongly against the use of contingent monetary
rewards within industrial organizations. He maintained that paying people contingently upon the performance of specific tasks may reduce intrinsic motivation
for these activities, and he recommended noncontingent reinforcers in their
stead. As we have seen, however, a decrease in intrinsic motivation does not
always occur following the administration of extrinsic rewards; certain necessary conditions must be present before there is a negative relationship between
intrinsic and extrinsic motivation. Generally, industrial work settings do not
meet these necessary conditions.

First, within industrial organizations, a large number of jobs are not inherently interesting enough to foster high intrinsic motivation. Persons would
not ordinarily perform many of the tasks of the industrial world (e.g., assembly
line work) without extrinsic inducements, and this initial lack of intrinsic interest
will probably preclude the effect of overly sufficient justification. Second, even
when an industrial job is inherently interesting, there exists a powerful norm
for extrinsic payment. Not only do workers specifically join and contribute
their labor in exchange for particular inducements, but the instrumental relationship between task behavior and extrinsic rewards is supported by both
social and legal standards. Thus the industrial work situation is quite unlike
that of either a voluntary organization or an educational system. In the latter
cases, participants may be initially interested in performing certain tasks without
external force, and the addition of overly sufficient rewards may convey information that the task is not intrinsically interesting. Within industrial organizations, on the other hand, extrinsic reinforcement *is* the norm, and tasks
may often be perceived to be even more interesting when they lead to greater
extrinsic rewards.

The very basic distinction between nonvoluntary work situations and other
task settings (e.g., schools and voluntary organizations) is that, without extrinsic

rewards, nonvoluntary organizations would be largely without participants. The important question for industrial work settings is therefore not one of payment versus nonpayment, but of the recommended degree of contingency between reward and performance. On the basis of current evidence, it would seem prudent to suggest that, within industrial organizations, rewards continue to be made contingent upon behavior. This could be accomplished through performance evaluation, profit sharing, or piece-rate incentive schemes. In addition, intrinsic motivation should be increased directly via the planned alteration of specific job characteristics (e.g., by increasing task variety, complexity, social interaction, task identity, significance, responsibility for results, and knowledge of results).

A FINAL COMMENT

Although the study of the interaction of intrinsic and extrinsic motivation is a relatively young area within psychology, it has been the intent of this paper to outline a theoretical model and provide some practical suggestions based upon the research evidence available to date. As we have seen, the effects of intrinsic and extrinsic motivation are not always simple, and several moderating variables must often be taken into account before specific predictions can be made. Thus in addition to providing "answers" to theoretical and practical problems, this paper may illustrate the complexities involved in drawing conclusions from a limited body of research data. The main caution for the reader is to regard these theoretical propositions and practical recommendations as working statements subject to the influence of future empirical evidence.

REFERENCES

Aronson, E. "The Psychology of Insufficient Justification: An Analysis of Some Conflicting Data." In *Cognitive Consistency: Motivational Antecedents and Behavior Consequences*, edited by S. Feldman. Academic Press, 1966.

Bem, D. J. "Self-perception: An Alternative Interpretation of Cognitive Dissonance Phenomena." *Psychological Review* 74 (1967): 183–200. (a)

———. "Self-perception: The Dependent Variable of Human Performance." *Organizational Behavior and Human Performance* 2 (1967): 105–21. (b)

———. "Self-perception Theory." In *Advances in Experimental Social Psychology*, vol. 6, edited by L. Berkowitz. New York: Academic Press, 1972.

Brehm, J. W., and Cohen, A. R. *Explorations in Cognitive Dissonance*. New York: Wiley, 1962.

Calder, B. J.; Ross, M.; and Insko, C. A. "Attitude Change and Attitude Attribution: Effects of Incentive, Choice, and Consequences." *Journal of Personality and Social Psychology* 25 (1973): 84–100.

———, and Staw, B. M. "The Interaction of Intrinsic and Extrinsic Motivation: Some Methodological Notes." *Journal of Personality and Social Psychology* 31 (1975): 76–80. (a)

———, and Staw, B. M. "Self-perception of Intrinsic and Extrinsic Motivation." *Journal of Personality and Social Psychology* 31 (1975): 599–605. (b).

Carlsmith, J. M.; Collins, B. E.; and Helmreich, R. L. "Studies in Forced Compliance: The Effect of Pressure for Compliance on Attitude Change Produced by Face-to-Face Role Playing and Anonymous Essay Writing." *Journal of Personality and Social Psychology* **4** (1966): 1–13.

Cherrington, D. J. "The Effects of a Central Incentive—Motivational State on Measures of Job Satisfaction." *Organizational Behavior and Human Performance* **10** (1973): 271–89.

———; Reitz, H. J.; and Scott, W. E. "Effects of Reward and Contingent Reinforcement on Satisfaction and Task Performance," *Journal of Applied Psychology* **55** (1971): 531–36.

Collins, B. E., and Hoyt, M. F. "Personal Responsibility-for-Consequences: An Integration and Extension of the Forced Compliance Literature." *Journal of Experimental Social Psychology* **8** (1972): 558–94.

de Charms, R. *Personal Causation: The Internal Affective Determinants of Behavior.* New York: Academic Press, 1968.

Deci, E. L. "The Effects of Externally Mediated Rewards on Intrinsic Motivation." *Journal of Personality and Social Psychology* **18** (1971): 105–15.

———. "The Effects of Contingent and Noncontingent Rewards and Controls on Intrinsic Motivation." *Organizational Behavior and Human Performance* **8** (1972): 217–29.

Festinger, L. *A Theory of Cognitive Dissonance*, Stanford University Press, 1957.

———, and Carlsmith, J. M. "Cognitive Consequences of Forced Compliance." *Journal of Abnormal and Social Psychology* **58** (1959): 203–10.

Freedman, J. L. "Attitudinal Effects of Inadequate Justification." *Journal of Personality* **31** (1963): 371–85.

Greene, C. N. "Causal Connections Among Managers' Merit Pay, Job Satisfaction, and Performance." *Journal of Applied Psychology* **58** (1974): 95–100.

Heider, F. *The Psychology of Interpersonal Relations.* New York: Wiley, 1958.

Jones, E. E., and Davis, K. E. "From Acts to Dispositions: The Attribution Process in Person Perception." In *Advances in Experimental Psychology*, vol. 2, edited by L. Berkowitz. New York: Academic Press, 1965.

———; Davis, K. E.; and Gergen, K. E. "Role Playing Variations and Their Informational Value for Person Perception." *Journal of Abnormal and Social Psychology* **63** (1961): 302–10.

———, and Harris, V. A. "The Attribution of Attitudes." *Journal of Experimental Social Psychology* **3** (1967): 1–24.

———, and Nisbett, R. E. *The Actor and the Observer: Divergent Perceptions of the Causes of Behavior.* New York: General Learning Press, 1971.

Kazdin, A. E., and Bootzen, R. R. "The Token Economy: An Evaluative Review." *Journal of Applied Behavior Analysis* **5** (1972): 343–72.

Kelley, H. H. "Attribution Theory in Social Psychology." In *Nebraska Symposium on Motivation*, vol. 15, edited by D. Levine. University of Nebraska Press, 1967.

Kruglanski, A. W.; Freedman, I.; and Zeevi, G. "The Effects of Extrinsic Incentives on Some Qualitative Aspects of Task Performance." *Journal of Personality* **39** (1971): 606–17.

Lepper, M. R., and Greene, D. "Turning Play into Work: Effects of Adult Surveillance and Extrinsic Rewards on Children's Intrinsic Motivation." *Journal of Personality and Social Psychology*, in press.

————; Greene, D.; and Nisbett, R. E. "Undermining Children's Intrinsic Interest with Extrinsic Rewards: A Test of the 'Overjustification' Hypothesis." *Journal of Personality and Social Psychology* **28** (1973): 129–37.

Linder, D. E.; Cooper, J.; and Jones, E. E. "Decision Freedom as a Determinant of the Role of Incentive Magnitude in Attitude Change." *Journal of Personality and Social Psychology* **6** (1967): 245–54.

Ross, M. "Salience of Reward and Intrinsic Motivation." *Journal of Personality and Social Psychology* **32** (1975): 245–254.

Staw, B. M. "Attitudinal and Behavioral Consequences of Changing a Major Organizational Reward: A Natural Field Experiment." *Journal of Personality and Social Psychology* **6** (1974): 742–51. (a)

————. "Notes Toward a Theory of Intrinsic and Extrinsic Motivation." Paper presented at Eastern Psychological Association, 1974. (b)

————; Calder, B. J.; and Hess, R. "Intrinsic Motivation and Norms about Payment." Working paper, Northwestern University, 1975.

Strickland, L. H. "Surveillance and Trust." *Journal of Personality* **26** (1958): 200–215.

Thibaut, J. W., and Riecken, H. W. "Some Determinants and Consequences of the Perception of Social Causality." *Journal of Personality* **24** (1955): 113–33.

Weick, K. E. "Reduction of Cognitive Dissonance Through Task Enhancement and Effort Expenditure." *Journal of Abnormal and Social Psychology* **68** (1964): 533–39.

————, and Penner, D. D. "Justification and Productivity." Unpublished manuscript, University of Minnesota, 1965.

NOTES

1 It is interesting to note that Kazdin and Bootzin (1972) have made a quite similar point in their recent review of research on token economies. They noted that while operant conditioning procedures have been quite effective in altering focal behaviors within a controlled setting, seldom have changes been found to generalize to natural, nonreinforcing environments.

2 The author wishes to express his gratitude to Bobby J. Calder and Greg R. Oldham for their critical reading of the manuscript, and to the Center for Advanced Study at the University of Illinois for the resources and facilities necessary to complete this work.

The Satisfaction-Performance Controversy—Revisited

Charles N. Greene
Robert E. Craft, Jr.

In a review of literature dealing with the relationship between satisfaction and performance, Brayfield and Crockett (1955) concluded, more than 20 years ago, that "there is little evidence that employee attitudes of the type usually measured in morale surveys bear any simple or, for that matter, appreciable, relationship to performance on the job." In another extensive review of the literature that closely followed that of Brayfield and Crockett (1955), Herzberg, Mausner, Peterson, and Capwell (1957) came to quite a different conclusion: "There is frequent evidence for the often suggested opinion that positive job attitudes are favorable to increased productivity."

Thus, more than two decades after the initial reviews of prior research addressing the satisfaction-performance relationship, and more than four decades after the first investigation of this relationship (Kornhauser and Sharp, 1932), there had developed considerably different viewpoints as to the proper nature of the relationships. Another one and one-half decades passed before Greene (1972a) found the controversy to be quite robust. He identified three essentially distinct positions regarding the relationship between satisfaction and performance: (a) satisfaction causes performance, (b) performance causes satisfaction, and (c) "rewards" as a causal factor. These positions very closely approximate the range of positions on the subject that remain extant, at this writing.

THEORY AND SUPPORT

Satisfaction Causes Performance

A proposition widely held among practitioners, and often identified with the so-called Human Relations Movement, is that a happy worker is a productive worker. According to this proposition, the degree of job satisfaction felt by an employee determines his performance; that is, satisfaction causes performance. This position has had a great deal of intuitive appeal, reflecting the notion that "all good things go together," and the relatively more pleasant approach of increasing an employee's happiness as opposed to dealing directly with his performance. Acceptance of the satisfaction-causes-performance proposition makes sense as a solution, particularly because it represents the path of least resistance in that the manager, by not making rewards contingent on performance, avoids the problems associated with creating dissatisfaction among low

Portions of this article are based on and, particularly in the "Implications" section, taken from an earlier article, C. N. Greene, "The Satisfaction-Performance Controversy," *Business Horizons,* 1972, **15**(2), 31–41. Used by permission of the publisher.

performing subordinates. Further, most modern managers view both high satisfaction and high performance as desirable outcomes—both are "good" and,
therefore, they *ought* to be related to one another.

The strength of this proposition is not relegated solely to the visceral or
"gut" reactions of the practicing manager. A number of academicians have
found it quite appealing as well. Vroom's valence-force model (Vroom, 1964)
is an example of theory-based support for the satisfaction-causes-performance
case. In Vroom's (1964) model, job satisfaction reflects the valence (attractiveness) of the job. It then follows from his theory that the force exerted on
an employee to remain on the job is an increasing function of the valence of
the job. Thus, satisfaction should be negatively related to absenteeism and
turnover, and at the empirical level, it is.

Whether or not this valence also leads to higher performance, however,
has less empirical support. Vroom's review of twenty-three field studies, which
investigated the relationship between satisfaction and performance, revealed
an insignificant median static correlation of 0.14; that is, satisfaction explained
less than two percent of the of the variance in performance. The statistically
insignificant results and lack of tests of the causality question have not produced
strong empirical support for his position.

However, Vroom's report (1964) has not laid this position to rest. Shaw
and Blum (1965) reported that group performance is, in part, a function of the
group's awareness of member satisfaction. Results of an investigation of direction of causation in the relationship between job satisfaction and work performance (Sheridan and Slocum, 1975) were inconclusive with respect to managers but need satisfaction was found to affect the performance of the operative
level employees included in the sample. Thus, there does remain the possibility
that satisfaction does lead to performance; for some employees, under some
conditions.

Evidence that the satisfaction-causes-performance proposition is alive (if
not well) in contemporary academic writing is also attested to by a recent article
by Organ (1976). Interpreting previous literature in terms of equity theory and
reciprocity in social exchange, Organ asks whether reconstruction of the logic
behind the satisfaction-causes-performance hypothesis will call for "a more
judicious consideration than we have recently accorded it." Organ further
argues that research findings relevant to the hypothesis offer more support than
one is usually led to believe, particularly if certain qualifying assumptions are
made. Although he presents a cogent and interesting viewpoint, the evidence
"reinterpreted" by Organ remains primarily correlational in nature and thus
does not overcome the paucity of causal evidence supporting a satisfaction-
causes-performance position.

Performance Causes Satisfaction

A second theoretical proposition has been advanced concerning the relationship
between satisfaction and performance. This view, represented by the work of
Porter and Lawler (1968) posits that satisfaction, rather than being a cause, is

an effect of performance; that is, performance *causes* satisfaction. Differential performance determines rewards, that, in turn, produce variation in employees' expressions of job satisfaction. In this view, rewards serve as a moderating variable and satisfaction is considered to be a function of performance related rewards.

At the empirical level, this position has received support from a number of studies. Using cross-lag correlational techniques, Bowen and Siegel (1970) and Greene (1972b) reported finding relatively strong correlations between performance in one period and subsequent expressions of satisfaction (the performance-causes-satisfaction condition). These correlations were significantly higher than the low correlations between satisfaction and performance which followed in a later period (the satisfaction-causes-performance condition). The dynamic correlation coefficients in these two studies were not strong and thus one could not rule out the possibility of a third or additional variables affecting satisfaction and performance and thus the relationship between them. Indeed, in an evaluation of causal models linking the perceived role with job satisfaction, Greene and Organ (1973) offered a revised model in which role perceptions lead to compliance which then lead to performance. Thus performance was mediated by rewards and only then resulted in variations in satisfaction. Thus Porter and Lawler's predictions that differential performance determines rewards and that rewards produce variance in satisfaction has received some support but that support is not unequivocal. Additional support for the Lawler and Porter (1967) model was offered by Slocum (1971). Farris and Lim (1969) and Kavanagh, MacKinney, and Wolins (1970) report performance leading to satisfaction but see the mediating variable as leader behavior. Leader behavior was also seen by Greene (1973b and 1975) and Downey, Sheridan, and Slocum (1976) as moderating the performance-satisfaction relationship. Other variables, such as occupational group (Doll & Gunderson, 1969), self-esteem (Greenhaus & Badin, 1974), job values (Locke, 1973), and ability (Carlson, 1969) have been suggested as variables moderating the relationship between performance and satisfaction.

Rewards as a Causal Factor

Rewards as causal factors are really a subset of a more general proposition that both satisfaction and performance are co-determined by a third (or more) variable(s). Brayfield and Crockett (1955) and Fournet, Distefano, and Pryer (1966) expressed the belief that the relationship between satisfaction and performance is one of concomitant variation rather than cause and effect. Katzell, Barrett, and Parker (1961) saw the correlation between satisfaction and performance as a function of the same situational characteristics; that is, in general mathematical terms, "A" and "B" are a function of "C."

Another form of this covariation proposition is that rewards cause satisfaction, and rewards that are based on current performance cause subsequent performance. According to this proposition, formulated by Cherrington, Reitz, and Scott (1971), there is no inherent relationship between satisfaction and performance. In an experimental investigation of this proposition, they found that "rewarded" subjects expressed significantly greater satisfaction than did "unrewarded" subjects. Further, when rewards (monetary bonuses, in this case) were granted on the basis of performance, the subjects' performances were significantly higher than those of subjects whose rewards were unrelated to their performance. For example, they reported finding that when a low performer was not rewarded, dissatisfaction was expressed but subsequent performance improved. On the other hand, when a low performer was in fact rewarded for low performance, high satisfaction was expressed but performance continued at a low level. A similar pattern of findings was reported in the case of the high performing subjects, except that, the high performing subjects who were not rewarded expressed dissatisfaction as expected, and subsequent performance declined significantly for these subjects. The correlation between satisfaction and subsequent performance, excluding the effects of rewards, was 0.00; that is, satisfaction does *not* cause improved performance.

A subsequent longitudinal field study (Greene, 1973a) investigating the source and direction of causal influence in satisfaction-performance relationships, supports the Cherrington, Reitz, and Scott (1971) findings. Merit pay was identified as a cause of satisfaction and contrary to some current beliefs, was found to be a significantly more frequent source of satisfaction than dissatisfaction. The results of this study further indicated significant relationships between: (a) merit pay and subsequent performance; and (b) current performance and subsequent merit pay. Given the Cherrington, Reitz, and Scott (1971) report that rewards based on current performance caused improvements in subsequent performance, Greene's (1973a) results suggest the possibility of reciprocal causation. In other words, merit pay based on current performance probably caused variations in subsequent performance. The company in this field study evidently was relatively successful in implementing its policy of granting salary increases to an employee based on his performance (as evidenced by the significant relationship found between current performance and subsequent merit pay). The company's use of a fixed annual merit increase schedule may have obscured some of the stronger reinforcing effects of merit pay on performance.

Unlike the Cherrington, Reitz, and Scott (1971) controlled experiment, the fixed merit increase schedule precluded (as it does in many organizations) giving an employee a monetary reward immediately after the successful performance of a major task. This constraint undoubtedly reduced the magnitude of the relationship between merit pay and subsequent performance.

Additional support of the Cherrington, Reitz and Scott position is found by Wanous (1974). In this causal-correlational analysis of the job satisfaction and performance relationship, Wanous concluded that:

> The results indicate that there probably is no single "correct" relationship between satisfaction and performance. Sometimes there appears to be no relationship at all, which is consistent with the view that situations can be created by reward systems that will support any causal model. (page 143)

Reporting elsewhere, Wanous (1973) posits that other variables besides reward systems can contribute to covariation in the satisfaction-performance relationship; i.e., type of satisfaction, work experience of the individual, and type of job situation. In this same vein, Bachman, Smith and Slesinger (1966) report:

> It seems clear that in the present setting neither variable (satisfaction or performance) is the direct cause of the other. A more likely explanation is that they are both caused in part by the high total control syndrome.

The study investigated the effects of various forms of social control on satisfaction and performance. Similarly, Greene (1972b) reported finding that:

> . . . accuracy of the subordinate's perceptions of what his superior expects of him (*role accuracy*) and the extent to which the subordinate complies with these expectations (*compliance*) were significantly related to: (a) job satisfaction expressed by the subordinate and (b) his performance evaluated by his superior.

Downey, Sheridan, and Slocum (1975) also found that variance in task structure significantly influenced satisfaction and performance relationships and, yet, Ivancevich and Donnelly's (1975) findings suggest that organizational structure does not have strong effects on the relationship between these two variables.

Kahn (1960) quite adamantly writes, "I would like to begin by asserting, without qualification, that productivity and job satisfaction do not necessarily go together." He found at International Harvester that intrinsic job satisfaction and satisfaction with the company, supervision, and with reward and mobility opportunities were either unrelated or moderately negatively related to productivity. Stronger evidence supporting Kahn's position was provided by Turcotte (1974), who found high satisfaction to be associated with low performance and even cases of high performing groups in which overall satisfaction was quite low.

IMPLICATIONS FOR MANAGEMENT

Although it is clear that both employee satisfaction and performance are the result of complex processes that have not yet been completely articulated, it is equally apparent that there are steps that management can take to significantly influence the relationship between these. It is now fairly well established that rewards can produce variance in satisfaction. For the manager who is desirous of enhancing the satisfaction of employees, whether for philosophical motives or to reduce absenteeism and turnover, this may be an end-state that is valued for its own merits. However, if the manager's goal is to increase employee performance, it is equally clear that increasing subordinate's satisfaction will have no effect, *pro forma*, on their performance.

Fortunately, for manager and subordinate alike, the evidence to date clearly supports the conclusion that performance and satisfaction are covariants of a third variable (or variables). Particularly promising is the finding that rewards based on current performance significantly affect subsequent performance. In other words, while the manager cannot hope that performance will inevitably follow satisfaction, he can be consoled by the fact that there is evidently no theoretical or empirical reason to settle for only satisfaction or for only performance. Indeed, there seems to be a great deal that the contemporary manager can do to influence concomitant increase in both employee satisfaction and employee performance. The route to this achievement is not, however, the path of least resistance for the manager. In addition to constraints arising from organizational patterns, resource limitations and collective bargaining agreements, it would seem that increasing numbers of today's employees subscribe to the egalitarian philosophy articulated by John Rawls (1975) and other disciples of the non-performance contingent view of man's rights to the fruits of industrial society. According to the egalitarian argument, the fruits of modern society are the accomplishment of society at large. Therefore, all members of society are entitled to enjoy these fruits without contingencies, or constraints, beyond their membership in society.

Granting differential rewards on the basis of differences in subordinate performance will cause subordinates to express varying degrees of satisfaction or dissatisfaction. And, even if the manager is successful in overcoming obstacles to the implementation of performance-contingent reward systems, an uncomfortable position will follow—particularly with respect to his relationship with the low performer. The manager will be forced, and repeatedly, to defend his performance evaluations until the low performer responds to the new contingencies or gives up and leaves the organization. Even so, substantial benefits should offset these short-run costs. Equity theory posits that performance-contingent rewards will result in equity since the most satisfied employees are the rewarded high performers and the organization will be more successful in retaining its most productive employees.

However, as one is often reminded, "There is, indeed, no such thing as a free lunch." Faced with constraints, limited resources for rewards and limited expertise in performance appraisal techniques, it is all too apparent that the manager's task here will not be easy. The relationship between rewards and performance is often not as simple or direct as one would think, for at least two reasons. *First*, there are other causes of performance that may have a more direct bearing on a particular problem. Wanous (1973) has suggested type of satisfaction (intrinsic job satisfaction, satisfaction with company, etc.), work experience, and the job environment might be significant causal variables. *Second* is the question of the appropriateness of the reward itself, that is, what is rewarding for one person may not be rewarding for another. In short, the manager will need to consider other potential causes of performance and a range of rewards in addressing any particular performance problem.

Non-motivational Factors

The element of performance that relates most directly to the discussion thus far is effort. Effort is that element which can produce the performance to which the rewards are to be linked. If the worker believes that the magnitude of the rewards forthcoming is contingent on performance and that this performance is a function of effort expended, then the motivational force developed in the job will be expressed in performance-related effort. Even so, however, there remain other nonmotivational considerations that might best be considered prior to an analysis of means by which the manager can effectuate the desired motivation.

Direction   Suppose, for example, that an employee works hard at the job, yet performance is inadequate. What can the manager do to alleviate the problem? The manager's first action should be to identify the cause. One likely possibility is what can be referred to as a "direction problem."

Several years ago, the Minnesota Vikings' defensive end, Jim Marshall, very alertly gathered up the opponent's fumble and then, with obvious effort and delight, proceeded to carry the ball some fifty yards into the wrong end zone. This is a direction problem in its purest sense. For the employee working under more usual circumstances, a direction problem generally stems from lack of understanding of what is expected or what a job well done looks like. The action indicated to alleviate this problem is to clarify or define in detail for the employee the requirements of the job. The manager's own leadership style may also be a factor. In dealing with an employee with a direction problem, the manager needs to exercise closer supervision and to initiate structure or focus on the task, as opposed to emphasizing consideration or relations with the employee (House, 1971).

In cases where this style of behavior is repugnant or inconsistent with the manager's own leadership inclinations, an alternative approach is to engage in mutual goal setting or management-by-objectives techniques with the employee. Here, the necessary structure can be established, but at the subordinate's own initiative, thus creating a more participative atmosphere. This approach, however, is not free of potential problems. The employee is more likely to make additional undetected errors before performance improves, and the approach is more time-consuming than the more direct route.

Ability   What can the manager do if the actions taken to resolve the direction problem fail to result in significant improvements in performance? The subordinate still exerts a high level of effort and undertstands what is expected—yet continues to perform poorly. At this point, the manager may begin, justifiably so, to doubt the subordinate's ability to perform the job. When this doubt does arise, there are three useful questions, suggested by Mager and Pipe (1970), to which the manager should find answers before treating the problem as an ability deficiency: Could the subordinate do it if really necessary? What if the subordinate's life depended on it? Are his present abilities adequate for the desired performance?

If the answers to the first two questions are negative, then the answer to the last question also will be negative. The obvious conclusion is that an ability deficiency does, in fact, exist. Most managers, upon reaching this conclusion, begin to develop some type of formal training experience for the subordinate. This is unfortunate and frequently wasteful. There is probably a simpler, less expensive solution, as will be noted shortly. Formal training is usually required only when the individual has never done the particular job in question or when there is no way in which the ability requirement in question can be eliminated from the job.

If the individual formerly used the skill but now uses it only rarely, systematic practice will usually overcome the deficiency without formal training. Alternatively, the job can be changed or simplified so that the impaired ability is no longer crucial to successful performance. If, on the other hand, the individual once had the skill and still rather frequently is able to practice it, the manager should consider providing greater feedback concerning the outcome of efforts. The subordinate may not be aware of the deficiency and its effect on performance, or may no longer know how to perform the job. For example, elements of the job or the relationship between the job and other jobs may have changed, and the subordinate simply is not aware of the change.

Where formal training efforts are indicated, systematic analysis of the job is useful for identifying the specific behaviors and skills that are closely related with successful task performance and that, therefore, need to be learned. Alternatively, if the time and expense associated with job analysis are considered excessive, the critical incidents approach, as Folley (1969) suggests, can be employed toward the end.[1] Once training needs have been identified and the appropriate training technique employed, the manager can profit by asking one last question: "Why did the ability deficiency develop in the first place?"

Ultimately, the answer rests with the selection and placement process. Had a congruent person-job match been attained at the outset, the ability deficiency would have never presented itself as a performance problem.[2]

Performance Obstacles   When inadequate performance is not the result of a lack of effort, direction, or ability, there is still another potential cause that needs attention. Custer's 7th Cavalry undoubtedly expended a great deal of effort at the Little Big Horn. Unambiguous direction of subordinates may well have been "Old Yellow Hair's" long suit and surely the veterans of the Plains Wars had developed some minimal ability to fight. Yet, the results of this apparently highly motivated effort (Custer is reported to have urged his men to "give no quarter" as they attacked the seemingly unprepared Indian camp), were probably not quite what our "manager"-hero desired. Obstacles beyond the control of the subordinates can arise to interfere with performance. Three thousand Sioux and Northern Cheyenne warriors presented such an obstacle. Though this is admittedly a dramatic example, the 103 odd years since have not led to the removal of all the potential obstacles to performance. Indeed, performance obstacles can take many forms to the extent that their number, independent of a given situation, is almost unlimited.

However, the contemporary manager might survey the scene with less dismay than did Custer's superior, General Crook. More common potential obstacles may include lack of time or conflicting demands on the subordinate's time, inadequate work facilities, restrictive policies or "right ways of doing it" that inhibit performance, lack of authority, insufficient information about other activities that affect the job, and lack of cooperation from others with whom he must work.

An additional obstacle, often not apparent to the manager in face-to-face interaction with a subordinate, is the operation of group goals and norms that run counter to organizational objectives. Where the work group adheres to norms of restricting productivity, for example, the subordinate will similarly restrict performance to the extent that identification is closer with the group than with management.

Many performance obstacles can be overcome either by removing the obstacle or by changing the subordinate's job so that the obstacle no longer impinges on his performance. When the obstacle stems from group norms, however, a very different set of actions is required. Here, the actions that should be taken are the same, essentially, as those that will be considered shortly in coping with lack of effort on the part of the individual. In other words, the potential causes of the group's lack of effort are identical to those that apply to the individual.

The Motivational Problem

Thus far, performance problems have been considered in which effort was not the source of the performance discrepancy. While reward practices constitute the most frequent and direct cause of effort, there are, however, other less direct causes. Direction, ability, and performance obstacles may indirectly affect effort through their direct effects on performance. For example, an individual may perform poorly because of an ability deficiency and, as a result, exert little effort on the job. Here, the ability deficiency produces low performance, and the lack of effort on the individual's part results from his expectations of failure. Thus, actions taken to alleviate the ability deficiency should result in improved performance and, subsequently, in higher effort.

Effort is that element of performance which links rewards to performance. The relationship between rewards and effort is, unfortunately, not a simple one. As indicated in the figure, effort is considered not only as a function of the (a) value and (b) magnitude of reward, but also as a function of the (c) individual's perceptions of the extent to which greater effort on his part will lead to higher performance, and (d) that his higher performance, in turn, will lead to rewards. Therefore, a manager who is confronted with a subordinate who exerts little effort must consider these four attributes of reward practices in addition to the more indirect, potential causes of the lack of effort. The key issues in coping with a subordinate's lack of effort—the motivation problem—or in preventing such a problem from arising, involve all four of the attributes of rewards just identified (Porter & Lawler, 1968).[3]

Appropriateness of the Reward Regardless of the extent to which the individual believes that hard work determines his own performance and subsequent rewards, little effort will expended unless these rewards are valued—that is, the rewards must have value in terms of the individual's own need state. An accountant, for example, may value recognition from the boss, an opportunity to increase the scope of the job, or a salary increase; however, it is unlikely that the same value would be ascribed to a ten-year supply of budget forms.

In other words, there must be consistency between reward and what the individual needs or wants and recognition that there are often significant differences among individuals in what they consider rewarding. Similarly, individuals differ in terms of the *magnitude* of that valued reward that is positively reinforcing. A seven or eight percent salary increase may motivate one person but have little or no positive effect on another person at the same salary level. Furthermore, a sizable reward in one situation might be considered small by the same individual in a different set of circumstances.

These individual differences, particularly those concerning what rewards are valued, raise considerable question about the adequacy of current organization reward systems, virtually none of which make any formal recognition of individual differences. Lawler, for example, has suggested that organizations could profit greatly by introducing "cafeteria-style" wage plans (Lawler, 1971). These plans allow an employee to select any combination of cash and fringe benefits desired. An employee would be assigned "X" amount in compensation, which may then be divided up among a number of fringe benefits and cash. This practice would ensure that employees receive only those fringe benefits they value; from the organization's point of view, it would reduce the waste in funds allocated by the organization to fringe benefits not valued by its members. As a personal strategy, however, the manager could profit even more by extending Lawler's plan to include the entire range of non-monetary rewards.

Rewards can be classified into two broad categories, extrinsic and intrinsic. Extrinsic rewards are those external to the job, but in the context of the job, such as job security, improved working facilities, praise from one's boss, status symbols, and, of course, pay, including fringe benefits. Intrinsic rewards, on the other hand, are rewards that can be associated directly with the "doing of the job," such as a sense of accomplishment after successful performance, opportunities for advancement, increased responsibility, and work itself.

Thus, intrinsic rewards flow immediately and directly from the individual's performance on the job and, as such, may be considered as a form of self-reward. For example, one essentially must decide for one's self whether the level of performance is worthy of a feeling of personal achievement. Extrinsic rewards, to the contrary, are administered by the organization; the organization first must identify good performance and then provide the appropriate reward.

Generally speaking, extrinsic rewards have their greatest value when the individual is most strongly motivated to satisfy what Maslow has referred to as lower level needs—basic physiological needs and needs for safety or security, and those higher level ego needs that can be linked directly to status. Pay, for

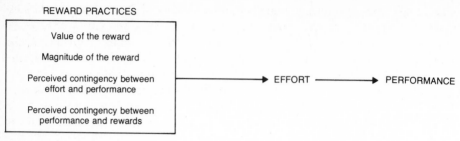

Figure 1 Rewards and effort.

example, may be valued by an individual because of a belief that it is a determinant of social position within the community or because it constitutes a means for acquiring status symbols.

Jorgenson, Dunnette, and Pritchard (1973) have reported that there was a general trend for subjects in their study to perceive money as more important over time relative to other outcomes. This is consistent with the reinforcement theory position that money is a powerful generalized, conditioned reinforcer in our society. That is, by its association with other desirable outcomes such as status, promotion, recognition, as well as what it can buy, money has acquired the effect of a powerful secondary reinforcer. Furthermore, at least one investigator, Schwab (1973), reported finding that ". . . males did not value pay more than females, older employees did not value pay less than younger employees and lower paid employees did not value pay more than higher paid employees as has been found previously." Indeed, it may well be the case that inappropriate appreciation for the subtleties of reinforcement contingencies has contributed to an apparently widespread tendency to disdain the effectiveness of monetary rewards.

The potency of pay as a reinforcer notwithstanding, there are other rewards potentially susceptible to the control of the manager. Intrinsic rewards are more likely to be valued by the individual after lower level needs have been satisfied. This is not, however, a "sufficient" condition for using intrinsic rewards since individuals vary significantly with respect to the extent to which higher order needs are motivating (e.g., Hackman and Lawler, 1971). In other words, for most people, there must be an adequate level of satisfaction with the extrinsic rewards before intrinsic rewards can be utilized effectively. For these employees, the manager needs to provide meaningful work assignments; that is, work with which the subordinate can identify and become personally involved. Challenging yet attainable goals can be established or, in some cases, it may be more advantageous to create conditions that greatly enhance the likelihood that the subordinate will succeed, thus increasing the potential for attaining feelings of achievement, advancement and recognition. The manager may also consider such means as increased delegation or other forms of job enlargement for extending the scope and depth of the jobs of subordinates shown to be motivated by higher level needs—thereby increasing these subordinates' sense of responsibility and providing greater opportunity to make the job into something more compatible with the higher level needs.

In short, managers should as closely as possible match the rewards at their disposal, both extrinsic and intrinsic rewards, with what the subordinate indicates a need or desire for. This must be done with a full appreciation for individual differences in response to various reinforcers. Second, the manager should, by varying the magnitude and timing of the rewards granted, establish clearly in the subordinate's mind the desired effort-performance-reward contingencies.

Establishing the Contingencies The contingency between effort and performance (that is, the extent to which the individual believes that working harder will improve performance) is largely a function of confidence in one's own ability and of perceptions of the difficulty of the task and absence of obstacles standing in the way of successful task performance. When the effort-performance contingency is not clear for these reasons, the manager should consider several actions. Perhaps work can be reassigned or the task made more consistent with individual perceptions of own ability; or the problem treated as "real" ability deficiency; or the apparent performance obstacles removed; or the individual simply reassured.

The second contingency, the individual's belief that the rewards received reflect accomplishments, is usually more difficult to establish. Here, two rather vexing predicaments are frequently encountered, both of which stem primarily from administration of extrinsic rewards. First, the instrument (usually a merit evaluation or performance appraisal device) may inaccurately measure the individual's contribution and thus performance is rewarded in error. Reward schedules constitute the source of the second problem. Given fixed reward schedules (that is, the ubiquitous annual salary increase) adopted by the great majority of organizations, there is more frequently than not a considerable delay between task accomplishment and bestowal of the reward. As a result, the individual may not only fail to perceive the intended contingency but may incorrectly associate the reward with behavior just prior to being rewarded. In other words, the individual may perceive a nonexistent contingency, and subsequent behavior will reflect that contingency and, this time, go unrewarded. As operant theory suggests, an important component of the performance-reward contingency is the time interval between performance and reward (Kesselman, Wood, & Hagen, 1974).

Reward Schedules The manner in which a given reward, or reinforcer, is scheduled is as strong a determinant of the effectiveness of that reward as is the value of the reward itself; or, for that matter, any other attribute of the reward. In organizations, the only plausible forms of reward schedules are intermittent as opposed to the continuous reward schedule in which the reward or punishment is administered after every behavioral sequence to be conditioned. In the case of the intermittent schedules, the behavior to be conditioned is reinforced only occasionally. There are four schedules of interest to the manager, each with varying degrees of effect on performance as a number of investigations in the field of experimental psychology have revealed.

1 *Fixed-interval schedule* Rewards bestowed after a fixed period, usually since the last time the reward was administered. This type of schedule is reflected in schedules where pay is earned on an hourly basis, generally paid on a weekly or monthly fixed schedule. Annual salary increases are also examples of this type of schedule. Typically, the individual will exhibit a "scalloped" performance pattern, with performance rising just prior to the time of reinforcement and then returning to a lower level until just before the next administration of reinforcement.

2 *Variable-interval schedule* Rewards are administered at designated time periods, but the intervals between the periods vary. For example, a reward may be given one day after the last rewarded behavior sequence, then three days later, then one week later, and so on, but only if the behavior to be conditioned actually occurs. This schedule results in fairly consistent rates of performance over long periods of time. Praise or other forms of social reinforcement from one's peers and superior, as an example, usually occur according to a variable-interval schedule, not by intention but simply because they are too involved with their own affairs to provide systematic reinforcement.

3 *Fixed-ratio schedule* Reinforcement is provided after a fixed number of responses or performances by the individual. Incentive wage plans so frequently utilized in organizations constitute the prime example of this type of schedule. It is characterized by higher rates of effort than the interval schedules unless the ratio is large. When significant delays do occur between rewards, performance, much like in the fixed schedule, declines immediately after the reward is bestowed and improves again as the time for the next reward approaches. In fact, it is more commonly the case that rewards (in this case wages) are "earned" and/or recorded on a fixed-ratio schedule but actually delivered on a fixed-interval schedule; i.e., paid once a week or once a month. This undoubtedly "dampens" the effect of the ratio schedule.

4 *Variable-ratio schedule* The reward is administered after a series of responses or performances, the number of which varies from the granting of one reward to the next.

For example, an individual on a 15:1 variable-ratio schedule might be reinforced after ten responses, then fifteen responses, then twenty responses, then ten responses, and so on, an average of one reinforcement for every fifteen responses. This schedule tends to result in performance that is higher than that of a comparable fixed-ratio schedule, and the variation in performance both before and after the occurrence of a reward or reinforcement is considerably less.

Virtually all managers must function within the constraints imposed by a fixed-interval schedule (weekly or monthly payday) or fixed-ratio schedule (wage incentives). It is unlikely that in a society where the security and phys-iological survival of the worker and dependents is tied to a predictable stream of income, that workers can live with the uneven timing of a basic wage delivered on a variable time or variable ratio schedule.

However, this fact should not preclude consideration of mixed or multiple schedules; that is, concomitant use of variable and fixed schedules. A basic wage, sufficient to provide the employee with a reliable, predictable ability to meet physiological and contractual needs such as food purchases, auto and home payments, etc., might well be used in conjunction with a bonus that is *delivered* on a variable interval or variable-ratio schedule. Even the "basic" wage can be made performance-contingent to the extent that its magnitude is determined by piece rate or level of performance. Further, other reinforcers may be even more susceptible to the use of variable schedules; such as praise, salary increases, time-off, feedback and so forth. The entire range of non-monetary rewards could be more effectively scheduled on a variable-interval (in some cases, variable-ratio) basis, assuming such scheduling is done in a systematic fashion.

CONCLUSIONS

This article has reviewed recent research concerning the relationship between satisfaction and performance and attempted to update an appraisal of its im-plications for the practicing manager. Three basic propositions were identified: (a) Satisfaction-causes-performance, (b) Performance-causes-satisfaction, and (c) Both satisfaction and performance are caused by an additional variable(s), primarily rewards.

The oldest of these propositions, that satisfaction-causes-performance, is still widespread, continuing to appeal to both practitioners and academicians. A more recent proposal is that performance-causes-satisfaction. This position has gained considerable following, especially in academic circles. However, empirical support for neither of these first two propositions is convincing, though more promising for the second than for the first.

Instead, recent evidence is more indicative of the third proposition, that satisfaction and performance are covariants of a third (or more) variable(s). The most significant co-determinant identified to date is the administration of rewards. Though complex, the relationship is essentially this: (a) rewards con-stitute a more direct cause of satisfaction than does performance and (b) not satisfaction, but rewards based on current performance, cause subsequent performance.

For the manager concerned with the well-being of subordinates, the im-plication of the finding that rewards cause satisfaction is quite clear. In order to achieve this end, the manager must provide rewards that have value in terms of the subordinate's own need state and provide them in sufficient magnitude and on an appropriate schedule as to be positively reinforcing.

The manager whose goal is to increase a subordinate's performance, on the other hand, is faced with a more difficult task for two reasons. First, the relationship between rewards and performance is not a simple one. Second, there are other causes of performance—direction, the subordinate's ability, and existence of performance obstacles standing in the way of successful task performance—which the manager must deal with, also.

The relationship between rewards and performance is complex because in reality there is at least one intervening variable and more than one contingency that need to be established. An employee exerts high level effort usually because of the valued rewards associated with high performance. Effort, the intervening variable, may be considered a function of the value and magnitude of the reward and the extent to which the individual believes that high effort will lead to high performance and that high performance, in turn, will lead to rewards.

Therefore, the manager in addition to providing appropriate rewards, must establish contingencies between effort and performance and between performance and rewards. The first contingency, the extent to which the individual believes that hard work determines performance, is perhaps the more readily established. This contingency is a function, at least in part, of the individual's confidence in his own abilities, perceptions of the difficulty of the task, and the presence of performance obstacles. When a problem does arise here, the manager can take those actions indicated earlier in this article to overcome an apparent ability deficiency or performance obstacle. The performance-reward contingency requires the manager, by means of accurate performance appraisals and appropriate reward practices, to clearly establish in the subordinate's mind the belief that performance determines the magnitude of the rewards received.

The establishment of this particular contingency, unfortunately, is becoming increasingly difficult as organizations continue to rely more heavily on fixed salary schedules and nonperformance-related factors (for example, seniority) as determinants of salary progression. However, the manager can, as a supplement to organizationally determined rewards, place more emphasis on nonmonetary rewards and both the cafeteria-style reward plans and variable-interval schedules for their administration.

It is apparent that the manager whose objective is to significantly improve subordinates' performance has assumed a difficult but by no means impossible task. The path of least resistance—that is, increasing subordinates' satisfaction—*simply will not work*.

However, the actions suggested concerning reward practices and, particularly, establishment of appropriate performance-reward contingencies, will result in improved performance, assuming that such improvement is not restricted by ability or direction problems or by performance obstacles. The use of differential rewards may require courage on the part of the manager, but failure to use them will have far more negative consequences. A subordinate will repeat that behavior which was rewarded, regardless of whether it resulted in high or low performance. A rewarded low performer, for example, will continue to perform poorly. With knowledge of this inequity, the high performer, in turn, will eventually reduce performance or seek employment elsewhere.

NOTES

1 See, for example, J. D. Folley, Jr., "Determining Training Needs of Department Store Personnel," *Training Development Journal*, 1969, Vol. 23, 24–27, for a discussion of how the critical incidents approach can be employed to identify job skills to be learned in a formal training situation.

2 For a useful discussion of how ability levels can be upgraded by means of training and selection procedures, the reader can refer to Larry L. Cummings and Donald P. Schwab, *Performance in Organizations: Determinants and Appraisal* (Glenview, Ill.: Scott, Foresman & Co.) 1972.

3 Portions of the discussion in this section are based in part on Cummings and Schwab, *Performance in Organizations*, and Lyman W. Porter and Edward E. Lawler, III, "What Job Attitudes Tell About Motivation," *Harvard Business Review*, LXVI (January-February, 1968), pp. 118–126.

REFERENCES

Bachman, J. G., C. Smith, and J. A. Slesinger, "Control, performance and satisfaction: An analysis of structural and individual effects," *Journal of Personality and Social Psychology*, 1966, Vol. 4, 127–136.

Bowen, D., and J. P. Siegel, "The relationship between satisfaction and performance: The question of causality," *Proceedings of the Annual Convention of the American Psychological Association*, 1970.

Brayfield, A. H., and W. H. Crockett, "Employee attitudes and employee performance," *Psychological Bulletin*, 1955, Vol. 52, 396–424.

Carlson, R. E., "Degree of job satisfaction as a moderator of the relationship between job performance and job satisfaction," *Personnel Psychology*, 1969, Vol. 22, 159–170.

Cherrington, D. L., H. J. Reitz, and W. E. Scott, Jr., "Effects of contingent and noncontingent reward on the relationship between satisfaction and task performance," *Journal of Applied Psychology*, 1971, Vol. 55, 531–537.

Cummings, L. L., and D. P. Schwab, *Performance in Organizations: Determinants and Appraisal* (Glenview, Ill.: Scott, Foresman & Co.) 1972.

Doll, R. E., and E. K. E. Gunderson, "Occupational group as a moderator of the job satisfaction-job performance relationship," *Journal of Applied Psychology*, 1969, Vol. 53, 359–361.

Downey, H. K., J. E. Sheridan, and J. W. Slocum, "Analysis of relationships between leader behavior and subordinate job," *Academy of Management Journal*, 1975, Vol. 18, 253–262.

Downey, H. K., J. E. Sheridan, and J. W. Slocum, Jr., "The path-goal theory of leadership: A longitudinal analysis," *Organizational Behavior and Human Performance*, 1976 (in press).

"Egalitarianism: Mechanisms for redistributing income," *Business Week*, December 8, 1975, pp. 86–90.

"Egalitarianism: Threat to a free market," *Business Week*, December 1, 1975, pp. 62–65.

"Egalitarianism: The corporation as villain," *Business Week*, December 15, 1975, pp. 86–88.

Farris, G. F., and F. G. Lim, Jr., "Effects of performance on leadership, cohesiveness, influence, satisfaction and subsequent performance," *Journal of Applied Psychology*, 1969, Vol. 53, 490–497.

Fournet, G. P., M. K. J. Distefano, and M. W. Pryer, "Job satisfaction: Issues and problems," *Personnel Psychology*, 1966, Vol. 19, 165–183.

Folley, J. D., Jr., "Determining training needs of department store personnel," *Training Development Journal*, 1969, Vol. 23, 24–27.

Greene, C. N., "The satisfaction-performance controversy," *Business Horizons*, 1972a, Vol. 15(5), 31–41.

Greene, C. N., "A causal interpretation of relationship among pay, performance, and satisfaction." Paper presented at *Annual Meeting of the Midwest Psychological Association*, 1972b, Cleveland, Ohio.

Greene, C. N., "Relationships among role accuracy, compliance, performance evaluation and satisfaction," *Academy of Management Journal*, 1972c, Vol. 15, 205–215.

Greene, C. N., "Causal connections among managers' pay, job satisfaction and performance," *Journal of Applied Psychology*, 1973a, Vol. 58, 95–100.

Greene, C. N., "A longitudinal analysis of relationships among leader behavior and subordinate performance and satisfaction," *Proceedings of the 33rd Annual Meeting of the Academy of Management*, 1973b.

Greene, C. N., "The reciprocal nature of influence between leader and subordinate," *Journal of Applied Psychology*, 1975, Vol. 60, 187–193.

Greene, C. N., and D. W. Organ, "An evaluation of causal models linking the perceived role with job satisfaction," *Administrative Science Quarterly*, 1973, Vol. 18, 95–103.

Greenhaus, J. H., and I. J. Badin, "Self-esteem, performance and satisfaction: Some tests of a theory," *Journal of Applied Psychology*, 1974, Vol. 59, 722–726.

Hackman, J. R., and E. E. Lawler, III, "Employee reactions to job characteristics," *Journal of Applied Psychology*, 1971, Vol. 55, 259–286.

Herzberg, F., B. Mausner, R. O. Peterson, and D. F. Capwell, "Job attitudes: A review of research and opinion," (Pittsburgh, Pa.: Psychological Service of Pittsburgh) 1957.

House, R. J., "A path goal theory of leader effectiveness," *Administrative Science Quarterly*, 1971, Vol. 16, 321–339.

Ivancevich, J. M., and J. H. Donnelly, Jr., "Relation of organizational structure to job satisfaction, anxiety-stress and performance," *Administrative Science Quarterly*, 1975, Vol. 20, 272–280.

Jorgenson, D. O., M. D. Dunnette, and R. D. Pritchard, "Effects of the manipulation of a performance-reward contingency on behavior in a simulated work setting," *Journal of Applied Psychology*, 1973, Vol. 57, 271–280.

Kahn, R. L., "Productivity and job satisfaction," *Personnel Psychology*, 1960, Vol. 13, 275.

Katzell, R. A., R. S. Barrett, and T. C. Parker, "Job satisfaction, job performance and situational characteristics," *Journal of Applied Psychology*, 1961, Vol. 45, 65–72.

Kavanagh, M. J., A. C. MacKinney, and L. Wolins, "Satisfaction and morale of foremen as a function of middle manager's performance," *Journal of Applied Psychology*, 1970, Vol. 54, 145–156.

Kesselman, G. A., M. T. Wood, and E. L. Hagen, "Relationships between performance and satisfaction under contingent and noncontingent reward systems," *Journal of Applied Psychology*, 1974, Vol. 59, 374–376.

Lawler, E. E., III, *Pay and Organizational Effectiveness: A Psychological View* (New York: McGraw-Hill Book Company) 1971.

Lawler, E. E., III, and L. W. Porter, "The effect of performance on job satisfaction," *Industrial Relations*, 1967, Vol. 7, 20–28.

Locke, E. A., "Job satisfaction and job performance: A theoretical analysis," *Organizational Behavior and Human Performance*, 1970, Vol. 5, 484–500.

Mager, R. F., and P. Pipe, *Analyzing Performance Problems* (Belmont, Cal.: Lear Siegler, Inc.) 1970.

Organ, D. W., "A reappraisal and reinterpretation of the satisfaction-causes-performance hypothesis," *Academy of Management Journal*, 1976.

Porter, L. W., and E. E. Lawler, III, *Management Attitudes and Performance* (Homewood, Ill.: Richard D. Irwin, Inc.) 1968.

Porter, L. W., and E. E. Lawler, III, "What job attitudes tell about motivation," *Harvard Business Review*, 1968, Vol. 66, 118–126.

Schwab, D. P., "Impact of alternative compensation systems on pay valence and instrumentality perceptions," *Journal of Applied Psychology*, 1973, Vol. 58, 308–312.

Shaw, M. E., and J. M. Blum, "Group performance as a function of task difficulty and the group's awareness of member satisfaction," *Journal of Applied Psychology*, 1965, Vol. 49, 151–154.

Sheridan, J. E., and J. W. Slocum, Jr., "The direction of the causal relationship between job satisfaction and work performance," *Organizational Behavior and Human Performance*, 1975, Vol. 14.

Slocum, J. W., Jr., "Motivation in managerial levels: Relationship of need satisfaction to job performance," *Journal of Applied Psychology*, 1971, Vol. 55, 312–316.

Turcotte, W. E., "Control systems, performance and satisfaction in two state agencies," *Administrative Science Quarterly*, 1974, Vol. 19, 60–73.

Vroom, V. H. *Work and Motivation* (New York: John Wiley & Sons) 1964.

Wanous, J. P., "A causal-correlational analysis of the job satisfaction and performance relationship," *Proceedings of the 33rd Annual Meeting of the Academy of Management*, 1973.

Wanous, J. P., "A causal-correlational analysis of the job satisfaction and performance relationship," *Journal of Applied Psychology*, 1974, Vol. 59, 139–144.

Satisfaction and Behavior

Edward E. Lawler III

Compared to what is known about motivation, relatively little is known about the determinants and consequences of satisfaction. Most of the psychological research on motivation simply has not been concerned with the kinds of affective reactions that people experience in association with or as a result of motivated behavior. No well-developed theories of satisfaction have appeared and little theoretically based research has been done on satisfaction. The influence of

Abridged from E. E. Lawler III, *Motivation in work organizations.* Monterey, Calif.: Brooks/Cole, 1973, 61–4, 74–87. Used by permission.

behaviorism on the field of psychology had a great deal to do with this lag in research. While psychology was under the influence of behaviorism, psychologists avoided doing research that depended on introspective self-reports. Behaviorists strongly felt that if psychology were to develop as a science, it had to study observable behavior. Since satisfaction is an internal subjective state that is best reported by the people experiencing it, satisfaction was not seen as a proper subject for study. Psychologists thought they should concentrate on those aspects of motivation that are observable (for example, performance, hours of deprivation, strength of response, and so on).

Most of the research on the study of satisfaction has been done by psychologists interested in work organizations. This research dates back to the 1930s. Since that time, the term "job satisfaction" has been used to refer to affective attitudes or orientations on the part of individuals toward jobs. Hoppock published a famous monograph on job satisfaction in 1935, and in 1939 the results of the well-known Western Electric studies were published. The Western Electric studies (Roethlisberger & Dickson, 1939) emphasized the importance of studying the attitudes, feelings, and perceptions employees have about their jobs. Through interviews with over 20,000 workers, these studies graphically made the point that employees have strong affective reactions to what happens to them at work. The Western Electric studies also suggested that affective reactions cause certain kinds of behavior, such as strikes, absenteeism, and turnover. Although the studies failed to show any clear-cut relationship between satisfaction and job performance, the studies did succeed in stimulating a tremendous amount of research on job satisfaction. During the last 30 years, thousands of studies have been done on job satisfaction. Usually these studies have not been theoretically oriented; instead, researchers have simply looked at the relationship between job satisfaction and factors such as age, education, job level, absenteeism rate, productivity, and so on. Originally, much of the research seemed to be stimulated by a desire to show that job satisfaction is important because it influences productivity. Underlying the earlier articles on job satisfaction was a strong conviction that "happy workers are productive workers." Recently, however, this theme has been disappearing, and many organizational psychologists seem to be studying job satisfaction simply because they are interested in finding its causes. This approach to studying job satisfaction is congruent with the increased prominence of humanistic psychology, which emphasizes human affective experience.

The recent interest in job satisfaction also ties in directly with the rising concern in many countries about the quality of life. There is an increasing acceptance of the view that material possessions and economic growth do not necessarily produce a high quality of life. Recognition is now being given to the importance of the kinds of affective reactions that people experience and to the fact that these are not always tied to economic or material accomplishments. Through the Department of Labor and the Department of Health, Education, and Welfare, the United States government has recently become active in trying to improve the affective quality of work life. Job satisfaction is one measure of the quality of life in organizations and is worth understanding and increasing even if it doesn't relate to performance. This reason for studying satisfaction is likely to be an increasingly prominent one as we begin to worry more about the effects working in organizations has on people and as our humanitarian concern for the kind of psychological experiences people have during their lives increases. What happens to people during the work day has profound effects both on the individual employee's life and on the society as a whole, and thus these events cannot be ignored if the quality of life in a society is to be high. As John Gardner has said:

> Of all the ways in which society serves the individual, few are more meaningful than to provide him with a decent job. . . . It isn't going to be a decent society for any of us until it is for all of us. If our sense of responsibility fails us, our sheer self-interest should come to the rescue [1968, p. 25].

As it turns out, satisfaction is related to absenteeism and turnover, both of which are very costly to organizations. Thus, there is a very "practical" economic reason for organizations to be concerned with job satisfaction, since it can influence organizational effectiveness. However, before any practical use can be made of the finding that job dissatisfaction causes absenteeism and turnover, we must understand what factors cause and influence job satisfaction. Organizations can influence job satisfaction and prevent absenteeism and turnover only if the organizations can pinpoint the factors causing and influencing these affective responses.

Despite the many studies, critics have legitimately complained that our understanding of the causes of job satisfaction has not substantially increased during the last 30 years (for example, see Locke, 1968, 1969) for two main reasons. The research on job satisfaction has typically been atheoretical and has not tested for causal relationships. Since the research has not been guided by theory, a vast array of unorganized, virtually uninterpretable facts have been unearthed. For example, a number of studies have found a positive relationship between productivity and job satisfaction, while other studies have found no evidence of this relationship. Undoubtedly, this disparity can be explained, but the explanation would have to be based on a theory of satisfaction, and at present no such theory exists. One thing the research on job satisfaction has done is to demonstrate the saying that "theory without data is fantasy; but data without theory is chaos!"

Due to the lack of a theory stating causal relationships, the research on job satisfaction has consistently looked simply for relationships among variables. A great deal is known about what factors are related to satisfaction, but very little is known about the causal basis for the relationships. This is a serious problem when one attempts to base change efforts on the research. This problem also increases the difficulty of developing and testing theories of satisfaction. Perhaps the best example of the resulting dilemma concerns the relationship between satisfaction and performance. If satisfaction causes performance, then organizations should try to see that their employees are satisfied; however, if performance causes satisfaction, then high satisfaction is not necessarily a goal but rather a by-product of an effective organization. . . .

A MODEL OF FACET SATISFACTION

Figure 1 presents a model of the determinants of facet satisfaction. The model is intended to be applicable to understanding what determines a person's satisfaction with any facet of the job. The model assumes that the same psychological processes operate to determine satisfaction with job factors ranging from pay to supervision and satisfaction with the work itself. The model in Figure 1 is a discrepancy model in the sense that it shows satisfaction as the difference between a, what a person feels he should receive, and b, what he perceives that he actually receives. The model indicates that when the person's perception of what his outcome level is and his perception of what his outcome level should be are in agreement, the person will be satisfied. When a person perceives his outcome level as falling below what he feels it should be, he will be dissatisfied. However, when a person's perceived outcome level exceeds what he feels it should be, he will have feelings of guilt and inequity and perhaps some discomfort (Adams, 1965). Thus, for any job factor, the assumption is that satisfaction with the factor will be determined by the difference between how much of the factor there is and how much of the factor the person feels there should be.

Present outcome level is shown to be the key influence on a person's

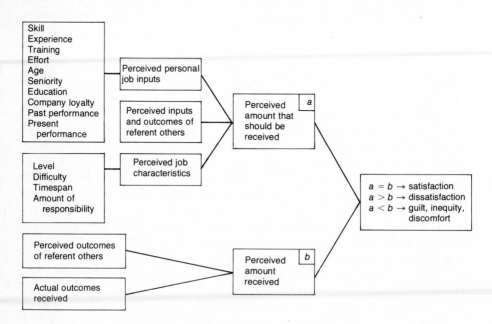

Figure 1   Model of the determinants of satisfaction.

perception of what rewards he receives, but his perception is also shown to be influenced by his perception of what his "referent others" receive. The higher the outcome levels of his referent others, the lower his outcome level will appear. Thus, a person's psychological view of how much of a factor he receives is said to be influenced by more than just the objective amount of the factor. Because of this psychological influence, the same amount of reward often can be seen quite differently by two people; to one person it can be a large amount, while to another person it can be a small amount.

The model in Figure 1 also shows that a person's perception of what his reward level should be is influenced by a number of factors. Perhaps the most important influence is perceived job inputs. These inputs include all of the skills, abilities, and training a person brings to the job as well as the behavior he exhibits on the job. The greater he perceives his inputs to be, the higher will be his perception of what his outcomes should be. Because of this relationship, people with high job inputs must receive more rewards than people with low job inputs or they will be dissatisfied. The model also shows that a person's perception of what his outcomes should be is influenced by his perception of the job demands. The greater the demands made by the job, the more he will perceive he should receive. Job demands include such things as job difficulty, responsibilities, and organization level. If outcomes do not rise along with these factors, the clear prediction of the model is that the people who perceive they have the more difficult, higher level jobs will be the most dissatisfied.

The model shows that a person's perception of what his outcomes should be is influenced by what the person perceives his comparison-other's inputs and outcomes to be. This aspect of the model is taken directly from equity theory and is included to stress the fact that people look at the inputs and outcomes of others in order to determine what their own outcome level should be. If a person's comparison-other's inputs are the same as the person's inputs but the other's outcomes are much higher, the person will feel that he should be receiving more outcomes and will be dissatisfied as a result.

The model allows for the possibility that people will feel that their outcomes exceed what they should be. The feelings produced by this condition are quite different from those produced by under-reward. Because of this difference, it does not make sense to refer to a person who feels over-rewarded as being dissatisfied. There is considerable evidence that very few people feel over-rewarded, and this fact can be explained by the model. Even when people are highly rewarded, the social-comparison aspect of satisfaction means that people can avoid feeling over-rewarded by looking around and finding someone to compare with who is doing equally well. Also, a person tends to value his own inputs much higher than they are valued by others (Lawler, 1967). Because of this discrepancy, a person's perception of what his outcomes should be is often not shared by those administering his rewards, and is often above what he actually receives. Finally, the person can easily increase his perception of his inputs and thereby justify a high reward level.

As a way of summarizing some of the implications of the model, let us briefly make some statements about who should be dissatisfied if the model is correct. Other things being equal:

1   People with high perceived inputs will be more dissatisfied with a given facet than people with low perceived inputs.

2   People who perceive their job to be demanding will be more dissatisfied with a given facet than people who perceive their jobs as undemanding.

3   People who perceive similar others as having a more favorable input-outcome balance will be more dissatisfied with a given facet than people who perceive their own balance as similar to or better than that of others.

4   People who receive a low outcome level will be more dissatisfied than those who receive a high outcome level.

5   The more outcomes a person perceives his comparison-other receives, the more dissatisfied he will be with his own outcomes. This should be particularly true when the comparison-other is seen to hold a job that demands the same or fewer inputs.

OVERALL JOB SATISFACTION

Most theories of job satisfaction argue that overall job satisfaction is determined by some combination of all facet-satisfaction feelings. This could be expressed in terms of the facet-satisfaction model in Figure 1 as a simple sum of, or average of, all $a - b$ discrepancies. Thus, overall job satisfaction is determined by the difference between all the things a person feels he should receive from his job and all the things he actually does receive.

A strong theoretical argument can be made for weighting the facet-satisfaction scores according to their importance. Some factors do make larger contributions to overall satisfaction than others. Pay satisfaction, satisfaction with the work itself, and satisfaction with supervision seem to have particularly strong influences on overall satisfaction for most people. Also, employees tend to rate these factors as important. Thus, there is a connection between how important employees say job factors are and how much job factors influence overall job satisfaction (Vroom, 1964). Conceptually, therefore, it seems worthwhile to think of the various job-facet-satisfaction scores as influencing total satisfaction in terms of their importance. One way to express this relationship is by defining overall job satisfaction as being equal to Σ (facet satisfaction $\times$ facet importance). However, as stressed earlier, actually measuring importance and multiplying it by measured facet satisfaction often isn't necessary because the satisfaction scores themselves seem to take importance into account. (The most important items tend to be scored as either very satisfactory or very dissatisfactory; thus, these items have the most influence on any sum score.) Still, on a conceptual level, it is important to remember that facet-satisfaction scores do differentially contribute to the feeling of overall job satisfaction.

A number of studies have attempted to determine how many workers are actually satisfied with their jobs. Our model does not lead to any predictions in this area. The model simply gives the conditions that lead to people experiencing feelings of satisfaction or dissatisfaction. Not surprisingly, the studies that have been done do not agree on the precentage of dissatisfied workers. Some suggest figures as low as 13 percent, others give figures as high as 80 percent. The range generally reported is from 13 to 25 percent dissatisfied. Herzberg et al. (1957) summarized the findings of research studies conducted from 1946 through 1953. The figures in their report showed a yearly increase in the median percentage of job-satisfied persons (see Table 1). Figure 2 presents satisfaction-trend data for 1948 through 1971. These data also show an overall increase in the number of satisfied workers, which is interesting because of recent speculation that satisfaction is decreasing. However, due to many measurement problems, it is impossible to conclude that a real decline in number of dissatisfied workers has taken place.

The difficulty in obtaining meaningful conclusions from the data stems from the fact that different questions yield very different results. For example, a number of studies, instead of directly asking workers "How satisfied are you?," have asked "If you had it to do over again, would you pick the same job?" The latter question produces much higher dissatisfaction scores than does the simple "how satisfied are you" question. One literature review showed that 54 percent of the workers tended to say that they were sufficiently dissatisfied with their jobs that they would not choose them again. On the other hand, the straight satisfaction question shows between 13 and 25 percent dissatisfied. However, even this figure is subject to wide variation depending on how the question is asked. When the question is asked in the simple form, "Are you satisfied, yes or no?," the number of satisfied responses is large. When the question is changed so that the employees can respond yes, no, or undecided—or satisfied, dissatisfied, or neutral—the number of satisfied responses drops.

Because of these methodological complexities, it is difficult to draw conclusions about the number of workers who are or are not satisfied with their jobs or with some facet of their jobs. This drawback does not mean, however,

Table 1   Median Percentage of Job-dissatisfied Persons Reported from 1946–1953

Year	Median percentage of job-dissatisfied
1953	13
1952	15
1951	18
1949	19
1948	19
1946–1947	21

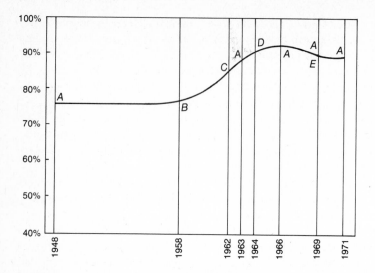

Figure 2 Percentage of "satisfied" workers, 1948–1971. (*From Quinn, Staines, & McCullough, 1973.*) *Note*: "Don't know" and "uncertain" have been excluded from the base of the percentages. *Sources*: A = Gallup, or Gallup as reported by Roper; B = Survey Research Center (Michigan); C = NORC; D = Survey Research Center (Berkeley); E = 1969–1970 Survey of Working Conditions.

that meaningful research on satisfaction is impossible. On the contrary, interesting and important research has been and can be done on the determinants of job satisfaction. For example, the relationship between personal-input factors—such as education level, sex, and age and seniority—and job or facet satisfaction can be ascertained by simply comparing those people who report they are satisfied with those people who report they are dissatisfied and checking the results to see if the two groups differ in any systematic manner. The number of people reporting satisfaction is not crucial for this purpose. What is important is that we distinguish those people who tend to be more satisfied from those people who tend to be less satisfied. This distinction can be made with many of the better-known satisfaction-measuring instruments, such as the Job Description Index (Smith, Kendall, & Hulin, 1969) and Porter's (1961) need-satisfaction instrument.

A number of studies have tried to determine the amount of employee dissatisfaction that is associated with different job facets. Although these studies have yielded interesting results, some serious methodological problems are involved in this work. As with overall job satisfaction, factors such as type of measurement scale used and manner of wording questions seriously affect the number of people who express dissatisfaction with a given facet. For example, a question about pay satisfaction can be asked in a way that will cause few people to express dissatisfaction, while a question about security satisfaction can be asked in a way that will cause many people to express dissatisfaction. In this situation, comparing the number of people expressing security satisfaction with the number of people expressing pay dissatisfaction might produce very misleading conclusions. This problem is always present no matter how carefully the various items are worded because it is impossible to balance the items so they are comparable for all factors.

Despite methodological problems, the data on relative satisfaction levels with different job factors are interesting. These data show that the factors mentioned earlier as being most important—that is, pay, promotion, security, leadership, and the work itself—appear in these studies as the major sources of dissatisfaction. Porter (1961) designed items using Maslow's needs as a measure of satisfaction. With these items, he collected data from various managers. The results of his study (see Table 2) show that more managers express higher order need dissatisfaction than express lower order need dissatisfaction. The results also show that a large number of managers are dissatisfied with their pay and with the communications in their organizations and that middle level managers tend to be better satisfied in all areas than lower level managers.

Porter's data also show that managers consider the areas of dissatisfaction to be the most important areas. It is not completely clear whether the dissatisfaction causes the importance or the importance causes the dissatisfaction. The research reviewed earlier suggests that the primary causal direction is from dissatisfaction to importance, although there undoubtedly is a two-way-influence process operating. The important thing to remember is that employees do report varying levels of satisfaction with different job factors, and the factors that have come out high on dissatisfaction have also been rated high on importance and have the strongest influence on overall job satisfaction.

A study by Grove and Kerr (1951) illustrates how strongly organizational conditions can affect factor satisfaction. Grove and Kerr measured employee satisfaction in two plants where normal work conditions prevailed and found that 88 percent of the workers were satisfied with their job security, which indicated that security was one of the least dissatisfying job factors for employees in these two plants. In another plant where layoffs had occurred, only

Table 2   Differences between Management Levels in Percentage of Subjects Indicating Need-Fulfillment Deficiencies *(Adapted from Porter, 1961)*

Questionnaire items	% Bottom management (N = 64)	% Middle management (N = 75)	% Difference
Security needs	42.2	26.7	15.5
Social needs	35.2	32.0	3.2
Esteem needs	55.2	35.6	19.6
Autonomy needs	60.2	47.7	12.5
Self-actualization needs	59.9	53.3	6.6
Pay	79.7	80.0	−0.3
Communications	78.1	61.3	16.8

17 percent of the workers said they were satisfied with the job security, and job security was one of the most dissatisfying job factors for this plant's employees.

The research on the determinants of satisfaction has looked primarily at two relationships: (1) the relationship between satisfaction and the characteristics of the job, and (2) the relationship between satisfaction and the characteristics of the person. Not surprisingly, the research shows that satisfaction is a function of both the person and the environment. These results are consistent with our approach to thinking about satisfaction, since our model (shown in Figure 1) indicates that personal factors influence what people feel they should receive and that job conditions influence both what people perceive they actually receive and what people perceive they should receive.

The evidence on the effects of personal-input factors on satisfaction is voluminous and will be only briefly reviewed. The research clearly shows that personal factors do affect job satisfaction, basically because they influence perceptions of what outcomes should be. As predicted by the satisfaction model in Figure 1, the higher a person's perceived personal inputs—that is, the greater his education, skill, and performance—the more he feels he should receive. Thus, unless the high-input person receives more outcomes, he will be dissatisfied with his job and the rewards his job offers. Such straightforward relationships between inputs and satisfaction appear to exist for all personal-input factors except age and seniority. Evidence from the study of age and seniority suggests a curvilinear relationship (that is, high satisfaction among young and old workers, low satisfaction among middle-age workers) or even a relationship of increasing satisfaction with old age and tenure. The tendency of satisfaction to be high among older, long-term employees seems to be produced by the effects of selective turnover and the development of realistic expectations about what the job has to offer.

CONSEQUENCES OF DISSATISFACTION

Originally, much of the interest in job satisfaction stemmed from the belief that job satisfaction influenced job performance. Specifically, psychologists thought that high job satisfaction led to high job performance. This view has now been discredited, and most psychologists feel that satisfaction influences absenteeism and turnover but not job performance. However, before looking at the relationship among satisfaction, absenteeism, and turnover, let's review the work on satisfaction and performance.

Job Performance

In the 1950s, two major literature reviews showed that in most studies only a slight relationship had been found between satisfaction and performance. A later review by Vroom (1964) also showed that studies had not found a strong relationship between satisfaction and performance: in fact, most studies had found a very low positive relationship between the two. In other words, better performers did seem to be slightly more satisfied than poor performers. A considerable amount of recent work suggests that the slight existing relationship is probably due to better performance indirectly causing satisfaction rather than the reverse. Lawler and Porter (1967) explained this "performance causes satisfaction" viewpoint as follows:

> If we assume that rewards cause satisfaction, and that in some cases performance produces rewards, then it is possible that the relationship found between satisfaction and performance comes about through the action of a third variable—rewards. Briefly stated, good performance may lead to rewards, which in turn lead to satisfaction; this formulation then would say that satisfaction rather than causing performance, as was previously assumed, is caused by it.
>
> Figure 3 shows that performance leads to rewards, and it distinguishes between two kinds of rewards and their connection to performance. A wavy line between performance and extrinsic rewards indicates that such rewards are likely to be imperfectly related to performance. By extrinsic rewards is meant such organizationally controlled rewards as pay, promotion, status, and security—rewards that are often referred to as satisfying mainly lower-level needs. The connection is relatively weak because of the difficulty of tying extrinsic rewards directly to performance. Even though an organization may have a policy of rewarding merit, performance is difficult to measure, and in dispensing rewards like pay, many other factors are frequently taken into consideration.
>
> Quite the opposite is likely to be true for intrinsic rewards, however, since they are given to the individual by himself for good performance. Intrinsic or internally mediated rewards are subject to fewer disturbing influences and thus are likely to be more directly related to good performance. This connection is indicated in the model by a semi-wavy line. Probably the best example of an intrinsic reward is the feeling of having accomplished something worthwhile. For that matter any of the rewards that satisfy self-actualization needs or higher order growth needs are good examples of intrinsic rewards [p. 23–24].[1]

Figure 3 shows that intrinsic and extrinsic rewards are not directly related

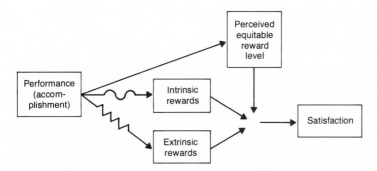

Figure 3 Model of the relationship of performance to satisfaction. (From Lawler, E. E., and Porter, L. W., The effect of performance on job satisfaction. *Industrial Relations,* 1967, **7**, 20–28. Reprinted by permission of the publisher, *Industrial Relations.*)

[1]Lawler, E. E., and Porter, L. W. The effect of performance on job satisfaction. *Industrial Relations*, 1967, **7**, 20–28. Reprinted by permission of the publisher, *Industrial Relations*.

to job satisfaction, since the relationship is moderated by perceived equitable rewards (what people think they should receive). The model in Figure 3 is similar to the model in Figure 1, since both models show that satisfaction is a function of the amount of rewards a person receives and the amount of rewards he feels he should receive.

Because of the imperfect relationship between performance and rewards and the important effect of perceived equitable rewards, a low but positive relationship should exist between job satisfaction and job performance in most situations. However, in certain situations, a strong positive relationship may exist; while in other situations, a negative relationship may exist. A negative relationship would be expected where rewards are unrelated to performance or negatively related to performance.

To have the same level of satisfaction for good performers and poor performers, the good performers must receive more rewards than the poor performers. The reason for this, as stressed earlier, is that performance level influences the amount of rewards a person feels he should receive. Thus, when rewards are not based on performance—when a poor performers receive equal rewards or a larger amount of rewards than good performers—the best performers will be the least satisfied, and a negative satisfaction-performance relationship will exist. If, on the other hand, the better performers are given significantly more rewards, a positive satisfaction-performance relationship should exist. If it is assumed that most organizations are partially successful in relating rewards to performance, it follows that most studies should find a low but positive relationship between satisfaction and performance. Lawler and Porter's (1967) study was among those that found this relationship; their study also found that, as predicted, intrinsic-need satisfaction was more closely related to performance than was extrinsic-need satisfaction.

In retrospect, it is hard to understand why the belief that high satisfaction causes high performance was so widely accepted. There is nothing in the literature on motivation that suggests this causal relationship. In fact, such a relationship is opposite to the concepts developed by both drive theory and expectancy theory. If anything, these two theories would seem to predict that high satisfaction might reduce motivation because of a consequent relation in the importance of various rewards that may have provided motivational force. Clearly, a more logical view is that performance is determined by people's efforts to obtain the goals and outcomes they desire, and satisfaction is determined by the outcomes people actually obtain. Yet, for some reason, many people believed—and some people still do believe—that the "satisfaction causes performance" view is best.

Turnover

The relationship between satisfaction and turnover has been studied often. In most studies, researchers have measured the job satisfaction among a number of employees and then waited to see which of the employees studied left during an ensuing time period (typically, a year). The satisfaction scores of the employees who left have then been compared with the remaining employees' scores. Although relationships between satisfaction scores and turnover have not always been very strong, the studies in this area have consistently shown that dissatisfied workers are more likely than satisfied workers to terminate employment; thus, satisfaction scores can predict turnover.

A study by Ross and Zander (1957) is a good example of the kind of research that has been done. Ross and Zander measured the job satisfaction of 2680 female workers in a large company. Four months later, these researchers found that 169 of these employees had resigned; those who left were significantly more dissatisfied with the amount of recognition they received on their jobs, with the amount of achievement they experienced, and with the amount of autonomy they had.

Probably the major reason that turnover and satisfaction are not more strongly related is that turnover is very much influenced by the availability of other positions. Even if a person is very dissatisfied with his job, he is not likely to leave unless more attractive alternatives are available. This observation would suggest that in times of economic prosperity, turnover should be high, and a strong relationship should exist between turnover and satisfaction; but in times of economic hardship, turnover should be low, and little relationship should exist between turnover and satisfaction. There is research evidence to support the argument that voluntary turnover is much lower in periods of economic hardship. However, no study has compared the relationship between satisfaction and turnover under different economic conditions to see if it is stronger under full employment.

Absenteeism

Like turnover, absenteeism has been found to be related to job satisfaction. If anything, the relationship between satisfaction and absenteeism seems to be stronger than the relationship between satisfaction and turnover. However, even in the case of absenteeism, the relationship is far from being isomorphic. Absenteeism is caused by a number of factors other than a person's voluntarily deciding not to come to work; illness, accidents, and so on can prevent someone who wants to come to work from actually coming to work. We would expect satisfaction to affect only voluntary absences; thus, satisfaction can never be strongly related to a measure of overall absence rate. Those studies that have separated voluntary absences from overall absences have, in fact, found that voluntary absence rates are much more closely related to satisfaction than are overall absence rates (Vroom, 1964). Of course, this outcome would be expected if satisfaction does influence people's willingness to come to work.

Organization Effectiveness

The research evidence clearly shows that employees' decisions about whether they will go to work on any given day and whether they will quit are affected by their feelings of job satisfaction. All the literature reviews on the subject have reached this conclusion. The fact that present satisfaction influences future absenteeism and turnover clearly indicates that the causal direction is from satisfaction to behavior. This conclusion is in marked contrast to our conclusion with respect to performance—that is, behavior causes satisfaction.

The research evidence on the determinants of satisfaction suggests that satisfaction is very much influenced by the actual rewards a person receives; of course, the organization has a considerable amount of control over these rewards. The research also shows that, although not all people will react to the same reward level in the same manner, reactions are predictable if something is known about how people perceive their inputs. The implication is that organizations can influence employees' satisfaction levels. Since it is possible to know how employees will react to different outcome levels, organizations can allocate outcomes in ways that will cause either job satisfaction or job dissatisfaction.

Absenteeism and turnover have a very direct influence on organizational effectiveness. Absenteeism is very costly because it interrupts scheduling, creates a need for overstaffing, increases fringe-benefit costs, and so on. Turnover is expensive because of the many costs incurred in recruiting and training replacement employees. For lower-level jobs, the cost of turnover is estimated at $2000 a person; at the managerial level, the cost is at least five to ten times the monthly salary of the job involved. Because satisfaction is manageable and influences absenteeism and turnover, organizations can control absenteeism and turnover. Generally, by keeping satisfaction high and, specifically, by seeing that the best employees are the most satisfied, organizations can retain those employees they need the most. In effect, organizations can manage turnover so that, if it occurs, it will occur among employees the organization can most afford to lose. However, keeping the better performers more satisfied is not easy, since they must be rewarded very well.

REFERENCES

Adams, J. S. Injustice in social exchange. In L. Berkowitz (Ed.), *Advances in experimental social psychology*, Vol. 2. New York, Academic Press, 1965.

Gardner, J. W. *No easy victories*. New York, Harper & Row, 1968.

Grove, E. A., & Kerr, W. A. Specific evidence on origin of halo effect in measurement of employee morale. *Journal of Social Psychology*, 1951, **34**, 165–170.

Herzberg, F., Mausner, B., Peterson, R. O., & Capwell, D. I. *Job attitudes: Review of research and opinion*, Pittsburgh, Psychological Service of Pittsburgh, 1957.

Lawler, E. E. The multitrait multirater approach to measuring managerial job performance. *Journal of Applied Psychology*, 1967, **51**, 369–381.

Lawler, E. E., & Porter, L. W. The effect of performance on job satisfaction. *Industrial Relations*, 1967, **7**, 20–28.

Locke, E. A. What is job satisfaction? Paper presented at the APA Convention, San Francisco, September 1968.

Locke, E. A. What is job satisfaction? *Organizational Behavior and Human Performance*, 1969, **4**, 309–336.

Porter, L. W. A study of perceived need satisfactions in bottom and middle management jobs. *Journal of Applied Psychology,* 1961, **45,** 1–10.

Quinn, R. P., Staines, G., & McCullough, M. Job satisfaction in the 1970's. Recent history and a look to the future, *Manpower Monograph,* 1973.

Roethlisberger, F. I., & Dickson, W. I. *Management and the worker.* Cambridge, Mass., Harvard University Press, 1939.

Ross, I. E., & Zander, A. F. Need satisfaction and employee turnover. *Personnel Psychology,* 1957, **10,** 327–338.

Smith, P., Kendall, I., & Hulin, C. *The measurement of satisfaction in work and retirement.* Chicago, Rand McNally & Company, 1969.

Vroom, V. H. *Work and motivation.* New York, John Wiley & Sons, 1964.

QUESTIONS FOR DISCUSSION

1 Why is it so difficult to measure such factors as performance and job satisfaction objectively?

2 What role do job attitudes play in effective job performance?

3 Is job satisfaction an objective or a subjective concept? Explain.

4 Exactly how might rewards such as pay, promotion, and positive feedback affect the determination of job satisfaction? How might they affect performance?

5 Do you think it likely that we will soon have one universally accepted theory of work motivation? Why or why not?

6 Is it necessary for line managers to select one theory of motivation and remain with it in their day-to-day supervisory activities or could they use several theories simultaneously? Explain.

7 Evaluate Deci's model of intrinsic and extrinsic motivation. What research evidence exists in regard to this issue (consult Staw)?

8 Evaluate Greene's argument concerning the performance-satisfaction controversy.

9 Critique Lawler's facet model of job satisfaction.

10 What are the consequences of job dissatisfaction?

Chapter 7

Attachment to Organizations

Up to this point, we have concentrated on what March and Simon (1958) term the "decision to produce." That is, we have been concerned with factors that appear to influence an individual's willingness or desire to perform well on the job. There also exists a second and equally important type of motivated work behavior, which has been called the "decision to participate." Here we focus on the processes by which individuals decide whether to form attachments, or linkages, with organizations or to sever such attachments.

We are concerned, then, with what organizations want from their employees and what employees want in exchange from their employers. It is important to recognize that an exchange relationship exists here. On the one hand, organizations want to be assured of receiving a certain quantity and quality of employee participation, or else they have little need of that employee. On the other hand, employees want to be sure that they can satisfy many of their own personal goals—such as adequate pay, promotion opportunities, co-worker interactions—or else there is little purpose in their coming to work. Thus, linkages between individuals and organizations are a process in which both parties agree to some compromise situation in which both organizational and personal goal attainment are facilitated.

The topic of employee attachment to organizations is indeed a broad one.

When loosely defined, it includes such topics as why and how people select their occupations or careers, why they shift occupations, why they choose a particular organization, why the organization chooses them, and why individuals decide to remain with or withdraw from an organization. Lawler (1973) has added a further dimension to this topic by suggesting the need for research into why people decide *not* to work at all!

ORGANIZATIONAL ENTRY

Conceptually, it is possible to distinguish three rather general stages in the attachment process, as shown in Exhibit 1. The first stage, *organizational entry*, concerns the manner in which employees choose which organization to join. Such a choice is obviously a two-way process; that is, both parties to the choice (the employer and the employee) must support the choice. Unfortunately, while problems of personnel selection (that is, how organizations select employees) have been studied for some time, our knowledge of how employees choose organizations is much more limited. Recently, efforts have been made to examine this process more fully (see, for example, Wanous, 1977; Hall, 1976).

ORGANIZATIONAL COMMITMENT

In the second stage, which may be termed *organizational commitment*, individuals decide the extent or depth of their attachment to the organization. Organizational commitment focuses on the extent to which employees identify with organizational goals, value organizational membership, and intend to work hard to attain the overall organizational mission (Porter, Steers, Mowday, & Boulian, 1974; Steers, 1977). In this sense, commitment differs from simple attachment, or membership, in that it involves an active relationship between an employee and his or her employer such that the employee is willing to go beyond normal required compliance behavior in order to contribute to the realization of the organization's goals. Recent findings have indicated that highly committed employees are less likely to be absent or turn over (Steers, 1977). Little relationship, however, has been found between commitment and sub-

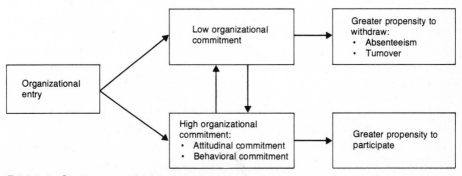

Exhibit 1 Stages in organizational attachment.

sequent performance. It thus appears that the major benefit of highly committed employees lies in increased attachment and not necessarily increased performance.

Commitment has been viewed in two ways in the literature. Staw (1977) distinguishes between *attitudinal* commitment and *behavioral* commitment. Consistent with the definition above, attitudinal commitment is viewed in terms of the extent to which employees identify with the organization and wish to remain a member. It represents a strong positive attitude toward the organization, accompanied by a behavioral intention to work hard on behalf of the organization (Porter et al., 1974).

Following this attitudinal definition of commitment, the literature suggests at least three separate sets of factors that can influence the degree of employee (attitudinal) commitment: (1) personal characteristics, (2) job characteristics, and (3) work experiences (Steers, 1977). More specifically, increased commitment has been found to be related to several *personal characteristics,* including age, need for achievement, and education (inversely). Similarly, commitment has also been found to be related to the following *job characteristics:* job challenge, opportunities for social interaction, task identity, and feedback. Finally, commitment has been shown to be related to the following *work experiences:* group attitudes toward the organization, organizational dependability, perceived personal importance to the organization, and the extent to which expectations have been met on the job. In all, then, attitudinal commitment has been shown to be influenced by a variety of both personal and organizational factors. These influences are shown in Exhibit 2.

The second approach to conceptualizing commitment suggested by Staw (1977; see also the reading selection by Salancik) is termed *behavioral* commitment. This approach views commitment as a process by which people make irrevocable decisions to the extent that they cannot "back out" of the orga-

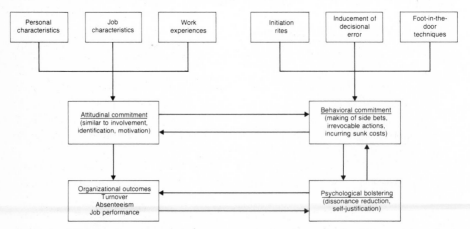

Exhibit 2 Two approaches to understanding organizational commitment. (*Adapted from Staw, 1977.*)

nization without extreme difficulty (see Exhibit 2). Through such techniques as initiation rites, errors in previous decisions, or "foot-in-the-door" techniques, individuals become committed to certain courses of action (such as joining a particular organization). That is, they incur sunk costs that make it difficult to take alternate courses of action. For example, a blue-collar employee who undergoes an apprenticeship program to be a skilled machinist (and who collects seniority in the process) may find that the sunk costs in time and seniority "commit" him or her to the organization; that is, he or she cannot afford to leave and go elsewhere. As can be seen, this second approach to commitment says little about an employee's agreement with organizational goals or a willingness to facilitate organizational goal attainment, only that the individual feels bound to the organization. Furthermore, as a result of this binding process, employees typically engage in some form of psychological bolstering. That is, such employees attempt to rationalize or self-justify their situation in an effort to demonstrate to themselves that they have indeed made the right choice by joining that particular organization. This bolstering could be done in a variety of ways. For instance, an employee may accentuate the value of the company's fringe benefits or retirement benefits. Through such accentuation, the employee attempts to convince himself or herself that a correct decision was made in joining the organization.

The two approaches to organizational commitment need not be seen as conflicting. Indeed, a better understanding of attachment processes can be obtained by examining attitudinal and behavioral commitments simultaneously. That is, it must be recognized that individuals do become bound to organizations as a result of past choices but that such a bond does not guarantee high levels of *attitudinal* commitment to the organization. Similarly, it is possible for employees to feel highly committed to an organization (attitudinally) and believe in the organization's mission, yet not be irrevocably bound to remain with the organization.

EMPLOYEE ABSENTEEISM AND TURNOVER

The final phase of the attachment process is the actual decision to participate or withdraw (see Exhibit 1). Here we are concerned about the problems of employee absenteeism and turnover. As indicated in Exhibit 1, high levels of organizational commitment tend to be associated with lower rates of turnover and absenteeism (Porter et al., 1974, 1976; Steers, 1977). However, as we shall see in the last two readings of this chapter, a variety of other important variables also influence the decision to withdraw.

The majority of research on this topic has emphasized turnover and treated absenteeism with subsidiary interest. Moreover, it is often argued that turnover and absenteeism share common antecedents and hence can be treated with similar techniques. However, a closer look at the available research cautions against this conclusion. As pointed out by Porter and Steers (1973), absenteeism as a category of behavior differs from turnover in three important aspects:

(1) the negative consequences associated with absenteeism are typically much less than those associated with turnover; (2) absenteeism is more likely to be a spontaneous and relatively easy decision, while turnover is generally thought through more carefully; and (3) absenteeism often represents a substitute for turnover, particularly during poor economic times when alternate forms of employment may be scarce.

In addition, in a review of 22 investigations that studied both turnover and absenteeism, it was found that only six demonstrated significant relationships in the same direction between the variables under study and *both* turnover and absenteeism. Hence, it appears justified to separate our analysis of turnover and absenteeism instead of treating one as the analog of the other. In this way, we will hopefully derive a clearer understanding of the causes (and cures) for both forms of withdrawal behavior.

OVERVIEW

Four reading selections follow on the topic of organizational attachment. First, John Wanous reviews the available material on organizational entry, including the processes by which people choose both careers and organizations. Next, Gerald Salancik provides an overview of the topic of organizational commitment, focusing primarily on behavioral (as opposed to attitudinal) commitment.

Following this are two selections dealing with withdrawal from organizational settings. First, Steers and Rhodes present a theoretical model that attempts to describe the processes leading up to absenteeism. Finally, Mobley proposes a similar model dealing with employee turnover. A comparison of these two models will highlight the different causes behind each form of withdrawal behavior.

REFERENCES AND SUGGESTED ADDITIONAL READINGS

Forest, C. R., Cummings, L. L., & Johnson, A. C. Organizational participation: A critique and model. *Academy of Management Review*, 1977, **2**, 586–601.

Hall, D. T. *Careers in organizations*. Pacific Palisades, Calif.: Goodyear, 1976.

Hall, D. T., & Schneider, B. Correlates of organizational identification as a function of career pattern and organizational type. *Administrative Science Quarterly*, 1972, **17**, 340–350.

Hrebiniak, L. G., & Alutto, J. A. Personal and role-related factors in the development of organizational commitment. *Administrative Science Quarterly*, 1972, **17**, 555–573.

Lawler, E. E., III. *Motivation in work organizations*. Monterey, Calif: Brooks/Cole, 1973.

March, J. G., & Simon, H. A. *Organizations*. New York: Wiley, 1958.

Muchinsky, P. M. Employee absenteeism: A review of the literature. *Journal of Vocational Behavior*, 1977, **10**, 316–340.

Pettman, B. O. *Labour turnover and retention*. London: Wiley, 1975.

Porter, L. W. Crampon, W. J., & Smith, F. J. Organizational commitment and managerial turnover: A longitudinal study. *Organizational Behavior and Human Performance*, 1976, **15**, 87–98.

Porter, L. W., & Steers, R. M. Organizational, work, and personal factors in employee turnover and absenteeism. *Psychological Bulletin*, 1973, **80**, 151–176.

Porter, L. W., Steers, R. M., Mowday, R. T., & Boulian, P. V. Organizational com-
     mitment, job satisfaction, and turnover among psychiatric technicians. *Journal of
     Applied Psychology*, 1974, **59**, 603–609.
Price, J. *The study of turnover*. Ames, Iowa: Iowa State University Press, 1977.
Schuh, A. The predictability of employee tenure: A review of the literature. *Personnel
     Psychology*, 1967, **20**, 133–152.
Sheldon, M. E. Investments and involvements as mechanisms producing commitment
     to the organization. *Administrative Science Quarterly*, 1971, **16**, 143–150.
Staw, B. M. Two sides of commitment. Paper presented at the National Meeting of the
     Academy of Management, 1977.
Steers, R. M. Antecedents and outcomes of organizational commitment. *Adminstrative
     Science Quarterly*, 1977, **22**, 46–56.
Super, E. E., & Bohn, M. J. *Occupational psychology*. Belmont, Calif.: Wadsworth,
     1970.
Vroom, V. H. *Work and motivation*. New York: Wiley, 1964.
Wanous, J. P. Organizational entry: Newcomers moving from outside to inside. *Psy-
     chological Bulletin*, 1977, **84**, 601–618.
Yolles, S. F., Carone, P. A., & Krinsky, L. W. *Absenteeism in industry*. Springfield,
     Ill.: Charles C Thomas, 1975.

Organizational Entry: The Individual's Viewpoint

John P. Wanous

All organizational systems import various types of energy: people, money, raw materials, information, and so forth. This paper is concerned with *human* energy sources, in particular new employees in organizations. Fundamentally, the "organizational entry process" can be viewed in two ways: (1) from the individual's viewpoint, and (2) from the organization's perspective. This paper focuses exclusively on the individual's viewpoint during the entry process and has four objectives. The first is to define the individual's view of organizational entry in general, and then identify four components of this process. The second objective is to describe why new employees are an important group to study. The third is to review what we know about each of the topic areas in organizational entry. The final objective is to point out what remains to be done for a better understanding of newcomers in organizations.

WHAT IS ORGANIZATIONAL ENTRY?

Organizational entry concerns how individuals move from outside to inside a new organization. Viewed from the perspective of the individual who enters, the entry process begins outside the organization as people think about possible

From Hackman, J. R., Lawler, E. E., III, and Porter, L. W. *Perspectives on behavior in organizations*. New York: McGraw-Hill, 1977, 126–135. Used by permission of the author and publisher.

entry. The process continues throughout the phase where an effort is made to join, when there is an acceptance of the individual by the organization, and when the individual makes the final decision to enter.

The topic of organizational entry continues to be important even after entry itself. In particular, it is important to consider the "aftereffects" of the entry process on both the individual and the organization. An examination of these entry consequences does *not* include what some have called "organizational socialization" (Bakke, 1953; Schein, 1968) or the "personalizing process" (Bakke, 1953). Both of these processes occur *after* entry, but are *not* necessarily *direct* consequences of the entry itself. Organizational socialization refers to how individuals learn: (1) the basic values and goals of the organization, (2) the means for attaining them, (3) individual job responsibilities, (4) acceptable behavior patterns for effective job performance, and (5) other guiding principles for maintaining the organization (Schein, 1968). The personalizing process refers to how each individual leaves his or her "mark" on the organization. Together these describe the character of mutual-influence processes that are set in motion when newcomers enter organizations.

Organizational entry does not focus on these two active processes, but it does include that postentry behavior of newcomers which has been caused by the entry process itself. It can perhaps be best understood by listing four specific components, each of which has become a question for research.

1 How do individuals choose new organizations?

2 How accurate and complete is the information that "outsiders" have about new organizations?

3 What is the impact of organizational recruitment on the "matching" of individual and organization?

4 What are the consequences of matching or mismatching individuals and organizations?

NEW EMPLOYEES AS AN IMPORTANT TOPIC

Implied by the above questions is a view of organizational entry from the individual's viewpoint, not the organization's. Viewing entry from an organizational perspective changes the way such questions are asked. For example, the selection and testing research in industrial psychology is the "flip side" of the first area. Concern over getting lots of data about job applicants is the organizational analogue of the second question. For the third area, organizations have been concerned with making themselves appear attractive for recruitment purposes, but have not investigated the impact of this recruitment strategy on newcomers. Thus, one reason why the study of new employees has merit is that we know so little about it from the individual's viewpoint. The second reason is closely related. Because organizations and researchers have viewed new employees primarily as passive figures, they have tended to concentrate on abilities and skills in the context of predicting job performance. This emphasis overlooks the fact that individuals choose new organizations and that the satisfaction of the individual's need is a crucial element in keeping effective employees from leaving.

A third reason for the significance of this area is that turnover in most organizations tends to be highest during the first six months or so of work experience. This varies from situation to situation, but tends to be fairly characteristic of most business organizations. In many cases this is quite costly to an organization, when there is a "revolving-door" effect for certain jobs. That is, there can be high turnover for some entry-level jobs because the newcomers are "testing" the work environment to see if it will be satisfactory. If it is not, they often leave quickly; hence the revolving-door phenomenon. A fourth point is that people who join new organizations are probably more open to influence than they will be at any other time spent in that particular organization. For example, the formation of a "psychological contract" (Schein, 1968) may revolve around how well matched are personal versus organizational values.

MATCHING INDIVIDUAL AND ORGANIZATION: A GENERAL FRAMEWORK FOR ORGANIZATIONAL ENTRY

Most organizations are constantly involved in a "matching process" between the individual and the organization. On the one hand, newcomers to an organization come with their own *individual talent* (such as skills, abilities, and knowledge), as well as important *human needs*. On the other hand, the typical organization can be viewed as having *talent requirements* for various jobs as well as its own particular *climate characteristics*. Thus, there are two important "match-ups" which occur during the process of new employees entering an organization: (1) individual talent with organizational talent requirements, and (2) human needs with organizational climate. This general process of matching individual and organization is *continuous* because both people and jobs change over time, and because there is constant labor force movement (hires, promotions, quits and fires).

It is fair to say that most organizations strongly emphasize the match between employees' talents and job demands. On the other hand, matching the needs of employees and the characteristics of jobs is typically underemphasized. In fact, rarely are efforts made to match newcomers to a specific job in a particular organization in terms of human needs and the job climate.

While both matches are probably important for motivation, performance, and job satisfaction, the match between an employee's talent and job-talent requirements probably has a more immediate and powerful effect on job performance than it does on job satisfaction or job tenure (Lofquist & Dawis, 1969). A poor match typically results in poor job performance. Sometimes, however, a mismatch of this first type can affect job tenure (i.e., absenteeism, turnover, or tardiness), especially when an individual is *over*-qualified for a job.

On the other hand, the match between human needs and organizational climate usually has a more immediate and potent effect on job satisfaction and tenure than on job performance. A poor matching can produce employees' dissatisfaction which results in tardiness, absenteeism, and turnover. There are exceptions to this, of course, because some individuals may use ineffective job performance as a way to "get back" at an organization for a job which is not psychologically rewarding (Argyris, 1964).

Two selection processes operate in the matching of people and jobs. One of these involves the organization selecting the individual and the other involves the individual selecting the organization. Research pertaining to the former abounds in industrial psychology, as it has been a major focus there. When the organization is selecting an individual the tendency has been to assess the *talents* of an applicant for placement on an appropriate type of job. On the other hand, when individuals select an organization they often look for a potentially satisfying climate in which to work (in a business organization), or study (in a university).

Thus, there has been a historical tendency for the matching of individual talent and organizational requirements to be associated with the organization's selection of individuals rather than vice versa. It is obvious that a complete treatment of organizational entry necessarily includes *both* match-ups, and should stress organizational selection of individuals as well as the individuals' choice of organizations. However, the present paper is intentionally slanted toward the relatively underresearched topics concerning organizational entry from the individual's viewpoint.

EXAMPLES OF RESEARCH ON ORGANIZATIONAL ENTRY

Although our present knowledge about organizational entry is highly asymmetrical, we do have a good start in all four of the areas listed above. Below are examples of what has been done to date.

How Do Individuals Choose New Organizations?

About one dozen studies of organizational choice can be found in today's literature. The procedures of each study vary. For example, one long-term study investigated how a group of forty-nine people studying for the master's degree at Carnegie-Mellon University chose their first full-time jobs (Vroom, 1966; Vroom & Deci, 1971). This study "tracked" the job expectations and goals these students held concerning the organizations they interviewed. For most students there was a very close correspondence between their *overall* ratings of "organizational attractiveness" and an *index* composed of their *specific expectations* (about each organization) multiplied by their *personal goals* for the job. When it came time to choose a particular job offer, 76 percent of them picked the organization which had been rated the highest on the index of "expectations × goals." This was felt to be strong confirmation of the "expectancy theory" of motivation (Vroom, 1964), upon which the study was based.

A number of other studies have also found that individuals tend to select those organizations which have the greatest personal attractiveness based on an index of their *expectations* multiplied by their *goals*. Perhaps the best way to characterize these studies is to distinguish among the various stages in the individual's choice of organization:

Stage 1: Initial Attractiveness of an Organization Most studies indicate that people are attracted to those organizations which are rated highest on a psychological index based on *both* an individual's *expectations* about what the organization will be like *and* each person's own values or goals (Huber, Daneshgar, & Ford, 1971; Lawler, Kuleck, Rhode, & Sorenson, 1975; Vroom, 1966; Wanous, 1975a).

Stage 2: Effort to Join a Particular Organization After deciding what organizations are most attractive, the field of possibilities is somewhat narrowed. From among those remaining, certain ones seem to be more highly sought out than others. An individual's greatest efforts to join a particular organization seem to be directed to those which not only are attractive, but which are seen as likely to offer an opening. In a nutshell, studies have shown that one's *expectations* of gaining entry *and* the *attractiveness* of an organization determine how hard most individuals try to join certain organizations (Glueck, 1974; Lawler et al., 1975; Wanous, 1975a).

Stage 3: Choice from among Organizations Offering Entry In between stages 2 and 3 the initiative returns to the organization, which selects or rejects the individual. Every organization that one tries to enter will not necessarily offer admission. Once again the range of possibilities is limited. From among those which do extend offers, most people choose the one which has the greatest attractiveness (Ford, Huber, & Gustafson, 1972; Huber et al., 1971; Lawler et al., 1975; Pieters, Hundert, & Beer, 1968; Soelberg, 1967; Vroom, 1966; Wanous, 1975a).

Although the art of organizational choice seems to be quite rational, and well understood, research has uncovered two interesting "twists." For example, the *act of choosing* seems to *distort* the perceptions of those engaged in the process. Immediately after deciding which organization to enter, most people tend to perceive it as even *more* attractive than before the choice. They also tend to perceive the rejected alternatives as even less attractive (Lawler et al., 1975; Soelberg, 1967; Vroom, 1966). This is an example of a basic human need to *justify* one's own choices, although it may not always occur (Sheridan, Richards, & Slocum, 1975).

The second "twist" to be found is that newcomers in organizations tend to be *less* satisfied with their choice than either before making it or immediately after choosing (Vroom & Deci, 1971; Wanous, 1975a). This result raises many questions, but especially those concerning the quality of information outsiders have when making choices and the impact of typical recruitment programs on such expectations. Both of these are taken up in the next two component areas of the organizational entry process.

How Accurate and Complete Is the Information of Outsiders about New Organizations?

Until recently, problems of misinformation were not considered serious enough to warrant much attention. The subsequent disappointment after entry clearly implies that some people were led to expect the wrong things about new organizations. The research to be discussed under topic 3 (see page 313) also points in the direction of inaccurate—especially inflated—expectations held by outsiders before entry.

A study of Harvard M.B.A. students (Ward & Athos, 1972) indicated that recruiters from various companies gave "glowing" rather than "balanced" descriptions, and glossed over details of organizational life. Research at an automotive manufacturer (Dunnette, Arvey, & Banas, 1973) examined two groups of employees: those who left within their first four years, and those who remained longer than four years. They found that most people's expectations were *not* realized in actual job situations. The problem of unfulfilled expectations was much more severe for those who "terminated early." Only such concrete expectations as pay levels were confirmed by actual experience, a finding documented by Wanous (1972b) earlier in a study of University of Minnesota graduating seniors.

The American Telephone and Telegraph study of newly entered managers (Bray, Campbell, & Grant, 1974) shows that expectations decline with increasing years in the same company. This study did not begin until after entry, but found that employees' expectations about the future continued to decline for the first seven years at AT&T work experience. This decline was about equal for both effective and ineffective performers.

A recent study of M.B.A. students in three New York City graduate business schools (Wanous, 1976) provides the most detailed information on the quality of information that outsiders have about new organizations. Students were asked to complete questionnaires about their school choices at three points in time: (1) outsiders—before entry, (2) newcomers—shortly after entry in the fall semester, and (3) insiders—during the spring after the first academic year. There was a *decline* from naive (inflated) expectations of outsiders to realistic (lower) beliefs on the part of insiders. Interestingly enough, the decline occurred only for those aspects "intrinsic" to the educational process itself (e.g., quality of teaching, school status, competition), and not for those "extrinsic" to learning (e.g., location, tuition, transfer credit, etc.). The Wanous (1976) study also looked at a smaller group of telephone operators who moved from outside to inside the Southern New England Telephone Company. As with the M.B.A. students, there was a decline for intrinsic job characteristics. Unlike the M.B.A. study, a decline also occurred for extrinsic factors, but it was not as strong as the decline for intrinsic job characteristics.

As the M.B.A. data from the Wanous (1976) study indicate, there may *not* be a problem of "total inaccuracy" on the part of outsiders. Nevertheless, those aspects considered intrinsic in this study, and in other studies (e.g., Dunnette, Campbell, & Hakel, 1967), are the ones *most* important to individuals.

This poses a very serious and interesting problem for organizational recruitment. Namely, outsiders tend to have inaccurately inflated expectations about those organizational characteristics (i.e., the intrinsic ones) which are the hardest ones to describe because they are the most abstract. Even if an organization tried to describe itself accurately to new recruits, it would not be easy. The next section discusses a series of studies where a variety of organizations tried to recruit newcomers with as much realism as possible.

What Is the Impact of Organizational Recruitment on the "Matching" of Individual and Organization?

One way to deal with the inflated expectations of outsiders is to give recruits a "realistic job preview" (Wanous, 1975b, c) to "set" initial expectations at a realistic level and to help individuals make better organizational choices. Over the last twenty years six experimental studies in organizations have compared the effectiveness of a realistic job preview with a more "traditional" approach.

The basic difference between the two strategies is that the realistic one emphasizes *specific* facts which are typical of *both* desirable *and* undesirable aspects of the organization. The traditional approach tries to maximize the number of recruitees for each opening by "selling" the job in its most positive light. Recruitment by the traditional approach also tends to overlook the costs associated with high quit rates.

The six experiments involved a variety of techniques to present a realistic job preview: four studies used a booklet, one a film, and another a two-hour "practice session." They involved a variety of individuals and jobs: insurance salesmen, West Point cadets, telephone operators, and sewing machine operators. The first two groups were all male, while the latter were all female.

A number of criteria were used to assess the impact of these realistic job previews. First, was the ability to recruit newcomers impaired by the use of realism? Four of the six studies directly addressed this issue and three show no impairment at all (Wanous, 1973; Weitz, 1956; Youngberg, 1963). A fourth study (Farr, O'Leary, & Bartlett, 1973) found a slightly higher rate of job offer refusals for those seeing the realistic job preview. Second, were initial job expectations really lowered due to the realistic preview? Two of the six directly addressed this issue, and the answer is clearly affirmative (Wanous, 1973; Youngberg, 1963). In fact, Wanous found that the preview was "selective," i.e., it lowered *only* those initial expectations that were discussed in the preview, and did not "spill over" to other aspects of the job.

A third question is whether realistic recruitment results in more positive attitudes on the part of newcomers. Two of the six studies did address this issue and both found such beneficial effects as higher satisfaction after three months (Youngberg, 1963) and fewer thoughts of quitting (Wanous, 1973). The fourth, and final, question is whether realism resulted in lower turnover. For many organizations this is the "bottom line" question concerning the effectiveness of realistic job previews. The typical way to assess it has been to compare the percentage of newcomers who "survive" (i.e., do *not* leave) with a similar percentage for those in the control group. The higher the survival percentage, the lower the turnover, and the more effective the preview. These results are listed below in chronological order, showing the realistic preview's percentage first, followed by the job survival rate of the control group.

- At Life and Casualty Insurance Company of Tennessee, 68 percent versus 53 percent over five months for life insurance agents (Weitz, 1956).
- At Prudential Insurance Company, 71 percent versus 57 percent over six months for life insurance agents (Youngberg, 1963).
- At West Point, 91 percent versus 86 percent over one year for first year cadets (Macedonia, 1969).
- At the Southern New England Telephone Company, 62 percent versus 50 percent over three months for telephone operators (Wanous, 1973).
- At Manhattan Industries, Inc., 88.9 percent versus 68.8 percent over six weeks for white sewing machine operators. No differences were found for Black operators, however.
- At West Point, 94 percent versus 88.5 percent over a three-month summer training period for first year cadets (Ilgen & Seely, 1974).

What Are the Consequences of Matching or Mismatching Individuals and Organizations?

Thus far we have seen that individuals *try* to "match" themselves to organizations, but they often make such decisions on the basis of incomplete and inaccurate information. A few organizations, however, have consciously tried to recruit newcomers using realistic job previews to effect better match-ups between human needs and organizational climate. The majority of organizations, whether businesses or universities, have not attempted systematic, realistic recruiting. Thus it is important to ask what the consequences are when mismatches between individuals and organizations occur.

Guiding this brief review are two assumptions. First, based on the "matching model" presented earlier, it is expected that the match between individual and organization will have a greater impact on job *satisfaction* and *tenure* than on actual job performance. Second, in most cases a good, or "close," match between an individual's needs and the organizational climate is desirable. The exceptions to these assumptions will be discussed last.

The match-up between individual and organization takes place in two related "levels": (1) the immediate job or task, and (2) general aspects of the climate other than the immediate job, such as pay, relationships with coworkers, the status of the organization, etc. (Schneider, 1975). This distinction is similar to the one Herzberg et al. have drawn between job content and the job's context (Herzberg, Mausner, & Snyderman, 1959).

Studies of the relationship between job characteristics and individual differences are good examples of research falling into the first type of matching category. Early studies in the area of task (or job) characteristics sought to identify the most important ones which influence employees' motivation, performance, tenure and satisfaction (e.g., Herzberg et al., 1959). Recent studies have gone beyond the mere identification of important job characteristics to include the influence of individual differences (in desires or needs). Several recent studies have shown that matching *actual* job characteristics to *desired* characteristics leads to high levels of employee motivation and satisfaction but not necessarily to performance (Hackman & Lawler, 1971; Wanous, 1974).

Besides the individual's match-up to the immediate job, studies have examined the consequences of the match-up between individuals and the broader context of organizational climate. Most of these do, in fact, support the assumption that organizational climate has a greater impact on satisfaction than on actual job performance (Friedlander & Margulies, 1969; Lawler, Hall, & Oldham, 1974; Pritchard & Karasick, 1973).

A recent study by Schneider (1975) tried to relate the match-up (or "fit," as he called it) between individual and organization to both performance and tenure among 1,125 life insurance agents. Initially he was unable to find any sizeable relationships. Further analysis revealed that some of the agencies studied had far "better" climates than others. That is, they were higher on supportiveness, concern, morale, and autonomy, and lower on conflict than other agencies. By then examining the match-up between individual and organization for both the "good" and "bad" agencies, he found differences which had been hidden when he examined all the agencies together. Among the "good" agencies the expected relationship was found (i.e., the closer matched individuals and organizations were, the higher the sales and the lower the turnover). On the other hand, in the "bad" (or "negative") climates the reverse was true. The *less* the individual was similar to the climate, the better were sales and turnover was lower. Although Schneider's study is one of the first to separate out the *type* of climate, it does suggest that a strict interpretation of matching individual to organization may have to be slightly modified. This is especially true for those organizations with basically "negative" climates.

WHERE DO WE GO FROM HERE?

For the future study of organizational entry the greatest single need is for an *integrated conceptual overview* of the entire process. The present paper should be considered as only suggestive in this regard. What needs to be done is to adopt a general "systems view" of this process by drawing on the relevant research from industrial, organizational, social, and vocational psychology, as well as from the relevant areas of other disciplines such as industrial sociology, labor economics, and industrial relations. In one way or another all these areas of research have something of relevance for the study of organizational entry.

Certainly, future efforts in this direction should look at organizational entry from *both* sides of the matching process, and should consider both organizational selection of individuals as well as organizational choice by individuals. The present paper did *not* do this because it was considered more urgent to emphasize the underdeveloped research areas.

The future may also hold different views of organizational entry depending on the *type* of organization concerned. Most of what we know today has been obtained from studies in business organizations, and less so from colleges, universities, or the military. The basic problem of matching individual and organization is common to all these organization types, but shows up in quite different ways. For example, some businesses experience high turnover in certain entry-level jobs. In university programs, however, students pay for the opportunity to study (rather than being paid for their services), and they can be influenced by the magnet of "sunk costs." That is, the length of time for getting a degree is predictable. Thus, the longer a student remains in a school, the greater is the investment in it, and the harder it is to leave before graduation. In the military, the situation is still different. Given the legal nature of commitment to such service, the major problem is to retain qualified personnel at reenlistment time.

REFERENCES

Argyris, C. *Integrating the individual and the organization*. New York: Wiley, 1964.

Bakke, E. W. *The fusion process*. New Haven: Labor and Management Center, Yale University, 1953.

Bray, D. W., Campbell, R. J., & Grant, D. L. *Formative years in business*, New York: Wiley, 1974.

Dunnette, M. D., Arvey, R. D., & Banas, P. A. Why do they leave? *Personnel*, 1973, 3, 25–39.

Dunnette, M. D., Campbell, J. P., & Hakel, M. D. Factors contributing to job satisfaction and job dissatisfaction in six occupational groups. *Organizational Behavior and Human Performance*, 1967, 2, 143–174.

Farr, J. L., O'Leary, B. S., & Bartlett, C. J. Effect of a work sample test upon self-selection and turnover of job applicants. *Journal of Applied Psychology*, 1973, 58, 283–285.

Ford, D. L., Huber, G. P., & Gustafson, D. H. Predicting job choices with models that contain subjective probability judgments: An empirical comparison of five models. *Organizational Behavior and Human Performance*, 1972, 7, 397–416.

Friedlander, F., & Margulies, N. Multiple impacts of organizational climate and individual value systems upon job satisfaction. *Personnel Psychology*, 1969, 22, 171–183.

Glueck, W. F. Decision-making: Organizational choice. *Personnel Psychology*, 1974, 27, 77–93.

Hackman, R. J., & Lawler, E. E., III. Employee reactions to job characteristics. *Journal of Applied Psychology*, 1971, 55, 259–286.

Herzberg, F. Mausner, B., & Snyderman, B. *The motivation to work*. New York: Wiley, 1959.

Huber, G. P., Daneshgar, R., & Ford, D. L. An empirical comparison of five utility models for predicting job preferences. *Organizational Behavior and Human Performance*, 1971, 6, 267–282.

Ilgen, D. R. & Seely, W. Realistic expectations as an aid in reducing voluntary resignations. *Journal of Applied Psychology*, 1974, 59, 452–455.

Lawler, E. E., III, Hall, D. T., & Oldham, G. R. Organizational climate: Relationship to organizational structure, process, and performance. *Organizational Behavior and Human Performance*, 1974, 11, 139–155.

Lawler, E. E., III, Kuleck, W. J., Rhode, J. G., & Sorenson, J. E. Job choice and post decision dissonance. *Organizational Behavior and Human Performance*, 1975, **13**, 133–145.

Lofquist, L. H., & Dawis, R. V. *Adjustment to work*. New York: Appleton-Century-Crofts, 1969.

Macedonia, R. M. Expectations—press and survival. Unpublished doctoral dissertation, New York University, Graduate School of Public Administration, 1969.

Pieters, G. R., Hundert, A. T., & Beer, M. Predicting organizational choice: A post hoc analysis. *Proceedings of the 76th Annual Convention of the American Psychological Association*, 1969, 573–574.

Pritchard, R. D., & Karasick, B. The effects of organizational climate on managerial job performance and job satisfaction. *Organizational Behavior and Human Performance*, 1973, **9**, 126–146.

Schein, E. H. Organizational socialization and the profession of management. *Industrial Management Review*, 1968, **9**, 1–16.

Schneider, B. Organizational climate: Individual preferences and organizational realities revisited. *Journal of Applied Psychology*, 1975, **60**, 459–465.

Sheridan, J. E., Richards, M. D., & Slocum, J. W. Comparative analysis of expectancy and heuristic models of decision behavior. *Journal of Applied Psychology*, 1975, **60**, 361–368.

Soelberg, P. Unprogrammed decision making. *Industrial Management Review*, 1967, **8**, 19–29.

Vroom, V. H. *Work and motivation*. New York: Wiley, 1964.

Vroom, V. H. Organizational choice: A study of pre and post decision processes. *Organizational Behavior and Human Performance*, 1966, **1**, 212–225.

Vroom, V. H., & Deci, E. L. The stability of post decisional dissonance: A follow-up study of the job attitudes of business school graduates. *Organizational Behavior and Human Performance*, 1971, **6**, 36–49.

Wanous, J. P. Occupational preferences: Perceptions of valence and instrumentality, and objective data. *Journal of Applied Psychology*, 1972, **56**, 152–155.

Wanous, J. P. Effects of a realistic job preview of job acceptance, job attitudes, and job survival. *Journal of Applied Psychology*, 1973, **58**, 327–332.

Wanous, J. P. Individual differences and reactions to job characteristics. *Journal of Applied Psychology*, 1974, **59**, 616–622.

Wanous, J. P. *Organizational entry: The transition from outsider to newcomer to insider* (Working Paper 75–14). New York University, Graduate School of Business Administration, 1975a.

Wanous, J. P. Tell it like it is at realistic job previews. *Personnel*, 1975b, **52** (4), 50–60.

Wanous, J. P. A job preview makes recruiting more effective. *Harvard Business Review*, 1975c, **53** (5), 16, 166–8.

Wanous, J. P. Organizational entry: From naive expectations to realistic beliefs. *Journal of Applied Psychology*, 1976, **61**, 22–29.

Ward, L. B., & Athos, A. G. *Student expectations of corporate life*. Boston: Division of Research, Graduate School of Business Administration, Harvard University, 1972.

Weitz, J. Job expectancy and survival. *Journal of Applied Psychology*, 1956, **40**, 245–247.

Youngberg, C. F. An experimental study of job satisfaction and turnover in relation to job expectations and self expectations. Unpublished doctoral dissertation, New York University Graduate School of Arts and Sciences, 1963.

Commitment and the Control of Organizational Behavior and Belief

Gerald R. Salancik

Most articles on organizational commitment extol the virtues of commitment. In them, you will find that the committed employee is the happy employee, the success of the organization is a matter of its members sacrificing their time and effort, and commitment to the values of the organization gives meaning to a person's life. In them commitment enhances productivity, assures quality in the final product, and guarantees the flow of adaptive innovation. In them, you will find, in short, a lot of nonsense mixed with a lot of common sense. But from them your understanding of commitment may not be enhanced. . . .

The view of commitment we present in this paper is one which is grounded in behavior and the implications of behavior in one situation for behavior in another. The view derives primarily from the model of commitment developed by Kiesler (1971), with intellectual roots going back to Festinger (1957; 1964) and Lewin (1947). We borrow considerably from Kiesler's work, and deviate in significant ways. As a working definition, "commitment is the binding of the individual to behavioral acts" (Kiesler and Sakumura, 1966). The important words are "binding" and "acts."

To act is to commit oneself. A person may talk about how important it is to keep the population growth rate down, but to be sterilized is to give eloquent, unshakeable force to the statement. An adulterer may proclaim unrelenting devotion to a lover, but to give up children, home, and joint bank accounts is to put meaning into the proclamation. Thus, at a minimum, a concept of commitment implies that behavior, or action, be a central focus.

DETERMINANTS OF COMMITMENT

While action is a necessary ingredient in commitment, all behaviors are not equally committing. There are degrees of commitment. A statement of a belief or attitude is a less committing action than the signing of a petition in favor of the belief, which in turn is less committing than actively advocating the belief to a hostile or skeptical audience.

The degree of commitment derives from the extent to which a person's behaviors are binding. Four characteristics of behavioral acts make them binding, and hence determine the extent of commitment: explicitness; revocability; volition; and publicity. The first is the *explicitness* or deniability of the act, and concerns the extent to which an action can be said to have taken place. Two contributors to explicitness are the observability of the act and the unequivocality of the act. Some acts are not observable and we may know them only

From B. M. Staw and G. R. Salancik (eds.), *New directions in organizational behavior*. Chicago: St. Clair Press, 1977, 1–21. Abridged with permission of the author and publisher.

by inference from assumed consequences. You leave a dollar bill on a check-out counter, turn away for a moment, then find it missing. The consequence is obvious, but do you know if the customer next to you took it or if it was carried away by a draft from the open door? Acts themselves can be equivocal, forgotten, or otherwise intractable. A person who says, "I sometimes think . . ." is behaving more equivocally than one who says, "I think. . . ."

A second characteristic of behavior affecting commitment is the *revocability* or reversibility of the action. Some actions are like trials. We try them out, see how they fit with us, and if they don't suit us we change our minds and do something else. Few actions are really irreversible. Even a vasectomy can be undone. Promises can be made and broken. Jobs can be quit. Marriages can be dissolved; engagements, broken. Contracts can be torn up. On the other hand, some actions are permanent and having occurred, they cannot be undone. They are committing. Slapping someone in the face can be excused, forgiven, forgotten or reciprocated, but it cannot be taken back. Consumption of food or drink may be regretted but not reversed. Pulling the trigger of a loaded gun pointed at a friend commits all to its gross reality.

The explicitness and irrevocability of an act link action to an indelible reality. *Volition*, a third characteristic of committing behaviors, links action to the individual. This is one of the more difficult characteristics of human action to define precisely, and is frequently associated with such concepts as freedom and personal responsibility. What makes definition difficult is that all human action is both free and constrained, being done under one's own volition and in response to contingencies. Even the most seemingly free and personal action can be perceived as constrained. Artists and writers, such as Dostoevski and George Bernard Shaw, describe their acts of creation as the result of compulsions and external forces. And even the most seemingly constrained acts can be considered free. A person with a gun to his head ultimately is free to choose, whether to comply or accept the consequences of noncompliance. The perception of volition, moreover, can vary with the consequences that follow acts. A manager who takes a decision which turns out to be a disaster for his firm may make every effort to divest himself of responsibility. And one can observe in the annual reports of most corporations the following simple relationship. When sales increase from the previous year, the annual report points out how management's ingenious investments and development programs are paying off; when, the next year, sales decrease, an astounding downturn in the economy is lugubriously noted.

Despite difficulties in developing a precise concept of volition, volition wields powerful influences on the attitudes and behaviors of people, at least in Western culture. Some major characteristics found to relate to the degree of perceived volition of action are: (1) choice; (2) the presence of external demands for action; (3) the presence of extrinsic bases for action; and (4) the presence of other contributors to action. Thus a person who works hard in order to make a lot of money is not perceived as having as much volition as a person who works hard for nothing. A person who works hard because his superior stands over him constantly is not perceived as having as much volition as one who does as much on his own. With regard to choice, a person who buys a Ford because that is the only car available for sale is not perceived as having as much volition as one who passes over a hundred other models to make the same purchase. . . .

A fourth characteristic of action affecting commitment is the *publicity* or publicness of the act. This characteristic links the action into a social context. While all action and behavior is by definition observable, publicity refers to the extent to which others know of the action and the kinds of persons who know of it. Some audiences are unimportant to us, as are their observations of our behavior. One of the simplest ways to commit yourself to a course of action is to go around telling all your friends that you are definitely going to do something. You will find yourself bound by your own statements. The same commitment will not develop from proclamations to strangers you meet on trains. The publicity of one's action places the action in a social context which is more or less binding and, as we shall describe, contributes to directing the effect of those behaviors on subsequent behaviors. . . .

COMMITMENT TO ORGANIZATIONS

A careless interpretation of the consistency assumption might lead one to infer that having chosen to join an organization or to do a job, individuals will be willing to stay with it and be quite satisfied. After all, one implication of taking a job is that the person likes it. Choice, however, is not enough. The choice itself must be committing. The person must be bound to this choice. . . .

Sacrifice and Initiation Rites

Some organizations prefer not to leave a member's commitment to the happenstance of his own decision process. Corporations frequently publicize the decisions of their new managers. The *Wall Street Journal* is crammed with advertisements by companies announcing that a particular individual has joined their firm, an act giving instant status to the manager's new role. Friends and past associates call in their congratulations and set into motion a climate of expectation that he is part of that firm. In recent years, insurance companies have been taking full spreads in such magazines as *Time* and *Newsweek* to publish the pictures of their sales personnel. Western Electric has done the same with television scans of their employees working on the job. For a few hundred dollars, an individual is identified with the organization. Next-door neighbors rush to ask, "Say, is this you?" One implication of the advertisement to both the employee and his friends is that the company really cares about its employees, and as a consequence it becomes more and more difficult to complain about it to friends. Harvard Business School uses a particularly effective method of maintaining long-term commitment from its graduates. Entering MBAs are immediately assigned to a group of classmates. This class does everything together from then on. They live in the same dormitories, hear the same lectures, and take the same exams. Virtually everything is scheduled for the class as a whole. Within each class, individuals are identified by namecards so that everyone knows the name of everyone else and is referred to by name in classroom discussions. Twenty years later, when the individuals have long departed the ivy-draped halls, the social network created there continues to operate. One of the things it is used for is to drum donations to the "B School," as it is fondly called.

In addition to advertising a person's commitment, some organizations take pains to make sure the individual is aware he has made a decision. Like the experiments with a well-constructed social psychological choice manipulation, the new employer commits the beginner: "Now, we want to be sure you're taking this job because you want to. We know you've given up a lot to come here and we're grateful. You left your home, your old friends. It must have been very difficult for you. And the salary we're offering, while more than you were making, is never enough to compensate for that."

The idea of giving up something to join the organization is one exploited in many ways. A common form is the initiation rites which still persist in college fraternities and sororities, fraternal clubs like the Masons or Elks, prisons, military organizations, revolutionary cadres, communal living experiments, police academies and religious organizations, orders and cults. An important part of the initiation process is the forcing of a sacrifice, in which members are asked to give up something as a price of membership (Karter, 1968). College fraternities require pledges to do hours of push-ups, to take verbal abuse, to have their privileges restricted, to accept subservient roles; in the end, those who endure love it. The effect is obvious. The individual in order to give meaning to his sacrifices is left to conclude they were made because of his devotion to the organization, a conclusion made more likely by his public pledge to enter the organization out of his own choosing. Other organizations have less colorful forms of sacrifice. Exclusive country clubs require their new members to make large initial donations in addition to yearly fees. The donations themselves provide for no services, and members pay for almost all services. But having given up an initial thousand, or a few thousand dollars, members feel a certain compulsion to spend $3.00 for a martini at the club's bar rather than half that at a public lounge.

Investments and Tenure

Many organizations do not exploit the idea of sacrifice as a price of membership. Instead they emphasize the instrumental or exchange bases for participation. Members are hired rather than invited into the organization. Commitment under such circumstances will obviously be more difficult.

Studies on commitment to organizations that emphasize the instrumental bases for membership—work organizations—have consistently found two factors as most reliably related to commitment. The two factors are position in the organization and tenure with the organization. Study after study on the issue comes down to: People with good jobs are willing to stay in them, and, the longer a person has been with an organization, the more he wants to stay. Unfortunately, most of the studies were done in such ways that it is difficult, and in many cases impossible, to interpret the meaning of the findings.

The relationship of tenure to organizational commitment is predictable from the model of commitment presented in this chapter and has been discussed in a related manner. Howard Becker (1960) suggested that individuals build up commitment over time through certain "side-bets" they make in the organization. One obvious form of accumulation investments in an organization is the build-up of pension benefits and credits over the course of a lifetime. Until recently, such employee benefits, often called the "golden padlock," were not transferable from one organization to another. If an individual terminated in one organization, he lost some of his future wealth or security and had to begin accumulating it again in another organization. The costs of leaving the organization thus increase the longer one's involvement and one becomes more and more likely to continue where one is.

Regardless of financial investments, mobility also declines with tenure in an organization. As time goes by, one becomes less employable. And one's expertise becomes increasingly specific to one's current organization. Some organizations purposely manipulate the costs of leaving for some individuals. Universities will promote some of their assistant professors at rapid rates, making it more costly for other organizations to entice them away. Some business organizations will give young managers attractive positions unusual for their age, knowing it would be difficult for them to obtain equivalent offers elsewhere and also knowing it is cheaper to buy their commitment at an early age than it would be when they become industry hot-shots. . . .

WORK ENVIRONMENTS AND ORGANIZATIONAL COMMITMENT

Thus far we have discussed commitment to the organization as the result of the constraints on an individual's ability to leave the organization, and the extent to which the individual himself has made a definite and committing choice. In reading this over, one gets the feeling that commitment to an organization is an entrapment: an individual is either cut off from other alternatives because no one else wants him or because his own situation doesn't allow him to change it. Thus, individuals rarely make job changes involving moves when their children are entrenched in a school. In all, it is a rather negative view of commitment. You are committed because the facts of your life have bound you.

What about more positive features? Do people become committed to their jobs because they are attracted to them and find them enjoyable? The research on this issue is unimpressive. Much is based on termination interviews which find that workers who quit say they quit because they didn't like the job or the pay. Having taken so decisive a step, it would be rather amusing to find them saying that they loved the job. Studies attempting to predict employee turnover or absenteeism from prior reports of job satisfaction have been notoriously unsuccessful from a practical point of view; that is, the studies report statistically reliable relationships of so low a magnitude that they predict little about behavior. Even superior measurement techniques do poorly (Newman, 1974).

The typical relationship found between job attitudes and turnover or absenteeism is clouded by other factors. We have already discussed that one of these factors is the tenure of the employee. Job satisfaction increases with age and tenure, as does commitment to the organization (see Grupp and Richards, 1975; Organ and Greene, 1974, Gow, Clark, and Dossett, 1974 for illustrative studies). Where investigators have bothered to make the necessary causal analyses, they have found that the change is a "real" one and not simply a function of changes in position, jobs, or salary (Stagner, 1975). As a person becomes more experienced in what he does he becomes more able to cope with the negative and positive features of his job. . . .

Commitment and Job Features

Despite the rather unpredictable relationship between job attitudes, absenteeism, turmoil, and turnover, the model of commitment presented here does suggest that certain features of a person's job situation will affect his commitment. In general, any characteristic of a person's job situation which reduces his felt responsibility will reduce his commitment. As for the relationship between commitment and satisfaction, our own view is that enjoyment is more likely to follow commitment than the reverse.

Many characteristics of job situations can affect a person's perception of responsibility. Some positions simply carry more responsibility, and persons in higher positions tend to be more committed. Similarly, some jobs offer more discretion and self-determination to their occupants, and it has been found that employees in autonomous positions generally have more favorable attitudes than those with little freedom to decide how to do their jobs (Hackman and Lawler, 1971; Hackman and Oldham, 1974).

In addition to the job and the freedom it permits, the manner by which the job is supervised or monitored can affect perceptions of responsibility. The supervisor who stands over a subordinate provides an excuse for the subordinate's behavior. When unpleasant aspects of the job become apparent, rather than coping with them, and finding some joy in the job, the subordinate can attribute his endurance to the supervisor's tenacious pressure. Lepper and Greene (1975) found that surveillance deteriorates interest in a task. Zanna (1970) found that when students are led to believe they worked very hard for a nasty supervisor, they enjoyed the task more than when they worked very hard for a nice supervisor. When they work for a nice person they attribute their effort to their liking for him, not the job. This would be an unrealistic attribution to a nasty boss, so they like the job more.

If a supervisor merely stands by without taking an active part in determining the subordinate's behavior, his presence may serve to reinforce the subordinate's felt responsibility. Maguire and Ouchi (1975) found that close output supervision improves employee satisfaction but that close behavioral supervision does not. Monitoring and providing an individual with feedback about his work performance can increase a person's felt responsibility. The person, knowing his outcomes and knowing his outcomes are known by others, may become more aware that the outcomes are his responsibility. Hackman and Oldham (1974) found workers' perception of responsibility was in part a function of feedback about their performance. While the precise effects of various supervisory conditions on commitment have not been well studied, we would expect that high output monitoring coupled with low behavioral control would lead to the greatest felt responsibility on the part of the worker. Whether or not these conditions will lead to greater satisfaction, would depend on whether or not the worker can handle the task. Maguire and Ouchi (1975) found more satisfaction among monitored workers who could do their jobs without depending on others (i.e., low interdependence), than those who could not.

Commitment also derives from the relation of an employee's job to those of others in the organization. Some jobs are rather isolated and can be done independently of other jobs in the organization. It has been found that jobs which are not integrated with the work activities of others tend to be associated with less favorable attitudes (Sheperd, 1973). Gow, Clark and Dossett (1974), for instance, find that telephone operators who quit tend to be those who are not integrated into the work group. Work integration can affect commitment by the fact that integrated jobs are likely to be associated with salient demands from others in the organization. If a person has a job which affects the work of others in the organization, it is likely that those others will communicate their expectations for performance of that job. Such expectations can be committing in that the other people implicitly or explicitly hold the person accountable for what he does. Earlier we mentioned that when individuals did not know what was expected of them they tended to be less committed to the organization. One reason an individual will not know what is expected is because no one is telling him. In general, we would expect that anything which contributes to creating definite expectations for a person's behavior would enhance his felt responsibility, and hence commitment. Integration may be one such contributor.

Perhaps the most pervasive condition of a job which affects commitment is its instrumentality, the fact that work is a means to some other end. While all jobs in industrial and commercial organizations are done in exchange for salary, there are perhaps great variations in the extent to which the instrumental basis for the work is salient or not. In general, we would expect that when the instrumental basis for work is salient it will reduce a person's felt responsibility. The attribution, "I am doing this job only for the money," should inhibit commitment. A similar point was raised by Ingham (1970), who analyzed absenteeism and turnover in light engineering firms in Bradford, England. Observing that larger organizations had more absenteeism (but lower turnover), he argued that workers were attracted to large firms because of the higher pay offered, but that this instrumental orientation led to little personal involvement with the organization. . . .

There is far too little empirical work on the nature of commitment to jobs, and how features of the work situation lead to or detract from feelings of personal responsibility for work. Much more detailed accountings of the particulars of job situations need to be made.

REFERENCES

Becker, H. S. Notes on the concept of commitment. *American Journal of Sociology*, 1960, **66**, 32–40.

Festinger, L. *A theory of cognitive dissonance*. Stanford, Calif.: Stanford University Press, 1957.

Festinger, L. *Conflict, decision, and dissonance*. Stanford, Calif.: Stanford University Press, 1964.

Gow, J. S., Clark, A. W., & Dossett, G. S. A path analysis of variables influencing labour turnover. *Human Relations*, 1974, **27**, 703–19.

Hackman, J. R., & Lawler, E. E. Employee reactions to job characteristics. *Journal of Applied Psychology*, 1971, **55**, 259–86.

Hackman, J. R., & Oldham, G. R. Motivation through the design of work: Test of a theory. Technical Report no. 6, Administrative Sciences, Yale University, 1974.

Ingham, G. K. *Size of industrial organizations and worker behavior*. Cambridge: Cambridge University Press, 1970.

Kanter, R. M. Commitment and social organizations. *American Sociological Review*, 1968.

Kiesler, C. A. *The psychology of commitment: Experiments linking behavior to belief*. New York: Academic Press, 1971.

Kiesler, C. A., & Sakumura, J. A test of a model for commitment. *Journal of Personality and Social Psychology*, 1966, **3**, 349–53.

Lepper, M. R., Greene, D., & Nisbett, R. E. Undermining children's intrinsic interest with extrinsic rewards: A test of the "overjustification" hypothesis. *Journal of Personality and Social Psychology*, 1973, **28**, 129–37.

Lewin, K. Group decision and social change. In T. M. Newcomb and E. L. Hartley (Eds.), *Readings in social psychology*. New York: Holt, Rinehart & Winston, 1947, pp. 330–44.

Maguire, M. A., & Ouchi, W. Organizational control and work satisfaction. Research Paper no. 278, Graduate School of Business, Stanford University, 1975.

Newman, J. E. Predicting absenteeism and turnover: A field comparison of Fishbein's model and traditional job attitude measures. *Journal of Applied Psychology*, 1974, **59**, 610–15.

Organ, D. W., & Greene, N. The perceived purposefulness of job behavior: Antecedents and consequences. *Academy of Management Journal*, 1974, **17**, 69–78.

Stagner, R. Boredom on the assembly line: Age and personality variables. *Industrial Gerontology*, 1975, **21**, 23–44.

Zanna, M. P. Attitude inference in a low choice setting. Ph.D. dissertation, Yale University, 1970.

Major Influences on Employee Attendance: A Process Model[1]

Richard M. Steers
Susan R. Rhodes

Each year, it is estimated that over 400 million work days are lost in the United States due to employee absenteeism, or about 5.1 days lost per employee (Yolles, Carone, & Krinsky, 1975). In many industries, daily blue-collar absenteeism runs as high as 10% to 20% of the workforce (Lawler, 1971). A recent study by Mirvis and Lawler (1977) estimates the cost of absenteeism among non-managerial personnel to be about $66 per day per employee; this estimate includes both direct salary and fringe benefit costs, as well as costs associated with temporary replacement and estimated loss of profit. While such figures are admittedly crude, combining the estimated total days lost with the costs associated with absenteeism yields an estimated annual cost of absenteeism in the U.S. of $26.4 billion! Even taking the more conservative minimum wage rate yields an estimated annual cost of $8.5 billion. Clearly, the phenomenon of employee absenteeism is an important area for empirical research and management concern. . . .

A review of existing research indicates that investigators of employee absenteeism have typically examined bivariate correlations between a set of variables and subsequent absenteeism (Muchinsky, 1977; Nicholson, Brown & Chadwick-Jones, 1976; Porter & Steers, 1973; Vroom, 1964). Little in the way of comprehensive theory-building can be found, with the possible exception of Gibson (1966). Moreover, two basic (and questionable) assumptions permeate the work that has been done to date. First, the current literature largely assumes that job dissatisfaction represents the primary cause of absenteeism. Unfortunately, however, existing research consistently finds only weak support for this hypothesis. Locke (1976), for example, points out that the magnitude of the correlation between dissatisfaction and absenteeism is generally quite low, seldom surpassing $r = .40$ and typically much lower. Moreover, Nicholson et al. (1976), in their review of 29 such studies, concluded that "at best it seems that job satisfaction and absence from work are tenuously related (p. 734)." Nicholson et al. also observed that the strength of this relationship deteriorates as one moves from group-based studies to individually-based studies. Similar weak findings have been reported earlier (Porter & Steers, 1973; Vroom, 1964). Implicit in these modest findings is the probable existence of additional variables (both personal and organizational) which may serve to moderate or enhance the satisfaction-attendance relationship.

[1]Support for this paper was provided by funds supplied under ONR Contract No. N00014-76-C-0164, NR 170-812.

The second major problem to be found in much of the current work on absenteeism is the implicit assumption that employees are generally free to choose whether or not to come to work. As noted by Herman (1973) and others, such is often not the case. In a variety of studies, important situational constraints were found which influenced the attitude-behavior relationship (Herman, 1973; Ilgen & Hollenback, 1977; Morgan & Herman, 1976; Smith, 1977). Hence, there appear to be a variety of situational constraints (e.g., poor health, family responsibilities, transportation problems) that can interfere with free choice in an attendance decision. Thus, a comprehensive model of attendance must include not only job attitudes and other influences on attendance motivation but also situational constraints that inhibit a strong motivation-behavior relationship.

In view of the multitude of narrowly-focused studies of absenteeism but the dearth of conceptual frameworks for integrating these findings, it appears useful to attempt to identify the major sets of variables that influence attendance behavior and to suggest how such variables fit together into a general model of employee attendance. Toward this end, a model of employee attendance is presented here. This model incorporates both voluntary and involuntary absenteeism and is based on a review of 104 studies of absenteeism (see Rhodes & Steers, Note 4). . . .

THE CONCEPTUAL MODEL

The model proposed here attempts to examine in a systematic and comprehensive fashion the various influences on employee attendance behavior. Briefly stated, it is suggested that an employee's attendance is largely a function of two important variables: (1) an employee's motivation to attend; and (2) an employee's ability to attend. Both of these factors are included in the schematic diagram presented in Figure 1 and each will be discussed separately as it relates to existing research. First, we shall examine the proposed antecedents of attendance motivation.

Job Situation, Satisfaction, and Attendance Motivation

A fundamental premise of the model suggested here is that an employee's motivation to come to work represents the primary influence on actual attendance, assuming one has the ability to attend (Herman, 1973; Locke, 1968). Given this, questions must be raised concerning the major influences on attendance motivation. Available evidence indicates that such motivation is determined largely by a combination of: (1) an employee's affective responses to the job situation; and (2) various internal and external pressures to attend (Vroom, 1964; Hackman & Lawler, 1971; Locke, 1976; Porter & Lawler, 1968). In this section, we will examine the relationship between an employee's satisfaction with the job situation and attendance motivation. The second major

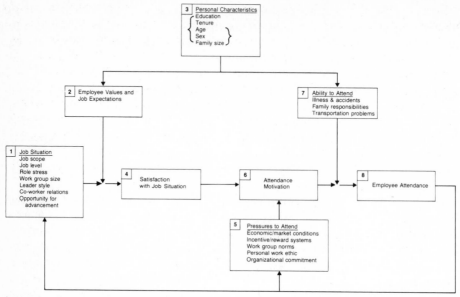

Figure 1 A model of employee attendance.

influence on attendance motivation, pressures to attend, will be dealt with subsequently.

Other things being equal, when an employee enjoys the work environment and.the tasks that characterize his or her job situation, we would expect that employee to have a strong desire to come to work (Hackman & Lawler, 1971; Lundquist, 1958; Newman, 1974; Porter & Steers, 1973; Vroom, 1964). Under such circumstances, the work experience would be a pleasurable one. In view of this relationship, our first question concerns the manner in which the job situation affects one's attendance motivation. The job situation (box 1 in Figure 1), as conceived here, consists of those variables that characterize the nature of the job and the surrounding work environment. Included in the job situation are such variables as: (1) job scope; (2) job level; (3) role stress; (4) work group size; (5) leader style; (6) co-worker relations; and (7) opportunities for advancement. In essence, available evidence suggests that variables such as these strongly influence one's level of satisfaction which, in turn, influences attendance motivation. . . .

The Role of Employee Values and Job Expectations

Considerable evidence suggests that the relationship between job situation variables and subsequent satisfaction and attendance motivation is not a direct one (Locke, 1976). Instead, a major influence on the extent to which employees experience satisfaction with the job situation is the values and expectations they have concerning the job (box 2). It has been noted previously that people come to work with differing values and job expectations; that is, they value different features in a job and expect these features to be present to a certain degree in order to maintain membership (Locke, 1976; Porter & Steers, 1973).

To a large extent these values and expectations are influenced by the personal characteristics and backgrounds of the employees (box 3). For example, employees with higher educational levels (e.g., a college degree) may value and expect greater (or at least different) rewards from an organization than those with less education (e.g., a private office, a secretary, a higher salary, greater freedom of action). Support for this contention can be found in Hedges (1973). Moreover, older and more tenured employees often value and expect certain perquisites because of their seniority (Baumgartel & Sobol, 1959; Cooper & Payne, 1965; Nicholson et al., 1976; Nicholson, Brown, & Chadwick-Jones, 1977; Hill & Trist, 1955; Martin, 1971).

Whatever the values and expectations that individuals bring to the job situation, it is important that these factors be largely met for the individual to be satisfied. In this regard, Smith (1972) found that realistic job previews created realistic job expectations among employees and led to a significant decline in absenteeism. Somewhat relatedly, Stockford (1944) found that absenteeism was higher among a sample of industrial workers whose previous training was not seen as relevant for their current positions than among a sample whose training was more closely aligned with the realities of the job situations (see also: Weaver & Holmes, 1972). Hence, based on the limited evidence that is available, it would appear that the extent to which an employee's values and expectations are met does influence the desirability of going to work.

Pressures to Attend

While satisfaction with the job situation thus apparently represents a major influence on attendance motivation, the relationship is indeed not a perfect one. Other factors can be identified which serve to enhance attendance motivation, probably in an additive fashion (Garrison & Muchinsky, 1977; Ilgen & Hollenback, 1977; Nicholson et al., 1976). These variables are collectively termed here "pressures to attend" and represent the second major influence on the desire to come to work. These pressures may be economic, social, or personal in nature and are represented in Figure 1 by box 5. Specifically, at least five major pressures can be identified: (1) economic and market conditions; (2) incentive/reward system; (3) work group norms; (4) personal work ethic; and (5) organizational commitment.

Economic and Market Conditions   The general state of the economy and the job market place constraints on one's ability to change jobs. Consequently, in times of high unemployment, there may be increased pressure to maintain a good attendance record for fear of losing one's job. Evidence suggests that there is a close inverse relationship between changes in unemployment levels within a given geographical region and subsequent absence rates (Behrend, Note 1; Crowther, 1957). Moreover, as the threat of layoff becomes even greater (e.g., when an employee's own employer begins layoffs), there is an even stronger decrease in absenteeism (Behrend, Note 1).

However, when an employee knows that *he* or *she* is to be laid off (as opposed to a knowledge that layoffs are taking place in general), the situation is somewhat different. Specifically, Owens (1966) found that railway repair employees in a depressed industry who had been given notice of layoff because of shop closure had significantly higher absence rates prior to layoffs than a comparable group of employees who were not to be laid off. Owens suggests that, in addition to being a reflection of manifest anxiety, the increased absenteeism allowed employees time to find new positions. On the other hand, Hershey (1972) found no significant differences in absence rates between employees who were scheduled for layoffs and employees not so scheduled. Hershey argued that the subjects in his study were much in demand in the labor market and generally felt assured of finding suitable jobs. (Improved unemployment compensation in recent years may also have been a factor in minimizing absenteeism among those to be laid off.)

Hence, economic and market factors may be largely related to attendance motivation and subsequent attendance through their effects on one's ability to change jobs. When *general* economic conditions are deteriorating, employees may be less likely to be absent for fear of reprisal. However, when the *individual* employee is to be laid off, absence rates are apparently influenced by one's perceptions of his or her ability to find alternate employment. Where such alternatives are readily available, no effect of impending layoff on absenteeism is noted; when such alternatives are not readily available, absence rates can be expected to increase as employees seek other employment.

Incentive/Reward System   A primary factor capable of influencing attendance motivation is the nature of the incentive or reward system used by an organization. Several aspects of the reward system have been found to influence attendance behavior.

When perceptual measures of pay and pay satisfaction are used, mixed results are found between such measures and absenteeism. Specifically, three studies among various work samples found an inverse relationship between pay satisfaction or perceived pay equity and absenteeism (Patchen, 1960; Dittrich & Carrell, 1976; Smith, 1977), while six other studies did not find such a relationship (Hackman & Lawler, 1971; Newman, 1974; Nicholson et al., 1976; Lundquist, 1958; Garrison & Muchinsky, 1977; Nicholson et al., 1977). Three other studies found mixed results (Waters & Roach, 1971, 1973; Metzner & Mann, 1953). In short, it is difficult to draw any firm conclusions about pay and absenteeism from these perceptual measures.

In contrast, when actual wage rates or incentive systems have been studied, the results are somewhat more definitive. Lundquist (1958), Fried et al. (1972), Beatty and Beatty (1975), and Bernardin (1977) all found a direct inverse relationship between wage rate and absenteeism. The Bernardin study is particularly useful here because several potentially spurious variables (e.g., age, tenure) were partialled out of the analysis and because the results were cross-validated. Moreover, the Lundquist study employed multiple absence measures with similar results. Other studies cited in Yolles et al. (1975) point to the same conclusion. However, studies by Fried et al. (1972) and Weaver and Holmes (1972), both using the less rigorous "total days absent" measure of absenteeism, did not support this relationship. In view of the objective nature of actual wage rates as opposed to perceptual measures, it would appear that greater confidence can be placed in them than in the perceptual studies mentioned above. Hence we would expect increases in salary or wage rates to represent one source of pressure to attend, even where the employee did not like the task requirements of the job itself.

Several factors must be kept in mind when considering the role of incentives or reward systems in attendance motivation. First, the rewards offered by the organization must be seen as being both attainable and tied directly to attendance. As Lawler (1971) points out, many organizations create reward systems that at least up to a point reward nonattendance. For instance, the practice of providing 12 days "sick leave" which employees lose if they fail to use only encourages people to be "sick" 12 days a year (see also: Morgan & Herman, 1976). In this regard, Garrison and Muchinsky (1977) found a negative relationship between job satisfaction and absenteeism for employees absent without pay but no such relationship for employees absent with pay. Hence there must be an expectancy on the part of the employee that attendance (and not absenteeism) will lead to desirable rewards. Moreover, the employees must value the rewards available. If an employee would prefer a three-day weekend to having additional pay, there is little reason to expect that employee to be motivated to attend. On the other hand, an employee with a strong financial need (perhaps because of a large family) would be expected to attend if attendance was financially rewarded.

Oftentimes, a major portion of an employee's income is derived from overtime work. Consequently, the effects of such overtime on absenteeism is important to note. Two studies found that the availability of overtime work among both male and female employees was *positively* related to absenteeism (Gowler, 1969; Martin, 1971), while two other studies found no such relationship (Buck & Shimmin, 1959; Flanagan, 1974). One could argue here that the availability of overtime with premium pay can lead to an incentive system that rewards absenteeism, not attendance. That is, if an employee is absent during regular working hours (and possibly compensated for this by sick leave), he or she can then work overtime later in the week to make up for the production lost earlier due to absenteeism. Clearly, such a reward system would operate differently than it was intended to. However, in view of the fact that all four relevant studies used either weak absence measures or unduly small samples, the influence of overtime availability on absenteeism must remain in the realm of conjecture pending further study.

Several attempts have been made to examine experimentally the effects of incentive or reward systems in work organizations. In one such study, Lawler and Hackman (1969; Scheflen, Lawler, & Hackman, 1971) experimentally introduced a bonus incentive plan to reward group attendance among a sample of part-time blue-collar employees. Two important findings emerged. First, the employees working under the bonus plan were found to have better attendance records than those not working under the plan. Moreover, the group that was allowed to participate in developing the bonus plan had higher attendance rates than the other experimental group that was given the bonus plan without an opportunity to participate in its design. (See also: Glaser, 1976.) Hence, both the adoption of a bonus incentive system to reward attendance and employee participation in the development of such a system appear to represent important influences on subsequent attendance.

A few studies have examined the role of punitive sanctions by management in controlling absenteeism. Results have been mixed. Two studies found that the use of stringent reporting and control procedures (e.g., keeping detailed attendance records, requiring medical verifications for reported illnesses, strict disciplinary measures) was related to lower absence rates (Baum & Youngblood, 1975; Seatter, 1961), while one found no such relationship (Rosen & Turner, 1971). Moreover, Buzzard and Liddell (Note 2) and Nicholson (1976) found that such controls did not influence average attendance rates, but did lead to fewer but longer absences. Such contradictory results concerning the use of punitive sanctions suggests that more effective results may be achieved through more positive reward systems than through punishment.

One such positive approach is the use of a lottery reward system, where daily attendance qualifies employees for an opportunity to win some prize or bonus. This approach is closely tied to the behavior modification approach to employee motivation (Hamner & Hamner, 1976). Four studies report such lotteries can represent a successful vehicle for reducing absenteeism (Nord, 1970; Tjersland, 1972; Pedalino & Gamboa, 1974; Johnson & Wallin, Note 3). However, in view of the very small magnitude of the rewards available for good attendance, it is possible here that results were caused more by the "Hawthorne effect" than the lottery itself. As Locke (1977) points out, in at least one of the lottery experiments (Pedalino & Gamboa, 1974), absenteeism in the experimental group declined even before anyone in the group had been, or could have been, reinforced. In addition, more conventional behavior modification techniques for reducing absenteeism, reviewed in Hamner and Hamner (1976), show only moderate results over short periods of time.

Finally, other approaches to incentives and rewards relate to modifying the traditional work week. For instance, Golembiewski et al. (1974) and Robison (Note 5) both reported a moderate decline in absenteeism following the introduction of "flexitime," where hours worked can be altered somewhat to meet employee needs. Moreover, while Nord and Costigan (1973) found favorable results implementing a four-day (4-40) work week, Ivancevich (1974) did not. Since both of these studies used similar samples, it is difficult to draw meaningful conclusions about the utility of such programs for reducing absenteeism.

Work Group Norms   Pressure for or against attendance can also emerge from one's colleagues in the form of work group norms. The potency of such norms is clearly established (Cartwright & Zander, 1968; Shaw, 1976). Where the norms of the group emphasize the importance of good attendance for the benefit of the group, increased attendance would be expected (Gibson, 1966). Recent findings by Ilgen and Hollenback (1977) support such a conclusion. This relationship would be expected to be particularly strong in groups with a high degree of work group cohesiveness (Whyte, 1969). In his job attractiveness model of employee motivation, Lawler (1971) points out that members of highly cohesive groups view coming to work to help one's co-workers as highly desirable; hence, job attendance is more attractive than absenteeism. In this regard, several uncontrolled field experiments have been carried out (summarized by Glaser, 1976) which found that the creation of "autonomous work groups" consistently led to increased work group cohesiveness and reduced absenteeism. It should be remembered, however, that work group norms can also have a detrimental impact on attendance where they support periodic absenteeism and punish perfect attendance.

Personal Work Ethic   A further influence on attendance motivation is the personal value system that individuals have (Rokeach, 1973). Recent research on the "work ethic" has shown considerable variation across employees in the extent to which they feel morally obligated to work. In particular, several investigations have noted a direct relationship between a strong work ethic and the propensity to come to work (Goodale, 1973; Ilgen & Hollenback, 1977; Feldman, 1974; Searls et al., 1974). While more study is clearly in order here, it would appear that one major pressure to attend is the belief by individuals that work activity is an important aspect of life, almost irrespective of the nature of the job itself.

Organizational Commitment   Finally, somewhat related to the notion of a personal work ethic is the concept of organizational commitment (Porter, Steers, Mowday, & Boulian, 1974). Commitment represents an agreement on the part of the employees with the goals and objectives of an organization and a willingness to work towards those goals. In short, if an employee firmly believes in what an organization is trying to achieve, he or she should be more motivated to attend and contribute toward those objectives. This motivation may exist even if the employee does not enjoy the actual tasks required by the job (e.g., a nurse's aide who may not like certain distasteful aspects of the job but who feels he or she is contributing to worthwhile public health goals). Support for this proposition can be found in Steers (1977) and Smith (1977), where commitment and attendance were found to be related for two separate samples of employees. On the other hand, where an employee's primary commitments lie elsewhere (e.g., to a hobby, family, home, or sports), less internal pressure would be exerted on the employee to attend (Morgan & Herman,

1976). This notion of competing commitments is an important one often over-looked in research on absenteeism.

Ability to Attend

A major weakness inherent in much of the current research on absenteeism is the failure to account for (and partial out) involuntary absenteeism in the study of voluntary absenteeism. This failure has led to many contradictions in the research literature that may be explained by measurement error alone. [In fact, in a comparison of five absenteeism measures, Nicholson and Goodge (1976) found an average intercorrelation of $r = .24$ between measures, certainly not an encouraging coefficient.] Thus, if we are serious about studying absenteeism, a clear distinction must be made between voluntary and involuntary attendance behavior and both must necessarily be accounted for in model-building efforts.

Even if a person wants to come to work and has a high attendance motivation, there are many instances where such attendance is not possible; that is, where the individual does not have behavioral discretion or choice (Herman, 1973). At least three such unavoidable limitations on attendance behavior can be identified: (1) illness and accidents; (2) family responsibilities; and (3) transportation problems (box 7).

Illness and Accidents   Poor health or injury clearly represents a primary cause of absenteeism (Hedges, 1973; Hill & Trist, 1955). Both illness and accidents are often associated with increased age (Baumgartel & Sobol, 1959; De La Mare & Sergean, 1961; Cooper & Payne, 1965; Martin, 1971). This influence of personal characteristics on ability to attend is shown in box 3 of Figure 1. Included in this category of health-related absences would also be problems of alcoholism and drug abuse as they inhibit attendance behavior. [See Yolles et al. (1975) for a review of the literature on health-related reasons for absenteeism.]

Family Responsibilities   The second constraint on attendance is often overlooked; namely, family responsibilities. As with health, this limitation as it relates to attendance is largely determined by the personal characteristics of the individual (sex, age, family size). In general, women as a group are absent more frequently than men (Covner, 1950; Hedges, 1973; Kerr et al., 1951; Kilbridge, 1961; Isambert-Jamati, 1962; Flanagan, 1974; Yolles et al., 1975). This finding is apparently linked, not only to the different types of jobs women typically hold compared to men, but also to the traditional family responsibilities assigned to women (that is, it is generally the wife or mother who cares for sick children). Support for this assumption comes from Naylor and Vincent (1959), Noland (1945), and Beatty and Beatty (1975). Hence, we would expect female absenteeism to increase with family size (Ilgen & Hollenback, 1977; Nicholson & Goodge, 1976; Isambert-Jamati, 1962).

It is interesting to note, however, that the available evidence suggests that the absenteeism rate for women declines throughout their work career (possibly because the family responsibilities associated with young children declines). For males, on the other hand, unavoidable absenteeism apparently increases with age (presumably because of health reasons), while avoidable absenteeism does not (Nicholson et al., 1977; Martin, 1971; Yolles et al., 1975). In any case, gender and family responsibilities do appear to place constraints on attendance behavior for some employees.

Transportation Problems Finally, some evidence suggests that difficulty in getting to work can at times influence actual attendance. This difficulty may take the form of travel distance from work (Isambert-Jamati, 1962; Martin, 1971; Stockford, 1944), travel time to and from work (Knox, 1961), or weather conditions that impede traffic (Smith, 1977). Exceptions to this trend have been noted by Hill (1967) and Nicholson and Goodge (1976), who found no relationship between either travel distance or availability of public transportation and absence. In general, however, increased difficulty of getting to work due to transportation problems does seem to represent one possible impediment to attendance behavior for some employees, even when the individual is motivated to attend.

Cyclical Nature of Model

Finally, as noted in Figure 1, the model as presented is a process model. That is, the act of attendance or absenteeism often influences the subsequent job situation and subsequent pressures to attend in a cyclical fashion. For example, a superior attendance record is often used in organizations as one indicator of noteworthy job performance and readiness for promotion. Conversely, a high rate of absenteeism may adversely affect an employee's relationship with his or her supervisor and co-workers and result in changes in leadership style and co-worker relations. Also, widespread absenteeism may cause changes in company incentive/reward systems, including absence control policies. Other outcomes could be mentioned. The point here is that the model, as suggested, is a dynamic one, with employee attendance or absenteeism often leading to changes in the job situation which, in turn, influence subsequent attendance motivation.

CONCLUSION AND DISCUSSION

Our review of the research literature on employee absenteeism reveals a multiplicity of influences on the decision and ability to come to work. These influences emerge both from the individuals themselves (e.g., personal work ethic, demographic factors) and from the work environment (e.g., the job situation, incentive/reward systems, work group norms). Moreover, some of these influences are largely under the control of the employees (e.g., organizational commitment), while others are clearly beyond their control (e.g., health).

We have attempted to integrate the available evidence into a systematic conceptual model of attendance behavior. In essence, it is suggested that the nature of the job situation interacts with employee values and expectations to determine satisfaction with the job situation (Locke, 1976; Porter & Steers, 1973). This satisfaction combines in an additive fashion with various pressures to attend to determine an employee's level of attendance motivation. Moreover, it is noted that the relationship between attendance motivation and actual attendance is influenced by one's ability to attend, a situational constraint (Herman, 1973; Smith, 1977). Finally, the model notes that feedback from the results of actual attendance behavior can often influence subsequent perceptions of the job situation, pressures to attend, and attendance motivation. Hence, the cyclical nature of the model should not be overlooked.

The importance of the various factors in the model would be expected to vary somewhat across employees. That is, certain factors may facilitate attendance for some employees but not for others. For instance, one employee may be intrinsically motivated to attend because of a challenging job; this individual may not feel any strong external pressures to attend because he or she likes the job itself. Another employee, however, may have a distasteful job (and not be intrinsically motivated) and yet may come to work because of other pressures (e.g., financial need). Both employees would attend, but for somewhat different reasons.

This interaction suggests a substitutability of influences up to a point for some variables. For instance, managers concerned with reducing absenteeism on monotonous jobs may change the incentive/reward system (that is, increase the attendance-reward contingencies) as a substitute for an unenriched work environment. In fact, it has been noted elsewhere that most successful applications of behavior modification (a manipulation of behavior-reward contingencies) have been carried out among employees holding unenriched jobs (Steers & Spencer, 1977). Support for this substitutability principle can be found in Ilgen and Hollenback (1977), who found some evidence that various factors influence attendance in an additive fashion, not a multiplicative one. Thus, the strength of attendance motivation would be expected to increase as more and more major influences, or pressures, emerged.

In addition, differences can be found in the manner in which the various influences on attendance affect such behavior. That is, a few of the major variables are apparently fairly *directly* related to desire to attend (if not actual attendance). For instance, highly satisfied employees would probably want strongly to attend, while highly dissatisfied employees would probably want strongly not to attend. On the other hand, certain other factors appear to serve a *gatekeeper* function and do not covary directly with attendance. The most prominent gatekeeper variable is one's health. While sick employees typically do not come to work, it does not necessarily follow that healthy employees will attend. Instead, other factors (e.g., attendance motivation) serve to influence a healthy person's attendance behavior.

In conclusion, the proposed model of employee attendance identifies several major categories of factors that have been shown to influence attendance behavior. Moreover, the model specifies, or hypothesizes, how these various factors fit together to influence the decision to come to work. Throughout, the model emphasizes the psychological processes underlying attendance behavior and in this sense is felt to be superior to the traditional bivariate correlational studies that proliferate on the topic. It remains the task of future research to extend our knowledge on this important topic and to clarify further the nature of the relationships among variables as they jointly influence an employee's desire and intent to come to work. It is hoped that the model presented here represents one useful step toward a better understanding of this process.

REFERENCE NOTES*

1 Behrend, H. Absence under full employment. Monograph A3, University of Birmingham Studies in Economics and Society, 1951.
2 Buzzard, R. B., & Liddell, F. D. K. Coal miners' attendance at work. NCB Medical Service, Medical Research Memorandum No. 3, 1958.
3 Johnson, R. D., & Wallin, J. A. Employee attendance: An operant conditioning intervention in a field setting. Paper presented at American Psychological Association annual meeting, Washington, D.C., 1976.
4 Rhodes, S. R., & Steers, R. M. Summary tables of studies of employee absenteeism. Technical Report No. 13, University of Oregon, 1977. This report is available from the second author at the Graduate School of Management, University of Oregon, Eugene, OR 97403.
5 Robison, D. Alternate work patterns: Changing approaches to work scheduling. Report of a conference sponsored by National Center for Productivity and Quality of Working Life and the Work in America Institute, Inc., June 2, 1976, Plaza Hotel, New York.

REFERENCES

Baum, J. F., & Youngblood, S. A. Impact of an organizational control policy on absenteeism, performance, and satisfaction. *Journal of Applied Psychology*, 1975, **60**, 688–694.
Baumgartel, H., & Sobol, R. Background and organizational factors in absenteeism. *Personnel Psychology*, 1959, **12**, 431–443.
Beatty, R. W., & Beatty, J. R. Longitudinal study of absenteeism of hard-core unemployed. *Psychological Reports*, 1975, **36**, 395–406.
Bernardin, H. J. The relationship of personality variables to organizational withdrawal. *Personnel Psychology*, 1977, **30**, 17–27.
Buck, L., & Shimmin, S. Overtime and financial responsibility. *Occupational Psychology*, 1959, **33**, 137–148.
Cartwright, D., & Zander, A. *Group dynamics*. New York: Harper & Row, 1968.
Cooper, R., & Payne, R. Age and absence: A longitudinal study in three firms. *Occupational Psychology*, 1965, **39**, 31–43.

*Reference Notes and References have been abridged.

Covner, B. J. Management factors affecting absenteeism. *Harvard Business Review*, 1950, **28**, 42–48.

Crowther, J. Absence and turnover in the divisions of one company—1950-55. *Occupational Psychology*, 1957, **31**, 256–270.

de la Mare, G., & Sergean, R. Two methods of studying changes in absence with age. *Occupational Psychology*, 1961, **35**, 245–252.

Dittrich, J. E., & Carrel, M. R. Dimensions of organizational fairness as predictors of job satisfaction, absence and turnover. *Academy of Management Proceedings '76*. Thirty-Sixth Annual Meeting of the Academy of Management, Kansas City, Missouri, August 11–14, 1976.

Feldman, J. Race, economic class, and the intention to work: Some normative and attitudinal correlates. *Journal of Applied Psychology*, 1974, **59**, 179–186.

Flanagan, R. J., Strauss, G., & Ulman, L. Worker discontent and work place behavior. *Industrial Relations*, 1974, **13**, 101–123.

Fried, J., Wertman, M., & Davis, M. Man-machine interaction and absenteeism. *Journal of Applied Psychology*, 1972, **56**, 428–429.

Garrison, K. R., & Muchinsky, R. M. Attitudinal and biographical predictors of incidental absenteeism. *Journal of Vocational Behavior*, 1977, **10**, 221–230.

Gibson, J. O. Toward a conceptualization of absence behavior of personnel in organizations. *Administrative Science Quarterly*, 1966, **11**, 107–133.

Glaser, E. M. *Productivity gains through worklife improvement*. New York: The Psychological Corporation, 1976.

Golembiewski, R. T., Hilles, R., & Kagno, M. S. A longitudinal study of flex-time effects: Some consequences of an OD structural intervention. *Journal of Applied Behavioral Science*, 1974, **10**, 503–532.

Goodale, J. G. Effects of personal background and training on work values of the hard-core unemployed. *Journal of Applied Psychology*, 1973, **57**, 1–9.

Gowler, D. Determinants of the supply of labour to the firm. *Journal of Management Studies*, 1969, **6**, 73–95.

Hackman, J. R., & Lawler, E. E., III. Employee reactions to job characteristics. *Journal of Applied Psychology Monograph*, 1971, **55**, 259–286.

Hamner, W. C., & Hamner, E. P. Behavior modification on the bottom line. *Organizational Dynamics*, 1976, **4**(4), 2–21.

Hedges, J. N. Absence from work—A look at some national data. *Monthly Labor Review*, 1973, **96**, 24–31.

Herman, J. B. Are situational contingencies limiting job attitude-job performance relationships? *Organizational Behavior and Human Performance*, 1973, **10**, 208–224.

Hershey, R. Effects of anticipated job loss on employee behavior. *Journal of Applied Psychology*, 1972, **56**, 273–274.

Hill, J. M., & Trist, E. L. Changes in accidents and other absences with length of service. *Human Relations*, 1955, **8**, 121–152.

Ilgen, D. R., & Hollenback, J. H. The role of job satisfaction in absence behavior. *Organizational Behavior and Human Performance*, 1977, **19**, 148–161.

Isambert-Jamati, V. Absenteeism among women workers in industry. *International Labour Review*, 1962, **85**, 248–261.

Ivancevich, J. M. Effects of the shorter workweek on selected satisfaction and performance measures. *Journal of Applied Psychology*, 1974, **59**, 717–721.

Kerr, W., Koppelmeier, G., & Sullivan, J. Absenteeism, turnover and morale in a metals fabrication factory. *Occupational Psychology*, 1951, **25**, 50–55.

Kilbridge, M. Turnover, absence, and transfer rates as indicators of employee dissatisfaction with repetitive work. *Industrial and Labor Relations Review*, 1961, **15**, 21–32.

Knox, J. B. Absenteeism and turnover in an Argentine factory. *American Sociological Review*, 1961, **26**, 424–428.

Lawler, E. E., III. *Pay and organizational effectiveness*. New York: McGraw-Hill, 1971.

Lawler, E. E., III, & Hackman, J. R. Impact of employee participation in the development of pay incentive plans: A field experiment. *Journal of Applied Psychology*, 1969, **53**, 467–471.

Locke, E. A. Toward a theory of task motivation and incentives. *Organizational Behavior and Human Performance*, 1968, **3**, 157–189.

Locke, E. A. The nature and causes of job satisfaction. In M. D. Dunnette (Ed.), *Handbook of industrial and organizational psychology*. Chicago: Rand McNally, 1976. Pp. 1297–1349.

Locke, E. A. The myths of behavior mod in organizations. *Academy of Management Review*, 1977, **2**, 543–553.

Lundquist, A. Absenteeism and job turnover as a consequence of unfavorable job adjustment. *Acta Sociologica*, 1958, **3**, 119–131.

Martin, J. Some aspects of absence in a light engineering factory. *Occupational Psychology*, 1971, **45**, 77–91.

Metzner, H., & Mann, F. Employee attitudes and absences. *Personnel Psychology*, 1953, **6**, 467–485.

Mirvis, P. H., & Lawler, E. E., III. Measuring the financial impact of employee attitudes. *Journal of Applied Psychology*, 1977, **62**, 1–8.

Morgan, L. G., & Herman, J. B. Perceived consequences of absenteeism. *Journal of Applied Psychology*, 1976, **61**, 738–742.

Muchinsky, P. M. Employee absenteeism: A review of the literature. *Journal of Vocational Behavior*, 1977, **10**, 316–340.

Naylor, J. E., & Vincent, N. L. Predicting female absenteeism. *Personnel Psychology*, 1959, **12**, 81–84.

Newman, J. E. Predicting absenteeism and turnover. *Journal of Applied Psychology*, 1974, **59**, 610–615.

Nicholson, N. Management sanctions and absence control. *Human Relations*, 1976, **29**, 139–151.

Nicholson, N., Brown, C. A., & Chadwick-Jones, J. K. Absence from work and job satisfaction. *Journal of Applied Psychology*, 1976, **61**, 728–737.

Nicholson, N., Brown, C. A., & Chadwick-Jones, J. K. Absence from work and personal characteristics. *Journal of Applied Psychology*, 1977, **62**, 319–327.

Nicholson, N., & Goodge, P. M. The influence of social, organizational and biographical factors on female absence. *Journal of Management Studies*, 1976, **13**, 234–254.

Nicholson, N., Wall, T., & Lischeron, J. The predictability of absence and propensity to leave from employees' job satisfaction and attitudes toward influence in decision-making. *Human Relations*, 1977, **30**, 499–514.

Noland, E. W. Attitudes and industrial absenteeism: A statistical appraisal. *American Sociological Review*, 1945, **10**, 503–510.

Nord, W. Improving attendance through rewards. *Personnel Administration*, November 1970, 37–41.

Nord, W. R., & Costigan, R. Worker adjustment to the four-day week: A longitudinal study. *Journal of Applied Psychology*, 1973, **58**, 660–661.

Owens, A. C. Sick leave among railwaymen threatened by redundancy: A pilot study. *Occupational Psychology*, 1966, **40**, 43–52.

Patchen, M. Absence and employee feelings about fair treatment. *Personnel Psychology*, 1960, **13**, 349–360.

Pedalino, E., & Gamboa, V. V. Behavior modification and absenteeism: Intervention in one industrial setting. *Journal of Applied Psychology*, 1974, **59**, 694–698.

Porter, L. W., & Lawler, E. E. *Managerial attitudes and performance*. Homewood, Ill.: Irwin, 1968.

Porter, L. W., & Steers, R. M. Organizational, work, and personal factors in employee turnover and absenteeism. *Psychological Bulletin*, 1973, **80**, 151–176.

Porter, L. W., Steers, R. M., Mowday, R. T., & Boulian, P. V. Organizational commitment, job satisfaction, and turnover among psychiatric technicians. *Journal of Applied Psychology*, 1974, **59**, 603–609.

Rokeach, M. *The nature of human values*. New York: The Free Press, 1973.

Rosen, H., & Turner, J. Effectiveness of two orientation approaches in hard-core unemployed turnover and absenteeism. *Journal of Applied Psychology*, 1971, **55**, 296–301.

Scheflen, K. C., Lawler, E. E., III, & Hackman, J. R. Long-term impact of employee participation in the development of pay incentive plans: A field experiment revisited. *Journal of Applied Psychology*, 1971, **55**, 182–186.

Searls, D. J., Braucht, G. N., & Miskimins, R. W. Work values and the chronically unemployed. *Journal of Applied Psychology*, 1974, **59**, 93–95.

Seatter, W. C. More effective control of absenteeism. *Personnel*, 1961, **38**, 16–29.

Shaw, M. E. *Group dynamics*. New York: McGraw-Hill, 1976.

Smith, A. L. Oldsmobile absenteeism/turnover control program. *GM Personnel Development Bulletin*, February 1972.

Smith, F. J. Work attitudes as predictors of specific day attendance. *Journal of Applied Psychology*, 1977, **62**, 16–19.

Steers, R. M. Antecedents and outcomes of organizational commitment. *Administrative Science Quarterly*, 1977, **22**, 46–56.

Steers, R. M., & Spencer, D. G. The role of achievement motivation in job design. *Journal of Applied Psychology*, 1977, **4**, 472–479.

Stockford, L. O. Chronic absenteeism and good attendance. *Personnel Journal*, 1944, **23**, 202–207.

Tjersland, T. *Changing worker behavior*. New York: Manpower Laboratory, American Telephone and Telegraph, December, 1972.

Vroom, V. *Work and motivation*. New York: Wiley, 1964.

Waters, L. K., & Roach, D. Relationship between job attitudes and two forms of withdrawal from the work situation. *Journal of Applied Psychology*, 1971, **55**, 92–94.

Waters, L. K., & Roach, D. Job attitudes as predictors of termination and absenteeism: Consistency over time and across organizations. *Journal of Applied Psychology*, 1973, **57**, 341–342.

Weaver, C. N., & Holmes, S. L. On the use of sick leave by female employees. *Personnel Administration and Public Personnel Review*, 1972, **1**(2), 46–50.

Whyte, W. F. *Organizational behavior*. Homewood, Ill.: Irwin, 1969.

Yolles, S. F., Carone, P. A., & Krinsky, L. W. *Absenteeism in industry*. Springfield, Ill.: Charles C Thomas, 1975.

Intermediate Linkages in the Relationship between Job Satisfaction and Employee Turnover

William H. Mobley

Reviews of the literature on the relationship between employee turnover and job satisfaction have reported a consistent negative relationship (Brayfield & Crockett, 1955; Locke, 1975; Porter & Steers, 1973; Vroom, 1964). Locke (1976) noted that while the reported correlations have been consistent and significant, they have not been especially high (usually less than .40).

It is probable that other variables mediate the relationship between job satisfaction and the act of quitting. Based on their extensive review, Porter and Steers (1973) concluded the following:

> Much more emphasis should be placed in the future on the psychology of the withdrawal *process*. . . . Our understanding of the manner in which the actual decision is made is far from complete. (p. 173)

The present paper suggests several of the possible intermediate steps in the withdrawal decision process (specifically, the decision to quit a job). Porter and Steers (1973) suggested that expressed "intention to leave" may represent the next logical step after experienced dissatisfaction in the withdrawal process. The withdrawal decision process presented here suggests that thinking of quitting is the next logical step after experienced dissatisfaction and that "intention to leave," following several other steps, may be the last step prior to actual quitting.

A schematic representation of the withdrawal decision process is presented in Figure 1. Block A represents the process of evaluating one's existing job, while Block B represents the resultant emotional state of some degree of satisfaction-dissatisfaction. A number of models have been proposed for the process inherent in Blocks A and B—for example, the value-percept discrepancy model (Locke, 1969, 1976), an instrumentality-valence model (Vroom, 1964), a met-expectations model (Porter & Steers, 1973), and a contribution/inducement ratio (March & Simon, 1958). Comparative studies that test the relative efficacy of these and other alternative models of satisfaction continue to be needed.

Most studies of turnover examine the direct relationship between job satisfaction and turnover. The model presented in Figure 1 suggests a number of possible mediating steps between dissatisfaction and actual quitting. Block C suggests that one of the consequences of dissatisfaction is to stimulate thoughts of quitting. Although not of primary interest here, it is recognized that other forms of withdrawal less extreme than quitting (e.g., absenteeism, passive job

Reprinted from *Journal of Applied Psychology*, 1977, **62**, 237–240. Copyright © American Psychological Association. Reprinted by permission.

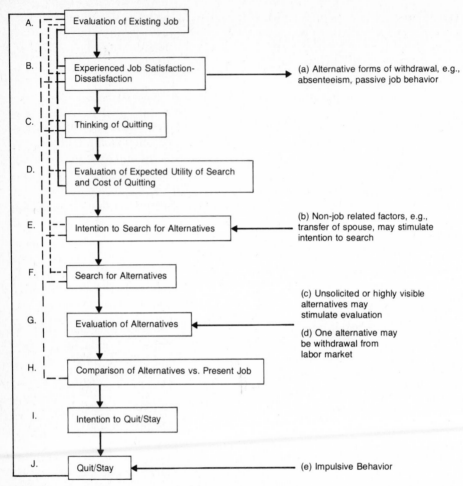

Figure 1   The employee turnover decision process.

behavior) are possible consequences of dissatisfaction (see e.g., Brayfield & Crockett, 1955; Kraut, 1975).

Block D suggests that the next step in the withdrawal decision process is an evaluation of the expected utility of search and of the cost of quitting. The evaluation of the expected utility of search would include an estimate of the chances of finding an alternative to working in the present job, some evaluation of the desirability of possible alternatives, and the costs of search (e.g., travel, lost work time, etc.). The evaluation of the cost of quitting would include such considerations as loss of seniority, loss of vested benefits, and the like. This block incorporates March and Simon's (1958) perceived ease of movement concept.

If the costs of quitting are high and/or the expected utility of search is low, the individual may reevaluate the existing job (resulting in a change in job satisfaction), reduce thinking of quitting, and/or engage in other forms of withdrawal behavior. Research is still needed on the determinants of alternative forms of withdrawal behavior and on how the expression of withdrawal behavior changes as a function of time and of changes in or reevaluation of the environment.

If there is some perceived chance of finding an alternative and if the costs are not prohibitive, the next step, Block E, would be behavioral intention to search for an alternative(s). As noted by Arrow (b) in Figure 1, non-job-related factors may also elicit an intention to search (e.g., transfer of spouse, health problem, etc.). The intention to search is followed by an actual search (Block F). If no alternatives are found, the individual may continue to search, reevaluate the expected utility of search, reevaluate the existing job, simply accept the current state of affairs, decrease thoughts of quitting, and/or engage in other forms of withdrawal behavior (e.g., absenteeism, passive job behavior).

If alternatives are available, including (in some cases) withdrawal from the labor market, an evaluation of alternatives is initiated (Block G). This evaluation process would be hypothesized to be similar to the evaluation process in Block A. However, specific job factors the individual considers in evaluating the present job and alternatives may differ. (See Hellriegel & White, 1973; and Kraut, 1975, for a discussion of this point.) Independent of the preceding steps, unsolicited or highly visible alternatives may stimulate this evaluation process.

The evaluation of alternatives is followed by a comparison of the present job to alternative(s) (Block H). If the comparison favors the alternative, it will stimulate a behavioral intention to quit (Block I), followed by actual withdrawal (Block J). If the comparison favors the present job, the individual may continue to search, reevaluate the expected utility of search, reevaluate the existing job, simply accept the current state of affairs, decrease thoughts of quitting, and/or engage in other forms of withdrawal behavior.

Finally, Arrow (e) gives recognition to the fact that for some individuals, the decision to quit may be an impulsive act involving few, if any, of the preceding steps in this model. The relative incidence and the individual and situational determinants of an impulsive versus a subjectively rational decision process presents yet another area of needed research.

The model being described is heuristic rather than descriptive. There may well be individual differences in the number and sequence of steps in the withdrawal decision process, in the degree to which the process is conscious, and as noted earlier, in the degree to which the act of quitting is impulsive rather than based on a subjectively rational decision process. One value of such an heuristic model is to guide thinking and empirical research toward a valid descriptive model that can account for such individual differences.

There is a lack of research evaluating all or even most of the possible steps in the withdrawal decision process. There have been a few studies that have tested one or two of the intermediate linkages proposed in the present note. Mobley (Note 1) found high negative correlations between satisfaction and frequency of thinking of quitting (Blocks B and C). Atkinson and Lefferts

(1972), who dealt with the association between Blocks C and J, found that the frequency with which people thought about quitting their job was significantly related to actual termination. Kraut (1975), looking at the associations among Blocks B, I, and J, found significant correlations between expressed intention to stay and subsequent employee participation. These correlations were much stronger than relationships between expressed satisfaction and continued participation. Finally, Armknecht and Early's (1972) review is relevant to the relationships between Blocks D and/or F and Block J. They concluded that voluntary terminations are closely related to economic conditions.

Each of these studies fails to look at a complete withdrawal decision process. Such research would appear to be sorely needed. Several researchable questions that follow from the withdrawal decision process described in the present note were mentioned earlier. Additional questions include the following. Do individuals evaluate the expected utility of search? If so, what are the determinants and consequences of this evaluation? What are the consequences and determinants of behavior in the face of an unsuccessful search? In such cases, do individuals persist in search, reevaluate their existing jobs, reevaluate the cost of search, or engage in other forms of withdrawal? Is the process and/ or content for evaluating alternative jobs the same as for evaluating the present job? Does satisfaction with the present job change as a function of the availability or evaluation of alternatives?

Attention to these sorts of questions rather than a continued replication of the direct relationship between job satisfaction and turnover would appear to be warranted. Particularly useful would be the longitudinal analysis of the variables and linkages suggested by the model. Such research would be responsive to Porter and Steers' (1973) conclusion that more emphasis should be placed on the psychology of the withdrawal decision process.

REFERENCE NOTE

1   Mobley, W. H. *Job satisfaction and thinking of quitting* (Tech. Rep. 75–3). Columbia: University of South Carolina, College of Business Administration, Management and Organizational Research Center, 1975.

REFERENCES

Armknecht, P. A., & Early, J. F. Quits in manufacturing: A study of their causes. *Monthly Labor Review*, 1972, 11, 31–37.

Atkinson, T. J., & Lefferts, E. A. The prediction of turnover using Herzberg's job satisfaction technique. *Personnel Psychology*, 1972, 25, 53–64.

Brayfield, A. H., & Crockett, W. H. Employee attitudes and employee performance. *Psychological Bulletin*, 1955, 52, 396–424.

Hellriegel, D., & White, G. E. Turnover of professionals in public accounting: A comparative analysis. *Personnel Psychology*, 1973, 26, 239–249.

Kraut, A. I. Predicting turnover of employees from measured job attitudes. *Organizational Behavior and Human Peformance*, 1975, 13, 233–243.

Locke, E. A. What is job satisfaction? *Organizational Behavior and Human Performance*, 1969, **4**, 309–336.

Locke, E. A. Personnel attitudes and motivation. *Annual Review of Psychology*, 1975, **26**, 457–480.

Locke, E. A. The nature and consequences of job satisfaction. In M. D. Dunnette (Ed.), *Handbook of industrial and organizational psychology*. Chicago: Rand-McNally, 1976.

March, J. G., & Simon, H. A. *Organizations*. New York: Wiley, 1958.

Porter, L. W., & Steers, R. M. Organizational, work, and personal factors in employee turnover and absenteeism. *Psychological Bulletin*, 1973, **80**, 151–176.

Vroom, V. H. *Work and motivation*. New York: Wiley, 1964.

QUESTIONS FOR DISCUSSION

1 What can managers do to decrease the kinds of problems employees have upon entry into a new organization?
2 How might the causes of turnover and absenteeism differ between managerial and blue-collar workers? How widespread do you feel such differences may be?
3 Why might the causes of turnover differ from the causes of absenteeism among the same group of employees?
4 Given the large number of empirical studies of turnover and absenteeism, why do you feel that withdrawal continues to be so widespread?
5 What would you consider the most important things a manager could do to reduce turnover and absenteeism?
6 List several of the more important disadvantages associated with high withdrawal rates from organizations. What are some advantages of high withdrawal rates?
7 Aside from monetary considerations, what specific factors in the organization milieu do you consider most important in keeping employees "attached" to their organization?
8 Can employees be physically attached to an organization, in that they continue to come to work for it, but not be psychologically attached? If so, does their lack of psychological attachment really make any difference?
9 How can the concept of organizational commitment be utilized by managers?

Chapter 8

Work Environment and Behavior

Dating from the early work of Allport (1924), Mayo (1933), and Roethlisberger and Dickson (1939), a considerable body of research data has accumulated on the effect of an employee's immediate work environment on motivation and behavior. In fact, under the initial leadership of Kurt Lewin, there has arisen a group dynamics school of thought, which views group processes as the basic unit of analysis in the study of organizations (see, for example, Cartwright & Zander, 1968). We intend in this chapter to examine such processes as they relate to performance and effectiveness in organizations.

This discussion will be divided into three sections. First, we shall examine the nature of groups and group processes. Next, the concept of organizational climate will be introduced. Finally, the role of the supervisor or manager in group behavior will be discussed.

NATURE OF GROUPS

Defining precisely what constitutes a "group" is no easy task. The boundaries of group membership tend to be rather permeable, with new members joining and old ones leaving at a fairly consistent rate. Moreover, members of one group are generally also members of several additional groups, thereby dividing their time and loyalties. Because of problems such as these, we tend to discuss and define groups more in terms of processes than in terms of specific members and their personal characteristics. Thus, a typical definition of a group would include the notion of a collectivity of people who share a set of norms (or common viewpoints), who generally have differentiated roles among members, and who jointly pursue common goals. While it is not possible to specify the "required" size of such a collectivity, the number usually averages between four and seven.

Groups form for a variety of reasons. Some groups result simply from proximity. The day-to-day interactions with one's immediate coworkers tend to facilitate group formation. Other groups form for economic reasons. For example, where bonuses are paid to workers based on *group* productivity, an incentive exists to band together for mutual gain. Still other groups form as the result of various social-psychological forces. Such groups can satisfy employees' social needs for interaction, reinforce feelings of self-worth, and provide emotional support in times of stress. Whatever the reason for their formation, they can be a potent factor in the determination of both individual job effort and individual job satisfaction.

Primarily as a result of the Hawthorne studies (Roethlisberger & Dickson, 1939) and the later research they stimulated, we have developed a fairly clear picture of some of the more common characteristics of a group. To begin with, as mentioned above, there are generally rather detailed norms, or shared beliefs, that are held by the group members and that guide their behavior. In addition, various members often have specific duties, or role prescriptions, for which they are responsible. Groups usually have acknowledged control procedures, such as ostracism, to minimize deviant behavior from their norms. They also develop their own systems or patterns of communications, which often include special or technical words (jargon). They tend to have an informal leader whose responsibility it is to enforce the norms and assure goal attainment. Finally, groups provide a useful source of support for their members. Employees who find little satisfaction in a dull, repetitive job may refrain from quitting because they really enjoy their coworkers, who provide comfort, support, and satisfaction on an otherwise meaningless job. Moreover, groups also provide support in a different sense where the group intends to regulate its rate of output. If one member restricts output, a very real possibility exists that he or she will be punished or even terminated by the organization. However, if all group members restrict output in unison, there is much less chance of "retribution" by the company.

From a motivational standpoint, perhaps the most important group process is the tendency toward conformity (Asch, 1939/1958; Sherif, 1936). One of the basic prerequisites for continued group membership is adherence to group standards, norms, and so forth. Once a work group has determined an acceptable rate of output, for example, it tends to punish or reject members whose output is above ("ratebusters") or below ("goldbrickers") this rate. If a company offers individual incentives for increased output but the group decides the new rate of output is too high (perhaps out of fear of working themselves out of a job), the group will exert force on its members not to increase output, despite the potential short-run monetary gain. On the other hand, however, if group support can be won for the new rate of output, conformity could then lead to increased output. The application of this latter example can be seen in such programs as the Lincoln Electric and the Scanlon plans, where workers have a significant voice in the determination of production rates and in the introduction of new production techniques. Under such plans, participation in program formulation *and* in the rewards from the new techniques appears to lead to group acceptance of the innovations, resulting in increased output.

In summary, then, research indicates that groups often serve useful functions for their members and must be taken into account as potential moderator variables in any program designed by the organization to increase employee effort and performance.

ORGANIZATIONAL CLIMATE

Central to a discussion of work environment is the concept of "organizational climate." Climate is a broad term designed to include the relatively constant variables in a work environment that are considered important to the efficient use of human resources. Examples of climate factors would be the type of supervision, the nature and direction of communication flows, the perceived reward-punishment structure, and so forth. These variables are assumed to be measurable and manipulatable at least to some extent and are considered the defining characteristics that distinguish one organization's working environment from another. Litwin and Stringer describe the concept as

> . . . a set or cluster of expectancies and incentives [that represent] . . . a property of environments that is perceived directly or indirectly by the individuals in the environment. It is a molar construct which (1) permits analysis of the determinants of motivated behavior in actual, complex social situations, (2) simplifies the problem of measurement of situational determinants by allowing the individuals in the situation to think in terms of bigger, more integrated chunks of their experience, and (3) makes possible the characterization of the total situational influence of various environments, so that they may be mapped and categorized, and so that cross-environmental comparisons can be made.[1]

In other words, organizational climate can be thought of in one sense as the "personality" of the organization. Moreover, climate is believed by many to serve as a basis for individuals to interpret situations, to act as a source of pressure and/or constraint for directing individual activity, and to determine in large measure the reward-punishment system within the organization (Forehand & Gilmer, 1964; Pritchard & Karasick, 1973).

It is generally held that climatic factors affect behavior—not by themselves, but rather to the extent that they interact with other individual or personal factors. The importance of this interrelationship was first discussed by Lewin (1938, 1951). Lewin proposed a model of human behavior, based upon his research, which took into account both individual or personal differences (P) and the climate or environment surrounding the individual (E). In brief, Lewin posited that human behavior (B) was a function of the interaction of both P and E. This hypothesis has been traditionally abbreviated $B = f(P,E)$. More recently, several management researchers, most notably Likert (1961, 1967), Katz and Kahn (1966), and Vroom (1964), have attempted to develop more complex models based upon this basic equation.

[1]G. H. Litwin & R. A. Stringer, Jr., *Motivation and organizational climate*. Boston: Harvard University, Graduate School of Business Administration, Division of Research, 1968, 29–30.

Organizational climate is created as the result of several forces (Litwin & Stringer, 1968). First, past experiences (including climate) play a major role in the determination of present climate. Second, climate is viewed as being affected by the constraints imposed by the formal organizational system and by the nature of the tasks required of the employees. Compare, for example, the climate of a highly structured, bureaucratic military organization with that of a free-form, unstructured R & D laboratory, or "think tank." Third, it is thought that the particular needs, expectations, and values of organizational members represent a significant input into climate determination. However, the most important determinant of climate is probably the leadership style of management. Litwin and Stringer (1968, p. 188) argue that "the emphasis a leader puts on adherence to rules, the kinds of goals and standards he sets, and perhaps most important, the nature of his informal relationships and communications with his people, have very great impact on the climate." Supervisors who foster open, two-way communications with their subordinates, for instance, may indeed create an environment where their employees feel comfortable in expressing their true feelings on matters of importance to the organization. The opposite type of supervisory behavior, on the other hand, may lead to the creation of a work group of rule-oriented "yes men" who tell their superiors what they want to hear and seldom suggest innovations that deviate significantly from company norms or policies.

THE ROLE OF THE MANAGER

The topic of managerial style and leadership has been consistently popular throughout the literature on organization behavior. Countless articles and books have appeared which attempted to prescribe the "correct" leadership style or approach to managing people at work. As one reviews this literature, however, at least two important conclusions emerge. First, it becomes evident that the amount of theoretical and/or prescriptive material on managerial behavior and leadership style far outweighs the amount of empirical research on the topic. One is easily led to the conclusion that almost every manager has strong feelings about the "best" way to lead subordinates and that such feelings are based more on past experiences and attitudes than on objective data.

Second, it becomes evident that there is little agreement as to what "leadership" as a concept really means. Some people use the term to describe a *position* in the organizational hierarchy. Under this definition, the president of a company is a "leader" by virtue of holding high office. Other people use the term to describe particular *personal characteristics*. How often have we heard the phrase "a natural-born leader"? Finally, a more recent definition has emerged in which leadership is described as a *category of behavior*. In this last description, leadership is seen as a dynamic process in which one person behaves in a certain manner, thereby causing others to follow. Phrasing this third definition in more formal terms, Katz and Kahn (1966, p. 302) state that leadership is "the influential increment over and above mechanical compliance with the routine directives of the organization." If we view leadership in a dynamic state, particularly as it relates to motivation, then it appears that this third approach is far more valuable for our purposes here.

Using such a definition, effective leadership is something beyond power or authority in that it implies some form of voluntary compliance on the part of the followers. That is, effective leadership can be understood in terms of an individual's ability to stimulate and direct subordinates to perform specific tasks deemed important by the leader. As such, the concept of leadership really reduces to a question of motivation. In other words, using the Katz and Kahn or similar definitions, leaders are effective only to the extent that they can motivate their subordinates or followers to perform.

This crucial relationship between motivation and leadership can also be seen when one considers the various "functions" leaders and managers are believed to serve within organizations at one time or another. Krech, Crutchfield, and Ballachey (1962) have provided a rather extensive list of these functions. They include (1) executive, or coordinator of group activities; (2) planner, or strategist; (3) policy maker; (4) expert, or source of information; (5) group representative to nongroup members; (6) controller of internal group relations; (7) purveyor of rewards and punishment; (8) arbitrator and mediator; (9) exemplar; (10) symbol of the group; (11) substitute for individual responsibility; (12) ideologist; (13) parent figure; and (14) scapegoat when things go wrong.

On a more abstract level, Katz and Kahn (1966) have argued that leadership serves four general functions in ongoing organizations: (1) it fills the voids left by the incompleteness and imperfections of organization design; (2) it maintains the stability of an organization in a turbulent environment, allowing the organization to respond and adjust to changing external conditions; (3) it maintains internal coordination and adjudication through periods of internal change and growth; and (4) it attempts to maintain human membership in the organization. Although these lists are not empirically derived, they should suggest that not only is the leadership function quite broad-based but also it is centrally related to the ability of the leader to motivate subordinates.

Having considered both various definitions of leadership and some functions leaders purportedly serve, we can now examine several general "theories" of leadership that have been prominent at one time or another. Viewed historically, the earliest theory is generally termed the "great man" theory. This approach dates from the time of the ancient Greeks, but it maintained its popularity into the early twentieth century. Briefly, it assumed that true leaders possessed two quite dissimilar characteristics: (1) they were capable of "instrumental" behavior, such as planning, organizing, controlling subordinates' activities and (2) they showed concern for their subordinates and fostered sound group interrelationships (Bales, Borgatta, & Couch, 1954). Persons who showed both of these traits simultaneously were considered "great" and it was generally believed that they would be effective leaders in *any* given situation. Moreover, it was assumed that such leaders were born with these qualities; learned behavior was not considered relevant.

With the emergence of the behavioral school of psychology in the early

1900s, researchers began to reexamine the great man theory. There were at least two reasons for this reexamination. First, it was argued that if there were in fact "great" people, or true leaders, it should be possible scientifically to investigate the qualities, or traits, that were common across such individuals. By so investigating, it was felt that valuable insight would be gained into the nature of leadership. This concern for the identification of "traits" closely paralleled the emergence of the instinct theory of motivation, both in time and in nature. Second, it was largely believed that if these traits could be identified accurately, it might be possible for individuals to acquire these leadership qualities through experience and learning. In other words, this newer trait theory of leadership rejected the more passive great man approach by arguing that leadership could to some degree be *learned*.

Between approximately 1930 and 1950, numerous studies were undertaken in search of universal traits (physical, mental, and personality) that might be related to leadership. In general, some support was found for the conclusion that good leaders tended (1) to have appealing physical characteristics (for example, they were physically dominating, and so on); (2) to have certain personality traits (such as high needs for achievement and dominance, social maturity, and the like); and (3) to be well above average in intelligence (Gibb, 1954; Mann, 1959; Stogdill, 1948). However, such findings were generally weak and often inconsistent. Partially because of this latter fact, researchers began to challenge the existence of universal traits. Based on the early work of Kurt Lewin (Lewin, Lippitt, & White, 1939/1958) and the later studies at the University of Michigan (Katz, Maccoby, Gurin, & Floor, 1951; Katz, Maccoby, & Morse, 1950) and Ohio State University (Fleishman, Harris, & Burtt, 1955; Shartle, 1952; Stogdill & Coons, 1957), important evidence began to emerge that one set of traits or one style of leadership might not be equally appropriate in all situations. In general, these studies, which formed the basis of the "behavioral" theory of leadership, suggested that there were two fairly distinct *styles* of leadership: task-oriented (also called "production centered," "instrumental," and "initiating structure") and employee-oriented (or "people centered," "expressive," and "consideration"). A third style of leadership, laissez faire, was used by Lewin and his associates but was later dropped from both theory and research after it was discovered to have no practical relationship to performance or satisfaction (Lewin et al., 1939/1958).

Some disagreement has existed in the literature concerning the nature of the relationship between task orientation and employee orientation. Some researchers believe the two are relatively independent factors, while others believe they are opposite ends of a single continuum. Evidence generally tends to support the former approach; that is, most research tends to indicate that leadership style may be high on both dimensions (task orientation *and* employee orientation), low on both dimensions, or high on one and low on the other. If we consider the relation of these styles of leadership to motivation, it appears that both styles have relevance. The task-oriented supervisor can increase motivation by clarifying the connection between successful task accomplishment and the receipt of desired rewards. The employee-oriented supervisor can increase motivation by providing as many rewarding situations as possible and by creating a supportive environment.

Most recently, a series of newer theories have emerged which use the environment, or situation, as the basic unit of analysis in a theory of leadership instead of the style itself. These theories, known generally as situational or contingency models, typically argue that effective leadership is really a function of the interaction of several variables. For example, under Fiedler's (1967) model, effective leadership is seen as largely a function of (1) the favorableness of superior-subordinate relations, (2) the power distribution between superior and subordinates, and (3) the degree of task structuring on the job. Other models of leadership could be mentioned (see, for example, Vroom & Yetton, 1973; House, 1971). However, instead of comparing various specific theories of leadership in this chapter, we shall focus on the larger issue of how supervisory behavior impacts upon subordinates. That is, we shall be examining general processes, not specific theories.

OVERVIEW

In the three selections that follow, various aspects of the work environment will be examined as they relate to employee motivation. The first selection, by Porter, Lawler, and Hackman, reviews several mechanisms by which groups influence individual employees to produce (or not to produce). Included in this discussion is consideration of how managers may try to change the work environment so group processes are more compatible with organizational goals. The second selection, by Steers, reviews our current level of knowledge concerning organizational climate. A model of organizational climate is proposed which incorporates both major influences on climate and major outcomes. In addition to reviewing relevant research, we discuss several criticisms of the climate construct. Finally, Locke discusses on a general level the various mechanisms by which managers and supervisors can influence employee motivation, performance, and satisfaction. Relevant research is reviewed where appropriate.

REFERENCES AND SUGGESTED ADDITIONAL READINGS

Allport, F. H. *Social psychology*. New York: Houghton Mifflin, 1924.

Asch, S. E. The effects of group pressure upon the modification and distortion of judgments. In E. E. Maccoby, T. E. Newcomb, & E. L. Hartley (Eds.), *Readings in social psychology*. New York: Holt, Rinehart & Winston, 1958. (First published in 1939.)

Bales, R. F., Borgatta, E. F., & Couch, A. S. Some findings relevant to the great-man theory of leadership. *American Sociological Review*, 1954, **19**, 755–759.

Cartwright, D., & Zander, A. (Eds.). *Group dynamics*, 3rd ed. Evanston, Ill.: Row, Peterson, 1968.

Cummings, L. L., & Berger, C. J. Organization structure: How does it influence attitudes and performance? *Organizational Dynamics*, 1976, **5**(2), 34–49.

Evans, M. G. The effects of supervisory behavior on the path-goal relationship. *Organizational Behavior and Human Performance*, 1970, **5**, 277–298.

Fiedler, F. E. *A theory of leadership effectiveness*. New York: McGraw-Hill, 1967.

Fiedler, F. E. Validation and extension of the contingency model of leadership effectiveness: A review of empirical findings. *Psychological Bulletin*, 1971, **76**, 128–148.

Fiedler, F. E., & Chemers, M. M. *Leadership and effective management*. Glenview, Ill.: Scott, Foresman, 1974.

Fleishman, E. A., Harris, E., & Burtt, H. E. *Leadership and supervision in industry*. Columbus, Ohio: Ohio State University, Bureau of Educational Research, 1955.

Forehand, G. A., & Gilmer, B. V. H. Environmental variation in studies of organizational behavior. *Psychological Bulletin*, 1964, **62**, 361–482.

Gibb, C. Leadership. In G. Lindzey (Ed.), *Handbook of social psychology*. Reading, Mass.: Addison-Wesley, 1954.

Guion, R. M. A note on organizational climate. *Organizational Behavior and Human Performance*, 1973, **9**, 120–125.

Halpin, A. W., & Crofts, D. B. *The organizational climate of schools*. Chicago: University of Chicago, Midwest Administration Center, 1963.

Hare, A. P. *Handbook of small group research*. New York: Free Press, 1976.

Hellriegel, D., & Slocum, J. W., Jr. Organizational climate: Measures, research, and contingencies. *Academy of Management Journal*, 1974, **17**, 255–280.

Hill, W. A. Leadership style: Rigid or flexible. *Organizational Behavior and Human Performance*, 1973, **9**, 35–47.

Hinton, B. L., & Reitz, H. J. (Eds.). *Groups and organizations*. Belmont, Calif.: Wadsworth, 1971.

Hollander, E. P. *Leaders, groups, and influence*. New York: Oxford University Press, 1964.

Homans, G. C. *The human group*. New York: Harcourt, Brace & World, 1950.

House, R. J. A path goal theory of leader effectiveness. *Administrative Science Quarterly*, 1971, **16**, 321–338.

Hunt, J. G., & Larson, L. L. (Eds.). *Contingency approaches to leadership*. Carbondale, Ill.: Southern Illinois University Press, 1974.

James, L. R., & Jones, A. P. Organizational climate: A review of theory and research. *Psychological Bulletin*, 1974, **81**, 1096–1112.

Kaczra, E. E., & Kirk, R. V. Managerial climate, work groups, and organizational performance. *Administrative Science Quarterly*, 1967, **12**, 253–272.

Katz, D., & Kahn, R. L. *The social psychology of organizations*. New York: Wiley, 1966.

Katz, D., Maccoby, N. M., & Morse, N. *Productivity supervision and morale in an office situation*. Ann Arbor, Mich.: University of Michigan, Survey Research Center, 1950.

Katz, D., Maccoby, N., Gurin, G., & Floor, L. *Productivity, supervision, and morale among railroad workers*. Ann Arbor, Mich.: University of Michigan, Institute for Social Research, 1951.

Kemp, C. G. *Perspectives on group processes*. Boston: Houghton Mifflin, 1970.

Krech, D., Crutchfield, R. S., & Ballachey, E. L. *Individuals in society*. New York: McGraw-Hill, 1962.

Lewin, K. *The conceptual representation and the measurement of psychological forces*. Durham, N. C.: Duke University Press, 1938.

Lewin, K. *Field theory in social science*. New York: Harper, 1951.

Lewin, K., Lippitt, R., & White, R. K. An experimental study of leadership and group life. In E. Maccoby, T. M. Newcomb, & E. L. Hartley (Eds.), *Readings in social psychology*. New York: Holt, Rinehart & Winston, 1958. (First published in 1939.)

Likert, R. *New patterns in management*. New York: McGraw-Hill, 1961.

Likert, R. *The human organization*. New York: McGraw-Hill, 1967.

Litwin, G. H., & Stringer, R. A. *Motivation and organizational climate*. Boston: Harvard University, Graduate School of Business Administration, Division of Research, 1968.

Mann, R. D. A review of the relationships between personality and performance in small groups. *Psychological Bulletin*, 1959, **56**, 241–270.

Mayo, E. *The human problems of an industrial civilization*. New York: Macmillan, 1933.

Olmstead, M. S. *The small group*. New York: Random House, 1959.

Payne, R. L., & Mansfield, R. Relationships of perceptions of organizational climate to organizational structure, context, and hierarchical position. *Administrative Science Quarterly*, 1973, **18**, 515–526.

Pervin, L. A. Performance and satisfaction as a function of individual-environmental fit. *Psychological Bulletin*, 1968, **69**, 56–68.

Porter, L. W., & Lawler, E. E., III. Properties of organizational structure in relation to job attitudes and job behavior. *Psychological Bulletin*, 1965, **64**, 23–51.

Prien, E. P., & Ronan, W. W. An analysis of organizational characteristics. *Organizational Behavior and Human Performance*, 1971, **6**, 215–234.

Pritchard, R. D., & Karasick, B. W. The effects of organizational climate on managerial job performance and job satisfaction. *Organizational Behavior and Human Performance*, 1973, **9**, 126–146.

Roethlisberger, F. J., & Dickson, W. J. *Management and the worker*. Boston: Harvard University Press, 1939.

Sales, S. M. Supervisory style and productivity: Review and theory. *Personnel Psychology*, 1966, **19**, 275–286.

Schachter, S. *The psychology of affiliation*. Palo Alto, Calif.: Stanford University Press, 1959.

Schneider, B. Organization climates: An essay. *Personnel Psychology*, 1975, **28**, 447–479.

Schneider, B. Organizational climate: Individual preferences and organizational realities. *Journal of Applied Psychology*, 1972, **56**, 211–217.

Schneider, B., & Bartlett, C. J. Individual differences and organizational climate as the multi-trait, multi-rater matrix. *Personnel Psychology*, 1970, **23**, 493–512.

Shartle, C. L. *Executive performance and leadership*. Columbus, Ohio: The Ohio State University Research Foundation, 1952.

Sherif, M. *The psychology of social norms*. New York: Harper, 1936.

Stogdill, R. M. Personal factors associated with leadership: A survey of the literature. *Journal of Psychology*, 1948, **25**, 35–71.

Stogdill, R. *Handbook of leadership*. New York: Free Press, 1974.

Stogdill, R. M., & Coons, A. E. *Leader behavior: Its description and measurement*. Columbus, Ohio: Ohio State University, Bureau of Business Research, 1957.

Tagiuri, R., & Litwin, G. H. (Eds.). *Organizational climate*. Boston: Harvard University, Division of Research, 1968.

Tannenbaum, A. S. *Social psychology of the work organization*. Belmont, Calif.: Wadsworth, 1966.

Tannenbaum, R., & Schmidt, W. H. How to choose a leadership pattern. *Harvard Business Review*, 1958, **36**, 95–101.

Thibaut, J., & Kelley, H. *The social psychology of groups*. New York: Wiley, 1959.

Vroom, V. *Work and motivation*. New York: Wiley, 1964.

Vroom, V. H., & Yetton, P. *Leadership and decision making*. Pittsburgh: University of Pittsburgh Press, 1973.

Whyte, W. F. *Organizational behavior: Theory and application*. Homewood, Ill.: Irwin-Dorsey, 1969.

Yukl, G. Toward a behavioral theory of leadership. *Organizational Behavior and Human Performance*, 1971, **6**, 414–440.

Ways Groups Influence Individual Work Effectiveness

Lyman W. Porter
Edward E. Lawler III
J. Richard Hackman

To analyze the diversity of group and social influences on individual work effectiveness, it may be useful to examine group effects separately on each of four summary classes of variables that have been shown to influence employee work behavior. These four classes of variables are:

1 The job-relevant knowledge and skills of the individual
2 The level of psychological arousal the individual experiences while working
3 The performance strategies the individual uses during his work
4 The level of effort the individual exerts in doing his work.

Below, we shall examine the ways in which work groups influence each of these four major influences on individual performance.

GROUP INFLUENCES BY AFFECTING MEMBER KNOWLEDGE AND SKILLS

Performance on many tasks and jobs in organizations is strongly affected by the job-relevant knowledge and skills of the individuals who do the work. Thus, even if an employee has both high commitment toward accomplishing a particular piece of work and a well-formed strategy about how to go about doing it, the implementation of that plan can be constrained or terminated if he does not know how to carry it out, or if he knows how but is incapable of doing so. While ability is relevant to the performance of jobs at all levels in an organization, its impact probably is somewhat reduced for lower-level jobs. The reason is that such jobs often are not demanding of high skill levels. Further, to the extent that organizational selection, placement, and promotion practices are adequate, *all* jobs should tend to be occupied by individuals who possess the skills requisite for adequate performance.

Discussion in the previous chapter focused on how groups can improve

Slightly revised from L. W. Porter, E. E. Lawler, & J. R. Hackman, *Behavior in organizations*. New York: McGraw-Hill, 1975, 411–422. Used by permission.

the job-relevant knowledge and skills of an individual through direct instruction, feedback, and model provision. For jobs in which knowledge and skill are important determiners of performance effectiveness, then, groups can be of help. Nevertheless, the impact of groups on member performance effectiveness by improving member knowledge and skill probably is one of the lesser influences groups can have—both because employees on many jobs tend already to have many or all of the skills needed to perform them effectively and because there are other sources for improving skills which may be more useful and more potent than the work group, such as formal job training programs and self-study programs.

GROUP INFLUENCES BY AFFECTING MEMBER AROUSAL LEVEL

A group can substantially influence the level of psychological arousal experienced by a member—through the mere presence of the other group members and by those others sending the individual messages which are directly arousal-enhancing or arousal-depressing. The conditions under which such group-promoted changes in arousal level will lead to increased performance effectiveness, however, very much depend upon the type of task being worked on (Zajonc, 1965).

In this case, the critical characteristics of the job have to do with whether the initially *dominant task responses* of the individual are likely to be correct or incorrect. Since the individual's output of such responses is facilitated when he is in an aroused state, arousal should improve performance effectiveness on well-learned tasks (so-called performance tasks) in which the dominant response is correct and needs merely to be executed by the performer. By the same token, arousal should impair effectiveness for new or unfamiliar tasks (learning tasks) in which the dominant response is likely to be incorrect.

It has sometimes been argued that the *mere* presence of others should heighten the arousal of individuals sufficiently for the predicted performance effects to be obtained. However, the evidence now seems to indicate that the *mere* presence of others may not result in significant increases in arousal. Instead, only when the other group members are—or are seen as being—in a potentially evaluative relationship vis-à-vis the performer are the predictions confirmed (cf. Zajonc & Sales, 1966; Cottrell et al., 1968; Hency & Glass, 1968).

Groups can, of course, increase member arousal in ways other than taking an evaluative stance toward the individual. Strongly positive, encouraging statements also should increase arousal in some performance situations—for example, by helping the individual become personally highly committed to the group goal, and making sure he realizes that he is a very important part of the team responsible for reaching that goal. What must be kept in mind, however, is that such devices represent a double-edged sword: while they may facilitate effective performance for well-learned tasks, they may have the opposite effect for new and unfamiliar tasks.

What, then, can be said about the effects on performance of group members when their presence (and interaction) serves to *decrease* the level of arousal of the group member—as, for example, when individuals coalesce into groups under conditions of high stress? When the other members of the group are a source of support, comfort, or acceptance to the individual (and serve to decrease his arousal level), it would be predicted that performance effectiveness would follow a pattern exactly opposite to that described above: the group would impair effectiveness for familiar or well-learned performance tasks (because arousal helps on these tasks, and arousal is being lowered) and facilitate effectiveness for unfamiliar or complicated learning tasks (because in this case arousal is harmful, and it is being lowered).

The relationships predicted above are summarized in Figure 1. As the group becomes increasingly threatening, evaluative, or strongly encouraging, effectiveness should increase for performance tasks and decrease for learning tasks. When the group is experienced as increasingly supportive, comforting, or unconditionally accepting, effectiveness should decrease for performance tasks and increase for learning tasks. And when no meaningful relationship at all is experienced by the individual between himself and the group, performance should not be affected. While some of these predictions have been tested and confirmed in small group experimental settings, others await research.

Even that research which has focused on these relationships has not been designed or conducted in actual organizational settings, and the findings must

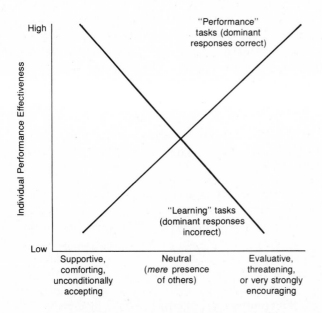

Figure 1 Individual performance effectiveness as a function of type of task and experienced relationship to the group.

be generalized with caution. It is clear, however, that individuals in organizations do use their group memberships as a means of achieving more comfortable levels of arousal. Individuals in high-pressure managerial jobs, for example, often find that they need to gather around themselves a few trusted associates who can and do provide reassurance and continuing acceptance when the going gets especially tough. This, presumably, should help reduce the manager's level of arousal and thereby increase the likelihood that he will be able to come up with *new and original* ways of perceiving and dealing with his immediate problem. If the theory is correct, however, this practice should not facilitate performance of the more "routine" (i.e., well-learned) parts of his job.

It is well known that overly routine jobs can decrease a worker's level of arousal to such an extent that his performance effectiveness is impaired. It seems quite possible, therefore, that the social environment of workers on such jobs can be designed so as to compensate partially for the deadening effects of the job itself and thereby lead to an increment in performance on well-learned tasks.

Finally, the supervisor probably has a more powerful effect on the level of arousal of a worker than any other single individual in his immediate social environment. By close supervision (which usually results in the worker's feeling more or less constantly evaluated) supervisors can and do increase the level of arousal experienced by workers. While this may, for routine jobs, have some potential for improving performance effectiveness, it also is quite likely that the worker's negative reactions to being closely supervised ultimately will result in his attention being diverted from the job itself and focused instead on ways he can either get out from "under the gun" of the supervisor or somehow get back at the supervisor to punish him for his unwanted close supervision.

GROUP INFLUENCES BY AFFECTING LEVEL OF MEMBER EFFORT AND MEMBER PERFORMANCE STRATEGIES

The level of effort a person exerts in doing his work and the performance strategies he follows are treated together here because both variables are largely under the performer's *voluntary* control.

Direct versus Indirect Influences on Effort and Strategy   We have used a general "expectancy theory" approach to analyze those aspects of a person's behavior in organizations which are under his voluntary control. From this perspective, a person's choices about his effort and work strategy can be viewed as hinging largely upon (1) his *expectations* regarding the likely consequences of his choices and (2) the degree to which he *values* those expected consequences. Following this approach, it becomes clear that the group can have both a direct and an indirect effect on the level of effort a group member exerts at his job and on his choices about performance strategy.

The *direct* impact of the group on effort and strategy, of course, is simply the enforcement by the group of its own norms regarding what is an "appropriate" level of effort to expend on the job and what is the "proper" performance strategy. We previously discussed in some detail how groups use their control of discretionary stimuli to enforce group norms, and thereby affect such voluntary behaviors. Thus, if the group has established a norm about the level of member effort or the strategies members should use in going about their work, the group can control individual behavior merely by making sure that individual members realize that their receipt of valued group-controlled rewards is contingent upon their behaving in accord with the norm.

The *indirect* impact of the group on the effort and performance strategies of the individual involves the group's control of information regarding the state of the organizational environment outside the boundaries of the group. Regardless of any norms the group itself may have about effort or strategy, it also can communicate to the group member "what leads to what" in the broader organization, and thereby affect the individual's *own* choices about his behavior.

For example, it may be the case in a given organization that hard work (i.e., high effort) tends to lead to quick promotions and higher pay; the group can influence the effort of the individual by helping him realize this objective state of affairs. Similarly, by providing individual members with information about what performance strategies are effective in the organization, the group can indirectly affect the strategy choices made by the person. Whether high quality of output or large quantities of output are more likely to lead to organizational rewards, for example, is information that the group can provide the individual with to assist him in making his own choices about work strategy.

Moreover, groups can affect the *personal preferences and values* of individual members—although such influences tend to occur relatively slowly and over a long period of time. When such changes do occur, the level of desire (or the valence) individuals have for various outcomes available in the organizational setting will change as well. And as the kinds of outcomes valued by the individual change, his behavior also will change to increase the degree to which the newly valued outcomes are obtained at work. The long-term result can be substantial revision of the choices made by the individual about the effort he will expend and the performance strategies he will use at work.

It should be noted, however, that such indirect influences on member effort and performance strategy will be most potent early in the individual's tenure in the organization when he has not yet had a chance to develop through experience his own personal "map" of the organization. When the individual becomes less dependent upon the group for data about "what leads to what" and "what's good" in the organization, the group may have to revert to direct norm enforcement to maintain control of the work behavior of individual members.

In summary, the group can and does have a strong impact on both the level of effort exerted by its members and the strategies members use in carrying out their work. This impact is realized both directly (i.e., by enforcement of group norms) and indirectly (i.e., by affecting the beliefs and values of the members). When the direct and indirect influences of a group are congruent—which is often the case—the potency of the group's effects on its members can be quite strong. For example, if at the same time that a group is enforcing its *own* norm of, say, moderately low production, it also is providing a group member with data regarding the presumably *objective* negative consequences of hard work in the particular organization, the group member will experience two partially independent and mutually reinforcing influences aimed at keeping his rate of production down.

Effort, Strategy, and Performance Effectiveness   What, then, are the circumstances under which groups can improve the work *effectiveness* of their members through influences on individual choices about level of effort and about strategy? Again, the answer depends upon the nature of the job. Unless a job is structured so that effort level or performance strategy actually can make a real difference in work effectiveness, group influences on effort or strategy will be irrelevant to how well individual members perform.

Strategy: In general, groups should be able to facilitate member work effectiveness by influencing strategy choices more for complex jobs than for simple, straightforward, or routine ones. The reason is that on simple jobs, strategy choices usually cannot make much of a difference in effectiveness; instead, how well one does is determined almost entirely by how hard one works. On jobs characterized by high variety and autonomy, on the other hand, the work strategy used by the individual usually is of considerable importance in determining work effectiveness. By helping an individual develop and implement an appropriate work strategy—of where and how to put in his effort—the group should be able to substantially facilitate his effectiveness.

Effort: In the great majority of organizational settings, most jobs are structured such that the harder one works, the more effective his performance is likely to be. Thus, group influences on the effort expended by members on their jobs are both very pervasive and very potent determiners of individual work effectiveness. There are, nevertheless, some exceptions to this generalization; the success of a complicated brain operation, for example, is less likely to depend upon effort expended than it is upon the strategies used and the job-relevant knowledge and skills of the surgeon.

When either effort or strategy or both are in fact important in determining performance effectiveness, the individual has substantial personal control over how well he does in his work. In such cases, the degree to which the group facilitates (rather than hinders) individual effectiveness will depend jointly upon (1) the degree to which the group has accurate information regarding the task and organizational contingencies which are operative in that situation and makes such information available to the individual and (2) the degree to which the norms of the group are congruent with those contingencies and reinforce them.

Participation   One management practice which in theory should contribute positively to meeting both of the above conditions is the use of group participation in making decisions about work practices. Participation has been widely advocated as a management technique, both on ideological grounds and as a direct means of increasing work effectiveness. And, in fact, some studies have shown that participation can lead to higher work effectiveness (e.g., Coch

& French, 1948; Lawler & Hackman, 1969). In the present framework, participation should contribute to increased work effectiveness in two different ways.

1 Participation can increase the amount and the accuracy of information workers have about work practices and the environmental contingencies associated with them. In one study (Lawler & Hackman, 1969), for example, some groups themselves designed new reward systems keyed on coming to work regularly (a task clearly affected by employee effort—i.e., trying to get to work every day). These groups responded both more quickly and more positively to the new pay plans than did groups which had technically identical plans imposed upon them by company management. One reason suggested by the authors to account for this finding was that the participative groups simply may have understood their plans better and had fewer uncertainties and worries about what the rewards were (and were not) for coming to work regularly.

2 Participation can increase the degree to which group members feel they "own" their work practices—and therefore the likelihood that the group will develop a norm of support for those practices. In the participative groups in the study cited above, for example, the nature of the work-related communication among members changed from initial "shared warnings" about management and "things management proposes" to helping members (especially new members) come to understand and believe in "our plan." In other words, as group members come to experience the work or work practices *as under their own control or ownership*, it becomes more likely that informal group norms supportive of effective behavior vis-à-vis those practices will develop. Such norms provide a striking contrast to the "group protective" norms which often emerge when control is perceived to be exclusively and unilaterally under management control.

We can see, then, that group participative techniques can be quite facilitative of individual work effectiveness—but only under certain conditions:

1 The topic of participation must be relevant to the work itself. There is no reason to believe that participation involving task-irrelevant issues (e.g., preparing for the Red Cross Bloodmobile visit to the plant) will have facilitative effects on work productivity. While such participation may indeed help increase the cohesiveness of the work group, it clearly will not help group members gain information or develop norms which are facilitative of high work effectiveness. Indeed, such task-irrelevant participation may serve to direct the attention and motivation of group members *away from* work issues and thereby even lower productivity (cf. French, Israel, & Ås, 1960).

2 The objective task and environmental contingencies in the work setting must actually be supportive of more effective performance. That is, if through participation group members learn more about what leads to what in the organization, then it is increasingly important that there be real and meaningful positive outcomes which result from effective performance. If, for example, group members gain a quite complete and accurate impression through participation that "hard work around here pays off only in backaches," then increased effort as a consequence of participation is most unlikely. If, on the other hand, participation results in a new and better understanding that hard work can lead to increased pay, enhanced opportunities for advancement, and the chance to feel a sense of personal and group accomplishment, then increased effort should be the result.

3 Finally, the work must be such that increased effort (or a different and better work strategy) objectively can lead to higher work effectiveness. If it is true—as argued here—that the main benefits of group participation are (1) increased understanding of work practices and the organizational environment and (2) increased experienced "ownership" by the group of the work and work practices, then participation should increase productivity only when the *objective determinants of productivity are under the voluntary control of the worker*. There is little reason to expect, therefore, that participation should have a substantial facilitative effect on productivity when work outcomes are mainly determined by the level of skill of the worker and/or by his arousal level (rather than effort expended or work strategy used) or when outcomes are controlled by objective factors in the environment over which the worker can have little or no control (e.g., the rate or amount of work which is arriving at the employee's station).

IMPLICATIONS FOR DIAGNOSIS AND CHANGE

This section has focused on ways that the group can influence the performance effectiveness of individual group members. While it has been maintained throughout that the group has a substantial impact on such performance effectiveness, it has been emphasized that the nature and extent of this impact centrally depends upon the characteristics of the work being done.

To diagnose and change the direction or extent of social influences on individual performance in an organization, then, the following three steps might be taken.

1 An analysis of the task or job would be made to determine which of the four classes of variables (i.e., skills, arousal, strategies, effort) objectively affect measured performance effectiveness. This might be done by posing this analytical question: "If skills (or arousal, or effort, or strategies) were brought to bear on the work differently than is presently the case, would a corresponding difference in work effectiveness be likely to be observed as a consequence?" By scrutinizing each of the four classes of variables in this way, it usually is possible to identify which specific variables are objectively important to consider for the job. In many cases, of course, more than one class of variables will turn out to be of importance.

2 After one or more "target" classes of variables have been identified, the work group itself would be examined to unearth any ways in which the group was blocking effective individual performance. It might be determined, for example, that certain group norms were impeding the expression and use of various skills which individuals potentially could bring to bear on their work.

Or it might turn out that the social environment of the worker created conditions which were excessively (or insufficiently) arousing for optimal performance on the task at hand. For effort and strategy, which are under the voluntary control of the worker, there are two major possibilities to examine: (a) that norms are enforced in the group which coerce individuals to behave in ineffective ways or (b) that the group provides information to the individual members about task and environmental contingencies in an insufficient or distorted fashion, resulting in their making choices about their work behavior which interfere with task effectiveness.

3   Finally, it would be useful to assess the group and the broader social environment to determine if there are ways that the "people resources" in the situation could be more fully utilized in the interest of increased work effectiveness. That is, rather than focusing solely on ways the group may be blocking or impeding performance effectiveness, attention should be given as well to any unrealized *potential* which resides in the group. It could turn out, for example, that some group members would be of great help to others in increasing the level of individual task-relevant skills, but these individuals have never been asked for help. Alternatively, it might be that the group could be assisted in finding new and better ways of ensuring that each group member has available accurate and current information about those tasks and environmental contingencies which determine the outcomes of various work behaviors.

The point is that the people who surround an individual at work can facilitate as well as hinder his performance effectiveness—and that any serious attempt to diagnose the social environment in the interest of improving work performance should explicitly address unrealized possibilities for enhancing performance as well as issues for which remedial action may be required.

What particular organizational changes will be called for on the basis of such a diagnosis—or what techniques should be used to realize these changes—will, of course, largely depend upon the particular characteristics of the organization and of the resources which are available there. The major emphasis of this section has been that there is *not* any single universally useful type of change or means of change—and that, instead, intervention should always be based on a thorough diagnosis of the existing social, organizational, and task environment. Perhaps especially intriguing in this regard is the prospect of developing techniques of social intervention which will help groups see the need for (and develop the capability of) making such interventions *on their own* in the interest of increasing the work effectiveness of the group as a whole.

REFERENCES

Coch, L., & French, J. R. P., Jr. Overcoming resistance to change. *Human Relations*, 1948, **1**, 512–532.

Cottrell, N. B., Wack, D. L., Sekerak, F. J., & Rittle, R. H. Social facilitation of dominant responses by the presence of an audience and the mere presence of others. *Journal of Personality and Social Psychology*, 1968, **9**, 245–250.

French, J. R. P., Jr., Israel, J., & Ås, D. An experiment on participation in a Norwegian factory. *Human Relations,* 1960, **19**, 3–19.

Hency, T., & Glass, D. C. Evaluation apprehension and the social facilitation of dominant and subordinate responses. *Journal of Personality and Social Psychology,* 1968, **10**, 446–454.

Lawler, E. E., & Hackman, J. R. The impact of employee participation in the development of pay incentive plans: A field experiment. *Journal of Applied Psychology,* 1969, **53**, 467–471.

Zajonc, R. B. Social facilitation. *Science,* 1965, **149**, 269–274.

Zajonc, R. B., & Sales, S. M. Social facilitation of dominant and subordinate responses. *Journal of Experimental Social Psychology,* 1966, **2**, 160–168.

Work Environment and Individual Behavior

Richard M. Steers

The issue of organizational climate is indeed a controversial one (Guion, 1973). Not only are there disagreements over what is meant by climate but in addition it is difficult to reach consensus concerning the exact role of climate in determining organizational performance. Therefore, we shall first examine what is meant by the concept itself—including its relevant dimensions—and how it relates to other organizational variables. Following this, a model is proposed concerning the role played by climate in determining individual behavior and job attitudes. Several examples of recent investigations of the topic are then examined to determine the appropriateness of the model. Finally, several critiques of the construct itself are considered in the light of current research evidence.

NATURE OF ORGANIZATIONAL CLIMATE

When we discuss the concept of organizational climate, we are talking about the perceived properties or characteristics found in the work environment that result largely from actions taken consciously or unconsciously by an organization and that presumably affect subsequent behavior. In other words, climate may be thought of as the "personality"of an organization as seen by its members. Several important things should be noted about this definition. First, we are dealing in a perceptual realm; the climate of a particular organization is that which its employees believe it to be, not necessarily what it "really" is. If employees perceive the climate to be highly authoritarian, for example, we would expect them to act accordingly, even if top management made every effort to be democratic or employee-centered.

From R. M. Steers, *Organizational effectiveness: A behavioral view*. Santa Monica, Calif.: Goodyear, 1977, 100–112. Used by permission.

A second important feature of this definition is the suggested relationship between other organizational characteristics and actions and resulting climate. It is generally believed that characteristics unique to a given organization, along with the actions and behavior of management, largely determine the climate of an organization. Finally, it is further believed that the climate that does emerge within an organization represents a major determinant of employee behavior. Given this central relationship between organizational characteristics and actions, climate, and behavior, it becomes readily apparent why climate has received such widespread attention in recent years.

The variables that constitute the climate construct are the defining characteristics that distinguish one working environment from another *as seen by* members of the organization. These variables are thought to be measurable and manipulable to some extent (Litwin & Stringer, 1968). Moreover, climate ostensibly serves as a basis for individuals to interpret and understand their surroundings and to determine reward-punishment relationships (Forehand & Gilmer, 1964; Pritchard & Karasick, 1973).

DIMENSIONS OF ORGANIZATIONAL CLIMATE

A major difficulty that has arisen in attempts to understand the role of climate in organizational settings has been a general inability among analysts to agree on what actually constitutes the construct. That is, although it is relatively easy to agree on a general definition, there is widespread disagreement concerning which specific dimensions or components are involved. Part of this problem lies in the diversity of environments that have been studied (for example, business organizations, R&D laboratories, elementary schools, government agencies). It is difficult to identify several core dimensions that have relevance for all these organizations. A second problem that exists in the work on climate is that a priori climate scales are typically set forth by one investigator with little concern for how this set of scales relates to other sets. Moreover, little concern has been shown in many cases for the validity and reliability of the various scales used in research projects. The result is that scales purporting to measure dimensions of climate proliferate while considerable difficulty is encountered in any attempt to draw meaningful conclusions or generalizations from the various sets of findings.

One of the more promising avenues of research on climate dimensions is represented by Campbell and his associates (Campbell & Beaty, 1971; Pritchard & Karasick, 1973) in their attempt to develop relatively independent scales of several climate dimensions. By using cluster analysis on their original questionnaire, these investigators identified ten dimensions of climate on an organization-wide basis. These dimensions are:

1 *Task structure*   The degree to which the methods used to accomplish tasks are spelled out by an organization.

2 *Reward-punishment relationship* The degree to which the granting of additional rewards such as promotions and salary increases are based on performance and merit instead of other considerations like seniority, favoritism, and so forth.

3 *Decision centralization* The extent to which important decisions are reserved for top management.

4 *Achievement emphasis* The desire on the part of the people in an organization to do a good job and contribute to the performance objectives of the organization.

5 *Training and development emphasis* The degree to which an organization tries to support the performance of individuals through appropriate training and development experiences.

6 *Security versus risk* The degree to which pressures in an organization lead to feelings of insecurity and anxiety on the part of its members.

7 *Openness versus defensiveness* The degree to which people try to cover their mistakes and look good rather than communicate freely and cooperate.

8 *Status and morale* The general feeling among individuals that the organization is a good place in which to work.

9 *Recognition and feedback* The degree to which an individual knows what his supervisor and management think of his work and the degree to which they support him or her.

10 *General organizational competence and flexibility* The degree to which an organization knows what its goals are and pursues them in a flexible and innovative manner. Includes the extent to which it anticipates problems, develops new methods, and develops new skills in people before problems become crises.

This set of climate dimensions is illustrative of the variety of factors commonly included in other conceptualizations of climate (see, for example, Halpin & Croft, 1962; Litwin & Stringer, 1968; Schneider & Bartlett, 1968; Taylor & Bowers, 1972). Although some differences exist between these formulations, the dimensions proposed by Campbell and his associates generally subsume the various dimensions found in earlier formulations. As such, this formulation will be used in the present discussion for the purpose of consistency. (The reader is referred to Campbell et al., 1974, for a detailed comparison of the various approaches to the study of climate.)

Before exploring the relationship between organizational climate and facets of effectiveness, it is important to understand how the notion of climate differs from that of organizational structure. Although some overlap obviously exists [for example, Campbell & Beaty's (1971) notion of "task structure"], it is still possible to differentiate the two concepts. Structure generally refers either to the physical arrangement of people in an organization (for example, work-group size, span of control, and so forth) or to the extent of work "structuring" that is imposed on individuals by an organization (Campbell et al., 1974). In both instances, we are concerned with the extent to which individual behavior in organizational settings is prescribed, standardized, and restricted or controlled.

Climate, on the other hand, refers principally to the prevalent attitudes, values, norms, and feelings employees have concerning the organization (Payne & Pugh, 1976). These affective responses result largely from the interaction of an organization's structure and the individual's (or group's) goals, needs, and abilities. Thus, on a conceptual level, structure, an objective phenomenon, is seen as a major influence on climate, a subjective phenomenon.

CLIMATE AND ORGANIZATIONAL EFFECTIVENESS

In order to understand the role of climate in organizational effectiveness, we can construct a hypothetical model on a general level that specifies the relationships between the major sets of variables. Such a model should provide a useful framework around which to analyze the various research findings as they relate to climate and effectiveness.

We have already mentioned the role of structure as a determinant of climate. Along with structure, we can also include technology, external environment, and managerial policies and practices as important influences on climate. (These relationships are schematically represented in Exhibit 1 and will be discussed in greater detail below.) The emerging climate, then, represents the arena where employee performance decisions are made. Where climate is conducive to the needs of individuals (for example, it is employee-centered and achievement-oriented), we would expect goal-directed behavior to be high. Conversely, where the emerging climate is in opposition to personal goals, needs, and motives, we would expect both performance and satisfaction to be diminished. In other words, ultimate behaviors or outcomes are determined by the interaction of individual needs and the perceived organizational environment. The resulting level of performance, satisfaction, and so forth, then feeds back to contribute not only to the climate of the particular work environment but also to possible changes in managerial policies and practices.

Following this viewpoint, structure, technology, external environment, and other organizational characteristics affect ultimate outcomes (such as performance, satisfaction) largely to the extent that they contribute to an appropriate climate. Climate is thus seen as an intervening variable. This intervening nature of climate may explain many of the weak or contradictory findings that result when the structure-performance or environment-performance relationships are examined irrespective of climate.

Several additional points need to be made concerning the role of climate in organizational effectiveness as viewed here. First, because climate is generally regarded as existing on an individual or group level (as opposed to an organization-wide level), outcome measures must also be considered on an individual or group level. Thus, instead of talking about climate leading to

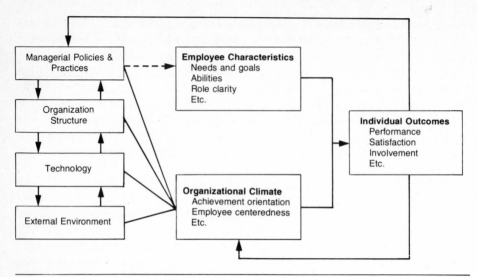

Note: The dotted line from managerial policies and practices to employee characteristics denotes the influence of management on such characteristics through employee selection and training.

Exhibit 1   A partial model of the determinants of effectiveness-related individual outcomes.

organizational effectiveness, it is probably more appropriate to talk in terms of individual or group-related facets of effectiveness (for example, job satisfaction, employee performance, organizational commitment, and so forth).

Second, the available information suggests that there is no best, or most suitable, climate. Instead, management must determine what its goals are and attempt to create a climate that is appropriate both for those goals and for the goals and objectives of its employees. If performance is the desired outcome, an achievement-oriented climate may be more suitable; an affiliation-oriented climate may be more suitable if job satisfaction were the desired outcome (Litwin & Stringer, 1968).

Third, it should be noted that the relationships we are discussing here (Exhibit 1) should hold only to the extent that employees have control over the attainment of the outcome variables. Where machines control productivity, for example, we would not expect climate to play as large a role in performance, although it most certainly would relate to resulting job attitudes and withdrawal behavior.

Consistent with the framework presented above, investigations of organizational climate have taken one of three approaches. First, some studies examined the potential *determinants* of climate in organizations. Questions were raised here regarding the "causes" of variations in climate dimensions across work environments. A second set of investigations looked at the various *outcomes* that resulted from variations in climate. Particular interest was focused here on how changes in climate affected employee performance and job attitudes. Finally, a third set of studies examined the *intervening* nature of climate as it moderated the relationship between such organizational characteristics as structure and technology and resulting job performance and satisfaction. After examining each of these aspects of the role of organizational climate in work settings, we shall attempt to draw some meaningful generalizations concerning how the research supports the model presented above (see also Hellriegel & Slocum, 1974; James & Jones, 1974).

DETERMINANTS OF CLIMATE

Exhibit 1 suggests that at least four sets of factors can influence in some fashion the climate of a particular organization or work group. In general, these factors originate either in the structure or technology of the organization, its external task environment, or the policies and practices set forth by top management.

The first set of variables that are thought to affect organizational climate are found in the structure of the organization. When taken together, the available evidence indicates that the more "structured" an organization (that is, the greater the degree of centralization, formalization, rules-orientation, and so on), the more rigid, closed, and threatening the perceived environment (see, for example, Marrow, Bowers, & Seashore, 1967; Payne & Pheysey, 1971). Apparently, the more individual autonomy and discretion that is permitted and the more concern management demonstrates for its employees, the more "favorable" (that is, open, trusting, responsible) the work climate. Moreover, this relationship is particularly evident concerning individual discretion in decision making. The results of several investigations indicate that achievement-oriented and trusting climates are highly influenced by the extent to which management allows subordinates to participate in the decisions affecting their jobs (Dieterly & Schneider, 1974; Lawler, Hall, & Oldham, 1974; Likert, 1961; Litwin & Stringer, 1968).

Other structural factors that can affect climate are organization size and the position of one's job in the hierarchy. For instance, one study in a school system found that smaller organizations were consistently associated with a more open, trusting, and dependent climate, although the larger (and more bureaucratized) organizations were perceived to be the opposite (George & Bishop, 1971). Moreover, several studies have found that the location of an employee's job in the organizational hierarchy or in a particular department can affect perceptions of climate to some degree (Hall & Lawler, 1969; Schneider & Bartlett, 1968; Schneider & Hall, 1972). Thus, although research scientists in their section of an organization may see the climate as open, flexible, and dynamic, accountants working for the same firm may view its climate as rigid, routinized, and static. Such findings reinforce the notion that one organization probably has several climates, rather than just one.

The nature of the job technology employed by an organization has also been shown to influence climate. For example, a study by Burns and Stalker

(1961) found that routine technologies (such as assembly lines) tended to create rules-oriented, rigid climates where trust and creativity were low. More dynamic or changing technologies (such as aerospace engineering), on the other hand, led to more open communications, trust, creativity, and acceptance of personal responsibility for task accomplishment (see also Litwin & Stringer, 1968).

We know very little about the impact of the external environment on internal organizational climate. One might expect, however, that external events or factors that have particular relevance for employees may indeed affect climate to no small extent. For example, when economic conditions are severe and organizations are forced to lay off (or even consider laying off) some of their employees, those who remain would probably be inclined to see the climate as a threatening one, with little warmth or support and no motivation to take moderate risks (as one would expect in an achievement-oriented climate). Instead, job security would become paramount and creativity, and perhaps productivity, would suffer as people wondered who would be the next to go. Support for such a view of environment as a determinant of climate is provided in a study by Golembiewski, Mungenvider, Blumbery, Carrigan, and Mead (1971), who found that economic and market uncertainties had detrimental effects on perceived openness of climate.

Finally, several investigators have indicated that the policies and practices of management can have a major bearing on climate. For example, it has been shown that managers who provide their subordinates with more feedback, autonomy, and task identity contribute to a significant degree to the creation of an achievement-oriented climate, where members feel more responsible for the attainment of organizational and group objectives (Lawler et al., 1974; Litwin & Stringer, 1968; Marrow et al., 1967; Schneider & Bartlett, 1968). On the other hand, where management emphasized standardized procedures, rules, and job specialization, the resulting climate was not found to lead to the acceptance of responsibility, creativity, or feelings of competence. In other words, it appears that management behavior towards employees, as reflected in the policies and practices that are implemented, does represent a major input into at least certain aspects of climate (such as achievement-orientation). In fact, based on their own research, Litwin and Stringer concluded that management or leadership style represented the single most important determinant of organizational climate.

In summary, the available evidence is consistent with the model outlined in Exhibit 1, particularly insofar as structure and management policies and practices are concerned. Such factors apparently represent major determinants of climate in work settings and, as such, represent important areas of management concern. If climate is related to performance and job satisfaction, then it is incumbent upon managers to consider those variables that can affect climate if changes are to be made that will ultimately contribute to organizational goal attainment. Here again, it becomes apparent that effective managers must exhibit the capacity to recognize clearly the interrelationships between major sets of organizational variables (structure and climate, for example) and to be able to respond to the particular needs of a given organization if they are to contribute to organizational success.

OUTCOMES OF CLIMATE

We now turn to a consideration of the consequences or outcomes of variations in organizational climate. Our focus here will be primarily on individual rather than organization-wide outcomes because of the paucity of information concerning the latter. The two most widely investigated outcomes in this regard are job satisfaction and job performance.

Available evidence indicates that a clear positive relationship exists between climate and job satisfaction. In particular, it has been found that more consultative, open, employee-centered climates are generally associated with more positive job attitudes (Frederickson, 1966; Friedlander & Margulies, 1969; Kaczka & Kirk, 1968; LaFollette & Sims, 1975). Such findings have emerged among a wide range of samples in a variety of institutional areas. Although the magnitude of the relationships between climate and satisfaction is not overly large (indicating that other factors also contribute significantly to overall satisfaction), the findings are consistently in the predicted direction. Thus, it appears that satisfaction on the job results to at least some extent from the manner in which managers show concern for and seek advice and participation from their subordinates. When employees feel that they are an integral part of the organization and that their superiors take a personal interest in their welfare, it is not surprising that they will experience higher degrees of job satisfaction.

The relationship between climate and job performance appears to be somewhat more complex. In a major investigation of this relationship, Litwin and Stringer (1968) concluded that authoritarian climates, in which decision making is centralized and employee behavior is governed largely by rules and standardized procedures, led not only to low productivity but also resulted in low satisfaction and creativity and negative attitudes toward the work group. An affiliative climate, on the other hand, in which good interpersonal relations among employees were stressed, generally led to high job satisfaction, positive attitudes toward the work group, and moderate creative behavior; job performance still remained low. Only in the achievement-oriented climate, where emphasis was placed on goal attainment, were both creative behavior and productivity high. The achievement climate also led to high job satisfaction, positive group attitudes, and high achievement motivation levels. More recent findings by Steers (1975; 1976) are consistent with these findings.

It has also been shown that employee-centered climates, with open communications, mutual support, and decentralized decision making, generally lead to increased employee performance, reduced turnover, lower manufacturing costs, and reduced training time (Frederickson, 1966; Friedlander & Greenberg, 1971; Hand, Richards, & Slocum, 1973; Marrow et al., 1967). When these findings are compared with those reviewed above, a picture emerges in which the most favorable climate for both production and satisfaction is generally one that emphasizes *both* employee achievement and employee consideration. That is, we can generally conclude that one way for managers to facilitate effectiveness is to bring about a climate that stresses the importance of goal attainment while at the same time encouraging mutual support, cooperation, and participation on the activities that contribute to goal attainment.

Although creating an achievement-oriented, employee-centered climate may facilitate the desired outcomes, however, it certainly does not guarantee them. Instead, it is also important to look at how the emerging climate interacts with the personal characteristics of employees (for example, needs, abilities, goals) as they jointly affect performance and satisfaction. If employees genuinely are not motivated to perform (perhaps because they see no relationship between performance and rewards) or if they lack the abilities to accomplish their tasks, the impact of climate on performance would be lessened. On the other hand, when the climate is such that it stimulates the achievement motive and provides a vehicle for the satisfaction of a variety of important employee needs, then the contribution of climate to performance and satisfaction would be expected to be substantial (Downey, Hellriegel, & Slocum, 1975; Pritchard & Karasick, 1973; Schneider & Bartlett, 1968; Steers, 1976).

In summary, climate does indeed represent an important influence on performance and satisfaction. This relationship is apparently enhanced by the creation of a climate that emphasizes achievement and consideration for employees. [Although research generally confirms the relationship between variations in climate and both performance and satisfaction, a few studies have indicated that climate has a much more profound influence on satisfaction than on performance (LaFollette & Sims, 1975; Lawler et al., 1974; Pritchard & Karasick, 1973).] Moreover, initial findings suggest that some personal characteristics (for example, individual need strengths) interact with certain climate dimensions to jointly affect various outcomes. These findings suggest that personal needs, goals, and values must be consistent with—or at least compatible with—the prevailing work environment if desired outcomes are to be maximized. Finally, the general magnitude of the relationships across the various studies suggests a more complex process than current research has demonstrated. It seems probable, therefore, to conclude that variables other than the ones encompassed in our partial model also affect performance and satisfaction.

CLIMATE AS AN INTERVENING VARIABLE

We now come to the third part of the model: the intervening nature of organizational climate. Little is known about this aspect of climate that would guide us in evaluating this facet of the model directly. However, indirect evidence (reviewed above) has demonstrated that several organizational factors (such as structure, managerial style) have an impact on climate and that climate, in turn, influences to no small degree resulting satisfaction and performance. In addition to this indirect evidence, two investigations have been carried out that specifically examined the potential intervening nature of climate. In one study, managerial policies and practices were altered (primarily by replacing top management in a small manufacturing firm), resulting in significant changes in climate (Marrow et al., 1967). The new management, which was described as being more people-oriented, created a climate in which employees felt more important and more responsible for their own actions. The new management style was also seen as being more supportive of employees and more participative on decisions affecting employees' jobs. As a result of such changes in climate, performance increased while manufacturing costs, training time, and turnover all declined.

In the second study, interest focused on how climate served to mediate the impact of both structure and management style on performance and satisfaction (Lawler et al., 1974). In general, it was found that climate was a strong mediator of the relationship between management style and the outcome variables; that is, style influenced climate, which, in turn, influenced performance and satisfaction. In addition, climate also appeared to moderate the impact of organizational structure on the same two outcome variables, although the magnitude of this second relationship was not as high as that concerning management style.

In general, then, the available evidence tends to support the proposed model of the role of climate in organizational dynamics. As shown in Exhibit 1, we may conclude that various organizational and environmental characteristics influence the emerging climate of a particular organization and that this climate, along with employee characteristics, influences performance and satisfaction. These outcomes, then, contribute to possible changes in the existing climate and in managerial practices in the form of a feedback loop. Moreover, it would appear that the most desirable climate from the standpoint of meeting both organizational and personal objectives would be one that emphasized both goal achievement and employee consideration. Such a climate represents an exchange relationship between employees and their employer where both work together to satisfy mutual objectives in the long run.

CRITICISM OF THE CLIMATE CONSTRUCT

Due to the rather controversial nature of the climate construct, it would be inappropriate to leave our discussion here without considering several criticisms that have been advanced recently relative to it. Such criticisms should be kept in mind when evaluating the role and utility of climate in modern organizations.

First, several researchers have noted that climate is exclusively a *perceptual* phenomenon. That is, the climate of a given organization is that which an employee *thinks* it is. As Johannesson (1971, p. 30) has pointed out, "there are potentially as many climates as there are people in the organization." Such criticism raises the possibility that organizations do not, in fact, have a climate at all, but rather only a set of feelings and perceptions on the part of the various employees that may change from time to time and from employee to employee (Guion, 1973).

Some have argued that this problem is easily overcome by collecting "objective" data concerning climate instead of using the more subjective self-report data of employees. In other words, we should measure the degree of employee participation, for example, by having trained observers rate quantitatively the extent to which employees have autonomy in decision making. By doing so, it is argued, managers would be more able to determine the precise nature of the climate with which they are dealing. Unfortunately, the problem is not so simple. As pointed out by Vroom (1964) and others, people tend to behave based on how they see their environment and not necessarily how it really is. If employees see their company as employee-centered, they will respond accordingly—even if the company is in fact authoritarian. In other words, whether or not perceptions are accurate, we would still expect them to strongly influence actual behavior. This fact, combined with the knowledge that there may be as many climates as there are employees, significantly increases the difficulty incurred by managers in trying to deal with climate as it relates to desired outcomes.

A second criticism of climate focuses on the relationship between climate and job satisfaction. Specifically, it has been suggested by several people (for example, Johannesson, 1973) that climate is redundant with respect to satisfaction. In short, questions have been raised as to whether or not climate and satisfaction really represent the same thing. Although theoretically climate represents objective descriptions of the work environment and satisfaction represents affective response (that is, positive or negative feelings) to the environment, it is suggested that when the two variables are measured both represent affective responses. LaFollette and Sims (1975) dispute this contention, however, and offer evidence in support of their position. They found that, although climate and satisfaction were related, the two constructs were not related to performance in the same fashion. If the two variables do not relate in a similar fashion to third variables, it is difficult to defend the contention that they do, in fact, represent the same construct. It was concluded by LaFollette and Sims (1975, p. 276) that assertions of redundancy between climate and satisfaction seem "premature and judgmental, and . . . contrary to the prevailing evidence to date."

As noted by Hellriegel and Slocum (1974), the primary criticisms of the climate construct appear to be directed not at the construct itself but rather at how the construct has been operationalized and measured in organizational settings. However weak the measures, our current understanding of organizational dynamics indicates clearly that there is "something" within an organization's cultural milieu that creates conditions that are conducive to certain attitudes and patterns of behavior. Whether these forces are called climate or something else, their existence and influence on organizational behavior must be recognized and dealt with if organizations are to become more effective in pursuing their chosen objectives.

REFERENCES

Burns, T., & Stalker, G. M. *The management of innovation*. London: Tavistock, 1961.

Campbell, J. P., & Beaty, E. E. Organizational climate: Its measurement and relationship to work group performance. Paper presented at the annual meeting of the American Psychological Association, Washington, D.C., 1971.

Campbell, J. P., Bownas, E. A., Peterson, N. G., & Dunnette, M. D. *The measurement of organizational effectiveness: A review of relevant research and opinion*. San Diego, Calif.: Naval Personnel Research and Development Center, 1974.

Dieterly, D., & Schneider, B. The effect of organizational environment on perceived power and climate: A laboratory study. *Organizational Behavior and Human Performance*, 1974, **11**, 316–37.

Downey, H. K., Hellriegel, D., & Slocum, J. W., Jr. Congruence between individual needs, organizational climate, job satisfaction and performance. *Academy of Management Journal*, 1975, **18**, 149–54.

Forehand, G., & Gilmer, B. Environmental variation in studies of organizational behavior. *Psychological Bulletin*, 1964, **22**, 361–82.

Frederickson, N. Some effects of organizational climates on administrative performance (ETS RM-66-21). Princeton, N.J.: Educational Testing Service, 1966.

Friedlander, R., & Greenberg, S. Effect of job attitudes, training and organizational climates on performance of the hard-core unemployed. *Journal of Applied Psychology*, 1971, **55**, 287–95.

Friedlander, F., & Margulies, N. Multiple impacts of organizational climate and individual value systems upon job satisfaction. *Personnel Psychology*, 1969, **22**, 171–83.

George, J., & Bishop, L. Relationship of organizational structure and teacher personality characteristics to organizational climate. *Administrative Science Quarterly*, 1971, **16**, 467–76.

Golembiewski, R., Mungenvider, R., Blumbery, A., Carrigan, S., & Mead, W. Changing climate in a complex organization: Interactions between a learning design and an environment. *Academy of Management Journal*, 1971, **14**, 465–83.

Guion, R. M. A note on organizational climate. *Organizational Behavior and Human Performance*, 1973, **9**, 120–25.

Hall, D. T., & Lawler, E. E., III. Unused potential in research and development organizations. *Research Management*, 1969, **12**, 339–76.

Halpin, A., & Croft, D. *The organizational climate of schools*. U.S. Office of Education, Department of Health, Education, & Welfare, Washington, D. C., 1962.

Hand, H., Richards, M., & Slocum, J. Organizational climate and the effectiveness of a human relations training program. *Academy of Management Journal*, 1973, **16**, 185–95.

Hellriegel, D., & Slocum, J. W., Jr. Organizational climate: Measures, research, and contingencies. *Academy of Management Journal*, 1974, **17**, 225–80.

James, L. R., & Jones, A. P. Organizational climate: A review of theory and research. *Psychological Bulletin*, 1974, **81**, 1096–1112.

Johannesson, R. E. Job satisfaction and perceptually measured organizational climate: Redundancy and confusion. *Proceedings*, Eastern Academy of Management, 1971, pp. 27–37.

Johannesson, R. E. Some problems in the measurement of organizational climate. *Organizational Behavior and Human Performance*, 1973, **10**, 118–44.

Kaczka, E., & Kirk, R. Managerial climate, work groups, and organizational performance. *Administrative Science Quarterly*, 1968, **12**, 252–71.

LaFollette, W. R., & Sims, H. P., Jr. Is satisfaction redundant with organizational climate? *Organizational Behavior and Human Performance*, 1975, **13**, 257–78.

Lawler, E. E., III, Hall, D. T., & Oldham, G. R. Organizational climate: Relationship to organizational structure, process, and performance. *Organizational Behavior and Human Performance*, 1974, **11**, 139–55.

Likert, R. *New patterns in management*. New York: McGraw-Hill Book Company, 1961.

Litwin, G., & Stringer, R. *Motivation and organizational climate*. Cambridge, Mass.: Harvard University Press, 1968.

Marrow, A., Bowers, D., & Seashore, S. *Management by participation*. New York: Harper & Row, 1967.

Payne, R. L., & Pheysey, D. G. Stern's Organizational Climate Index: A reconceptualization and application to business organizations. *Organizational Behavior and Human Performance*, 1971, **6**, 77–98.

Payne, R. L., & Pugh, D. Organizational structure and climate. In M. D. Dunnette (Ed.), *Handbook of industrial and organizational psychology*. Chicago: Rand McNally & Company, 1976.

Pritchard, R., & Karasick, B. The effects of organizational climate on managerial job performance and job satisfaction. *Organizational Behavior and Human Performance*, 1973, **9**, 110–19.

Schneider, B., & Bartlett, C. Individual differences and organizational climate 1: The research plan and questionnaire development. *Personnel Psychology*, 1968, **21**, 323–34.

Schneider, B., & Hall, D. T. Toward specifying the concept of work climate: A study of Roman Catholic Diocesan priests. *Journal of Applied Psychology*, 1972, **56**, 447–56.

Steers, R. M. Task-goal attributes, *n* achievement, and supervisory performance. *Organizational Behavior and Human Performance*, 1975, **13**, 392–403.

Steers, R. M. Factors affecting job attitudes in a goal-setting environment. *Academy of Management Journal*, 1976, **19**, 6–16.

Taylor, J. C., & Bowers, D. *Survey of organizations: A machine scored standardized instrument*. Ann Arbor: University of Michigan, Institute for Social Research, 1972.

Vroom, V. H. *Work and motivation*. New York: John Wiley & Sons, Inc., 1964.

The Supervisor as "Motivator":
His Influence on Employee Performance
and Satisfaction

Edwin A. Locke[1]

It is widely recognized that supervisors can influence the "motivation" of their subordinates. However, the precise nature and mechanism of this influence (and its limitations) have not been clearly identified in the literature.

There are two interrelated aspects of motivation that must be considered in this context: satisfaction with the job (and supervisor) and work performance. Let us first consider how a supervisor can influence employee satisfaction.

THE SUPERVISOR AND SATISFACTION

An individual's degree of satisfaction with his job reflects the degree to which he believes (explicitly or implicitly) that it fulfills or allows the fulfillment of his job values (Locke, 1969a). It follows that a supervisor can influence employee satisfaction by facilitating or blocking subordinate value attainment. There are two broad categories of job values over which a supervisor may have some control.[2]

1 Task Values Individuals have different degrees of intrinsic interest in different task activities. If a supervisor has any options with respect to task assignment, he can facilitate satisfaction by assigning workers tasks which they enjoy doing. Within limits he may even allow or promote restructuring of the job to increase its interest to the worker.

Furthermore, most employees have implicit or explicit performance goals in their work (quantity, quality, time limits, deadlines, quotas, budgets, etc.). Work goal achievement has been found repeatedly to be a major source of satisfaction on the job (Friedlander, 1964; Herzberg, 1966; Hoppock, 1935; Wernimont, 1966). A supervisor can either help or hinder his subordinates in the pursuit of their work goals and will affect their satisfaction accordingly.

A study by Hahn of several hundred Air Force officers found that when actions of superiors were judged to be responsible for causing a "good day on the job" these actions entailed work goal facilitation 33% of the time. When the actions of superiors were seen as causing a "bad day on the job," it was

From B. M. Bass, R. Cooper, & J. A. Haas (eds.), *Managing for accomplishment*, 57–67. Copyright 1970 by Lexington Books, D. C. Heath and Company. Reprinted by permission.

[1]Preparation of this paper was facilitated by Grant No. 10542 from the American Institutes for Research.

[2]These categories are discussed in more detail in Locke (1970).

perceived to be caused by work goal blockage or hindrance 56% of the time.[3]

There is a crucial respect in which a supervisor has more *potential* for causing employee dissatisfaction than for causing satisfaction, as implied by the above data. A supervisor can help an employee attain his work goals but he cannot attain them for him. The subordinate himself must be at least *one* of the agents responsible for the accomplishment of his own work. However, the converse is not necessarily true. A supervisor can hinder or prevent goal attainment regardless of the actions of his subordinates—such as by refusing to give him the permission, or time, or facilities, money, helpers, authority, etc., needed to achieve them.

Similarly a supervisor can allow a subordinate to work on tasks which the subordinate finds intrinsically interesting but he cannot create interests himself. However, a supervisor can prevent an employee from working on tasks which interest him without the latter's consent or participation.

The above should not be taken as supporting Herzberg's (1966) theory of motivation as it now stands. Herzberg claims that supervision can cause only dissatisfaction with the job whereas task factors such as achievement can only cause satisfaction. Herzberg's supporting data, however, are virtually meaningless since his classification system confuses *events* (what happened) with *agents* (who made it happen). When incidents reported as causing satisfaction and dissatisfaction on the job are classified separately as to agent and event, it is found that the *same class of events* (namely, task-related events, such as achievement and failure) are seen as the main cause of *both* satisfaction and dissatisfaction, but that *different agents* are judged to be predominantly responsible for these events. The self is typically given credit for good day events (successes) while others (supervisors) are usually blamed for bad day events (failures). It must be added that the latter relationship is only statistical. Some individuals do blame themselves for failures and give others (partial) credit for their successes.[4] Furthermore defensiveness could lead them to underestimate their actual degree of responsibility for failures.

2 Non-Task Values   A supervisor also administers rewards and punishments for performance, both directly and indirectly. He has direct control, for example, over the giving of praise and recognition for a job well done and of criticism for a poor job. By recommending or criticizing an employee to his own superiors, a supervisor can indirectly affect a subordinate's chances for raises and promotions.

Employees value supervisors who have influence in the organization (Mann and Hoffman, 1960; Pelz, 1952). Influence is what enables a supervisor to gain values for his subordinates from the organization, e.g., raises, promotions, time off, good equipment, better working conditions, etc.

---

[3]These percentages were computed from unpublished data supplied by Clifford P. Hahn of the American Institutes for Research.

[4]Much of this data has been gathered and analyzed by Joseph Schneider of the University of Maryland in partial fulfillment of his Master's degree. The unpublished data of Hahn, some of which were referred to above, yielded similar results.

Rosen (1969) found that two of the characteristics which best differentiated between the most and least-liked foremen in a furniture factory were the ability to "get things for his men" and to "organize the work." Since these workers were on a piece-rate incentive, there is little doubt that money was one thing a good foreman could help his men to get, especially if he knew how to organize the work.

There is an interconnection between task and non-task values in that the former can be a means to attaining the latter. By helping his subordinates attain high production, solve problems, and do competent work, a supervisor can help them make high earnings and gain promotions.

If an employee sees his supervisor as instrumental in gaining him important job values, he will not only like the job, he will like the supervisor as well. Employees also like supervisors who are "pleasant," "considerate" and "friendly" (Mann and Hoffman, 1960; Rosen, 1969; Vroom, 1964). At first glance these traits might seem to be completely unrelated to the idea of functional utility; but a closer look suggests otherwise. A supervisor may be described as unpleasant and inconsiderate because in the past he has blocked value attainment by subordinates or he projects the kind of personality that *would* do so if given the chance. An unfriendly supervisor is typically one who does not acknowledge or reward work or who unjustly condemns or punishes marginal work or who looks as though he might do these things.

Individuals also like people who are like themselves, with whom they have important traits in common. This too can be interpreted (partly) in functional terms. A supervisor who values the same things as his subordinates, for example, is more likely to be of benefit to them than one whose values are opposite to theirs.

The functional (utility) implications of being pleasant or having values similar in one's subordinates do not exhaust the reasons a supervisor could be liked. Individuals may value each other not only as a means to an end but as ends in themselves. The value in such a case is associated with the person rather than in what he can do for you. One can respond to a supervisor *qua* individual as well as *qua* supervisor.

A discussion of the reasons individuals value those who respond to them as persons is beyond the scope of this paper.[5] Suffice it to say that this principle is probably less crucial to an understanding of supervisor-subordinate relationships than is the principle of functional utility.

THE SUPERVISOR AND PERFORMANCE

A subordinate who likes his supervisor will desire to approach (interact with) him, to seek or take his advice, and/or (within limits) to do favors for him. There is nothing inherent in the fact of liking a supervisor, however, that necessarily leads to high production.

[5]The basic psychological principle involved here was first discussed, to the author's knowledge, in N. Branden's "Self-esteem and Romantic Love," *The Objectivist,* 1967, VI, No. 12, 1–8.

A subordinate who dislikes his supervisor will want to avoid him, or persuade him to change his ways, or file a grievance against him or refuse to do favors for him or possibly quit the job altogether. There is nothing inherent in fact of disliking, however, that necessitates low production, although such a reaction is possible (if the employee sees it as an appropriate means of "getting even" with the supervisor and thinks he can get away with it).

In short there is no causal connection—divorced from the individuals' other values, his beliefs and expectations and his understanding of the total job— between satisfaction with the job or supervisor and productivity (for a detailed theoretical discussion of this issue, see Locke, 1969b).

I have argued previously (Locke, 1970) that the most direct motivational determinant of an individual's performance on the job is his specific performance goal or intention (Locke, Cartledge and Knerr, 1970). Let us now discuss the relationship between goals and performance.

GOAL CONTENT AND PERFORMANCE

Goals and values have two major attributes: content and intensity (Rand, 1966). The attribute of content pertains to the *what*, to the nature of the activity or end sought. The attribute of intensity pertains to the *how much*, to the importance of the goal or value in the individual's value hierarchy.

The effects of goal content are most fundamentally directive in nature. This is true with respect to both mental and physical action. If a (normal) individual's purpose is to think about how he will spend his next pay check, he will think of that topic rather than about something else. A man whose goal is to walk across the street will walk there rather than to another location.

This is not to claim that all goals lead to the activity or end specified by the goal. To attain a desired goal successfully an individual must possess sufficient ability and mental health and be given sufficient opportunity. Goal attainment may be prevented by lack of knowledge, capacity or determination on his part, or by external interference. Furthermore, goal conflicts may render efficacious action and efficacious thinking impossible.

Even when action is abortive or unsuccessful, it is typically set in motion and guided by some goal or intention. For example, a person who accidentally hits a shot out of bounds in tennis still intended to hit the ball, even if it did not go where he wanted it to go. Further, the degree of discrepancy between the place he intended to hit the ball and the place he did hit it might be only a matter of inches.

If an individual's goal is long range, or difficult, or complex, he may have to establish a series of *subgoals* and develop a coordinated *plan of action* in order to reach it. The *means* by which a goal can be attained may not be known initially and may have to be discovered. For this reason goals may indirectly stimulate creativity and the seeking of new knowledge. This was illustrated in a study done at General Electric by Stedry and Kay (1964; see also a study by

Chaney, 1969). A group of foremen were assigned quantitative production goals with respect to both quantity and quality. Some of these who were assigned difficult goals, rather than simply exhorting their subordinates to work harder, made an effort to discover the causes of and to eliminate unproductive time. The latter procedure generally led to greater performance improvement than the former. A laboratory study by Eagle and Leiter (1964) found that individuals who had an intention to memorize certain materials did so more effectively if they developed a specific learning plan than if they simply "tried" to learn the material.

The pursuit of any goal requires action, whether it be mental or physical, and action requires effort. A second function of goal content, which is necessarily entailed in the directive function, is the *regulation of energy expenditure*. Different goals require different amounts of effort. More energy is required to run the marathon than to walk across the room; more mental concentration is needed to write a book than to write one's name. Typically, a person mobilizes an amount of energy that is appropriate to the perceived difficulty of the goal sought. For instance, Bryan and Locke (1967) found that when people are given different amounts of time to complete the same task, those given the shorter time limits worked faster than those given longer time limits. These authors noted that:

> Because the phenomenon [of adjusting effort level to the perceived difficulty of the task] is so much a part of our everyday life, it is often taken for granted and we do not always think about it consciously. But it can become particularly salient when errors of . . . [judgment] occur. For example, if a weight lifter's weights are secretly replaced by wooden blocks painted to resemble the real weights, he will be likely to jerk [them] right through the ceiling [on his first try] . . . (Bryan and Locke, 1967, p. 259).

Goal importance may also influence direction and level of effort by affecting the individual's degree of commitment to his goal. The greater a man's commitment, the longer he should persist at a task in the face of failure, fatigue and stress.

Most studies of the effect of goals have focused on the relationship of goal content to performance on simple laboratory tasks. (See Locke, 1968a, for a review.) In these tasks, performance could be influenced relatively directly by effort or choice; the acquisition of new knowledge and long range planning were not required. Two categories of studies have stressed the directing function of goals, while two other categories have stressed the energizing as well as the directing effects of goal content. Studies representative of each category are described below:

1 Intentions and Response Selection   In these studies, typified by the work of Dulany (1962, 1968) and Holmes (1967), subjects had to select (on each trial) one of a number of possible verbal responses and were "rewarded" or "punished" according to their choices. It was found that the individual's intentions with respect to responses were correlated as high as .94 with his actual responses, regardless of the "reinforcements" given for performance.

2   Intentions and Task Choice   In another group of studies subjects could choose, on each trial, the difficulty of the task they would work on and were offered various monetary incentives for succeeding at their chosen task. Correlations in the .70's and .80's were typically found between intentions with respect to future choices and actual choice distributions regardless of incentive condition (Locke, Bryan and Kendall, 1968).

3   Qualitatively Different Goals and Performance   Two types of studies fall into this category. In one, all subjects worked on the same task but tried to minimize or maximize their scores on different performance dimensions on different trials. The interest was in whether subjects could modify their scores on the various dimensions as intended. Locke and Bryan (1969) found that subjects could lower their scores on two dimensions of automobile driving performance as intended 100% of the time. They also found that subjects committed fewer errors on an addition task when trying to minimize errors than when trying to maximize the number of problems correct.

In the second subcategory of studies only one performance dimension was involved (number of correct answers). Individuals trying to do "as well as possible" on a task were compared to those trying to reach difficult, quantitative goals. Subjects trying for the latter type of goal typically outperformed subjects trying for the former (Locke, 1968a; Mace, 1935). One effect of trying for specific hard goals is to prevent performance from dropping below one's previous best level more often than is the case with the abstract goal of "do your best" (Locke and Bryan, 1966).

4   Goal Level and Performance Level (Output)   Most studies of the effects of goals have focused on the relationship between the individual's level of aspiration (quantitative goal level) and his performance level on a task. A consistent finding has been that high, difficult goals lead to a higher level of performance than moderate or easy goals. The evidence thus far suggests that, provided the individual has the requisite ability, there is a positive, linear relationship between goal level and performance level (Locke, 1968a). No claim is made that this linear relationship would hold across all possible levels of goal difficulty; some goals are obviously impossible to reach.

Let us now summarize the findings with respect to goals and performance. The results indicate that on simple repetitive tasks goals usually lead to the behavior specified by the goal, or else to outcomes correlated with the intended goal. Goals guide performance by determining the direction or content of mental and/or physical action; as a result they energize action by leading the individual to mobilize the effort necessary to attain the goal.

It should be stressed that the above findings presuppose that the individual has really *accepted* (is actually committed to) the goal(s) in question. This issue will be discussed further below.

Considerable research evidence indicates that the effects of external incentives on action depend on the goal and intentions individuals set in response to them. For it has been found in a number of laboratory studies that: (a) when incentives do affect behavior, they also affect goals and intentions; (b) when differential goal-setting is controlled or partialled out, there is no relationship of incentive condition to choice behavior or to level of performance; and (c) partialling out or controlling incentive differences does not vitiate the relationship between goals and performance.

These findings are most well documented with respect to three external incentives: *money* (Locke, Bryan and Kendall, 1968); *feedback* regarding overall task performance ("knowledge of results," Locke, 1967, 1968b; Locke and Bryan, 1968, 1969; Locke, Cartledge and Koeppel, 1968); and so-called *verbal reinforcement* (Dulany, 1962, 1968; Holmes, 1967). There is some documentation with respect to three other incentives: *instructions* (Eagle, 1967; Locke, Cartledge and Koeppel, 1968); *time limits* (Bryan and Locke, 1967); and *participation* (Locke, 1968a; Meyer, Kay and French, 1965). Experimental evidence is still lacking for incentives such as competition, and praise and reproof. (See Locke, 1968a, for a theoretical analysis of these incentives.)

GOAL COMMITMENT AND PERFORMANCE

Very few studies have explored either the determinants or the effects of goal commitment. Theoretically, strength of goal commitment should be a function of the importance of the goal in the individual's value hierarchy. The importance of goal attainment should be a function of the importance of success and efficacy as ends in themselves and of the importance of the other values to which goal attainment leads (money, promotion) and/or of the disvalues which it avoids (lack of money, being fired, losing a promotion, etc.).

One procedure that may promote goal commitment is *participation* in the goal-setting process. A possible explanation for this is that making an overt agreement to strive for or attain a certain goal engages a value not previously engaged. It implies an overt test of one's *integrity:* (loyalty to one's stated values in action). Participation may also allow subordinates to choose tasks or methods of work which interest and challenge them to a greater extent than would be the case if supervisors made assignments on their own.

HOW THE SUPERVISOR INFLUENCES GOAL-SETTING

The implication of the above is that in order for a supervisor to influence the job performance of his subordinates, he must implicitly or explicitly influence the goals they set and/or their commitment to them. There are at least four ways he can try to do this, differing in degree of directness:

1 Instructions The simplest and most direct method is to tell the subordinate what is expected of him on the job, not only with respect to the content of the work but also with respect to the speed or proficiency level desired.

The effect of instructions on performance will depend upon their content and upon whether or not the employee *accepts* them. When goals assigned by a supervisor (or experimenter) are judged to be unreasonable or impossible, they may be rejected by the individual and easier ones (overtly or covertly) substituted in their place. (See Stedry, 1960; Stedry and Kay, 1964.) Or barring this, the individual may leave the situation (e.g., job) altogether.

Whether or not an employee accepts an assigned goal will depend upon other factors as well: whether he believes the demands to be morally legitimate; whether he sees them as just in the context of his ability and the nature of the job; whether the goal is congruent with his personal preferences; his desire to help or hurt the supervisor; the anticipated outcomes of compliance and non-compliance; the amount of "pressure" exerted, etc.

A study at General Electric by Miller (1965) found that direct instructions to production workers to improve the quality of their work sometimes resulted in an initial improvement in performance; but this improvement was not maintained unless it was made clear that punishments (loss of income) would be administered for noncompliance with this request. In other words, the instructions had to be backed up by (the threat of) sanctions for them to be effective.

2 Participation Rather than assigning goals to employees a supervisor may let his subordinates participate in the goal-setting process. It was mentioned earlier that such a procedure can enhance goal commitment by engaging the employee's integrity and his personal interests.

It must be stressed, however, that simply using the *method* of participation does not guarantee either increased job satisfaction or higher productivity as is often implied by advocates of the "human relations" approach to motivation. Its outcome will depend on such factors as: (a) the particular values of the employees (whether they want to participate); (b) the nature of the job (size of work group; need for rapid decisions); and (c) the content of the participation sessions. (The first factor is discussed in Vroom, 1964.)

With respect to the last point, a close examination of several experimental studies of participation by Locke (1968a) revealed that employees in the "participation" conditions were typically urged to aim for higher production goals than they had previously whereas employees in the "control" conditions received no such request. In other studies, supervisors of participation groups were given special training designed to correct their weaknesses and deficiencies (Chaney, 1969). In a recent field study Meyer, Kay and French (1965) found that the goals employees set (or failed to set) during conferences with their supervisors had far more influence on subsequent performance than participation as such.

3 Rewards and Punishments Money is the most widely used incentive in industry. Not only is it an incentive to take a job or to switch jobs, it may be an incentive to perform competently on the job. The effectiveness of money in motivating effective performance will depend on such things as: (a) how the incentive system is structured; (b) what the employee believes it is given (or withheld) for; and (c) the degree to which he values money (in comparison to other rewards).

Many years ago F. W. Taylor (1911) argued that ordinary piece-rate incentives were not optimal for increasing production because workers often failed to set their output goals as high as they were capable of achieving. A key element of Taylor's Scientific Management system was to assign workers specific (and high) production quotas and to make monetary bonuses (and remaining on the job) contingent upon their attaining these quotas. Locke, Bryan and Kendall (1968) found this method to produce higher output than offering piece-rate incentives alone in some recent laboratory studies.

Other studies have shown that the effectiveness of monetary incentives depends upon the degree to which workers believe that high effort and high performance will "pay-off" in higher earnings and on the degree to which they value money (Georgopoulos, Mahoney and Jones, 1957; Porter and Lawler, 1968). Dalton (in Whyte, 1955) found that incentive pay was not very effective for workers who valued the approval of their coworkers (which was contingent upon moderate to low production) more than maximizing earnings.

Praise and criticism are also commonly used incentives, but their effects on subsequent performance are far from simple. (See the review article by Kennedy and Willcatt, 1964.) A crucial determinant of the effect of praise is the subordinate's interpretation of what it *means*. If he interprets it to mean that his performance is adequate and he sees no other values to be gained by increasing production, it may be an incentive to maintain his present level of production. If the employee understands it to mean that if he keeps up the good work, he may be promoted, and he values promotion, it may encourage him to work even harder. If praise is seen as being insincere or manipulative in its intent, it may have no effect at all (or a negative effect) on performance.

The effects of criticism on subsequent performance also depend upon how the employee interprets it. For example, an individual may deliberately refrain from performance improvement after being criticized because it would be an implicit admission that the criticism was justified—which admission would threaten his self-esteem. Meyer, Kay and French (1965) found criticism by supervisors to inhibit subsequent performance improvement by subordinates because it produced defensiveness rather than constructive goal-setting.

Even if a man believed criticism to be justified (in the sense that performance was not up to the minimum requirements of the job), he would become apathetic if he believed that further improvement was totally impossible. Many individuals have implicit deterministic premises (to the effect that certain abilities are impossible to acquire or that certain things are not open to their understanding or that certain personality traits or emotional reactions are beyond their control). Such premises can severely undercut a man's motivation to persist in the face of difficulty and failure.

Under certain conditions, criticism will spur a man on to greater efforts. The necessary conditions for such an effect are not yet known but they would no doubt include: (a) the individual's belief that his performance was, in fact, inadequate; (b) his conviction that he can do better; and (c) his desire to improve.

4 Setting an Example   Some results reported by Cooper[6] suggest a relatively indirect way that supervisors may influence subordinate goals. He found positive correlations between the degree to which supervisors were rated by their superiors as "task oriented" and high work quality and low absence on the part of subordinates. Although several interpretations of these correlations are possible, the one suggested by Cooper is that employees implicitly adopted (some of) the work attitudes and standards of their supervisors.

It is not difficult to imagine how this might happen. A supervisor who comes late, who is frequently absent, who takes numerous coffee breaks, who is careless in his work and unconcerned with its outcome could not help but convey to a subordinate that the work is not very important, that he does not value it, and that low standards of performance are acceptable. (The employee may adopt such standards without any explicit purpose to do so, in the same way that a student may absorb or adopt the values of his teachers.)

Similarly, a supervisor who loves his job, who sets himself high standards and works to achieve them, who creates an atmosphere of dedication to hard work and high standards may help instill similar attitudes in his subordinates.

SATISFACTION WITH SUPERVISION AND PRODUCTIVITY

The foregoing discussion indicated that high production (ability and knowledge being equal) was the result of setting high or hard work goals. It follows that the supervisor with high producing subordinates (ability being equal) will be the one whose subordinates set and attain high goals.

A supervisor may try to achieve high production by direct instructions backed up by threats of punishment. If employees see no short-run alternative to accepting hard goals, high production may result. But such high production would be accompanied by low satisfaction with the job and with supervision to the degree that: (a) employees fail to achieve fully their hard goals or goal attainment fails to gain them just extrinsic rewards; (b) supervisors interfere with their task performance, and/or (c) the supervisors' pressures are perceived as excessive and/or illegitimate. In the long run, of course, such actions as the above may lead to increased absences, grievances and turnover, depending on the workers' other values and the job market (Locke, 1970).

Alternatively, a supervisor could offer positive incentives (monetary bonuses, recognition, increased responsibility) to employees who reached (or approached) high work goals. If high goals were set as a result, high production could occur. To the extent that the supervisor was perceived as helping his subordinates to achieve these goals and as giving just rewards for success, he

---

[6]R. Cooper, "Task-oriented Leadership and Subordinate Response," in B. M. Bass, R. Cooper, & J. A. Haas (Eds.) *Managing for accomplishment*. Lexington, Mass.: Heath-Lexington, 1970.

would be liked. In this case, production and satisfaction with supervision would both be high.

An individual could also set high work goals on his own and not interact with his supervisor at all. If the person preferred to be left alone, high production would be accompanied by indifference toward the supervisor.

Many other patterns are possible. A supervisor might reward his subordinates for low production. If they actually set low goals as a result and personally valued low productivity, high satisfaction with supervision would accompany low production. Or, if a supervisor prevented his employees from achieving their work goals through interference and harassment, and then penalized them for their failure, low satisfaction and low production would result.

To repeat, there is no direct causal relationship between satisfaction with supervision (on the job) and productivity. The two effects are the results of different causes. Production level, to the degree that it is affected by motivation, depends (in the short run) upon the production goal the individual is actually trying for, *regardless of how or why he chose that goal.* (The reasons why an employee has a particular goal, of course, have long range implications, since these factors determine how susceptible the goal is to change and under what conditions.) Satisfaction with supervision depends (in the short run) upon the degree to which the supervisor is perceived as achieving or helping the employee to achieve his work and other goals *regardless of the particular content (level) of these goals.*[7]

Satisfaction is an outcome of action and an incentive to further action; thus it fulfills a crucial motivational function. But a man's emotional reactions do not determine the content of his values, or his goals, or his knowledge, or his thinking (Locke, 1970).

CONCLUSION

A supervisor can contribute in important ways to an individual's satisfaction and his motivation to produce. But there is a fundamental respect in which he cannot "motivate" an employee. To perform adequately on a job, an individual must choose to pursue values; he must gain the knowledge needed to perform the work; he must set goals; he must expend effort. A supervisor can help fulfill an employee's desires but he cannot provide him with desires; he can offer him new knowledge or the chance to gain new knowledge but he cannot force him to learn; he can assign goals to a worker but he cannot compel him to accept those goals. In short, a supervisor's influence is *limited*; what he can accomplish depends not simply on his own actions but on the values, knowledge, and goals of his subordinates.

To put the matter more generally, man is not a passive responder to external

[7]One important qualification must be made to this statement. If an individual's goals and values are irrational (anti-life) or if he has value conflicts, he will not derive the same quality or duration or intensity of pleasure from attaining them as compared with rational values. This issue is discussed in Locke (1969a) based on Rand (1964).

stimulation but an active agent. He is not an effect of the actions of others but a cause in his own right.

REFERENCES

Bryan, J. F., & Locke, E.A. Parkinson's law as a goal-setting phenomenon. *Organizational Behavior and Human Performance*, 1967, **2**, 258–275.

Chaney, F.B. Employee participation in manufacturing job design. *Human Factors*, 1969, **11**, 101–106.

Dulany, D. E., Jr. The place of hypotheses and intentions: An analysis of verbal control in verbal conditioning. In C. W. Eriksen (Ed.), *Behavior and awareness*, Durham, N.C.: Duke University Press, 1962, 102–129.

Dulany, D. E., Jr. Awareness, rules and propositional control: A confrontation with S-R behavior theory. In D. Horton and T. Dixon (Eds.), *Verbal behavior and general behavior theory*, Englewood Cliffs, N.J.: Prentice-Hall, 1968, 340–348.

Eagle, M. N. The effect of learning strategies upon free recall. *American Journal of Psychology*, 1967, **80**, 421–425.

Eagle, M., & Leiter, E. Recall and recognition in intentional and incidental learning. *Journal of Experimental Psychology*, 1964, **68**, 58–63.

Friedlander, F. Job characteristics as satisfiers and dissatisfiers. *Journal of Applied Psychology*, 1964, **48**, 388–392.

Georgopoulos, B. S., Mahoney, G. M., & Jones, N. W. A path-goal approach to productivity. *Journal of Applied Psychology*, 1957, **41**, 345–353.

Herzberg, F. *Work and the nature of man*. Cleveland: World Publishing Company, 1966.

Holmes, D. S. Verbal conditioning or problem solving and cooperation? *Journal of Experimental Research in Personality*, 1967, **2**, 289–294.

Hoppock, R. *Job satisfaction*. New York: Harper, 1935.

Kennedy, W. A., & Willcatt, H. C. Praise and blame as incentives. *Psychological Bulletin*, 1964, **62**, 323–332.

Locke, E. A. The motivational effects of knowledge of results: Knowledge or goal-setting? *Journal of Applied Psychology*, 1967, **51**, 324–329.

Locke, E. A. Toward a theory of task motivation and incentives. *Organizational Behavior and Human Performance*, 1968, **3**, 157–189. (a)

Locke, E. A. The effects of knowledge of results, feedback in relation to standards and goals on reaction time performance. *American Journal of Psychology*, 1968, **81**, 566–574. (b)

Locke, E. A. What is job satisfaction? *Organizational Behavior and Human Performance*, 1969, **4**, 309–336. (a)

Locke, E. A. Job satisfaction and job performance: A theoretical analysis. Unpublished manuscript. Washington, D.C.: American Institutes for Research, 1969. (b)

Locke, E. A. Studies of the relationship between satisfaction, goal-setting, and performance. *Organizational Behavior and Human Performance*, 1970, **5**, 135–158.

Locke, E. A., & Bryan, J. F. Cognitive aspects of psychomotor performance: The effects of performance goals on level of performance. *Journal of Applied Psychology*, 1966, **50**, 286–291.

Locke, E. A., & Bryan, J. F. Goal-setting as a determinant of the effect of knowledge of score on performance. *American Journal of Psychology*, 1968, **81**, 398–406.

Locke, E. A., & Bryan, J. F. Knowledge of score and goal difficulty as determinants of work rate. *Journal of Applied Psychology*, 1969, **53**, 59–65.

Locke, E. A., Bryan, J. F., & Kendall, L.M. Goals and intentions as mediators of the effects of monetary incentives on behavior. *Journal of Applied Psychology*, 1968, **52**, 104–121.

Locke, E. A., Cartledge, N., & Koeppel, J. The motivational effects of knowledge of results: A goal-setting phenomenon? *Psychological Bulletin*, 1968, **70**, 474–485.

Locke, E. A., Cartledge, N., & Knerr, C. Studies of the relationship between satisfaction, goal-setting and performance. *Organizational Behavior and Human Performance*, 1970, **5**, 135–158.

Mace, C. A. Incentives: Some experimental studies. Industrial Health Research Board (Great Britain), 1935, Report No. 72.

Mann, F. C., & Hoffman, L. R. *Automation and the worker*. New York: Holt, 1960.

Meyer, H. H., Kay, E., & French, J. R. P., Jr. Split roles in performance appraisal. *Harvard Business Review*, 1965, **43**, 123–129.

Miller, L. The use of knowledge of results in improving the performance of hourly operators. General Electric Co., Behavioral Research Service, 1965.

Pelz, D. C. Influence: A key to effective leadership in the first-line supervisor. *Personnel*, 1952, **3**, 209–217.

Porter, L. W., & Lawler, E. E. *Managerial attitudes and performance*. Homewood, Ill.: R. D. Irwin, 1968.

Rand, A. The objectivist ethics. In A. Rand (Ed.), *The virtue of selfishness*. New York: Signet, 1964, 13–35.

Rand, A. Concepts of consciousness. *The Objectivist,* 1966, **5**(9), 1–8.

Rosen, N. A. *Leadership change and work-group dynamics*. Ithaca, N.Y.: Cornell University Press, 1969.

Stedry, A. C. *Budget control and cost behavior*. Englewood Cliffs, N.J.: Prentice-Hall, 1960.

Stedry, A. C., & Kay, E. The effects of goal difficulty on performance. General Electric Co., Behavioral Research Service, 1964.

Taylor, F. W. *The principles of scientific management*. New York: Harper, 1911.

Vroom, V. H. *Work and motivation*. New York: Wiley, 1964.

Wernimont, P. F. Intrinsic and extrinsic factors in job satisfaction. *Journal of Applied Psychology*, 1966, **50**, 41–50.

Whyte, W. F. *Money and motivation.* New York: Wiley, 1955.

QUESTIONS FOR DISCUSSION

1 What relationships exist between group aspiration level and individual performance on the job?
2 What motivationally relevant functions do groups serve in organizations?
3 What role do group processes play in equity theory?
4 How can group processes influence motivation to perform, as analyzed using expectancy/valence theory?
5 What does achievement motivation theory say about the influence of the group on employee motivation?

6 What influence might the nature of the task have on the effectiveness of participative decision making?

7 If you were a manager trying to increase performance among your subordinates, would you use group or individual incentives? Why?

8 What is the role of group norms in the motivational process?

9 Under what circumstances would you expect competition among group members for rewards to result in higher performance than cooperation? When might cooperation lead to higher performance than competition? Explain why such differences can occur.

10 Do you feel the concept of organizational climate is a useful one for managers? Explain.

11 What is the general process by which a particular climate is created?

12 Is it fair to say that there is a universally desirable climate for all work organizations? Why or why not?

13 How might organizational climate affect expectancies and/or valences under expectancy/valence theory?

14 Why have some people argued that supervisory style is the most important climate factor? Do you agree or disagree?

15 Specifically, how might climate affect work behavior?

16 How might different climates (a) be more effective in terms of job performance; and (b) be more satisfying for employees?

17 How does the concept of organizational climate relate to equity theory?

18 Is the concept of organizational climate really different from the sum of employees' various job attitudes?

19 How are the concepts of leadership and supervision related? How are these two concepts different?

20 What role does leadership play in motivating employees in general?

21 Where might differing styles of leadership be equally effective under different circumstances? Give examples.

22 Critically evaluate Locke's comments on the role of the supervisor as motivator. Are his comments universally applicable or only relevant under particular circumstances?

23 Assume you are a middle manager in an organization. What type of leader or supervisor do you honestly believe you would be?

Chapter 9

Job Design Factors in Motivation

Early managerial approaches to job design (discussed in Chapter 1) focused primarily on attempts to simplify an employee's required tasks insofar as possible in order to increase production efficiency. It was felt that, since workers were largely economically motivated, the best way to maximize output was to reduce tasks to their simplest forms and then reward workers with money on the basis of units of output—a piece-rate incentive plan. In theory, such a system would simultaneously satisfy the primary goals of both the employees and the company. Evidence of such a philosophy can be seen in the writings of Taylor and other scientific management advocates.

This approach to simplified job design reached its zenith from a technological standpoint in assembly-line production techniques such as those used by automobile manufacturers. (Piece-rate incentive systems have been largely omitted here, however.) On auto assembly lines, in many cases, the average length of "work cycle" (that is, the time allowed for an entire "piece" of work) ranges between 30 seconds and 1½ minutes. This means that workers would repeat the same task on an average of at least 500 times per day. Such a technique, efficient as it may be, is not without its problems, however. As workers have become better educated and more organized, they have begun demanding more from their jobs. Not only is this demand shown in recurrent requests for shorter hours and increased wages, it is also shown in several undesirable behavior patterns, such as higher turnover, absenteeism, dissatisfaction, sabotage, and so on.

While organizational psychologists and practicing managers have long sought ways of reducing such undesirable behavior, only recently have they begun to rigorously study it in connection with the task performed. As pointed out by Porter (1969, p. 415), ". . . at best, prior to the last few years, task factors have been underemphasized, if considered at all, in attempts to reveal the motivational and cognitive explanations for job behaviors." This omission has been largely alleviated by a series of recent investigations into ways to attack the problem of job redesign as it affects motivation, performance, and satisfaction. Somewhat surprisingly, many of the new "solutions" bear striking resemblance to the old craft-type of technology of pre-assembly-line days.

Considerable evidence has come to light recently in support of positive behavioral and attitudinal consequences of such job enrichment efforts (Ford, 1969; Lawler, 1973; Maher, 1971; Myers, 1970; Special Task Force, HEW, 1973; Vroom, 1964). In general, such efforts have tended to result in (1) significantly reduced turnover and absenteeism; (2) improved job satisfaction; (3) improved quality of products; and (4) some, though not universal, improvements in productivity and output rates. On the negative side, the costs often associated with such programs are generally identified as (1) increased training time and expense and (2) occasionally, additional retooling costs where dramatic shifts toward group assembly teams have been instituted.

A major thrust of many of the contemporary efforts at job redesign research represents a blend of two central factors. On the one hand, researchers are concerned with studying the motivational processes associated with redesigning jobs. On the other hand, they are equally concerned with the practical applications of such knowledge as it affects attempts to improve the work environment. In this sense, investigations in this area have generally represented applied research in the truest sense.

HERZBERG'S TWO-FACTOR THEORY

One of the earliest researchers in the area of job redesign as it affected motivation was Frederick Herzberg (Herzberg, Mausner, & Snyderman, 1959). Herzberg and his associates began their initial work on factors affecting work motivation in the mid-1950s. Their first effort entailed a thorough review of existing research to that date on the subject (Herzberg, Mausner, Peterson, & Capwell, 1957). Based on this review, Herzberg carried out his now famous survey of 200 accountants and engineers from which he derived the initial framework for his theory of motivation. The theory, as well as the supporting data, was first published in 1959 (Herzberg, Mausner, & Snyderman, 1959) and was subsequently amplified and developed in a later book (Herzberg, 1966).

Based on his survey, Herzberg discovered that employees tended to describe satisfying experiences in terms of factors that were intrinsic to the content of the job itself. These factors were called "motivators" and included such variables as achievement, recognition, the work itself, responsibility, advancement, and growth. Conversely, dissatisfying experiences, called "hygiene" factors, largely resulted from extrinsic, non-job-related factors, such as company policies, salary, coworker relations, and supervisory style (see Exhibit 1). Herzberg argued, based on these results, that eliminating the causes of

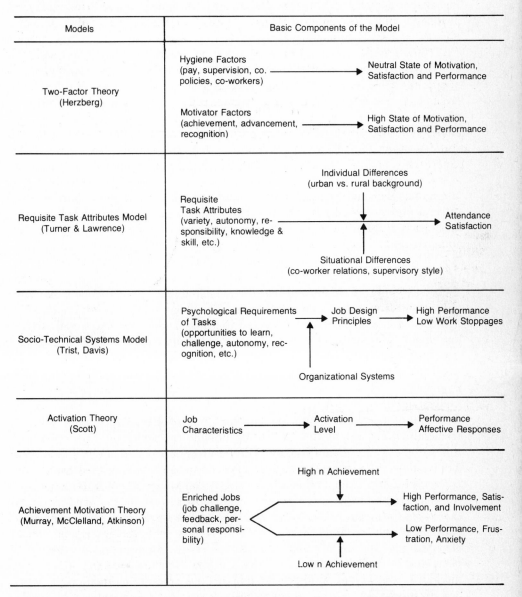

Exhibit 1 Conceptual models of the motivational properties of tasks. *(From R. M. Steers and R. T. Mowday. The motivational properties of tasks.* Academy of Management Review, *1977,* **2,** *645– 658. Reprinted by permission.)*

dissatisfaction (through hygiene factors) would not result in a state of satisfaction. Instead, it would result in a neutral state. Satisfaction (and motivation) would occur only as a result of the use of motivators.

The implications of this model of employee motivation are clear: motivation can be increased through basic changes in the nature of an employee's job (that is, job enrichment). Thus, jobs should be redesigned to allow for increased challenge and responsibility, opportunities for advancement and personal growth, and recognition.

Herzberg differentiated between what he described as the older and less effective job redesign efforts, known as job *enlargement*, and the newer concept of job *enrichment* (Paul, Robertson, & Herzberg, 1969). The term "job enlargement," as used by Herzberg, means a *horizontal* expansion of an employee's job, giving him or her more of the same kinds of activities but not altering the necessary skills. "Job enrichment," on the other hand, means a *vertical* expansion of an employee's job, requiring an increase in the skills repertoire which ostensibly leads to increased opportunities. As Paul et al. (1969, p. 61) described it, job enrichment "seeks to improve both efficiency and human satisfaction by means of building into people's jobs, quite specifically, a greater scope for personal achievement and recognition, more challenging and responsible work, and more opportunity for individual advancement and growth."

Since its inception, Herzberg's theory has been subject to several troubling criticisms. For example, King (1970) noted that the model itself has five different theoretical interpretations and that the available research evidence is not consistent with any of these interpretations. This suggests that Herzberg failed to provide an unambiguous statement of the model. Second, the model ignores individual differences and assumes that job enrichment benefits all employees. Research evidence suggests this assertion is in error. Finally, research has also failed to support the existence of two independent factors (motivators and hygiene factors). Even so, the model has made significant contributions to our understanding of motivation at work.

One of the most significant contributions of Herzberg's work was the tremendous impact it had on stimulating thought, research, and experimentation on the topic of motivation at work. This contribution should not be overlooked. Before 1959, little research had been carried out in the area of *work* motivation (with the notable exception of Viteles, 1953, and Maier, 1955), and the research that did exist was largely fragmentary. Maslow's work on the need hierarchy theory and Murray, McClelland, and Atkinson's work on achievement motivation theory were largely concerned with laboratory-based findings or clinical observations, and neither had seriously addressed the problems of the workplace at that time. Herzberg filled this void by specifically calling attention to the need for increased understanding of the role of motivation in work organizations.

Moreover, he did so in a systematic manner and in language that was easily understood by a large body of managers. He advanced a theory that was simple to grasp, based on some empirical data, and—equally important—offered specific action recommendations for managers to improve employee motivational levels. In doing so, he forced organizations to examine closely a number of possible misconceptions concerning motivation. For example, Herzberg argued that money should not necessarily be viewed as the most potent force on the job. Moreover, he stated that other "context" factors in addition to money which surround an employee's job (such as fringe benefits and supervisory style) should not be expected to markedly affect motivation either. He advanced a strong case that managers must instead give considerable attention to a series of "content" factors (such as opportunities for achievement, recognition, and advancement) that have an important bearing on behavior. According to Herzberg, it is these content factors, and not money or other context factors, that are primarily related to work motivation. These contributions are often overlooked in the heated debates over the validity of the empirical data behind the theoretical formulations.

Herzberg, in addition, probably deserves a good deal of credit for acting as a stimulus to other researchers who have advocated alternative theories of work motivation. A multitude of research articles have been generated as a result of the so-called "Herzberg controversy." Some of these articles (e.g., Bockman, 1971; Whitset & Winslow, 1967) strongly support Herzberg's position, while others (e.g., House & Wigdor, 1967; Vroom, 1964) seriously question the research methodology underlying the theory. Such debate is healthy for any science. The serious student of motivation should consider Herzberg's theory—just as any other theory—to be one attempt at modeling work behavior. As such, the theory should be dissected and/or modified in a continuing effort to develop comprehensive and accurate predictors of human behavior on the job. In other words, it appears that a fruitful approach to this "controversial" theory would be to learn from it that which can help us to develop more improved models, rather than to accept or reject the model totally.

ADDITIONAL EARLY MODELS OF JOB DESIGN

In addition to Herzberg's model, several other early models of job design can be identified (see Exhibit 1). These are (1) the requisite task attributes model, (2) the sociotechnical systems model, (3) activation theory, and (4) achievement motivation theory. While a detailed examination of these models is beyond the scope of this chapter (see Steers and Mowday (1977) for a review), we can briefly review how these various approaches differ in their approach to the motivational properties of tasks.

The *requisite task attributes model*, proposed by Turner and Lawrence (1965) argued that an enriched job (that is, a job characterized by variety, autonomy, responsibility, etc.) would lead to increased attendance and job satisfaction. The model is similar to Herzberg's in that it viewed job enrichment as a motivating variable. It differed from Herzberg's in that Turner and Lawrence included absenteeism as a dependent variable. Moreover, Turner and Lawrence acknowledged the existence of two sets of important moderators in the job scope-outcome relationship. First, it was found in their study that workers from urban settings were more satisfied with low-scope jobs than were workers from rural settings. Second, it was found that situational factors (such as supervisory style or coworker relations) also moderated the impact of job scope on satisfaction and absenteeism. This acknowledgment of the role of individual and situational variables represents a significant contribution to our understanding of the ways in which job redesign affects employee attitudes and behavior. In fact, much of the subsequent work on the topic has taken the lead from the work of Turner and Lawrence.

A second and popular model, advanced by Eric Trist and Lou Davis, is known as the *sociotechnical systems model*. This model suggests that an appropriate starting point for understanding job design is to consider the psychological requirements of tasks in order for them to be motivating. These principles include the need for a job to provide (1) reasonably demanding content, (2) an opportunity to learn, (3) some degree of autonomy or discretion in decisions affecting one's job, (4) social support and recognition, and (5) a feeling that one's job leads to a desirable future.

Based on these principles, job design principles are derived which suggest, in brief, that enriched jobs meet these psychological requirements. As a consequence, enriched jobs would be expected to lead to such outcomes as high job performance and low labor stoppages. An important aspect of the sociotechnical model is that it clearly acknowledges the role of the social context (or organizational system) in which job redesign attempts are made. That is, the model argues that such changes cannot be successfully implemented without acknowledging and taking into account various social and organizational factors that also influence people's desire to perform on the job (e.g., reward system, work group norms, supervisory relations, etc.). Hence, the sociotechnical systems approach attempts to be a truly systematic (that is, comprehensive) approach to work design.

Activation theory focuses on the physiological processes involved in job redesign (Scott, 1966). Activation, defined as the degree of excitation of the brain stem reticular formation, has been found in laboratory experiments to have a curvilinear relationship to performance. Research has demonstrated that performance suffers at very low or very high levels of activation. Hence, jobs that are dull or repetitive may lead to low levels of performance because they fail to activate. On the other hand, more enriched jobs should lead to a state of activation with a resulting increase in performance. While many questions remain concerning the empirical support for activation theory, it does suggest how job design can affect employees physiologically, a relationship ignored in previous research.

Finally, the *achievement motivation model* proposed by Murray (1938) and refined by McClelland and Atkinson (see Chapter 2) also examines the process by which changes in the job situation influence behavior. The focus of this approach, however, is on employee personality, specifically, an employee's need for achievement. In essence, achievement motivation theory posits that employees with a high need for achievement will be more likely to respond favorably to enriched jobs than will employees with a low need for achievement. Enriched jobs cue, or stimulate, the achievement motive, typically leading to higher levels of performance, involvement, and satisfaction. For low need achievers, however, an enriched job may be threatening; that is, the low need achiever may feel overchallenged. As a result, he or she may experience increased frustration, anxiety, and lower performance. Recent findings by Steers and Spencer (1977) support this conclusion.

In conclusion, we have seen that several models of job design exist. Each model tends to focus on one aspect of the job situation (e.g., personality, social context, physiological response, etc.) and, as such, makes a useful contribution by expanding our understanding of the relevant variables that must be included in a comprehensive model of work design.

OVERVIEW

The readings that follow attempt to present a more comprehensive approach to job design than those reviewed above. Initially, J. Richard Hackman examines in some detail the concept of job redesign, with particular attention to job design as a change strategy. The Job Characteristics Model is presented, along with supporting evidence. Moreover, several principles for enriching jobs are reviewed. Finally, guidelines for instituting job redesign are suggested.

Second, Pehr Gyllenhammar, the president of Volvo, reviews the application of job redesign principles at Volvo. The special problems surrounding the early redesign attempts are examined. Moreover, cultural differences between various countries that may impinge on the success of job redesign efforts are mentioned. Finally, several guidelines that have proved useful at Volvo in their change efforts are reviewed.

Third, Mitchell Fein, an industrial engineer, takes a more pessimistic view of current job redesign efforts. It is argued that most successes represent special cases that are not easily replicated in run-of-the-mill factories and businesses. Several limitations on job enrichment are noted. The issue of management and union support for such efforts is discussed. Finally, Fein points to several alternatives to job design.

Finally, a second selection by Hackman examines the future of job redesign in the 1980s. Our progress to date is summarized. Next, two divergent courses of future action are identified, along with opinions concerning where the field is headed.

REFERENCES AND SUGGESTED ADDITIONAL READINGS

Bockman, V. M. The Herzberg controversy. *Personnel Psychology*, 1971, **24**, 155–189.

Dowling, W. Job redesign on the assemblyline: Farewell to blue-collar blues? *Organizational Dynamics*, 1973, **2**(2), 51–67.

Fitzgerald, T. H. Why motivation theory doesn't work. *Harvard Business Review*, 1971, **49**(4), 37–44.

Ford, R. N. *Motivation through the work itself*. New York: American Management Association, 1969.

Foulkes, F. *Creation of more meaningful work*. New York: American Management Association, 1969.

Grigaliunas, B. S., & Herzberg, F. Relevance in the test of motivator-hygiene theory. *Journal of Applied Psychology*, 1971, **55**, 73–79.

Hackman, J. R. Nature of the task as a determiner of job behavior. *Personnel Psychology*, 1969, **22**, 435–444.

Hackman, J. R., & Lawler, E. E., III. Employee reactions to job characteristics. *Journal of Applied Psychology*, 1971, **55**, 259–286.

Hackman, J. R., & Oldham, G. R. Development of the job diagnostic survey. *Journal of Applied Psychology*, 1975, **60**, 159–170.

Hackman, J. R., & Oldham, G. R. Motivation through the design of work: Test of a theory. *Organizational Behavior and Human Performance*, 1976, **16**, 250–279.

Hackman, R. C. *The motivated working adult*. New York: American Management Association, 1969.

Herzberg, F. The motivation-hygiene concept and problems of manpower. *Personnel Administration*, 1964, **27**(1), 3–7.

Herzberg, F. *Work and the nature of man*. Cleveland: World, 1966.

Herzberg, F., Mausner, B., Peterson, R. O., & Capwell, D. F. *Job attitudes: Review of research and opinion*. Pittsburgh: Psychological Services of Pittsburgh, 1957.

Herzberg, F., Mausner, B., & Snyderman, B. *The motivation to work*. New York: Wiley, 1959.

House, R. J., & Wigdor, L. A. Herzberg's dual-factor theory of job satisfaction and motivation. *Personnel Psychology*, 1967, **20**, 369–390.

Hulin, C. L., & Blood, M. R. Job enlargement, individual differences, and worker responses. *Psychological Bulletin*, 1968, **69**, 41–55.

King, N. Clarification and evaluation of the two-factor theory of job satisfaction. *Psychological Bulletin*, 1970, **74**, 18–31.

Lawler, E. E., III. *Motivation in work organizations*. Monterey, Calif.: Brooks/Cole, 1973.

Lawler, E. E., Hackman, J. R., & Kaufman, S. Effects of job design: A field experiment. *Journal of Applied Social Psychology*, 1973, **3**, 46–62.

Locke, E. A. In defense of defense mechanisms: Some comments on Bobbitt and Behling. *Journal of Applied Psychology*, 1972, **56**, 297–298.

Maher, J. R. (Ed.). *New perspectives in job enrichment*. New York: Van Nostrand Reinhold, 1971.

Maier, N. R. F. *Psychology in industry*, 2d ed. Boston: Houghton Mifflin, 1955.

Miner, J. B., & Dachler, H. P. Personnel attitudes and motivation. In P. H. Mussen & M. R. Rosenzweig (Eds.), *Annual review of psychology*. Palo Alto, Calif.: Annual Reviews, Inc., 1973.

Murray, H. A. *Explorations in personality*. New York: Oxford University Press, 1938.

Myers, M. S. *Every employee a manager*. New York: McGraw-Hill, 1970.

Paul, W. J., Robertson, K. B., & Herzberg, F. Job enrichment pays off. *Harvard Business Review*, 1969, **47**(2), 61–78.

Porter, L. W. Effects of task factors on job attitudes and behavior. *Personnel Psychology*, 1969, **22**, 415–418.

Reif, W. E., & Luthans, F. Does job enrichment really pay off? *California Management Review*, 1972, **14**, 30–37.

Rush, H. M. F. *Job design for motivation*. New York: The Conference Board, Report No. 515, 1971.

Schneider, J., & Locke, E. A. A critique of Herzberg's incident classification system and a suggested revision. *Organizational Behavior and Human Performance*, 1971, **6**, 441–457.

Schwab, D. P., & Cummings, L. L. A theoretical analysis of the impact of task scope on employee performance. *Academy of Management Review*, 1976, **1**, 23–35.

Schwab, D. P., DeVitt, H. W., & Cummings, L. L. A test of the adequacy of the two-factor theory as a predictor of self-report performance effects. *Personnel Psychology*, 1971, **24**, 293–303.

Scott, W. E. Activation theory and task design. *Organizational Behavior and Human Performance*, 1966, **1**, 3–30.

Special Task Force to the Secretary of Health, Education, and Welfare. *Work in America*. Cambridge, Mass.: MIT, 1973.

Steers, R. M., & Mowday, R. T. The motivational properties of tasks. *Academy of Management Review*, 1977, **2**, 645–658.

Steers, R. M., & Spencer, D. G. The role of achievement motivation in job design. *Journal of Applied Psychology*, 1977, **62**, 472–479.

Turner, A. N., & Lawrence, P. R. *Industrial jobs and the worker*. Boston: Harvard University, Graduate School of Business Administration, 1965.

Viteles, M. S. *Motivation and morale in industry*. New York: Norton, 1953.

Vroom, V. H. *Work and motivation*. New York: Wiley, 1964.

Waters, L. K., & Roach, D. The two-factor theories of job satisfaction: Empirical tests for four samples of insurance company employees. *Personnel Psychology*, 1971, **24**, 697–705.

Waters, L. K., & Waters, C. W. An empirical test of five versions of the two-factor theory of job satisfaction. *Organizational Behavior and Human Performance*, 1972.

Whitset, D. A., & Winslow, E. K. An analysis of studies critical of the motivation-hygiene theory. *Personnel Psychology*, 1967, **20**, 391–416.

Work Design

J. Richard Hackman

Every five years or so, a new behavioral science "solution" to organizational problems emerges. Typically such a solution is first tried out—with great success—in a few forward-looking organizations. Then it is picked up by the management journals and the popular press and spreads across the country. And finally, after a few years, it fades away as disillusioned managers, union leaders, and employees come to agree that the solution really does not solve much of anything.

Reprinted from J. R. Hackman and J. L. Suttle (eds.), *Improving life at work*. Santa Monica, Calif.: Goodyear Publishing Company, 1976, 96–104, 128–133, 136–140, 148–162. Reprinted by permission.

It looks as if the redesign of work is to be the solution of the mid-1970s. The seeds of this strategy for change were planted more than two decades ago, with the pioneering research of Charles Walker and Robert Guest (1952), Frederick Herzberg and his associates (Herzberg, Mausner, and Snyderman, 1959; Herzberg, 1966), Louis Davis (1957, 1966), and a few others. Successful tests of work redesign were conducted in a few organizations and were widely reported. Now, change programs involving work redesign are flooding the nation, stories on "how we profited from job enrichment" are appearing in management journals, and the labor community is struggling to determine how it should respond to the tidal wave that seems to be forming (Gooding, 1972).

The question of the moment is whether the redesign of work will evolve into a robust and powerful strategy for organizational change—or whether, like so many of its behavioral science predecessors, it will fade into disuse as practitioners experience failure and disillusionment in its applications. The answer is by no means clear.

Present evidence regarding the merits of work redesign can be viewed as optimistic or pessimistic, depending on the biases of the reader. On the one hand, numerous published case studies of successful work redesign projects show that work redesign can be an effective tool for improving both the quality of the work experience of employees and their on-the-job productivity. Yet it also is true that numerous failures in implementing work redesign have been experienced by organizations around the country—and the rate of failure shows no sign of diminishing. Reif and Luthans (1972), for example, summarize a survey, conducted in the mid-1960s, in which only four of forty-one firms implementing job enrichment described their experiences with the technique as "very successful." Increasingly, other commentators are expressing serious doubts about whether job enrichment is really as effective as it has been cracked up to be (Fein, 1974; Gomberg, 1973; Hulin and Blood, 1968).

Unfortunately, existing research findings and case reports are not very helpful in assessing the validity of the claims made by either the advocates or the skeptics of work redesign. In particular, an examination of the literature cited in Hackman (1975a) leads to the following conclusions:

1   Reports of work redesign successes tend to be more evangelical than thoughtful; for example, little conceptualizing is done that would be useful either as a guide to implementation of work redesign in other settings or as a theoretical basis for research on its effects.

2   The methodologies used in evaluating the effects of changes in work design often are weak or incomplete. Therefore, findings reported may be ambiguous and open to alternative explanations.

3   Although informal sources and surveys suggest that the failure rate for work redesign projects is moderate to high, few documented analyses are available of projects that failed. This is particularly unfortunate because careful analyses of failures often are among the most effective tools for exploring the

applicability and the consequences of this or any other organizational change strategy.

4 Most published reports focus almost exclusively on assessing the positive and negative effects of specific changes in work content. Conclusions are then drawn about the general worth of work redesign as a change strategy. Yet there is an *interaction* between the content of the changes and the organizational context in which they are installed; identical job changes may have quite different effects in different organizational settings (or when installed using different processes). Existing literature has little to say about the nature or dynamics of such interactions.

5 Rarely are economic data (that is, direct and indirect dollar costs and benefits) analyzed and discussed when conclusions are drawn about the effects of work redesign projects, even though many such projects are undertaken in direct anticipation of economic gains.

In sum, it appears that despite the abundance of writing on the topic, there is little definite information about why work redesign is effective when it is, what goes wrong when it is not, and how the strategy can be altered to improve its general usefulness as an approach to personal and organizational change.

This paper attempts to advance current understanding about such questions. It reviews what is known about how the redesign of work can help improve life in organizations and attempts to identify the circumstances under which the approach is most likely to succeed. It reviews current practice for planning and installing work redesign and emphasizes both the pitfalls that may be encountered and the change strategies that have been shown to be especially effective. And, at the most general level, it asks whether this approach to organizational change is indeed worth saving, or whether it should be allowed to die.

WHAT IS WORK REDESIGN?

Whenever a job is changed—whether because of a new technology, an internal reorganization, or a whim of a manager—it can be said that work redesign has taken place. The present use of the term is somewhat more specialized. Throughout this paper, work redesign is used to refer to any activities that involve the alteration of specific jobs (or interdependent systems of jobs) with the intent of increasing both the quality of the employees' work experience and their on-the-job productivity. This definition of the term is deliberately broad, to include the great diversity of changes that can be tried to achieve these goals. It subsumes such terms as *job rotation, job enrichment*, and *sociotechnical systems design*, each of which refers to a specific approach to or technique for redesigning work.

There are no simple or generally accepted criteria for a well-designed job, nor is there any single strategy that is acknowledged as the proper way to go about improving a job. Instead, what will be an effective design for one specific job in a particular organization may be quite different from the way the job should be designed or changed in another setting. There are, nonetheless, some commonalities in most work redesign experiments that have been carried out to date. Typically changes are made that provide employees with additional responsibilities for planning, setting up, and checking their own work; for making decisions about methods and procedures; for establishing their own work pace within broad limits; and sometimes for relating directly with the client who receives the results of the work. Often the net effect is that jobs which previously had been simplified and segmented into many small parts (in the interest of efficiency from an engineering perspective) are put back together again and made the responsibility of individual workers (Herzberg, 1974).

An early case of work redesign (reported by Kilbridge, 1960) is illustrative. The basic job involved the assembly of small centrifugal pumps used in washing machines. Prior to redesign, the pumps were assembled by six operators on a conveyor line, with each operator performing a particular part of the assembly. The job was changed so that each worker assembled an entire pump, inspected it, and placed his own identifying mark on it. In addition, the assembly operations were converted to a batch system in which workers had more freedom to control their work pace than they had had under the conveyor system. Kilbridge reports that after the job had been enlarged, total assembly time decreased, quality improved, and important cost savings were realized.

In another case, the responsibilities of clerks who assembled information for telephone directories at Indiana Bell Telephone Company were significantly expanded (Ford, 1973). Prior to the change, a production line model was used to assemble directory information. Information was passed from clerk to clerk as it was processed, and each clerk performed only a very small part of the entire job. There were a total of twenty-one different steps in the workflow. Jobs were changed so that each qualified clerk was given responsibility for all the clerical operations required to assemble an entire directory—including receiving, processing, and verifying all information. (For large directories, clerks were given responsibility for a specific alphabetical section of the book.) Not only did the new work arrangement improve the quality of the work experience of the employees, but the efficiency of the operation increased as well—in part because clerks made fewer errors, and so it was no longer necessary to have employees who merely checked and verified the work of others.

In recent years, work redesign increasingly has been used as part of a larger change package aimed at improving the overall quality of life and productivity of people at work. A good example is the new General Foods pet food manufacturing plant in Topeka, Kansas (Walton, 1972, 1975b). When plans were developed for the facility in the late 1960s, corporate management decided to design and manage the plant in full accord with state-of-the-art behavioral science knowledge. Nontraditional features were built into the plant from the beginning—including the physical design of the facilities, the management style, information and feedback systems, compensation arrangements, and career paths for individual employees. A key part of the plan was the organization of the work force into teams. Each team (consisting of from seven to fourteen members) was given nearly autonomous responsibility for a significant organizational task. In addition to actually carrying out the work required to complete that task, team members performed many activities that traditionally had been reserved for management. These included coping with manufacturing problems, distributing individual tasks among team members, screening and selecting new team members, and participating in organizational decision-making (Walton, 1972). The basic jobs performed by team members were designed to be as challenging as possible, and employees were encouraged to further broaden their skills in order to be able to handle even more challenging work. Although not without problems, the Topeka plant appears to be prospering, and many employees experience life in the organization as a pleasant and nearly revolutionary change from their traditional ideas about what happens at work.

The Uniqueness of Work Redesign as a Strategy for Change

The redesign of work differs from most other behavioral science approaches to changing life in organizations in at least four ways (Hackman, 1975b). Together, these four points of uniqueness make a rather compelling case for work redesign as a strategy for initiating organizational change.

1 Work Redesign Alters the Basic Relationship between a Person and What He or She Does on the Job When all the outer layers are stripped away, many organizational problems come to rest at the interface between *people* and the *tasks* they do. Frederick Taylor realized this when he set out to design and manage organizations "scientifically" at the beginning of this century (Taylor, 1911). The design of work was central to the scientific management approach, and special pains were taken to ensure that the tasks done by workers did not exceed their performance capabilities. As the approach gained credence in the management community, new and more sophisticated procedures for analyzing work methods emerged, and industrial engineers forged numerous principles of work design. In general, these principles were intended to maximize overall production efficiency by minimizing human error on the job (often accomplished by partitioning the work into small, simple segments), and by minimizing time and motion wasted in doing work tasks.

It turned out, however, that many workers did not like jobs designed according to the dictates of scientific management. In effect, the person-job relationship had been arranged so that achieving the goals of the organization (high productivity) often meant sacrificing important personal goals (the opportunity for interesting, personally rewarding work). Taylor and his associates attempted to deal with this difficulty by installing financial incentive programs intended to make workers want to work hard toward organizational goals, and by placing such an elaborate set of supervisory controls on workers that they scarcely could behave otherwise. But the basic incongruence between the person and the work remained, and people-problems (such as high absenteeism and turnover, poor quality work, and high worker dissatisfaction) became increasingly evident in work organizations.

In the past several decades, industrial psychologists have carried out a

large number of studies intended to overcome some of the problems that accompanied the spread of scientific management. Sophisticated strategies for
identifying those individuals most qualified to perform specific jobs have been
developed and validated. New training and attitude change programs have been
tried. And numerous motivational techniques have been proposed to increase
the energy and commitment with which workers do their tasks. These include
development of human relations programs, alteration of supervisory styles, and
installation of complex piece-rate and profit-sharing incentive plans. None of
these strategies have proven successful. Indeed, some observers report that
the quality of the work experience of employees today is more problematic
than it was in the heyday of scientific management (cf., *Work in America*, 1973).

Why have behavioral scientists not been more successful in their attempts
to remedy motivational problems in organizations and improve the quality of
work life of employees? One reason is that psychologists (like managers and
labor leaders) have traditionally assumed that the *work itself was inviolate*—
that the role of psychologists is simply to help select, train, and motivate people
within the confines of jobs as they have been designed by others. Clearly, it
is time to reject this assumption and to seek ways to change both people and
jobs in order to improve the fit between them.

The redesign of work as a change strategy offers the opportunity to break
out of the "givens" that have limited previous attempts to improve life at work.
It is based on the assumption that the work itself may be a very powerful
influence on employee motivation, satisfaction, and productivity. It acknowledges (and attempts to build on) the inability of people to set aside their social
and emotional needs while at work. And it provides a strategy for moving away
from extrinsic props to worker motivation and to move instead toward *internal*
work motivation that causes the individual to do the work because it interests
him, challenges him, and rewards him for a job well done.

**2 Work Redesign Directly Changes Behavior—and It Tends to Stay
Changed** People do the tasks they are given. How well they do them depends
on many factors, including how the tasks are designed. But no matter how the
tasks are designed, people do them.

On the other hand, people do *not* always behave in ways that are consistent
with their attitudes, their levels of satisfaction, or what they cognitively know
they should do. Indeed, it is now well established that one's attitudes often are
determined by the behaviors one engages in—rather than vice versa, as traditionally has been thought (Bem, 1970; Kiesler, Collins, and Miller, 1969).
This is especially true when individuals perceive that they have substantial
personal freedom or autonomy in choosing how they will behave (Steiner, 1970).

Enriching jobs, then, may have twin virtues. First, behavior is changed;
and second, because enriched jobs usually bring about increased feelings of
autonomy and personal discretion, the individual is likely to develop attitudes
that are supportive of his new on-the-job behaviors (cf. Taylor, 1971). Work
redesign does not, therefore, rely on changing attitudes first (for example,

inducing the worker to care more about the work outcomes, as in zero defects programs) and hoping that the attitude change will generalize to work behavior. Instead, the strategy is to change the *behavior*, and to change it in a way that gradually leads to a more positive set of attitudes about the work, the organization, and the self.

Moreover, after jobs are changed, it usually is difficult for workers to slip back into old ways. The old ways simply are inappropriate for the new tasks, and the structure of those tasks reinforces the changes that have taken place. Thus, one need not worry much about the kind of backsliding that occurs so often after training or attitude modification activities, especially those that occur off-site. The task-based stimuli that influence the worker's behavior are very much on-site, every hour of every day. And once those stimuli are changed, behavior is likely to stay changed—at least until the job is again redesigned.

3 Work Redesign Offers—and Sometimes Forces into One's Hands— Numerous Opportunities for Initiating Other Organizational Changes When work is redesigned in an organization so that many people are doing things differently than they used to, new problems inevitably surface and demand attention. These can be construed solely as *problems*, or they can be treated as *opportunities* for further organizational change activities. For example, technical problems are likely to develop when jobs are changed—offering opportunities to smooth and refine the work system as a system. Interpersonal issues also are likely to arise, almost inevitably between supervisors and subordinates and sometimes between peers who now have to relate to one another in new ways. These issues offer opportunities for developmental work aimed at improving the social and supervisory aspects of the work system.

Because such problems are literally forced to the surface by the job changes, all parties may feel a need to do something about them. Responses can range from using the existence of a problem to justify that "job enrichment doesn't work," to simply trying to solve the problem quickly so the work redesign project can proceed, to using the problem as a point of entry for attacking other organizational issues. If the last stance is taken, behavioral science professionals may find themselves pleasantly removed from the old difficulty of selling their wares to skeptical managers and employees who are not really sure there is anything wrong. Eventually a program of organizational change and development may evolve that addresses organizational systems and practices that, superficially at least, seem unrelated to how the work itself is designed (Beer and Huse, 1972).

4 Work Redesign, in the Long Term, Can Result in Organizations That Rehumanize Rather than Dehumanize the People Who Work in Them Despite the popular inflation of the work ethic issue in recent years, there is convincing evidence that organizations can and do sometimes stamp out part of the humanness of their members—especially people's motivations toward growth and personal development (cf. Kornhauser, 1965).

Work redesign can help individuals regain the chance to experience the kick that comes from doing a job well, and it can encourage them to once again *care* about their work and about developing the competence to do it even better. These payoffs from work redesign go well beyond simple job satisfaction. Cows grazing in the field may be satisfied, and employees in organizations can be made just as satisfied by paying them well, by keeping bosses off their backs, by putting them in pleasant work rooms with pleasant people, and by arranging things so that the days pass without undue stress or strain.

The kind of satisfaction at issue here is different. It is a satisfaction that develops only when individuals are stretching and growing as human beings, increasing their sense of competence and self-worth. Whether the creation of opportunities for personal growth is a legitimate goal for work redesign activities is a value question deserving long discussion; the case for the value of work redesign strictly in terms of *organizational* health easily can rest on the first three points discussed above. But personal growth is without question a central component of the overall quality of work life in organizations, and the impact of work redesign on the people who do the work, as human beings, should be neither overlooked nor underemphasized. . . .

DESIGNING WORK FOR INDIVIDUALS

A model specifying how job characteristics and individual differences interact to affect the satisfaction, motivation, and productivity of individuals at work has been proposed by Hackman and Oldham (1976). The model is specifically intended for use in planning and carrying out changes in the design of jobs. It is described below and then is used as a guide for discussion of diagnostic procedures and change principles that can be used in redesigning the jobs of individuals.

The Job Characteristics Model

The basic job characteristics model is shown in Figure 1. As illustrated in the figure, five core job dimensions are seen as creating three critical psychological states that, in turn, lead to a number of beneficial personal and work outcomes. The links among the job dimensions, the psychological states, and the outcomes are shown to be moderated by individual growth need strength. The major classes of variables in the model are reviewed briefly below.

Psychological States   The three following psychological states are postulated as critical in affecting a person's motivation and satisfaction on the job:

1   Experienced meaningfulness: The person must experience the work as generally important, valuable, and worthwhile.

2   Experienced responsibility: The individual must feel personally responsible and accountable for the results of the work he performs.

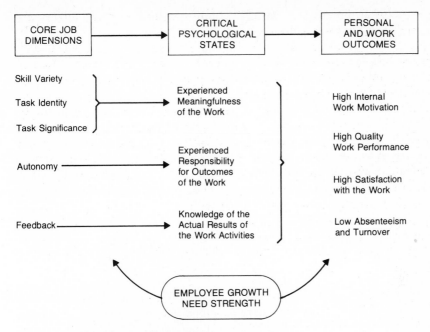

Figure 1   The job characteristics model of work motivation.

   3   Knowledge of results: The individual must have an understanding, on a fairly regular basis, of how effectively he is performing the job.

   The more these three conditions are present, the more people will feel good about themselves when they perform well. Or, following Hackman and Lawler (1971), the model postulates that internal rewards are obtained by an individual when he *learns* (knowledge of results) that he *personally* (experienced responsibility) has performed well on a task that he *cares about* (experienced meaningfulness). These internal rewards are reinforcing to the individual and serve as incentives for continued efforts to perform well in the future. When the person does not perform well, he does not experience reinforcement, and he may elect to try harder in the future so as to regain the rewards that good performance brings. The net result is a self-perpetuating cycle of positive work motivation powered by self-generated rewards. This cycle is predicted to continue until one or more of the three psychological states is no longer present, or until the individual no longer values the internal rewards that derive from good performance.

   Job Dimensions   Of the five job characteristics shown in Figure 1 as fostering the emergence of the psychological states, three contribute to the experienced meaningfulness of the work, and one each contributes to experienced responsibility and to knowledge of results.

The three job dimensions that contribute to a job's *meaningfulness* are skill variety, task identity, and task significance.

Skill variety—the degree to which a job requires a variety of different activities that involve the use of a number of different skills and talents.

When a task requires a person to engage in activities that challenge or stretch his skills and abilities, that task almost invariably is experienced as meaningful by the individual. Many parlor games, puzzles, and recreational activities, for example, achieve much of their fascination because they tap and test intellectual or motor skills. When a job draws on several skills of an employee, that individual may find the job to be of very high personal meaning even if, in any absolute sense, it is not of great significance or importance.

Task identity—the degree to which the job requires completion of a whole and identifiable piece of work—that is, doing a job from beginning to end with a visible outcome.

If an employee assembles a complete product or provides a complete unit of service, he should find the work more meaningful than if he were responsible for only a small part of the whole job, other things (such as skill variety) being equal.

Task significance—the degree to which the job has a substantial impact on the lives or work of other people, whether in the immediate organization or in the external environment.

When an individual understands that the results of his work may have a significant effect on the well-being of other people, the experienced meaningfulness of the work usually is enhanced. Employees who tighten nuts on aircraft brake assemblies, for example, are much more likely to perceive their work as meaningful than are workers who fill small boxes with paper clips—even though the skill levels involved may be comparable.

The job characteristic predicted to prompt employee feelings of personal *responsibility* for the work outcomes is autonomy, which is defined as follows:

Autonomy—the degree to which the job provides substantial freedom, independence, and discretion to the individual in scheduling the work and in determining the procedures to be used in carrying it out.

To the extent that autonomy is high, work outcomes will be viewed by workers as depending substantially on their *own* efforts, initiatives, and decisions, rather than on the adequacy of instructions from the boss or on a manual of job procedures. In such circumstances, individuals should feel strong personal responsibility for the successes and failures that occur on the job.

The job characteristic that fosters *knowledge of results* is feedback, which is defined as follows:

> Feedback—the degree to which carrying out the work activities required by the job results in the individual obtaining direct and clear information about the effectiveness of his performance.

It often is useful to combine the scores of a job on the five dimensions described above into a single index reflecting the overall potential of the job to prompt self-generated work motivation in job incumbents. Following the model diagrammed in Figure 1, a job high in motivating potential must be high on at least one (and hopefully more) of the three dimensions that lead to experienced meaningfulness, *and* high on autonomy and feedback as well. The presence of these dimensions creates conditions for all three of the critical psychological states to be present. Arithmetically, scores of jobs on the five dimensions are combined as follows to meet this criterion:

$$\begin{array}{l} \text{Motivating} \\ \text{Potential} \\ \text{Score (MPS)} \end{array} = \left[\frac{\begin{array}{c}\text{Skill}\\\text{Variety}\end{array} + \begin{array}{c}\text{Task}\\\text{Identity}\end{array} + \begin{array}{c}\text{Task}\\\text{Significance}\end{array}}{3} \right] \times \text{Autonomy} \times \text{Job Feedback}$$

As can be seen from the formula, a near-zero score of a job on either autonomy or feedback will reduce the overall MPS to near-zero; a near-zero score on one of the three job dimensions that contribute to experienced meaningfulness cannot, by itself, do so.

Individual Growth Need Strength   Growth need strength is postulated to moderate how people react to complex, challenging work at two points in the model shown in Figure 1: first at the link between the objective job dimensions and the psychological states, and again between the psychological states and the outcome variables. The first link means that high growth need individuals are more likely (or better able) to *experience* the psychological states when their objective job is enriched than are their low growth need counterparts. The second link means that individuals with high growth need strength will respond more positively to the psychological states, when they are present, than will low growth need individuals.

Outcome Variables   Also shown in Figure 1 are several outcomes that are affected by the level of self-generated motivation experienced by people at work. Of special interest as an outcome variable is internal work motivation (Lawler and Hall, 1970; Hackman and Lawler, 1971). This variable taps directly the contingency between effective performance and self-administered affective rewards. Typical questionnaire items measuring internal work motivation include: (1) "I feel a great sense of personal satisfaction when I do this job well''; (2) ''I feel bad and unhappy when I discover that I have performed poorly on this job''; and (3) ''My own feelings are *not* affected much one way or the other by how well I do on this job'' (reversed scoring).

Other outcomes listed in Figure 1 are the quality of work performance, job satisfaction (especially satisfaction with opportunities for personal growth and development on the job), absenteeism, and turnover. All of these outcomes are predicted to be affected positively by a job high in motivating potential.

Validity of the Job Characteristics Model

Empirical test of the job characteristics model of work motivation is reported in detail elsewhere (Hackman and Oldham, 1976). In general, results are supportive, as suggested by the following overview:

1 People who work on jobs high on the core job characteristics are more motivated, satisfied, and productive than are people who work on jobs that score low on these characteristics. The same is true for absenteeism, although less strongly so.

2 Responses to jobs high in objective motivating potential are more positive for people who have strong needs for growth than for people with weak growth needs. The moderating effect of individual growth need strength occurs both at the link between the job dimensions and the psychological states and at the link between the psychological states and the outcome measures, as shown in Figure 1. (This moderating effect is not, however, obtained for absenteeism.)

3 The job characteristics operate *through* the psychological states in influencing the outcome variables, as predicted by the model, rather than influencing the outcomes directly. Two anomalies have been identified, however: (a) results involving the feedback dimension are in some situations less strong than results obtained for the other dimensions (perhaps in part because individuals receive feedback at work from many sources—not just the job), and (b) the linkage between autonomy and experienced responsibility does not operate exactly as specified by the model in affecting the outcome variables (Hackman and Oldham, 1976). . . .

Principles for Enriching Jobs

The core job dimensions specified in the job characteristics model are tied directly to a set of action principles for redesigning jobs (Hackman, Oldham, Janson, and Purdy, 1975; Walters and Associates, 1975). As shown in Figure 2, these principles specify what types of changes in jobs are most likely to lead to improvements in each of the five core job dimensions, and thus to an increase in the motivating potential of the job as a whole.

Principle #1: Forming Natural Work Units   A critical step in the design of any job is the decision about how the work is to be distributed among the

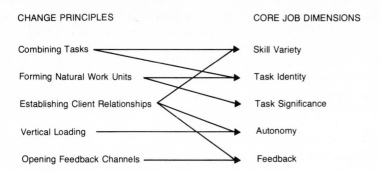

Figure 2 Principles for changing jobs.

people who do it. Numerous considerations affect that decision, such as technological constraints, level of worker training and experience, efficiency from an industrial or systems engineering perspective, and equity of individual work loads. Work designed on the basis of these factors usually is distributed among employees rationally and logically. The problem is that the logic used often does not include the needs of employees for personally meaningful work.

Consider, for example, a typing pool consisting of one supervisor and ten typists who do all the typing for one division of an organization. Jobs are delivered in rough draft or dictated form to the supervisor, who distributes them as evenly as possible among the typists. In such circumstances the individual letters, reports, and other tasks performed by a given typist in one day or week are randomly assigned. There is no basis for identifying with the work or with the person or department for whom it is performed, or for placing any personal value on it.

By contrast, creating natural units of work increases employee "ownership" of the work and improves the chances that employees will view their work as meaningful and important rather than as irrelevant and boring. In creating natural units of work, one must first identify the basic work items. In the typing pool example, that might be "pages to be typed." Then these items are grouped into natural and meaningful categories. For example, each typist might be assigned continuing responsibility for all work requested by a single department or by several smaller departments. Instead of typing one section of a large report, the individual will type the entire piece of work, with knowledge of exactly what the total outcome of the work is. Furthermore, over time the typist will develop a growing sense of how the work affects co-workers or customers who receive the completed product. Thus, as shown in Figure 2, forming natural units of work increases two of the core dimensions that contribute to experienced meaningfulness—task identity and task significance.

Because it is still important that work be distributed so that the system as a whole operates efficiently, work loads must be arranged so that they are divided equitably. The principle of natural work units simply requires that these traditional criteria be supplemented so that, as far as possible, the tasks that arrive at an employee's work station form an identifiable and meaningful whole.

Principle #2: Combining Tasks   The very existence of a pool made up entirely of persons whose sole function is typing reflects a fractionalization of jobs that sometimes can lead to such hidden costs as high absenteeism and turnover and extra supervisory time. The principle of combining tasks is based on the assumption that such costs often can be reduced by taking existing and fractionalized tasks and putting them back together again to form a new and larger module of work. At the Medfield, Massachusetts plant of Corning Glass Works, for example, the job of assembling laboratory hot plates was redesigned by combining a number of tasks that had been separate. After the change, each hot plate was assembled from start to finish by one operator, instead of going through several separate operations performed by different people.

Combining tasks (like forming natural work units) contributes in two ways to the experienced meaningfulness of the work. First, task identity is increased. The hot plate assembler, for example, can see and identify with a finished product ready for shipment, rather than with a nearly invisible junction of solder. Moreover, as more tasks are combined into a single worker's job, the individual must use a greater variety of skills in performing the job, further increasing the meaningfulness of the work.

Principle #3: Establishing Client Relationships   Jobs designed according to traditional criteria often provide workers with little or no contact with the ultimate user of their product or service. As a consequence, workers may have difficulty generating high commitment and motivation to do the job well.

By establishing direct relationships between workers and their clients, jobs often can be improved in three ways. First, feedback increases because additional opportunities are created for the employees to receive direct praise or criticism of their work outputs. Second, skill variety may increase, because of the need to develop and exercise one's interpersonal skills in managing and maintaining the relationship with the client. Finally, autonomy will increase to the degree that individuals are given real personal responsibility for deciding how to manage their relationships with the people who receive the outputs of their work.

Creating client relationships can be viewed as a three-step process: (1) identifying who the client actually is; (2) establishing the most direct contact possible between the worker and the client; and (3) establishing criteria and procedures so that the client can judge the quality of the product or service received and relay his judgments directly to the worker. Especially important (and, in many cases, difficult to achieve) is identification of the specific criteria by which the work output is assessed by the client, and ensuring that both the worker and the client understand these criteria and agree with them.

Principle #4: Vertical Loading   In vertical loading, the intent is to partially close the gap between the "doing" and the "controlling" aspects of the job.

Thus, when a job is vertically loaded, responsibilities and controls that formerly were reserved for management are given to the employee as part of the job. Among ways this might be achieved are the following:

- Giving job incumbents responsibility for deciding on work methods and for advising or helping to train less experienced workers;
- Providing increased freedom in time management, including decisions about when to start and stop work, when to take breaks, and how to assign work priorities;
- Encouraging workers to do their own troubleshooting and to manage work crises, rather than calling immediately for a supervisor;
- Providing workers with increased knowledge of the financial aspects of the job and the organization, and increased control over budgetary matters that affect their work.

Vertically loading a job inevitably increases *autonomy*. And, as shown in Figure 1, this should lead to increased feelings of personal responsibility and accountability for the work outcomes.

Principle #5: Opening Feedback Channels   In virtually all jobs there are ways to open channels of feedback to individuals, to help them learn not only how well they are performing their jobs but also whether their performance is improving, deteriorating, or remaining at a constant level. Although there are various sources from which information about performance can come, it usually is advantageous for a worker to learn about his performance directly as he does the job—rather than from management on an occasional basis.

Job-provided feedback is more immediate and private than supervisor-supplied feedback, and it increases workers' feelings of personal control over their work. Moreover, it avoids many of the potentially disruptive interpersonal problems that can develop when a worker can find out how he is doing only from direct messages or subtle cues from the boss.

Exactly what should be done to open channels for job-provided feedback varies from job to job and from organization to organization. Often the changes involve simply removing existing blocks that isolate the individual from naturally occurring data about performance, rather than generating entirely new feedback mechanisms. For example:

- Establishing direct client relationships (discussed above) often removes blocks between the worker and natural external sources of data about the work.
- Quality control efforts often eliminate a natural source of feedback, because all quality checks are done by people other than the individuals responsible for the work. In such situations, any feedback that workers do receive may be belated and diluted. Placing most quality control functions in the hands of workers will dramatically increase the quantity and quality of data available to them about their performances.

• Tradition and established procedure in many organizations dictate that records about performance be kept by a supervisor and transmitted up (not down) the organizational hierarchy. Sometimes supervisors even check the work and correct any errors themselves. The worker who made the error never knows it occurred and is therefore denied the very information that could enhance both internal work motivation and the technical adequacy of his performance. In many cases, it is possible to provide standard summaries of performance records directly to the workers. This would give the employees personally and regularly the data they need to improve their effectiveness.

• Computers and other automated machines sometimes can be used to provide individuals with data now blocked from them. Many clerical operations, for example, are now performed on computer consoles. These consoles often can be programmed to provide the clerk with immediate feedback in the form of a CRT display or a printout indicating that an error has been made. Some systems even have been programmed to provide the operator with a positive feedback message when a period of error-free performance has been sustained.

The principles for redesigning jobs reviewed above, although illustrative of the kinds of changes that can be made to improve the jobs of individuals in organizations, obviously are not exhaustive. They were selected for attention here because of the links (Figure 2) between the principles and the core job dimensions in the motivational model presented earlier. Other principles for enriching jobs (which, although often similar to those presented here, derive from alternative conceptual frameworks) are presented by Ford (1969), Glaser (1975), Herzberg (1974), and Katzell and Yankelovich (1975). . . .

GUIDELINES FOR INSTALLING PLANNED CHANGES IN JOBS

We move now to exploration of issues that arise in the actual installation of changes in the design of work. The material presented below is based on observations and interviews conducted by the author and his associates over the past three years in numerous organizations where work redesign activities were being planned, implemented, or evaluated.

In general, we have found job enrichment to be failing at least as often as it is succeeding. And the reasons for the failures, in many cases, appear to have more to do with the way planned changes are *implemented* in organizations than with the intrinsic merit of the changes. Again and again we have seen good ideas about the redesign of work die because the advocates of change were unable to gain acceptance for their ideas or because unexpected roadblocks led to early termination of the change project.

Our findings are summarized below as six prescriptive guides for implementing changes in jobs. Each guide includes a discussion of pitfalls that frequently are encountered in work redesign projects, as well as ingredients that were common to many of the more successful projects we observed.

Guide 1: Diagnose the Work System Prior to Change

It now is clear that work redesign is not effective in all organizational circumstances. Yet rarely is a systematic diagnosis carried out beforehand to determine whether meaningful change is feasible, given the jobs being considered, the people who will be involved, and the social, organizational, or cultural environment in which the work is performed. As a result, faulty initial assumptions often go uncorrected, and the change project may be doomed before it is begun.

The choice of the job to be changed, for example, often seems to be almost random. Perhaps a manager will decide that a given job seems right for enrichment. Or he will settle on a job because it is peripheral to the major work done in the organization—thereby minimizing the risk of severe disruption if something should go wrong. Or a job will be selected because everything seems wrong with it—the work is not getting done on time or correctly, employees are angry about everything from their pay to the cleanliness of the restrooms, grievances are excessive, and so on. The hope, apparently, is that somehow redesigning the job will fix everything all at once.

Yet it must be recognized that some jobs, given existing technological constraints, are about as good as they ever can be. Work redesign in such situations is at best a waste of time. Other jobs have so much wrong with them that is irrelevant to how enriched they are that job enrichment could not conceivably bring about a noticeable improvement—and instead might add even more complexity to an already chaotic situation. When such matters are overlooked in planning for work redesign, the result often is a change effort that fails simply because it is aimed at an inappropriate target.

Similarly, differences in employee readiness to handle contemplated changes in jobs only infrequently are assessed before a project is installed. Line managers often express doubts that employees can handle proposed new responsibilities or skepticism that employees will enjoy working on an enriched job. Sometimes, as planning for work redesign proceeds, managers become convinced of the contrary. But only rarely are change projects designed with full cognizance that employees are likely to differ in their psychological readiness for enriched work.

Even less frequently is explicit assessment made of the readiness of managers to deal with the kinds of problems that inevitably arise when a major organizational change is made. In one case, the management team responsible for a job enrichment project nearly collapsed when the first serious change-related problem emerged. Time and energy that were needed for the project were spent instead working on intrateam issues that had been flushed out by the problem. And another "job enrichment failure" occurred while the managers talked and talked. An adequate diagnosis of the readiness of the management team for change-management would have increased the likelihood that the problematic intrateam issues would have been dealt with *before* the work redesign activities were initiated.

The commitment of middle and top management to job enrichment also rarely received diagnostic attention in the organizations we observed. Whether organizational change activities must begin at the top—or whether work redesign is a strategy for change that can spread from the bottom up—remains an important and unresolved question (Beer and Huse, 1972). It is almost always true, however, that middle and top management can terminate a project they find unsatisfactory, whether for good reasons or on a whim. In one case, a high-level executive agreed to serve as sponsor for a project without really understanding what the changes would involve. When difficulties in implementation developed, the executive concluded that he had been misled—and the project found itself out from under its protective umbrella and in serious organizational jeopardy. In another case, a single vice-president was counted on to protect a fledgling project from meddling by others who favored alternative approaches to organizational change. When the vice-president departed the organization to attend a several-month executive development program, his temporary replacement terminated job enrichment activities and substituted a training program more to his own liking. In both cases, an early assessment of the attitudes of key top managers would have revealed the need to develop a broader and better informed base of high-level support for the projects.

A number of organizations we studied did conduct diagnoses of the work system before changes were installed. Almost invariably these studies identified problems or issues that required attention prior to the beginning of the job changes. Such diagnoses are not easy to make. They involve the raising of anxieties at a time when most participants in a project are instead seeking comfort and assurance that everything will turn out all right. Moreover, the tools and methodologies required for undertaking such diagnoses only now are beginning to become available (cf. Hackman and Oldham, 1975; Jenkins, Nadler, Lawler, and Cammann, 1975; Sirota and Wolfson, 1972). Our observations suggest, however, that the diagnostic task may be one of the most crucial in a work redesign project.

Guide 2: Keep the Focus on the Work Itself

Redesigning a job often appears seductively simple. In practice, it is a rather challenging undertaking. It requires a good deal more energy than most other organizational development activities, such as attitude improvement programs, training courses, and objective-setting practices (Ford, 1971).

There are many reasons why it is so hard to alter jobs. At the purely bureaucratic level, the entire personnel-and-job-description apparatus often must be engaged to get the changes approved, documented, and implemented. If the organization is unionized, the planned changes often must be negotiated beforehand—sometimes a formidable task. Simple inertia often tempts managers to add lots of window dressing to make things appear different, rather than actually to change what people do on their jobs. Finally, when even one job in an organization is changed, many of the interfaces between that job and related ones must be dealt with as well. In even moderately complex work systems, this is no small matter.

Because of these and other forces against change, work redesign projects frequently are carried out that have very little impact on the work itself. A project carried out in the stock transfer department of a large bank is illustrative (Frank and Hackman, in press). At the end of the project the informal word among managers was, "We tried job enrichment and it failed." But our research data (which measured the objective characteristics of jobs before and after the change) showed that, although all manner of things did change as part of the job enrichment project, the work itself was not among them. Our correlational analyses of data collected in that organization showed that there were very positive relationships between the amount of skill variety, autonomy, and feedback in various jobs and the satisfaction, motivation, performance, and attendance of the job incumbents. These across-job relationships were present prior to the change project and they were there afterwards. But it was also true that those people who held the "good" jobs before the change also held them afterward, and those people whose jobs originally were routine, repetitive, and virtually without feedback had essentially identical jobs after the work was "redesigned." Workers had been formed into small groups, supervision had been changed, names of jobs and work units had been altered, and a general stirring about had taken place. But the *jobs* were not changed much, and the effect (after about six months) was a slight deterioration in worker satisfaction and motivation. This deterioration, apparently, was due more to the failure of the project to live up to expectations than to the changes that had actually taken place.

It is easy, apparently, for those responsible for work redesign activities to delude themselves about what is actually being altered in such projects, and thereby to avoid the rather difficult task of actually changing the structure of the work people do. One way of ensuring that a project stays focused on the work is to base change activities firmly on a theory of work design.

No doubt some theories are better than others. Our observations suggest, however, that the specific details of various theories may not be as important as the fact that *some* theory is used to guide the implementation of change. In addition to keeping the changes focused on the original objective of restructuring the work, a good theory can help identify the kinds of data needed to plan and evaluate the changes and can alert implementors to special problems and opportunities that may develop as the project unfolds.

The theory must, however, be appropriate for the changes that are contemplated. Therein lies one of the major difficulties of the stock transfer project described above. The project originally was designed on the basis of motivation-hygiene theory, which deals exclusively with the enrichment of jobs performed by individuals. The changes that actually were made, however, involved the creation of enriched *group* tasks. Because the theory did not address the special problems of designing work for groups (how to create conditions that encourage members to share with one another their special task-relevant skills), those responsible for implementation found the theory of limited use as a guide for planning and installing the changes. Gradually the theory dropped from their attention. Without the benefit of theory-specified guidelines for change, the project became increasingly diffuse and eventually addressed many issues that had little or nothing to do with the work. All this is not to imply that these other issues were unrelated to the change or were improper. However, they cannot be made as substitutes for changes in the work itself.

Guide 3: Prepare Ahead of Time for Unexpected Problems

When substantial changes are made in jobs, shock waves may be created that reverberate throughout adjacent parts of the organization. If insufficient attention is given to such spin-off effects of job changes, they may backfire and create problems that negate (or even reverse) expected positive outcomes.

The site of the backfire varies from case to case. In one company, employees who prepared customer accounts for computer processing were given increased autonomy in scheduling their work and in determining their own work pace. This resulted in a less predictable schedule of data input to the computer system. Because the data processing department had not been involved in the project until the changes were already made, serious computer delays were encountered while data processing managers struggled to figure out how to respond to the new and irregular flow of work. The net result was an increase in antagonism between computer operations and the employees whose jobs had been enriched—and a decrease in the promptness of customer service.

In another company work was redesigned to give rank-and-file employees a number of responsibilities that previously had been handled by their supervisors. The employees (who dealt with customers of the company by telephone) were given greater opportunities for personal initiative and discretion in dealing with customers, and initially seemed to be prospering in their new responsibilities. But later observations revealed a deterioration in morale, especially in the area of supervisor-subordinate relationships. Apparently the supervisors had found themselves with little work to do after the change (because the employees were handling much of what the supervisors had done before). When supervisors turned to higher management for instructions, they were told to "develop your people—that's what a manager's job is." The supervisors had little idea what "developing your people" involved, and many of them implemented that instruction by looking over the employees' shoulders and correcting each error they could find. Resentment between the supervisor and the employee groups soon developed, and more than overcame any positive benefits that had accrued from the changes in the job (Lawler, Hackman, and Kaufman, 1973).

Problems such as those described above often can be avoided by developing contingency plans ahead of time to deal with the inevitable spin-off problems that crop up whenever jobs are changed. Such plans can be advantageous in at least two ways. First, employees, managers, and consultants all will share an awareness that problems are likely to emerge elsewhere in the work system as the change project develops. This simple understanding may help keep surprise and dismay at manageable levels when the problems do appear and so may decrease the opportunity for people to conclude prematurely that "the project failed."

Second, preplanning for possible problems can lead to an objective increase in the readiness of all parties to deal with those problems that do emerge. Having a few contingency plans filed away can increase the chances that change-related problems will be dealt with before they get out of hand—and before they create a significant drain on the energy and morale needed to keep the change project afloat.

Not all contingency plans can be worked out in detail beforehand. Indeed, they probably should not be. Until a project is underway one cannot know for sure what the specific nature of the most pressing needs and problems will be. But one can be ready to deal with common problems that may appear. For example, the training department can be alerted that some training may be required if managers find themselves in difficulty supervising the employees after the work is redesigned. And those responsible for the reward system can be asked to engage in some contingency planning on the chance that the new work system may require nontraditional compensation arrangements. One does not *begin* with these matters. But one is well advised to anticipate that some of them will arise, and to be prepared to deal with them when and if they do.

Guide 4: Evaluate Continuously

When managers or consultants are asked whether a work redesign project has been evaluated, the answer nearly always is affirmative. But when one asks to see the evaluation, the response frequently is something like, "Well, let me tell you . . . only one week after we did the actual job changes this guy who had been on the lathe for fifteen years came up to me, and he said. . . ." Such anecdotes are interesting, but they provide little help to managers and union officials as they consider whether work redesign is something that should be experimented with further and possibly diffused throughout the organization. Nor is it the stuff of which generalizable behavioral science knowledge is made.

Sometimes hard data are pointed to, such as financial savings resulting from reductions in personnel in the unit where the work redesign took place. Such data can validly document an improvement in worker productivity, but they are of little value in understanding the full richness of what has happened, or why. And, of great importance in unionized organizations, they are hardly the kind of data that will engage the enthusiasm of the bargaining unit for broader application of work redesign.

There are many good reasons why adequate evaluations of work redesign projects are not done—not having the capability to translate human gains into dollars and cents, not being able to separate out the influence of the job changes on measured productivity and unit profitability from the many other factors that influence these outcomes, having an organization-wide accounting system that cannot provide data on the costs of absenteeism, turnover, training, and extra supervisory time, not really trusting measures of job satisfaction, and so on.

These reasons can be convincing, at least until one asks what was done to try to overcome the problems and gets as a response, "Well, we really didn't think we could get the accountants to help out, so. . . ." And one is left with several unhappy hypotheses: (1) nobody knows how to do a decent evaluation—nor how to get help in doing one; or (2) management does not consider systematic evaluation an essential part of the change activity; or (3) the desire of the people responsible for the program to have it appear successful is so strong that they cannot afford the risk of an explicit evaluation.

In a retailing organization, for example, job enrichment was sold to top management by a single individual. And soon the program came to be known throughout the organization as "Joe's program." Joe, understandably, developed a considerable personal interest in managing the image of the program within the organization. When offered the chance for a systematic evaluation of the project to be conducted at no cost to the organization, Joe showed considerable initial hesitation, and finally declined the offer. Later discussions revealed that although he recognized the potential usefulness of the information he would gain from an outside evaluation, that benefit was more than countered by the risk of losing his personal control over the image of the project that eventually would emerge.

Because of the pressure on lower-level managers and consultants to make job enrichment programs at least *appear* successful, it often is necessary for top management or union leaders to insist that serious and systematic evaluations of such programs take place. For such evaluations to be valid and useful, management must attempt to create an organizational climate in which the evaluation is viewed as an occasion for *learning*—rather than as an event useful mainly for assessing the performance and competence of those who actually installed the changes.

Such a stance permits interim disappointments and problems to be used as times for reconsideration and revision of the change project, rather than as a cause for disillusionment and abandonment. And it encourages those responsible for managing the change to learn as they go how most effectively to design, install, and manage enriched jobs. This is a matter of considerable importance, because there is no neat package for redesigning work in organizations and there probably never will be.

Taking a learning orientation to work redesign is, however, a costly proposition. It is expensive to collect trustworthy data for use in monitoring a project throughout its life, and to experiment actively with different ways of changing jobs. It is painful to learn from failure, and to try again. Yet such costs may actually be among the better investments an organization contemplating work redesign can make. Paying such costs may be the only realistic way for the organization to develop the considerable knowledge and expertise it will need to reap the full benefits of work redesign as a strategy for change.

Guide 5: Confront the Difficult Problems Early

Individuals responsible for work redesign projects often find it tempting to get the project sold to management and union leadership, and only then to begin negotiations on the difficult problems that must be solved before the project can actually be carried out. This seems entirely reasonable. If such problems are raised *before* the project is agreed to, the chances are increased that it will never get off the ground. It appears, nevertheless, that in the long run it may be wiser to risk not doing a project for which the tough issues cannot be resolved beforehand than to do one under circumstances that require compromise after compromise to keep the project alive after it has begun.

Vigilance by those responsible for the change is required to ensure that the tough issues are not swept under the rug when the project is being considered. Among such issues (that too often are reserved for later discussion) are:

- The nature and extent of the commitment of management and union leaders, including the circumstances under which a decision may be made to terminate the project. It is especially important to make sure that both management and union leadership realize that problems will emerge in the early stages of a project, and that a good deal of energy may be required to protect and nurture the project during such down phases.
- The criteria against which the project ultimately will be evaluated and the means by which the evaluation will be done, including measures that will be used. Given that there are serious measurement difficulties in assessing any work redesign project, it is important to make sure that all parties, including management and union sponsors, are aware of these difficulties and are committed at the outset to the evaluation methodology.
- The way that learnings gained in the project (whether they are "successful tactics we discovered" or "roadblocks we unexpectedly encountered") will be made available to people who can use them as guides for future action, in the same or in other organizations.

Guide 6: Design Change Processes That Fit with Change Objectives

Most work redesign projects provide employees with increased opportunities for autonomy and self-direction in carrying out the work of the organization. Employees are allowed to do their work with a minimum of interference, and they are assumed to have the competence and sense of responsibility to seek appropriate assistance when they need it. The problem is that far too often the process of *implementing* job enrichment is strikingly incongruent with that intended end state.

It appears unrealistic to expect that a more flexible, bottom-loaded work system can be created using implementation procedures that are relatively rigid and bureaucratic, and that operate strictly from the top down. Yet again and again we observed standard, traditional, organizational practices being used to install work redesign. More often than not employees were the last to know what was happening, and only rarely were they given any real opportunity to actively participate in and influence the changes. In many situations they were never told the reasons why the changes were being made.

What happens during the planning stages of a work redesign project is illustrative of such incongruence between means and ends. Typically, initial planning for work redesign (including decision-making about what jobs will be changed) is done privately by managers and consultants. Diagnostic work, if performed at all, is done using a plausible cover story—such as telling employees that they are being interviewed "as part of our regular program of surveying employee attitudes." (The rationale is that employee expectations about change should not be raised prematurely; the effect often is that suspicions are raised instead.) Eventually managers appear with a fully determined set of changes that are installed in traditional top-down fashion. If employees resist and mistrust the changes, managers are surprised and disappointed. As one said: "I don't understand why they did not respond more enthusiastically. Don't they realize how we are going to make their work a lot more involving and interesting?" Apparently he did not see the lack of congruence between the goals being aspired to and the means being used, between "what we want to achieve" and "how we're going to achieve it."

As an alternative approach, managers might choose to be public and participative in translating from theory through diagnosis to the actual steps taken to modify jobs. Such an approach could be advantageous for a number of reasons.

First, when diagnostic data are collected and discussed openly, everyone who will be affected by the changes has the chance to become involved in the redesign activities and knowledgeable about them, and so everyone is less threatened. In one organization, managers initially were very skeptical about employee participation in planning for job changes. After employees had become involved in the project, however, a number of managers commented favorably on the amount of energy employees contributed to the planning activities and on the constructive attitudes they exhibited.

Second, the quality of the diagnostic data may be improved. If employees know that changes in their own work will be made partly on the basis of their responses to the diagnostic instruments, they may try especially hard to provide valid and complete data.

Third, chances are increased that learnings will emerge from the project that can be used to develop better action principles of work redesign for future applications. The involvement of people from a diversity of organizational roles in diagnostic and change-planning activities should facilitate attempts to piece together a complete picture of the change project—including the reasons that various changes were tried, what went wrong (and what went right), and what might be done differently next time.

Fourth, expectations about change will be increased when employees are involved in diagnostic and change-planning processes. Rather than being something to be avoided, therefore, heightened employee expectations can serve as a positive force for change. For example, such expectations might counter the conservatism that inevitably creeps into changes planned and implemented downwards through several hierarchical levels in an organization.

Despite these potential advantages, it is not easy to carry off a fully participative work redesign project. Nor do openness and employee participation guarantee success. Indeed, some experienced commentators have argued explicitly against employee participation in planning job changes, because (1) participation may contaminate the change process with "human relations hygiene" (Herzberg, 1966), (2) employees are not viewed as competent to redesign their own jobs, or (3) job design is viewed solely as a management function (Ford, 1969).

Our observations of work redesign projects turned up few projects in which employee participation was actively used in the change process. And the ideas for change that employees proposed in these cases did focus mainly on the removal of roadblocks from the work and on the improvement of hygiene items. This is consistent with the predictions of Ford (1969) that employee suggestions usually deal more with the context of work than with its motivational core.

The circumstances under which employees participated in work redesign activities in these organizations, however, were far from optimal. Often employees simply were asked, "What would you suggest?" and given little time to consider their responses. In no case were employees provided with education in the theory and strategy of job redesign before being asked for suggestions. And in all cases we studied, employees had no real part in the final decision-making about what changes actually would be made. They were contributors to the change process, but not partners in it.

To develop and utilize the *full* potential of employees as resources for change would be an exciting undertaking, and a major one. It could require teaching employees the basics of motivation theory, discussing with them state-of-the-art knowledge about the strategy and tactics of work redesign, and providing them with training and experience in planning and installing organizational innovations. Such an approach would be costly, perhaps too much so to be practical. But it would have the advantage of encouraging employees to become full collaborators in the redesign of their own work, thereby creating a process for improving jobs that is consistent with the ultimate objectives of the change. Moreover, and of special importance to the quality of work life in organizations, the approach would provide employees with greatly increased opportunities for furthering their own personal growth and development—and at the same time would significantly increase their value as human resources to the organization.

REFERENCES

Bakan, P., Belton, J. A., & Toth, J. C. Extraversion-introversion and decrement in an auditory vigilance task. In *Vigilance: A symposium*, edited by D. N. Buckner and J. J. McGrath. New York: McGraw-Hill, 1963.

Beer, M., & Huse, E. F. A systems approach to organization development. *Journal of Applied Behavioral Science* **8** (1972): 79–101.

Bem, D. J. *Beliefs, attitudes, and human affairs.* Monterey, Calif.: Brooks/Cole, 1970.

Berlyne, D. E. Arousal and reinforcement. *Nebraska Symposium on Motivation* **15** (1967).

Best, F. Flexible work scheduling: Beyond the forty-hour impasse. In *The future of work*, edited by F. Best. Englewood Cliffs, N.J.: Prentice-Hall, 1973.

Blood, M. R., & Hulin, C. L. Alienation, environmental characteristics, and worker responses. *Journal of Applied Psychology* **51** (1967): 284–290.

Calame, B. E. Wary labor eyes job enrichment. *Wall Street Journal,* February 26, 1973, p. 12.

Davis, L. E. Toward a theory of job design. *Journal of Industrial Engineering* **8** (1957): 19–23.

Davis, L. E. The design of jobs. *Industrial Relations* **6** (1966): 21–45.

Davis, L. E. Developments in job design. In *Personal goals and work design,* edited by P. B. Warr. London: Wiley, 1975.

Davis, L. E., & Trist, E. L. Improving the quality of work life: Sociotechnical case studies. In *Work and the quality of life,* edited by J. O'Toole. Cambridge, Mass.: MIT Press, 1974.

Dunnette, M. D., Campbell, J. P., & Hakel, M. D. Factors contributing to job satisfaction and dissatisfaction in six occupational groups. *Organizational Behavior and Human Performance* **2** (1967): 143–174.

Emery, F. E., & Trist, E. L. Socio-technical systems. In *Systems thinking,* edited by F. E. Emery. Middlesex, England: Penguin, 1969.

Engelstad, P. H. Socio-technical approach to problems of process control. In *Design of jobs,* edited by L. E. Davis and J. C. Taylor. Middlesex, England: Penguin, 1972.

Fein, M. Job enrichment: A reevaluation. *Sloan Management Review* **15** (1974): 69–88.

Fiss, B. *Flexitime in federal government.* Washington, D.C.: Government Printing Office, 1974.

Ford, R. N. *Motivation through the work itself.* New York: American Management Association, 1969.

Ford, R. N. A prescription for job enrichment success. In *New perspectives in job enrichment,* edited by J. R. Maher. New York: Van Nostrand-Reinhold, 1971.

Ford, R. N. Job enrichment lessons from AT&T. *Harvard Business Review,* January–February, 1973, pp. 96–106.

Frank, L., & Hackman, J. R. A failure of job enrichment: The case of the change that wasn't. *Journal of Applied Behavioral Science,* in press.

Friedlander, F., & Brown, L. D. Organization development. *Annual Review of Psychology* **25** (1974): 313–341.

Glaser, E. M. *Productivity gains through worklife improvement.* New York: The Psychological Corp., 1975.

Gomberg, W. Job satisfaction: Sorting out the nonsense. *AFL-CIO American Federationist,* June 1973.

Gooding, J. *The job revolution.* New York: Walker, 1972.

Graen, G. B. Testing traditional and two-factor hypotheses concerning job satisfaction. *Journal of Applied Psychology* **52** (1968): 343–353.

Gulowsen, J. A measure of work group autonomy. In *Design of jobs,* edited by L. E. Davis and J. C. Taylor. Middlesex, England: Penguin, 1972.

Hackman, J. R. *Improving the quality of work life: Work design.* Washington, D.C.: Office of Research, ASPER, U.S. Dept. of Labor, 1975(a).

Hackman, J. R. On the coming demise of job enrichment. In *Man and work in society,* edited by E. L. Cass and F. G. Zimmer. New York: Van Nostrand-Reinhold, 1975(b).

Hackman, J. R., & Lawler, E. E. Employee reactions to job characteristics. *Journal of Applied Psychology Monograph* **55** (1971): 259–286.

Hackman, J. R., & Oldham, G. R. Development of the job diagnostic survey. *Journal of Applied Psychology* **60** (1975): 159–170.

Hackman, J. R., & Oldham, G. R. Motivation through the design of work: Test of a theory. *Organizational Behavior and Human Performance* **16** (1976): 250–279.

Hackman, J. R., Oldham, G. R., Janson, R., & Purdy, K. A new strategy for job enrichment. *California Management Review*, Summer 1975, pp. 57–71.

Herbst, P. G. *Autonomous group functioning*. London: Tavistock, 1962.

Herzberg, F. *Work and the nature of man*. Cleveland: World, 1966.

Herzberg, F. The wise old turk. *Harvard Business Review*, September-October 1974, pp. 70–80.

Herzberg, F., Mausner, B., & Snyderman, B. *The motivation to work*. New York: Wiley, 1959.

Hinton, B. L. An empirical investigation of the Herzberg methodology and two-factor theory. *Organizational Behavior and Human Performance* **3** (1968): 286–309.

House, R. J., & Wigdor, L. Herzberg's dual-factor theory of job satisfaction and motivation: A review of the evidence and a criticism. *Personnel Psychology* **20** (1967): 369–398.

Hulin, C. L. Individual differences and job enrichment. In J. R. Maher (Ed.), *New perspectives in job enrichment*. New York: Van Nostrand-Reinhold, 1971.

Hulin C. L., & Blood, M. R. Job enlargement, individual differences and worker responses. *Psychological Bulletin* **69** (1968): 41–55.

Jenkins, G. D., Jr., Nadler, D. A., Lawler, E. E. III, & Cammann. C. Standardized observations: An approach to measuring the nature of jobs. *Journal of Applied Psychology* **60** (1975): 171–181.

Katzell, R. A., & Yankelovich, D. *Work, productivity and job satisfaction*. New York: The Psychological Corporation, 1975.

Kiesler, C. A., Collins, B. E., & Miller, N. *Attitude change*. New York: Wiley, 1969.

Kilbridge, M. D. Reduced costs through job enrichment: A case. *The Journal of Business* **33** (1960): 357–362.

King, N. A clarification and evaluation of the two-factor theory of job satisfaction. *Psychological Bulletin* **74** (1970): 18–31.

Kornhauser, A. *Mental health of the industrial worker*. New York: Wiley, 1965.

Lawler, E. E. III, Hackman, J. R., & Kaufman, S. Effects of job redesign: A field experiment. *Journal of Applied Social Psychology* **3** (1973): 49–62.

Lawler, E. E. III, & Hall, D. T. The relationship of job characteristics to job involvement, satisfaction and intrinsic motivation. *Journal of Applied Psychology* **54** (1970): 305–312

Oldham, G. R. The motivational strategies used by supervisors: Relationships to effectiveness indicators. *Organizational Behavior and Human Performance* **15** (1976): 66–86.

Paul, W. J., Jr., Robertson, K. B., & Herzberg, F. Job enrichment pays off. *Harvard Business Review*, March-April 1969, pp. 61–78.

Reif, W. E., & Luthans, F. Does job enrichment really pay off? *California Management Review*, Fall 1972, pp. 30–37.

Rice, A. K. *Productivity and social organization: The Ahmedabad experiment*. London: Tavistock, 1958.

Scott, W. E. Activation theory and task design. *Organizational Behavior and Human Performance* **1** (1966): 3–30.

Scott, W. E. The behavioral consequences of repetitive task design: research and theory. In *Readings in organizational behavior and human performance*, edited by L. L. Cummings and W. E. Scott. Homewood, Ill.: Irwin-Dorsey, 1969.

Scott, W. E., & Rowland, K. M. The generality and significance of semantic differential scales as measures of 'morale.' *Organizational Behavior and Human Performance* **5** (1970): 576–591.

Sirota, D., & Wolfson, A. D. Job enrichment: Surmounting the obstacles. *Personnel*, July-August 1972, 8–19.

Special Task Force to the Secretary of the U.S. Dept. of Health, Education, and Welfare. *Work in America*. Boston, Mass.: MIT Press, 1973.

Steiner, I. D. Perceived freedom. In *Advances in experimental social psychology*, edited by L. Berkowitz. Vol. 5. New York: Academic Press, 1970.

Taylor, F. W. *The principles of scientific management*. New York: Harper, 1911.

Taylor, J. C. Some effects of technology in organizational change. *Human Relations* **24** (1971): 105–123.

Thayer, R. E. Measurement of activation through self-report. *Psychological Reports* **20** (1967): 663–678.

Thayer, R. E. Activation states as assessed by verbal report and four psychophysiological variables. *Psychophysiology* **7** (1970): 86–94.

Trist, E. L., Higgin, G. W., Murray, H., & Pollock, A. B. *Organizational choice*. London: Tavistock, 1963.

Turner, A. N., & Lawrence, P. R. *Industrial jobs and the worker*. Boston: Harvard Graduate School of Business Administration, 1965.

Vernon, H. M. *On the extent and effects of variety in repetitive work*. Industrial Fatigue Research Board Report No. 26. London: H. M. Stationary Office, 1924.

Vroom, V. *Work and motivation*. New York: Wiley, 1964.

Walker, C. R., & Guest, R. H. *The man on the assembly line*. Cambridge, Mass.: Harvard University Press, 1952.

Walters, R. W. A long-term look at the shorter work week. *Personnel Administrator*, July-August 1971.

Walters, R. W. & Associates. *Job enrichment for results*. Reading, Mass.: Addison-Wesley, 1975.

Walton, R. E. How to counter alienation in the plant. *Harvard Business Review*, November-December 1972, pp. 70–81.

Walton, R. E. The diffusion of new work structures: Explaining why success didn't take. *Organizational Dynamics*, Winter 1975, pp. 3–22.(a)

Walton, R. E. From Hawthorne to Topeka and Kalmar. In *Man and work in society*, edited by E. L. Cass and F. G. Zimmer. New York: Van Nostrand-Reinhold, 1975.(b)

Whitsett, D. A., & Winslow, E. K. An analysis of studies critical of the motivator-hygiene theory. *Personnel Psychology* **20** (1967): 391–415.

Worthy, J. C. Organizational structure and employee morale. *American Sociological Review* **15** (1950): 169–179.

How Volvo Adapts Work to People

Pehr G. Gyllenhammar

In any industrialized country today, more than half the working population still works in companies with less than 50 employees. At the same time, however, very large organizations are growing even larger—too large to be comfortable for employees. Inside a large modern company too often the individual feels lost, unimportant in the overall scheme, merely a replaceable cog in the industrial system, with little or no control over his or her own life until he or she retires.

Inside government, too, as departments grow to cope with social problems and the growth itself creates new and different ills, the same anonymity occurs. In some countries the government employs directly or indirectly, at least one-third of the working population.

Much of our growth resulted from the discovery that a larger unit could get access to resources—notably capital—that were unavailable to smaller units. We found ways to produce in large factories more efficiently than we could in small workshops where a small team of employees was the basic manufacturing unit. We found ways to move our goods to more distant markets. We began to move people as well, creating new demands for products and an international flow of attitudes and values, as well as what we at Volvo refer to as "technology transfer."

In these circumstances, it is not surprising that the idea that if a little bigness is good, a lot of it must be better, seems to have flourished. This concept has given rise to such phenomena as conglomerates, 1,000-desk offices, and mile-long factories and assembly lines.

Like other good things, economy of scale turns out to have subtle limits. We begin to find today the symptoms of a new industrial illness. We invent machines to eliminate some of the physical stresses of work, and then we find that psychological tensions cause even more health and behavior problems. People don't want to be subservient to machines and systems. They react to inhuman conditions in very human ways: by job-hopping, absenteeism, apathetic attitudes, antagonism, and even malicious mischief.

From the employee's viewpoint this behavior is perfectly reasonable. The younger he or she is, the stronger his or her reactions are likely to be. The people entering the work force today have received more education than ever before in history. Society has educated them to regard themselves as mature adults, capable of making their own choices. By offering them jobs in our overorganized industrial units we offer them jobs where they have virtually no choices. For eight hours a day managers regard them as children, ciphers, or potential problems—and manage or control them accordingly.

Today a new element enters the picture—permanent unemployment. Technical advances in the industrial world have been so rapid that just at a time when more people are entering the job market, we can produce more with less people. Employees whose jobs are threatened in the name of "progress" cluster together under union or government umbrellas to protect the status quo. The featherbedding that follows not only hastens the demise of their organizations but also creates polarized "them and us" attitudes that make it impossible for management to propose retraining, work reorganization, and diversification that might help create new jobs and new business. The more employees try to protect their endangered jobs, the more planners and managers find reason to design people out of the industrial system.

If the industrial society succeeds in putting people to one side, what will happen to them and thus to society itself? A humane answer to this crucial question depends on the cultural and economic framework in which industry operates and on the commitment of the people making the decisions that will affect employment in the future. Instead of doing away with jobs, they will have to ask themselves how to make the jobs meaningful to the people as well as to the organization.

Managers need to find ways to capture the personal involvement of each employee. Management cannot be based on power. In any show of power, the employees today will "win" and management will "lose," though the inevitable result is that everyone loses. Instead of an adversary game, I hope we can rewrite the rules to make business the kind of game in which everybody wins.

THE SWEDISH WAY

For reasons of its own, Sweden has spent a great deal of time and energy in the last few years looking at some of these problems and trying to find ways to make work more livable and life more workable. We have stringent new laws for job security and work safety. A 1977 law calls for full consultation with employees and full participation by their representatives in decision making from board level to the shop floor. Employee organizations have the right to all financial information about a company. More important than the laws are the attitudes of managers who, in spite of the discomforts of change, seem to share the conviction that greater employee participation is good and necessary.

Sweden has a unique demography, with a population less than that of Los Angeles spread over an area larger than the state of California. The country is more dependent on its success in world markets than are many larger countries. The population is fairly homogeneous, mainly Nordic. This coherence gives rise to a culture in which social change can sweep more swiftly than it can in countries that have more heterogeneous populations and cultures within their borders.

Industrially, Sweden's situation is quite different from that of the United States, for example. While the United States has a pool of unemployed that, in effect, buffers staffing problems, Sweden has relatively full employment and is to some extent dependent on "guest workers" from other countries. Like other industrialized nations, though, Sweden and the United States share a similar need to involve people in their work to achieve better productivity.

Sweden has its labor laws, a body of practice, a union/employer structure, and an entire industrial culture based on cooperative rather than contentious models. Blue-collar union membership is approaching 90%, and wage agreements are worked out from a national viewpoint. The United States model is based more on arm's length negotiations, with different unions having different demands and union membership comprising considerably less than half the work force (though the membership is high in manufacturing industries).

Factories in both countries have fairly efficient unions and clear-cut ways for managers and unions to communicate with relatively strike-free results. Both countries experience employee absenteeism, but a major difference between the two is that Swedish companies had the problem sooner and have treated it as a more serious matter. Many U.S. companies, on the other hand, consider the problem less important as there are available people waiting hopefully for jobs. These distinct experiences of employee absenteeism underlie the differences between Swedish and American attitudes toward employee participation.

THE VOLVO EXPERIENCE

Just as Sweden's situation differs from that of other countries, so Volvo's differs from that of other companies. The events at Volvo's factories need to be seen in that perspective. By today's international standards, Volvo is a medium-sized company, but in its home country, it is a large company. Ranking between sixtieth and seventieth in the list of non-U.S. companies, Volvo's share of the world automotive market has doubled in the last ten years to about 2.5%. Deriving 70% of its sales from outside Sweden, Volvo accounts for between 8% and 9% of Sweden's total export.

Like other auto manufacturers, at its inception Volvo had a production system that was technically oriented and planned in detail, and it used the Methods Time Measurement system (MTM). When labor unrest became visible in 1969, it became necessary for us to adapt the way we controlled production to new attitudes in the work force.

In 1972, to increase exports and build further volume and profit in the noncar divisions, Volvo went through a major reorganization. We cut headquarters staff from 1,800 to 100 people. Each major product group became an independent division, and all major market units became independent profit centers within the divisions. The new organization took on a more international flavor, recognizing the fact that more than 100 countries provided its income. To balance the income from the dominant car activities, we made major investments in trucks, buses, and industrial equipment.

Although Sweden's labor costs have become the highest in the world, Volvo remains a profitable company. In recent years, the company's cash flow as a percentage of sales was one of the three highest in the automotive industry. The corporate strategy today is to add strength and reduce vulnerability by diversifying within the transportation field.

When we started thinking about reorganizing the way we worked, the first bottleneck seemed to be production and technology. We couldn't really reorganize the work to suit the people unless we also changed the technology that chained people to the assembly line. But in an industry like ours such changes are risky and irreversible. Volvo's Kalmar plant, for example, is designed for a specific purpose: car assembly in working groups of about 20 people. If it didn't work, it would be a costly and visible failure, in both financial and social terms. We would lose credibility with our own people as well as with those who are watching from outside.

It was also clear that technical changes would be fruitless if they were not accompanied by organizational changes and evolution toward a climate of co-operation and partnership. So the second major change over the last five years has been Volvo's investment of tens of millions of dollars to improve the physical working environment for employees. That was simply part of the cost of achieving cleaner, more pleasant surroundings. This is our responsibility as an employer. It demonstrates in concrete, visible ways that we value the people who work for Volvo.

But this investment does not create better jobs. It only helps give us the conditions in which people can work together to organize their jobs in more human ways. The third part of our change strategy, then, concerned the jobs themselves. In some cases we have built entirely new factories, where work can be organized more flexibly. In other cases we have tried to mechanize unpleasant jobs and change or enrich those that can't be automated.

In addition to physical change and job redesign, the change process requires participation from the employees and a consultation structure that permits their voices to be heard. Therefore, the fourth element of our change strategy, one that grows increasingly important as we make progress on the other three fronts, is personal development. Volvo wants individuals to have a chance to learn more and to enhance their personal lives and careers through opportunities available within the company.

In both Sweden and Volvo, the structure for consultation already existed. Throughout the company we have a hierarchy of works councils with representatives from both management and the employees. Some of these councils, one per plant, have been required by law since 1948. Others, like the Corporate Works Council, were created to meet our own needs for consultation. Given these councils, the physical changes quite naturally led to improvements in the work itself and to greater individual involvement.

INNOVATION AT THE WORKPLACE

A new factory presents a unique opportunity to try out entirely new approaches to work design, and many of the changes Volvo has adopted in the last five years were first tried at the Kalmar factory in the south of Sweden.

Kalmar: The Catalyst

In designing the Kalmar plant, we decided to break up the inexorable assembly line to which the people are subservient and to use instead individual carriers that move under control of the employees. An assembly line is essentially a set of conveyors going through a warehouse full of materials. The materials, not the employees, are the focus of the system. People are continually having to run after their work as it moves past their stations. We thought perhaps people could do a better job if the product could stand still while they worked on it.

Another problem in factory life is that there is an antisocial atmosphere built into the production line. People want to have some social contact, a chance to look at each others' faces now and then. But in an assembly line, people are physically isolated from each other. If they do manage to get together to discuss something, people in the traditional auto plant typically have to yell over the sound of machines. Furthermore, people performing jobs of very short duration (perhaps 30 to 60 seconds) seldom get a chance to stop between tasks to think or talk.

We believed the human-scaled work group would be more effective. If work were patterned according to people, rather than the other way around, we thought people could act in cooperation, discuss more, and decide among themselves how to organize the work. In essence, our approach is based on stimulation rather than restriction. If one views the employees as adults, then one must assume they will respond to stimulation. If one views them as children, then the assumption is that they will need restriction. The intense emphasis in most factories on measurement and control seems to be a manifestation of the latter viewpoint.

The design for Kalmar incorporated pleasant, quiet surroundings, arranged for group working, with each group having its own individual rest and meeting areas. The work itself is organized so that each group is responsible for a particular, identifiable portion of the car—electrical systems, interiors, doors, and so on. Individual cars are built up on self-propelling "carriers" that run around the factory following a movable conductive tape on the floor. Computers normally direct the carriers, but manual controls can override the taped route. If someone notices a scratch in the paint on a car, he or she can immediately turn the carrier back to the painting station. Under computer control again, the car will return later to the production process wherever it left off.

Each work group has its own buffer areas for incoming and outgoing carriers so it can pace itself as it wishes and organize the work inside its own area so that its members work individually or in subgroups to suit themselves. Most of the employees have chosen to learn more than one small job; the individual increase in skills also gives the team itself added flexibility.

To gain a sense of identification with its work, a group must also take responsibility for its work. The myriad inspection stations with "watchdog" overtones that characterize most factories have been abandoned at Kalmar. Instead, each team does its own inspection. After a car passes about three work group stations, it passes through a special inspection station where people with special training test each car. A computer-based system takes quality information reports from these stations and, if there are any persistent or recurring problems, flashes the results to the proper group station, telling them also how they solved similar problems the last time. The computer also informs the teams when their work has been particularly problem-free.

When we started at Kalmar, we made the assumption that the productivity could equal that of any comparable traditional plant. Today we have not one but five new plants, organized in a nontraditional way, all scaled for 600 employees or less. These new plants cost a little bit more to build than traditional factories of similar size, but they are already showing good productivity. We believe productivity will continue to increase because the people who work in them have better jobs. One of the most important measures of our success came in autumn 1976 when we received the results of a union survey of all Kalmar employees. Almost all of them were in favor of the new working patterns; one result of the survey has been to increase our focus on working groups at other plants.

Torslanda: Breaking Down Bigness

At Kalmar where there is a maximum of 600 employees, organized in groups that control the auto carrier system, change was part of the design. At a place like our 8,000-employee Torslanda factory, just outside Gothenburg, introducing change is quite a different matter. Built in 1964, at the zenith of the technical era, Torslanda is tied to a large-scale assembly line. Furthermore, it remains the source of our "bread-and-butter" production, the mother factory for the cars that are the company's primary product. This means, too, that we can't make sweeping changes that might disrupt production, as we might be able to do in a new place where we were adding capacity.

While to a large extent central management spurred the Kalmar plan, most of the changes in the last five years at Torslanda have been locally generated. For this we must give considerable credit not only to the managers there but also to the 55 works council groups and subgroups, to a number of active union officials, and to the more than 8,000 employees themselves.

A factor that seems to permeate our experience, at Torslanda and throughout the company in Sweden, is the serious, mature attitude of union officials, who have often initiated or supported changes that caused them short-term inconveniences and required adjustments in such basic items as wage structures. Group working, for example, means that the basis for incentive or bonus payments shifts from individual production to group production; yet it is the union as much as the company that has made group working a primary goal for Torslanda.

Although the consultation structure has always been strong at Torslanda, real changes in the work itself began to come to light as the planning for Kalmar got under way. Torslanda was in some ways the cradle for Kalmar. The carrier was developed by people borrowed from Torslanda; its tilting device, which eliminates the need to work in pits on cars overhead, was tested at Torslanda, and 20 of the tilters replace pits in assembly there today.

One of the first change steps at Torslanda was to make the four main departments (pressing, body work, painting, and assembly) as autonomous as possible. Each department has its own problems and its own style. In 1973, for example, the body shop formed a working group to consider problems of noise and dust. The working group enlisted some architects from the Gothenburg School of Applied Art, and from their suggestions employees selected schemes for cutting noise, eliminating dirt, and brightening their environment. It took several years to implement all the proposals, but today the body shop is one of the brightest spots in the corporation.

Starting change and keeping it going is a challenge in a place like Torslanda. Most of the works councils, consultation groups, and project groups have money to spend on such things as improving their working conditions. Changes to cut the dust or noise require little outside impetus. Changes of work structure that can take place within a single working group also occur naturally. But we have discovered that most real changes of work structure affect other groups, at least indirectly. So the problem has been to draw the boundaries for single working groups wherever we could, and to make them as clear-cut as possible.

Job rotation was the opening wedge. It started around 1964 in the upholstery department for practical reasons—to eliminate the muscular aches and pains the employees got from doing the same operation over and over. Some of the employees, however, disliked the change of pace, and reactions were mixed for several years. In 1966, when the upholstery employees themselves helped plan a rotation system, the results were much better. Each employee learned the work for all 15 stations; and each checked and corrected his or her own work. The employees noticed a sharp drop in the aches and pains, and new signs of team spirit began to show up. Eventually they took responsibility for planning their own work as well as for checking it. Employee turnover and absenteeism in the group dropped, and the upholstery quality improved.

The evolution of this group from 1964 to 1968 has many of the characteristics of other successful changes that have occurred in more recent years. People often resist change at first, and this is overcome only when there has been sufficient time and contact among members for a real group to begin crystallizing. This contact is difficult to achieve on a rapidly moving assembly line with short-cycle tasks. As the upholstery example shows, a group creates itself; it cannot be created by someone else. And the process does not take place overnight.

Once a real group does exist, though, it can take on other tasks well beyond its original purpose. As later groups also learned, rotating jobs was often more satisfying than continually performing a single short-cycle task, even though it entailed a lot of job-hopping. If group members could enlarge jobs, taking in neighboring tasks, they could turn a two-minute station time into four, or eight, or ten minutes, and have more satisfaction in handing on a fairly finished product. Enrichment, whereby the group took on supervision, control, and planning, usually came later when the group was quite well formed.

Although we had a good example in the upholstery group on hand, and a deep interest in job content, job rotation at Torslanda nonetheless crept on very slowly. By the end of 1970 about 3% of our 3,000 assembly people were rotating jobs. We hit 10% in 1971, 18% in 1972, and then began to see momentum when

30% of the assembly people were rotating by the end of 1973. Today it is well over 60%, with employees showing more interest in job enlargement or job enrichment, and we know that interest will grow until we gradually reach the point where employees make the natural demand for change in jobs. There will always be a few people, however, especially older ones, who don't want to change at all.

In the body and paint shops it was fairly natural for the employees to be organized in groups, and enrichment occurred in different forms in different areas. Assembly in the shops, though, is still paced by the speed of the line. In late 1976, we began a new kind of work within Torslanda to replace the traditional line. Two groups, each with nine people, do final assembly in docks. The nine group members do everything including chassis assembly, body work, mating the chassis and body, final trimming, and checkout. The dock employees have production meetings every week to discuss their situation, which includes the usual technical problems that occur with new equipment.

It takes each group about an hour to make a car. Thus the production costs remain competitive, and we think the additional investment for the dock equipment and more material-handling support (such as fork-lift drivers, who already have fairly interesting jobs) is justified. We are convinced that improved working conditions and work content result in lower employee turnover and absenteeism, and thus in less expense to the company as well as the community.

We wouldn't invest in dock assembly if we couldn't see economic as well as social justification for it. We can already see that it is possible to cut the standard assembly line production time sharply. When work is split as in normal MTM, each employee has unused time between tasks. With larger job cycles more work is done in total, and the work is more satisfying for the person doing it.

Does It Work outside Sweden?

Volvo management realizes that the easy acceptance of joint union and company projects is uniquely Swedish. Our emphasis on improving work content was also early in terms of the current worldwide trend. When we bought a controlling interest in the Dutch auto manufacturer DAF in 1975, we found the company was experiencing some of the same problems we had observed at the beginning of the 1970s and was thinking about similar solutions. The association with Volvo simply added impetus to a trend that was already there.

The factory at Born in the Netherlands, which now manufactures our smaller model 343 car, employs about 3,700 people, about a third of whom are not Dutch. When absenteeism and employee turnover rose in 1973, a steering committee of managers and technical people set out to improve work on the assembly line. Starting with a relatively difficult mixture of people, 12 employees of both sexes, all ages, and varied nationalities, they explored job enlargement. Involvement grew rapidly as members taught each other their jobs. By the end of 1973, most people had learned from 3 to 11 of the 12 jobs, and then they could work in longer cycles. The foreman together with the group took the planning task formerly done by the foreman's supervisor.

While management was officially reviewing and evaluating these results during most of 1974, similar activities started spontaneously in other parts of the plant. In early 1975, a new steering committee, including employee representatives, set up discussion groups regarding job enlargement and problem solving. Today about 150 groups, each containing 15 or so people, involving more than 80% of the blue-collar employees, meet regularly, about once a month. Also, managers at Born are planning management development courses, concentrating on interpersonal relations and communications, for people starting at the foreman level.

One outgrowth of the Born activities is a new assembly hall, where the conveyor belt, which the employees control, is divided into small overhead conveyors with intermediate buffers between them. The conveyor idea is now being studied at Torslanda. The managers consult the employees regarding all new equipment or layouts; they have published a "letter of intent" setting out their desire to improve the work structure not just as a project but as an ongoing process. There is at Born now a useful strategy for the future.

At Volvo's own Ghent factory in Belgium, which is less troubled by absenteeism and employee turnover, the reexamination of work structure happened somewhat later than at Born, but managers there are pleased by recent progress. In April 1974, influenced by changes in the Belgian social climate, growing demand from employees for better conditions, and the rapid progress in most of Volvo's Swedish plants, the management at Ghent decided there was a need to make the individual more central to the production process.

Ghent managers initiated a program focusing on a better arrangement of the relief people (a ratio of 1 relief person to 14 employees instead of the former 1 to 25) and installation of buffer areas. Storage now provides 20-minute production coverage; fixed stations and group working replace the pits in the assembly factory and the merry-go-rounds in the body assembly shop. In the upholstery area the line was abandoned entirely in favor of group working. Today an employee assembles an entire seat and takes responsibility for the quality.

In the second phase at Ghent, managers saw that those areas where factory employees gave some input to the change process were obviously running more smoothly than those that had been changed entirely by managers and engineers. Now top managers are looking for better ways to keep in touch with employees, and management education has a higher priority today at Ghent. A "group working" project team is investigating further changes. Ghent managers say the results so far are convincing.

WORK TEAMS AND MANAGEMENT

At every level, management of group working is a different phenomenon. I think the change is healthy. Instead of giving orders the manager has to listen, argue, motivate, and often compromise. This process takes longer. Decisions are slower. But it works out better in the long run because, once they are made, the decisions are accepted and implemented rapidly.

We have learned something else from the group working at Torslanda and other factories. The success or failure of an idea is often attributable to whose idea it was, rather than to any intrinsic goodness or badness of the idea. If it is the union's idea, or if it comes from a work group, an innovation has a good chance of working. If it is a management idea, its chances are slimmer. (In the United States it seems to be the other way around.)

So the function of management at Volvo is not so much having ideas as creating an environment, a climate where the people who matter will be able to have ideas and try them out. Joint consultation on an informal basis—best exemplified in group working—gives the best chance for a group to develop ownership of an idea and, therefore, find good reasons to make sure it succeeds.

In this environment leadership is crucial. Participation actually demands better leadership, as well as more self-discipline from everyone involved. Some foreigners talk about Sweden as if management control, in the traditional sense, may be lost in the new industrial environment. Outsiders also worry that participation by employees will lead to reduced efficiency for corporations. Examples of reduced efficiency, however, and there will be some, are more likely to be due to poor management than to changes in the system.

I don't believe the new values and the new laws call for "permissiveness." Instead, I think managers have to be stronger and more disciplined. It is the weak people in management who have difficulties dealing with employee representatives. Until the manager can earn the respect of employees, there will be mutual suspicion, and too little information will flow between them. Leaders who have the strength and self-confidence to respect their employees and the strength to talk about their own mistakes will earn respect. Once the employees trust and respect a manager, real progress is possible. That kind of strength is the focus for selection, training, and development of Volvo managers.

The new climate we have achieved at Volvo clearly demands a different type of leadership at all levels. Foremen, who had been the focus of our production achievements in the past, are now faced with a new situation. The new approach means that they risk being squeezed between higher management and the plant employees. Also, today, foremen carry the heaviest responsibility in implementing changes.

For decades we told them, in essence, that they had two main functions. The first was to supervise the pace of the work, to keep the line moving. The second was to give technical advice and assistance wherever necessary. Thus most of the people promoted to foremen's positions had been skilled employees who could solve technical problems. To keep people working, they became disciplinarians, expert at saying "thou-shalt-not."

Suddenly we asked foremen to develop a rather different set of skills. We wanted them to be "good managers of people." Instead of people receiving discipline from the supervisor, the new climate emphasizes self-discipline. We redefined the foreman's role rapidly, and this created problems during the change. The problems were exacerbated by the fact that formal training for foremen was traditionally less important than on-the-job training, so they tended to be reluctant to take courses at first.

Yet in the new circumstances foremen needed considerable training to regard themselves as information-gatherers, as aides to the employees, as teachers and consultants, rather than as bosses. And in many cases the attitude change was only partial, stimulated and, at the same, hampered because it was forced by pressure from employees and management, rather than from the foremen's own convictions. The situation is better today, but it was a problem at first because of the speed with which we implemented changes and the fact that we did not consult with foremen enough in planning for the changes.

In a sense top management can act as an enzyme, a catalyst, to speed up the process of change—but it has not been an easy process even in Sweden where the social and political values supported the directions we chose. In the mid-1960s there weren't many managers who could uphold what we're doing now.

Today's managers have moved a long way from the attitude they held ten years ago for several reasons. Because people had such bad experiences with existing systems, there was force from the bottom. And because we insisted on change, there was also force from the top. Furthermore, if a middle manager wakes up every morning wondering whether he will have to replace or do without 15% to 20% of his work force, he will grow more willing to change.

Numbers are important, and the manager has to produce the numbers. The pressure builds up, resulting in change much more rapid than the normally conservative culture of a corporation would permit.

We have no "management development" chief at Volvo. The task is too important to put into a specialist department. Instead, I consider it one of my most important duties. This view is increasingly shared by line managers throughout the company. Their foremen, supervisors, managers, and employees are resources for which they are accountable, just as they are accountable for investments in buildings and machines.

In this atmosphere of employee participation and rapid change, management is an exacting task. If you don't manage tautly, you can drift into inefficiency that endangers the entire venture. It is the manager's job to create an atmosphere of urgency. But tight management need not be authoritative. Today's manager must be able to talk to people, and to listen as well. If the manager is alert to every opportunity for improvement and full of zest for his job, this communicates itself to others.

Participation demands more work, not less, from everybody. Idle people become bored and sloppy, so it is an important part of the manager's job to be taking the temperature all the time, injecting some of his or her own alertness whenever he or she senses signs of apathy or boredom. As other companies have learned—and so have we—the manager who is reluctant or just gives lip service to the idea of participation can hold back employee-based changes that are actually in the best interests of both the corporation and its employees.

Volvo's Guidelines

Our experiences with change in our various plants have produced a few rules of thumb that may be helpful to others:

- Each unit should be free to develop individually, without detailed control or interference from headquarters.

- An active and positive top management attitude toward change is a prerequisite for positive results. However, when this attitude turns into a drive from above to install programs, projects, and plans, management tends to fail.

- Headquarters is most effective when its role is sanctioning investments for new approaches and challenging local managers to take more radical initiatives and risks.

- Our positive achievements seem related to the extent our managers understand that the change process will sooner or later affect several organizational levels, regardless of where it started.

- We encounter problems if we formalize change and request targets, minutes, and figures too early. Change requires time and freedom of action. When people view it as a continuing search-and-learning process of their own, the chances of lasting effects are increased.

- The initiative for change should be a line responsibility, with specialists as supporters rather than initiators. Changes line managers initiate seldom have lasting effects. Managers can, however, act as sounding boards and catalysts, carrying know-how from one place to another.

- Progress seems to be fastest when a factory or company starts by forming a joint management and union steering committee to look at its own problems.

- Steering committee members should be the strongest possible people, sharing commitment to change.

- The fastest way to get ideas flowing seems to be to set up discussion groups in each working area. A working area in this sense (and in a group-working sense) should probably contain fewer than 25 people.

- Groups that have money to spend on their own facilities and a mandate to list their own problems seem to achieve cohesion and cooperation most rapidly. It need not cost the corporation more money to apportion facilities or safety budgets to the groups themselves than to experts.

- A new plant, a new product, or a new machine is an opportunity to think about new working patterns.

- An investment in one new facility or one group area often results in spontaneous changes in related facilities or groups. These can be encouraged by alert managers.

- Most factories have a number of tasks that need not be done on assembly lines. Once a few have been found and changed, others will reveal themselves.

- So that the change suggestions will emerge from inside, changes of work organization must be integrated with a structure of employee consultation.

Job Enrichment: A Reevaluation

Mitchell Fein

INTRODUCTION

The quality of working life, work humanization, job enrichment, restructure of work, and other such concerns are increasingly the subject of discussions and articles in the management literature and the press. A vocal school of social scientists is pressing government officials, legislators, and management to give serious attention to the signs of unrest in industry. Their proposals are summarized in *Work in America*, a study written for the Department of Health, Education, and Welfare.[1]

To a large extent this article disagrees with the findings of that study. In the first part of the article, the theory of job enrichment is examined in detail. It is suggested that job enrichment does not work as well as has been claimed. The second part of the article develops a more balanced framework for thinking about worker motivation and job enrichment.

THE THEORY BEHIND JOB ENRICHMENT

According to the study *Work in America*, the primary cause of the dissatisfaction of white- and blue-collar workers is the nature of their work: ". . . significant numbers of American workers are dissatisfied with the quality of their working lives. Dull, repetitive, seemingly meaningless tasks, offering little challenge or autonomy, are causing discontent among workers at all occupational levels."[2] The study reports that the discontent of women, minorities, blue-collar workers, youth, and older adults would be considerably less if these Americans had an active voice in decisions at the work place that most directly affect their lives. "The redesign of jobs is the keystone of this report, . . ."; work must be made more meaningful to the workers.[3] The presumption is that blue-collar employees will work harder if their jobs are enriched or expanded to give them greater control over the order of their work or its content, or to allow them more freedom from direct supervision. Far too many variations on the theme of job enrichment have appeared in the last ten years to attempt to describe even a small proportion of them. The following discussion therefore assumes that the reader is familiar with the basic ideas of job enrichment.

DO THE STUDIES SUPPORT THE THEORY?

Claims for the success and usefulness of job enrichment are based primarily on a number of job enrichment case histories and studies conducted over the

[1]See *Work in America* [24].
[2]See *Work in America* [24], p. xv.
[3]See *Work in America* [24], p. xvii.

From *Sloan Management Review*, Winter 1974, 69–88. Reprinted by permission.

past ten years. These studies attempt to prove that workers really want job enrichment. However, when they are examined closely, it is found that:

1 What actually occurred in the cases was often quite different from what was reported to have occurred.

2 Most of the cases were conducted with hand-picked employees, who were usually working in areas or plants isolated from the main operations and thus did not represent a cross section of the working population. Practically all experiments have been in nonunion plants.

3 Only a handful of job enrichment cases have been reported in the past ten years, despite the claims of gains obtained for employees and management through job changes.

4 In *all* instances the experiments were initiated by management, never by workers or unions.

A review of some the more prominent studies illustrates these points.

Survey of Working Conditions[4]

This large scale study of workers' attitudes toward work and working conditions, conducted for the Department of Labor by the Survey Research Center at the University of Michigan, is cited in numerous articles and is a mainstay of the HEW study. When examined closely, however, several errors are revealed which cast serious doubt upon the validity of its conclusions.

In the study, the workers polled were asked to rank twenty-five aspects of work in order of importance to them. They ranked interesting work first; pay, fifth; and job security, seventh. The researchers neglected, however, to indicate that these rankings averaged together the survey results for all levels of workers, from managers and professionals to low skilled workers. The researchers created a composite image that they called a "worker." The study, however, was based on a cross section of the United States work force rather than just lower-level workers.

When separated into the basic occupational categories and analyzed separately, the data show that blue-collar workers rank pay and job security higher than interesting work. Interesting work was ranked so high in SRC's results because the responses of managers, professionals, and skilled people were averaged with the responses of lower-level workers.[5]

It seems reasonable to suspect that the attitudes of managers and professionals toward their jobs might be different from those of factory workers, and that there also might be differences between skilled and unskilled workers' attitudes within occupational groupings. When the data were compiled by SRC, each subject's occupation was identified, but the results presented in the final report were lumped together for all subjects.

[4]See "Survey of Working Conditions" [26].
[5]See, for example, Fein [4].

The new data obtained by reanalyzing the SRC data by occupational categories is supported by a large scale study that was conducted abroad. In the first phase of a study covering 60,000 people in more than fifty countries (excluding the Communist bloc), Sirota and Greenwood found that there was considerable similarity in the goals of employees around the world and that the largest and most striking differences are between jobs rather than between countries. Most interestingly, the security needs of people in lower-skilled jobs were found to be highest.[6] The final phase of the study is even more illuminating because the data include the full range of occupations, from managers to unskilled workers, reported separately by seven occupational groups. Unskilled workers in manufacturing plants abroad ranked their needs in this order: physical conditions first, security second, earnings third, and benefits fourth. A factor labeled "interesting work" was not included, but there were several which in total encompass this factor. These were ranked far below the workers' top four needs.[7]

General Foods-Topeka

General Foods-Topeka has been widely cited to show how, when jobs are enriched according to organization development principals, productivity and employee satisfaction will rise. However, Walton's reporting of this case omits critical information which greatly affects the interpretation of what actually occurred and why.[8]

Walton attributes the success of the Topeka plant to the ". . . autonomous work groups . . . integrated support functions . . . challenging job assignments . . . job mobility and rewards for learning . . . facilitative leadership . . . managerial decision making for operations . . . self-government for the plant community . . . congruent physical and social context . . . learning and evolution . . ." which were established for the employees.[9] He does not mention that the sixty-three Topeka employees are a group of very special people who were carefully selected from 700 applicants in five screening interviews. The fourth screening was an hour-long personal interview, and the fifth was a four-hour session that included a complex two-hour personality test.[10]

General Foods-Topeka is a controlled experiment in a small plant with conditions set up to achieve desired results. The employees are not a cross section of the larger employee population, or even of Topeka. The plant and its operations are not typical of those in industry today. The results obtained are valid only for this one plant. What are other managers to do? Should they screen out nine of ten possible candidates and hire only from the select group that remains? What happens to the other nine who were not selected?

---

[6]See Sirota and Greenwood [18].
[7]See Hofstede [9].
[8]See Walton [27].
[9]See Walton [28], p. 9.
[10]See King [12], p. 9.

If the investigators had shown how they converted a plant bursting with labor problems into one where management and employees told glowingly of their accomplishments, the study would truly merit the praise it has received. Instead they turned their backs on the company's parent plant in Kankakee, which has many of the problems of big city plants. Even worse, they tantalize management with the prospect that, in building a new plant with new equipment, carefully selected employees, and no union, productivity will be higher.

Many managers have dreamed of relocating their plants in the wheat fields or the hills to escape from the big city syndrome. Is this Walton's message to managers in his article, "How to Counter Alienation in the Plant?"[11]

Writers who extol the GF-Topeka case do not understand that what makes this plant so unique is not only the management style but the workers themselves, who were hand-picked. These are highly motivated workers who were isolated from the mainstream of workers and now are free to do their work in their own way. One wonders how these hand-picked workers would produce without any changes at all in management practices.

Procter & Gamble

Procter & Gamble is cited by Jenkins. "Without doubt the most radical organizational changes made on a practical, day-to-day basis in the United States have taken place at Procter & Gamble, one of America's largest companies, well known for its hardboiled, aggressive management practices."[12] What generally is not mentioned in any of the laudatory articles about P&G's organizational development practices is that P&G is an unusual company with a history of concern for its employees that is matched by few other firms in this country. In 1923 William C. Procter, then president of the company, recognized that the workers' problems were caused in large part by seasonal employment, and he established genuine job security. He guaranteed forty-eight weeks of employment a year. P&G has a long history of good wages and working conditions; they also have pioneered in old age pensions and profit sharing. Since P&G has a good reputation among workers, its plants attract some of the best workers in their areas. In seeking the reasons for P&G's success, one must not overlook their excellent bread and butter policies, among the best in the nation. Would their organizational development and job enrichment practices work without such policies?

Other Studies on Job Enrichment

Texas Instruments   The intensive job enrichment efforts of Texas Instruments management is unequaled in this country. Since 1952 the TI management has tried diligently to gain acceptance of its enrichment program by its workers. In 1968 the management announced that its goal was to involve 16 percent of

[11]See Walton [27].
[12]See Jenkins [10].

its employees in job enrichment. Their data show that the actual involvement was 10.5 percent.[13] This is far from the huge success claimed in the numerous articles describing the program.

Polaroid Corporation   Experiments involve only job rotation, not job enrichment. Foulkes reports that from 1959 to 1962, 114 employees out of 2000 were involved in changing their jobs.[14] Although management had guaranteed that employees could change their jobs and be assured of a return to their original jobs if they wished, less than 6 percent of the employees actually became involved. It does not appear that the employees favored the plan or that it was broadly successful.

Texas Instruments Cleaning and Janitorial Employees   The version of this report in *Work in America* states that when Texas Instruments took over the cleaning work formerly done by an outside contracting firm, the employees were ". . . given a voice in planning, problem solving, and goal setting for their own jobs . . . the team (had the) responsibility to act independently to devise its own strategies, plans, and schedules to meet the objective . . . the cleanliness level rating improved from 65 percent to 85 percent, personnel . . . dropped from 120 to 71, and quarterly turnover dropped from 100 percent to 9.8 percent . . . cost savings for the entire site averaged $103,000 per annum."[15]

What was not reported by the study was that the outside contractor's employees received only $1.40 per hour. When TI took over the program, the starting pay was raised to $1.94 per hour for the first shift, with $.10 extra added for the second shift and $.20 extra added for the third. The janitorial employees were given good insurance programs, profit sharing, paid vacations, sick leave, a good cafeteria, and working conditions similar to those of other employees at Texas Instruments. *Work in America* does not mention that in raising the pay by 46 percent and adding benefits worth one-third of their pay, TI was able to recruit better qualified employees. Yet the study insists on attributing the improved performance to job enrichment. The omission of this pay data is strange, since the data appear prominently in the report from which the HEW task force obtained the case material.[16]

American Telephone and Telegraph   Space does not permit a discussion of the various cases reported by Robert Ford.[17] To a large degree, he redesigned jobs at AT&T which had been ineffectively set up in the first place. To label such changes "job enrichment" is to render the phrase meaningless.

The Scandinavian Experience   *Work in America* suggests that worker initiative is inhibited by a lack of democracy at the work place. The study points

[13]See Fein [2].
[14]See Foulkes [7].
[15]See *Work in America* [24], p. 100.
[16]See Rush [15], pp. 39–45.
[17]See Ford [5].

to Europe and especially to the Scandinavian countries as examples of productivity gains through democracy in the plants.[18] The assumption is that European experience in industrial relations is directly transferable to this country. In fact, it may not be. Nat Goldfinger, Research Director of the AFL-CIO, believes ". . . that industrial democracy was not needed in America: 'The issue is irrelevant here. I would suspect that most of the issues that are bugging Europeans are taken care of here in collective bargaining.' "[19]

The study of worker participation councils covering fifty different countries cited earlier supports this position. It shows clearly that this movement is the European workers' way of institutionalizing union plant locals and of establishing collective bargaining on the plant floor. It is not a new form of worker democracy as described by the behaviorists.[20]

The examples discussed above are only a sampling of the job enrichment studies. Many more could be cited, but most of them are subject to criticisms already voiced. Only lack of space prevents a fuller discussion.

Job Enrichment or Common Sense?

Admittedly there are some cases where jobs have actually been productively enriched. Much more common, however, is the masquerading of common sense as job enrichment. Many studies have simply involved the elimination of an obviously bothersome problem, which hardly warrants the use of the term job enrichment. This paper is not directed toward the common sense applications of job enrichment. Rather this analysis is aimed at the broader claims of job enrichment success.

LIMITS TO JOB ENRICHMENT

One reason that job enrichment has not been widely implemented is that there are many factors operating within the work place to constrain its applicability. Several of these factors are discussed below.

Technology

The structure of jobs in American industry today is dictated largely by the technology employed in the production process. The size of the parts used, the equipment required for the operations, and the volume of production are all important determinants. When the blacksmith of a century ago shaped a piece of metal, his only capital equipment was a forge. He was the operator and the forge press. Today there are even large, specialized machines for parts which are viewed under a microscope. Much of the job redesign called for by proponents of job enrichment neglects the constraints imposed by technology.

There are few decisions on what to do in mass production. A piece is put

[18]See *Work in America* [24], pp. 103–105.
[19]See Jenkins [11], p. 315.
[20]See Roach [14].

into a press and hit. Two pieces or fifty are assembled in a given manner, simply because the pieces do not fit together in another way. In typing a letter or keypunching, the operators strike certain keys, not just any they wish. Even in the highly praised experimental Volvo plant where a small team assembles an engine, the workers have no choice in the selection of parts to be installed, and they must assemble the parts in a given sequence. While they may rotate their jobs within the group and thus obtain variety, this is not job enrichment or autonomy but job rotation.

In most instances it is impossible to add to jobs decision making of the kind that job enrichment theorists call for, simply because of the technology of the work. The job shops which produce only a small number of an item can provide true decision making for many of its employees, but these shops have not attracted the attention of job enrichers. They are worried about the mass production plants where work has been grossly simplified.

Another view of the technological constraints on job enrichment is offered by workers themselves. A full page article in a union newspaper recently denounced attempts by General Electric to combine the tasks of a thirty-two operator line producing steam irons into a single work station, with a headline: "Makes no difference how you slice it, it's still monotony and more speed up." Jim Matles, an officer of the United Electrical Workers, derides management's efforts, pointing out that, "As monotonous as that job was on that continuous assembly line, they were able to perform it practically without having to keep their minds on the job . . . they could talk to each other. On the new assembly line, however, the repetitiveness of the job was there just as much, but . . . they no longer could do it without being compelled to keep their minds on the job." Another union leader in the plant said, "I've finally been able to show [management] that the more repetitive or rhythmic the job, the less unhappy the worker. On jobs where the rhythm is broken and unrepetitive, the employees are unhappy and must constantly fight these jobs [rather] than do them by natural reflex."[21]

It is not intended that technological constraints be thought of as structural barriers to job enrichment. In the long run technology can be changed. Workers and managers are by no means forever locked into the present means of production. At the very least, however, proponents of job enrichment have neglected badly the immediate problems posed by technology. At their worst they have intentionally ignored them. The purpose of this section is to restore a more balanced perspective to the relationship of technology to job enrichment.

Cost

Giving workers job rotation opportunities or combining jobs can increase costs. This occurred recently at the General Motors Corporation Truck and Coach Division. Early this year they initiated an experiment using teams of workers to assemble motor homes. *Business Week* reported that, "Six-member teams

[21]See Matles [13].

assembled the body while three-member teams put the chassis together. The move was an attempt to curb assembly line doldrums and motivate workers. Last month, the experiment was curtailed. The complexity of assembly proved too difficult for a team approach, which was too slow to meet GM's production standards.''[22]

Increased costs from combining jobs and in job rotation also occurred in a case reported by Louis E. Davis, a prominent advocate of job redesign. He made studies to compare the levels of output obtained with a mechanically-paced conveyor line, a line with no pacing, and a line with individuals performing all of the jobs as a ''one-man line.'' Using the average output of the nine-operator paced line as 100 percent. Davis found that the same non-paced line operated at 89 percent, and the ''one-man line'' operated at 94.0 percent. Translated into unit costs, the non-paced line cost 12.4 percent more and the individual line 6.4 percent more than the conventional paced line.[23] Suppose that the workers liked the non-pacing or the built up job better (although this did not happen to be true). Would the consumer be willing to pay the additional cost?

Relative Levels of Skill

The possibility of making enriching changes in jobs increases with the skill level of the jobs. However, relatively few jobs have a high skill content, and relatively few workers occupy these jobs. If widespread benefits are derived from job enrichment, these are most needed for workers in the low level jobs, where boredom presumably is highest. The work of skilled workers already has challenge and interest built into the jobs, requiring judgment, ingenuity and initiative. Adding job enrichment responsibilities in some cases may only be gilding the lily. What are managers to do with low-skilled workers who make up the great majority of the work force? That is the essence of the problem confronting managers. When tested in the plant, enrichment programs do not operate as predicted. They usually can be applied only to the wrong people, to those who do not need them because their jobs potentially provide the necessary enrichment.

Work Group Norms

Studies from around the world, including the communist countries, demonstrate that the concepts of McGregor and Herzberg regarding workers' need to find fulfillment through work hold only for those workers who choose to find fulfillment through their work. Contrary to the more popular belief, the vast majority of workers seek fulfillment outside their work.[24] After almost twenty years of active research in job enrichment, it is clear that only a minority of workers is attracted to it. These workers are mostly in the skilled jobs or on

[22]See ''GM Zeroes in on Employee Discontent'' [8], p. 140.
[23]See Davis and Canter [1], p. 279.
[24]See, for example, Fein [2].

their way up. However the social pressure in the plant from the workers who are not involved in job enrichment sets the plant climate, and they apparently oppose job changes. The effect of this opposition is minimal on the active minority, because they find their enrichment by moving up to the skilled jobs where they have greater freedom to exercise their initiative. Obviously, the isolation of small groups of workers is not possible in the real world industry. In the main plant, the pervasive social climate controls what goes on, and job enrichment may not be permitted to work.

Contrasting Employer and Employee Goals

Proponents of job enrichment often forget that management and workers are not motivated in the same direction; they have different goals, aspirations, and needs. The fact of life which workers see clearly, but which often is obscured to others, is that *if workers do anything to raise productivity, some of them will be penalized.*

Job enrichment predicts that increased job satisfaction will increase motivation and raise productivity. However workers know that if they increase production, reduce delays and waiting time, reduce crew sizes or cooperate in any way, less overtime will be available, some employees will be displaced, and the plant will require fewer employees. The remaining workers will receive few financial benefits. What employee will voluntarily raise his production output, only to be penalized for his diligence?

This phenomenon does not occur with "exempt" employees, the executives, administrators, professionals, and salesmen. Have you ever heard of a manager who worked himself out of a job by superior performance? Have you ever heard of a salesman whose security was threatened because he sold too much or an engineer who caused the layoff of other engineers because he was too creative? These employees usually can anticipate rewards for their creativity and effectiveness.

When workers excel and raise productivity, the company benefits and management is pleased, but the workers usually do not benefit. On the contrary, in the short term their economic interests may be threatened; some suffer loss of income. When exempt employees are more effective, they cover themselves with glory; their economic security is enhanced not threatened. Ironically, the relationship between workers and management actually provides workers with the incentive not to cooperate in productivity improvement. Most companies offer their employees the opportunity to reduce their earnings and job security as they raise productivity. Management does not, of course, intend such results, but the system often operates that way in this country.

A recent study by the Harris organization, conducted for the National Commission on Productivity, provides support for this contention.

Nearly 7 in 10 feel that stockholders and management would benefit a lot from increased productivity, compared with scarcely more than 1 in 3 who see the same gains for the country as a whole.

The term "increased productivity" does not have a positive connotation for most people who work for a living.

A majority believes the statement 'companies benefit from increased productivity at the expense of workers.' Hourly workers believe this by 80–14 percent.[25]

Is it any wonder that workers are alienated from their work? Would company executives improve the effectiveness of their work if they believed it would not benefit them, and more, that it would reduce their income and even cause their layoff?[26]

DO MANAGERS SUPPORT THE THEORY?

If job enrichment were the panacea it is so often claimed to be, then somewhere in this country some aggressive, farsighted manager should have been able, in the past ten years, to have made it operational on a large scale basis. The claims that large productivity gains will be made through job redesign should have spurred many companies to implement it. Yet there are few successful examples. Given this lack of acceptance, it is reasonable to assume that managers do not support job enrichment.

DO THE WORKERS SUPPORT THE THEORY?

Those advocating that work should be redesigned start with the premise that such changes are socially desirable and beneficial to workers. Curiously, however, these investigators are not supported in their claims by many workers or unions. There is a sharp difference of opinion between what workers say they want and what proponents of job enrichment say workers should want.[27]

Workers' opinions on the enrichment of jobs are expressed by William W. Winpisinger, Vice-President of the Machinist Union.

In my years as a union representative and officer I've negotiated for a lot of membership demands. I've been instructed to negotiate on wages . . . noise . . . seniority clauses; fought for health and welfare plans, . . . and everything else you find in a modern labor-management contract. But never once have I carried into negotiations a membership mandate to seek job enrichment. In fact, quite to the contrary, working people want management to leave their jobs alone.[28]

The question of job enrichment and boredom on the job was discussed at last year's United Auto Workers convention and significantly was not made

---

[25]See the Harris Survey published in *The Record* (Bergen, N.J.), 19 February 1973, p. A-3.

[26]A most ironic turn of events has occurred in plants with supplementary unemployment benefits (SUB). Unions are asking that layoffs occur in *inverse seniority*, with the highest seniority employees going first. By inverting seniority and giving the senior employees a choice, a layoff under SUB becomes a reward, not a penalty. For working diligently and working himself out of a job, a worker is rewarded by time off with pay.

[27]This divergence of opinion is explored in more detail by Fein [3].

[28]See Winpisinger [30].

an issue in the following auto negotiations. Leonard Woodcock, President of the UAW, was sharply critical of the HEW report and a number of its suggestions. "Mr. Woodcock was very outspoken in his denunciation of government officials, academic writers and intellectuals who contend that boredom and monotony are the big problems among assembly workers. He said 'a lot of academic writers . . . are writing a lot of nonsense' . . . [he] expressed resentment over a recent government report on work as 'elitist' in its approach, describing assembly line workers as if they were 'subhumans'."[29]

A similar attitude on the part of European workers is reported by Basil Whiting of the Ford Foundation. He visited Europe to study their job enrichment efforts ". . . in terms of the experiments on job redesign: By and large all these experiments were initiated by management. We found no cases where they were initiated by unions and other forces in society."[30]

Despite the urgings for increased participation by workers, Strauss and Rosenstein also found that workers all over the world have failed to respond: " 'Participation' is one of the most overworked words of the decade. Along with 'meaningful' and 'involvement' it appears in a variety of forms and contexts." "Participation in many cases has been introduced from the top down as symbolic solutions to ideological contradictions," especially in the countries with strong socialist parties.[31] "In general the impetus for participation has come more from intellectuals, propagandists and politicians (sometimes all three combined) than it has from the rank-and-file workers who were supposed to do the participating."[32] There is obviously a lack of worker interest in participation despite claims by intellectuals that the work place is dehumanizing.

A MORE BALANCED APPROACH TO WORKER MOTIVATION AND JOB ENRICHMENT

Studying satisfied and dissatisfied workers, job enrichment theory contends that the intrinsic nature of the work performed is the main cause of the differences between them. The job enrichment theorists propose to change the work of the dissatisfied workers to more closely resemble the work performed by the satisfied workers. There is, however, a large "if" to this approach. What if the nature of the work is not what primarily satisfies all satisfied workers? Restructuring the work and creating work involvement opportunities may ignite a small flame under some people, but to what extent is the nature of the work the determinant of a person's drive? *The simple truth is that there are no data which show that restructuring and enriching jobs will raise the will to work.*

The essential assumption of job enrichment theory is that the nature of the work performed determines to a large extent worker satisfaction or dissatis-

[29]See "UAW Indicates It Will Seek to Minimize Local Plant Strikes in Talks Next Fall" [22].
[30]See his testimony before the Senate Subcommittee on Employment, Manpower, and Poverty [23].
[31]See Strauss and Rosenstein [21], pp. 197, 198.
[32]See Strauss and Rosenstein [21], p. 199.

faction. It is argued here that this is not always so. *The intrinsic nature of the work is only one factor among many that affect worker satisfaction.* Moreover, the available evidence suggests that its influence is very often subordinate to that of several other variables: pay, job security, and job rules. The inconclusive performance of job enrichment to date stems largely from those programs that have neglected to consider these factors.

A useful starting point in understanding how workers feel about their jobs is to look at how they choose their jobs. A "natural selection" model of job choice proves very fruitful in examining this process.

A "NATURAL SELECTION" MODEL OF JOB CHOICE

There is greater selection by workers of jobs than is supposed. The selection process in factories and offices often occurs without conscious direction by either workers or management. The data for white- and blue-collar jobs show that there is tremendous turnover in the initial employment period, which drops sharply with time on the job. Apparently what happens is that a worker begins a new job, tries it out for several days or weeks, and decides whether the work suits his needs and desires. Impressions about a job are a composite of many factors: pay, proximity to home, the nature of the work, working conditions, the attitude of supervision, congeniality of fellow workers, past employment history of the company, job security, physical demands, opportunities for advancement, and many other related factors. A worker's choice of job is made in a combination of ways, through evaluating various trade-offs. Working conditions may be bad, but if pay and job security are high, the job may be tolerable. There are numerous combinations of factors which in total influence a worker's disposition to stay on the job or not.

There is a dual screening which culls out those who will be dissatisfied with the work. The worker in the first instance decides whether to stay on the job, and management then has the opportunity to determine whether to keep him beyond the trial period. The combination of the worker's choice to remain and management's decision that the worker is acceptable initially screens out workers who might find the work dissatisfying.

INTRINSIC AND EXTRINSIC JOB CHARACTERISTICS

As a result of this selection process, workers are able to exert much control over the nature of the work which they finally accept. They can leave jobs that they do not like and only accept jobs which they find rewarding. The major constraint on the variety of work available to them is the intrinsic nature of the work itself. However, if there are no intrinsically rewarding jobs but a worker still must support his family, he will have to take an intrinsically unsatisfactory job.

Unlike the intrinsic nature of the work that he accepts, the worker has much less control over the extrinsic characteristics of his job. There may be many different kinds of jobs for which he is qualified, but most of them will pay about the same maximum salary or wage. Similarly, there will be few options regarding the different kinds of job security and work rule combinations which he can find. The suggested hypothesis is that the influence of extrinsic factors, particularly pay, job security, and work rules, on worker satisfaction has been obscured and neglected by job enrichment. Undoubtedly some workers are distressed by the highly routinized work that they may be performing, but to what extent is dissatisfaction caused by the intrinsic nature of their work? What proportion is caused by their insufficient pay? Would workers have a greater interest in the work if their living standards were raised and they could see their jobs as contributing to a good life?

Individual Differences in Job Preference

Work that one person views as interesting or satisfying may appear boring and dissatisfying to another. There are significant differences among workers, and their needs vary. Some workers prefer to work by rote without having to be bothered with decisions. Some workers prefer more complicated work. It is really a matter of individual preference.

There would undoubtedly be far greater dissatisfaction with work if those on the job were not free to make changes and selections in the work they do. Some prefer to remain in highly repetitive, low skill jobs even when they have an opportunity to advance to higher skill jobs through job bidding. A minority of workers strives to move into the skilled jobs such as machinists, maintenance mechanics, set-up men, group leaders, utility men, and other such positions where there is considerable autonomy in the work performed.

The continued evaluation of workers by management and the mobility available to workers to obtain jobs which suit them best refine the selection process. A year or two after entering a plant, most workers are on jobs or job progressions which suit them or which they find tolerable. Those who are no longer on the job have been "selected" out, either by themselves or by management. Given the distinction between intrinsic and extrinsic job characteristics and the greater degree of control which workers exert over the former, those who are left on the job after the selection process can be expected to be relatively more satisfied with the nature of their work than with their pay, job security, or work rules. In fact this prediction proves to be correct.

WORKERS' ATTITUDES TOWARD THEIR WORK

Work in America cites a Gallup Poll which found that 80 to 90 percent of American workers are satisfied with their jobs.[33] A more recent poll found that from 82 to 91 percent of blue- and white-collar workers like their work. The workers were asked, "If there were one thing you could change about your job, what would it be?" Astonishingly, very few workers said that they would make their jobs "less boring" or "more interesting."[34]

[33]See *Work in America* [24], p. 14.
[34]See Sorenson [20].

In a recent study, David Sirota was surprised to find that the sewing operators in one plant found their work interesting. Since the work appeared to be highly repetitive, he had expected that they would say they were bored and their talents underutilized.[35] These workers' views are supported in a large scale study by Weintraub of 2535 female sewing machine operators in seventeen plants from Massachusetts to Texas. He found that "Most of the operators like the nature of their work. Of those who were staying (65%), 9 out of 10 feel that way. Even of those who would leave (35%), 7 out of 10 like their work."[36]

For the most part workers are satisfied with the nature of their work. What they find most discomforting is their pay, their job security, and many of the work rules with which they must cope. They can find their work engrossing and still express dissatisfaction because of other job related factors such as pay, working conditions, inability to advance, and so on. When a person says his work is satisfying, he implies that his work utilizes his abilities to an extent *satisfactory to him*.

EXTRINSIC DETERMINANTS OF WORKER SATISFACTION

As the studies cited above indicate, most workers appear relatively more satisfied with the intrinsic nature of their jobs than with the extrinsic job factors. The major extrinsic factors are examined below.

Pay

Pay is very important in determining job satisfaction. This is hardly a novel observation, but it is one that is too often overlooked or forgotten in job enrichment programs. Sheppard and Herrick, both of whom served on the *Work in America* task force, analyzed the SRC and other data and provided a cross section of feelings by workers about their jobs. The following quotations concerning pay are from their study.[37]

> It was found that dissatisfaction with work decreases steadily as pay rises. When earnings exceed $10,000 per year, dissatisfaction drops significantly.

> If we knew why this occurs, we would probably have a major part of the answer to the question of why there is dissatisfaction at the work place. There is a cause and effect relationship involved in which it is difficult to evaluate

---

[35]Personal communication.

[36]See Weintraub [29], p. 349. The auto workers' jobs have been cited by many writers as the extreme of monotonous and dehumanizing work. However, a recent study of auto workers in the United States, Italy, Argentina, and India by W. H. Form found that "Most workers believe that their work integrates their lives . . . that their jobs are satisfying. Nowhere did assemblyline workers dwell upon monotony. . . . Machine work does not make workers more unhappy at any industrial stage. Nor do workers heed the lament of the intellectuals that the monotony of the job drives them mad" (See Form [6], pp. 1, 15).

[37]See Sheppard and Herrick [16].

how the various factors affect the employee. The higher the social value of the work performed, the higher is the pay. The higher the skill required of the employee, the higher is his opportunity for involvement in his work. As pay rises, to what extent does the pay level produce higher satisfaction with the affluence it brings? To what extent does the interesting content of the work cause higher satisfaction?

Construction workers are the highest paid of the blue-collar workers and have unexcelled benefits. Many professionals and managers earn less than construction workers. These workers are among the last of the craftsmen who still largely work with their hands and still may own their own tools. Their satisfaction may well come from their creative work, but to what extent does their high pay influence their attitudes?

In the managerial, professional and technical occupations only 1 in 10 were dissatisfied.

Is it the attraction of their work or their pay which affords them their satisfaction?

Slightly less than 1 in 4 manufacturing workers were dissatisfied. The data for workers in the service occupations and the wholesale-retail industry are about the same.

In 1971, Bureau of Labor Statistics data for blue-collar workers showed that 58.7 percent earned less than $150 per week, 24.6 percent earned from $150 to $199, and 16.8 percent earned over $200. In 1971, the BLS "lower level" budget for a family of four was $7214 per year.[38] The SRC data showed that 56.2 percent of the subjects reported having inadequate incomes. Considering the earnings statistics, it is a wonder that more workers are not dissatisfied.

Experience reveals that increasing the availability of interesting work will not compensate for a desire for increased pay, whereas increasing pay can go far to compensate for poor working conditions. This was vividly demonstrated by the workers who collect garbage in New York City. They perform their work in all kinds of weather. Their job is highly accident-ridden and is not held in high esteem by society. Ten years ago few people were interested in the job. Then the pay scale was raised to $10,500 per year with good benefits, and a long waiting line formed for the jobs. The nature of the work had not changed. It was the same dirty, heavy work, but now the pay was attractive.[39]

Job Security

A second critical component of the work environment is job security, the continuity of income. Pay must be not only sufficiently high but also fairly regular. No one can budget for a family if he is not reasonably sure of his

[38] See *Handbook of Labor Statistics* [25].
[39] The average annual pay is now $12,886.

income for some time into the future. Most people become distressed when faced with a layoff. Reduced employment affects the morale of everyone in the organization. When employment finally is stabilized and the threat of further reductions passes, fears and memories still linger.

Because it is such an important component of the work environment, *job security is an essential precondition to enhancing the will to work*. While the idea is not new that economic insecurity is a restraint on the will to work, its effect often is minimized by managers, behavioral scientists, and industrial engineers involved in productivity improvement. Job security is as vital to productivity improvement as advanced technical processes and new equipment.

What happens to feelings of identity and loyalty when employees see their increased productivity contributing to their layoff? It is hard to conceive of a manager who would cooperate in designing his own job out of existence, as might occur when several managerial jobs are combined and one person is no longer required. When managers consider their own job security, they quite expectedly have empathy for James F. Lincoln's truism: "No man will willingly work to throw himself out of his job, nor should he." Yet managers do not extend this obvious logic to their work force.

Managers must view job security not only in the social sense of how it affects workers' lives, but as absolutely essential to high levels of productivity. In the plants without job security, workers stretch out the work if they do not see sufficient work ahead of them.[40] They will not work themselves out of their jobs. When workers stretch out their jobs, though it is hidden from view, it is reflected in costs.

Managers historically have considered job security as a union demand to be bargained as are other issues. This has been a tragic error because whenever job security is lacking, labor productivity is restrained. Paradoxically, job security must be established as a demand of *management* if it hopes to increase productivity. What would happen in contract negotiations if management started off by demanding that the new contract include job protection for the employees? This radical act might encourage profound changes in employees' attitudes.

Unduly Restrictive Plant Rules

There are many other factors beside the work itself which affect workers' attitudes. In many companies workers still are considered "hands," hired by the hour with little consideration given to their needs and desires as "people." Some managers find it easier to lay workers off with four to eight hours notice than to plan production and avoid plant delays. In many plants, the plant rules, which management calls its prerogatives and guards jealously, are insulting to human sensibilities.

A worker's self-esteem is affected by how he is treated and how he rates with the others around him. Increasingly, workers want fair treatment for

---

[40] In a very fundamental way, work *does* expand to fill time (Parkinson's Law).

everyone. However, the "hands" concept still separates the white-collar from the blue-collar workers. White-collar workers are generally paid a weekly salary and often do not punch a time clock. They have more leeway in lateness and often do not lose pay when absent. Most factory workers have few of these benefits. A white-collar worker often has a telephone available and can make personal calls during the day. Factory workers have great difficulty in making calls. Receiving calls usually is reserved for extreme emergencies. When a worker has a problem, he stays out.

The penned-in feeling of workers, which is stylishly called their blues, comes in large part from their inability to take care of these daily personal problems and needs. Any job enrichment program which hopes to succeed must effectively address the problems posed to workers by plant rules. Until now very few programs have acknowledged their importance.

WHAT SHOULD BE DONE?

Everyone will accept the idea that improvement of the quality of working life is a desirable social goal. However, how should this be done? David Sirota provides a concise statement of the problem. "I can't get it through some thick skulls that [many] people may want both—that they would like to finish a day's work and feel that they had accomplished something and still get paid for it."[41] A logical approach to formulating the problem must begin with a determination of who is now dissatisfied and why and with the recognition that people have individual needs and desires.

The *Work in America* task force believes that "... pay ... is important," it must support an "adequate" standard of living, and be perceived as equitable—but high pay alone will not lead to job (or life) satisfaction.[42] They conclude that work must provide satisfaction and must be restructured to become the *raison d'etre* of people's lives. Their statement of the problem is correct, but their conclusion that work alone must provide satisfaction is wrong. Satisfaction can come from wherever people choose. It need not be only from their work.

The blues of many workers are due less to the nature of their work and more to what their work will not bring them in their pay envelopes. Increasingly, workers also want freedom on their jobs. Some workers prefer enriched jobs with autonomy. Most workers want more freedom to act on personal things outside of their work place. Some may want the freedom to just "goof off" once in a while. In short, workers' blues are not formed solely around the work place. Blues are partly work place reaction to non-work related problems.

Solving problems in the plants must start with the question why should workers want enriched jobs? It is readily apparent that management and the

[41]Panel discussion between Louis E. Davis, Mitchell Fein, and David Sirota, Annual Convention of the American Institute of Industrial Engineers, 24 May 1973.

[42]See *Work in America* [24], p. 95.

stockholders benefit from increased worker involvement which leads to reduced costs. For their part, if all the workers get is reduced hours or even layoffs, they must resist it. It is futile to expect that workers willingly will create more for management without simultaneously benefiting themselves. *The most effective productivity results will be obtained when management creates conditions which workers perceive as beneficial to them.* The changes must be genuine and substantial and in forms which eventually are turned into cash and continuity of income. Psychic rewards may look good on paper, but they are invisible in the pocketbook. If workers really wanted psychic job enrichment, management would have heard their demands loud and clear long ago.

Change must start with management taking the first steps, unilaterally and without *quid pro quo*. There must not be productivity bargaining at first. Management must provide the basic conditions which will motivate workers to raise productivity: job security, good working conditions, good pay and financial incentives. There must be a diminution of the win-lose relationship and the gradual establishment of conditions in which workers know that both they and management gain and lose together. Labor, management, and government leaders are very concerned that rising wages and costs are making goods produced in this country less competitive in the world markets. Increasingly all three parties are engaging in meaningful dialogue to address these problems.

There are unquestionably enormous potentials for increased productivity which workers can unleash—if they want to. The error of job enrichment is that it tries to talk workers into involvement and concern for the nature of their work when their memories and experiences have taught them that increased productivity only results in layoffs. Only management can now create conditions which will nullify the past.

Companies which are experimenting with new work methods probably will increase their efforts. As viable methods and approaches are developed, more companies will be tempted to innovate approaches suited to their own plants. The greatest progress will come in companies where workers see that management protects their welfare and where productivity gains are shared with the employees.

In the ideal approach, management should leave to workers the final choice regarding what work they find satisfying. In real life, this is what occurs anyway. Workers eschew work that they find dissatisfying or they find ways of saying loudly and clearly how they feel about such work. We should learn to trust workers' expressions of their wants. Workers will readily signal when they are ready for changes.

REFERENCES

[1]   Davis, L. E., and Canter, R. R. "Job Design Research." *The Journal of Industrial Engineering* 7 (1956): 275–282.
[2]   Fein, M. "Motivation for Work." In *Handbook of Work, Organization and Society*, edited by R. Dubin. Chicago: Rand McNally, 1973.

[3]   ———. "The Myth of Job Enrichment." *The Humanist*, September-October 1973, pp. 30–32.

[4]   ———. "The Real Needs of Blue Collar Workers." *The Conference Board Record*, February 1973, pp. 26–33.

[5]   Ford, R. N. *Motivation Through Work Itself*. New York: American Management Association, 1969.

[6]   Form, W. H. "Auto Workers and Their Machines: A Study of Work, Factory, and Job Satisfaction in Four Countries." *Social Forces* **52** (1973): 1–15.

[7]   Foulkes, F. K. *Creating More Meaningful Work*. New York: American Management Association, 1969.

[8]   "GM Zeroes in on Employee Discontent." *Business Week*, 12 May 1973, pp. 140–144.

[9]   Hofstede, G. H. "The Colors of Collars." *Columbia Journal of World Business*, September-October 1972, pp. 72–80.

[10]   Jenkins, D. "Democracy in the Factory." *The Atlantic*, April 1973, pp. 78–83.

[11]   ———. *Job Power: Blue and White Collar Democracy*. New York: Doubleday, 1973.

[12]   King, D. C. "Selecting Personnel for a Systems 4 Organization." Paper read at NTL Institute for Applied Behavioral Science Conference, 8–9 October 1971.

[13]   Matles, J. "Humanize the Assembly Line?" *UE News*, 13 November 1972, p. 5.

[14]   Roach, J. M. "Worker Participation: New Voices in Management." The Conference Board, Report 594, 1973.

[15]   Rush, H. M. F. *Job Design for Motivation*. New York: The Conference Board, 1971.

[16]   Sheppard, H. L., and Herrick, N. Q. *Where Have All the Robots Gone?* New York: New Press, 1972,

[17]   Sirota, D. "Job Enrichment—Another Management Fad?" *The Conference Board Record*, April 1973, pp. 40–45.

[18]   Sirota, D., and Greenwood, J. M. "Understand Your Overseas Work Force." *Harvard Business Review*, January-February 1971, pp. 53–60.

[19]   Sorcher, M. "Motivating the Factory Workers." In *The Failure of Success*, edited by A. J. Morrow. New York: American Management Association, 1972.

[20]   Sorenson, T. C. "Do Americans Like Their Jobs?" *Parade*, 3 June 1973, pp. 15–16.

[21]   Strauss, G., and Rosenstein, E. "Workers' Participation: A Critical View." *Industrial Relations* **9** (1970): 197–214.

[22]   "UAW Indicates It Will Seek to Minimize Local Plant Strikes in Talks Next Fall." *Wall Street Journal*, 20 February 1973, p. 5.

[23]   U.S., Congress, Senate, Subcommittee on Employment, Manpower, and Poverty, Labor and Public Welfare Committee. *Worker Alienation, 1972*, 92d Cong., 2d sess., S. 3916, July 25 and 26, 1972.

[24]   U.S., Department of Health, Education, and Welfare. *Work in America*. Report of a Special Task Force to the Secretary of Health, Education, and Welfare. Prepared under the Auspices of the W. E. Upjohn Institute for Employment Research. Cambridge: MIT Press, 1973.

[25]   U.S., Department of Labor. *Handbook of Labor Statistics 1972*. Bulletin 1735. Bureau of Labor Statistics. Washington, D.C.: Government Printing Office, 1972.

[26]   ———. "Survey of Working Conditions, November 1970." Prepared by the Survey Research Center of the University of Michigan. Washington, D.C.: Government Printing Office, 1971.

458CENTRAL ISSUES IN MOTIVATION AT WORK

[27] Walton, R. E. "How to Counter Alienation in the Plant." *Harvard Business Review*, November-December 1972, pp. 70–81.
[28] ———. "Work Place Alienation and the Need for Major Innovation." Paper prepared for a Special Task Force to the Secretary of Health, Education, and Welfare (for *Work in America*), May 1972. Unpublished.
[29] Weintraub, E. "Has Job Enrichment Been Oversold?" Address to the 25th Convention of the American Institute of Industrial Engineers, May 1973. Reprinted in the technical papers of the convention.
[30] Winpisinger, W. P. Paper presented to University Labor Education Association, 5 April 1973, at Black Lake, Michigan.

The Design of Work in the 1980s
J. Richard Hackman

Many observers are concerned these days about the quality of work life in organizations, about organizational productivity, and about possible changes in the work ethic of people in contemporary Western society. Indeed, there recently has been a clamor in the popular press that we are in the midst of a major "work ethic crisis" that has its roots in work that is designed more for robots than for mature, adult human beings (e.g., Garson, 1972; Sheppard & Herrick, 1972; *Work in America*, 1973). Even the very idea of work has taken on negative connotations for some commentators. Studs Terkel begins his book *Working* (1974), in which the thoughts and feelings of workers from many occupations are reflected, as follows:

> This book, being about work, is, by its very nature, about violence—to the spirit as well as to the body. It is about ulcers as well as accidents, about shouting matches as well as fistfights, about nervous breakdowns as well as kicking the dog around. It is, above all (or beneath all) about daily humiliations. To survive the day is triumph enough for the walking wounded among the great many of us. (p. xi)

IS THERE A CRISIS?

Those who perceive that we are in the midst of a crisis in the world of work tend to argue along the following lines. No less than a revolution in the way productive work is done has occurred in the U.S. in this century. Organizations have steadily increased the use of technology and automation in attaining organizational objectives. Consistent with this trend (and with the dictates of the "scientific management" approach to work design as espoused by F. W. Taylor (1911) at the turn of the century), work has become dramatically more spe-

This essay was written for the Visiting Scholars Program of the College of Business Administration, University of Houston, and was presented there in March 1977. It is based on research supported by the Organizational Effectiveness Research Program, Psychological Sciences Division, Office of Naval Research, under Contract No. N00014-75C-0269, NR 170-744. Used by permission.

cialized, simplified, standardized and routinized. Moreover, organizations themselves have become larger in size and more bureaucratic in function. Partly as a consequence of the increase in organizational size, managerial and statistical controls are used more and more to direct and enforce the day-to-day activities of organization members.

The efficiencies of advanced technology, the economies of scale, and the benefits of increased managerial control have generated substantial increases in the productive efficiency of organizations, and substantial economic benefits for both the owners of organizations and society as a whole. These economic benefits, in turn, have contributed to a general increase in the affluence, education and personal level of aspiration of individuals in American society. As a result, people today want jobs that allow them to use their education, that provide "intrinsic" work satisfactions, and that meet their expectations that work should be personally meaningful (Kanter, in press). No longer will people accept routine and monotonous work as their legitimate lot in life.

According to this line of thinking, we now have arrived at a point where the way most organizations function is in direct conflict with the talents and aspirations of the people who work in them. Such conflict manifests itself in increased personal alienation from work and in decreased organizational effectiveness. That which worked for Taylor early in this century, it is argued, simply cannot work now because the people who populate organizations, especially well-educated younger workers, will not put up with it.

Other observers have a contrary view (e.g., Fein, 1972; Strauss, 1974). Reports of worker discontent and demands for fulfilling work activities, they suggest, have been greatly exaggerated in the popular press and behavioral science journals. The work ethic "crisis" may be more manufactured than real, they say, and probably represents a serious misapprehension of the actual needs and aspirations of people at work.

Considerable evidence can be marshalled in support of this contention. Perhaps most widely-publicized is a project sponsored by the Ford Foundation to test how satisfied U.S. automobile workers would be working on highly "enriched" team assembly jobs in a Swedish automobile plant. Six Detroit auto workers were flown to Sweden and spent a month working as engine assemblers in a Saab plant. At the end of the month, five of the six workers reported that they preferred the traditional U.S. assembly line. As one put it: "If I've got to bust my ass to be meaningful, forget it; I'd rather be monotonous" (Goldmann, 1976, p. 31). Arthur Weinberg, a Cornell labor relations expert who accompanied the six workers to Sweden, summarized their negative reactions:

> They felt it was a deprivation of their freedom and it was a more burdensome task which required more effort which was more tedious and stressful. They preferred the freedom the assembly line allowed them, the ability to think their own thoughts, to talk to other workers, sing or dance on the assembly line, which you can't do at Saab. There is a freedom allowed on the assembly line not possible in more complex work. The simplified task allows a different kind of freedom. The American

workers generally reacted negatively to doing more than one task. They were not accustomed to it and they didn't like it. (quoted by Gainor, 1975)

Other studies support the results of this trans-Atlantic experiment, and cast doubt on the popular notion that people who work on routine and repetitive tasks invariably experience psychological and emotional distress as a consequence (Hulin & Blood, 1968; Siassi, Crocetti & Spiro, 1974). Perhaps most supportive of the ''no crisis'' view are the data reported in a U.S. Department of Labor Monograph titled ''Job Satisfaction: Is There a Trend?'' (Quinn, Staines & McCullough, 1974). Researchers examined findings from national surveys of job satisfaction from 1958-1973 and found no decline in job satisfaction over the past two decades.The present level of employee satisfaction is, as it has been, quite high: better than 80% of the workforce consistently report being ''satisfied''with their jobs.

The findings do show that younger workers are more dissatisfied with work than older workers. Yet younger workers also were more dissatisfied than their older colleagues 25 years ago, just as they are at present, casting doubt on the hypothesis that contemporary young workers are at the cutting edge of a trend toward increasing job alienation and dissatisfaction. A crisis in job satisfaction? No. Data such as those summarized above suggest that the ''crisis'' may lie more in the minds of journalists and behavioral scientists than in the hearts of people who perform the work of contemporary organizations.

WHAT TO CONCLUDE?

Both the argument for and the argument against a crisis in job satisfaction can be persuasive, and both sides of the question can be argued forcefully and with ample supportive data. How can we come to terms with this seeming conflict in the evidence as we attempt to generate some predictions about how work will be designed and managed in the 1980s? My own resolution of the issue takes the form of two complementary conclusions. Each of the conclusions strikes me as valid and as consistent with existing evidence about the state of work and workers in contemporary society. Yet, as will be seen, the conclusions provide quite different bases for decisions about how to proceed with the design of work in the decades to come.

Conclusion One: Many Individuals Are Presently Under-Utilized and Under-Challenged at Work   It seems to me an indisputable fact that numerous jobs in the bowels of organizations have become increasingly simplified and routinized in the last several decades, even as members of the U.S. workforce have become better educated and more ambitious in their expectations about what life will hold for them. The result is a poor fit between large numbers of people and their work. These people, who O'Toole (1975) calls ''the reserve army of the under-employed,'' have more to offer their employers than those employers seek, and they have personal needs and aspirations that cannot be satisfied by the work they do.

It also is indisputable that there are many people who do *not* seek challenge and meaning in their work, who instead aspire to a secure job and a level of income that permits them to pursue personal interests and satisfactions off the job. Do the under-utilized and under-challenged workers comprise three-quarters of the workforce, or only a quarter?

We cannot say for sure. What we can say—and what may be much more important—is that for some unknown millions of people work is neither a challenge nor a personally fulfilling part of life. And the organizations that employ these individuals are obtaining only a portion of the contribution that these people could be making at work.

Conclusion Two: People Are Much More Adaptable Than We Often Assume   When they must do so, people show an enormous capacity to adapt to their environments. Almost whatever happens to them, people survive and make do: gradually going blind, winning the lottery, losing one's home to fire or flood, gaining a spouse and children—or losing them. The same is true for work. Some of us adjust to challenging, exciting jobs; others of us to a petty routine and dull state of affairs. But we adapt. Not to do so would open us to constant feelings of distress and dissatisfaction, noxious states that we are well-motivated to avoid.

This plasticity often goes unrecognized by those who argue loudly on one or the other side of the "work ethic" debate. Part of the reason is that it is very hard to see adaptation happening, except when the environment changes dramatically and suddenly. When change is gradual, as it is when a young person adjusts to his or her job, it can be almost invisible. We tend, in our studies of work and workers, to catch people after they have adapted to their work situation, or before they have done so, rather than right in the middle of it. It is tough to figure out what is happening (or what has happened) to a person at work if you look only once.

Precisely because we adapt to our work environment, it is dangerous to take at face value self-reports of how "satisfied" people are with their work. Consider the case of Ralph Chattick, a 44-year-old worker in a metal fabrication shop on the outskirts of a large midwestern city. Ralph (not his real name) has worked in the same department of his company since graduating from high school, and is being interviewed about his job.

> *Are you satisfied with your work?*
> Yes, I guess so.
> *Would you keep working if you won a million dollars in the lottery?*
> Sure. *(Why?)* Well, you have to do something to fill the day, don't you? I don't know what I'd do if I didn't work.
> *Do you work hard on your job?*
> I do my job. You can ask them if I work hard enough.
> *Is it important to you to do a good job?*
> Like I said, I do my job.
> *But is it important to you personally?*
> Look, I earn what I'm paid, okay? Some here don't, but I do. They pay me to

cut metal, and I cut it. If they don't like the way I do it, they can tell me and I'll change. But it's their ball game, not mine.

Ralph is telling us that he is basically satisfied with his work. But how are we to interpret that? Take it at face value, and conclude that he is a "satisfied worker"? No, there are some signs in this interview excerpt that all is not well with Ralph. Yet it also would be inappropriate to take a "yes" such as that provided by Ralph and routinely assume that he *really* isn't satisfied. Ralph is not lying to us. He *is* satisfied, as he understands what we are asking.

The phenomenon of job satisfaction becomes clearer, and the diagnostic task more difficult, when we put ourselves in Ralph's person and consider the alternatives he has in responding. In fact, things are not awful, which is part of the reason for responding affirmatively. Moreover, Ralph has made numerous small choices over the years (such as deciding not to change jobs or to quit work and attend school) that have increased his personal commitment to his job. To answer other than affirmatively would raise for Ralph the spectre that perhaps these choices were poor ones, that in fact he has done a bad job in managing his career: "If I'm dissatisfied with this job, then what the hell have I been doing here all these years? Why haven't I done something about it?" That is an anxiety-arousing issue to face and not one that most of us would readily choose to engage. So the easiest response, and one that fairly represents Ralph's present feelings about his work situation, is to say, "Sure, I guess I'm satisfied with my job."

Because, like Ralph, most people do adapt to their work, responses to questions about job satisfaction can be misleading, especially among people who have considerable tenure in their jobs. For the same reason, self-reports of satisfaction do not provide a sturdy enough basis on which to erect plans for organizational change—let alone national policy about quality of work life issues.

CHOICES FOR THE 1980s

The conclusions drawn above cast doubt on the usefulness of trying to decide whether or not we are now in the midst of a work ethic "crisis." They also highlight two quite different routes that can be taken as choices are made about how to design and manage work in the next decade and beyond. One route, which derives from the conclusion that many people are under-utilized by the work they do, leads to increases in the level of challenge that is built into jobs, and in the degree of self-control job-holders have in managing their own work. In effect, we would attempt to change jobs to make them better fits for the people who do them.

The other route derives from the second conclusion; namely, that people gradually adapt and adjust to almost any work situation, even one that initially seems to greatly under-utilize their talents. This route leads to greater control of work procedures and closer monitoring of work outcomes by management to obtain increases in the productive efficiency of the workforce. Technological and motivational devices would be used to attempt to change the behavior of people to fit the demands of well-engineered jobs. The expectation is that in a carefully designed work environment employees gradually will adjust to having little personal control of their work, and that the efficiencies gained by using sophisticated managerial controls of work and workers will more than compensate for any temporary dissatisfactions the people experience.

Route One: Fitting Jobs to People

The core idea of Route One is to build into the work increased challenge and autonomy for the people who perform it. By designing jobs so they create conditions under which employees can develop *internal* motivation to do well, gains might be realized both in the productive effectiveness of the organization and in the personal satisfaction and well-being of the workforce.

Specifically, the aspiration would be to design work so that employees (a) experience the work as inherently meaningful, (b) feel personal responsibility for the outcomes of the work, and (c) receive, on a regular basis, trustworthy knowledge about the results of their work activities. Research has suggested that when all three of these conditions are met, most people experience internal motivation to do a good job—that is, they get a positive internal "kick" when they do well, and feel bad when they do poorly (Hackman & Oldham, 1976). Such feelings provide an incentive for trying to perform well and, when performance is excellent, lead to feelings of satisfaction with the work and with one's self.

How might jobs be designed to create these conditions? In the article cited above, Oldham and I have attempted to specify in detail the attributes of jobs that provide a basis for internal work motivation; here I will suffice with two examples of such jobs. Consider first the assembly of a small electrical appliance, such as a toaster. Following traditional dictates of engineering efficiency, such devices usually are manufactured using some form of a production line: one individual attaches the heating element to the chassis, another solders on the line cord, a third attaches the mechanical apparatus for handling the bread to be toasted, another inspects the assembled product, and so on.

An alternative design would be to make each employee, in effect, an autonomous toaster manufacturer. All necessary parts would be available at the employee's work station and the individual would be skilled in all aspects of toaster assembly, inspection and repair. The individual would perform the whole assembly task, would inspect his or her own work, and then (when satisfied that the apparatus was in perfect working order) would place a sticker on the bottom of the toaster. The sticker would say something along these lines: "This toaster was made by Andrew Whittier, an employee at the San Diego plant of General Toasters, Inc. I believe that it is in perfect condition and will give you years of reliable service. If, however, your toaster should malfunction in any way, please call me at my toll-free number, (800) 555-1217. We will see if we can clear up your problem over the telephone, and if not, I will authorize you to send the toaster to me and I will either repair it or send you a replacement, under the terms of the limited warranty that I packed in the box with the toaster.''

What would such a design achieve? Meaningful work? Yes, I'm making a useful household appliance all on my own. Personal responsibility for the work outcomes? Yes, I am personally accountable for the performance of any toaster I release for shipping; there is no one to blame but myself if I ship a bad product. Knowledge of results? Yes, for two reasons. First, I do my own inspection and testing before shipping, which means I can self-correct any assembly problems. And I obtain as well direct and personal feedback from customers about any problems they have with my work (not to mention the slight embarrassment of having it announced on the shop loudspeaker that "Andy, you have another call on the 800 line . . . !").

Surely such a design would lead to quite high internal motivation to perform effectively, and, for able employees who value the internal rewards that can be obtained from doing a demanding job well, high satisfaction with the work. The quality of work done also should improve. However, there might be some decrease in the *quantity* of the work done by a given worker on a given day, as compared to the more technically efficient production line design.

The hypothetical design for toaster manufacturing described above has much in common with many "job enrichment" experiments carried out in numerous organizations in the last decade (see, for example, reviews by Glaser, 1975 and Herzberg, 1976). Although the changes made in such projects inevitably involve alterations of many aspects of the work organization, not just the task itself, the focus clearly is on the work that is done by individual employees.

A different approach, but one that has many objectives in common with individual job enrichment, is to design work to be done by a more-or-less autonomous *group* of employees. Use of the work group as a design device requires that attention be given simultaneously to the technical and the social aspects of the work system, which often is advantageous. Indeed, the group may be the *only* feasible design alternative for creating a whole and meaningful piece of work in some cases, such as the assembly of automobile transmissions where coordinated activity among several individuals is essential because of the weight of the materials and the complexity of the assembly.

Probably the best-known application of group work design in a U.S. organization is the Topeka petfood plant of General Foods, where an entire new manufacturing organization was designed around the concept of the semi-autonomous work group. Each work team at Topeka (consisting of seven to fourteen members) was given responsibility for a significant organizational task. In addition to actually carrying out the work required to complete the task, team members performed many activities that traditionally had been reserved for management—such as coping with manufacturing problems, distributing individual tasks among team members, screening and selecting new team members, participating in organizational decision-making, and so on. Moreover, employees in each team were encouraged to broaden their skills on a continuous basis so that they and their teams would become able to handle even more responsibility for carrying out the work of the organization. Early reports from Topeka indicated that the innovative project has generated numerous beneficial outcomes, both for the organization and for the people who do the work (Walton, 1972; 1975a).

While autonomous work teams and job enrichment interventions have been carried out successfully in many organizations, we still have much to learn about how most effectively to design, install and diffuse such innovations. If that learning proceeds at a rapid rate in the next few years, then the shape of work in the next decade could turn out to be quite different from what it is today. Assuming that we follow Route One, and do so competently and successfully, here are some speculations about the design and management of work in the mid-1980s.

1   Responsibility for work will be clearly pegged at the organizational level where the work is done. No longer will employees experience themselves as people who merely execute activities that ''belong'' to someone else (such as a line manager). Instead, they will feel, legitimately, that they are both responsible and accountable for the outcomes of their own work. Moreover, the resources and the information needed to carry out the work (including feedback about how well the work is getting done) will be provided directly to employees, without being filtered first through line and staff managers. As a result, we will see an increase in the personal motivation of employees to perform well and a concomitant increase in the quality of the work that is done.

2   Questions of employee motivation and satisfaction will be considered explicitly when new technologies and work practices are invented and engineered, as is presently the case for the employee's intellectual and motor capabilities. No longer will equipment and work systems be designed solely to optimize technological or engineering efficiency, with motivational problems left in the laps of managers and personnel consultants after work systems are put in place. Moreover, there will be no single ''right answer'' about how best to design work and work systems. Sometimes tasks will be arranged to be performed by individuals working more-or-less alone; other times they will be designed to be performed by interacting teams of employees. Choices among such design options will take into account the character of the work itself (e.g., any technological imperatives that may exist), the nature of the organization in which the work will be done, and the needs, goals and talents of the people who will do the work. In many cases work will be ''individualized'' to improve the fit between the characteristics of an employee and the tasks that he or she performs. Standard managerial practices that apply equally well to all individuals in a work unit will no longer be appropriate. Instead, managers will have to become as adept at adjusting jobs to people as they now are at adjusting people to fit the demands and requirements of fixed jobs.

3   Organizations will be leaner, with fewer hierarchical levels and fewer managerial and staff personnel whose jobs are primarily documentation, supervision and inspection of work done by others. This will require a new way of managing people at work, and will give rise to new kinds of managerial problems. For example, to the extent that significant motivational gains are realized by enriched work in individualized organizations, managers will no longer have the problem of "how to get these lazy incompetents to put in a decent day's work." Instead, the more pressing problem may be what to do *next* to keep people challenged and interested in their work. For as people become accustomed to personal growth and learning at their work, what was once a challenge eventually becomes routine—and ever more challenge may be required to keep frustration and boredom from setting in. How to manage an organization so that growth opportunities are continuously available may become a difficult managerial challenge—especially if, as predicted, there is shrinkage in the number of managerial slots into which employees can be promoted.

4   Finally, if the previous predictions are correct, there eventually will be a good deal of pressure on the broader political and economic system to find ways to use effectively human resources that no longer are needed to populate the bowels of work organizations. Imagine that organizations eventually do become leaner and more effective and, at the same time, the rate of growth of society as a whole is reduced to near-zero. Under such circumstances, there will be large numbers of people who are "free" for meaningful employment outside traditional private and public work organizations. To expand welfare services and compensate such individuals for not working (or for working only a small portion of the time they have available for productive activities) would be inconsistent with the overall thrust of Route One. But what, then, is to be done with such individuals? Can we imagine groups of public philosophers, artists and poets, compensated by society for contributing to the creation of an enriched intellectual and aesthetic environment for the populace? An interesting possibility, surely, but one that would require radical rethinking of public decision-making about the goals of society and the way shared resources are to be allocated toward the achievement of those goals.

Route Two: Fitting People to Jobs

If we take Route Two, the idea is to design and engineer work for maximum economic and technological efficiency, and then do whatever must be done to help people adapt and adjust in personally acceptable ways to their work experiences. No great flight of imagination is required to guess what work will be like in the 1980s if we follow Route Two, as the sprouts of this approach are visible at present. Work is designed and managed in a way that clearly subordinates the needs and goals of people to the demands and requirements of fixed jobs. External controls are employed to ensure that individuals do in fact behave appropriately on the job. These include close and directive supervision, financial incentives for correct performance, tasks that are engineered to minimize the possibility of human mistakes, and information and control systems that allow management to monitor the performance of the work system as closely and continuously as possible. And, throughout, productivity and efficiency tend to dominate quality and service as the primary criteria for assessing organizational performance.

If we continue down Route Two, what might we predict about the design and management of work in the 1980s? Here are my guesses.

1   Technological and engineering considerations will dominate decision-making about how jobs are designed. Technology is becoming increasingly central to many work activities, and that trend will accelerate. Also, major advances will be achieved in techniques for engineering work systems to make them ever more efficient. Together, these developments will greatly boost the productivity of individual workers and, in many cases, result in tasks that are nearly "people proof" (that is, work that is arranged to virtually eliminate the possibility of error due to faulty judgment, lapses of attention, or mis-directed motivation). Large numbers of relatively mindless tasks, including many kinds of inspection operations, will be automated out of existence. The change from person to machine not only will further increase efficiency, but also will eliminate many problems that arise from human frailties, as suggested by Oliver (1977, p. 183) in an essay on the future of automated instrumentation and control:

> Automatic test systems do not fudge the data or make mistakes in recording it or get tired or omit tests or do any of the dozens of troublesome things human beings are apt to do. Whatever tests the program specifies will be made regardless of the time of day or the day of the week; no front office pressure to ship goods by a certain date can compromise the computer's inspection.

Simultaneous with these technological advances will be a further increase in the capability of industrial psychologists to analyze and specify in advance the knowledge and skills required for a person to perform satisfactorily almost any task that can be designed. Sophisticated employee assessment and placement procedures will be used to select people and assign them to tasks, and only rarely will an individual be placed on a job for which he or she is not fully qualified.

The result of all of these developments will be a quantum improvement in the efficiency of most work systems, especially those that process physical materials or paper. And while employees will receive more pay for less work than they presently do, they also will experience substantially less discretion and challenge in their work activities.

2   Work performance and organizational productivity will be closely monitored and controlled by managers using highly sophisticated information systems. Integrated circuit microprocessors will provide the hardware needed to gather and summarize performance data for work processes that presently defy cost-efficient measurement. Software will be developed to provide managers with data about work performance and costs that are far more reliable, more valid, and more current than is possible with existing information systems. Managers increasingly will come to depend on these data for decision-making, and will use them to control production processes vigorously and continuously.

Because managerial control of work will increase substantially, responsibility for work outcomes will lie squarely in the laps of managers, and the gap between those who do the work and those who control it will grow. There will be accelerated movement toward a two-class society of people who work in organizations, with the challenge and intrinsic interest of managerial and professional jobs increasing even as the work of rank-and-file employees becomes more controlled and less involving.

3   Desired on-the-job behavior will be elicited and maintained by extensive and sophisticated use of extrinsic rewards. Since (if my first prediction is correct) work in the 1980s will be engineered for clarity and simplicity, there will be little question about what each employee should (and should not) do on the job. Moreover, (if my second prediction is correct) management will have data readily at hand to monitor the results of the employee's work on a more-or-less continuous basis. All that is required, then, are devices to ensure that the person *actually* does what he or she is *supposed* to do. Because many jobs will be routinized, standardized, and closely controlled by management, it is doubtful that employee motivation to perform appropriately can be created and maintained using intrinsic rewards (i.e., people working hard and effectively because they enjoy the tasks, or because they obtain internal reinforcement from doing them well). So it will be necessary for management to use extrinsic rewards (such as pay or supervisory praise) to motivate employees by providing such rewards contingent on behavior that is in accord with the wishes of management.

In recent years the fine old principle of contingent rewards has been dressed up in the rather elaborate and sophisticated clothes of "behavior modification" as espoused by B.F. Skinner (see, for example, Luthans and Kreitner, 1975). Research evidence shows that in many circumstances, contingent rewards do powerfully shape individual behavior. If we follow Route Two, I predict that behavior modification programs will be among the standard motivational techniques used in work organizations in the 1980s.

4   Most organizations will sponsor programs to aid employees in adapting to life at work, including sophisticated procedures for helping employees and their families deal with alcohol and drug abuse problems. Such programs will become much more widely offered (and needed) than they are at present, I believe, because of unintended spin-offs of the movement toward the rainbow of productive efficiencies promised at the end of Route Two.

Consider, for example, a person working in an organization this year, in the mid-1970s, whose work is undemanding, repetitive and routine. It might be someone who matches checks and invoices, and then clips them together to be processed by another employee. Imagine that we asked that individual the following question: "What happens to you, what outcomes do you receive, when you try to work especially hard and effectively on your job?" The answers are likely to be far from inspiring. Probably they will have more to do with headaches and feelings of robothood than with any sense of meaningful personal accomplishment from high on-the-job effort. Clearly, such perceived outcomes reveal a lack of any positive, internal motivation to work hard and effectively.

Now let us transport that employee via time machine to the mid-1980s, and place him on a very similar job under full-fledged Route Two conditions. The work is just as routine and undemanding as it was before. But now there is greater management control over hour-by-hour operations, and valued external rewards are available—but only when the employee behaves in close accord with explicit management specifications. How will our hypothetical employee react to that state of affairs?

At first, he is likely to feel even more like a small cog in a large wheel than he did before. Whereas prior to the introduction of the new management controls he could get away with some personal games or fantasies on the job, that is now much harder to do. Moreover, the problem is exacerbated, not relieved, by the addition of the performance-contingent rewards. The negative intrinsic outcomes that were contingent on the hard work in the 1970s are still felt—but they have been supplemented (not replaced) by a set of new and positive *extrinsic* outcomes. So the employee is faced with contingencies that specify "The harder I work, the more negative I feel about myself and what I'm doing, the more likely I am to get tired and headachy on the job, *and* the more likely I am to get praise from my supervisor and significant financial bonuses."

That state of affairs is precisely what we might devise if we wished deliberately to drive someone insane—that is, arranging the work and its rewards such that strong positive and strong negative outcomes are *simultaneously contingent on the same behavior* (in this case, working hard). Some of the problems of drug usage, alcoholism, and industrial sabotage that presently are observed in work organizations appear to derive from this kind of no-win state of affairs. And if we move vigorously down Route Two, we can predict with some confidence that signs of employee "craziness" will increase.

Only a small proportion of the workforce will exhibit severely maladaptive behaviors, however, even under full-fledged Route Two conditions. As suggested earlier, people have a good deal of resilience and usually can adjust and adapt to almost any work situation if given enough time and latitude to do so. So although we can predict that numerous individuals will feel tension and stress in adjusting to work in the 1980s, and that their aspirations for personal growth and development at work may be significantly dampened, major overt problems will be observed infrequently.

Yet because *any* "crazy" employee behavior is an anathema to management (and clearly dysfunctional for organizational effectiveness), managers will attempt to head off such behaviors before they occur. When they do occur, management will deal with them as promptly and as helpfully as possible. So we should see in the 1980s a substantial elaboration of organizational programs to help people adapt in healthy ways to their work situations, and to minimize the personal and organizational costs of maladaptive responses to the work. All will applaud such programs, because they will benefit both individual human beings and their employing organizations. Few will understand that the need for such programs came about, in large part, as a result of designing work and managing organizations according to the technological and motivational "efficiencies" of Route Two.

AT THE FORK IN THE ROAD

Which will it be in the 1980s—Route One, or Route Two? There will be no occasion for making an explicit choice between the two. Instead, the choice will be enacted as seemingly insignificant decisions are made about immediate questions such as how to design the next generation of a certain technology, how to motivate employees and increase their commitment to their present jobs, or how best to use the sophisticated information technologies that are becoming available.

My view, based on the choices that even now are being made, is that we are moving with some vigor down Route Two. That direction, moreover, is unlikely to change in the years to come, for at least two reasons.

First, we know how to operate according to Route Two rules, and we're fumbling at best when we try to design a work unit in accord with Route One (Hackman, 1975). Present theory about how to design enriched jobs and autonomous work groups is still primitive, and is depressingly uninformative about how the properties of people, jobs and organizational units *interact* in determining the consequences of a given innovative design for work. Moreover, we are only just beginning to develop procedures for assessing the economic costs and benefits of innovative work designs (Macy & Mirvis, 1976), and for reconciling the dual criteria of efficiency and quality of work life in designing work systems (Lupton, 1975).

While it is not surprising given the paucity of theory and research on work redesign, it also is significant that there exists no trained, competent cadre of managers and behavioral scientists primed to create innovative work systems in contemporary organizations. We do have a substantial and growing set of case studies describing successful work redesign projects, but little *systematic* knowledge about how to proceed with such work redesign activities has emerged from these studies. Moreover, there are very few instances in which even a highly successful program has been successfuly diffused throughout the larger organization in which it was developed—let alone from organization to organization (Walton, 1975). Even the much-touted Topeka experiment has not had much of an impact on the broader General Foods organization, and is now being viewed with a good deal of skepticism by some commentators (see, for example, "Stonewalling Plant Democracy," *Business Week,* 28 March 1977, pp. 78–82).

Secondly, even if we *did* know how to design and manage work according to Route One dictates, my guess is that we would decide not to do so. There are many reasons. For one, Route One is heavily dependent on behavioral science knowledge and techniques, whereas Route Two depends more on "hard" engineering technology and traditional economic models of organizational efficiency. If behavioral science has ever won out over an amalgam of engineering and economics, the case has not come to my attention. Moreover, Route One solutions, if they are to prosper, require major changes in how organizations themselves are designed and managed; Route Two solutions, on the other hand, fit nicely with traditional hierarchical organizational models and managerial practices. Again, it seems not to be much of a contest.

But perhaps most telling is the fact that Route Two is much more consistent with the behavioral styles and values of both employees and managers in contemporary organizations. Experienced employees know how to adapt and survive on relatively routine, unchallenging jobs. Would such individuals, most of whom are comfortable and secure in their work lives, leap at the chance for a wholly different kind of work experience in an organization designed in accord with the principles of Route One? Some would, to be sure, especially among the younger and more adventurous members of the workforce; but I suspect that many would not. Learning how to function within a Route One organization would, for many, be a long and not terribly pleasant process, and it is unclear how many would be willing to tolerate the upset and the anxiety of the change process long enough to gain a sense of what work in a Route One organization might have to offer.

Managers, too, have good reasons to be skeptical about Route One and its implications. The whole idea flies in the face of beliefs and values about people and organizations that have become very well-learned and well-accepted by managers of traditional organizations. For example: that organizations are supposed to be run from the top down, nor from the bottom up. That many employees have neither the competence nor the commitment to take real responsibility for carrying out the work of the organization on their own. That organizational effectiveness should be measured primarily, if not exclusively, in terms of the economic efficiency of the enterprise. That more management control of employee behavior is better management.

Am I being too pessimistic? Perhaps. There are documented instances where employees and managers alike have responded with enthusiasm to work redesign projects that had many of the trappings of the Route One approach. Yet it is troublesome to note that very few of these experiments have persisted and diffused widely throughout the organizations where they took place. Why? The optimistic reason is that we do not yet have sufficient knowledge and skill about maintaining and diffusing innovations in organizations—but, with additional research, we soon will learn how to create conditions necessary for Route One innovations to catch on and spread. The pessimistic reason is that, without being fully aware of the fact, we have already progressed so far down Route Two that it may be nearly impossible to turn back.

As should be apparent from my remarks, I'm very favorably disposed to the ideas and the aspirations of Route One. But as may also be apparent, I suspect that my pessimistic explanation may have validity, that it may be too late to change directions, and that my description of Route Two may turn out to be a good characterization of what work will be like in the 1980s and beyond.

REFERENCES

Fein, M. The real needs and goals of blue collar workers. *The Conference Board Record*, February 1972, 26–33.

Gainor, P. Do blue collar workers really have blues? *Detroit News*, January 5, 1975.

Garson, B. Luddites in Lordstown. *Harper's Magazine*, June 1972, 68–73.

Glaser, E. M. *Improving the quality of worklife . . . And in the process, improving productivity*. Los Angeles: Human Interaction Research Institute, 1975.

Goldmann, R. B. *A work experiment: Six Americans in a Swedish plant*. New York: The Ford Foundation, 1976.

Hackman, J. R. On the coming demise of job enrichment. In E. L. Cass & F. G. Zimmer (Eds.), *Man and work in society*. New York: Van Nostrand Reinhold, 1975.

Hackman, J. R. & Oldham, G. R. Motivation through the design of work: Test of a theory. *Organizational Behavior and Human Performance*, 1976, **16**, 250–279.

Herzberg, F. *The managerial choice*. Homewood, Ill.: Dow Jones-Irwin, 1976.

Hulin, C. L. & Blood, M. R. Job enlargement, individual differences, and worker responses. *Psychological Bulletin*, 1968, **69**, 41–55.

Kanter, R. M. Work in a new America. *Daedalus*, in press.

Lupton, T. Efficiency and the quality of worklife: The technology of reconciliation. *Organizational Dynamics*, Autumn 1975, 68–80.

Luthans, F. & Kreitner, R. *Organizational behavior modification*. Glenview, Ill.: Scott, Foresman, 1975.

Macy, B. A. & Mirvis, P. H. Measuring the quality of work and organizational effectiveness in behavioral-economic terms. *Administrative Science Quarterly*, 1976, **21**, 212–226.

Oliver, B. M. The role of microelectronics in instrumentation and control. *Scientific American*, 1977, **237**(3), 180–190.

O'Toole, J. The reserve army of the underemployed: I—The world of work. *Change*, May 1975.

Quinn, R. P., Staines, G. L., & McCullough, M. R. *Job satisfaction: Is there a trend?* Washington, D.C.: Manpower Research Monograph No. 30, U.S. Dept. of Labor, 1974.

Sheppard, H. L. & Herrick, N. Q. *Where have all the robots gone?* New York: Free Press, 1972.

Siassi, I., Crocetti, G., & Spiro, H. R. Loneliness and dissatisfaction in a blue collar population. *Archives of General Psychiatry*, 1974, **30**, 261–265.

Strauss, G. Is there a blue-collar revolt against work? In J. O'Toole (Ed.), *Work and the quality of life*. Cambridge: MIT Press, 1974.

Taylor, F. W. *The principles of scientific management*. New York: Harper, 1911.

Terkel, S. *Working*. New York: Pantheon, 1974.

Walton, R. E. How to counter alienation in the plant. *Harvard Business Review*, November-December 1972, **50**, 70–81.

Walton, R. E. From Hawthorne to Topeka and Kalmar. In E. L. Cass & F. G. Zimmer
(Eds.), *Man and work in society*. New York: Van Nostrand Reinhold, 1975.(a)
Walton, R. E. The diffusion of new work structures: Explaining why success didn't
take. *Organizational Dynamics*, Winter 1975, 3–22.(b)
Work in America. Cambridge, Mass.: The MIT Press, 1973.

QUESTIONS FOR DISCUSSION

1 How might variations in job design affect employee motivation? Explain using (a)
Maslow's need hierarchy theory, and (b) expectancy/valence theory.

2 Why might individual differences among employees play an important role in the
determination of the impact of job characteristics on motivation?

3 What are several potential drawbacks to job enrichment and job redesign efforts?

4 How might job enrichment efforts differ between managerial and blue-collar jobs?

5 How would you go about enriching an assembly-line worker's job without actually
doing away with the assembly line?

6 How important a factor do you feel an individual's task requirements really are in
determining his or her motivation to perform? In determining his or her level of job
satisfaction? Why?

7 What role do various cultural factors play in employee reactions to job redesign?

8 Describe several cultural differences between countries that may influence both the
nature of a job design program and its potential success.

9 What future do you see for job design efforts?

Chapter 10

Goal-Setting and Performance

In this chapter, we discuss the role of goals and goal-setting in organizations as they affect employee motivation and performance. The notion of goals in organizations is receiving increased attention in work organizations as managers attempt to find ways to maximize the return on investment from limited resources. Goals and goal-setting provides one way in which such limited resources can be allocated with some degree of rationality. Before analyzing this role, however, we should first consider what is meant by the concept of goals itself.

THE GOAL CONCEPT

Traditionally, there have been two definitional approaches. First, goals can be conceptualized as future states of desired affairs (Etzioni, 1964; Vroom, 1960). In this sense, they are statements of where the individual or organization wants to be at some future time. Second, goals can be seen as constraints placed on present and future behavior as a result of past and present decisions and commitments (Cyert & March, 1963; Simon, 1964).

Although the literature on goals has generally treated these approaches as two distinct entities (Porter, Lawler, & Hackman, 1975; Steers, 1977), it appears that they are more complementary than mutually exclusive. That is, it is possible to envision the concept of goals as a dynamic process by which individuals and organizations determine their future aspirations within certain known limitations. Once these aspirations (or objectives) have been set, however, they tend to rule out the possibility of pursuing other potential goals because of the limit of resources. Hence, goal-setting really becomes a process of allocating one's resources—such as manpower, money, time. Such a dynamic approach to goals—viewing goal-setting as a continual decision and reevaluation process—subsumes both of the definitional approaches discussed above.

FUNCTIONS OF GOALS

Once goals have been formulated, they tend to serve several *functions* for the goal-setter (Steers, 1977). First—and perhaps most important—goals guide and direct behavior; they focus attention and effort in specific directions. In this sense, they provide a rationale for organizing resources. Second, goals often serve as a standard against which judgments can be made as to the relative effectiveness and efficiency with which individuals or organizations achieve (or fail to achieve) their purposes. Third, goals may also serve as a source of legitimacy, justifying various activities and the use of resources necessary to pursue them. Fourth, on an organizational level, goals often significantly affect the structure of the organization itself. The activities, practices, and technological processes necessary for goal attainment can impose restrictions on the activities of the membership, as well as on the acquisition and distribution of resources. Such basic social phenomena as communication patterns, authority and power relations, division of labor, and status orderings can thus be directly affected. Fifth, the study of goals can provide significant insight that is not found elsewhere into the underlying motives and character—and thus behavior—of both individuals and organizations. In this sense, goals are statements of what the goal-setter thinks is important and worthy of pursuit.

TYPES OF GOALS

When specifically viewing the role of goals in employee motivation and performance, it is important to ask which *type* of goals we are considering. There appear to be at least three important types that have a bearing on the individual's effort and performance. First, there are organizationwide (or, at least, departmentwide) goals. These goals represent statements concerning future directions for large segments of the organization's population. Making a suitable profit or increasing a company's market share might be examples of organizational goals. (See the Steers and Porter selection, immediately following, for a discussion of official versus operational organizational goals.) Such goals may affect employee effort by giving individuals a general idea of the types of performance desired. Moreover, they may serve as a source of identification for employees, enhancing to some extent their feelings of self-worth through such identification. (How often have we heard people, when asked what they do, respond by saying they work for such-and-such corporation?)

A second major type of goal is the task-goal. Task-goals are specific objectives assigned to an individual, or small group of individuals. Broad organizational goals may lack significant influence for employees unless they are translated into task-goals so that each employee knows the extent of his or her own responsibilities.

A third distinct type of goal is the personal goal, or level of aspiration. Personal goals differ from task-goals in that they are internally generated; they are the goals set by the individual. For example, salespersons who have been assigned a task-goal of increasing their sales by 10 percent may think that, realistically, they can increase their sales by only 5 percent. This 5 percent goal, then, becomes their personal goal (or aspiration level)—the goal for which they are really *trying*.

When these three types of goals are taken into consideration, goal-setting behavior at the level of the individual employee can be viewed as a bargaining process between the individual and the organization (usually represented by the employee's immediate supervisor). On the one hand, management attempts to set employee task-goals that are consistent with the larger organizational purpose and of sufficient scope and magnitude to justify hiring the employee. On the other hand, the employees themselves must ultimately determine what level of aspiration on assigned tasks they think is fair or desirable and worth pursuing. This bargaining process—whether overt or implicit—is an important force in the determination of individual performance in complex organizations. In theory, the closer an employee's aspiration levels are to his or her assigned task-goals, the greater is the likelihood that the task-goal will be realized.

MANAGEMENT BY OBJECTIVES

The clearest organizational application of goal-setting processes is management-by-objectives (MBO). MBO is the process by which employees of an organization, working together, identify common objectives or goals and coordinate their efforts toward goal attainment. The major focus in this process is on the future—where the organization wants to go—not on the past. Objectives are set forth for purposes of planning and coordination of available resources. It is hoped that the identification of specific objectives and goals allows employees at all levels of the organization to raise questions concerning the ways in which their particular jobs contribute toward larger organizational purposes.

Objectives are generally divided into two categories: performance objectives and personal development objectives. Performance objectives focus on goals and activities that relate to an employee's position in the organization. For example, a salesperson may have a goal of increasing sales in his or her territory by 10 percent over the next year. Personal development goals, on the other hand, deal with improving an employee's skills and abilities so they are better able to perform on the job and move up in the hierarchy. Personal development goals for a manager could include taking public speaking courses, earning an MBA, or improving various social and interpersonal skills.

In theory, the specific goals set forth by each employee will be aimed at contributing ultimately toward the attainment of organizationwide goals and objectives. In this way, maximum effort is concentrated and coordinated on important organizational problems and aspirations. However, such a scheme assumes (sometimes incorrectly) that employees identify with and wish to pursue the goals and objectives of the organization. Where employees see personal benefit in pursuing such goals (that is, when there is a strong integration of personal and organizational goals), we would expect MBO techniques to be successful. On the other hand, when organizational goals conflict with personal goals, there is little reason to believe that MBO would sustain improved employee effort over the long run.

GOAL-SETTING VERSUS JOB DESIGN

Both goal-setting and job design represent techniques that purportedly influence employee behavior and attitudes. As such, it is useful to ask how these two techniques differ in their effects. One recent study, by Umstot, Bell, and Mitchell (1976), compared the respective influence of the two techniques on both behavior and attitudes.

To carry out this comparative analysis, Umstot and associates set up a unique experiment in which some workers were exposed to job enrichment, while others were exposed to goal-setting. Each group was responsible for carrying out a series of tasks. The results of the experiment showed clearly that job enrichment had a substantial impact on job satisfaction but little effect on productivity. On the other hand, goal-setting techniques resulted in a major improvement in productivity, but had little effect on job satisfaction.

Based on these results, Umstot suggests that goal-setting and job enrichment can be used jointly in many work situations with beneficial results. Ostensibly, the increased autonomy, feedback, variety, and task identity that typically accompany job enrichment programs should facilitate higher levels of employee job satisfaction. Concomitantly, the increased goal specificity and goal difficulty of the goal-setting program should enhance subsequent task performance. Taken together, then, both techniques represent potentially useful methods for improving employee motivation in work situations.

OVERVIEW

In the three selections that follow, we shall examine in detail the nature of goal-setting processes in organizations. First, the role of personal aspiration level in performance is reviewed by Locke, Cartledge, and Knerr. Locke and his associates propose a model of motivation that posits that behavior is largely the result of intentional actions taken by individuals. In short, it is argued that people set personal goals on various activities and that these goals guide their behavior. Locke reviews several laboratory experiments which are largely consistent with his basic theoretical formulations. Moreover, he compares his model to other motivational theories, pointing out several unique features of his own model.

Following this, Latham and Yukl review the field research that has a bearing on Locke's theory of goal-setting. In general, strong support is found for the contention that goal-setting represents an effective means of enhancing employee performance.

Finally, Steers and Porter analyze the role of goal-setting not only in the context of employee performance, but also as it relates to the larger issue of organizational effectiveness. Using expectancy/valence theory, the available research evidence on goal-setting is examined to see how goals influence the cognitive processes leading up to the decision to produce.

REFERENCES AND SUGGESTED ADDITIONAL READINGS

Bryan, J. F., & Locke, E. A. Goal-setting as a means of increasing motivation. *Journal of Applied Psychology*, 1967, **51**, 274–277.

Carroll, S. J., Jr., & Tosi, H. L., Jr. Goal characteristics and personality factors in a management-by-objective program. *Administrative Science Quarterly*, 1970, **15**, 295–305.

Carroll, S. J., Jr., & Tosi, H. L., Jr. *Management by objectives: Applications and research*. New York: Macmillan, 1973.

Cyert, R. M., & March, J. G. *A behavioral theory of the firm*. Englewood Cliffs, N. J.: Prentice-Hall, 1963.

Etzioni, A. *Modern organizations*. Englewood Cliffs, N. J.: Prentice-Hall, 1964.

French, J. R., Kay, E., & Meyer, H. H. Participation and the appraisal system. *Human Relations*, 1966, **19**, 3–19.

Humble, J. W. *Management by objectives in action*. London: McGraw-Hill, 1970.

Ivancevich, J. M. A longitudinal assessment of management by objectives. *Administrative Science Quarterly*, 1972, **17**, 126–138.

Latham, G. P., & Yukl, G. A. Effects of assigned and participative goal setting on performance and job satisfaction. *Journal of Applied Psychology*, 1976, **61**, 166–171.

Locke, E. A. The motivational effects of knowledge of results: Knowledge or goal-setting? *Journal of Applied Psychology*, 1967, **51**, 324–329.

Locke, E. A. Toward a theory of task performance and incentives. *Organizational Behavior and Human Performance*, 1968, **3**, 157–189.

Locke, E. A., & Bryan, J. F. The directing function of goals in task performance. *Organizational Behavior and Human Performance*, 1969, **4**, 35–42.

Meyer, H. H., Kay, E., & French, J. R. Split roles in performance appraisal. *Harvard Business Review*, 1965, **43**, 123–129.

Porter, L. W., Lawler, E. E., III, & Hackman, J. R. *Behavior in organizations*. New York: McGraw-Hill, 1975.

Raia, A. P. Goal setting and self control. *Journal of Management Studies*, 1965, **2**, 34–53.

Raia, A. P. A second look at goals and controls. *California Management Review*, 1966, **8**(4), 49–58.

Simon, H. A. On the concept of organizational goal. *Administrative Science Quarterly*, 1964, **9**, 1–22.

Stedry, A. C., & Kay, E. The effects of goal difficulty on performance: A field experiment. *Behavioral Science*, 1966, **11**, 459–470.

Steers, R. M. Task goal attributes, n achievement, and supervisory performance. *Organizational Behavior and Human Performance*, 1975, **13**, 392–403.

Steers, R. M. Factors affecting job attitudes in a goal-setting environment. *Academy of Management Journal*, 1976, **19**, 5–16.

Steers, R. M. *Organizational effectiveness: A behavioral view*. Santa Monica, Calif.: Goodyear, 1977.

Tosi, H. L., Jr., & Carroll, S. J., Jr. Managerial reaction to management by objectives. *Academy of Management Journal*, 1968, **11**, 415–426.

Umstot, D. D., Bell, C. H., & Mitchell, T. R. Effects of job enrichment and task goals on satisfaction and productivity: Implications for job design. *Journal of Applied Psychology*, 1976, **61**, 379–394.

Vroom, V. H. The effects of attitudes on perception of organizational goals. *Human Relations*, 1960, **13**, 229–240.

Studies of the Relationship between Satisfaction, Goal-Setting, and Performance

Edwin A. Locke
Norman Cartledge
Claramae S. Knerr

In several previous papers (Locke, 1968a, 1969; Locke, Bryan, & Kendall, 1968), a partial model of task motivation has been proposed which may be summarized as follows: (*a*) the most immediate, direct motivational determinant of task performance is the individual's goal or intention; (*b*) external incentives affect action through their effects on the individual's goals and intentions; (*c*) affective reactions are the result of evaluations, which consist of estimating the relationship between the existents one perceives and one's values or value standards. The model is schematized in the following:

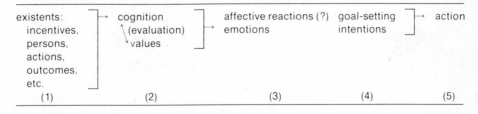

Revised and abridged from *Organizational Behavior and Human Performance*, 1970, *5*, 135–139 and 151–158. Copyright by Academic Press. Reprinted by permission of the authors and publisher.

This model is organized in terms of the functions of consciousness: cognition, evaluation, and the regulation of action.[1]

(a) Cognition. In order to survive man has to act. In order to act he has to know the world, i.e., know something about the nature and properties of things which exist. Man gains knowledge through perception and the exercise of reason. The present model is not concerned with the problem of the validity of man's cognitions. It is assumed that he acts on the basis of his interpretation of the tasks and situations which confront him.

(b) Evaluation. Man's existence is conditional; it depends upon taking actions which will fulfill his needs. To survive man has to judge the significance of the existents he perceives for his own life and well-being. Furthermore, at any given time man holds far more information "in his head" than he could possibly act upon. His capacity to act is limited; thus, he needs a means of choosing among alternative courses of action (Locke, Cartledge, & Koeppel, 1968). To make choices he must make value judgments. Certain value judgments are biologically programmed; the physical sensations of pleasure and pain inform man as to whether a particular on-going course of action or object is physically harmful or beneficial. Physical sensations, however, will not guide a man's actions through the course of a lifetime. To do this man must acquire an (explicit or implicit) code of values: a set of standards by which to judge what is good or bad, right or wrong, for or against his interests (Rand, 1964).

A "value is that which one acts to gain and/or keep" (Rand, 1964, p. 25). In making evaluations man estimates (subconsciously) the relationship between what he perceives and his value standards. He asks, in effect, "Is this (object, situation, incentive, person) for me or against me (according to my values)?"

The form in which one experiences one's value judgments are emotions (Rand, 1964). Man's most basic emotions are those of joy and suffering. (For a related view of the nature of emotions, see Arnold, 1960.)

(c) Regulation of action. Most human action is purposive; it is regulated by goals and intentions. The most fundamental effects of goals on (mental and/or physical) action are directive in nature. They guide man's thoughts and overt acts to one end rather than another. Since the pursuit of some goals require greater mental concentration and/or physical effort than others, goals, in the process of directing action, also regulate energy expenditure. For example, if a man decides to mow his lawn rather than watch television, this action necessarily entails the expenditure of more effort than would have been required to watch TV.

This is not to claim that every goal leads to the activity or end specified by the goal. A particular goal may not lead to efficacious action because it conflicts with the individual's other goals. Or the situation at a given time may be perceived as inappropriate for action. An individual may not have sufficient knowledge, ability, or determination to carry out his plan of action. Further, external factors may interfere with his performance. Even abortive action,

[1]This research was supported by Grants No. MH 12103-01 and 12103-02 from the National Institutes of Mental Health to the American Institutes for Research.

however, is (typically) initiated and guided by goals, and such action may still be highly correlated with the action intended.

Previous research has focused on several aspects of the above model:

(i) The directing function of goals and intentions has been emphasized in studies of choice behavior. In these studies individuals had to choose among alternative responses (Dulany, 1968) or among alternative tasks (Locke, Bryan, & Kendall, 1968), or had to decide which of the number of performance dimensions to maximize or minimize (Locke & Bryan, 1969a). In all cases, substantial correlations were found between intended choices or goals and actual behavior.

(ii) A second category of studies stressed the energizing function of goals. All individuals worked on the same task and only their performance with respect to a single dimension was considered (e.g., output quantity). It was found that with simple, repetitive tasks, there was a positive linear correlation between goal level and performance level, i.e., the higher the goal, the higher the performance (see Locke, 1968a, for a summary of these studies). Even when individuals tried for goals which were so high that they rarely, if ever, were reached, they performed better than individuals with easy goals. (There is a point, of course, at which an increment in one's goal level would not lead to further improvement, i.e., there are limits to human performance.)

(iii) Other studies have shown that external incentives motivate action through their effects on the individual's goals and intentions. This is evidenced by the facts that: *(a)* when incentives do effect changes in performance, they bring about corresponding changes in the individual's goals and intentions; *(b)* when goal and intention differences are controlled or partialed out, the correlation between incentive condition and performance is vitiated. Thus far, the above relationships are most well documental with respect to three incentives: money (Locke, Bryan, & Kendall, 1968); feedback regarding one's overall score on a task (Locke, 1967a, 1968b; Locke & Bryan, 1968b, 1969b); and "verbal reinforcement" (Dulaney, 1962, 1968).

(iv) Another series of studies have explored the effect of the judged relationship between the individual's values and what he perceives on his affective reactions (Locke, 1969). For example, work satisfaction was shown to be a function of the relationship between (or discrepancy between) what one perceives one's work as being like and what one wants from it (or wants it to be like). Satisfaction with performance was shown to be the result of perceiving one's performance as fulfilling or facilitating the fulfillment of one's performance goals. Job and performance dissatisfaction were shown to be the result of perceiving one's job as frustrating one's job values or perceiving one's performance as being discrepant from one's performance goals, respectively.

Referring to the numbers in the above schematic, research to date has focused on relationships between: *(a)* Steps 4 and 5: goals and action; *(b)* Steps 1, 4, and 5: incentives, goals, and action; and *(c)* Steps 2 and 3: value judgments and emotional reactions. A missing link in this research is that between Steps 3 and 4; namely, how, specifically, are goals generated?

Arnold (1960) has argued that emotions contain inherent action tendencies, these action tendencies being experienced as desires. The basic desires are those of approach and avoidance. An unpleasant emotion entails the desire to avoid the object or situation that caused it, while a pleasant emotion entails the desire to approach or retain the object or situation that caused it.

If one is dissatisfied with one's performance on a task (and is constrained from leaving the situation altogether), one should desire and thus set a goal to change one's level of performance. Conversely, satisfaction with one's past performance should produce the desire and thus the goal to maintain this previous performance level.

In most real life situations, the process of setting a specific goal is enormously complex. It is the result of one's integration of numerous separate value judgments and cognitions. For the purposes of the present research, therefore, it was necessary to severely limit the range of phenomena investigated and the number of alternatives permitted.

Previous studies of the determinants of goal-setting (known generally as "level of aspiration" studies) have dealt primarily with situations where: (a) probability of success or difficulty was a major determinant of goal selection; and (b) the individual was free to set virtually any goal he wanted on the task, i.e., there were no external constraints on goal-setting. (For a summary and discussion of typical studies in this area, see Atkinson, 1964.) . . .

THE REVISED MODEL

(1) Satisfaction. Our findings confirm previous work (Locke, 1969) showing that satisfaction with performance is a function of the degree to which one's performance achieves one's desired goal or is discrepant from one's value standard. The present results also extend the earlier findings which dealt only with goals as ends in themselves to include goals which are a means to an end. Subgoal attainment is valued to the extent that it is seen as instrumental in achieving one's overall (end) goal.

In Studies 3, 4, and 5 the use of goal-performance discrepancy to predict satisfaction added significantly (F tests) to the variance in satisfaction accounted for by instrumentality alone. Evidently the subjects valued hitting their subgoals as ends in themselves and not just as a means to an end. The wider or more general value that probably accounts for both relationships is that of "efficacy." In order to achieve values (and therefore to survive) man has to be able to predict and control (to some extent) the outcomes of his actions. In attaining the goals he sets for himself, he develops and reinforces the conviction that he is competent to pursue and attain values in general.

(2) Goal-setting. When an individual's goal level remains constant, dissatisfaction with previous performance will correlate highly with the difference between previous performance level and subsequent goal level.

When a person has an overall end goal on a task, he will set subgoals according to their judged instrumentality in achieving this end goal. Judged instrumentality will correlate highly with anticipated satisfaction.

(3) Performance. To the degree that performance is affected by motivational factors, it is a result of the goals and intentions individuals set on the task. Goals guide action (and thought) and indirectly regulate energy expenditure. The revised model is illustrated schematically in the following:

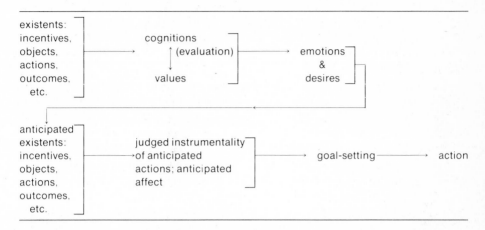

This model is by no means complete, but only outlines the major processes that lead to goal setting and task performance.

(1) The model is not intended to be "hedonistic." It should be stressed that we do not assert that people pursue pleasure as such, but that they pursue goals. Goals are chosen with an awareness of their affective consequences, but these immediate consequences are not (typically) the sole criterion used in selecting them.

It is true that a "pure hedonist" would focus only on the immediate pleasures and displeasures to be gained from his actions. But few (if any) individuals follow this pattern. Most men choose subgoals as a means to an end goal. Their focus in choosing a subgoal is not on the immediate pleasure to be gained from it but on its instrumentality in achieving their long-range goals.

Men differ enormously in the time span across which they project their actions and in the criteria they use to choose their goals. An important individual difference variable in this context would be the degree to which an individual stresses immediate affective consequences as opposed to long-range instrumentality in selecting goals. The latter type should be willing to endure many more hardships and persist far longer in the face of frustration and dissatisfaction than the hedonist type.

(2) It should not be assumed that individuals precede their every action with an exhaustive "rational analysis" of all possible alternatives and their outcomes. Men differ greatly in the degree to which they think before they act, in the number of alternatives they consider before acting, in the degree to which they are aware of their own values, and in the number of value conflicts they experience.

Furthermore, over time a given individual may encounter the same situation over and over. When this happens, he becomes habituated to the outcomes and alternatives. The more familiar he becomes with a situation the less reflection and foresight are necessary in order to make a choice. Considerations which were initially conscious and deliberate become subconscious and automatic.

We would argue that even in these cases, however, the same basic processes are occurring as specified above, the main difference being in the speed with which they take place, and the degree to which the individual is aware of them.

(3) The model does not delineate the factors which influence the establishment and acceptance of (end) goals and general values (e.g., "achievement") in the first place. In the studies reported here end goals were assigned and acceptance was facilitated by the "demand characteristics" of the experimental situation. In industrial situations, however, instructions are not always accepted. ("Participation" is one method that has been used to help insure goal acceptance by work-group members.) A series of studies by Miller (1965) at General Electric found that workers did not continue to try for assigned goals unless the instructions were backed up with rewards and punishments for goal attainment and failure, respectively.

The problem of where goals come from is often dismissed with the assertion that they are absorbed unthinkingly from "significant others." We believe that this is a somewhat over-simplified and misleading view of the matter. Individuals are often highly selective in the values they accept from society and with respect to whom they consider significant. Furthermore, some individuals generate their own goals and values.

(4) As stated earlier, the process by which an individual, in real life, decides to pursue a given goal and/or to change goals is enormously complex. For example, new knowledge (cognitions) from external sources and new insights based on self-generated thinking may intrude at any stage of this model and hence change the outcome. Subconscious value conflicts and premises may make actions difficult to predict from direct questioning of the individual. Our model, therefore, is only a very rough sketch of the major processes which appear to be involved in choosing a goal. The above experiments were able to show certain interconnections among the stages only because all or most extraneous factors were controlled.

RELATION TO OTHER THEORIES

There are a number of other theories of task performance which are similar in one or more respects to our model. It will only be possible to discuss some of them briefly here.

Dulany (1968) has proposed a theory to explain verbal response selection in laboratory studies of "verbal conditioning." The immediate determinant of response selection in this model is the "behavioral intention" which is similar to our "goal." Behavioral intentions are viewed as determined by the subject's hypotheses about what the experimenter wants him to do, what responses will gain him (sensory) reinforcement, and his desire to comply with the experimenter and to get the (sensory) reinforcement.

Dulany explicitly includes cognitive anticipations (i.e., hypotheses) in his model, but does not use the term "anticipated satisfaction." However, this idea is implicit in his concept of "desire." The desires to please the experimenter and to get (sensory) "reinforcement" (in this case, puffs of air to the face) are not the only types of rewards men will seek. But it might be possible to extend Dulany's model to cover other (real life) situations.

Atkinson and Feather (1966) have offered a theory based on individual differences in the desire to "achieve" or perform well on tasks (which they call "need for achievement"). They view achievement-motivated action as a joint function of the strength of the motivation to achieve, the anticipated satisfaction to be gained from success, and the estimated probability that a given course of action will produce success.

The subjective value of success is defined as the product of the importance of the motive to achieve and the anticipated satisfaction to be attained from achievement. The justification for this definition is questionable; it was argued in an earlier paper (Locke, 1969), that valid ratings of satisfaction already reflect value importance, so that multiplying one by the other is redundant.

Atkinson and Feather assume that the value of success is an inverse function of the probability (frequency) of success; however, their assumption has not always been empirically supported (e.g., see Locke, 1967b). Further, their model does not include goal-setting as a part of the process leading to action. This has led to different predictions as to the effects of difficult goals or tasks on performance. Atkinson and Feather argue that moderately difficult tasks lead to the highest level of performance, while Locke (1968a) has found that hard goals or tasks produce a higher level of performance than moderately difficult tasks or goals.

Vroom (1964) and Porter and Lawler (1968) see action as the result of cognitive and affective anticipations (i.e., the instrumentality of a given course of action in achieving valued goals), and view satisfaction as a function of the attainment of rewards (reward appears similar in meaning to what we call values). Porter and Lawler, however, see satisfaction as the result of value-percept discrepancy only, rather than value-percept discrepancy and value importance (see Locke, 1969, for a discussion of this issue).

Porter and Lawler view anticipated satisfaction and perceived probability of success as leading directly to the expenditure of effort; explicit goal-setting is not incorporated into the model. We would argue that the individual, on the basis of his anticipations, first chooses a goal and then mobilizes or expends the amount and type of effort that is appropriate to the goal or task he has chosen.

Like Atkinson and Feather, Vroom and Porter and Lawler appear to view performance as a multiplicative function of anticipated satisfaction and the probability of success in attaining the desired outcome. We would agree that probability of success is taken into account in any decision to try for a goal. But, the empirical problem is how to combine measures of satisfaction and probability which are measured in very different units. Further, as noted above, we now believe that instrumentality is a more appropriate predictor of goal-setting than satisfaction.

Miller, Galanter, and Pribram (1960) view action as guided by plans, a concept which resembles what we call subgoals. Plans represent the sequence and order of actions to be taken so as to attain some end. The equivalent term to our end goal, or value, is Miller *et al.*'s concept of image (the image, however, also includes all stored knowledge and memories). These authors write that: "A motive is comprised of two independent parts: value and intention. A value refers to an Image, whereas an intention refers to a Plan" (1960, p. 62). According to Miller *et al.* each action outcome is compared to the image and the degree of "match" or similarity noted. Then new action is taken, guided by the plan, and the process is repeated until a match is obtained. The procedure of testing outcomes against the image and modifying future actions accordingly is called a "TOTE" (test-operator-test-exit) unit.

The similarity of the above model to ours is obvious. Our major reservation with Miller *et al.*'s position concerns their overly literal use of a computer analogy. We view conscious experience as being fundamentally different from the operation of a machine, whereas they (evidently) do not.

Finally, our interest in goals and intentions as determinants of performance is related to the approach to motivation advocated by Ryan (1958)[2] some years ago (see also Mace, 1935). Historically, interest in the effects of goals and tasks on behavior arose from the work of the Wurzburg School (Kulpe, Watt, Ach) around the turn of the century. Due primarily to the influence of behaviorism, this work has received limited attention from American psychologists to date.

REFERENCES

Arnold, M. B. *Emotion and personality*. Vol. I. *Psychological aspects*. New York: Columbia University Press, 1960.

Atkinson, J. W. *An introduction to motivation*. New York: Van Nostrand, 1964.

Atkinson, J. W., & Feather, N. T. *A theory of achievement motivation*. New York: Wiley, 1966.

Cartledge, N. Some determinants of goal-setting. Unpublished Master's Thesis, U. of Georgia, 1968.

Dulany, D.E., Jr. The place of hypotheses and intentions: An analysis of verbal control in verbal conditioning. In. C. W. Eriksen (Ed.), *Behavior and awareness*. Durham, N.C.: Duke University Press, 1962. Pp. 102–129.

Dulany, D. E., Jr. Awareness, rules and propositional control: A confrontation with S-R behavior theory. In D. Horton and T. Dixon (Eds.), *Verbal behavior and general behavior theory*. Englewood Cliffs, N.J.: Prentice Hall, 1968. Pp. 340–388.

Dunnette, M. *Personnel selection and placement*. Belmont, Cal.: Wadsworth, 1966.

[2] A book by Ryan giving his expanded views on this subject is now in press.

Eagle, M. N. The effect of learning strategies upon free recall. *American Journal of Psychology*, 1967, **80**, 421–425.

Locke, E. A. The motivational effects of knowledge of results: Knowledge or goal-setting? *Journal of Applied Psychology*, 1967, **51**, 324–329. (a)

Locke, E. A. The relationship of success and expectation to affect on goal-seeking tasks. *Journal of Personality and Social Psychology*, 1967, **7**, 125–134. (b)

Locke, E. A. Toward a theory of task motivation and incentives. *Organizational Behavior and Human Performance*, 1968, **3**, 157–189. (a)

Locke, E. A. The effects of knowledge of results, feedback in relation to standards and goals on reaction time performance. *American Journal of Psychology*, 1968, **81**, 566–574. (b)

Locke, E. A. What is job satisfaction? *Organizational Behavior and Human Performance*, 1969, **4**, 309–336.

Locke, E. A., & Bryan, J. F. Grade goals as determinants of academic achievement. *Journal of General Psychology*, 1968, **79**, 217–228. (a)

Locke, E. A., & Bryan, J. F. Goal-setting as a determinant of the effect of knowledge of score on performance. *American Journal of Psychology*, 1968, **81**, 398–407. (b)

Locke, E. A., & Bryan, J. F. The directing function of goals in task performance. *Organizational Behavior and Human Performance*, 1969, **4**, 35–42. (a)

Locke, E. A., & Bryan, J. F. Knowledge of score and goal difficulty as determinants of work rate. *Journal of Applied Psychology*, 1969, **53**, 59–63. (b)

Locke, E. A., Cartledge, N., & Koeppel, J. The motivational effects of knowledge of results: A goal-setting phenomenon? *Psychological Bulletin*, 1968, **70**, 474–485.

Locke, E. A., Bryan, J. F., & Kendall, L. M. Goals and intentions as mediators of the effects of monetary incentives on behavior. *Journal of Applied Psychology*, 1968, **52**, 104–121.

Mace, C. A. Incentives: Some experimental studies. Report No. **72**, 1935, Industrial Health Research Board (Great Britain).

Miller, L. The use of knowledge of results in improving the performance of hourly operators. General Electric Co., Behavioral Research Service, 1965.

Miller, G., Galanter, E., & Pribram, K. *Plans and the structure of behavior*. New York: Holt, 1960.

Porter, L., & Lawler, E. *Managerial attitudes and performance*. Homewood, Illinois: Dorsey, 1968.

Rand, Ayn. The objectivist ethics. In Ayn Rand (Ed.), *The virtue of selfishness*. New York: Signet, 1964. Pp. 13–35.

Ryan, T. A. Drives, tasks, and the initiation of behavior. *American Journal of Psychology*, 1958, **71**, 74–93.

Vroom, V. *Work and motivation*. New York: Wiley, 1964.

A Review of Research on the Application of Goal Setting in Organizations

Gary P. Latham
Gary A. Yukl

Locke's (36) theory of goal setting deals with the relationship between conscious goals or intentions and task performance. The basic premise of the theory is that an individual's conscious intentions regulate his actions. A goal is defined simply as what the individual is consciously trying to do. According to the theory, hard goals result in a higher level of performance than do easy goals, and specific hard goals result in a higher level of performance than do no goals or a generalized goal of "do your best." In addition, the theory states that a person's goals mediate how performance is affected by monetary incentives, time limits, knowledge of results (i.e., performance feedback), participation in decision making, and competition. Goals that are assigned to a person (e.g., by a supervisor) have an effect on behavior only to the degree that they are consciously accepted by the person. Thus, Locke states, "It is not enough to know that an order or request was made; one has to know whether or not the individual heard it and understood it, how he appraised it, and what he decided to do about it before its effects on his behavior can be predicted and explained" (36, p. 174).

Locke's theory is based primarily on a series of well-controlled laboratory experiments with college students who performed relatively simple tasks (e.g., adding numbers) for short periods of time. Some psychologists legitimately have questioned whether something so deceptively simple as setting specific hard goals can increase the performance of employees in real organizational settings, where experimental "demand effects" are absent and acceptance of goals cannot be obtained so easily (5, 15). Although Locke (36) cites a large number of laboratory studies in support of his theory, only four field studies are discussed in his article. Most of the field research on goal setting has been conducted since Locke's 1968 theoretical article was published.

The purpose of the present article is to review research on the application of goal setting in organizations, particularly in industry. The article is concerned with evaluating the practical feasibility of goal setting as well as with evaluating Locke's theory. The review includes 27 published and unpublished reports of field research. The major characteristics of these studies are summarized in Table 1.

A few laboratory studies conducted since 1968 also are discussed when the research appears to be particularly relevant for evaluating the theory. The review is divided into sections corresponding to the following aspects of Locke's theory: (a) the effects of specific goals versus generalized goals or no goals; (b) the effects of goal difficulty on performance; and (c) goals as mediators of performance feedback, monetary incentives, and time limits. Some research

From *Academy of Management Journal*, 1975, **18**, 824–845. Reprinted by permission.

Table 1   Summary of Goal Setting Field Studies

Investigators	Type of study[a]	Sample	Criterion	Goal measure or manipulation
Blumenfield and Leidy (2)	C	55 vending machine servicemen	Supervisor report of typical output quantity	Supervisor report of assigned goal level or absence of goals
Burke and Wilcox (4)	C	323 female telephone operators	Self-rated performance improvement	Employee perception that specific goals were set and perceived participation
Carroll and Tosi (6, 7, 8, 9)	C	150 managers	Self-reported goal attainment and effort increase	Self-reported goal difficulty, participation, and feedback
Dachler and Mobley (14)	C	596 production employees	Output quantity[b]	Employees' stated goals
Duttagupta (16)	C	18 R&D managers	Self-reported motivation	Self-reported participation and feedback
French, Kay, and Meyer (17)	E	92 managers	Self-rated goal acceptance, self and superior-rated goal attainment	Assigned vs. participative goal setting in MBO and perceived participation
Ivancevich (22)	QE	166 managers	Change in self-rated need satisfaction	Goal setting in MBO programs
Ivancevich (23)	QE	181 groups of salesmen and production workers	Sales; output quantity and quality[b]	MBO with and without reinforcement vs. comparison group
Ivancevich, Donnelly, and Lyon (24)	QE	166 managers	Change in self-rated need satisfaction	Goal setting in MBO programs
Kolb and Boyatzis (26)	C	111 management students in T-groups	Self- and trainer-rated behavior change	Self-reported goal for behavior change
Kolb, Winters, and Berlew (27)	E-C	79 management students in T-groups	Self- and trainer-rated behavior change	Self-reported goal for behavior change
Latham and Baldes (29)	QE	36 truck drivers	Net weight of truck loads[b]	Assigned individual goals vs. prior no-goal condition
Latham and Kinne (30)	E	20 logging crews	Quantity of output[b]	Assigned group goals vs. no-goal control condition
Latham and Yukl (32)	E	48 logging crews	Quantity of output[b]	Assigned group goals, participative group goals, and no-goal control condition

Table 1   Summary of Goal Setting Field Studies (Continued)

Investigators	Type of study[a]	Sample	Criterion	Goal measure or manipulation
Latham and Locke (31)	QE	379 logging crews	Quantity of output[b]	Time limitations on output disposal
Lawrence and Smith (33)	E	22 office and garment factory workers	Improvement in output quantity[b]	Participative group goal setting vs. discussion without goal setting
Mendleson (42)	C	25 superior-subordinate pairs in 8 companies	Superior ratings of subordinate performance	Superior-subordinate reported degree of goal setting
Raia (48)	QE	112 managers and supervisors	Output quantity[b]	MBO participative goal setting vs. prior no-goal condition
Raia (49)	QE	74 managers and supervisors	Output quantity[b]	(See above)
Ronan, Latham, and Kinne (50)	C	1184 logging crews	Quantity of output[b]	Supervisor reported goal specificity
Shetty and Carlisle (52)	C	109 professors in a public university	Perceived improvement in performance and commitment	Goal setting in MBO
Sorcher (53)	QE	14 assembly work groups	Improvement in output quality[b]	Participative goal setting vs. prior no-goal condition
Stedry and Kay (54)	E-C	19 manufacturing work groups	Productivity and rework costs[b]	Assigned goals for two performance criteria
Steers (55)	C	133 female first-line supervisors	Superior ratings of performance	Perceived goal specificity, goal difficulty, and participation
Wexley and Nemeroff (58)	E	27 managers and 125 subordinates	Absenteeism,[b] LBDQ, and JDI	Assigned goals vs. no goals
Zander, Forward, and Albert (63)	C	255 members of 64 United Fund campaigns	Dollars collected[b]	Official annual goal set by each local committee
Zander and Newcomb (62)	C	149 United Fund campaign	Dollars collected[b]	Official annual goal set by each local committee

[a]E = experiment, C = correlational study, QE = quasi-experimental study.
[b]Denotes "hard" objective criterion.

on goal setting within the context of a management by objectives (MBO) program also is examined. Finally, studies on the relative effectiveness of assigned versus participative goal setting are reviewed. The article concludes with a general evaluation of the theory and a discussion of desirable directions for future research on goal setting.

SPECIFIC VERSUS GENERALIZED GOALS OR NO GOALS

One of the earliest field studies providing information on the effects of goal setting was conducted by Lawrence and Smith (33). The objective of the study was to investigate the effects of employee participation in decision making and goal setting, rather than to determine the effects of setting specific goals. However, since the researchers compared a participative goal setting condition with a condition in which work problems and company policy were discussed without any explicit goal setting, the study can appropriately be interpreted as an assessment of the effects of goal setting. Lawrence and Smith found that employees were equally satisfied in both conditions, but production (quantity) increased significantly more in the goal setting condition than in the no-goal condition.

Sorcher (53) conducted a study to evaluate the effects of a program consisting of employee participation in goal setting together with "role training" (i.e., an explanation of the importance of each employee's job). This program resulted in substantial improvement in the quality of production, as well as in some increases in quantity of production. A possible limitation of both this and the preceding study is the difficulty in determining the extent to which the improvements were due to the goal setting rather than to other features of the experimental treatment, such as the role training.

A study by Burke and Wilcox (4) assessed the effects of goal setting during the appraisal interview. Data were obtained by means of a questionnaire survey of a sample of nonmanagerial female employees. Burke and Wilcox found that employee perception of the extent to which an employee and her supervisor set mutual goals was correlated with the employee's self-reported desire to improve her performance ($r = .45$) and her self-ratings of actual performance improvement ($r = .29$).

In another correlational study, Blumenfeld and Leidy (2) found that soft drink salesmen and servicemen checked more vending machines when specific hard goals were assigned than when no goals were assigned. However, assignment of easy goals did not result in better performance than no goals.

In a factor analysis of data obtained from 292 independent pulpwood producers, Ronan, Latham, and Kinne (50) found that the effects of goal setting depended on the extent to which logging crews were closely supervised. Goal setting was correlated with high performance only when it was accompanied by close supervision. Goal setting without supervision correlated with labor turnover but not with performance. Supervision that did not include goal setting was not correlated with any performance criterion. In a follow-up study by the same authors, an analysis of variance was performed on the man-day production of 892 producers. These producers were classified on the basis of the three factor patterns cited above: (a) producers who supervise their men and set production goals; (b) "absentee" producers who set production goals only; and (c) producers who supervise their men but do not set production goals. The results indicated that producers who supervise their employees and set production goals have higher productivity than do producers who supervise their men but do not set production goals. The difference between "absentee producers" who set production goals only, and producers who set production goals and supervise their men was in the expected direction. In summarizing the results of these two studies, Ronan, Latham, and Kinne (50) interpreted their findings as supporting the conclusion that setting a specific task goal does not affect performance in an industrial setting unless a supervisor is present to encourage goal acceptance.

A limitation of the studies on pulpwood producers is that they were correlational in nature, and inferences about causality could not be made with confidence. In order to overcome this limitation, Latham and Kinne (30) matched and randomly assigned 20 pulpwood producers and their crews to either a one day training program in goal setting or to a control condition. Data on cords per man-hour production, turnover, absenteeism, and injuries then were collected for 12 consecutive weeks. Analyses of variance revealed that those individuals who received training in goal setting had a significant increase in production and a decrease in absenteeism compared to workers in the control condition. No significant trend effects over time were found. There were no significant differences between conditions with respect to injuries or turnover, which were very low in both conditions.

Latham and Baldes (29) conducted a quasi-experimental study of a goal setting program with unionized truck drivers. The goal setting program was designed to increase the net weight of truckloads of logs, which previously had been considerably below the legal limit. A specific hard goal of 94 percent of the legal maximum was assigned to the drivers, which resulted in an immediate increase in average net weight from approximately. 60 percent of the legal maximum to approximately 94 percent. Performance remained relatively stable at this improved level over the nine month study period, resulting in a cost savings of over a quarter of a million dollars for the company. Although the performance improvement was attributed primarily to goal specificity, anecdotal information suggested that goal setting also led to informal competition among drivers, and this competition probably helped to maintain goal commitment over the nine month period.

Latham and Yukl (32) conducted an experiment in which two methods of goal setting were compared to a control condition in which no specific goals were set. Goal setting resulted in higher performance of logging crews in only one of the four goal setting conditions. Some problems in the implementation of the goal setting program, such as a lack of support by local management, were cited as the likely reason for the failure of goal setting in the other three conditions. This study is discussed in more detail in the section "Assigned Versus Participative Goal Setting."

Mendleson (42) conducted a questionnaire survey of goal setting in eight companies and analyzed the responses of 25 pairs of superior-subordinate managers. The extent of goal setting, as perceived by both the superior and the subordinate was positively correlated with superior ratings of subordinate promotability, but not with superior ratings of subordinate performance. Due to the lack of consistency in these results, and the low reliability of the goal setting measure developed by Mendleson for use in this study, it is difficult to draw firm conclusions.

In a study differing in several respects from those preceding, Kolb and Bayatzis (26) examined the effect of goal setting on behavior change and attainment of personal development goals, rather than on performance and task goal attainment. In a management course requiring extensive T-group participation, each student established a personal development goal relevant to his behavior in groups and formulated a method for measuring goal attainment. At the end of each T-group session, the students filled out a form recording relevant feedback received from other group members during the session. Behavior change after the 30 hours of T-group sessions was reported by each student and was rated by the group trainers. Positive behavior change was greater for behavior dimensions related to the students' goals than for behavior dimensions not related to the goals.

Wexley and Nemeroff (58) evaluated the effects of goal setting and feedback when used in conjunction with role playing exercises in a two day supervisory training program. In two variations of the experimental treatment, hospital supervisors were assigned goals for behavior improvement, and they received coaching and feedback regarding their performance as leaders in the role playing exercises. The supervisors also were assigned specific behavioral goals after the first and third weeks back on the job, and additional feedback and coaching were provided. A control group of supervisors participated in the role playing, but were not assigned goals or given feedback either during or after the training. Wexley and Nemeroff found that supervisors in the experimental conditions had less subordinate absenteeism and more positive improvement in leadership behavior than did supervisors in the control group.

In summary, eleven studies in organizations have examined the effects of setting specific goals. In ten of these studies, evidence in support of the effectiveness of setting specific goals was obtained, although some possible limiting conditions also were discovered. Only one study (42) failed to find any support for the goal specificity proposition of Locke's theory, and the measure of goal setting in this study was of dubious validity.

EFFECTS OF SPECIFIC GOALS IN MBO PROGRAMS

Indirect evidence on the effectiveness of setting specific goals is provided by studies of MBO programs in organizations. Management by objectives is an approach to planning and performance appraisal that attempts to clarify employee role requirements, relate employee performance to organization goals, improve manager-subordinate communication, facilitate objective evaluation of employee performance, and stimulate employee motivation. An essential feature of the MBO approach is the setting of specific performance goals and, in many cases, goals for personal development of the employee. Employees are expected to be more committed to goals as a result of participating in setting them and involvement in the development of criteria for assessing goal attainment. Most of the published literature on MBO consists of anecdotal reports about employee reactions and the problems encountered in implementing an MBO program in a particular organization, or of discussions about the best procedures for implementing MBO (e.g., 3, 18, 19, 20, 25, 28, 46, 59). Only eight studies were found in which the effects of specific goals versus generalized goals or no goals were assessed with an acceptable degree of scientific rigor.

The first of these studies was conducted by Raia (48) in 15 plants of the Purex Corporation. The MBO program resulted in an increase in productivity over a 10-month period, even though the goals had to be revised downward several times during the fiscal year. Some improvements in absenteeism, accidents, grievances, turnover, and customer service also were noted in the plants that set goals for these criteria. The percentage of plants reporting an improvement for these criteria ranged from 33 percent for absenteeism to 80 percent for accident reduction.

Raia (49) obtained an additional 12 months of data from a follow-up study in the same company. These data indicated a stabilization of productivity at the higher level attained during the earlier period, and the attainment of budgetary goals continued to improve. The major weakness of Raia's research is that, with neither a control group nor an immediate large improvement in the performance curve following implementation of the MBO program, it is impossible to determine if the improvement was due to MBO. The gradual improvements in performance could have been due to extraneous conditions unrelated to the MBO program.

French, Kay, and Meyer (17) conducted an experiment on goal setting within an MBO program at General Electric Company. The sample consisted of 92 low-level managers who either participated in goal setting with their boss or were assigned goals during an appraisal interview. Regardless of how the goals were set, when criticisms of the subordinate manager were translated into specific goals, both the subordinate and the boss reported that twice as much improvement in performance occurred than when criticisms were made without being formulated as specific goals. No objective criterion measures were obtained in this study, however.

Shetty and Carlisle (52) evaluated an MBO program in a public university by means of a questionnaire survey of faculty opinions. There was no indication that the MBO program resulted in any substantial improvement in performance or commitment to the university. However, it should be noted that the criterion measures were entirely subjective and of questionable validity, and no measure of the extent of goal setting was obtained.

Ivancevich, Donnelly, and Lyon (24) did a comparative study of two companies with an MBO program. Managers in both companies were asked to complete a Porter-type job satisfaction questionnaire before the MBO programs were initiated and again after the programs were in effect for a year. Need satisfaction improved in one company but not in the other. Interviews with the managers to obtain their reactions to the program revealed that MBO was used primarily at the top management level in the second company. The MBO program was never effectively implemented with lower level managers, due in part to a lack of top management involvement in setting up the program. Some problems also were found in the first company, despite the improvement in need deficiency scores. The most frequent complaints were an excess of paperwork and the difficulty of stating quantitative goals for all aspects of the job. These same problems have been noted in some of the case study and discussion articles on MBO; they also were found by Raia (49).

In what was essentially a follow-up study, Ivancevich (22) measured need satisfaction again in the two companies 18 to 20 months after the MBO program had been initiated. He found that any improvements in need satisfaction were short-lived and had disappeared by the time of his final measurement. This extinction phenomenon was attributed to a lack of sustained top management commitment to the program and the absence of any additional training or reinforcement after the program was initiated. Although this research by Ivancevich and his associates suggests some conditions which may prevent an MBO program from being implemented and maintained, the absence of a performance criterion makes it impossible to determine whether MBO ever really had an effect on the behavior and performance of the managers in these companies.

In a more recent study, Ivancevich (23) used objective measures of employee performance to evaluate an MBO program in a manufacturing company. The performance of production departments in three plants was compared. One plant had an MBO program for supervisors which included encouragement and support from top management in the form of letters, memos, telephone conversations, and meetings. The second plant had an MBO program that was not given encouragement and support by top management. The third plant did not have an MBO program and served as a control condition. Only the production department in the first plant had a sustained improvement in quantity and quality of performance over the course of the three year study. In addition, there was a significant decrease in absenteeism and grievances in this one plant.

Ivancevich also compared the performance of marketing departments in the three plants. Unlike the production workers, salesmen in the two plants with an MBO program were involved in the goal setting process along with their supervisors. The results indicated that sales performance improved in both MBO programs, but there was no improvement in the plant without an MBO program.

In the final MBO study, by Steers (55), questionnaire data on task-goal perceptions and need strength were obtained from 133 female first-line supervisors in a company with an ongoing MBO program. In addition, ratings of goal effort and performance for the supervisors were obtained from each supervisor's boss. Steers found that a supervisor's perception of goal specificity was significantly correlated with goal effort but not with the rating of overall performance. Steers also found that these relationships were moderated by the supervisor's need for achievement. Goal specificity was significantly correlated with goal effort and overall performance only for those supervisors with a high need for achievement.

In summary, the eight studies on MBO appear to provide a diverse set of findings. However, if we disregard the studies which had no measure of performance or goal attainment, the results are more consistent. French et al. (17), Ivancevich (23), Steers (55), and Raia (48, 49) all found some support for the proposition that setting specific goals can result in improved performance although some limiting conditions were present. The major problem with this MBO research as a means of evaluating goal setting is that MBO programs typically involve other changes besides the introduction of goal setting. Therefore, it is difficult to determine the extent to which performance improvements in these studies were due to goal setting rather than to other changes.

THE EFFECTS OF GOAL DIFFICULTY ON PERFORMANCE

Locke (36) proposed that, as long as goals are accepted, the more difficult the goals the higher the level of performance. This proposition is supported by results from a number of laboratory studies reported by Locke (36), including correlations between stated goals and subsequent performance and experiments with different levels of assigned goals. Seven field studies also have attempted to determine the effects of goal difficulty.

In the first study, by Stedry and Kay (54), goal difficulty was manipulated for two different performance criteria: productivity and rework cost. Performance goals were set either at the average level of performance attained during the previous six months (easy goal) or at a level substantially higher than average previous performance (difficult goal). The 19 foremen were assigned in a nonrandom manner to one of the following four experimental conditions: (a) easy productivity goal and difficult rework goal; (b) difficult productivity goal and easy rework goal; (c) both goals easy; (d) both goals difficult. In addition to the experimental manipulation, Stedry and Kay measured the extent to which the foremen actually perceived the assigned goals to be easy, challenging or impossible, and these perceptions corresponded closely to actual difficulty. Performance improvement was defined as the difference between average performance during the 13 weeks after the manipulation and the 13 weeks before the manipulation. The data were analyzed first for each criterion separately. Performance improved more for the goals perceived to be easy or challenging than for the goals perceived to be impossible; and for the impossible goals, performance actually decreased. This finding is consistent with Locke's theory if it can be assumed that impossible goals are not accepted. Performance improvement was not significantly related to the difficulty of the productivity goal or the difficulty of the rework goal when analyzed separately. However, the theory may be tested more appropriately by an analysis of the combined difficulty of both goals since they are independent and a person must decide how to allocate his effort between them. Stedry and Kay conducted a regression analysis and found that total perceived difficulty for both goals was significantly related to a composite criterion of performance improvement ($R^2 = .59$), which is clearly in support of Locke's theory.

Zander and Newcomb (62) examined the effects of goals set in United Fund campaigns in 149 communities. They found a significant relationship between the difficulty of the goal, in terms of how far it was above the previous year's performance, and subsequent performance improvement. When the sample was subdivided according to the frequency of goal attainment success in the previous four years, prior success was found to be a moderator of the effects of goal difficulty. Goal difficulty was significantly correlated with subsequent performance improvement for communities with more prior successes than failures ($r = .76$) and for communities with an equal number of successes and failures ($r = .73$). However, for communities with more prior failures than successes in goal attainment, goal difficulty was not significantly correlated with performance improvement.

One explanation for these results is provided in a follow-up study by Zander, Forward, and Albert (63). They compared consistently successful and consistently unsuccessful United Funds and found that the successful Funds set higher absolute goals and attained a higher absolute level of performance. However, expressed as a percentage of the prior year's performance, the goals of successful Funds were more reasonable than were those of unsuccessful Funds. Furthermore, members of the successful Funds attributed more importance to attainment of the goal than did members of failing Funds. The unreasonableness of the goal and the lack of importance attributed to it by the members of consistently failing Funds suggest that there was little goal acceptance and commitment in these Funds. Therefore, it is not surprising that goal difficulty was unrelated to performance for the unsuccessful Funds.

Blumenfeld and Leidy (2) evaluated the effect of goal difficulty in an incentive program designed to motivate salesmen and servicemen to check and adjust soft drink vending machines to an optimal temperature. Employees who were assigned hard goals checked more vending machines than did employees who were assigned easy goals.

Steers (55) surveyed female first-line supervisors in a company with an MBO program and analyzed the relationship between perceived goal difficulty and performance ratings made by each supervisor's boss. No significant correlation was obtained, even when the sample was subdivided according to measures of supervisor needs.

In another survey of managers in an MBO program, Carroll and Tosi (6,7) found that perceived goal difficulty was positively correlated with the self-rated effort of managers who were high in self-assurance ($r = .26$) and maturity ($r = .31$) and who perceived rewards to be contingent upon performance ($r = .26$).

For managers with low scores on self-assurance and maturity or who did not perceive a strong contingency between rewards and performance, goal difficulty was negatively correlated ($r = -.25, -.26, -.19$) with self-rated effort. For the combined sample of managers, there was no significant correlation between goal difficulty and self-rated effort. Although Carroll and Tosi used a different criterion measure from that used by Steers (55), these results suggest that Steers also might have found significant correlations if he had used similar moderator variables.

Dachler and Mobley (14) examined the relationship between stated performance goals and objective performance of production workers in two organizations. Performance was measured in terms of piece rate earnings in the first organization and work rate as a percentage of standard in the second organization. A significant positive correlation ($r = .46$) between an employee's stated current goal and his performance was found in the first organization. This relationship was moderated by employee tenure. The correlation was significant ($r = .44$) for employees who had been on the job for more than two years but not for employees who had been on the job for less than two years ($r = .13$). This difference was consistent with the additional finding that long tenure employees perceived desirable outcomes to be contingent upon performance, whereas short tenure employees did not, presumably because of their limited experience in their current job situation.

The current performance goal stated by an employee also was significantly correlated with performance in the second organization. However, the correlation was very low ($r = .16$), and the relationship was not moderated by job tenure. The difference in magnitude of relationships between goal level and performance for the two organizations may have been due to differences in criterion measures, but more likely it is due to the lower perceived contingency of desirable outcomes on performance in the second organization, in which jobs were less structured and where there was no incentive system. This interpretation is consistent with the tenure results found in the first organization and with the findings of Carroll and Tosi (6,7) summarized earlier.

In summary, seven studies have examined the relationship between goal difficulty and performance. With one exception (55), support was found in each study for Locke's (36) proposition that hard goals lead to greater performance than do easy goals, as long as the goals are accepted. The major limitation of this research is that, except for the study by Stedry and Kay (54), the effects of goal difficulty were assessed by means of a correlational design rather than by manipulation of goal difficulty. Some of the correlational studies attempted to deal with the problem of determining causality when there is likely to be an influence of prior performance on goals by measuring both difficulty and performance in relation to prior performance. Since the results from these studies, most other correlational studies, the experiment by Stedry and Kay (54), and a large number of laboratory experiments are generally consistent, it can be concluded that there is strong support for Locke's goal difficulty proposition.

Because goal acceptance is a necessary condition of this proposition, it is important to identify the factors that determine whether employees will accept hard goals. Some of the studies reviewed in this section provide insights into the nature of these determinants. The variables found to moderate the effects of goal difficulty probably also influence goal acceptance. These variables include the employee's perception that the goal is reasonable, and the perceived contingency between goal attainment and desirable outcomes. Hard goals are more likely to be perceived as challenging rather than impossible if the employee has a high degree of self-assurance and has previously had more successes in goal attainment than failures. The perceived instrumentality of goal attainment depends largely upon the type of incentive systems and the objectivity of performance appraisal in the organization.

GOALS AS MEDIATORS OF PERFORMANCE FEEDBACK, MONETARY INCENTIVES, AND TIME LIMITS

Locke's (36) theory proposes that the effects of performance feedback, monetary incentives, and time limits are mediated by goal setting and conscious intentions. Performance feedback or "knowledge of results" can lead to an increase in effort and performance for at least four different reasons: (a) feedback may induce a person who previously did not have specific goals to set a goal to improve performance by a certain amount; (b) feedback may induce a person to raise his goal level after attaining a previous goal; (c) feedback that informs a person that his current level of effort is insufficient to attain his goal may result in greater effort; and (d) feedback may inform a person of ways in which to improve his methods of performing the task. Locke's theory is concerned primarily with the first three "motivational" aspects of feedback and not with the final "cueing" aspect. Locke also proposed that the form or quality of feedback partly determines what effect the feedback will have. These feedback propositions are supported by a substantial number of laboratory studies that are reviewed in the article by Locke, Cartledge, and Koeppel (38). Some recent laboratory studies have provided additional support and insight (e.g., 13, 37, 60).

Field studies in which goal setting and performance feedback are independently manipulated, or feedback is manipulated and the effects of goals are controlled, would provide evidence as to the validity of Locke's feedback propositions in real organizations. Unfortunately, no studies of this type were found. In fact, only a few field studies have investigated the effects of performance feedback on subsequent performance. Since use of feedback alone may be viewed by some persons as an alternative approach to goal setting, it is worthwhile to briefly review studies on the effects of feedback in comparison to no feedback. In addition, since the amount and frequency of feedback necessary for an effective goal setting program have not been established, it also is useful to examine studies on the effects of feedback in combination with goal setting.

Three studies investigated the effects of feedback on performance in the absence of explicit goal setting. Hundal (21) found that feedback resulted in increased productivity of industrial workers with a repetitive task; productivity also was higher than was that of a no-feedback control group. However, Chapanis (11) failed to find any effect of feedback on the performance of students hired to work an hour per day for 24 days on a repetitive job. Miller (44) found that feedback regarding errors resulted in only a temporary improvement in performance quality for manufacturing employees, unless used in conjunction with incentives or the threat of negative consequences for failure to improve. The improvement that occurred with feedback plus incentives may well have been due to employees setting goals to reduce errors. However, since the subjects in these studies were not asked if they set private goals, no firm conclusions can be drawn in relation to Locke's theory. With so few studies and the inconsistent results, it also would be premature to reach any conclusions about the effectiveness of feedback as a motivational technique when used without explicit goal setting. Of course, the importance of feedback for learning, as opposed to motivation, has been well established in the literature on training research.

A study on the effects of feedback in conjunction with goal setting was conducted by Kolb, Winters, and Berlew (27). Explicit goals for behavior change were set by students in a management course with extensive T-group participation. In T-groups instructed to provide relevant feedback, more positive change (self-rated and trainer-rated) occurred than in T-groups instructed not to discuss the behavior change projects of their members. The results also supported the importance of feedback quality (e.g., timing, relevance, and manner of presentation) for goal attainment. In a study of managers in a company with an MBO program, Carroll and Tosi (8) found that the amount and frequency of perceived feedback were positively correlated with self-rated goal attainment, but not with an increase in self-rated effort level. Duttagupta (16) found that frequency and amount of feedback were associated with greater self-reported motivation and a better perceived understanding of job requirements by the R&D managers in a company with an MBO program. Finally, Steers (55) found that the amount of perceived feedback in a company with an MBO program was positively correlated with goal effort and overall performance ratings for supervisors with high achievement motivation, but not for supervisors with low achievement motivation. Although these results tend to support the conclusion that frequent, relevant feedback is needed for a successful goal setting program, the evidence is limited, and further research clearly is warranted.

In contrast to performance feedback, monetary incentives are more likely to increase goal acceptance and commitment than to induce a person to set a harder goal. "Offering an individual money for output may motivate him to set his goals higher than he would otherwise, but this will depend on how much money he wishes to make and how much effort he wishes to expend to make it" (36, p. 185). Locke's propositions about goals as mediators of monetary incentives are based on a series of five laboratory studies in which he found that, when goal level was controlled or partialled out, incentives did not affect performance. Also, a particular goal level resulted in the same performance, regardless of whether monetary incentives were provided. A similar type of field study would provide evidence regarding the generalizability of these findings to real organizations. Unfortunately, no studies of this type have been conducted in an organizational setting. However, a recent laboratory study by Pritchard and Curtis (47) appears to be relevant to evaluating Locke's proposition. Pritchard and Curtis point out that Locke used small incentives with little potential for motivating his subjects. In a study designed to overcome this potential limitation, the effects of assigned goals were compared for three levels of incentive (large, small, and no incentive). Pritchard and Curtis found, as did Locke, that small incentives did not increase performance in comparison to no incentive when goal level was held constant. However, contrary to Locke, large incentives resulted in higher performance than did small or no incentives when goal level was held constant. Moreover, the self-reported commitment of subjects to the goal was not greater in the large incentive condition than in the small and no-incentive conditions. In other words, Pritchard and Curtis found that incentives can affect performance independently of goal level and goal commitment.

Latham and Locke (31) conducted a study which provided evidence in support of Locke's theory that time limits affect performance only to the degree that they lead to goal setting. The authors found that when pulp and paper mills limited their buying of wood to one or two days per week, they implicitly urged a higher production goal (per man-hour) on independent harvesting crews. To minimize income loss, the crews tried to harvest as much wood in one or two days as they normally harvested in five days. Thus logging crews with limitations on the number of days they could sell timber had higher productivity than crews without such restrictions. These findings are in basic agreement with the results of the early British studies (51) which found that a reduction in the work week led to a higher hourly rate of production.

In summary, there is little relevant data for evaluating Locke's proposition that goals mediate the effects of performance feedback. The few field studies on the effects of feedback alone or in combination with goal setting are not directly relevant for testing the mediation hypothesis. The three studies on the consequences of feedback without explicit goal setting do not yield consistent results. The four studies on feedback in combination with goal setting tend to support the importance of frequent, relevant feedback for goal setting effectiveness. No field studies have been conducted to provide a direct test of Locke's mediation proposition concerning monetary incentives, but one laboratory study provides evidence contrary to the proposition and raises doubts about the external validity of the earlier supporting results found by Locke and associates. One field study provides indirect support for the hypothesis that goals mediate the effects of time limits on performance.

ASSIGNED VERSUS PARTICIPATIVE GOAL SETTING

Locke's (36) theory specifies that goals mediate the effects of employee participation in decision making. The theory is not directly concerned with the manner in which goals are set. However, the most appropriate manner of setting goals is an important practical question. The consequences of subordinate participation in decision making have been the subject of considerable speculation in the leadership and management literature. According to the classical management theories (40), it is the leader's responsibility to assign goals and ensure that they are attained. Humanistic organization theories (35, 41) favor substantial subordinate participation in decision making, and such participation is believed to increase acceptance of the decision and commitment to implement it. More recently, various contingency theories (39, 45, 56, 57, 61) have proposed that participation is effective in some situations but not in others. Leadership research on the effects of employee participation in decision making tends to support the contingency approach.

Several studies have attempted to assess the effects of different amounts of subordinate participation in goal setting. In the first of these studies, French, Kay, and Meyer (17) compared assigned and participative goal setting during performance appraisal interviews with lower-level managers. In addition to the experimental manipulation of participation, the perceived participation of the managers and observer judgments of the amount of participation during the appraisal interview also were measured, as well as the managers' perception of the usual amount of participation they previously had been allowed. Perception of the usual amount of participation, which was measured prior to the appraisal interview, was positively related to acceptance of job goals. However, goal acceptance and goal attainment were not significantly related to the other participation measures and were not affected by the experimental manipulation. A number of limitations of this study make it difficult to reach any clear conclusions. The participation manipulation was not always successful, the participation treatment was somewhat confounded with the usual level of participation that occurred between the supervisor and his subordinates, and no objective performance measures were obtained. Despite these problems and the scarcity of significant differences, the authors reach the following conclusions in another report of this research (43): (a) subordinates who received a high participation level in the performance interview in most cases achieved a greater percentage of their improvement goals; (b) men who usually worked under high participation levels performed best on goals they set for themselves, and men who usually worked under low participation levels performed best on goals that their boss set for them.

Carroll and Tosi (6, 7) included a measure of perceived influence in establishing goals in their questionnaire survey of managers in an MBO program. The results indicate that participation in goal setting was not significantly correlated with the amount of goal attainment or effort increase. However, there was some indication that a manager's self-assurance moderated the effects of participation. Participation in goal setting tended to be positively correlated (r = .33) with effort increase for managers with high self-assurance but not for managers with low self-assurance (r = .08).

In a study by Duttagupta (16) R&D managers in an MBO program were interviewed and answered a short questionnaire. No relationship was found between self-reported motivation and perceived influence in the goal setting process.

In a questionnaire survey of first-line supervisors, Steers (55) found that perceived participation was significantly correlated with goal effort and overall performance ratings for supervisors with low need for achievement (r = .41), but was not significantly correlated for supervisors with a high need for achievement. For the overall sample, there was only a low correlation (r = .20). The major limitation of this study and the study by Carroll and Tosi is the subjective nature of the participation in goal setting measures. The leadership literature suggests that subordinate judgments about their influence in decision making are of questionable accuracy. Furthermore, since the conclusions reached in these studies are based on a large number of correlations and correlational comparisons, there also is a strong possibility that some significant findings occurred by chance. Therefore, the results should be regarded as tentative until they are replicated.

Latham and Yukl (32) conducted a field experiment on the effects of assigned and participative goal setting. Specifically, they attempted to determine which method of goal setting was most effective for independent logging crews with different levels of education. Twenty-four "educated" crews were randomly assigned to a participative goal setting condition, an assigned goal setting condition, or a "do your best" condition. Twenty-four educationally disadvantaged crews in another geographical location were randomly assigned to the same three conditions. In the sample of educationally disadvantaged crews, the participative goal setting condition yielded higher performance and more frequent goal attainment during the eight week period of the study than did the assigned goal setting condition. The average goal level was significantly higher for the participative condition than for the assigned goal condition, which suggests that the performance difference was due in part to greater goal difficulty in the participative condition. The fact that goal attainment was higher in the participative condition than in the assigned condition, despite more difficult goals, suggests that goal acceptance was increased by participation in the goal setting process.

In the sample of educated crews, performance, goal attainment, and average goal level were not significantly different for the participative and assigned conditions. Due to the unavoidable confounding of education level with geographical region and other factors in this study, it is not clear whether the failure to find a significant difference in the educated sample was due to education level or to other factors. Anecdotal evidence suggested that the goal setting program was not effectively implemented for this sample due to the lack of support by local management.

In summary, five studies in organizations provide data on the effects of participation in goal setting, but each of these studies has major limitations or problems. None of the studies provides an adequate test of Locke's mediation proposition regarding the effects of participation. With respect to the more applied question of whether participative goal setting results in higher performance than assigned goals, the results are not consistent. Although most of the studies found some evidence supporting the superiority of participative goal setting, a significant difference is found only under certain conditions or with certain types of employees. The most satisfactory way of explaining these discrepancies probably is in terms of a contingency model, but further research is needed to clarify the nature of the limiting conditions and the manner in which the moderating variables operate.

DISCUSSION AND CONCLUSIONS

The organizational research reviewed in this article provides strong support for Locke's (36) propositions that specific goals increase performance and that difficult goals, if accepted, result in better performance than do easy goals. The field studies do not provide relevant evidence concerning Locke's propositions that goal setting mediates the effects of participation, monetary incentives, and performance feedback. With respect to monetary incentives, the results from a laboratory experiment by Pritchard and Curtis (47) are contrary to the mediation proposition. Field research designed to test the mediation propositions and to investigate the possibility that participation, monetary incentives, and feedback affect performance independently of goal setting, or interact with goal setting, is clearly desirable.

Perhaps the greatest deficiency of Locke's theory is the failure to specify the determinants of goal acceptance and goal commitment. In recent research, investigators have used expectancy theory concepts to aid in explaining how goal acceptance is determined. In field studies by Dachler and Mobley (14) and Steers (55) and in a laboratory study by Cartledge (10), goal acceptance and performance appeared to be predictable from measures of a person's expectancy that effort will lead to goal attainment, his expectancy that goal attainment will lead to various outcomes, and the subjective values (valence) assigned to those outcomes. These studies and the accompanying efforts to develop a model integrating goal theory with expectancy theory appear to be the most promising direction for further elaboration of goal theory.

Another important gap in theory development and research is the manner in which goal acceptance, goal difficulty, and other aspects of goal setting combine to determine a person's task effort. This subject takes on added complexity as a history of successes or failures in goal attainment is accumulated. For example, if pressures exist to set excessively hard goals or to prevent a downward revision of goals that have proved to be unreasonable, a series of failures in goal attainment is likely and this in turn will greatly reduce the likelihood of subsequent goal acceptance by subordinates. There clearly is a need for more longitudinal research on the complex interactions that determine if goal setting will be effective. An understanding of *why* goal setting affects employee performance has only begun.

Another promising approach for elaboration of Locke's theory is the inclusion of propositions concerning the cueing function of goals. The usefulness of goal setting for clarifying role requirements and the effects of goals on the employee's allocation of effort to different aspects of his job have been emphasized in the MBO literature. The effects of goals and feedback on learning as well as motivation, specifically the development of better job procedures by employees, also have been noted in one of the goal setting studies. As yet, these processes have not been incorporated into Locke's goal setting theory in any systematic fashion.

As for the practical feasibility of goal setting as a means of improving employee performance, the research shows goal setting programs to be effective over an extended time period in a variety of organizations, at both the managerial and nonmanagerial levels. Substantial increases in performance were obtained in some of the studies without any special prizes or incentives for goal attainment, although in other studies reward contingencies were an important consideration. Assigned goal setting and participative goal setting each was effective in several studies. In the few studies where the relative effectiveness of these two goal setting methods could be compared, the results were not conclusive. Further research on the consequences of subordinate participation in goal setting and on variables moderating these effects is highly desirable.

Although goal setting was found to be effective in many situations, some limiting conditions and moderating variables also were identified. One determinant of goal setting feasibility may be the complexity of the job and the availability of reasonably accurate performance measures. Goal setting for simple jobs with only one or two important performance dimensions may be much easier and more effective than goal setting for jobs with many performance dimensions, especially when some of these dimensions cannot be measured quantitatively. Since managerial jobs usually are of this complex nature, it is not surprising that goal setting programs with managers have encountered more problems and have been less successful than goal setting with nonmanagerial employees. One problem found by Levinson (34) is the tendency to neglect aspects of the job that are not easily quantified, such as customer service. The way in which multiple goals direct behavior and effort allocation is an important applied question that has received little attention except for the initial exploration of this subject by Charnes and Stedry (12) and Stedry and Kay (54). Additional research is needed to determine what goal setting procedures are most effective for very complex jobs, and to determine if there are some jobs for which goal setting may be impractical or even dysfunctional.

Another type of limiting condition found in several studies is the degree of managerial attention and support received by a goal setting program. In some of the studies in which goal setting was unsuccessful, the failure was attributed to a lack of strong support by key managerial personnel. The importance of management support and involvement in all types of organizational interventions has been emphasized in the organization development literature as well as the MBO literature.

The interrelationships among jobs in an organization are another possible limiting condition for effective goal setting. There first is the problem of evaluating individual performance and goal attainment by employees with highly interdependent jobs. As Levinson has pointed out, "The more a man's effectiveness depends upon what other people do, the less he himself can be held responsible for the outcome of his efforts" (34, p. 127). Group goals can be used instead of individual goals for some types of interdependent jobs, but this remedy would not be applicable to many types of jobs. An additional problem with setting specific goals for interdependent jobs was found by Baumler (1). He conducted a laboratory study of simulated organizations with either independent or interdependent jobs and compared the effects of defined criteria (i.e., specific goals) and no defined criteria in both types of organizations. Specific goals facilitated performance when jobs were independent but inhibited performance when jobs were interdependent. The inhibiting effects in the latter case were attributed to coordination difficulties and a preoccupation with individual goals at the expense of overall organizational effectiveness. The possibility that individual goal setting can be dysfunctional for interdependent jobs is important enough to warrant further investigation in actual as opposed to simulated organizations.

Even when goal setting is feasible for a job, it may not be effective for all types of employees who hold that job. Individual traits were found to be moderators of goal setting effectiveness in several studies. Needs, attitudes, personality, and perhaps education and cultural background may determine whether an employee will respond favorably to goal setting, and such traits also may moderate the effects of goal difficulty and participation in goal setting. However, the research to date on this subject should be regarded as exploratory rather than definitive, and additional studies on employee traits as moderators of goal setting effectiveness are clearly needed.

In conclusion, the laboratory and field research on goal setting has provided impressive support for portions of Locke's theory and has demonstrated the practical feasibility of goal setting programs as a means of improving employee performance. Nevertheless, much still remains to be learned, and several lines of research are essential for further validation and elaboration of the theory. Such research is likely to result eventually in the formulation of a contingency model of goal setting effectiveness.

REFERENCES

1 Baumler, J. V. "Defined Criteria of Performance in Organizational Control," *Administrative Science Quarterly*, Vol. 16 (1971), 340–350.
2 Blumenfeld, W. E., and T. E. Leidy. "Effectiveness of Goal Setting as a Management Device: Research Note," *Psychological Reports*, Vol. 24 (1969), 24.

3   Brady, R. H. "MBO Goes to Work in the Public Sector," *Harvard Business Review*, Vol. 51 (1973), 65–74.

4   Burke, R. J., and D. S. Wilcox. "Characteristics of Effective Employee Performance Reviews and Developmental Interviews," *Personnel Psychology*, Vol. 22 (1969), 291–305.

5   Campbell, J. P., M. D. Dunnette, E. E. Lawler, and K. E. Weick, Jr. *Managerial Behavior, Performance and Effectiveness* (New York: McGraw-Hill, 1970).

6   Carroll, S. J., and H. L. Tosi. "Relationship of Goal Setting Characteristics as Moderated by Personality and Situational Factors to the Success of the Management by Objectives Approach," *Proceedings of the 77th Annual Convention*, American Psychological Association, 1969.

7   Carroll, S. J., and H. L. Tosi. "Goal Characteristics and Personality Factors in a Management by Objectives Program," *Administrative Science Quarterly*, Vol. 15 (1970), 295–305.

8   Carroll, S. J., and H. L. Tosi. "Relationship of Characteristics of the Review Process to the Success of the MBO Approach," *Journal of Business*, Vol. 44 (1971), 299–305.

9   Carroll, S. J., and H. L. Tosi. *Management by Objectives: Applications and Research* (New York: Macmillan, 1973).

10 Cartledge, N. D. *An Experimental Study of the Relationship Between Expectancies, Goal Utility, Goals, and Task Performance* (Ph. D. dissertation, University of Maryland, 1973).

11 Chapanis, A. "Knowledge of Performance as an Incentive in Repetitive, Monotonous Tasks," *Journal of Applied Psychology*, Vol. 48 (1964), 263–267.

12 Charnes, A., and A. C. Stedry. "Exploratory Models in the Theory of Budgetary Control," in W. W. Cooper, H. J. Leavitt, and M. W. Shelly (Eds.), *New Perspectives in Organizational Research* (New York: Wiley, 1964).

13 Cummings, L. L., D. P. Schwab, and M. Rosen. "Performance and Knowledge of Results as Predeterminants of Goal Setting," *Journal of Applied Psychology*, Vol. 55 (1971), 526–530.

14 Dachler, H. P., and W. H. Mobley. "Construct Validation of an Instrumentality-Expectancy-Task-Goal Model of Work Motivation," *Journal of Applied Psychology*, Vol. 58 (1973), 397–418.

15 Dobmeyer, T. W. "A Critique of Edwin Locke's Theory of Task Motivation and Incentives," in H. L. Tosi, R. J. House, and M. D. Dunnette (Eds.), *Managerial Motivation and Compensation* (East Lansing, Mich.: MSU Business Studies, 1971), pp. 244–259.

16 Duttagupta, D. *An Empirical Evaluation of Management by Objectives* (Master's thesis, Baruch College, 1975).

17 French, J. R. P., E. Kay, and H. H. Meyer. "Participation and the Appraisal System," *Human Relations*, Vol. 19 (1966), 3–19.

18 Gell, T., and C. F. Molander. "Beyond Management by Objectives," *Personnel Management*, Vol. 2 (1970), 18–20.

19 Howell, R. A. "A Fresh Look at Management by Objectives," *Business Horizons*, Vol. 10 (1967), 51–58.

20 Howell, R. A. "Managing by Objectives—A Three Stage System," *Business Horizons*, Vol. 13 (1970), 41–45.

21 Hundal, P. S. "Knowledge of Performance as an Incentive in Repetitive Industrial Work," *Journal of Applied Psychology*, Vol. 53 (1969), 214–226.

22   Ivancevich, J. M. "A Longitudinal Assessment of Management by Objectives,"
      Administrative Science Quarterly, Vol. 17 (1972), 126–138.
23   Ivancevich, J. M. "Changes in Performance in a Management by Objectives Pro-
      gram," *Administrative Science Quarterly*, Vol. 19 (1974), 563–574.
24   Ivancevich, J. M., J. H. Donnelly, and H. L. Lyon. "A Study of the Impact of
      Management by Objectives on Perceived Need Satisfaction," *Personnel Psychol-
      ogy*, Vol. 23 (1970), 139–151.
25   Kirchoff, B. A. "Using Objectives: The Critical Variable in Effective MBO,"
      Michigan Business Review, Vol. 26 (1974), 17–21.
26   Kolb, D. A., and R. E. Boyatzis. "Goal Setting and Self-Directed Behavior
      Change," in D. A. Kolb, I. M. Rubin, and J. M. McIntyre (Eds.), *Organizational
      Psychology: A Book of Readings* (Englewood Cliffs, N. J.: Prentice-Hall, 1971), pp.
      317–337.
27   Kolb, D. A., S. Winters, and D. Berlew. "Self-Directed Change: Two Studies,"
      Journal of Applied Behavioral Science, Vol. 4 (1968), 453–473.
28   Lasagna, J. B. "Make Your MBO Pragmatic," *Harvard Business Review*, Vol. 49
      (1971), 64–69.
29   Latham, G. P., and J. J. Baldes. "The Practical Significance of Locke's Theory
      of Goal Setting," *Journal of Applied Psychology*, Vol. 60 (1975), 122–124.
30   Latham, G. P., and S. B. Kinne, III. "Improving Job Performance Through Training
      in Goal Setting," *Journal of Applied Psychology*, Vol. 59 (1974), 187–191.
31   Latham, G. P., and E. A. Locke. "Increasing Productivity with Decreasing Time
      Limits: A Field Replication of Parkinson's Law," *Journal of Applied Psychology*,
      Vol. 60 (1975), 524–526.
32   Latham, G. P., and E. A. Locke. "Assigned Versus Participative Goal Setting with
      Educated and Uneducated Woods Workers," *Journal of Applied Psychology*, Vol.
      60 (1975), 299–302.
33   Lawrence, L. C., and P. C. Smith. "Group Decision and Employee Participation,"
      Journal of Applied Psychology, Vol. 39 (1955), 334–337.
34   Levinson, H. "Management By Whose Objectives?" *Harvard Business Review*,
      Vol. 48, No. 4 (1970), 125–134.
35   Likert, R. *The Human Organization* (New York: McGraw-Hill, 1967).
36   Locke, E. A. "Toward a Theory of Task Motivation and Incentives," *Organiza-
      tional Behavior and Human Performance*, Vol. 3 (1968), 157–189.
37   Locke, E. A., N. Cartledge, and C. S. Knerr. "Studies of the Relationship Between
      Satisfaction, Goal Setting and Performance," *Organizational Behavior and Human
      Performance*, Vol. 5 (1970), 135–158.
38   Locke, E. A., N. Cartledge, and J. Koeppel. "Motivational Effects of Knowledge
      of Results: A Goal Setting Phenomenon," *Psychological Bulletin*, Vol. 70 (1968),
      474–485.
39   Lowin, A. "Participative Decision-Making: A Model, Literature Critique and Pre-
      scription for Research," *Organizational Behavior and Human Performance*, Vol. 3
      (1968), 68–106.
40   Massie, J. L. "Management Theory," in J. G. March (Ed.), *Handbook of Orga-
      nizations* (Chicago: Rand McNally, 1965), pp. 387–422.
41   McGregor, D. *The Human Side of Enterprise* (New York: McGraw-Hill, 1960).
42   Mendleson, J. L. *Managerial Goal Setting: An Exploration into Meaning and
      Measurement* (Ph.D. dissertation, Michigan State University, 1967).
43   Meyer, H. H., E. Kay, and J. R. P. French. "Split Roles in Performance Appraisal,"
      Harvard Business Review, Vol. 43 (1965), 123–129.

44 Miller, L. *The Use of Knowledge of Results in Improving the Performance of Hourly Operators* (Crotonville, N. Y.: General Electric Company, Behavioral Research Service, 1965).

45 Morse, J. H., and J. W. Lorsch. "Beyond Theory Y," *Harvard Business Review,* Vol. 48 (1970), 61–68.

46 Murray, R. K. "Behavioral Management Objectives," *Personnel Journal,* Vol. 52 (1973), 304–306.

47 Pritchard, R. D., and M. I. Curtis. "The Influence of Goal Setting and Financial Incentives on Task Performance," *Organizational Behavior and Human Performance,* Vol. 10 (1973), 175–183.

48 Raia, A. P. "Goal Setting and Self-Control: An Empirical Study," *Journal of Management Studies,* Vol. 2 (1965), 32–53.

49 Raia, A. P. "A Second Look at Management by Goals and Controls," *California Management Review,* Vol. 8 (1966), 49–58.

50 Ronan, W. W., G. P. Latham, and S. B. Kinne. "Effects of Goal Setting and Supervision on Worker Behavior in an Industrial Situation," *Journal of Applied Psychology,* Vol. 58 (1973), 302–307.

51 Ryan, T. A. *Work and Effort* (New York: Ronald, 1947).

52 Shetty, Y. K., and H. M. Carlisle. "Organizational Correlates of a Management by Objectives Program," *Academy of Management Journal,* Vol. 17 (1974), 155–159.

53 Sorcher, M. *Motivating the Hourly Employee* (Crotonville, N. Y.: General Electric Company, Behavioral Research Service, 1967).

54 Stedry, A. C., and E. Kay. "The Effects of Goal Difficulty On Performance," *Behavioral Science,* Vol. 11 (1966), 459–470.

55 Steers, R. M. "Task-Goal Attributes, n Achievement, and Supervisory Performance," *Organizational Behavior and Human Performance,* Vol. 13 (1975), 392–403.

56 Tannenbaum, R., and W. Schmidt. "How to Choose a Leadership Pattern," *Harvard Business Review,* Vol. 36 (1958), 95–101.

57 Vroom V. H., and P. Yetton. *Leadership and Decision-Making* (Pittsburgh, Pa.: University of Pittsburgh Press, 1973).

58 Wexley, K. N., and W. F. Nemeroff. "Effects of Positive Reinforcement and Goal Setting as Methods of Management Development," *Journal of Applied Psychology,* Vol. 60 (1975), 446–450.

59 Wickens, J. D. "Management by Objectives: An Appraisal," *Journal of Management Studies,* Vol. 5 (1968), 365–379.

60 Wilsted, W. D., and H. H. Hand. "Determinants of Aspiration Levels in a Simulated Goal Setting Environment of the Firm," *Academy of Management Journal,* Vol. 6 (1971), 414–440.

61 Yukl, G. A. "Toward a Behavioral Theory of Leadership," *Organizational Behavior and Human Performance,* Vol. 6 (1971), 414–440.

62 Zander, A., and T. T. Newcomb, Jr. "Group Levels of Aspiration in United Fund Campaigns," *Journal of Personality and Social Psychology,* Vol. 6 (1967), 157–162.

63 Zander, A., J. Forward, and R. Albert. "Adaptation of Board Members to Repeated Failure or Success by the Organization," *Organizational Behavior and Human Performance,* Vol. 4 (1969), 56–76.

The Role of Task-Goal Attributes in Employee Performance

Richard M. Steers
Lyman W. Porter[1]

Organizational researchers and practicing managers have long been concerned with discovering methods for improving the effectiveness and efficiency of on-going organizations. The determination of organizational effectiveness has traditionally been seen as the extent to which an organization is successful in accomplishing its operative goals, while organizational efficiency is typically defined as the cost-benefit ratio incurred in pursuit of those goals (Barnard, 1938). Considerable theory exists on an abstract level concerning the nature of organizational goal formulation and goal attainment, particularly as it relates to the external environment (Cyert & March, 1963; Etzioni, 1964; Lawrence & Lorsch, 1967; March & Simon, 1958; Perrow, 1961, 1970; Simon, 1964; Thompson & McEwen, 1958). However, little attempt has been made empirically to understand how such broad-based objectives become translated into specific activities which can be carried out by the individual members of an organization; that is, our knowledge of the relationship between the pursuit of *organizational* goals and the required tasks of *individuals* appears lacking in several respects. What is needed is a clearer understanding of the factors which eventually go to determine how well an organization achieves its stated intentions.

It is the purpose of this paper to review systematically the relevant research dealing with the role played by *task*-goals in employee performance. The findings of these investigations will be placed in the larger organizational context as they ultimately relate to the attainment of organization-wide goals. We first briefly consider the association between organizational goals and task-goals. Next, we review the research relating various aspects of task-goals to individual performance on the job. Finally, the role of task-goals will be discussed within the theoretical context of an employee's motivational force to perform and how such performance relates to the larger issue of organizational effectiveness.

To begin with, it is important to consider, at least in theory, how the goals of an organization become translated into manageable tasks for employees to perform. A typical formalized goal-setting program designed to maximize organizational goal attainment, while simultaneously minimizing unnecessary expenditure of human resources, can be seen as proceeding on two levels. The first step in this (ideal) process would involve what March and Simon (1958) term a "means-ends analysis." Briefly defined, such an analysis represents an

Abridged from *Psychological Bulletin*, 1974, **81**, 434–452. Copyright 1974 by the American Psychological Association. Reprinted by permission.

[1]This paper was supported in part by a grant from the Graduate Division, University of California, Irvine, and by funds supplied under Office of Naval Research Contract No. N00014-69-0200-9001, NR 151–315.

attempt on an organization-wide basis to refine operative goals (i.e., the real objectives or intentions of the organization) into operational (i.e., specific, manageable, and measurable) goals. This means-ends analysis, which would finally culminate in fairly specific and tangible organizational goals, is generally *horizontal* in nature; that is, goal refinements typically would remain organization-wide, or at least department-wide, in scope and responsibility.

Next, a vehicle must be found to translate these organization-wide, operational goals into smaller segments which are of sufficient size to be suitably managed by individuals or sub-groups in the organization. In other words, the second step in the process involves extending the means-ends chain *vertically* down through the various levels of the organization in such a way as to marshall organizational resources efficiently for goal-directed activities. When this sequential process becomes formalized into a goal-setting system where each member, or small group, has specific goals and time parameters for task accomplishment, it often goes under the rubric of "Management-By-Objectives," or MBO. The basic motivational *assumption* of such goal-setting programs is that effort—and consequently performance—is increased by providing individuals with clear targets toward which to direct their energies. Thus, search behavior is theoretically reduced, allowing for greater effort to be concentrated in a single direction. Such a system has as its major purpose, then, the maximization of organizational goal attainment through the efficient use of an organization's resources. In other words, the contribution of each member to organizational effectiveness is theoretically maximized.

It becomes clear from the foregoing discussion that the common denominator of such a goal-setting system is the individual "task-goals" assigned to the various members of the organization. *Task-goals* may be defined as relatively specific targets or objectives which an employee (or a small group of employees) is responsible for accomplishing within a specified time period. Typically, task-goals are tied to some form of systematic performance appraisal and review. Assuming that such goals have been set with reference to the larger organizational purpose, the degree to which these task-goals are met (or not met) in large measure should determine the ultimate success or failure of an organization in meeting its overall objectives.

While formalized goal-setting programs had their beginnings among managerial and supervisory personnel, the techniques have more recently been applied to blue-collar workers. Myers (1970) argues that meaningful goals can provide a sense of purpose for almost any type of activity. He describes goals which potentially have maximum motivational value as those task-goals which are influenced by the employee and which are visible, desirable, challenging, and attainable. Such goals are hypothesized to lead to the satisfaction of an individual's needs for growth, achievement, responsibility, recognition, affiliation, and security (1970:42). Thus, *in theory,* goal-setting techniques, such as those employed in MBO-type programs, should have a significant and beneficial impact not only upon performance but also upon employee attitudes and need satisfaction. Unfortunately, much of this theory remains largely untested.

The books written on formalized goal-setting systems are legion in number (e.g., Batten, 1966; Beck & Hillmar, 1972; Drucker, 1954; Hughes, 1965; Koontz, 1971; E. Miller, 1968; Morrisey, 1970; Odiorne, 1965; Schleh, 1961; Valentine, 1966; Wikstrom, 1968). By and large, these works represent "how-to-do-it" manuals based primarily on anecdotal evidence and are often void of empirical support for the theories expounded. (A notable exception to this trend is a recent book by Carroll and Tosi [1973].) This situation leaves both the researcher and the organizational decision-maker in a position of either accepting the utility of goal-setting programs on face value or rejecting them out of hand due to an absence of supportive evidence. Neither of these positions appears desirable. In an attempt to resolve this dilemma, an effort will be made here to bring together in an integrated fashion the available research that does exist to provide a better understanding of the performance implications of various aspects of such systems.

RESEARCH ON TASK-GOALS AND PERFORMANCE

When the research on task-goals is considered *in toto*, strong and consistent evidence emerges that the act of setting clear goals on an individual's job (as opposed to only broadly defining his areas of responsibility) does generally result in increased performance. Such findings have been demonstrated both in the laboratory (Bryan & Locke, 1967a; Fryer, 1964; Mace, 1935) and in the field (French, Kay & Meyer, 1966; Humble, 1970a, 1970b; Lawrence & Smith, 1955; Meyer, Kay & French, 1965; Raia, 1965, 1966). However, knowing that goal-setting techniques are relatively successful does not explain *why* they work or *what* can be done to improve their effectiveness. A more complete picture of the nature of goal-setting may be obtained by studying the role played by various attributes of a goal-setting system as they relate to performance.

Toward this end, studies relating various "task-goal attributes" to performance will be reviewed. A *task-goal attribute* is defined here as a characteristic or dimension of an employee's task-goals. While research has been carried out on numerous—and often overlapping—attributes, a recent study using factor analytic techniques (Steers, 1973) demonstrated the existence of five relatively autonomous attributes: (1) goal specificity; (2) participation in goal-setting; (3) feedback on goal progress; (4) peer competition for goal attainment; and (5) goal difficulty. In addition, we shall include "goal acceptance" here as a sixth attribute. While the goal acceptance dimension was not derived from the factor analytic study, recent research has pointed to its potential importance for employee performance under goal-setting conditions. The relevant research relating to each of these attributes will be analyzed separately. . . .[2]

DISCUSSION AND CONCLUSIONS

It has been argued throughout this review that the simple knowledge that goal-setting "works" is insufficient for our understanding of the goal-setting process;

[2]Due to space limitations, the review section of the paper has been omitted. The interested reader is referred to the original source for a more detailed analysis of the specific investigations.

we must know how and why it works. Toward this end, some 80 empirical studies relating to six factor-analytically derived attributes of task-goals were examined. Based on this review, several specific conclusions can be drawn.

To begin with, increases in goal specificity were found to be consistently and positively related to performance across both field and laboratory investigations. We would expect such a finding in view of the centrality of goal specification in formalized goal-setting programs; in fact, goal specificity may in many ways be considered a defining characteristic of such programs. In addition, the available research indicates that acceptance of task-goals is also strongly and positively related to performance. However, this conclusion rests on only a few empirical studies, and final judgment must await further investigation.

Less consistent findings have been demonstrated for the three attributes of goal difficulty, participation in goal-setting, and feedback on goal effort. While the majority of findings concerning each of these attributes tends to indicate positive relationships with performance, a number of important exceptions exist. For example, while the laboratory studies of goal difficulty consistently point to a positive relationship with performance, the field studies generally indicate either more complex or null relationships. Moreover, many investigations of these three attributes found important intervening variables which influenced performance relationships. Thus, while the tendencies for all three task-goal attributes are in the direction of positive associations with performance, no definitive relationships were found. Finally, no consistent relationship emerged between the degree of peer competition and employee performance, again suggesting the existence of important intervening variables which influence the relationship.

From these data, a possible case could be made that the "key" to successful goal-setting programs in work situations, such as MBO, lies primarily in discovering those specific task-goal attributes most closely associated with performance and then "loading" an employee's task-goals with these attributes. This approach has often been taken in some of the more prescriptive literature on goal-setting. However, such actions by themselves appear less than desirable for at least two reasons. First, the singular attention to the role of task-goal attributes in performance ignores several additional factors which have been shown to have an important bearing on performance. Second, and perhaps more important from a psychological standpoint, such action really tells us very little about the dynamics behind the effects of goal-setting. That is, knowing that goal specificity, for example, is consistently related to task performance does not explain the process by which it affects such performance.

A more comprehensive analysis of the role of task-goal attributes in employee performance can be derived by analyzing from a theoretical standpoint the psychological processes involved in such activities. The question posed here, then, is how various attributes in a goal-setting program affect an individual's motivational force to perform. We shall consider this question by viewing the effects of goal-setting programs within an Expectancy/Valence motivational framework. While many theories of motivation exist, the Expectancy/Valence model has been selected as a framework for analysis for several reasons. First, it represents a reasonably well-developed and comprehensive approach to explaining human behavior at work. It attempts to account for important variables not only within the individual but also within the work environment in which he finds himself. Second, some research has begun to emerge which generally provides some support for the effectiveness of this model in explaining the decision to perform at a given level (Campbell, et al., 1970; Galbraith & Cummings, 1967; Georgopoulos, Mahoney, & Jones, 1957; Graen, 1969; Heneman & Schwab, 1972; Mitchell & Biglan, 1971; Porter & Lawler, 1968; Vroom, 1964).

In simplified form, Expectancy/Valence theory posits that the motivational force of an individual to perform is a multiplicative function of his subjective probability that effort will lead to the receipt of certain rewards and the valence he places on those rewards. For example, if an individual really believes that increasing his effort will lead to the receipt of a pay raise, and if he values having this additional income, we would expect his effort on the job to be high. (It should be noted that, while more complex elaborations of this theory exist, this simplified form will suffice for our purposes here.)

When the major findings of this review are placed within such a framework, it becomes possible to understand more fully—at least on a theoretical level— why certain task-goal attributes can play such important roles at times in the determination of employee performance under a goal-setting system. Under this conceptualization, it would appear that the various task-goal attributes affect performance because—and to the extent that—they affect the components comprising the motivational force equation. In other words, varying the amounts of certain of these attributes on the job may serve to alter an employee's expectancies, valences, or both, thereby affecting his motivation to perform. Three brief examples should serve to clarify this point.

First, consider the example of goal specificity. Giving an employee a set of goals that are highly specific in nature should allow him to know more precisely what is expected of him on the job. Such reduced search behavior should, in turn, make it easier for the individual to see the relationship between effort and resulting performance (and presumably rewards), thus clarifying his level of expectations on that job.

A second example can be seen by examining the potential motivational effects of allowing employee participation in goal-setting. It is possible that such participation may at times affect the valence an individual places on goal attainment. If an employee is allowed to play a central role in the determination of his task-goals, he may become more ego-involved in the outcome of those goals (Vroom, 1960) and place a higher value on goal attainment. Thus, assuming constant expectancies, increasing an employee's valence for potential rewards should lead to increased effort. We would expect, however, that these participation effects would be affected at least to some extent by the personality traits exhibited by the employee. For example, an employee with a high need for achievement might be more prone to become ego-involved in performance outcomes (and increase his valences accordingly) when allowed greater participation than someone who has a low need for achievement.

Finally, take the more complex example of peer competition for goal attainment. Where a situation approaches a zero-sum game (i.e., where there can be only one "winner"), we might expect a competitive atmosphere to lead to somewhat increased valences concerning outcomes, while at the same time lowering certain expectancy levels. A salesman, for instance, generally realizes that there are attractive benefits (e.g., bonuses, etc.) for ranking first among his peers in sales and that, simultaneously, there are undesirable penalties for ranking last (e.g., the possibility of termination). Under such circumstances, we would expect such competitive effects to lead to an increase in the valence attached to the available (and scarce) rewards. However, realization that one's peers are probably also putting forth maximum effort to gain such desirable rewards (and avoid such severe penalties) may tend to reduce one's expectancies that increased effort will, in fact, lead to increased performance and rewards. We may thus have a situation where increased peer competition would lead to increased valences, but the impact of such a change may be largely negated by a concomitant reduction in expectancies.

On the other hand, when the situation tends toward a non-zero-sum game (i.e., where there can be more than one "winner"), there is little reason to believe that perceived competitive effects would have a substantial influence on either expectancies or valences. The removal of both the extreme positive *and* the extreme negative consequences in the above example would tend to reduce in large measure the valence attached to goal attainment in and of itself. Subjective perceptions of the ease of goal attainment (expectancies) may be somewhat higher, however, because the individual may not perceive his peers as trying quite so hard, thereby making *relative* performance somewhat easier. Thus, while certain expectancies here may be somewhat higher, the corresponding reward valences would probably tend to be lower, again cancelling out any substantive gains in employee effort.

We have attempted here to provide three hypothetical examples of how goal-setting effects can be better understood by placing them within a specific motivational framework. Other examples could be provided. It is important to realize, however, that these examples are conjectural in nature and are meant simply to be illustrative of how a framework like the Expectancy/Valence model could be utilized to learn more about the processes behind goal-setting dynamics. It is argued here that one explanation for such a process is that variations in the attributes of an employee's task goals tend to affect effort and performance to the extent that they alter his level of path-goal expectancies or the valences he attaches to expected outcomes on the job. More specific description of such a process awaits further investigation.

Viewing formalized goal-setting programs, like MBO, within such a motivational model leads to several fairly specific implications for the practicing manager. To begin with, it appears as though greater consideration should be given in the design and application of such programs to the nature of the particular attributes which characterize an employee's task-goals. For example, it was generally found in the above review that goal specificity was positively associated with task performance. Following this finding, greater attention could be paid in the formulation of task-goals to insuring that such goals are clearly specified and well understood by the employee. Similarly, increased effort on the part of management could be directed toward securing employee acceptance of these goals in the form of personal levels of aspiration. In short, greater care should be given to insuring that the final goal-setting program design is consistent with existing knowledge concerning the performance implications of the various task-goal attributes. Such a practice has apparently not been the case in many existing MBO-type programs (Carroll & Tosi, 1973; Raia, 1965, 1966).

In addition, increased attention could be paid to drawing a suitable linkage between existing programs and relevant motivational theories of work behavior. For example, consideration should be directed toward a better understanding of the consequences to be obtained from a clarification for employees of the relationship between task performance and potential rewards. Moreover, increased attention could be focused on improving our knowledge as to which rewards employees truly value. If employees consistently attach a low valence to the traditional rewards offered for goal attainment, the motivational value of such rewards would tend to be less than desirable.

Third, some concern appears in order as to the potential negative attitudinal consequences which may be associated with certain aspects of goal-setting programs that could hamper program effectiveness. Some research has indicated that when goals are perceived as being far too difficult or far too rigid, the credibility of the program itself may be seriously jeopardized, leading to poor performance. Care must be taken, in other words, to insure that the general parameters of the program are fairly widely accepted by program participants.

Finally, it would appear highly desirable if management would increase their willingness to subject their MBO-type programs to continual empirical examination in an effort to monitor both attitudinal and performance consequences of such programs. Some research has demonstrated that goal-setting programs tend to lose their potency over time but little effort has been directed toward discovering why such a phenomenon occurs. A continuing monitoring system could hopefully assist in the identification of such trends and possibly point to potential remedies.

Assuming that such factors are taken into account, we would expect this increased understanding of the nature of goal-setting and of the role played by the various task-goal attributes to lead to at least some improvement in program effectiveness. However, one cannot assume that variations in the nature of task-goals would account solely for performance variances related to goal-setting. Sufficient evidence exists to demonstrate that several other factors must be taken into account if we are to more fully understand how level of effort is determined. For example, many studies point to the importance of certain additional situational and environmental factors (e.g., openness of communication, leadership style, etc.) in determining effort (French et al., 1966;

Ivancevich, 1972; Litwin & Stringer, 1968). Moreover, characteristics unique to the individual employee must be considered. Not only have some individual difference factors (e.g., need for achievement, level of aspiration) been shown to be somewhat effective predictors of performance by themselves (Cummin, 1967; E. French, 1955, 1958a, 1958b; Locke, 1968), but such factors have also been shown to represent important modifiers of the effects of certain task-goal attributes on performance (Carroll & Tosi, 1970, 1973; French et al., 1966; Steers, 1973; Vroom, 1960). These considerations must not be overlooked when attempting to understand more fully formalized goal-setting systems.

Thus, performance under goal-setting conditions appears to be a function of at least three important variables: the nature of task-goals, additional situational-environmental factors, and individual differences. Certainly, only when all three factors are duly considered can a greater understanding result concerning the extent of the role played by task-goals in employee performance. Such a conclusion must caution against the casual use of the *ceteris paribus* assumption when analyzing the performance implications of various task-goal attributes. We must begin to view the role of task-goal attributes within more complex frameworks which can adequately account for several additional variables which have been shown to represent important factors in employee performance. Moreover, there is a clear need to carry out these analyses within well-developed conceptualizations of the motivational process. One attempt at such a synthesis of empirical evidence with current work motivation theory has been made here, but more work is needed to test the applicability of such models to the goal-setting environment.

Finally, in addition to viewing individual performance on task-goals within a motivational framework, the role of task-goals must also be considered within the larger organizational context. More information is needed, for example, about the relation between task-goals and organizational goals. While much theorizing exists concerning such a relationship, in point of fact the bodies of research data on these two "types" of goals are virtually unrelated. Sound empirical investigation—as opposed to exhortative prescriptions—is needed on how (or whether) operational organizational goals become translated into employee task-goals and how such a process affects employee performance. Conversely, and equally important, we need to know how (or whether) task-goals impact upon organizational goals. Findings from such research should help us understand better how both types of goals affect the larger issue of organizational effectiveness.

REFERENCES[3]

Barnard, C. *The functions of the executive*. Cambridge, Mass.: Harvard University Press, 1938.

Batten, J. D. *Beyond management by objectives*. New York: American Management Association, 1966.

   [3]References abridged.

Beck, A. C., Jr., & Hillmar, E. D. *A practical approach to organization development through MBO—Selected readings.* Reading, Mass.: Addison-Wesley, 1972.

Bryan, J. F., & Locke, E. A. Goal setting as a means of increasing motivation. *Journal of Applied Psychology,* 1967, **51,** 274–277.

Campbell, J. P., Dunnette, M. D., Lawler, E. E., III, & Weick, K. E. *Managerial behavior, performance and effectiveness.* New York: McGraw-Hill, 1970.

Carroll, S. J., Jr., & Tosi, H. L. Goal characteristics and personality factors in a management-by-objectives program. *Administrative Science Quarterly,* 1970, **15,** 295–305.

Carroll, S. J., & Tosi, H. L., Jr. *Management by objectives: Applications and research.* New York: Macmillan, 1973.

Cummin, P. C. TAT correlates of executive performance. *Journal of Applied Psychology,* 1967, **51,** 78–81.

Cyert, R. M., & March, J. G. *A behavioral theory of the firm.* Englewood Cliffs, N.J.: Prentice-Hall, 1963.

Drucker, P. *The practice of management.* New York: Harper, 1954.

Etzioni, A. *Modern organizations.* Englewood Cliffs, N. J.: Prentice-Hall, 1964.

French, E. G. Some characteristics of achievement motivation. *Journal of Experimental Psychology,* 1955, **50,** 232–236.

French, E. G. Effects of the interaction of motivation and feedback on task performance. In J. W. Atkinson (Ed.), *Motives in fantasy, action, and society.* Princeton, N.J.: Van Nostrand, 1958. (a)

French, E. G. The interaction of achievement motivation and ability in problem solving success. *Journal of Abnormal Social Psychology,* 1958, **57,** 306–309. (b)

French, J. R., Kay, E., & Meyer, H. H. Participation and the appraisal system. *Human Relations,* 1966, **19,** 3–19.

Fryer, F. W. *An evaluation of level of aspiration as a training procedure.* Englewood Cliffs, N. J.: Prentice-Hall, 1964.

Galbraith, J., & Cummings, L. L. An empirical investigation of the motivational determinants of task performance: Interactive effects between instrumentality-valence and motivation-ability. *Organizational Behavior and Human Performance,* 1967, **2,** 237–257.

Georgopoulos, B., Mahoney, G., & Jones, N. A path-goal approach to productivity. *Journal of Applied Psychology,* 1957, **41,** 345–353.

Graen, G. Instrumentality theory of work motivation: Some experimental results and suggested modifications. *Journal of Applied Psychology Monograph,* 1969, **53** (2, Pt. 2).

Heneman, H. G., III, & Schwab, D. P. An evaluation of research on expectancy theory predictions of employee performance. *Psychological Bulletin,* 1972, **78,** 1–9.

Hughes, C. L. *Goal setting: Key to individual and organizational effectiveness.* New York: American Management Association, 1965.

Humble, J. W. *Improving business results.* London: McGraw-Hill, 1970. (a)

Humble, J. W. *Management by objectives in action.* London: McGraw-Hill, 1970. (b)

Ivancevich, J. M. A longitudinal assessment of management by objectives. *Administrative Science Quarterly,* 1972, **16,** 126–138.

Koontz, H. *Appraising managers as managers.* New York: McGraw-Hill, 1971.

Lawrence, L. C., & Smith, P. C. Group decision and employee participation. *Journal of Applied Psychology,* 1955, **39,** 334–337.

Lawrence, P. R., & Lorsch, J. *Organization and environment.* Boston: Division of Research, Graduate School of Business Administration, Harvard University, 1967.

Litwin, G. H., & Stringer, R. A., Jr. *Motivation and organizational climate*. Boston: Division of Research, Graduate School of Business Administration, Harvard University, 1968.

Locke, E. A. Toward a theory of task performance and incentives. *Organizational Behavior and Human Performance*, 1968, **3**, 157–189.

Mace, C. A. Incentives: Some experimental studies. London: Industrial Health Research Board, 1935, Report No. 72.

March, J. G., & Simon, H. A. *Organizations*. New York: Wiley, 1958.

Meyer, H., Kay, E., & French, J. R. Split roles in performance appraisal. *Harvard Business Review*, 1965, **43**, 123–129.

Miller, E. C. *Objectives and standards of performance in financial management*. New York: American Management Association, 1968.

Mitchell, T. R., & Biglan, A. Instrumentality theories: Current uses in psychology. *Psychological Bulletin*, 1971, **76**, 432–454.

Morrisey, G. L. *Management by objectives and results*. Reading, Mass.: Addison-Wesley, 1970.

Myers, M. S. *Every employee a manager*. New York: McGraw-Hill, 1970.

Odiorne, G. *Management by objectives*. New York: Pitman, 1965.

Perrow, C. The analysis of goals in complex organizations. *American Sociological Review*, 1961, **26**, 859–866.

Perrow, C. *Organizational analysis: A sociological view*. Belmont, Cal.: Wadsworth, 1970.

Porter, L. W., & Lawler, E. E., III. *Managerial attitudes and performance*. Homewood, Ill.: Irwin, 1968.

Raia, A. P. Goal setting and self control. *Journal of Management Studies*, 1965, **2**, 34–53.

Raia, A. P. A second look at goals and controls. *California Management Review*, 1966, **8** (4), 49–58.

Schleh, E. C. *Management for results*. New York: McGraw-Hill, 1961.

Simon, H. A. On the concept of organizational goal. *Administrative Science Quarterly*, 1964, **9**, 1–22.

Steers, R. M. *Task goals, individual need strengths, and supervisory performance*. Unpublished doctoral dissertation, Graduate School of Administration, University of California, Irvine, June 1973.

Thompson, J. D., & McEwen, W. J. Organizational goals and environment. *American Sociological Review*, 1958, **23**, 23–30.

Valentine, R. F. *Performance objectives for managers*. New York: American Management Association, 1966.

Vroom, V. H. *Some personality determinants of the effects of participation*. Englewood Cliffs, N.J.: Prentice-Hall, 1960.

Vroom, V. *Work and motivation*. New York: Wiley, 1964.

Wikstrom, W. S. *Managing by and with objectives*. New York: National Industrial Conference Board, 1968.

QUESTIONS FOR DISCUSSION

1 How does Locke's theory of task motivation differ from the theories discussed earlier?

2 How can Locke's model be integrated with an MBO program?

3 Discuss the role of goal-setting in the determination of employee attitudes.

4 What role does goal-setting play in equity theory?

5 In general, why do goal-setting and MBO often result in increased performance?

6 Under what circumstances might MBO-type programs be more successful? Less successful? Why?

7 What effects might an MBO program have on organizational climate?

8 How could you use expectancy/valence theory in designing MBO-type programs?

9 What are some negative *consequences* that could arise from the implementation of goal-setting or MBO?

10 What are some of the major problems that might arise in trying to implement an MBO program?

11 How can goal-setting be integrated into a job redesign program?

12 Evaluate the research evidence in support of goal-setting techniques in organizations.

Chapter 11

Money and Motivation

For reasons not fully understood, the role of financial compensation in employee motivation and performance remains one of the most frequently discussed but most underresearched areas in organizational psychology. All too often, writers have tended to set forth data-free pronouncements on the role of money at work, and investigators have employed less-than-rigorous research methodologies to test relatively simplistic models of such relationships. Similarly, in work settings, managers have tended to use reward systems that are based primarily on past practices or current fads (Dunnette & Bass, 1963), thus apparently trying both to save themselves time and yet find effective methods of compensation that are simple to administer. In many cases little concern is given to discovering the underlying relationships between organizational compensation practices and resulting motivation and performance. Such a trend has led to the creation of a series of myths concerning the exact role that is played by money.

EARLY APPROACHES TO COMPENSATION

A primary reason for the emergence of these myths—or misconceptions—about money and motivation can be found by tracing the history of the research efforts on the topic. The earliest systematic effort to study compensation practices in relation to productivity dates from the scientific management movement around the turn of the century. During this period, Frederick Taylor and his associates emphasized the use of piece-rate incentive systems for blue-collar workers, feeling that these systems provided the most efficient way to simultaneously maximize both productivity and worker income. Taylor saw such systems, when used in conjunction with his work redesign techniques, as being the fairest for both the organization and its employees. These scientific management notions had their roots in the "economic man" assumption that people work only (or primarily) for money. Thus, according to this line of reasoning, efforts to increase productivity meant using money as the basic incentive.

Most research during this period focused on comparative studies of various types of piece-rate incentive systems as each was related to improved work performance. Little or no concern was shown for possible variations across individuals, such as differences in personality, need strengths, and the like. In fact, it was primarily this failure to acknowledge the role of psychological variables in motivation and performance that led to the demise of the scientific management movement (Lawler, 1971; Schein, 1972) and allowed for the emergence of the human relations philosophy.

The human relations theorists, writing primarily in the 1930s and 1940s, substituted the concept of "social man" for "economic man." They contended that people in work settings were generally motivated by group forces, such as group pressures, social relations, and organizational structure. Pay was seen as less important. Unfortunately, little sound research was carried out to support such a proposition, and the data that did emerge were often misinterpreted. For example, when one reexamines the data from the classic Hawthorne studies (specifically the relay-assembly test-room experiments), it becomes apparent that almost half of the performance improvement that occurred was attributable to manipulations of the wage incentive system (Roethlisberger & Dickson, 1939). Such facts were often lost in the philosophical statements of the human relationists.

Beginning in the early 1960s and continuing until the present, money again emerged as an important topic of concern—this time to the behavioral scientists. During this period, it was realized how little hard data really existed on the role of money in motivation. These contemporary theorists and researchers argued that any comprehensive theory of work motivation must take into account the role of financial compensation practices. In contrast to the early scientific management proponents, however, contemporary theorists tend to view money as only one of *several* important influences. They hold that such additional factors as perceived equity of pay, group influences, and individual need strength differences may also play important roles in determining performance levels on the job. Considerable disagreement still exists, however, over the relative importance of all these factors.

IMPORTANCE OF MONEY IN MOTIVATION

According to Opsahl and Dunnette (1966), there are at least five theories, or explanations, of the role of money in employee motivation and performance. To begin with, many feel that money acts as a generalized conditioned reinforcer since it is repeatedly paired with primary reinforcers. This view of the role of money is consistent with the position advanced by advocates of behavior modification (see Chapter 4). Others suggest that money is a conditioned incentive. That is, it is felt by some that the repeated pairing of money with primary incentives helps to establish a new learned drive for money.

A third explanation for the role of money in employee motivation focuses on anxiety. Specifically, it is suggested here that people learn to become anxious in the presence of a variety of cues that signify an absence of money. Such cues include being told "That costs too much money" or "We can't afford that." Such cues lead to feelings of anxiety (and perhaps feelings of insecurity) which money can satisfy.

Fourth, money can be seen as a "hygiene" factor, according to Herzberg's two-factor theory (see Chapter 9). In this model, it is suggested that the absence of money causes dissatisfaction, although the presence of money does not satisfy. It merely eliminates the source of dissatisfaction and brings someone to a neutral state of satisfaction.

Finally, according to expectancy/valence theory, money can serve as an instrument for gaining other desired outcomes (e.g., purchasing a new car, a vacation, etc.). As discussed in Chapter 5, money acquires value for an individual to the extent that it can help to fulfill these other desires and needs. Hence, money would probably be an instrumental reward for someone wanting a new car, but may not be either an instrumental reward or a motivator for someone seeking escape from the pressures of a routine, dead-end job.

OVERVIEW

The two selections that follow attempt to provide a broad introduction into the nature of financial compensation as a motivator of employee behavior and performance. First, Lawler reviews the experience of several organizations that attempted to tie pay to performance. He then discusses methods of relating pay to performance and evaluates the effectiveness of each method. Next, several factors are identified that can often influence the success of various compensation plans. Finally, Lawler describes several instances in which organizations may prefer not to use money to motivate performance, and ends with a brief note on the behavioral and attitudinal implications of pay secrecy.

In the second selection, Hamner considers a variety of reasons why merit pay systems fail. This discussion is particularly interesting in view of the fact that most motivation theorists advocate the use of such merit systems. Recommendations are then offered for overcoming many of the potential hurdles to effective merit pay systems.

REFERENCES AND SUGGESTED ADDITIONAL READINGS

Andrews, I. R. *Managerial compensation.* Ann Arbor, Mich.: Foundation for Research on Human Behavior, 1965.

Andrews, I. R., & Henry, M. M. Management attitudes toward pay. *Industrial Relations,* 1963. **3**, 29–39.

Dunnette, M. D. The motives of industrial managers. *Organizational Behavior and Human Performance*, 1967, **2**, 176–182.

Dunnette, M. D., & Bass, B. M. Behavioral scientists and personnel management. *Industrial Relations*, 1963, **2**, 115–130.

Haire, M., Ghiselli, E. E., & Porter, L. W. Psychological research on pay: An overview. *Industrial Relations*, 1963, **3**, 3–8.

Lawler, E. E., III. The mythology of management compensation. *California Management Review*, 1966, **9**, 11–22.

Lawler, E. E., III. Secrecy about management compensation. *Organizational Behavior and Human Performance*, 1967, **2**, 182–189.

Lawler, E. E., III. *Pay and organizational effectiveness: A psychological view*. New York: McGraw-Hill, 1971.

Lawler, E. E., III, & Porter, L. W. Perceptions regarding management compensation. *Industrial Relations*, 1963, **3**, 41–49.

Lawler, E. E., III, & Porter, L. W. Predicting managers' pay and their satisfaction with their pay. *Personnel Psychology*, 1966, **19**, 363–373.

McClelland, D. C. Money as a motivator: Some research insights. *The McKinsey Quarterly*, Fall 1967.

Opsahl, R. L. Managerial compensation: Needed research. *Organizational Behavior and Human Performance*, 1967, **2**, 208–216.

Opsahl, R. L., & Dunnette, M. D. The role of financial compensation in industrial motivation. *Psychological Bulletin*, 1966, **66**, 94–96.

Porter, L. W., & Lawler, E. E., III. *Managerial attitudes and performance*. Homewood, Ill.: Irwin, 1968.

Roethlisberger, F. J., & Dickson, W. J. *Management and the worker*. Cambridge, Mass.: Harvard, 1939.

Schein, E. H. *Organizational psychology*. Englewood Cliffs, N.J.: Prentice-Hall, 1972.

Tosi, H. J., House, R. J., & Dunnette, M. D. (Eds.). *Managerial motivation and compensation: A selection of readings*. East Lansing, Mich.: Michigan State University, 1972.

Vroom, V. H. *Work and motivation*. New York: Wiley, 1964.

Weick, K. E. Dissonance and task enhancement: A problem for compensation theory. *Organizational Behavior and Human Performance*, 1967, **2**, 189–208.

Wernimont, P. F., & Fitzpatrick, S. The meaning of money. *Journal of Applied Psychology*, 1972, **56**, 218–226.

Using Pay to Motivate Job Performance

Edward E. Lawler III

The research evidence . . . clearly indicates that under certain conditions pay can be use to motivate good performance. The required conditions are deceptively simple . . . in the sense that establishing the conditions is easier said than done. Theory and research suggest that for a pay plan to motivate people, it must (1) create a belief among employees that good performance will lead to high pay, (2) contribute to the importance of pay, (3) minimize the perceived negative consequences of performing well, and (4) create conditions such that positive outcomes other than pay will be seen to be related to good performance. In this section, we shall consider some of the problems an organization confronts when it tries to set up a pay system that will satisfy these four conditions. . . .

TYING PAY TO PERFORMANCE

One obvious means of creating the perception that pay is tied to performance is actually to relate pay closely to job performance and to make the relationship as visible as possible. Several studies have attempted to determine the degree to which this is done in organizations and have come up with some unexpected results. Their evidence indicates that pay is not very closely related to performance in many organizations that claim to have merit increase salary systems. Lawler and Porter (1966) show that pay is related to job level, seniority, and other non-performance factors. Svetlik, Prien, and Barrett (1964) show that there is a negative relationship between amount of salary and performance as evaluated by superiors. Lawler (1964) shows that managers' pay is relatively unrelated to superiors' performance evaluations. Meyer, Kay, and French (1965) show that managers' raises are not closely related to what occurs in their performance appraisal sessions.

Studies by Haire, Ghiselli, and Gordon (1967) and by Brenner and Lockwood (1965) also indicate that at the managerial level, pay is not always related to performance. The evidence in both these studies consists of salary history data; they point up some interesting tendencies. Haire et al., for example, have established that the raises managers get from one year to another often show no correlation with each other. If the companies were tying pay to performance, the lack of correlation would mean that a manager's performance in one year was quite different from his performance in another year. This assumption simply does not fit with what is known about performance: A manager who is a good performer one year is very likely to be a good performer the next. Thus, we must conclude that the companies studied were not tying pay to performance. Apparently, pay raises were distributed on a random basis, or the criteria for awarding raises were frequently changed. As a result, recent raises were often not related to past raises or to performance.

Overall, therefore, the studies suggest that many business organizations do not do a very good job of tying pay to performance. This conclusion is rather surprising in light of many companies' very frequent claims that their pay systems are based on merit. It is particularly surprising that pay does not seem to be related to performance at the managerial level. Here there are no unions to contend with, and one would think that if organizations were effectively relating pay to performance for any group of employees, it would be at the managerial level. Admittedly this conclusion is based on sketchy evidence, and future research may prove it to be wrong. It may be, for instance, that pay is indirectly tied to performance and that the tie is obscured by promotion policies. All the studies reviewed here looked at the relationship between pay and performance within one management level. Even though there is no relationship between pay and performance within a level, there may actually be a relationship if the better performing managers are promoted and because of this receive higher pay. There is little evidence, however, to suggest that this is true.

Failure to tie pay closely to performance in many companies could mean that pay is not motivating job performance. In order for pay to motivate performance, it must appear to be related to performance; and employees are not likely to believe that pay is related to performance if it actually is not. Lawler (1967a) has shown that in one instance where pay was not related to performance, managers were aware of this fact and, consequently, were not motivated by pay. This study also showed that in a group of organizations where measurements indicated that pay was only marginally tied to performance, managers had a fairly high belief that pay was related to performance. Thus, the data suggest that, given some positive indicators, employees are willing to believe that pay is based upon performance. Often, however, the positive indicators are missing, and as a result, pay does not motivate the employees to perform effectively.

METHODS OF RELATING PAY TO PERFORMANCE

There are virtually as many methods of relating pay to performance as there are organizations, and at times it seems that every organization is in the process of changing its approach. The R.I.A. (1965) study found, for example, that one out of every three companies has "recently" changed its method of paying salesmen. Campbell, Dunnette, Lawler, and Weick (1970) report that their survey of company personnel practices showed widespread dissatisfaction with current pay systems. Such dissatisfaction is hardly surprising in light of the previously reported finding that pay is not closely related to performance in many companies. It is doubtful, however, that the problems and the dissatisfaction can be corrected simply by changing the mechanics of the plan already in use. Many plans seem to fail not because they are mechanically defective, but because they were ineffectually introduced, there is a lack of trust between superiors and subordinates, or the quality of supervision is too low. No plan can succeed in the face of low trust and poor supervision, no matter how valid it may be from the point of view of mechanics.

Still, some types of plans clearly are more capable than others of creating the four conditions mentioned at the beginning of the [section]. Some plans certainly do a better job of relating pay to performance than others, and some are better able to minimize the perceived negative consequences of good performance and to maximize the perceived positive consequences. One of the reasons pay often is not actually related to performance is that many organizations simply do not have pay plans that are correctly set up in order to accomplish this. Often this comes about because the particular conditions in the organization itself may not have been taken into account when the plan was developed. No plan is applicable to all situations. In a sense, one may say that a pay plan should be custom-tailored. Companies often try to follow the latest fads and fashion in salary administration, not recognizing that some plans simply do not fit their situation (Dunnette & Bass, 1963). Let us stress again, however, that mechanical faults are by no means the only reason that pay plans fail to relate pay to performance. Many of those which fail are not only well designed mechanically but also appropriate to the situation where they are used.

In looking at the mechanics of various types of pay programs, we shall group them together according to the way they differ on three dimensions. First, pay plans distribute rewards on different bases: individual, group, or organizationwide. Second, they measure performance differently: The measures typically vary from admittedly subjective (i.e., based on superiors' judgments or ratings) to somewhat objective (i.e., based on costs, sales, or profits). Third, plans differ in what they offer as rewards for successful performance: salary increases, bonuses, piece rates, or—in rare cases—fringe benefits. Table 1 presents a breakdown of the various plans, following this classification system. This classification yields some eighteen different types of incentive plans. A more detailed classification system would, of course, yield more. The table shows where the better-known plans fit in. It also shows a number of plans that are seldom used, and thus do not have a commonly known name. For example, companies do not typically base salary increases to individuals on the cost effectiveness of their work group. This does not mean that such a plan is a bad approach to distributing pay; it just means that it is not used very often.

EVALUATING THE DIFFERENT APPROACHES TO MERIT-BASED PAY

It is possible to make some general statements about the success of the different merit pay plans. We shall evaluate the plans in terms of how capable they have proved to be in establishing three of the conditions that are necessary if pay

Table 1 A Classification of Pay-Incentive Plans

| | Performance measure | Reward offered | |
		Salary increase	Cash bonus
Individual plans	Productivity Cost effectiveness Superiors' rating	Merit rating plan	Sales commission Piece rate
Group plans	Productivity Cost effectiveness Superiors' rating		Group incentive
Organizationwide plans	Productivity Cost effectiveness Profit	Productivity Bargaining	Kaiser, Scanlon Profit sharing (e.g., American Motors)

is to motivate performance. Such an evaluation must, of course, reflect actual experience with the different approaches in a number of situations. Here we are ignoring for the moment the effect of situational factors on the effectiveness of the plans in order to develop general ratings of the plans.

Table 2 lists the different types of incentive plans and provides a general effectiveness rating for each plan on three separate criteria. First, each plan is evaluated in terms of how effective it is in creating the perception that pay is tied to performance. In general, this indicates the degree to which the approach actually ties pay closely to performance, chronologically speaking, and the degree to which employees believe that higher pay will follow good performance. Second, each plan is evaluated in terms of how well it minimizes the perceived negative consequences of good performance. This criterion refers to the extent to which the approach eliminates situations where social ostracism and other negative consequences become associated with good performance. Third, each plan is evaluated in terms of whether it contributes to the perception that important rewards other than pay (e.g., recognition and acceptance) stem from good performance. The ratings range from $+3$ to -3, with $+3$ indicating that the plan has generally worked very well in terms of the criterion, while -3 indicates that the plan has not worked well. A 0 rating indicates that the plan has generally been neutral or average.

A number of trends appear in the ratings presented in Table 2. Looking just at the criterion of tying pay to performance, we see that individual plans

Table 2   Ratings of Various Pay-Incentive Plans

	Type of plan	Performance measure	Tie pay to performance	Minimize negative side effects	Tie other rewards to performance
Salary reward	Individual plan	Productivity	+2	0	0
		Cost effectiveness	+1	0	0
		Superiors' rating	+1	0	+1
	Group	Productivity	+1	0	+1
		Cost effectiveness	+1	0	+1
		Superiors' rating	+1	0	+1
	Organizationwide	Productivity	+1	0	+1
		Cost effectiveness	+1	0	+1
		Profits	0	0	+1
Bonus	Individual plan	Productivity	+3	−2	0
		Cost effectiveness	+2	−1	0
		Superiors' rating	+2	−1	+1
	Group	Productivity	+2	0	+1
		Cost effectiveness	+2	0	+1
		Superiors' rating	+2	0	+1
	Organizationwide	Productivity	+2	0	+1
		Cost effectiveness	+2	0	+1
		Profit	+1	0	+1

tend to be rated highest, while group plans are rated next, and organizationwide plans are rated lowest. This reflects the fact that in group plans to some extent and in organizationwide plans to a great extent, an individual's pay is not directly a function of his *own* behavior. The pay of an individual in these situations is influenced by the behavior of others with whom he works and also, if the payment is based on profits, by external market conditions.

Bonus plans are generally rated higher than pay raise and salary increase plans. Under bonus plans, a person's pay may vary sharply from year to year in accordance with his most recent performance. This does not usually happen with salary increase programs, since organizations seldom cut anyone's salary; as a result, pay under the salary increase plan reflects not recent performance but performance over a number of years. Consequently, pay is not seen to be closely related to present behavior. Bonuses, on the other hand, typically depend on recent behavior, so that if someone performs poorly, it will show up immediately in his pay. Thus, a person under the bonus plan cannot coast for a year and still be highly paid, as he can be under the typical salary merit pay program.

Finally, note that approaches which use objective measures of performance are rated higher than those which use subjective measures. In general, objective measures enjoy higher credibility; that is, employees will often grant the validity of an objective measure, such as sales or units produced, when they will not accept a superior's rating. Thus, when pay is tied to objective measures, it is usually clear to employees that pay is determined by their performance. Objective measures such as sales volume and units produced are also often publicly measurable, and when pay is tied to them, the relationship is often much more visible than when it is tied to a subjective, nonverifiable measure, such as a superior's rating. Overall, then, the suggestion is that individually based bonus plans which rely on objective measures produce the strongest perceived connection between pay and performance.

The ratings with respect to the ability of pay programs to minimize the perceived negative consequences of good performance reveal that most plans are regarded as neutral. That is, they neither contribute to the appearance of negative consequences nor help to eliminate any which might be present. The individual bonus plans receive a negative rating on this criterion, however. This negative rating reflects the fact that piece rate plans often lead to situations in which social rejection, firing, and running out of work are perceived by individuals to result from good performance. Under a piece rate system, the perceived negative consequences of good performance may cancel out the positive motivational force that piece rate plans typically generate by tying pay closely to performance.

With respect to the final criterion for pay plans, tying nonpay rewards to performance, the ratings are generally higher for group and organizationwide plans than for individual plans. Under group and organizationwide plans, it is generally to the advantage of everyone for an individual to work effectively. Thus, good performance is much more likely to be seen to result in esteem, respect, and social acceptance, than it is under individual plans. In short, if a person feels he can benefit from another's good performance, he is much more likely to encourage his fellow worker to perform well than if he will not benefit, and might even be harmed.

It should be clear from this short review that not one pay plan presents a panacea for a company's job motivation problems. Unfortunately, no one type of pay program is strong in all areas. Thus, no organization probably ever will be satisfied with its approach, since it will have problems associated with it. It is therefore not surprising to find that companies are usually dissatisfied with their pay programs and are constantly considering changing them. Still, the situation is not completely hopeless. Clearly, some approaches are generally better than others. We know, for example, that many of the approaches not mentioned in the table, such as stock option plans, across-the-board raises, and seniority increases, have no real effect on the performance motivation of most employees. In addition, the evidence indicates that bonus-type plans are generally superior to wage increase plans and that individually based plans are generally superior to group and organizationwide plans. This suggests that one widely applicable model for an incentive plan might take the following form.

Each person's pay would be divided into three components. One part would be for the job the employee is doing, and everyone who holds a similar job would get the same amount. A second part of the pay package would be determined by seniority and cost-of-living factors; everyone in the company would get this, and the amount would be automatically adjusted each year. The third part of the package, however, would not be automatic; it would be individualized so that the amount paid would be based upon each person's performance during the immediately preceding period. The poor performer in the organization should find that this part of his or her pay package is minimal, while the good performer should find that this part of his or her pay is at least as great as the other two parts combined. This would not be a raise, however, since it could vary from year to year, depending on the individual's performance during the last performance period. Salary increases or raises would come only with changes in responsibility, cost of living, or seniority. The merit portion of the pay package would be highly variable, so that if a person's performance fell off, his or her pay would also be decreased by a cut in the size of the merit pay. The purpose of this kind of system is, of course, to make a large proportion of an individual's pay depend upon performance during the current period. Thus, performance is chronologically closely tied to large changes in pay.

The really difficult problem in any merit pay system, including this one, is how to measure performance. A valid measure of performance must meet several requirements. Not only must it be valid from the point of view of top management, but it must lead to promotion and pay decisions that are accepted by people throughout the organization: Supervisors, subordinates, and peers must all accept the results of the system. Without this wide acceptance, pay raises will not be seen to reflect merit. Employees gain much of their knowledge about how pay systems operate by watching what happens to other people in the organization. If people whom they feel are doing good work get raises, then they accept the fact that a merit pay system exists. On the other hand, if workers they do not respect get raises, their belief in the system breaks down. Obviously the more the appraisal system yields decisions that are congruent with employee consensus about performance, the more the employees will believe that a merit system exists. The performance measure should also be such that employees feel that their contributions to the organization show up in it very directly. They must feel that they have control over it, rather than feeling that it reflects so many other things that what they do has little weight. . . . Finally, the performance measure or measures should be influenced by all the behaviors that are important for the job holder to perform. People perform those behaviors that are measured, and thus it is important that the measure be sufficiently inclusive.

The performance appraisal systems that are actually used by organizations range all the way from superiors' subjective judgments to the complicated "objective" accounting-based systems that are used to measure managers' effectiveness. The problems with the simple, subjective, superiors' judgments are obvious—the subordinates often see them as arbitrary, based upon inadequate information, and simply unfair. The more objective systems are appealing in many ways. Where they can be installed, they are the best, but even they often fail to reflect individual efforts. Stock option plans are a good example. With these plans, pay is tied to the price of the stock on the market, and this presumably motivates managers to work so that the price of the stock will go up. The problem with this approach is that for most managers the connection between their effort and the price of the stock is very weak.

Plans that base bonuses or pay increases on profit centers or on the effectiveness of certain parts of the business may work, but all too often much of the profitability of one part of the organization is controlled more by outside than by inside forces. Another problem with this kind of system is illustrated by the fate of most piece rate incentive plans used at the worker level. They give the false illusion that objective, highly measureable rates can be "scientifically" set and that trust between superiors and subordinates is not necessary, since the system is objective. Experience has shown that effective piece rate systems simply cannot be established where foremen and workers do not trust each other and have a participative relationship. No completely "objective" system has ever been designed, nor will one ever be. Unexpected contingencies will always come up and have to be worked out between superiors and subordinates. Such events can be successfully resolved only when trust based upon mutual influence exists. Where poor relationships exist, workers strive to get rates set low and then they restrict their production, because they do not believe that good performance will in fact lead to higher pay in the long run.

Thus the answer in many organizations must rest in a reasonable combination of the simple, superior-based rating system and a system which uses more objective measures. First, we must accept the fact that no system can ever be 100 percent objective and that subjective judgments will always be important. Second, we must realize that the key to general acceptance of the decisions that the appraisal system yields lies in having as broad as possible participation in the system.

What would such a system look like? It would be based upon superior-subordinate appraisal sessions where subordinates feel that they have a real opportunity to influence their boss. Obviously, such a system cannot operate, nor can any other for that matter, unless superior-subordinate relations are such that mutual influence is possible. In the first appraisal session the superior and subordinate would jointly decide on three things. First, they would decide on the objectives the subordinate should try to achieve during the ensuing time period. This period might last from three months to several years, depending on the level of the job. Second, they would decide on how the subordinate's progress toward these objectives will be measured. Objective measures might be used as well as subjective ratings by peers and others. Third, they would decide what level of reward the subordinate should receive if he accomplishes his objectives. A second meeting would be held at the end of the specified time period in order for the superior and subordinate to jointly assess the progress of the subordinate and decide upon any pay actions. Finally, a few weeks later the whole process would begin again with another objectives-setting session. The advantages of this kind of system extend far beyond pay administration. It can create a situation where superiors and subordinates jointly become much more certain of what the subordinate's actual job duties and responsibilities are. Some recent studies suggest that there is often greater than 70 percent disagreement between superior and subordinate about what constitutes the subordinate's job, so agreement on this score would not be an insignificant step forward. The fact that the subordinate has a chance to set goals and that he commits himself to a certain level of performance may have an impact on his motivation that is independent of rewards like pay. There is evidence that when people commit themselves to challenging goals, needs like esteem and self-realization can come into play and motivate them to achieve the goals. This system also offers the subordinate a chance to become involved in important decisions about his own future and thereby encourages a kind of give and take that seldom exists between superiors and subordinates.

Despite the fact that it is possible to state some general conclusions about the effectiveness of different pay plans, perhaps the most important conclusion arising from the discussion so far is that it is vital to fit the pay plan to the organization. What might be a wonderful plan for one organization may for a whole series of reasons be a bad plan for another. Thus, although it is tempting to say that X approach is always best, it is wiser to turn now to a consideration of the factors that determine which kind of plan is likely to be best in a given situation.

FACTORS INFLUENCING THE EFFECTIVENESS OF DIFFERENT PAY PLANS

In selecting a plan for a particular organization, what situational factors must be considered? . . . One factor that must be considered when an organization is deciding what type of pay plan to use is the degree of cooperation that is needed among the individuals who are under the plan. When the jobs involved are basically independent from one another, it is perfectly reasonable to use an individual-based plan. Independent jobs are quite common: examples are outside sales jobs and certain kinds of production jobs. In these jobs, employees contribute relatively independently to the effectiveness of the total group or organization, and thus it is appropriate to place them on an incentive scheme that motivates them to perform at their maximum and to pay little attention to cooperative activities.

As organizations become more complex, however, more and more jobs demand that work be done either successively (i.e., work passes from one person to another) or coordinately (i.e., work is a function of the joint effort of all employees) (Ghiselli & Brown, 1955). With successive jobs and especially with coordinate jobs, it is doubtful that individual incentive plans are appropriate. For one thing, on these jobs it is often difficult to measure the contribution of a given individual, and therefore difficult to reward individuals differentially. The organization is almost forced to reward on the basis of group performance. Another problem with individual plans is that they typically do not reward cooperation, since it is difficult to measure and to visibly relate to pay. Cooperation is essential on successive and coordinate jobs, and it is vital that the pay plan reward it. Thus, the strong suggestion is that group and organizationwide plans may be best in situations where jobs are coordinate or successive.

A related issue has to do with the degree to which appropriate inclusive subgoals or criteria can be created for individuals. An example was cited earlier of an individual pay plan that motivated salesmen to sell but did not motivate them to carry out other necessary job activities such as stocking shelves. The problem was that pay was tied to the most obvious and most measurable goal in the job, and some of the less measurable activities were overlooked and unrewarded. This situation occurs frequently; for many jobs, it is quite difficult to establish criteria that are both measurable quantitatively and inclusive of all the important job behaviors. The solution to the problem with the salesmen was to establish a group incentive plan. Indeed, inclusive criteria may often be possible at the group and organizational level but not at the individual level. It is quite easy to think of jobs for which a criterion like productivity might not be inclusive enough when individuals are looked at, but might be inclusive enough when a number of jobs or employees are grouped together. The point, of course, is that in choosing an incentive plan, an organization must consider whether the performance measures that are related to pay include all the important job activities. One thing is certain: If an employee is not evaluated in terms of an activity, he will not be motivated to perform it.

The point has often been made that, wherever possible, objective performance measures should be used. There are, however, many situations where objective measures do not exist for individual or even group performance. One way of dealing with such situations is to measure performance on the basis of larger and larger groups until some objective measures can be found. Another approach is to measure performance on the individual or small group level and to use admittedly subjective measures. This is possible in some situations but not in others. The key factor in determining whether this approach is feasible is the degree of superior-subordinate trust. The more subjective the measure, the higher the degree of trust needed, because without high trust there is little chance that the subordinate will believe that his pay is really fairly based upon performance. Figure 1 illustrates the relationship between trust and the objectivity of the performance criteria. Note that it indicates that, even with the most objective system, some trust is still required if the individual is going to believe in the system. It also shows that unless a high degree of trust exists, pay plans based on subjective criteria have little chance of success.

One further issue must be considered when an organization is installing a pay plan: will the individuals under the plan actually be able to control the criteria on which they will be evaluated? All too often the criteria are unrelated to the individual worker's efforts. A good example of this is the American Motors Corporation profit-sharing plan: The individual worker is not in a position to influence the profits of the company, yet this is a criterion upon which part of his pay is based. If a pay system is going to motivate employees, the criteria must be such that the employees can directly influence them. The criteria must, in short, be within the employees' control. This point, of course, argues for the use of individual criteria where possible, since they best reflect an individual's efforts.

Pay systems may also be results or process-oriented; that is, they may reward employees chiefly for results (e.g., actual production) or for the way the task or job is carried out. There are usually problems with any system that rewards process only, just as there are problems with systems that reward results only. Perhaps the ultimate example of what can happen in the process-oriented system can be seen in the large bureaucracies that grow up in many civil service and other large organizations. In these bureaucracies people seem motivated to follow the rules, and not to accomplish the objectives for which the organization was established. On the other hand, a salesman may be motivated only by a short-term desire to maximize results. His behavior may lead to a sale, but it may be such that his organization never makes another sale to that buyer. A pay system must be designed to reward both process and results. This may be difficult in many situations; process is particularly difficult to measure objectively, and thus subjective measures may have to be used. As

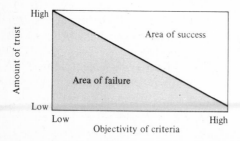

Figure 1 Relationship of trust and the objectivity of performance criteria to success of the program.

has already been pointed out, subjective measures can only be used effectively where a high degree of trust exists.

SHOULD PAY BE USED TO MOTIVATE?

Although we have not said so explicitly, it is clear that there are many situations in which pay should not be used to motivate job performance. In many jobs, it is impossible to develop adequate criteria for relating pay to performance. There may be no objective measures of performance, so that very subjective measures are needed but cannot be used because of the low level of trust between superiors and subordinates. On the other hand, the problem may be that objective measures are available but the level of trust is not even sufficient to allow their use. As was illustrated in Figure 1, there are situations where it simply may not be wise to measure performance for the purpose of relating it to pay. As has already been pointed out, it may be possible to measure some but not all of the relevant aspects of performance. A number of new problems can be created if pay is tied only to those aspects of performance that are measurable: The measurable aspects may receive all the employee's attention, while the others are neglected. In this situation it may well be better not to try to use pay to motivate performance.

Often, profit-sharing plans are used where individual performance measures are not appropriate, and the organization desires to use pay to motivate performance. There is some doubt whether this is worthwhile in large organizations. The larger the organization, the less likely it is that a companywide profit-sharing or cost effectiveness plan will work. The reason for this is simple: The larger the organization, the less influence any one individual has over companywide results, and the less an individual feels that his pay is related to performance. Thus, where individual-based pay plans are not possible, it is not always advisable to use an organizationwide plan. It may in fact be better to have no incentive pay plan at all. Often when organizationwide plans are installed in large organizations, they produce no extra motivation but do produce quite a few extra costs for the company: thus, the suggestion that the cost effectiveness of each plan should be considered.

Finally, motivating people with financial rewards is not a piker's game. Large amounts of money must be given to the good performers if employees are to place a high value on good performance and the raises to which it leads. A company must be willing and able to give certain employees very large raises and/or bonuses if pay is to motivate performance. If a company cannot afford to do this or is not willing to, it should probably forget about using pay to motivate performance. Even if they are willing to spend large amounts of money it may be that pay is not important to the employees and because of this not a possible source of motivation. In this case some other reward may be more appropriate. For example, in one factory that employed large numbers of unmarried women, time off the job was more important than money so when the women were told they could go home after a certain amount of work was done productivity increased dramatically. Several earlier attempts to use pay to motivate high productivity had failed.

In summary, serious thought should be given to *not* using pay as an incentive in organizations where:

1 The trust level is low.
2 Individual performance is difficult to measure.
3 Performance must be measured subjectively.
4 Inclusive measures of performance cannot be developed.
5 Large pay rewards cannot be given to the best performers.

PAY SECRECY

Secrecy about pay rates seems to be an accepted practice in organizations, regardless of whether they use individual or group plans, bonus or salary increases, objective or subjective performance measures. Secrecy seems to be particularly prevalent with respect to management pay (Lawler, in press). Some research suggests that one of the effects of secrecy may be to reduce the ability of pay to motivate (Lawler, 1965; Lawler, 1967b). . . . The argument that has been presented against secrecy is that it makes accurate social comparisons impossible (Festinger, 1954). Secrecy thus makes it difficult to conclusively and visibly establish that pay is tied to performance. Further, it is argued that because social comparisons are difficult, employees often get incorrect feedback about their own performance.

One of the findings that has consistently appeared in the research on pay secrecy is that managers tend to have incorrect information about the pay of other managers in the organization. Specifically, there is a general tendency for them to overestimate the pay of managers around them. For example, in one organization the average raise given was 6 percent, yet the managers believed that it was 8 percent, and the larger their raise was, the larger they believed other people's raises were (Lawler, in press). This had the effect of wiping out much of the motivational force of the differential reward system that was actually operating in the company. Almost regardless of how well the individual manager was performing, he felt that he was getting less than the average raise. This problem was particularly severe among the high performers, since they believed that they were doing well yet receiving a minimal reward. They did not believe that pay was in fact based upon merit. This was ironical, since their pay did reflect their performance. What actually existed did not matter as far as the motivation of the managers was concerned; they responded to what they thought existed. Thus, even though pay was tied to performance, these managers were not motivated because they could not see the connection.

There is another way in which pay secrecy may affect motivation. Several studies have shown that accurate feedback about quality of work is a strong stimulus to good performance (Vroom, 1964). People work better when they know how well they are doing in relation to some meaningful standard. For a manager, pay is one of the most meaningful pieces of feedback information. High pay means good performance. Low pay is a signal that he is not doing well and had better improve. The research shows that when managers do not really know what other managers earn, they cannot correctly evaluate their own pay and the feedback implications of it for their own performance. Since they tend to overestimate the pay of subordinates and peers and since they overestimate the raises others get, the majority of them consider their pay low; in effect, they receive negative feedback. Moreover, although this feedback suggests that they should change their work behavior, it does not tell them what type of change to make. When managers are not doing their jobs well, negative feedback is undoubtedly what they need. But it is doubtful that it is what managers who are working effectively need.

Note that one recommendation that appears in the discussion of factors affecting the importance of pay as well as in the discussion of factors affecting the belief that pay depends upon performance is that pay information should be more public. Unless this condition exists, pay is not likely to motivate performance, because it will be seen neither as an important satisfier of higher-order needs nor as something that is obtainable from good performance. Making pay information public will not itself establish the belief that pay is based upon merit or ensure that people will get accurate performance feedback. All it can do is clarify those situations where pay actually *is* based upon merit but where it is not obvious because relative salaries are not accurately known. This point is apparent in some unpublished data collected by the author. An organization was studied that had a merit-based plan and pay secrecy. At the beginning of the study, the data collected showed that the employees saw only a moderate relationship between pay and performance. Data collected after the company became more open about pay showed a significant increase in the employees' perceptions of the degree to which pay and performance were related. The crucial factor in making this change to openness successful was that pay was actually tied to performance. Making pay rates public where pay is not tied to performance will only serve to emphasize more dramatically that it is not, thereby further reducing the power of pay to motivate.

REFERENCES

Brenner, M. H., & Lockwood, H. C. Salary as a predictor of salary: A 20-year study. *Journal of Applied Psychology*, 1965, **49**, 295–298.

Campbell, J. P., Dunnette, M. D., Lawler, E. E., & Weick, K. E. *Managerial behavior, performance, and effectiveness*. New York: McGraw-Hill, 1970.

Dunnette, M. D., & Bass, B. M. Behavioral scientists and personnel management. *Industrial Relations*, 1963, **2**, 115–130.

Festinger, L. A theory of social comparison processes. *Human Relations*, 1954, **7**, 117–140.

Ghiselli, E. E., & Brown, C. W. *Personnel and industrial psychology*. New York: McGraw-Hill, 1955.

Haire, M., Ghiselli, E. E., & Gordon, M. E. A psychological study of pay. *Journal of Applied Psychology Monograph*, 1967, **51**(4), (Whole No. 636).

Lawler, E. E. *Managers' job performance and their attitudes toward their pay*. Unpublished doctoral dissertation, University of California, Berkeley, 1964.

Lawler, E. E. Managers' perceptions of their subordinates' pay and of their superiors' pay. *Personnel Psychology*, 1965, **18**, 413–422.

Lawler, E. E. The multitrait-multirater approach to measuring managerial job performance. *Journal of Applied Psychology*, 1967, **51**, 369–381. (a)

Lawler, E. E. Secrecy about management compensation: Are there hidden costs? *Organizational Behavior and Human Performance*, 1967, **2**, 182–189. (b)

Lawler, E. E. Secrecy and the need to know. In R. House, M. Dunnette, and H. Tosi (Eds.), *Readings in managerial motivation and compensation*, in press.

Lawler, E. E., & Porter, L. W. Predicting managers' pay and their satisfaction with their pay. *Personnel Psychology*, 1966, **19**, 363–373.

Meyer, H. H., Kay, E., & French, J. R. P. Split roles in performance appraisal. *Harvard Business Review*, 1965, **43**(1), 123–129.

R.I.A. *Sales compensation practices, an RIA survey*. New York: Research Institute of America, File No. 32, 1965.

Svetlik, B., Prien, E., & Barrett, G. Relationships between job difficulty, employee's attitudes toward his job, and supervisory ratings of the employee effectiveness. *Journal of Applied Psychology*, 1964, **48**, 320–324.

Vroom, V. H. *Work and motivation*. New York: Wiley, 1964.

How to Ruin Motivation with Pay

W. Clay Hamner

MERIT PAY—SHOULD IT BE USED?

Most behavioral scientists believe in the "law of effect," which states simply that behavior which appears to lead to a positive consequence tends to be repeated. This principle is also followed by most large organizations which have a merit pay system for their management team. Merit pay or "pay for performance" is so widely accepted by compensation managers and academic researchers that criticizing it seems foolhardy.

Despite the soundness of the principle of the law of effect on which merit pay is based, academic researchers have criticized the merit system as being detrimental to motivation rather than enhancing motivation as designed. These criticisms generally fall into one of two categories. The first group of reseachers criticize the failure of the merit plan to increase the motivation of the work force because of mismanagement or lack of understanding of the merit program by managers. The second group of researchers criticize the use of merit pay because it utilizes externally mediated rewards rather than focusing on a system where individuals can be motivated by the job itself. This second criticism centers on the proposition that employees who enjoy their job (i.e., are intrinsically motivated) will lose interest in the job when a merit pay plan is introduced because they soon believe they are doing the job for the money and not because they enjoy their job. Therefore, for the first group of researchers, the recommendation is that compensation managers need to examine ways to improve the introduction of merit plans, while the second group of researchers, albeit fewer in number, would recommend that compensation managers need to de-emphasize the merit pay plan system and concentrate on improving other aspects of the job.

The purpose of this presentation will be to examine the research behind both of these positions and then present recommendations which, it is hoped, will enable the compensation manager to utilize a "pay performance" plan as a method of improving the quality and quantity of job performance. Let's begin the discussion by examining possible reasons why merit pay systems fail.

REASONS WHY MERIT PAY SYSTEMS FAIL

As noted earlier, one group of researchers has concluded that the failure of merit pay plans is due not to a weakness in the law of effect, but to a weakness in its implementation by compensation managers and the line managers involved in the merit increase recommendations. For example, after reviewing pay research from General Electric and other companies, H. H. Meyer (1975) concluded that despite the apparent soundness of the simple principle on which merit pay is based, experience tells us that it does not work with such elegant simplicity. Instead, managers typically seemed to be inclined to make relatively small discriminations in salary treatment among individuals in the same job regardless of perceived differences in performance. As a matter of fact, Meyer notes, when discriminations are made, they are likely to be based on factors other than performance—such as length of service, future potential, or perceived need for "catch up," where one employee's pay seems low in relation to others in the group.

Michael Beer (see Beer & Gery, 1972), Director of Organizational Development at Corning Glass, explains why the implementation of the merit system has lost its effectiveness when he states that pay systems evolve over time and administrative considerations and tradition often override the more important considerations of behavioral outcomes in determining the shape of the system and its administration. Therefore, both of these researchers seem to say that it is not the merit pay theory that is defective. Rather, the history of the actual implementation of the theory is at fault. Let us look at the shortcomings—noted in the literature—that may cause low motivation to result from a merit pay program.

Pay Is Not Perceived as Being Related to Job Performance

Edward E. Lawler III, a leading researcher on pay and performance, has noted that one of the major reasons managers are unhappy with their wage system is that they do not perceive the relationship between how hard they work (productivity) and how much they earn. Lawler (1966), in a survey of 600 middle and lower level managers, found virtually no relationship between their pay and their rated performance. Of the managers studied, those who were most highly motivated to perform their jobs effectively were characterized by two attitudes: (1) they said that their pay was important to them and (2) they felt that good job performance would lead to higher pay for them.

There are several reasons why managers do not perceive their pay as being related to performance even when the company claims to have a merit pay plan. First, many rewards (e.g., stock options) are *deferred payments*, and the time horizon is so long that the employee loses sight of its relationship to performance. Second, the *goals* of the organization on which performance appraisals are based are either unclear, unrealistic, or unrelated to pay. W. H. Mobley (1974) found only 36 percent of the managers surveyed from a company using an MBO program saw goal attainment as having considerable bearing on their merit increase, while 83 percent of their bosses claim that they used the goal attainments to determine their pay increase recommendations. Third, the *secrecy* of the annual merit increases may lead managers to conclude that their recommended pay increase has no bearing on their past year's performance. R. L. Opsahl and M. D. Dunnette (1966) claimed that secrecy is due in part to a fear by salary administrators that they would have a difficult time mustering convincing arguments in favor of many of their practices. E. E. Lawler (1971) summarized his extensive research on secrecy of pay by stating that managers did not have an accurate picture of what other managers were earning. There was a general tendency for the managers to overstate the pay of managers at their own level (thereby reducing their own pay, relatively speaking) and at one level below them (again reducing their own pay, relatively speaking), while they tended to underestimate the pay of managers one level above them (thus reducing the value of future promotions).

Performance Ratings Are Seen as Biased

While many managers working under a merit program believe that the program is a good one, they are dissatisfied with the evaluation of their performance given them by their immediate superior. A merit plan is based on the assumption that managers can make objective (valid) distinctions between good and poor performance. Unfortunately, most evaluations of performance are subjective in nature, and consist of a "summary score" from a general (and sometimes dated) performance evaluation form. As H. H. Meyer (1975) notes, the supervisor's key role in determining pay creates a problem in that it reminds the employee very clearly that he or she is dependent on the supervisor for rewards. Therefore, the merit plan should, whenever possible, be based on objective measures (e.g., group sales, cost reduction per unit, goal obtainment, etc.) rather than subjective measures (e.g., cooperation, attitude, future potential, etc.).

As an aside, it should be noted that in the area of fair employment of minorities, both the courts (e.g., see *Rowe v. General Motors Corporation*, 1972) and the new EEOC (1974) guidelines recognize the potential of bias in subjective performance appraisals, and organizations must begin examining the validity of their performance ratings to see if they are, in fact, job related. My recent research has shown that, even when objective measures of job performance are clearly spelled out, supervisors have a tendency to rate blacks differently than whites and females differently than males even though their performance levels are identical (e.g., see Scott & Hamner, 1975; Hamner, Kim, Baird, & Bigoness, 1974). E. E. Lawler III feels that the complaints of managers and employees about the subjective nature of their performance evaluations may be a sign of a system of poor leadership. Lawler (1971) notes that many plans seem to fail not because they are mechanically defective, but because they are ineffectively introduced, there is a lack of trust between superiors and subordinates, or the quality of the supervisor is too low. He adds that no plan can succeed in the face of low trust and poor supervision, no matter how well-constructed it may be. L. W. Gruenfeld and P. Weissenberg (1966) reported support for this theory of poor leadership espoused by Lawler when they found that good managers are much more amenable than poor managers to the idea of basing pay on performance.

Rewards Are Not Viewed as Rewards

A third problem in administering a merit increase deals with management's inability to communicate accurately to the employee the information that they are trying to communicate through the pay raise. There is no doubt that the pay raise is more than money; it tells the employee "You're loved a lot," "You're only average," "You're not appreciated around here," "You'd better get busy," etc. Often management believes it is communicating a positive message to the employee, but the message being received by the employee is negative. This may have a detrimental effect on his or her future potential. Opsahl and Dunnette (1966) warn us that the relation between performing certain desired behaviors and attainment of the pay-incentive must be explicitly specified.

The reasons that the reward message may not be seen as a reward include the following: (1) Conflicting reward schedules may be operating. (2) A problem of inequity among employees is perceived to exist. (3) The merit increase is threatening to the self-esteem of the employee. All three of these problems center on the fact that the pay increases are generally kept secret—thus causing the employees to draw erroneous conclusions—or on the fact that there is little or no communication in the form of coaching and counselling coming from the supervisor during the year, or following the performance appraisal. Instead, the employee is "expected to know" what the supervisor thinks about his or her performance. As Beer and Gery (1972) stated, the more frequent the formal and informal reviews of performance and the more the individual is told about reasons for an increase, the greater his preference for a merit increase and the lower his preference for a seniority system.

Conflicting Reward Schedules Such schedules come about because of a defect in the merit plan itself. For example, individual rewards (e.g., the best manager will get a free trip to Hawaii) are set up in such a way that cooperation with other managers is discouraged, or perhaps a cost-reduction program is introduced at the expense of production, and one department (sales) suffers while another department (manufacturing) benefits in the short run. As Kenneth F. Foster, Manager of Composition at Xerox, has noted (see *Harvard Business Review*, July-August 1974), pay plans must be constantly changing because of general business conditions, shifts in management philosophy, competitive pressures, participant feedback, and modification in the structure and objectives of the organization. Nevertheless, these changes should be designed in such a way that the negative side effect of reduced cooperation does not result. For this reason, many companies are using a company-wide merit plan (e.g., the Scanlon Plan; see Frost, Wakeley, & Ruh, 1974) where there is a financial incentive to everyone in the organization based on the performance of the total organization.

Inequity Inequity in pay can come about for one of two reasons. First, the employee perceives the merit increase to be unfair relative to his own past year's performance. That is, he is dissatisfied with the performance evaluation, or else feels the performance evaluation is fair, but believes his supervisor failed to reward him in a manner consistent with his rating. A much more common problem is that while the employee may agree with the dollar amount of his pay, he perceives that others who are performing at levels below him are receiving as large an increase as he, or else those who are performing at his same level are receiving higher raises. For example, an employee who was rated as above average receives an 8 percent pay increase. He perceives this to be low since he believes that the average increase was 9 percent, when in fact it was 6½ percent. In order to avoid the feeling of inequity, which will contribute to dissatisfaction with pay and possible lower job performance, Lawler (1973) recommends that managers tell their employees how the salary raises were derived (e.g., 50 percent based on cost of living and 50 percent on merit) and tell them the range and mean of raises given in the organization for people at their job level. Lawler (1965) advocated the abandonment of secrecy policies: "There is no reason why organizations cannot make salaries public information."

Threat to Self-Esteem H. H. Meyer, in an excellent paper, argues that the problem with merit pay plans may be more than a problem of equity. Drawing on his previous research (Meyer, Kay, & French, 1965), he concluded that 90 percent of the managers at General Electric rated themselves as above average. Bassett and Meyer (1968) and Beer and Gery (1972) found similar results. Meyer concludes that the inconsistency in the information of the merit raise with the employee's evaluation of his or her performance will be a threat to the manager's *self-esteem*, and the manager may cope with this threat by either denying the importance of hard work or disparaging the source. Meyer (1975) concludes:

The fact that almost everyone thinks he is an above average performer probably causes most of our problems with merit pay plans. Since the salary increases most people get do not reflect superior performance (as determined by interpersonal comparisons, or as defined in the guide book for the pay plan), the effects of the actual pay increases on motivation are likely to be more negative than positive. The majority of the people feel discriminated against because, obviously, management does not recognize their true worth.

Managers of Merit Increases Are More Concerned with Satisfaction with Pay than Job Performance

Most studies which survey managers' satisfaction with their pay have shown high levels of dissatisfaction. Porter (1961) found that 80 percent of the managers surveyed from companies throughout the United States reported dissatisfaction with their pay. These same findings have been reported in surveys at General Electric (Penner, 1967) and a cross-section of managers from many companies (Lawler, 1965). Beer (Beer & Gery, 1972) points out that too often dissatisfaction with pay is assumed to mean dissatisfaction with amount. However, his research suggests that a change to a merit system with no increase in amount paid out by the company will increase satisfaction if the reasons for the increases are explained.

Opsahl and Dunnette (1966) noted that while there is a great deal of research on satisfaction with pay, there is less solid research in the area of the relationship between pay and job performance than any other field. Because of this failure to deal with the role of pay, Lawler (1966) notes that many managers have come to the erroneous conclusion that the experts in "human relations" have shown that pay is a relatively unimportant incentive.

In fact, Cherrington, Reitz, and Scott (1971) found that the magnitude of the relationship between satisfaction and performance depends primarily upon the performance-reinforcer contingencies that have been arranged (i.e., people who were appropriately reinforced were satisfied with their pay, while those people who were dissatisfied with their pay were those who were inappropriately rewarded). Likewise, Hamner and Foster (1974) found that the best performers working under a contingent (piece rate) pay plan were more satisfied than the poorer performers, but that there was no relationship between satisfaction and performance for those paid under a noncontingent (across the board) pay plan.

Managers need to be concerned with two questions. First, *is the merit raise being based on performance?* Numerous studies (e.g., see Lee, 1969; Belcher, 1974) show that pay is not closely related to performance in many organizations that claim to have merit raises. Typically, these studies show that pay is much more closely related to job level and seniority than performance. In fact, Belcher (1974) reports that low, zero, and even negative correlations between pay and supervisory ratings of performance occur even among managers where the correlation would be expected to be high.

Second, *who is doing the complaining?* Donald Finn, Compensation Manager at J. C. Penney, says we are often "hung up" as managers about the satisfaction of employees with our pay recommendations. He says:

> So who is complaining and why? If low producers are low earners, the pay plan is working—but there will be complaints. If a company wants an incentive plan in which rewards are commensurate with risk, it must be willing to accept a relatively broad range of earnings and corresponding degrees of manager satisfaction. (*Harvard Business Review*, July-August, 1974, pg. 8)

Beer agrees with Finn when he says:

> A merit system can probably be utilized effectively by management in motivating employees. This concept has been in disfavor lately, but our findings indicate that more might be done with money in motivating people, particularly those who are work and achievement oriented in the first place.
>   While a merit system would seem to be less need satisfying to the security-oriented individual and, therefore, potentially less motivating, there is probably a net gain in installing a merit system. Those who are high in achievement oriented needs will be stimulated by such a system to greater heights of performance, while those high in security-oriented needs will become more dissatisfied and it is hoped, will leave. (Beer & Gery, 1972, p. 330)

Trust and Openness about Merit Increases Is Low

A merit system will not be accepted and may not have the intended motivational effects if managers do not actively administer a performance appraisal system, practice good human relations, explain the reasons for the increases and ensure that employees are not forgotten when eligibility dates come and go. The organization must provide an open climate with respect to pay, and an environment where work and effort are valued (Beer & Gery, 1972).

The Xerox Corporation has recognized the problem of trust and openness and states a philosophy that "If pay and satisfaction is to be high, pay rates must vary according to job demands in such a way that each perceived increment in a job demand factor will lead to increased pay" (*Xerox Compensation Planning Model,* June 1972). This same document at Xerox notes that organizations expect extremely high levels of trust on the part of their employees, in that:

(a) Only 72% of 184 employing organizations had a written statement of the firm's basic compensation policy covering such matters as paying competitive salaries, timing of wage and salary increases, and how raises are determined.

(b) Only 51% of these same organizations communicate their general compensation policies directly to all employees, while 21% communicate the policy only to managers.

(c) Contrarily, 69% of the firms do not provide their employees with wage and salary schedules or progression plans that apply to their own categories, thus indicating a low trust level toward employees.

(d)   Over 50% of the firms do not tell their employees where this information is available.

(e)   In only 48% of the firms do managers have access to salary schedules applying to their own level in the organization, and in only 18% of the companies do managers have knowledge of the salaries of other managers at their own level or higher levels. (*Xerox Compensation Planning Model,* June, 1972, pp. 68–69)

Some Organizations View Money as the Primary Motivator, Ignoring the Importance of the Job Itself

The first five shortcomings deal with the criticism of researchers that the failure of the merit plan is due to poor implementation, and not due to a weakness in the theory of the "law of effect." However, the sixth shortcoming under discussion now centers on the second criticism that employees who have intrinsically interesting jobs will lose interest in the job when a merit pay plan is introduced. An intrinsically motivating job can be defined as one that is interesting and creative enough that certain pleasures or rewards are derived from completing the task itself. Until recently, most theories dealing with worker motivation (e.g., Porter & Lawler, 1968) have assumed that the effects of intrinsic and extrinsic reinforcement (e.g., merit pay) are additive; i.e., a worker will be more motivated to complete a task which combined both kinds of rewards than a task where only one kind of reward is present.

Deci (1971, 1972a, b), among others (Likert, 1967; Vroom & Deci, 1970), criticizes behavioral scientists who advocate a system of employee motivation that utilizes externally mediated rewards, i.e., rewards such as money administered by someone other than the employee. In so doing, according to Deci, management is attempting to control the employee's behavior so he or she will do as told. The limitations of this method of worker motivation, for Deci, is that it only satisfies a person's "lower order" needs (Maslow, 1943) and does not take into account "higher order" needs for self-esteem and self-actualization.

Deci recommends that we should move away from a method of external control, and toward a system where individuals can be motivated by the job itself. He says that this approach will allow managers to focus on higher-order needs where the rewards are mediated by the recipient (intrinsically motivated). To motivate employees intrinsically, tasks should be designed which are interesting, creative, and resourceful, and workers should have some say in decisions which concern them "so they will feel like causal agents in the activities which they engage in" (Deci, 1972b, p. 219).

Deci has introduced evidence which reportedly shows that a person's intrinsic motivation to perform an activity decreases when he or she receives contingent monetary payment for performing an interesting task. Deci concludes from these findings that:

> Interpreting these results in relation to theories of work motivation, it seems clear that the effects of intrinsic motivation and extrinsic motivation are not additive. While extrinsic rewards such as money can certainly motivate behavior, they appear

to be doing so at the expense of intrinsic motivation; as a result, contingent payment systems do not appear to be comparable with participative management systems. (1972b, pp. 224–225)

Deci brings out an important point: Managers should not use pay to offset a boring or negative task. However, like Herzberg before him, his results don't appear to completely support his conclusion about the effect of money as a motivator. Research by both Hamner and Foster (1974) and Calder and Staw (1975) has shown that the effect of intrinsic and extrinsic monetary rewards is additive and that even Deci's results themselves, on close examination, support this more traditional argument. In addition, I am not sure that merit pay plans are incompatible with a participative management system. The noted psychologist B. F. Skinner offers advice to managers on both of these last two arguments.

Skinner recommends that the organization should design feedback and incentive systems in such a way that the dual objective of getting things done and making work enjoyable are met. He says:

> It is important to remember that an incentive system isn't the only factor to take into account. How pleasant work conditions are, how easy or awkward a job is, how good or bad tools are—many things of that sort make an enormous difference in what a worker will do for what he receives. One problem of the production-line worker is that he seldom sees any of the ultimate consequences of his work. He puts on left front wheels day in and day out and he may never see the finished car. . . . (1973, p. 39)

Skinner also suggested that people be involved in the design of the contingencies of reinforcements (in this case, merit pay plans) under which they live. This way the rewards come from the behavior of the worker in the environment, and not the supervisor. Both Kenneth F. Foster at Xerox and Joe W. Rogers, Chairman of the Board of Waffle House, agree. Foster, commenting on the McDonald pay plan said, "McDonald's management is to be commended for recognizing a number of important incentive reward axioms. Foremost, the reward system must be meaningful to the recipient. They must also see it as equitable and its financial outcomes and rewards as within their power to control" (*Harvard Business Review*, July-August 1974, p. 5). Rogers agreed, saying, "In the restaurant industry, a bonus system must be self-monitoring and deal only with the facts. All areas of judgment by a friendly or unfriendly superior should be absent in a bonus system. . . . Let people participate in the design of the new pay. Credibility with the participants is much more critical" (Ibid., p. 6).

Deci's recommendation that jobs be designed so that they are interesting, creative, and resourceful should be wholeheartedly supported by proponents of a merit pay plan. Skinner warns managers that too much dependency on force and a poorly designed monetary reward system may actually reduce performance, while designing the task so that it is automatically reinforcing can have positive effects on performance. He says:

> The behavior of an employee is important to the employer, who gains when the employee works industriously and carefully. How is he to be induced to do so? The standard answer was once physical force; men worked to avoid punishment or death. The by-products were troublesome, however, and economics is perhaps the first field in which an explicit change was made to positive reinforcement. Most men now work, as we say, "for money."
>
> Money is not a natural reinforcer; it must be conditioned as such. Delayed reinforcement, as in a weekly wage, raises a special problem. No one works on Monday morning because he is reinforced by a paycheck on Friday afternoon. The employee who is paid by the week works during the week to avoid losing the standard of living which depends on a weekly system. Rate of work is determined by the supervisor and special aversive contingencies maintain quality. The pattern is therefore still aversive. It has often been pointed out that the attitude of the production-line worker toward his work differs conspicuously from that of the craftsman, who is envied by workers and industrial managers alike. One explanation is that the craftsman is reinforced by more than monetary consequences, but another important difference is that when a craftsman spends a week completing a given set object, each of the parts produced during the week is likely to be automatically reinforcing because of its place in the completed object. (Skinner, 1969, p. 18)

RECOMMENDATIONS FOR OVERCOMING FAILURES IN MERIT PAY SYSTEM

In the discussion of the shortcomings of merit pay plans, my suggestions for overcoming these deficiencies have been implied or suggested. Let us briefly review and outline several of these suggestions as a point of departure for our discussion.

1 *Openness and trust should be stressed by the compensation manager.* As a minimum, employees should know the formula for devising the merit increases and should be told the range and mean of the pay increases for people at their job level. This alone should reduce some of the feeling of low self-esteem and inequity present in many organizations today.

2 *Supervisors should be trained in rating and feedback techniques.* Compensation managers should help personnel design and carry out training programs which emphasize the necessity of having consistency between performance ratings, other forms of feedback, and pay increases. In addition, managers should be trained to emphasize objective rather than subjective areas of job performance. Skinner sees one of the greatest weaknesses in the motivation of workers through reinforcement principles as due to poor training of managers. He says that what must be accomplished, and what he believes is currently lacking, is an effective training program for managers. "In the not

too distant future, a new breed of industrial managers may be able to apply the principles of operant conditioning effectively" (*Organizational Dynamics*, 1973, p. 40).

3 *Components of the annual pay increase should be clearly and openly specified.* Compensation managers need to allocate a certain percentage for a cost-of-living increase (not to cover the total cost of living, however) and a percentage for merit. The percentage for merit should be an average and not a maximum, and the manager should be able to distribute this percentage in any way he or she deems appropriate. In other words, it should not be an either-or situation where the worker either gets the full amount of the merit increase or none at all. Any pay increase due to an adjustment for past inequities and pay increases due to promotions should come out of the payroll increase first, but should not be included in the stated average pay increase. Frequently, if the organization can afford a 10 percent increase in wages and benefits, it might take 2 percent of wages and benefits to use for the adjustments mentioned above, and then allocate an 8 percent average increase to cost of living (e.g., 4 percent) and merit (e.g., 4 percent). Therefore, the range of pay increases would be from 4 percent to 12 percent—not including adjustments—where the average for the department would be 8 percent. Along these same lines, I feel it is important to give the increases in percentages and not dollar amounts since managers have a tendency to "cheat" long-term good performers (i.e., high pay managers) when a dollar amount is used.

4 *Each organization should tailor its pay plan to the needs of the organization and individuals therein—with participation a key factor in the merit pay plan design.* One of the reasons the Scanlon plan has been so successful is that it combines participation with the company's ability to afford a merit increase. Workers understand how they get the increase they do and why it is the amount it is. In addition each company using a Scanlon approach has a unique pay plan designed especially for that organization by the members of the organization.

5 *Don't overlook other rewards.* Compensation managers should work with other staff people in the organization to improve the climate of the organization, the task design, and other forms of feedback to ensure that an employee has as much chance of success as possible.

ETHICAL IMPLICATIONS: EXCHANGE, NOT CONTROL

No discussion of effective uses of merit pay plans would be complete without a discussion of the compensation manager's ethical responsibilities in using pay as a motivator. There is no doubt that poorly designed reward structures can interfere with the development of spontaneity and creativity. Reinforcement systems which are deceptive and manipulative are an insult to everyone's integrity. The employee should be a willing party to any attempt to influence, with both parties benefiting from the relationship.

Nord (1974), referring to a well designed incentive plan, says:

I would add that to the degree that such approaches increase the effectiveness of man's exchanges with his environment, the potential for expanding freedom seems undeniable. To me these outcomes seem highly humanistic, although, for some reason this approach is labeled anti-humanistic and approaches which appear to have less potential for human advancement are labeled humanistic.

I concur with Nord, and think the ethical responsibility of compensation managers is clear. The first step in the ethical use of monetary control in organizations is the understanding by managers of the determination of behavior (see Hamner, 1974). Since reinforcement is the single most important concept in the learning process, managers must learn how to design effective reinforcement programs that will encourage productive and creative employees. This presentation has attempted to outline the knowledge and research available for this endeavor.

REFERENCES

Bassett, G. L., & Meyer, H. H. Performance appraisal based on self review. *Personnel Psychology*, 1968, **21**, 421–430.

Beer, M., & Gery, G. J. Individual and organizational correlates of pay system preferences. In H. L. Tosi, R. House, & M. D. Dunnette (Eds.), *Managerial Motivation and Compensation*. East Lansing, Michigan: Michigan State University Press, 1972.

Belcher, D. W. *Compensation Administration*. Englewood Cliffs, N.J.: Prentice-Hall, 1974.

Blood, M. R. Applied behavioral analysis from an organizational perspective. Paper presented at the 82nd Annual Convention of the American Psychological Association, New Orleans, August 1974.

Calder, B. J., & Staw, B. M. The interaction of intrinsic and extrinsic motivation: Some methodological notes. *Journal of Personality and Social Psychology*, 1975, **31**, 599–605.

Case of Big Mac's pay plans. *Harvard Business Review*, July–August 1974, 1–8.

Cherrington, D. L., Reitz, H. J., & Scott, W. E. Effects of reward and contingent reinforcement on satisfaction and task performance. *Journal of Applied Psychology*. 1971, **55**, 531–536.

Deci, E. L. Effects of externally mediated rewards on intrinsic motivation. *Journal of Personality and Social Psychology*, 1971, **18**, 105–115.

Deci, E. L. Work: Who does not like it and why? *Psychology Today*, August 1972 (a), **92**, 57–58.

Deci, E. L. The effects of contingent and noncontingent rewards and controls on intrinsic motivation. *Organizational Behavior and Human Performance*, 1972(b), **8**, 217–229.

Drucker, P. F. Beyond the stick and carrot: Hysteria over the work ethic. *Psychology Today*, November 1973, **87**, 89–93.

Employer survey finds most like their work. *Equinews*, March 18, 1974 (Vol. III, No. 6).

Equal Employment Opportunity Commission Guidelines (Rev. ed.). Washington, D.C.: U.S. Government Printing Office, 1974.

Frost, C. F., Wakeley, J. H., & Ruh, R. A. *The Scanlon Plan for Organization Development: Identity, Participation and Equity.* East Lansing: Michigan State University Press, 1974.

Gruenfeld, L. W., & Weissenberg, P. Supervisory characteristics and attitudes toward performance appraisals. *Personnel Psychology*, 1966, 143–152.

Hamner, W. Clay. Reinforcement theory and contingency management in organizational settings. In H. L. Tosi & W. C. Hamner (Eds.), *Management and Organizational Behavior: A Contingency Approach.* Chicago: St. Clair Press, 1974.

Hamner, W. Clay, Kim, J., Baird, L., & Bigoness, W. Race and sex as determinants of ratings by "potential" employees in a simulated work sampling task. *Journal of Applied Psychology,* 1974, **59**, 705–711.

Hamner, W. Clay, & Foster, L. W. Are intrinsic and extrinsic rewards additive? A test of Deci's cognitive evaluation theory. Paper presented at the National Academy of Management, Seattle, 1974.

Lawler, E. E. Managers' perceptions of their subordinates' pay and of their superiors' pay. *Personnel Psychology*, 1965, **18**, 413–422.

Lawler, E. E. The mythology of management compensation. *California Management Review*, 1966, **9**, 11–22.

Lawler, E. E. *Pay and Organizational Effectiveness.* New York: McGraw-Hill, 1971.

Lawler, E. E. *Motivation in Work Organization.* Monterey, Calif.: Brooks/Cole, 1973.

Lee, S. M. Salary equity: Its determination, analysis and correlates. Unpublished doctoral dissertation, University of Georgia, 1969.

Likert, R. *New Patterns of Management* (2nd ed.). New York: McGraw-Hill, 1967.

Maslow, A. H. A theory of human motivation. *Psychological Review*, 1943, **50**, 370–396.

Meyer, H. H. The pay for performance dilemma. *Organizational Dynamics*, 1975, **3**(3), 39–50.

Meyer, H. H., Kay, E., & French, J. R. P. Split roles in performance appraisals. *Harvard Business Review,* January-February 1965, 123–129.

Mobley, W. H. The link between MBO and merit compensation. *Personnel Journal*, June 1974, 423–427.

Nord, W. R. Some issues in the application of operant conditioning to the management of organizations. Paper presented at the National Academy of Management, Seattle, 1974.

Opsahl, R. L., & Dunnette, M. D. The role of financial compensation in industrial motivation. *Psychological Bulletin*, 1966, **66**, 94–118.

Penner, D. D. A study of the causes and consequences of salary satisfaction. *Behavioral Research Service Report*, General Electric Company, 1967.

Porter, L. W. A study of perceived need satisfactions in bottom and middle management jobs. *Journal of Applied Psychology,* 1961, **45**, 1–10.

Porter, L. W., & Lawler, E. E. *Managerial Attitudes and Performance.* Homewood, Ill.: Irwin-Dorsey, 1968.

Rowe vs. General Motors Corporation, 457 F 2d. 348 (5th Cir. 1972).

Scott, W. E., & Hamner, W. Clay. The influence of variations in performance profiles on the performance evaluation process: An examination of the validity of the criteria. *Organizational Behavior and Human Performance,* 1975, **14**, 360–370.

Skinner, B. F. *Contingencies of Reinforcement.* New York: Appleton-Century-Crofts, 1969.

Skinner, B. F. Conversations with B. F. Skinner. *Organizational Dynamics*, Winter
      1973, 31–40.
Vroom, V. H., & Deci, E. L. An overview of work motivation. In V. H. Vroom & E. L.
      Deci (Eds.), *Management and Motivation*. Baltimore: Penguin Press, 1970.
Xerox Compensation Planning Model. Rochester, N.Y.: Xerox Corporation, June 1972.

QUESTIONS FOR DISCUSSION

1   How would you design a program to increase the motivational levels of employees
    without using additional money? What factors would you think most important and
    how would you use such factors in your program design?
2   What role does money play in each of the five motivational models discussed in the
    beginning of this book?
3   Why might you expect pay and promotional opportunities to have different moti-
    vational effects on blue- and white-collar employees?
4   Under what circumstances might money be a stronger influence on the decision to
    participate than on the decision to produce?
5   What are some advantages and disadvantages of group incentive plans?
6   Differentiate between extrinsic rewards and intrinsic rewards. Which type do you
    feel would generally be a stronger motivating force? Why?
7   What are Hamner's major criticisms of merit pay systems?

Part Four

Motivation Theory
in Perspective

Chapter 12

Work and Motivation: An Evaluative Summary

The concept of the organization has long symbolized the efficient, effective, and rational allocation of resources for task accomplishment. As such, many attempts have been made by managers and researchers to define the optimal balance of financial, physical, and human resources as they help determine the growth and development of business, governmental, and educational institutions. The present volume has focused on the human aspects associated with such concerns. Specifically, we have reviewed in a systematic fashion the current level of knowledge concerning motivational processes as they affect work behavior.

Before attempting to summarize the current status of motivation theory and research, however, we should review briefly what we know about the nature of work itself. After all, if one objective of an increased knowledge of motivational processes is to improve both work attitudes and work performance, then we must be aware of the functions served by work activities in a modern society.

THE MEANING OF WORK

Work is important in the lives of individuals for several reasons. First, there is the notion of reciprocity, or exchange. Whether we are talking about a corporate executive, an assembly-line worker, or a Red Cross volunteer, each worker receives some form of reward in exchange for his or her services. These rewards may be primarily extrinsic, such as money, or they may be purely intrinsic, such as the personal satisfaction that comes from providing the service. In either case, a worker has certain personal expectations concerning the type and amount of reward he or she should receive for services rendered. The extent to which such expectations are met would presumably affect in large measure the inclination of the worker to continue at the current level of performance and, indeed, might even ultimately affect the decision of whether to remain with the organization.

Second, work generally serves several social functions. The workplace provides opportunities for meeting new people and developing friendships. In fact, many employees appear to spend more time interacting with their fellow employees than they do with their own families!

Third, a person's job is often a source of status, or rank, in society at large. For example, a carpenter who is trained in a specific craft is generally considered to be on a higher social plane than an unskilled ditchdigger. And a bank president would generally be accorded higher status than the carpenter. A point not to be overlooked here is the fact that work, or more precisely what one does at work, often transcends the boundaries of the work organization. The bank president in our example can have status in the *community* because of his or her position within the organization. Thus, work can be simultaneously a source of social differentiation as well as a source of social integration.

Fourth, and an aspect of work of special concern to the study of motivation, is the personal meaning that work has for the individual. From a psychological standpoint, it can be an important source of identity, self-esteem, and self-actualization. It can provide a sense of fulfillment by giving an employee a sense of purpose and by clarifying his or her value to society. Conversely, however, it can also be a source of frustration, boredom, and feelings of meaninglessness, depending on the characteristics of the individual and on the nature of the task. People tend to evaluate themselves according to what they have been able to accomplish. If they see their job as hampering the achievement of their full potential, it often becomes difficult for them to maintain a sense of purpose at work. Such feelings can then lead to a reduced level of job involvement, decreased job satisfaction, and a lowered desire to perform. Hence, the nature of the job—and the meaning it has for the employee—can have a profound impact on employee attitudes and work behavior.

As our society has increased in both complexity and affluence, so, too, have the problems associated with such developments. Alcoholism and drug abuse at work are prevalent, as are problems of turnover and absenteeism. Moreover, by several indications, worker productivity appears to be declining in many areas. Managers have often tried to explain away such problems by reverting to the old scientific management, or theory X, assumptions about human nature—namely, that people are basically lazy and have little desire to perform well on a job. However, a more realistic explanation for such problems may be found by looking at the type of work most employees are asked to perform.

Consider, for example, the case of younger workers just entering the job market. With higher educational levels as well as greater expectations concerning their work, many young workers have shown a strong aversion toward many of the more traditional (and well-paying) jobs at both the blue- and the white-collar levels. However, these same workers are largely in agreement with the notion that one should "work hard" on a job (Yankelovich, 1972). How are these two points reconciled? Perhaps the answer lies in the nature of the tasks. That is, rather than simply rebelling against the traditional (hard) work ethic, many younger workers appear to be demanding greater substance in the *nature* of their job activities. In this sense, it is a qualitative revolt, not a quantitative one. What they object to, it seems, is being placed on jobs which are essentially devoid of intrinsic worth.

Other examples could be cited (minority-group workers, women employees, even corporate executives). In all cases, a common denominator appears to be a reduced level of employee motivation to perform his or her job or even to remain with the organization. If we are to understand more clearly the nature and extent of such work-related problems and, better still, if we are to be able to find appropriate solutions to these problems, we must begin by understanding the very basic role played by motivation as it affects job behavior.

IMPORTANCE OF MOTIVATION IN WORK BEHAVIOR

Review of Major Variables

Perhaps the most striking aspect of the study of work motivation is the all-encompassing nature of the topic itself. Consider again our definition of motivation: that which energizes, directs, and sustains behavior. Following such a definition, it becomes readily apparent how many divergent factors can affect in some way the desire of an employee to perform. In Chapter 1, a conceptual framework, or model, was proposed (after Porter & Miles, 1974) to assist us in organizing these factors for detailed study and analysis throughout this book (see Exhibit 3 in Chapter 1).

By way of review, the model suggested that variables affecting motivation can be found on three levels in organizational settings. First, some variables were unique to the individual himself or herself (such as attitudes, interests, specific needs). Second, other variables arose from the nature of the job (such as degree of control over the particular job, level of responsibility, and so forth). Third, still other variables were found in the larger work situation, or organizational environment. Factors falling into this third category would include such things as peer group relations, supervisory practices, systemwide rewards, and organizational climate. In addition, it was emphasized in the model that a systems perspective was necessary. That is, instead of viewing these variables as three static lists of items, consideration had to be given to how they affected one another and changed over time in response to circumstances. The individual was thus seen as potentially being in a constant state of flux vis-à-vis his or her motivational level, based on the nature, strength, and interactive effects of these three groups of variables.

Let us consider briefly how some of the more important findings reviewed in this book relate to this conceptual framework, beginning with those variables unique to the individual. Only highlights of the major findings will be mentioned here. An analysis of the data presented throughout this volume reveals that several *individual* characteristics can represent a significant influence on employee performance. For instance, there is fairly consistent evidence that individuals who have higher needs for achievement generally perform better than those who have lower needs (as shown, for example, in Steers & Spencer, 1977; and Weiner & Kukla, 1970). Moreover, other evidence (see, for example, Porter & Steers, 1973; Porter et al., 1976; Steers, 1977) indicates that individuals who have strong negative attitudes toward an organization are less inclined to continue their involvement in organizational activities. Locke and his associates (Locke, Cartledge, & Knerr, 1970) present laboratory evidence and Latham and Yukl (1975) review field evidence indicating that personal aspiration level on a task (the level of performance for which an individual is actually trying) can be an accurate predictor of subsequent performance. Finally, investigations by Adams (1965) and others (e.g., Pritchard et al., 1972) found that *perceived* inequity in an organizational exchange situation was associated with changes (up or down) in performance levels. While many other examples could be cited, these kinds of findings generally support the proposition that personal characteristics unique to an individual can have an important impact on his or her work behavior.

A similar pattern emerges when we consider *job-related* characteristics. Evidence presented by Hackman (1976), Steers and Porter (1974), and others indicates that variations in the nature of the task itself can influence performance and satisfaction. For example, several studies have found that "enriching" an employee's job by allowing him or her more variety, autonomy, and responsibility can result in somewhat improved performance. However, many of these findings are not overly strong. Stronger evidence concerning the impact of job- or task-related variables emerges when we simultaneously consider the role of individual differences in such a relationship. That is, when variations across individuals are also taken into account, evidence indicates that certain task attributes are more strongly related to performance only for specific "types" of people, such as, say, high need achievers. For other persons, such attributes appear to have diminished effects (Hackman & Lawler, 1971; Hulin, 1971; Steers, 1975; Hackman & Oldham, 1976; Vroom, 1960). In other words, as stressed in Fein's (1974) article, it appears that not everyone wants *to the same degree* to have an enriched job, nor does everyone necessarily perform better when assigned to one. Recognition must be given, therefore, to the background characteristics of individual employees when considering job design changes.

Finally, let us review *work environment* effects on motivation and performance. Articles earlier in the book in Chapter 8 focused on these effects and reviewed much of the research on environmental impact and noted the importance of such variables as group influences, leadership styles, and organizational climate in the determination of employee performance. Again, however, we must consider the interactive dynamics between such factors and other individuals and job-related factors. Thus, it is possible that high group cohesion (a work environment characteristic) may be a much more potent influence on behavior for a person with a high need for affiliation (an individual characteristic) than for a person with a low need for affiliation. Persons with high needs for achievement may be less influenced by the degree of group cohesion and more interested in potential economic rewards. Moreover, a job that lacks enrichment (a job-related characteristic) may be eased somewhat by a supervisor who shows a good deal of consideration toward his or her subordinates (another work environment characteristic).

The important point, then, is that when we consider the variables involved in work motivation we must take a strong, integrative approach. We must study *relationships* among variables rather than focus on one specific topic. Only then can we achieve a greater understanding of the complexities of the motivational process.

REVIEW OF MAJOR THEORIES

A central purpose of any theory is to organize in a meaningful fashion the major sets of variables associated with the topic under study. In fact, one test of the usefulness of a theory or model is the degree to which it can account for a wide diversity of variables while simultaneously integrating them into a cohesive—and succinct—unifying framework. Such a theory of work motivation would ideally account for variables from the three major areas discussed above (individual, job, and work environment), as well as consider the implications of interactive effects among these areas. Unfortunately, such a totally unifying theory does not appear to exist at this time. What does exist are a set of different theories that address themselves to one or more of these sets of variables but none of which are completely and thoroughly comprehensive (both in terms of hypothesized interaction effects among the variables, and in terms of accounting for a diverse array of evidence).

In the absence of a "master" theory, it may be well to review briefly the several major theories that were discussed in the early chapters of the book. In this way, we can see to what extent they do deal with different sets of variables and thus compare their relative explanatory power. As was stated at the end of Chapter 1, however, many of the theoretical approaches are complementary rather than contradictory. Thus it is often not just a matter of choosing which is the "best" theory, but rather one of deciding which approaches are, *relatively speaking*, the most helpful for understanding particular aspects of employee work behavior.

The need theories of Maslow, Alderfer, and Murray and McClelland, while not entirely ignoring job-related and work environment variables, are primarily individual theories of motivation. Strong emphasis is placed on the character-istics of the individual, and these models represent highly developed statements concerning the role played by personal need strengths in the determination of work behavior. While the influences of the job and work environment are not central themes, it is easy to see how such factors could play a major role in these models. For example, for employees with a strong need for self-actual-ization, providing a work environment that would promote fulfillment of this need should increase their propensity to remain with the organization and respond positively to organizational objectives. A similar argument could be advanced for creating an achievement-oriented work environment under the Murray-McClelland-Atkinson model for individuals with a high need for achievement. Even so, although a good deal of speculation is possible con-cerning how such job and environmental variables might affect personal need satisfaction and performance, it should be recognized that such considerations are dealt with relatively lightly in these models (see, for example, the critique of need theories by Salancik and Pfeffer).

Equity theory (as delineated by Adams) centers around the relationship between individual characteristics—attitudes toward inputs and outcomes, tol-erance for feelings of inequity, and the like—and work environment charac-teristics (especially systemwide reward practices). This process-oriented ap-proach does place considerable stress on the individual's *perceptual* reactions to environmental variables, and in that sense the theory considers interactive effects. The approach does not, however, provide a comprehensive framework for integrating the major sets of variables affecting motivation at work, and in particular fails to consider many of the other impacts of these variables (besides producing feelings of equity or inequity).

Of all the theoretical approaches considered in this book, reinforcement theory (behavior modification) is the one that places by far the heaviest emphasis on the work environment cluster of variables. For those who advocate this approach, the response of the work environment—including its various elements such as the work group, the supervisor, company reward practices—is *the* controlling factor in affecting employee behavior (assuming a given level of ability). The notion of individual differences, and particularly the notion of individual needs and attitudes, is virtually ignored by this approach. Rather, as stressed earlier in the book, the reinforcement approach to explaining be-havior is epitomized by the phrase "behavior is a function of its consequences." Thus, it is clear that this kind of orientation to understanding motivated behavior in the organizational setting deliberately focuses on, basically, only one set of variables—the reaction of the environment to specific behaviors.

Finally, expectancy/valence theory can be examined in terms of how it deals with the three major sets of variables—individual, job, and work envi-ronment. To begin with, the theory is specific in dealing with the role of in-dividual differences. It recognizes individual variations in need strengths by acknowledging that not everyone values the same rewards equally; people attach different valences to potential outcomes. People also differ in their per-ceptions of how equitable a given level of rewards is (in relation to the individual's own standard of comparison). Moreover, the model particularly emphasizes that individuals have differing beliefs, or expectancies, that certain actions on their part will ultimately lead to desired rewards. Expectancy/valence theory also encompasses job-related variables by pointing to how these factors can affect future expectancies, and by arguing that job attributes can at times serve as sources of intrinsically valued rewards. The more sophisticated versions of the model have also included the notion of role clarity; that is, performance can often be improved by specifying more carefully the direction of behavior. Finally, expectancy/valence theory focuses fairly explicitly on several work environment influences on performance, particularly those relating to reward structures. Throughout, this model stresses the necessity of analyzing relationships among variables as a prerequisite to an understanding of the motivational *process*. It does, however, place heavy (some would say too heavy) emphasis on individuals' cognitions about how their own behavior will or will not lead to particular outcomes potentially available in the work situation. Whether individuals actually engage in the kinds of thought processes implied by the theory is the major issue to be raised with this conceptual approach.

In summary, each of these theories has something to offer in the attempt to understand motivation in the work situation. Also, as we have emphasized several times, various parts of the theories are, in many ways, complimentary. For example, individuals who have particularly strong needs (e.g., need for achievement) may also be inclined to make equity comparisons with regard to how their peers are being rewarded in relation to the types and amounts of rewards that they themselves are receiving. Not only that, but they will likely be sensitive to what it is that they do that results in "good" responses (from supervisors, peers, the organization, etc.) and thus will likely form ideas (i.e., "expectancies") that a certain action (behavior) on their part will, or will not, result in a "good response" (i.e., reward) next time. In other words, it seems clear that each of the major approaches to motivation provides an important *perspective* from which to view motivation, and—and this is *crucial*—these perspectives are not necessarily contradictory but rather provide a comprehensive viewpoint that permits an increased and (it is hoped) sophisticated understanding. If there is any utility to studying motivational theories it is exactly this fact: One can obtain more meaning about the events and situations that one observes or takes part in by knowing something about the theories than if one is not familiar with them. In this sense, improved knowledge about motivational processes is requisite not only for management but also for the employees themselves if all members are to contribute more effectively to the goals of the organization and simultaneously receive greater personal satisfaction.

IMPLICATIONS FOR MANAGEMENT

As we have found, the level of understanding concerning work motivation has increased considerably in the past several decades. However, when we survey current practice in this area we soon discover that there is a sizable discrepancy in a number of organizations between such practice and many of the more advanced theories of motivation. Why does such a discrepancy exist? There are several possible explanations.

First, many managers still hold conservative beliefs about how much employees really want to contribute on a job (Porter et al., 1975). They still tend to view motivation as largely a "carrot-and-stick" process, despite the fact that current research has demonstrated that employees by and large want active involvement in organizational activities.

Second, owing primarily to increased automation and machine-placed technology, some managers apparently feel that motivation is no longer a critical issue, since production control is often largely out of the employee's hands. Such a position ignores, however, the impact that turnover, absenteeism, strikes, output restrictions, and the like have on productivity, even with machine-paced technology. And, of course, the potential effects of motivation levels on performance are greatly increased as we move toward a more service-oriented economy (and, indeed, as one considers the *management* sector of organizations; if motivation differences have an impact anywhere, it is among *managers* themselves).

Third, considering the attitudes of some labor union leaders, we find that a few such leaders apparently still feel that increasing motivational and performance levels might ultimately lead to fewer jobs. Such attitudes in the past have led to the strengthening of the status quo insofar as potential changes in the performance environment were concerned.

It is our contention that such reasoning is somewhat superficial and is, to a large extent, unfounded. The creation of a stimulating, productive, and satisfying work environment can be beneficial for both management and workers if honest concern is shown for all parties involved. If everyone is to derive some benefit from such an environment, however, the problems of the *employee* must be clearly recognized and taken into account. The pivotal role in this process belongs to managers (and, particularly, to upper-level managers) because of their influence in determining the characteristics of the performance environment. If improvements are to be made, management must take the first step. Assuming such an orientation, several implications for managerial practices can be drawn from the material presented here. While this list does not pretend to be all-inclusive, we do feel that it points to several of the more important conclusions to be drawn:

1 Perhaps one of the most important lessons to be learned from the data reviewed here is that, if managers truly want to improve performance and work attitudes, they must take an active role in *managing* motivational processes at work. Managing motivation is conscious, intentional behavior; it is not something that just happens. Any organization desiring to improve attitudes or work behavior must therefore accept responsibility for active involvement and participation if such changes are to be successful.

2 Any attempt by managers to improve the motivational levels of their

subordinates should be prefaced by a self-examination on the part of the managers themselves. Are they aware of their major strengths *and* their major limitations? Do they have a clear notion of their own wants, desires, and expectations from their jobs? Are their perceptions of themselves consistent with the perceptions others have of them? In short, before managers attempt to deal with others, they should have a clear picture of their own role in the organizational milieu.

3 The importance of recognizing individual differences across employees has been pointed to time and again throughout the studies reviewed here. Managers should be sensitive to variations in employees' needs, abilities, and traits. Similarly, they should recognize that different employees have different preferences (valences) for the rewards available for good performance. Research has shown, for example, that money as a reward is much more important to some than to others. A greater awareness of such variations allows managers to utilize most efficiently the diversity of talents among their subordinates and, within policy limitations, to reward good performance with those things most desirable to the employees.

4 Somewhat relatedly, it is important that employees (i.e., anyone in the organization) see a clear relation between successful performance on their part and the receipt of their desired rewards. It therefore becomes incumbent upon management to be able to identify superior performers and reward them accordingly. When this is done, employee expectations generally increase, and this in turn should lead to greater effort toward goal attainment. Such an implication raises questions about the use of non-merit-based compensation systems and of seniority as a major factor in promotions. Where rewards are not based upon performance, we would expect motivational levels to be markedly reduced.

5 A further factor to consider is the nature of the tasks which employees are asked to perform. Questions should be raised by management concerning the feasibility of providing employees with jobs that offer greater challenge, diversity, and opportunities for personal need satisfaction. Managers might begin by putting themselves in the place of their subordinates and asking themselves what they would get out of doing such a job. Similarly, questions should be raised as to whether employees understand exactly what is expected of them. Research has shown that increasing role clarity on a job generally increases the likelihood of improving task performance.

6 In a broader sense, managers could give increased attention to the quality of the overall work environment. How are group dynamics affecting performance? Are the current styles of leadership effective, or would other styles be preferable? In short, is the "climate" within the work group such that it would facilitate task accomplishment or do obvious barriers exist that can be remedied?

7 In many cases greater efforts could be made to assess worker attitudes on a continual basis. In the past, attitude surveys have received little attention outside of personnel departments, or sometimes they have been used as a tool of last resort when managers have noted a decline in performance. Perhaps a more effective strategy would be to monitor job attitudes and to use such information as a motivational barometer to identify potential trouble spots. It is essential for managers to become intelligent consumers of behavioral data so that they can act more from a position of knowledge and understanding than from one of uncertainty or ignorance.

8 Finally, if employee motivational levels—and consequently performance—are to be increased, it becomes especially important to involve the employees themselves in a cooperative venture aimed at improving output for after all they too have a stake in what happens to the organization. Thus, one key factor in motivating employees is to engage them more fully in the processes aimed at attaining organizational effectiveness. Without employee cooperation and support, a great deal of managerial energy can be wasted.

In summary, it is our belief that theories of motivation, as with research in the behavioral sciences in general, are useful for practicing managers and employees, and are not solely for academicians. Their value lies primarily in their capacity to sensitize managers and researchers to specific factors and processes that can have an important bearing on the behavior of people at work. In this sense, theories and research data in the area of motivation are one more tool available to managers—and to employees—in the performance of their jobs.

REFERENCES

Adams, J. S. Inequity in social exchange. In L. Berkowitz (Ed.), *Advances in experimental social psychology*, vol. 2. New York: Academic Press, 1965.

Hackman, J. R. Work design. In J. R. Hackman & J. L. Suttle (Eds), *Improving life at work*. Santa Monica, Calif.: Goodyear Publishing Co., 1976.

Hackman, J. R., & Lawler, E. E., III. Employee reactions to job characteristics. *Journal of Applied Psychology*, 1971, **55**, 259–286.

Hackman, J. R., & Oldham, G. R. Motivation through the design of work: Test of a theory. *Organizational Behavior and Human Performance*, 1976, **16**, 250–279.

Hulin, C. L. Individual differences and job enrichment—The case against general treatments. In J. R. Maher (Ed.), *New perspectives in job enrichment*. New York: Van Nostrand Reinhold, 1971.

Latham, G. P., & Yukl, G. A. A review of research on the application of goal setting in organizations. *Academy of Management Journal*, 1975, **18**, 824–845.

Locke, E. A., Cartledge, N., & Knerr, C. S. Studies of the relationship between satisfaction, goal-setting, and performance. *Organizational Behavior and Human Performance*, 1970, **5**, 135–158.

Porter, L. W., Crampon, W. J., & Smith, F. J. Organizational commitment and managerial turnover: A longitudinal study. *Organizational Behavior and Human Performance*, 1976, **15**, 87–98.

Porter, L. W., Lawler, E. E., & Hackman, J. R. *Behavior in organizations*. New York: McGraw-Hill, 1975.

Porter, L. W., & Miles, R. E. Motivation and management. In J. W. McGuire (Ed.), *Contemporary management: Issues and viewpoints*. Englewood Cliffs, N. J.: Prentice-Hall, 1974.

Porter, L. W., & Steers, R. M. Organizational, work, and personal factors in employee turnover and absenteeism. *Psychological Bulletin*, 1973, **80**, 151–176.

Pritchard, R. D., Dunnette, M. D., & Jorgenson, D. O. Effects of perceptions of equity and inequity on worker performance and satisfaction. *Journal of Applied Psychology,* 1972, **56**, 75–94.

Steers, R. M. Antecedents and outcomes of organizational commitment. *Administrative Science Quarterly,* 1977, **22**, 46–56.

Steers, R. M. Task-goal attributes, achievement, and supervisory performance. *Organizational Behavior and Human Performance,* 1975, **13**, 392–403.

Steers, R. M., & Porter, L. W. The role of task-goal attributes in employee performance. *Psychological Bulletin*, 1974, **81**, 434–452.

Steers, R. M., & Spencer, D. G. The role of achievement motivation in job design. *Journal of Applied Psychology*, 1977, **62**, 472–479.

Vroom, V. H. *Some personality determinants of the effects of participation*. Englewood Cliffs, N. J.: Prentice-Hall, 1960.

Weiner, B., & Kukla, A. An attributional analysis of achievement motivation. *Journal of Personality and Social Psychology*, 1970, **15**, 1–20.

Yankelovich, D. *The changing values on campus: Political and personal attitudes on campus*. New York: Washington Square, 1972.

Name Index

Subject Index